MARYLANDERS AND DELAWAREANS IN THE FRENCH AND INDIAN WAR 1756–1763

Henry C. Peden, Jr.

HERITAGE BOOKS
2019

HERITAGE BOOKS

AN IMPRINT OF HERITAGE BOOKS, INC.

Books, CDs, and more—Worldwide

For our listing of thousands of titles see our website
at
www.HeritageBooks.com

Published 2019 by
HERITAGE BOOKS, INC.
Publishing Division
5810 Ruatan Street
Berwyn Heights, Md. 20740

International Standard Book Number
Paperbound: 978-1-68034-962-7

PREFACE

This book contains genealogical and historical information about the men and women of Maryland and Delaware who served in the military or in civil service and rendered aid to British and American soldiers during the war against the French and Indians in North America between 1756 and 1763.

Information, as shown in the list of references, was gleaned from original records, microfilm of original and transcribed records, and published books (many of which contained errors and omissions which have been corrected herein). The end result of this effort is that approximately 6,000 soldiers, sailors and civilian supporters (styled herein as patriots) have been identified and brought together in one easy to use volume. In many cases genealogical information has been included about the soldier or patriot and his family. Names have been cross-referenced within the text, thus precluding the need for a separate index.

This book should be a useful research tool for those seeking information about their colonial Maryland and Delaware ancestors and principally for those interested in joining such hereditary societies as the Society of Colonial Wars, National Society of Colonial Dames of America, and Daughters of American Colonists.

Henry C. Peden, Jr.
May 23, 2004

Introduction

The ***French and Indian War*** (1756-1763) was fought by Frenchmen, French Canadians, and Indians on the one side against Englishmen, Irishmen, Scots, British Colonials, and Indians on the other side.

The British still refer to this as the Seven Year's War, and while the battles may have begun in the colonies, it eventually became a global conflict drawing in other countries and playing on other battlefields.

The triggering event for the French and Indian War was the dispute over the French versus British territories on the frontier. While the English had always intended to settle the frontier, the French were more interested in trade. This influenced many of the Indian tribes to side with the French.

The Indians who fought with the French introduced a different type of warfare. Notably, their frequent scalping of soldiers who had officially surrendered, and their policy of intimidating frontier settlements by murdering men, women, and children and destroying animals and crops. Many settlers abandoned crops in the field and fled for protection to the local garrisons or returned to counties in more populated areas. Some even went so far as Great Britain.

The British (finally) won, and the war ended with the Treaty of Paris in 1763. The terms of peace stripped France of most of her North American possessions. Great Britain now ruled the territory of what would be eastern Canada and the United States.

Time Line of Events

1754 - George Washington is sent to destroy Fort Duquesne (held by the French) but is forced to surrender to superior forces. Washington is blamed for Fort Necessity and resigns his commission rather than be demoted. He will later return as a volunteer under the British authority of General Braddock.

June 17, 1755 - The British seize Acadia (Nova Scotia).

July 9, 1755 - British General Braddock's forces are defeated in the Battle of the Wilderness near Fort Duquesne in Pennsylvania, leaving colonists in the backwoods of British territory defenseless.

September 9, 1755 - British Colonel William Johnston's forces win the Battle of Lake George. Johnson had raised an army of about three thousand volunteers from New York and New England, plus about five hundred Mohawks.

May 8-9, 1756 - Great Britain declares war on France. France declares war on Great Britain.

August 14, 1756 - The French capture Fort Oswego on the banks of the Great Lakes.

August 8/9, 1757 - The commander-in-chief of the French forces Louis-Joseph de Montcalm takes Fort William Henry on Lake George. Many British soldiers and civilians are slaughtered by the Indians after they surrender in the infamous "Fort Henry Massacre."

8 July 1758 – The British lose 2000 soldiers in a failed attack led by General Abercromby on Fort Ticonderoga, New York.

July 26, 1758 - The British, led by Generals Jeffrey Amherst and James Wolfe, seize Louisbourg, opening the route to Canada.

August 27, 1758 - The French surrender a major store of supplies at Fort Frontenac on Lake Ontario to Lt. Colonel John Bradstreet of the Royal Americans, after being taken by surprise. Bradstreet's army is made up of mostly colonials including 1,112 New Yorkers, 675 from Massachusetts, 412 from New Jersey, 318 from Rhode Island, and 135 regulars.

October 21, 1758 - The British make peace with the Iroquois, Shawnee, and Delaware Indians.

November 26, 1758 - The British recapture Fort Duquesne - It is renamed Fort Pitt.

July 25, 1759 - The British under Sir William Johnson take Fort Niagara; the French abandon Crown Point. After these two victories, the British control the entire western frontier.

September 13, 1759 - The British win the decisive Battle of Quebec. Marquis de Montcalm and General James Wolfe, the commanding generals of both armies, die in battle.

May 16, 1760 - French Siege of Quebec fails.

September 8, 1760 - Montreal falls to the British led by Sir William Johnson; letters are signed finishing the surrender of Canada.

Circa September 15, 1760 - The British flag is raised over Detroit, effectively ending the war.

1761 - The British make peace with the Cherokee Indians.

September 18, 1762 – The French attempt to retake Newfoundland and fail.

1762 - Pontiac's War begins. In the wake of French defeat, Pontiac, the Ottowa Chief, sends messengers to all the tribes between the Alleghenies and the Mississippi, seeking their united support against the British.

February 10, 1763 - Treaty of Paris is signed, ending the French and Indian War. All French possessions east of the Mississippi including Canada, except New Orleans, are given to the British.

April 27, 1763 - Pontiac proposes a coalition of Ottowas, Potawatomies and Hurons for the purpose of attacking the British at Detroit.

May 9, 1763 - Pontiac's forces lay siege to Detroit. His allies later destroy forts at Venango, Le Boeuf and Presque Isle.

July 1763 - Fort Pitt army infects besieging chiefs with blankets from the smallpox hospital. Faced with an epidemic, the Indians retreat.

October 31, 1763 - Pontiac capitulates at Detroit.

Delawareans in the War

By the end of 1756, all three counties of Delaware had organized their militia for the protection of the region, in accordance with the acts of the Assembly.

The returns for the militia of the lower counties are summarized as follows: The Upper Regiment of New Castle County contained eleven companies, with the officers named and two servants for each company, with an average of sixty privates. The Lower Regiment of New Castle County consisted of nine companies, averaging about fifty privates, but with the same officers as the Upper Regiment. Kent and Sussex Counties furnished twelve and eight companies respectively, and the officers and privates in each were the same as in the various companies of the Lower Regiment of New Castle County. From this it appears that the lower counties organized a force of over two thousand troops.

By 1757 they had nearly 4,000 troops organized and a battery and barracks were begun late in the year. [1]

It doesn't appear that the Delaware militias were ever called into the battle, but they stood ready to defend their communities for the duration of the war.

Marylanders in the War

The border areas of Maryland and Virginia suffered increased raids by hostile Indians after Colonel George Washington's defeat at Fort Necessity. Volunteer militia units were formed to protect settlements like Elizabeth Town near Antietam Creek and Frederick Town in Western Maryland. Colonel Thomas Cresap received a commission to raise a company of rangers who were then positioned at Fort Cumberland. Horatio Sharpe, the governor of Maryland, was temporarily placed in command of the entire Royal forces after Colonel Washington resigned. He brought with him one Maryland company to Fort Cumberland in November of 1754 and drilled the militia to prepare for a spring campaign and the arrival of General Edward Braddock from England.

A large number of recruits from Maryland were included in the regiments who fought under Braddock. His later defeat at Fort Duquesne and the ensuing abandonment of the western territory including Fort Cumberland by the British Army left the Maryland settlers in even worse position than after Washington's rout. Maryland farmers were murdered and their farms burned in Cumberland in Allegheny County and other towns further east. Residents as far away as Annapolis were warned of Indian attacks. Scalping parties approached within 30 miles of Baltimore.[2]

During this time, Governor Sharpe ordered into service the militia of Frederick, Prince George's, Baltimore, Cecil, Anne Arundel, Calvert, Charles and St. Mary's counties to meet in Frederick and march to Colonel Cresap's blockhouse residence on the Conococheague to assist in the protection of the frontier settlers.

Some notables from Maryland who aided in the war include Christopher Gist, an avid explorer whose experience and talents were used to aide General Braddock in his expedition. He was with Braddock on the fatal field of Monongahela

---

[1] Most of the information on Delawareans comes from *History of Delaware* by J. Thomas Scharf.

[2] Most of the information on Marylanders comes from the *History of Western Maryland* by J. Thomas Scharf.

along with his own sons Nathaniel and Thomas. A brief genealogy of the Gist family is included as a footnote in *The History of Western Maryland*, p. 75.

Colonel Thomas Cresap of Maryland and his son Michael also played major roles in defending the colonists during this period. The *History of Western Maryland* includes a brief biography and genealogy of them on pp. 76-77. The author also includes a defense of the Cresaps against charges made by Thomas Jefferson that they murdered Chief Logan's family, in a separate chapter following the section on the French and Indian War.

REFERENCES

AACR: *Anne Arundel County Church Records of the 17th and 18th Centuries*, by F. Edward Wright (1990)
ARDE: *Archives of Delaware*
ARMD: *Archives of Maryland*
ARPA: *Archives of Pennsylvania*
BCF: *Baltimore County Families, 1659-1759*, by Robert W. Barnes (1989)
BDML: *A Biographical Dictionary of the Maryland Legislature, 1635-1789*, by Edward C. Papenfuse, et al. (1979)
CDSS: *Colonial Delaware Soldiers and Sailors, 1638-1776*, by Henry C. Peden, Jr. (1995)
CFD: *Colonial Families of Delaware*, by F. Edward Wright (1998-2002)
CMSP: *Calendar of Maryland State Papers-The Black Books* (1934)
CSOS: *Colonial Soldiers of the South, 1732-1774*, by Murtie J. Clark (1983)
ESVR: *Maryland Eastern Shore Vital Records, 1726-1750*, by F. Edward Wright (1983)
FCLR: *Frederick County, Maryland Land Records, Liber F Abstracts, 1756-1761*, by Patricia A. Andersen (1995)
GRSD: *Governor's Register, 1674-1851, State of Delaware* (1926)
HCC: *A History of Calvert County, MD*, by Charles F. Stein (1976)
HDE: *History of Delaware, 1609-1888*, by J. Thomas Scharf (1888)
MCW: *Maryland Calendar of Wills*
MDG: *Maryland Genealogies* (1980)
MHM: *Maryland Historical Magazine*
MHS: Maryland Historical Society (Manuscript Division)
MSA: Maryland State Archives (Special Collections)
MSR: *Maryland Source Records, Volume 1*, by Bettie Carothers (1975)
PGCR: *Prince George's County, Maryland, Indexes of Church Registers, 1686-1885*, by Prince George's County Historical Society (1988)
RPDE: *Revolutionary Patriots of Delaware, 1775-1783*, by Henry C. Peden, Jr. (1996)
SCWM: *Society of Colonial Wars in the State of Maryland, Volume III* (1995)
SLMH: *Side-Lights on Maryland History*, by Hester D. Richardson (1903)
TWL: *This Was the Life*, by Millard M. Rice (1979)
WMG: *Western Maryland Genealogy*

ABBREVIATIONS

admin.	administrator
b.	born
bapt.	baptized
bttn.	battalion
c.	circa
capt.	captain
co.	county
col.	colonel
cpl.	corporal
d.	died
dau.	daughter
DE	Delaware
exec.	Executor
gen.	general
lieut.	lieutenant
m.	married
maj.	major
MD	Maryland
(N)	name unknown
PA	Pennsylvania
P. E.	Protestant Episcopal
poss.	possibly
prob.	probably
pvt.	private
q.v.	"where see" (within)
regt.	regiment
sgt.	sergeant
VA	Virginia

MARYLANDERS AND DELAWAREANS IN THE FRENCH AND INDIAN WAR, 1756-1763

ABBOTT, JAMES (Delaware), pvt., Capt. French Battell's Company of Lower County Provincials, enlisted 20 May 1758. {Ref: ARDE I:16; ARPA (2nd Series) 2:555}

ABERCROMBIE, GENERAL, see "Morris Dickson," q.v.

ACKLAND, SARAH, see "Michael Raimon," q.v.

ADAIR, ROBERT (Maryland), b. c1720, Calvert Co., son of Dr. Alexander Adair and Christian Sterling, m. Martha (N), had no children, and d. 22 Oct 1768, Baltimore Town; patriot, merchant, gentleman by 1750, county justice (1752-1767), sheriff (1764-1766), and member of MD Assembly (1768); no known military service, but he served as one of the representatives of Baltimore Co. who assisted French and Indian War veterans in collecting their pay in 1767. {Ref: BDML I:97-98; *MD Gazette*, 27 Oct 1768} See "Henry Tarr" and "Philip Wilkinson" and "William Rowles" and "Abraham Eagleston" and "Samuel Sergeant" and "Edward Pack" and "Robert Davis" and "Darby Henly" and "Abel Peacock," q.v.

ADAMS, ALEXANDER, see "John Adams" and "William Adams," q.v.

ADAMS, BENJAMIN (Maryland), pvt., Capt. Joshua Beall's Company Muster Roll, Prince George's Co., circa 1757-1758, exact dates not given; bill of credit issued or paid to him for £0.9.0 in 1767, exact date not given. {Ref: MSA S960 or S752, p. 184}

ADAMS, JOHN (Maryland), b. c1730, Somerset Co., son of Rev. Alexander Adams and Sarah Horsey, m. Sarah Piper (widow of Clement Dashiell) on 14 Feb 1760, had sons John and William, and d. intestate after 1783; captain by 1763, member of MD Assembly (1762-1771), county judge (1766-1777), commissioner of the tax (1777-1783), Justice of the Court of Oyer and Terminer (commissioned 1772), and Judge of the Court of Appeals (appointed 1778). {Ref: BDML I:98}

ADAMS, NATHANIEL (Maryland), patriot, Annapolis, Anne Arundel Co., pay account submitted for quartering soldiers in 1757 or 1758, exact dates not given. {Ref: MHM 9:3, p. 260}

ADAMS, THOMAS (Maryland), b. c1733, MD (age 23 in 1756); pvt., Capt. Christopher Gist's Company of VA Militia, 13 Jul 1756, enlisted at Baltimore. {Ref: MSR I:37}

ADAMS, VALENTINE (Maryland), pvt., Capt. Peter Butler's Company Muster Roll, Frederick Co., circa 1757-1758, exact dates not given (served 34 days); bill of credit or order issued in his behalf for £1.14.0 and paid to Casper Shaff on 2 Mar 1767. {Ref: MSA S960 or S752, p. 166; CSOS:96}

ADAMS, WILLIAM (Maryland), b. Somerset Co., son of Rev. Alexander Adams and Sarah Horsey, m. 1st to Leah (N) by 1763 and 2nd to Ann (N), had no surviving children, and d. 1795; patriot, miller, and member of MD Assembly (served on Arms and Ammunition Committee, 1762-1766). {Ref: BDML I:99}

ADAMS, WILLIAM, see "John Adams," q.v.

ADDAM, JOHN (Delaware), b. c1738, Holland (age 21 in 1759); drummer, enlisted in Capt. John Wright's Company and mustered on 11 May 1759. {Ref: ARDE I:25; ARPA (2nd Series) 2:592}

ADDAMS, OSWALD (Maryland), alias William Addams *[sic]*, b. c1725, private soldier, enlisted in the MD Forces in 1757 (age about 32); reported as deserted by Robert Hanson, at Port Tobacco. {Ref: *MD Gazette*, 26 May 1757}

ADDISON, JOHN (Maryland), b. 16 Sep 1713, Prince George's Co., son of Thomas Addison and Elinor Smith, m. Susannah Wilkinson (d. 1774), had children Thomas, John, and Eleanor, and d. testate in 1764; captain by 1747 and colonel by 1760; member of MD Assembly (served on Arms and Ammunition Committee, 1751-1757). {Ref: BDML I:100-101}

ADDISON, REBECCA, see "George Plater " q.v.

ADDISON, THOMAS, see "George Plater," q.v.

ADGATE, ELIAS (Maryland), b. 12 Jan 1735/6, Prince George's Co., son of Able Adgate and Joneacre Cook, of Queen Anne's P. E. Parish. {Ref: PGCR 1:163} Pvt., Capt. Alexander Beall's Company of MD Troops, Frederick Co., from 9 Oct 1757 to 23 Oct 1758 when he reportedly deserted; however, payment to him was recorded in Col. Dagworthy's account book on 7 Mar 1763 for work on Fort Cumberland. {Ref: MHS MS.375.1; CSOS:79; MHS MS.375}

AISQUITH, THOMAS (Maryland), b. St. Mary's Company, son of William Aisquith and Elizabeth (N), m. 1st to Ann Hopewell (dau. of Hugh Hopewell and widow of Adam Bell) by 1724 and m. 2nd to Eleanor (N), had sons George, John, and an unborn child at the time he wrote his will, and d. testate in 1761; patriot, merchant, member of MD Assembly, county justice (1736-1761), and deputy commissary (1724-1761); styled colonel by 1760. {Ref: BDML I:101-102}

AKIN (AIKEN), ALEXANDER (Delaware), b. c1739 (birth place not given; laborer, age about 20 in 1759); pvt., enlisted by Capt. James Armstrong for the PA Regt. on 14 May 1759. {Ref: ARDE I:25; ARPA (2nd Series) 2:585}

ALDER, BOWLES (Maryland), pvt., Capt. Joshua Beall's Company Muster Roll, Prince George's Co., circa 1757-1758, exact dates not given; bill of credit issued or paid in his behalf to Francis King for £2.3.0 on 25 Feb 1767. {Ref: MSA S960 or S752, p. 184}

ALDER, JOHN (Maryland), b. c1729, Reading, County Berkshire, England; soldier in the Royal American Regt. (age 27 in 1756), reported by Lieut. McBean at Annapolis as being a deserter from His Majesty's Royal American Regiment. {Ref: *MD Gazette*, 25 Nov 1756}

ALDRIDGE, NICHOLAS (Maryland), cpl., Capt. Peter Bainbridge's Company Muster Roll, Frederick Co., circa 1757-1758, exact dates not given (served 36 days); bill of credit issued or paid in his behalf to Joseph Chaplin on 5 Mar 1767 for £2.8.0. {Ref: MSA S960 or S752, p. 181; CSOS:110} Pvt., Capt. Joseph Chapline's Company Muster Roll No. 1, Frederick Co., circa 1757-1758, exact dates not given (served 30 days); bill of credit issued or paid in his behalf to Joseph Chaplin for £1.10.0 on 5 Mar 1767. {Ref: MSA S960 or S752, p. 191; CSOS:102} Cpl., Capt. Moses Chapline's Company Muster Roll No. 3, Frederick Co., circa 1757-1758, exact dates not given (served 6 days); bill of credit issued or paid in his behalf to Joseph Chaplin for £0.8.0 on 5 Mar 1767. {Ref: MSA S960 or S752, p. 198; CSOS:114}

ALEXANDER, HENRY (Maryland), cpl., Capt. Henry Casson's Company Muster Roll, Queen Anne's Co., circa 1757-1758, exact dates not given; bill of credit issued or paid in his behalf to Capt. Casson on 8 Jun 1767 for £1.17.3. {Ref: MSA S960 or S752, p. 178}

ALL (AWL, AULL), WILLIAM (Delaware), b. c1724, Ireland (laborer, age 34 in 1758); pvt., recruited by Capt. Benjamin Noxon and enlisted on 1 May 1758. {Ref: ARDE I:18; ARPA (2nd Series) 2:566}

ALLASBOUGH, ADAM (Maryland), pvt., Capt. John Middaugh's Company Muster Roll, Frederick Co., circa 1757-1758, exact dates not given (served 30 days); bill of credit issued or paid in his behalf to Thomas Beatty, Jr. for £1.10.0 on 3 Apr 1767. {Ref: MSA S960 or S752, p. 172; CSOS:101}

ALLEE, SABRAH, see "Thomas Tilton," q.v.

ALLEN, DAVID (Delaware), pvt., Capt. Henry Vanbibber's Company of the Lower Counties on Delaware Troops at New Castle, enlisted on 5 May 1759. {Ref: ARDE I:26; ARPA (2nd Series) 2:594}

ALLEN, JAMES (Maryland), pvt., Capt. Elias Delashmutt's Company Muster Roll, Frederick Co., circa 1757-1758, exact dates not given (served 30 days); bill of credit issued or paid in his behalf to Elias Delashmut, Jr. on 16 Mar 1767 for £1.10.0. {Ref: MSA S960 or S752, p. 162; CSOS:94}

ALLEN, JOHN (Maryland), pvt., Capt. Joshua Beall's Company of MD Troops, Prince George's Co., circa 9 Oct 1757 to 30 Dec 1758; payment to him was recorded in Col. Dagworthy's account book on 7 Mar 1763. {Ref: MHS MS.375; CSOS:83; MHS MS.375.1} Bill of credit issued or paid to him for £1.19.0 in 1767, exact date not given. {Ref: MSA S960 or S752, p. 184}

ALLEN, MICHAEL, see "Michael Allix," q.v.

ALLEN, THOMAS (Maryland), pvt., Capt. Joshua Beall's Company Muster Roll, Prince George's Co., circa 1757-1758, exact dates not given; bill of credit issued or paid in his behalf to Thomas Richardson for £2.1.0 on 9 Jun 1767. {Ref: MSA S960 or S752, p. 184}

ALLISON, HENRY (Maryland), pvt., Capt. William Luckett's Company Muster Roll, Frederick Co., circa 1757-1758, exact dates not given (served 30 days); bill of credit issued or paid in his behalf to William Luckett, Jr. for £1.10.0 on 6 Apr 1767. {Ref: MSA S960 or S752, p. 170; CSOS:100}

ALLIX (ALEX), MICHAEL (Maryland), pvt., Capt. Peter Butler's Company Muster Roll, Frederick Co., circa 1757-1758, exact dates not given (served 34 days); bill of credit or order issued in his behalf for £1.14.0 and paid to Casper Shaff on 2 Mar 1767; name mistakenly transcribed once as "Michael Allen." {Ref: MSA S960 or S752, p. 166; CSOS:96} Soldier (rank not specified), Frederick Co., militia pay account submitted in 1758, exact date not given. {Ref: MHM 9:4, p. 367}

ALLNUTT, WILLIAM (Maryland), b. c1711, Calvert Co. (aged about 59 in 1770 deposition), son of William Allnutt and Sarah (Mears) Talbott, m. Mary (N) circa 1736 (poss. m. 2nd to Margaret Dare), had children Mary Jr., James Jr., Zacheus or Zachariah (b. 2 Sep 1745), William Jr., poss. Margaret and others (N), and d. testate by August 1781; served as a Justice of the Peace (1760-1777), Deputy Surveyor in 1763, Surveyor in 1766, was elected one of the representatives to carry out the Association agreed by the Continental Congress in 1774, was a Justice of the Orphans Court (1777-1780), and subscribed to the Oath of Fidelity and Allegiance in 1778. (Ref: "William Allnutt and wife Sarah (Mears) Talbott, widow of John Talbott, of Calvert County, Maryland: The Progenitors of the American Colonial Family of Allnutt with One Line of Their Descendants in Montgomery County, Maryland," by Ernest C. Allnutt, Jr., 1992). {Ref: MGSB 33:4, pp. 712-766} Ensign in Capt. Sutton Isaac's Company, Upper Hundred of the Cliffs, Calvert Co., 1748; he was poss. among those in Capt. Isaac's Company who were sent to the Western Frontier to help defend against the Indians circa 1756 (exact dates not given). {Ref: HCC:121-122}

ALLWINKLE, ISAAC (Maryland), farmer; pvt., Capt. Peregrine Brown's 7th Co. of Foot Militia, Kent Co., on 19 Feb 1758, by which time he had enlisted, but reportedly refused to appear and serve in arms against the enemy. {Ref: ARMD 31:283, 288}

ALLWINKLE, JOSEPH (Delaware), b. c1736, MD (laborer, age 22 in 1758); pvt., recruited by Capt. Benjamin Noxon and enlisted on 21 Apr 1758; pvt., Capt. Henry Vanbibber's Company of the Lower Counties on Delaware Troops at New Castle, enlisted on 1 May 1759. {Ref: ARDE I:18, 26; ARPA (2nd Series) 2:485, 566, 594}

ALRICKS (ALDRICKS), SAMUEL (Delaware), lieut., New Castle Hundred, Upper Regt. of Militia, South Division, New Castle Co., 1756. {Ref: ARDE I:11; ARPA (2nd Series) 2:526; HDE I:141}

ALTUM, JAMES (Delaware), pvt., Capt. French Battell's Company of Lower County Provincials, enlisted 28 May 1758. {Ref: ARDE I:16; ARPA (2nd Series) 2:555}

AMBRIES, FREEMAN (Maryland), b. c1734, MD (age 23 in 1757); pvt., 2nd Co. of VA Rangers under Capt. John Ashby on 21 Oct 1757. {Ref: MSR I:37}

ANDERSON, DANIEL (Maryland), pvt., Capt. John Dagworthy's Company of MD Troops, Frederick Co., from 9 May 1758 to 4 Jun 1758 (served 26 days) and noted as a "deserter from Virginia Rgt." {Ref: MHS MS.375.1; CSOS:75} Payment to him was recorded in Col. Dagworthy's account book on 8 Mar 1763. {Ref: MHS MS.375}

ANDERSON, EDWARD (Delaware), b. c1735, VA (age 24 in 1759); pvt., enlisted in Capt. John Wright's Company and mustered on 11 May 1759. {Ref: ARDE I:25; ARPA (2nd Series) 2:592}

ANDERSON, EDWARD (Delaware), b. c1738, Sussex, DE (laborer, age 20 in 1758); pvt., enlisted 9 May 1758 "for the campaign in the lower counties" by Capt. John McClughan. {Ref: ARDE I:17; ARPA (2nd Series) 2:570}

ANDERSON, JOHN (Delaware), ensign, St. George's Hundred, Lower Regt. of Militia, New Castle Co., 1756. {Ref: ARDE I:11; ARPA (2nd Series) 2:525; HDE I:141}

ANDERSON, JOHN (Delaware), pvt., Capt. Richard McWilliams' Company of Foot, New Castle Co., enlisted 28 Dec 1757. {Ref: ARDE I:15}

ANDERSON, JOHN (Maryland), patriot, Annapolis, Anne Arundel Co., pay account submitted for his exec. (unnamed) for his quartering soldiers in 1757 or 1758, exact dates not given. {Ref: MHM 9:3, p. 261}

ANDERSON, JOHN (Maryland), pvt., Capt. Richard Pearis' Company of MD Troops, Frederick Co., circa 9 Oct 1757 to 31 May 1758); pvt., Capt. John Dagworthy's Company of MD Troops, Frederick Co., from 1 Jun 1758 to 8 Dec 1758 (served 190 days) and reportedly deserted; however, payment to him was recorded in Col. Dagworthy's account book on 15 Jul 1762. {Ref: MHS MS.375.1; CSOS:75, 90; MHS MS.375}

ANDERSON, THOMAS (Maryland), pvt., Capt. Joseph Chapline's Company Muster Roll No. 4, Frederick Co., circa 1757-1758, exact dates not given (served 6 days); bill of credit issued or paid in his behalf to Joseph Chaplin for £0.6.0 on 13 Jun 1768. {Ref: MSA S960 or S752, p. 195; CSOS:105}

ANDERSON, WILLIAM (Maryland), pvt., Capt. Joseph Chapline's Company Muster Roll No. 1, Frederick Co., circa 1757-1758, exact dates not given (served 57 days); bill of credit issued or paid to him for £0.8.8 in 1767 (exact date not given) and order paid to Joseph Chaplin for £3.16.0 on 13 Jun 1768. {Ref: MSA S960 or S752, pp. 192, 194; CSOS:102} Cpl., Capt. Joseph Chapline's Company Muster Roll No. 4, Frederick Co., circa 1757-1758, exact dates not given (served 6 days); bill of credit issued or paid in his behalf to Joseph Chaplin for £0.8.0 on 5 Mar 1767. {Ref: MSA S960 or S752, p. 194; CSOS:104}

ANDERSON, WILLIAM (Maryland), sgt., Capt. Moses Chapline's Company Muster Roll No. 3, Frederick Co., circa 1757-1758, exact dates not given (served 6 days); bill of credit issued or paid in his behalf to Joseph Chaplin for £0.8.0 on 5 Mar 1767. {Ref: MSA S960 or S752, p. 198; CSOS:114}

ANDERSON, WILLIAM (Maryland), cpl., Capt. Peter Bainbridge's Company Muster Roll, Frederick Co., circa 1757-1758, exact dates not given (served 36 days); bill of credit issued or paid in his behalf to Joseph Chaplin on 5 Mar 1767 for £2.8.0. {Ref: MSA S960 or S752, p. 181; CSOS:110}

ANGIER, JOHN (Maryland), pvt., Capt. Peregrine Brown's Company Muster Roll, Kent Co., circa 1757-1758, exact dates not given (served 15 days); bill of credit issued or paid in his behalf to Robert Buchanan on 20 May 1767 for £0.15.0. {Ref: MSA S960 or S752, p. 179; CSOS:110} John Angier m. (N) and had children Thomas, John Jr., Unit, Araminta, Mary, and two other (N) daus. (siblings named in the will of John Angier, Jr. in 1794). {Ref: Kent Co. Wills 7:474}

ANGLIN, ATHANASIUS (Maryland), b. c1731, Anne Arundel Co.; soldier, Royal American Regt. (planter, age 25 in 1756), reported by Lieut. McBean at Annapolis as being a deserter from His Majesty's Royal American Regiment. {Ref: *MD Gazette*, 25 Nov 1756}

ANGLIN, JOHN (Maryland), b. c1741 on the Severn River in Anne Arundel Co.; pvt. (labourer, about age 18 in 1759), reported by Lieut. Harrington Baudin, at Annapolis, as having deserted from Capt. John Leland's recruiting party. {Ref: *MD Gazette*, 15 Mar 1759}

ANSLOW (ONSLOW), RICHARD (Delaware), b. c1725, Ireland; pvt., enlisted in Capt. John Wright's Company (age 34 in 1759) and mustered on 11 May 1759. {Ref: ARDE I:25; ARPA (2nd Series) 2:592}

ANSTILL, ISAAC (Delaware), b. c1737, VA (laborer, age 21 in 1758); pvt., recruited by Capt. Benjamin Noxon and enlisted on 21 Apr 1758. {Ref: ARDE I:18; ARPA (2nd Series) 2:566}

ANTHONY, JOSEPH (Maryland), pvt., Capt. Henry Casson's Company Muster Roll, Queen Anne's Co., circa 1757-1758, exact dates not given (served 27 days). {Ref: CSOS:109}

ANTHONY, WILLIAM (Delaware), b. c1739, Sussex, DE (age 20 in 1759); pvt., enlisted in Capt. John Wright's Company and mustered on 11 May 1759. {Ref: ARDE I:25; ARPA (2nd Series) 2:592}

APPLE (APPEL), PETER (Maryland), pvt., Capt. Stephen Rensburg's or Rensburger's Company Muster Roll, Frederick Co., circa 1757-1758, exact dates not given (erved 34 days); bill of credit or order issued to Casper Shaff and paid to David Cumming for £1.14.0 on 18 Apr 1767. {Ref: MSA S960 or S752, p. 183; CSOS:113} *Identification problem:* There were two men with this name who could have served in the war: (1) Peter Aple *[sic]* m. Catherina (N), had children Eve, Charlot, Mary, and Magdalena, and d. testate by 20 Apr 1779; and, (2) Peter Appel (Jr.?) *[sic]* m. (N), had a dau. Susanna, and d. testate by 10 May 1775. {Ref: WMG 4:4, p. 181; WMG 5:3, p. 134}

APPLE, SUSANNAH, see "Thomas Perkins," q.v.

APPLEGATE, THOMAS (Maryland), pvt., Capt. Joseph Chapline's Company Muster Roll No. 1, Frederick Co., circa 1757-1758, exact dates not given; bill of credit issued or paid in his behalf to Joseph Chaplin for £0.7.0 on 5 Mar 1767. {Ref: MSA S960 or S752, p. 191}

ARCHER, THOMAS, see "Patrick Mara," q.v.

ARMSTRONG, ARCHIBALD (Delaware), gent., b. c1727, Tyrone, Ireland (laborer, age 32 in 1759), m. Ann (N), had children William, John, Rebecca, and Margaret, d. testate by 18 May 1775 in Christiana Hundred, New Castle Co.; sgt., enlisted by Capt. James Armstrong for the PA Regt. on 26 Apr 1759. {Ref: ARDE I:25; ARPA (2nd Series) 2:585; CDSS:7}

ARMSTRONG, JAMES (Delaware), b. c1730, Fermanagh, Ireland (shoemaker, age 25 in 1758); sgt., enlisted 20 Apr 1758 "for the campaign in the lower counties" by Capt. John McClughan. {Ref: ARDE I:17; ARPA (2nd Series) 2:570}

ARMSTRONG, JOHN (Delaware), lieut., Christiana Hundred, Upper Regt. of Militia, North Division, New Castle Co., 1756; captain and recruiting officer for PA Troops in the "Three Lower Counties on Delaware" in 1759. {Ref: ARDE I:11, 27; ARPA (2nd Series) 2:526; HDE I:141}

ARMSTRONG, JOHN, see "George McSwain," q.v.

ARMSTRONG, WILLIAM (Delaware), colonel, New Castle Co. Regt., 1747-1748, during King George's War against Canada; colonel, Upper Regt. of Militia, New Castle Co., 1756. {Ref: CDSS:8; ARDE I:11; ARPA (2nd Series) 2:526; HDE I:141} Patriot who served as a Justice of the Peace, Justice of the Court of Oyer and Terminer, and Justice of the Court of Common Pleas, 1756-1761. {Ref: GRSD 1:13, 15}

ARMSTRONG, WILLIAM (Delaware), b. c1730, Fermanagh, Ireland (laborer, age 28 in 1758); cpl., enlisted 20 Apr 1758 "for the campaign in the lower counties" by Capt. John McClughan. {Ref: ARDE I:17; ARPA (2nd Series) 2:570}

ARNETT, JAMES (Delaware), b. c1737, Dorset, MD (laborer, age 22 in 1759); pvt., recruited by Capt. John Martin and enlisted on 18 May 1759 in Delaware (list of recruits dated 15 Jun 1759). {Ref: ARPA (2nd Series) 2:504}

ARNOLD, JOHN (Maryland), patriot and poss. soldier (rank not specified), Frederick Co., militia pay account submitted in 1758, exact date not given. {Ref: MHM 9:4, p. 368}

ARROWOOD (ARRAWOOD), JAMES (Maryland), pvt., Capt. Thomas Norris' Company, Frederick Co., circa 1757-1758, exact dates not given (served 30 days); bill of credit issued or paid in his behalf to Michael McGuire on 11 Apr 1767 for £1.10.0. {Ref: MSA S960 or S752, p. 176; CSOS:107}

ARSHCRAFT, RICHARD (Maryland), pvt., Capt. William McClellan's Company of MD Volunteers, Frederick Co., circa 1763-1764; on muster roll dated 15 Nov 1764 at Camp at the Forks of Muskingham. {Ref: ARMD 32:99}

ARVEN (ARVIN), WILLIAM (Maryland), pvt., Capt. Francis Ware's Company of MD Troops, Charles Co., from 9 Oct 1757 to 14 Sep 1758 (served 340 days) and was reported as killed; however, payment to him was recorded in Col. Dagworthy's account book on 7 Mar 1763 for work on Fort Cumberland. {Ref: MHS MS.375; CSOS:87; MHS MS.375.1}

ASBURY, JOSEPH (Maryland), pvt., Capt. Peregrine Brown's Company Muster Roll, Kent Co., circa 1757-1758, exact dates not given (served 15 days); bill of credit issued or paid in his behalf to Robert Buchanan on 20 Feb 1767 for £0.15.0; name listed once as "Joseph Ashbur." {Ref: MSA S960 or S752, pp. 179-180; CSOS:110}

ASHBY, ---- (Maryland), capt., Frederick Co., had five men (not named) who were killed by Indians in 1756 (exact date not given) about 4 or 5 miles from Fort Cumberland. {Ref: *MD Gazette*, 8 Apr 1756}

ASHBY, JOHN, see "Freeman Ambries" and "James Bell" and "Robert Goldsbarry" and "William Goldsbarry," q.v.

ASHBY, RUDY (Maryland), pvt., Capt. John White's Company Muster Roll, Frederick Co., circa 1757-1758, exact dates not given (served 6 days); bill of credit issued or paid to him for £0.6.0 in 1767, exact date not given. {Ref: MSA S960 or S752, p. 164: CSOS:95}

ASHLEY, ANN, see "James Smith," q.v.

ASHTON, GRACE, see "Richard Lee," q.v.

ASPERSHIP, RUDOLPH (Maryland), pvt., Capt. Joseph Chapline's Company Muster Roll No. 1, Frederick Co., circa 1757-1758, exact dates not given (served 21 days); bill of credit issued or paid in his behalf to Joseph Chaplin for £1.1.0 on 24 Apr 1767. {Ref: MSA S960 or S752, p. 192; CSOS:103}

ATHY, GEORGE (Maryland), pvt., Capt. Elias Delashmutt's Company Muster Roll, Frederick Co., 13 Aug 1757, exact dates not given (served 52 days); bill of credit issued or paid in his behalf to Elias Delashmut, Jr. on 16 Mar 1767 for £2.12.0. {Ref: MSA S960 or S752, p. 163; CSOS:98}

ATKINSON, ANNE, see "William Thomas," q.v.

ATKINSON, CHARLES (Maryland), pvt., Capt. John Dagworthy's Company of MD Troops, Frederick Co., from 9 Oct 1757 to 22 Jan 1759 (served 470 days) and reportedly deserted; however, payment to him was recorded in Col. Dagworthy's account book on 22 Jul 1763. {Ref: MHS MS.375.1; CSOS:75; MHS MS.375}

ATKINSON, JOHN (Maryland), patriot and poss. soldier (rank not specified), Queen Anne's Co., militia pay account submitted in 1758, exact date not given. {Ref: MHM 9:4, p. 367}

ATKINSON, WILLIAM, see "William Thomas," q.v.

AUGNER, WILLIAM (Maryland or Pennsylvania), b. America (date not given); pvt. in 1757 who was hanged at Carlisle for desertion. {Ref: *MD Gazette*, 10 Nov 1757}

AVART, ADAM or JOHN ADAM (Maryland), pvt., Capt. Peter Butler's Company Muster Roll, Frederick Co., circa 1757-1758, exact dates not given; bill of credit or order issued in his behalf for £1.14.0 and paid to Casper Shaff on 2 Mar 1767; name listed once as "Adam Evartt." {Ref: MSA S960 or S752, p. 166; CSOS:97}

AVEY, JACOB (Maryland), pvt., Capt. Moses Chapline's Company Muster Roll No. 3, Frederick Co., circa 1757-1758, exact dates not given (served 6 days); bill of credit issued or paid in his behalf to Joseph Chapline for £0.6.0 on 8 Jun 1767. {Ref: MSA S960 or S752, p. 198; CSOS:115}

AVEY, JOHN (Maryland), pvt., Capt. Moses Chapline's Company Muster Roll No. 3, Frederick Co., circa 1757-1758, exact dates not given (served 6 days); bill of credit issued or paid in his behalf to Joseph Chapline for £0.6.0 on 8 Jun 1767. {Ref: MSA S960 or S752, p. 198; CSOS:115}

AVEY, JOSEPH (Maryland), pvt., Capt. Moses Chapline's Company Muster Roll No. 3, Frederick Co., circa 1757-1758, exact dates not given (served 6 days); bill of credit issued or paid in his behalf to Joseph Chapline for £0.6.0 on 8 Jun 1767. {Ref: MSA S960 or S752, p. 198; CSOS:115}

AWBRY, FRANCIS (Maryland), pvt., Capt. Elias Delashmutt's Company Muster Roll, Frederick Co., 13 Aug 1757, exact dates not given (served 52 days); bill of credit issued or paid in his behalf to Elias Delashmut, Jr. on 16 Mar 1767 for £2.12.0. {Ref: MSA S960 or S752, p. 163; CSOS:98}

AYLER, ELECHART (Maryland), patriot and poss. soldier (rank not specified), Frederick Co., militia pay account submitted in 1758, exact date not given. {Ref: MHM 9:4, p. 366}

BACCHUS, RICHARD (Maryland), indentured servant and soldier who served in the French and Indian War some time between 1756 and 1763 (exact dates not known); his master Alexander Lawson, iron manufacturer, requested compensation from the Baltimore County Court due to the loss of use of Bacchus while in the service. {Ref: MHM 94:4, p. 426, citing Baltimore Co. Court Minutes}

BACK, JOHN (Maryland), pvt., Capt. Henry Sneavely's Company Muster Roll, Frederick Co., circa 1757-1758, exact dates not given; bill of credit issued or paid to him for £0.8.0 in 1767, exact date not given. {Ref: MSA S960 or S752, p. 190}

BACKER, ANDREW, see "Andrew Barker," q.v.

BACON, JOHN (Maryland), lieut., Capt. John Dagworthy's Company, Frederick Co., was killed and scalped by Indians in 1756 (exact date not given) about 4 or 5 miles from Fort Cumberland. {Ref: *MD Gazette*, 8 Apr 1756}

BADAMS, JOHN (Maryland), pvt., Capt. Moses Chapline's Company Muster Roll No. 3, Frederick Co., circa 1757-1758, exact dates not given (served 6 days); bill of credit issued or paid in his behalf to Joseph Chaplin for £0.6.0 on 5 Mar 1767. {Ref: MSA S960 or S752, p. 198; CSOS:115}

BAILEY, EDWARD (Delaware), b. c1738, Kent, DE (age 21 in 1759); pvt., enlisted in Capt. John Wright's Company and mustered on 11 May 1759. {Ref: ARDE I:25; ARPA (2nd Series) 2:592}

BAILEY, ENOCH, see "William Bailey," q.v.

BAILEY, GEORGE, see "William Bailey," q.v.

BAILEY, JABEZ, see "William Bailey," q.v.

BAILEY, JOHN (Maryland), pvt., Capt. John Dagworthy's Company of MD Troops, Frederick Co., from 9 Oct 1757 to 26 Dec 1758 (served 442 days) and reportedly deserted; however, payment to him was recorded in Col. Dagworthy's account book on 8 Mar 1763. {Ref: MHS MS.375.1; CSOS:75; MHS MS.375}

BAILEY, JOHN JR. (Maryland), pvt., Capt. Joseph Chapline's Company Muster Roll No. 1, Frederick Co., circa 1757-1758, exact dates not given (served 10 days); bill of credit issued or paid in his behalf to Joseph Chaplin for £0.10.0 on 13 Jun 1768. {Ref: MSA S960 or S752, p. 192; CSOS:102}

BAILEY, KERRENHAPPUCK, see "William Bailey," q.v.

BAILEY, MARY, see "William Bailey," q.v.

BAILEY, THOMAS (Delaware), pvt., Capt. French Battell's Company of Lower County Provincials, enlisted 19 May 1758. {Ref: ARDE I:16; ARPA (2nd Series) 2:555}

BAILEY, WILLIAM (Maryland), pvt., Capt. Tobias Stansbury's Company Muster Roll, Baltimore Co., circa 1757-1758, exact dates not given; bill of credit issued or paid in his behalf to Alexander Wells for £1.15.0 on 27 Mar 1767. {Ref: MSA S960 or S752, p. 186} *Identification problem:* There were four men with this name who could have served in the war: (1) William Bailey, b, 28 Oct 1735, son of George and Mary Bailey; (3) William Bailey, son of Jabez Bailey (d. 1769); (3) William Bailey, son of Enoch (d. 1766) and wife Kerrenhappuck Bailey; d. in Nottoway Co., VA by 1806, leaving a widow Prudence who sold land in Baltimore Co.; and, (4) William Bailey, shoemaker, who was a runaway servant in 1753. {Ref: BCF:17-19}

BAILEY, WILLIAM (Maryland), pvt., Capt. Joseph Chapline's Company Muster Roll No. 1, Frederick Co., circa 1757-1758, exact dates not given (served 14 days); bill of credit issued or paid in his behalf to Joseph Chaplin for £0.14.0 on 5 Mar 1767. {Ref: MSA S960 or S752, p. 191; CSOS:103}

BAINBRIDGE, PETER (Maryland), captain, Frederick Co., circa 1757-1758, exact dates not given; bill of credit issued or paid to him on 13 Apr 1767 for £6.16.7½; name listed once as "Peter Bambridge." {Ref: MSA S960 or S752, p. 181}

BAIRD (BARD), JOHN (Maryland), pvt., Capt. John White's Company Muster Roll, Frederick Co., circa 1757-1758, exact dates not given (served 6 days); bill

of credit issued or paid to him for £0.6.0 in 1767, exact date not given. {Ref: MSA S960 or S752, p. 164; CSOS:95}

BAKER, ---- (Maryland), lieut., Frederick Co., paid £218.19.5½ by the MD Assembly in 1756 "for the support of the ranging parties on the Western Frontier" from 9 Feb to 20 May 1756. {Ref: ARMD 52:674} Lieutenant on duty with Capt. John Dagworthy at Fort Cumberland in 1757. {Ref: ARMD 31:227}

BAKER, ABRAM (Maryland), pvt., Capt. Henry Sneavely's Company Muster Roll, Frederick Co., circa 1757-1758, exact dates not given; bill of credit issued or paid in his behalf to Joseph Chaplin for £0.8.0 on 13 Jun 1768. {Ref: MSA S960 or S752, p. 190}

BAKER, EARNEST (Maryland), pvt., Capt. Henry Sneavely's Company Muster Roll, Frederick Co., circa 1757-1758, exact dates not given; bill of credit issued or paid in his behalf to Joseph Chaplin for £0.8.0 on 9 Jun 1767. {Ref: MSA S960 or S752, p. 190} Pvt., Capt. Joseph Chapline's Company Muster Roll No. 1, Frederick Co., circa 1757-1758, exact dates not given (served 55 days); bill of credit issued or paid in his behalf to Joseph Chaplin for £2.4.0 on 5 Mar 1767. {Ref: MSA S960 or S752, p. 191; CSOS:103}

BAKER, ELIZABETH, see "Nathan Baker," q.v.

BAKER, ELIZABETH, see "Henry Baker," q.v.

BAKER, FRANCIS, see "Henry Baker," q.v.

BAKER, HENRY (Maryland), b. c1710, Cecil Co., son of Nathan Baker and Sarah Collet, m. Elizabeth (N), had sons Jeremiah, Jethro, Francis and Samuel, and d. 1768; patriot, merchant, member of MD Assembly (served on Arms and Ammunition Committee, 1758-1761), and captain by 1757. {Ref: BDML I:109-110; ARMD 55:44} Pay account submitted for quartering soldiers in 1757 or 1758, exact dates not given. {Ref: MHM 9:3, p. 262}

BAKER, ISAAC (Maryland), pvt., Capt. William Luckett's Company Muster Roll, Frederick Co., circa 1757-1758, exact dates not given (served 30 days); bill of credit issued or paid in his behalf to William Luckett, Jr. for £1.10.0 on 6 Apr 1767. {Ref: MSA S960 or S752, p. 169; CSOS:100} Militia pay account submitted in 1758, exact date not given; pay account submitted "for provisions found for Capt. Joseph Chapline's Company for 1,791 days" (exact dates not given). {Ref: MHM 9:4, pp. 367-368} He was paid £4.10.0 at Fort Frederick "for his wagon's attendance on the New Road" and £6 "for liquor dld. the parties that made the road from Pawlins' to Fort Frederick" on 30 Aug 1758. {Ref: ARMD 55:774-775}

BAKER, JACOB (Maryland), pvt., Capt. William Luckett's Company Muster Roll, Frederick Co., circa 1757-1758, exact dates not given (served 30 days); bill of credit issued or paid in his behalf to William Luckett, Jr. for £1.4.0 on 6 Apr 1767. {Ref: MSA S960 or S752, p. 169; CSOS:100}

BAKER, JEREMIAH, see "Henry Baker," q.v.

BAKER, JETHRO, see "Henry Baker," q.v.

BAKER, NATHAN (Maryland), b. c1715, Cecil Co., son of Nathan Baker and Sarah Collet, m. Joyce Yardley on 12 Jan 1736/7, had a dau. Elizabeth, and d. after 1778; miller, county justice (1741-1758), captain by 1755, and member of MD Assembly in 1763. {Ref: BDML I:111}

BAKER, NATHANIEL (Maryland), pvt., Capt. Joshua Beall's Company of MD Troops, Prince George's Co., from 9 Oct 1757 to 29 Jan 1758 when he was discharged. {Ref: MHS MS.375.1; CSOS:83} Payment to him was recorded in Col. Dagworthy's account book on 12 Jul 1762. {Ref: MHS MS.375}

BAKER, PETER (Maryland), pvt., Capt. John White's Company Muster Roll, Frederick Co., circa 1757-1758, exact dates not given (served 6 days); bill of credit issued or paid to him for £0.6.0 in 1767, exact date not given. {Ref: MSA S960 or S752, p. 164; CSOS:95}

BAKER, PHILIP (Maryland), pvt., Capt. John White's Company Muster Roll, Frederick Co., circa 1757-1758, exact dates not given (served 6 days); bill of credit issued or paid to him for £0.6.0 in 1767, exact date not given. {Ref: MSA S960 or S752, p. 164; CSOS:95}

BAKER, SAMUEL, see "Henry Baker," q.v.

BAKER, WILLIAM (Maryland), pvt., Capt. John White's Company Muster Roll, Frederick Co., circa 1757-1758, exact dates not given (served 6 days); bill of credit issued or paid to him for £0.6.0 in 1767, exact date not given. {Ref: MSA S960 or S752, p. 164; CSOS:95}

BALL, WILLIAM (Delaware), ensign, Mill Creek Hundred, Upper Regt. of Militia, North Division, New Castle Co., 1756. {Ref: ARDE I:11; ARPA (2nd Series) 2:526; HDE I:141}

BANING, NANCY, see "Solomon Downes," q.v.

BANIER, GEORGE, see "George Barrier," q.v.

BANKS, JOHN (Maryland), m. Barbara (N), had no children, and d. testate by 14 Jul 1776. {Ref: WMG 5:1, p. 19} Pvt., Capt. Moses Chapline's Company Muster Roll No. 3, Frederick Co., circa 1757-1758, exact dates not given (served 6 days); bill of credit issued or paid in his behalf to Joseph Chaplin for £0.6.0 on 5 Mar 1767. {Ref: MSA S960 or S752, p. 198; CSOS:115}

BARBER, DOROTHY, see "Thomas Greenfield," q.v.

BARD, NICHOLAS (Maryland), pvt., Capt. John White's Company Muster Roll, Frederick Co., circa 1757-1758, exact dates not given (served 6 days); bill of credit issued or paid to him for £0.6.0 in 1767, exact date not given. {Ref: MSA S960 or S752, p. 164; CSOS:95}

BARD, SAMUEL (Delaware), b. c1734, Ireland (age 25 in 1759); pvt., enlisted in Capt. John Wright's Company and mustered on 11 May 1759. {Ref: ARDE I:25; ARPA (2nd Series) 2:592}

BARE, JACOB (Maryland), pvt., Capt. Peter Butler's Company Muster Roll, Frederick Co., circa 1757-1758, exact dates not given (served 34 days); bill of credit or order issued in his behalf for £1.14.0 and paid to Casper Shaff on 2 Mar 1767. {Ref: MSA S960 or S752, p. 166; CSOS:96}

BARGAR, CHRISTOPHER (Maryland), pvt., Capt. Peter Butler's Company Muster Roll, Frederick Co., circa 1757-1758, exact dates not given (served 34 days); bill of credit or order issued in his behalf for £1.14.0 to Casper Shaff and paid to David Cumming on 18 Apr 1767. {Ref: MSA S960 or S752, p. 168; CSOS:96}

BARGAR, GEORGE (Maryland), pvt., Capt. Peter Butler's Company Muster Roll, Frederick Co., circa 1757-1758, exact dates not given (served 34 days). {Ref: CSOS:96}

BARGAR, PHILIP, see "Philip Berger," q.v.

BARKER (BACKER?), ANDREW, (Maryland), pvt., Capt. Peter Bainbridge's Company Muster Roll, Frederick Co., circa 1757-1758, exact dates not given (served 30 days); bill of credit issued or paid to him for £1.10.0 in 1767, exact date not given. {Ref: MSA S960 or S752, p. 180; CSOS:111}

BARKER, THOMAS (Maryland), pvt., Capt. Alexander Beall's Company of MD Troops, Frederick Co., from 9 Oct 1757 to 30 Dec 1758 when he received bounty for his service. {Ref: MHS MS.375.1; CSOS:80} Payment to him was recorded in Col. Dagworthy's account book on 16 Jul 1762. {Ref: MHS MS.375}

BARKER, THOMAS (Maryland), pvt., Capt. Richard Pearis' Company of MD Troops, Frederick Co., circa 9 Oct 1757 to 31 May 1758; pvt., Capt. Joshua Beall's Company of MD Troops, Prince George's Co., from 1 Jun 1758 to 8 Nov 1758. {Ref: MHS MS.375.1; CSOS:83, 90} Payment to him was recorded in Col. Dagworthy's account book on 14 Jul 1762; name listed once as "Thomas Barker or Parker." {Ref: MHS MS.375}

BARKMAN, PETER, see "Peter Barrickman," q.v.

BARLOW, SAMUEL (Delaware), b. c1725, Lancaster, England (dyer, age 33 in 1758); pvt., enlisted 12 May 1758 "for the campaign in the lower counties" by Capt. John McClughan. {Ref: ARDE I:17; ARPA (2nd Series) 2:570}

BARNES, ABRAHAM (Maryland), b. c1690, England, emigrated to MD from VA in 1740's, m. 1st to Mary Elizabeth King (1715-1739) and 2nd to Elizabeth Rousby by 1743, had children John, Richard and Mary, and d. testate in 1778, St. Mary's Company; merchant, member of MD Assembly (1745-1754), major by 1751 and colonel by 1756. {Ref: BDML I:114-115; ARMD 56:287}

BARNES, GEORGE (Maryland), sgt., Capt. Francis Ware's Company of MD Troops, Charles Co., from 9 Oct 1757 to 16 Feb 1758 (served 131 days) when he was discharged; payment to him was recorded in Col. Dagworthy's account book on 7 Mar 1763. {Ref: MHS MS.375.1; CSOS:87; MHS MS.375}

BARNES, JOHN, see "Abraham Barnes," q.v.

BARNES (BARNS), JOHN (Delaware), of Little Creek Hundred, m. (N), had children John, William, Stephen, and Percilla, and d. testate by 10 Jan 1767. {Ref: CDSS:10} Captain, Upper Part of Little Creek Hundred, Militia of Kent Co. on Delaware, 1756. {Ref: ARDE I:12; ARPA (2nd Series) 2:527-529; HDE I:141}

BARNES, MARY, see "Abraham Barnes," q.v.

BARNES, RICHARD, see "Abraham Barnes," q.v.

BARNES, WILLIAM (Maryland), pvt., Capt. Stephen Rensburg's or Rensburger's Company Muster Roll, Frederick Co., circa 1757-1758, exact dates not given (served 42 days); bill of credit issued or paid in his behalf to Stephen Rensburg or Rensburger for £2.2.0 on 27 Mar 1767. {Ref: MSA S960 or S752, p. 182; CSOS:112}

BARNETT, JAMES (Maryland), b. c1732, MD (age 24 in 1756); pvt., Capt. Christopher Gist's Company of VA Militia, 13 Jul 1756, enlisted at Baltimore. {Ref: MSR I:37}

BARNETT, JOHN (Maryland or Pennsylvania), pvt., Capt. Culbertson's Company, was wounded in "a recent battle with the Indians" in 1756 (exact date not given) in Cumberland Co., PA, after the burning of McCord's Fort. {Ref: *MD Gazette*, 29 Apr 1756}

BARNETT, MATTHIAS (Maryland), pvt., Capt. Jonathan Hagar's Company Muster Roll, Frederick Co., circa 1757-1758, exact dates not given (served 6 days); bill of credit issued or paid to him for £0.6.0 in 1767, exact date not given. {Ref: MSA S960 or S752, p. 173; CSOS:106}

BARR, DAVID (Delaware), b. c1705, m. (N), had a dau. Francina, and d. 2 Jul 1787; lieut., Pencader Hundred, Lower Regt. of Militia, New Castle Co., 1756; subscribed to the Oath of Fidelity and Allegiance in 1778 in Elkton, MD; buried in Head of Christiana Cem., New Castle Co., DE. {Ref: RPDE:12; ARDE I:12; ARPA (2nd Series) 2:525; HDE I:141}

BARRANCE, GEORGE (Maryland), sgt., Capt. Alexander Beall's Company of Foot, Frederick Co., by August 1757 at which time he was stationed at Fort Frederick. {Ref: FCLR: 30} See "John Boston" and "Adam Coonce" and "John Harlin" and "Joseph Hughes" and "William Kimboll" and "Aron Lee" and "Benjamin Martin" and "Henry Pitnar" and "William Smith" and "Henry Yea," q.v.

BARRETT (BARRET), BENJAMIN (Maryland), soldier (rank not specified), Calvert Co.; on 10 May 1756 a petition was submitted to the Governor of MD by sundry inhabitants of the county for commuting the death sentence of Benjamin Barret who was convicted of stealing, stating clemency was due him as a veteran of the French and Indian War. {Ref: CMSP-The Black Books:131}

BARRETT, JAMES (Delaware), b. c1735, Ireland (laborer, age 23 in 1758); pvt., "formally with ye Royal Americans," recruited by Capt. Benjamin Noxon and enlisted on 24 Apr 1758. {Ref: ARDE I:18; ARPA (2nd Series) 2:566}

BARRETT (BARRITT), JONATHAN (Maryland), patriot and poss. soldier (rank not specified), Kent Co., militia pay account submitted in 1758, exact date not given. {Ref: MHM 9:4, p. 369}

BARRETT (BARRET), THOMAS (Maryland), pvt., Capt. Richard Pearis' Company of MD Troops, Frederick Co., circa 9 Oct 1757 to 31 May 1758; pvt., Capt. Joshua Beall's Company of MD Troops, Prince George's Co., from 1 Jun 1758 to 30 Dec 1758. {Ref: MHS MS.375.1; CSOS:83, 90} Payment to him was recorded in Col. Dagworthy's account book on 12 Jul 1762. {Ref: MHS MS.375}

BARRICK, CHRISTIAN (Maryland), pvt., Capt. John Middaugh's Company Muster Roll, Frederick Co., circa 1757-1758, exact dates not given (served 30 days); bill of credit issued or paid in his behalf to Thomas Beatty, Jr. for £0.17.0 on 3 Apr 1767. {Ref: MSA S960 or S752, p. 172; CSOS:100}

BARRICK, EDWARD (Maryland), pvt., Capt. Henry Casson's Company Muster Roll, Queen Anne's Co., circa 1757-1758, exact dates not given (served 27 days); bill of credit issued or paid in his behalf to Capt. Casson on 27 Mar 1767 for £1.7.0; name listed once as "Edward Berwick." {Ref: MSA S960 or S752, pp. 177-178; CSOS:109}

BARRICK, HANDEL (Maryland), pvt., Capt. John Middaugh's Company Muster Roll, Frederick Co., circa 1757-1758, exact dates not given (served 30 days); bill of credit issued or paid in his behalf to Robert Wood for £0.17.0 on 4 Mar 1767; name listed once as "Handle Barrack." {Ref: MSA S960 or S752, p. 171; CSOS:102}

BARRICK, JOHN (Maryland), pvt., Capt. John Middaugh's Company Muster Roll, Frederick Co., circa 1757-1758, exact dates not given (served 30 days); bill of credit issued or paid in his behalf to Thomas Beatty, Jr. for £0.17.0 on 3 Apr 1767. {Ref: MSA S960 or S752, p. 172; CSOS:101}

BARRICK, PETER (Maryland), pvt., Capt. John Middaugh's Company Muster Roll, Frederick Co., circa 1757-1758, exact dates not given (served 30 days); bill of credit or order issued to Casper Shaff and paid to David Cumming for £1.10.0 on 18 Apr 1767. {Ref: MSA S960 or S752, p. 172; CSOS:100}

BARRICK, WILLIAM (Maryland), pvt., Capt. John Middaugh's Company Muster Roll, Frederick Co., circa 1757-1758, exact dates not given (served 30 days); bill of credit or order issued to Casper Shaff and paid to David Cumming for £1.10.0 on 18 Apr 1767. {Ref: MSA S960 or S752, p. 172; CSOS:100}

BARRICKMAN (BARRACKMAN), GEORGE (Maryland), pvt., Capt. Alexander Beall's Company of MD Troops, Frederick Co., from 9 Oct 1757 to 10 Jan 1758 when he was discharged. {Ref: MHS MS.375.1; CSOS:80} Payment to him was recorded in Col. Dagworthy's account book on 26 Feb 1763. {Ref: MHS MS.375}

BARRICKMAN, JOHN (Maryland), pvt., Capt. Alexander Beall's Company of Foot, 1757-1758, recorded his discharge in Frederick Co. Court on 12 Jan 1758. Capt. Beall certified that "John Barrickham *[sic]* served as a private soldier for 12 months and is hereby discharged, having received clothing and other necessaries, and also has full pay to the 8th of October last, as appears by receipt 10 Jan 1757." John Barrickman signed with his "X" mark. {Ref: FCLR:37}

BARRICKMAN (BARKMAN), PETER (Maryland), pvt., Capt. Moses Chapline's Company Muster Roll No. 3, Frederick Co., circa 1757-1758, exact dates not given (served 6 days); bill of credit issued or paid in his behalf to Joseph Chaplin for £0.6.0 on 24 Apr 1767. {Ref: MSA S960 or S752, p. 198; CSOS:114}

BARRIER (BANIER?), GEORGE (Maryland), pvt., Capt. Alexander Beall's Company of MD Troops, Frederick Co., from 9 Oct 1757 to 27 Jan 1758 when he was discharged. {Ref: MHS MS.375.1; CSOS:80} Payment to him was recorded in Col. Dagworthy's account book on 12 Jul 1762. {Ref: MHS MS.375}

BARTLETT, SAMUEL (Maryland), pvt., Capt. Henry Casson's Company Muster Roll, Queen Anne's Co., circa 1757-1758, exact dates not given (served 27 days); bill of credit issued to him for £1.7.0 in 1767, exact date not given. {Ref: MSA S960 or S752, p. 177; CSOS:109}

BARTON, JACOB (Maryland), pvt., Capt. John Middaugh's Company Muster Roll, Frederick Co., circa 1757-1758, exact dates not given (served 30 days); bill of credit issued or paid in his behalf to John Beatty for £1.10.0 on 1 Apr 1767. {Ref: MSA S960 or S752, p. 172; CSOS:100}

BASSET, JOHN (Delaware), b. c1732, Wales (laborer, age 26 in 1758); pvt., recruited by Capt. Benjamin Noxon and enlisted on 29 Apr 1758; subscribed to the Oath of Fidelity and Allegiance in 1778. {Ref: ARDE I:18; ARPA (2nd Series) 2:566; RPDE:13}

BASTON, JOHN (Delaware), b. c1730, America (laborer, age 28 in 1758); pvt., recruited by Capt. Benjamin Noxon and enlisted on 7 May 1758. {Ref: ARDE I:18; ARPA (2nd Series) 2:566}

BATELY, HENRY, see "Henry Butler," q.v.

BATEMAN, MARTHA, see "Henry Hall," q.v.

BATT, WALTER (Maryland), patriot, Annapolis, Anne Arundel Co., pay account submitted for quartering soldiers in 1757 or 1758, exact dates not given. {Ref: MHM 9:3, p. 260}

BATTELL (BATTLE), FRENCH (Delaware), ensign in Capt. David Finney's Company, New Castle Co., 1747-1748, during King George's War against Canada; lieut., militia, Town of Dover, Kent Co., 1756. {Ref: ARDE I:12; ARPA (2nd Series) 2:527-529; HDE I:141} 1st lieut., 20 Apr 1758; quartermaster and adjutant "of the lower government on Delaware" on 7 Jun 1758; capt., Lower County Provincials Co., 1758; commissioned capt. in 3rd Bttn., PA Regt., on 22 May 1759; major, Kent Co. militia, 1775; lieut. colonel, 1st Bttn., 1777; colonel, 1779; d. by January 1782 at which time admin. of the estate of "French Battle, Colonel, Town of Dover" was granted to Elizabeth Battle (who d. by March 1794 and the heirs were John F., French, James, and Cornelius Battell). {Ref: ARDE I:16, 20; ARPA (2nd Series) 2:555, 579, 582; RPDE:13; CDSS:11-12}

BAUDIN, HARRINGTON (Maryland), lieut., 58th Regt., stationed at Annapolis, 1759; reported deserters from Capt. John Leland's recruiting party to the local newspaper. {Ref: *MD Gazette*, 15 Mar 1759}

BAUMAN, JACOB (Maryland), indentured servant and soldier who served in the French and Indian War some time between 1756 and 1763 (exact dates not known); his master Andrew Stiger, innkeeper and butcher, requested compensation from the Baltimore County Court due to the loss of use of Bauman while in the service. {Ref: MHM 94:4, p. 426, citing Baltimore Co. Court Minutes}

BAXTER, EDWARD (Maryland), b. c1733, Baltimore Co., son of Edmund and Mary Baxter; d. after 1768 (date of father's will). {Ref: BCF:32} Pvt., Capt. Tobias Stansbury's Company Muster Roll, Baltimore Co., circa 1757-1758, exact dates not given; bill of credit or order issued and assigned to William Lux paid to Robert Adair for £2.12.0 on 1 Apr 1767. {Ref: MSA S960 or S752, p. 186}

BAXTER, ELIZABETH, see "James Baxter," q.v.

BAXTER, GRACE, see "James Baxter," q.v.

BAXTER, JAMES (Maryland), b. c1720, m. Elizabeth (N), had children William, Joseph, Elizabeth, Grace, Mary Waugh, and Rachel, and d. 24 Feb 1763, Cecil Co.; merchant, sheriff, county justice (1747-1763), member of MD Assembly (1750-1751), and colonel by 1763. {Ref: BDML I:118; *MD Gazette*, 10 Mar 1763}

BAXTER, JOHN (Maryland), pvt., Capt. William Luckett's Company Muster Roll, Frederick Co., circa 1757-1758, exact dates not given (served 30 days); bill of credit issued or paid in his behalf to William Luckett, Jr. for £1.10.0 on 6 Apr 1767. {Ref: MSA S960 or S752, p. 169; CSOS:100}

BAXTER, JOSEPH, see "John Baxter," q.v.

BAXTER, MARY, see "Edward Baxter" and "James Baxter," q.v.

BAXTER, RACHEL, see "James Baxter," q.v.

BAXTER, WILLIAM, see "John Baxter," q.v.

BAYARD, PETER (Maryland), b. 10 Jul 1702, Cecil Co., son of Samuel Bayard and Susanna Bouchelle, m. Susanna Richardson, had daus. Susanna, Elizabeth, and Nansey (Ann), and d. testate by 26 Nov 1766; farmer, merchant, captain by 1739, county justice (1744-1757), member of MD Assembly (1745-1749), and colonel by 1756. {Ref: BDML I:118-119; ARMD 31:244} Militia pay account submitted in 1758, exact date not given. {Ref: MHM 9:4, p. 370}

BEADLES, WILLIAM (Maryland), pvt., Capt. William McClellan's Company of MD Volunteers, Frederick Co., circa 1763-1764; on muster roll dated 15 Nov 1764 at Camp at the Forks of Muskingham. {Ref: ARMD 32:99}

BEAKE, MARGARET, see "Horatio Sharpe," q.v.

BEALE, ELIZABETH, see "Richard Dorsey," q.v.

BEALL, ALEXANDER (Maryland), captain, Frederick Co., paid £152.17.4 by the MD Assembly in 1756 "for the support of the ranging parties on the Western Frontier" from 13 Mar to 21 May 1756. {Ref: ARMD 52:674} "Major Prather and Capt. Alexander Beall are to raise more men for the defense of the frontier regions of Maryland." {Ref: *MD Gazette*, 11 Mar 1756} Capt., MD Troops, Frederick Co., from 9 Oct 1757 to 30 Dec 1758 (muster roll); payment to his estate was recorded in Col. Dagworthy's account book on 20 Jul 1762. {Ref: MHS MS.375.1; ARMD 55:614; MHS MS.375; CSOS:79}

BEALL, AMELIA, see "Joshua Beall" and "Samuel Beall," q.v.

BEALL, ANN, see "Samuel Beall," q.v.

BEALL, BASIL, see "Samuel Beall," q.v.

BEALL, BROOKE, see "Samuel Beall," q.v.

BEALL, CHARLES, see "Joshua Beall," q.v.

BEALL, EDWARD (Maryland), pvt., Capt. Alexander Beall's Company of MD Troops, Frederick Co., from 9 Oct 1757 to 30 Dec 1758 when he received bounty for his service. {Ref: MHS MS.375.1; CSOS:80} Payment to him was recorded in Col. Dagworthy's account book on 11 Jul 1762. {Ref: MHS MS.375}

BEALL, ELEANOR, see "Joshua Beall," q.v.

BEALL, ELIZABETH, see "Joshua Beall" and "Samuel Beall," q.v.

BEALL, ESTHER, see "Joseph Belt," q.v.

BEALL, FRANCES, see "Samuel Beall," q.v.

BEALL, GEORGE (Maryland), drummer, Capt. Peter Bainbridge's Company Muster Roll, Frederick Co., circa 1757-1758, exact dates not given (served 41 days); bill of credit issued or paid in his behalf to Casper Shaff on 2 Mar 1767 for £2.14.3; name listed once as "George Belt." {Ref: MSA S960 or S752, p. 180; CSOS:110} See "Joshua Beall," q.v.

BEALL, GEORGE (Maryland), b. 1695, son of Ninian Beall and Ruth Moore, m. Elizabeth Brooke, had children George, Thomas, and Elizabeth, and d. 1780; colonel by 1757, Frederick Co. (stated he was aged about 60 in a 1757 deposition). {Ref: BDML I:122, 125; FCLR:79}

BEALL, ISAAC, see "Samuel Beall," q.v.

BEALL, JEREMIAH, see "Samuel Beall," q.v.

BEALL, JOHN (Maryland), pvt., Capt. William Luckett's Company Muster Roll, Frederick Co., circa 1757-1758, exact dates not given (served 30 days); bill of credit issued or paid in his behalf to William Luckett, Jr. for £1.10.0 on 6 Apr 1767. {Ref: MSA S960 or S752, p. 170; CSOS:99}

BEALL, JOSHUA (Maryland), b. c1719, Prince George's Co., son of Capt. Charles Beall and Mary Wolstad, m. 1st to Eleanor Smith Greenfield by 1748 and 2nd to Elizabeth Waring (widow of Basil Waring) on 3 Feb 1787, had children George and Amelia by first wife, and d. testate in 1796; gentleman, planter, county justice (1751-1759, 1762-1787), county sheriff (1759-1762), captain of troops at Fort Frederick and Fort Duquesne (1756-1758, received £200 from the MD Assembly in December 1765 for his services and expenses during the French and Indian War), colonel of militia (1775-1776), and attended Provincial Conventions (1774-1775). {Ref: BDML I:122-123; ARMD 59:251} Capt., MD Troops, Prince George's Co., from 9 Oct 1757 to 30 Dec 1758 (muster roll). {Ref: MHS MS.375.1; ARMD 59:196; CSOS:83} Payment to him was recorded in Col. Dagworthy's account book on 14 Jul 11762. {Ref: MHS MS.375} Capt., Prince George's Co. Muster Roll, bill of credit issued or paid to him for £24.3.1½ on 23 Feb 1767. {Ref: MSA S960 or S752, p. 184} See "Anguish Shaw," q.v.

BEALL, JOSIAS, see "Charles King" and "David Flint" and "John Rofman," q.v.

BEALL, LEVEN (Maryland), 2nd lieut., Capt. John Dagworthy's Company of MD Troops, Frederick Co., from 9 Oct 1757 to 8 Nov 1758 (served 264 days); 1st lieut., Capt. Alexander Beall's Company of MD Troops, Frederick Co., from 9 Nov 1758 to 30 Dec 1758 (served 52 days). {Ref: MHS MS.375.1; CSOS:75, 79}

BEALL, MORDECAI (Maryland), company clerk, Capt. Stephen Rensburg's or Rensburger's Company Muster Roll, Frederick Co., circa 1757-1758, exact dates not given (served 42 days); bill of credit issued or paid in his behalf to Casper Shaff for £1.14.0 on 2 Mar 1767. {Ref: MSA S960 or S752, p. 182; CSOS:112}

BEALL (BELL), NINIAN (Maryland), patriot, Frederick Co., pay account submitted for 1 hogshead of beef supplied for the use of the militia in 1758, exact date not given. {Ref: MHM 9:4, p. 370}

BEALL, NINIAN (Maryland), son of Ninian Beall; patriot and poss. soldier (rank not specified), Frederick Co., militia pay account submitted in 1758, exact date not given. {Ref: MHM 9:4, p. 367}

BEALL, NINIAN (Maryland), son of William Beall; pvt., Capt. Joshua Beall's Company Muster Roll, Prince George's Co., circa 1757-1758, exact dates not given; bill of credit issued to Casper Shaff and paid to David Cumming for Beall's exec. (unnamed) for £1.11.0 on 18 Apr 1767. {Ref: MSA S960 or S752, p. 184}

BEALL, NINIAN, see "George Beall," q.v.

BEALL, REBECCA, see "Nathan Magruder," q.v.

BEALL, REZIN (Maryland), pvt., Capt. Joshua Beall's Company Muster Roll, Prince George's Co., circa 1757-1758, exact dates not given; bill of credit issued or paid to him for £2.3.0 on 20 Mar 1767. {Ref: MSA S960 or S752, p. 184} See "Thomas Brightwell," q.v.

BEALL, REZIN (Maryland), ensign in Capt. Francis Ware's Company of MD Troops, Charles Co., from 9 Oct 1757 to 8 Nov 1758 (served 396 days). {Ref: MHS MS.375} "Ensign Beall was wounded in the late battle" (date not given). {Ref: *MD Gazette*, 2 Nov 1758} 2nd lieut., Capt. Francis Ware's Company of MD Troops, Charles Co., from 9 Nov 1758 to 30 Dec 1758; account paid 15 Jul 1762. {Ref: MHS MS.375.1; CSOS:87; MHS MS.375} Also received £100 from the MD Assembly in December 1765 for his services and expenses during the French and Indian War. {Ref: ARMD 59:196, 251}

BEALL, RICHARD (Maryland), pvt., Capt. Joshua Beall's Company Muster Roll, Prince George's Co., circa 1757-1758, exact dates not given; bill of credit issued or paid in his behalf to David Ross for £2.1.0 on 16 Mar 1767. {Ref: MSA S960 or S752, p. 184} See "Samuel Beall," q.v.

BEALL, SAMUEL (Maryland), b. c1713, Prince George's Co. (now Frederick Co.), son of John Beall and Verlinda Magruder, m. Eleanor Brooke (b. 7 Mar 1717/8) circa 1735, had children Samuel, Richard, Walter, Thomas, Brooke, Isaac, Basil, Jeremiah, Verlinda, Amelia, Eleanor, Ann, Rebecca, and Frances, and d. testate by 10 Jan 1778, Washington Co.; planter, ironmaster, sheriff of Frederick Co. (1753-1756, 1759-1762), county justice (1763-1775), colonel by 1761, and member of MD Assembly (1775-1777). {Ref: BDML I:124-125; MDG I:105}

BEALL, THOMAS (Maryland), recruiting officer, Prince George's Co., 1757; Gov. Horatio Sharpe wrote to the MD Assembly on 7 Dec 1757, stating in part: "One Thomas Beall, a young fellow of Prince George's Co. (who was empowered by me to enlist men for his Majesty's Service, in consequence of several Acts of Assembly lately passed in this province) is accused of having pretended to enlist the said [Edward] Seares, [Thomas] Hill and [David] Mackelfish, of treating them afterwards as deserters, of compelling Seares to pay £10 for a discharged, which he could not give, and of endeavouring to oblige the other two to purchase their discharges likewise. Mr. Beall is not present to hear what is alleged against him, yet I don't think it would be right to condemn him unheard; he is no officer that I know of, neither is he in the least dependent on me; and if the complainants can prove that he has acted illegally, I hope they may redress themselves without applying to any branch of the Legislature; but if it should, on further enquiry, appear that they were duly enlisted, you will not, I am persuaded, take it amiss if they are apprehended and delivered up to one of his Majesty's Officers." {Ref: ARMD 55:320} See "Samuel Beall," q.v.

BEALL, VERLINDA, see "Samuel Beall," q.v.

BEALL, WALTER, see "Samuel Beall," q.v.

BEALL, WILLIAM (Maryland), pvt., Capt. Thomas Norris' Company, Frederick Co., circa 1757-1758, exact dates not given; bill of credit issued or paid in his behalf to Michael McGuire on 11 Mar 1767 for £1.10.0; name mistakenly listed once as "William Boalt." {Ref: MSA S960 or S752, p. 176; CSOS:107}

BEALL, WILLIAM (Maryland), pvt., Capt. Stephen Rensburg's or Rensburger's Company Muster Roll, Frederick Co., circa 1757-1758, exact dates not given (served 42 days); bill of credit issued or paid in his behalf to Casper Shaff for £1.14.0 on 2 Mar 1767. {Ref: MSA S960 or S752, p. 182; CSOS:112}

BEALL (BELL), WILLIAM (Maryland), pvt., Capt. Henry Casson's Company Muster Roll, Queen Anne's Co., circa 1757-1758, exact dates not given (served 27 days); bill of credit issued or paid in his behalf to Capt. Casson on 27 Feb 1767 for £1.7.0. {Ref: MSA S960 or S752, p. 177; CSOS:109} He may have been the William Bell who m. Ann Hardcastle on 14 Apr 1755 at St. John's Parish, Queen Anne's Co., and had children Samuel, Ann, Thomas, and Margarett. {Ref: MGSB 16:2, pp. 73, 79}

BEAN, JOHN (Maryland), pvt., Capt. Moses Chapline's Company Muster Roll No. 3, Frederick Co., circa 1757-1758, exact dates not given (served 6 days); bill of credit issued or paid in his behalf to Joseph Chaplin for £0.6.0 on 24 Apr 1767; one source listed the name twice on this muster roll. {Ref: MSA S960 or S752, p. 198; CSOS:114}

BEAN, RICHARD (Maryland), pvt., Capt. Joshua Beall's Company Muster Roll, Prince George's Co., circa 1757-1758, exact dates not given; bill of credit issued or paid to him for £2.3.0 in 1767, exact date not given. {Ref: MSA S960 or S752, p. 184}

BEANE, WILLIAM (Delaware), b. c1733, MD (cordwainer, age 25 in 1758); pvt., recruited by Capt. Benjamin Noxon and enlisted on 29 Apr 1758. {Ref: ARDE I:18; ARPA (2nd Series) 2:485, 566}

BEANES, COLMORE, see "Philip Connoly" and "Aaron Holdsworth," q.v.

BEARD, JAMES (Maryland), pvt., Capt. Joshua Beall's Company of MD Troops, Prince George's Co., circa 9 Oct 1757 to 30 Dec 1758; pvt., Capt. John Dagworthy's Company of MD Troops, Frederick Co., from 31 Dec 1758 to 27 Jan 1759 (served 27 days) and reportedly deserted; however, payment to him was recorded in Col. Dagworthy's account book on 12 Jul 1762. {Ref: MHS MS.375.1; CSOS:75, 83; MHS MS.375}

BEARD, PAUL (Maryland), pvt., Capt. Thomas Norris' Company, Frederick Co., circa 1757-1758, exact dates not given (served 30 days); bill of credit issued or paid in his behalf to Jacob Yingland on 10 Apr 1767 for £1.10.0. {Ref: MSA S960 or S752, p. 176; CSOS:108}

BEARD, PHILIP (Maryland), pvt., Capt. Thomas Norris' Company, Frederick Co., circa 1757-1758, exact dates not given (served 30 days); bill of credit issued or paid in his behalf to Valentine Rinehart on 6 May 1767 for £1.10.0. {Ref: MSA S960 or S752, p. 176; CSOS:108}

BEARDY, CHRISTIAN, see "Samuel Saunders," q.v.

BEATON, THOMAS (Maryland), pvt., Capt. William Luckett's Company Muster Roll, Frederick Co., circa 1757-1758, exact dates not given (served 30 days); bill of credit issued or paid in his behalf to William Luckett, Jr. for £1.10.0 on 6 Apr 1767. {Ref: MSA S960 or S752, p. 169; CSOS:100}

BEATTY, CHARLES (Maryland), pvt., Capt. Peter Butler's Company Muster Roll, Frederick Co., circa 1757-1758, exact dates not given (served 34 days); militia pay account submitted in 1758, exact date not given. {Ref: MHM 9:4, p. 368;

CSOS:96} Bill of credit or order issued in his behalf for £1.14.0 and paid to Thomas Beatty, Jr. on 3 Apr 1767. {Ref: MSA S960 or S752, p. 168}

BEATTY, GEORGE (Maryland), pvt., Capt. Peter Butler's Company Muster Roll, Frederick Co., circa 1757-1758, exact dates not given (served 34 days); bill of credit or order issued in his behalf for £1.14.0 and paid to Robert Wood on 4 Mar 1767. {Ref: MSA S960 or S752, p. 167; CSOS:96}

BEATTY, JOHN (Delaware), b. c1734, Ireland (weaver, age 24 in 1758); pvt., recruited by Capt. Benjamin Noxon and enlisted on 1 May 1758; pvt., New Castle Co. militia, 1778. {Ref: ARDE I:18; ARPA (2nd Series) 2:566; RPDE:14}

BEATTY, JOHN (Maryland), pvt., Capt. John Middaugh's Company Muster Roll, Frederick Co., circa 1757-1758, exact dates not given (served 30 days); bill of credit issued or paid to him for £1.10.0 on 1 Apr 1767. {Ref: MSA S960 or S752, p. 172; CSOS:100} See "Jacob Barton," q.v.

BEATTY, THOMAS JR. (Maryland), ensign in Capt. John Middaugh's Company Muster Roll, Frederick Co., circa 1757-1758, exact dates not given (served 30 days); bill of credit issued or paid to him for £3 on 23 Feb 1767. {Ref: MSA S960 or S752, p. 171; CSOS:100} See "Philip Coonce," q.v.

BEATTY, WILLIAM (Maryland), patriot and poss. soldier (rank not specified), Frederick Co., militia pay account submitted in 1758, exact date not given. {Ref: MHM 9:4, p. 368}

BEAVER, PETER (Maryland), pvt., Capt. Peter Bainbridge's Company Muster Roll, Frederick Co., circa 1757-1758, exact dates not given (served 28 days); bill of credit issued or paid in his behalf to Jacob Young on 4 Mar 1767 for £1.8.0. {Ref: MSA S960 or S752, p. 181; CSOS:111}

BEDDOES, SARAH, see "Godfrey Vine," q.v.

BEDFORD, GUNNING (Delaware), b. 1742, m. Mary Read (dau. of Col. John Read), had no children, and d. 20 Sep 1797; buried in Episcopal Cem. in New Castle; lieut., militia, 1756; major, militia, 1775; commissioned lieut. colonel, DE Bttn. of Continental Troops, 19 Jan 1776; colonel, 2nd Regt. of Militia, 1778; Attorney General of DE, 1783; member of Continental Congress, 1783-1787; and, Governor of Delaware, 1796-1797. {Ref: CDSS:12; RPDE:14}

BEDWELL, JAMES (Delaware), pvt., Kent Co. Militia, Capt. John Caton's Company, 25 Apr 1757 (date of muster roll). {Ref: ARDE I:13} *Identification problem:* There were two men with his name who could have served in the war: (1) James Bedwell, son of James Bedwell, b. by 1740 in Kent Co., may have been in Pasquotank Co., NC by 1790 and Union Co., SC by 1800; and, (2) James Bedwell d. intestate in Kent Co., DE by 15 Feb 1771 at which time Robert Bedwell, next of kin, was granted letters of admin. {Ref: CFS 1:24-25; CDSS:12}

BEDWELL, THOMAS (Delaware), b. by 1735, Kent Co., son of James Bedwell, m. Jemima (N), poss. Jemima Johnson, had children Thomas, George, James, Preston, Caleb, Sarah, and Elizabeth, removed to Pasquotank Co., NC, returned to Kent Co., DE in 1775, and d. testate by 17 Apr 1794. {Ref: CFD 1:24-25; CDSS:13} Pvt., Kent Co. Militia, Capt. John Caton's Company, by 25 Apr 1757 (date of muster roll). {Ref: ARDE I:14}

BEEKENBOCK (BEEKENBOK), GASPER (Maryland), pvt., Capt. Peter Bainbridge's Company Muster Roll, Frederick Co., circa 1757-1758, exact dates not given (served 28 days); bill of credit issued or paid in his behalf to Casper Shaff on 4 Mar 1767 for £1.8.0. {Ref: MSA S960 or S752, p. 180; CSOS:111}

BELL, ADAM, see "Thomas Aisquith," q.v.

BELL, JAMES (Maryland), b. c1737, MD (age 20 in 1757); pvt., 2nd Co. of VA Rangers under Capt. John Ashby on 21 Oct 1757. {Ref: MSR I:37}

BELL, JUDITH CARY, see "Nathaniel Gist," q.v.

BELL, MARY, see "Nicholas Orrick," q.v.

BELL, WILLIAM (Delaware), b. c1740, MD (tanner, age 18 in 1758); pvt., recruited by Capt. Benjamin Noxon and enlisted on 5 May 1758. {Ref: ARDE I:18; ARPA (2nd Series) 2:485, 566}

BELL, WILLIAM, see "William Beall," q.v.

BELLER, CHRISTIAN, see "Christian Better," q.v.

BELLVILLE, JOHN (Delaware), b. c1742, DE (tailor, age 16 in 1758); pvt., recruited by Capt. Benjamin Noxon and enlisted on 26 Apr 1758. {Ref: ARDE I:18; ARPA (2nd Series) 2:566}

BELLVILLE, NICHOLAS (Delaware), b. c1723, NY (weaver, age 35 in 1758); pvt., recruited by Capt. Benjamin Noxon and enlisted on 29 Apr 1758. {Ref: ARDE I:18; ARPA (2nd Series) 2:566}

BELLVILLE, PHILIP (Delaware), b. c1739, DE (tailor, age 19 in 1758); pvt., recruited by Capt. Benjamin Noxon and enlisted on 25 Apr 1758. {Ref: ARDE I:18; ARPA (2nd Series) 2:566}

BELT, GEORGE, see "George Beall," q.v.

BELT, JOSEPH (Maryland), b. 19 Dec 1717, Prince George's Co., son of Joseph Belt and Esther Beall, of Queen Anne's P. E. Parish, m. his stepsister Anne Sprigg, had children Thomas, Joseph, Charles, William, Elizabeth, Anne, and Mary, and d. testate on 6 Jun 1761; captain, Prince George's Co. militia, by 1760. {Ref: BDML I:127; MDG I:32-33; PGCR 1:164; ARMD 56:288; SLMH:II:11} Joseph Belt, Jr., "aged a little above 40 years, after a long indisposition," d. 11 Jun 1761 at his home near Upper Marlborough, leaving a wife and children (names not given in obituary). Col. Joseph Belt, father of Capt. Joseph Belt, d. 26 Jun 1761, age 81 [not 86 as stated in the newspaper], "his death supposed to have been occasioned by grief for the death of his son a few weeks before." {Ref: MDG I:30-33; *MD Gazette*, 2 Jul 1761 and 17 Sep 1761}

BELT, MIDDLETON (Maryland), mate and mariner (age 20 when deposed on 14 Mar 1761) on the brigantine *Duke of Marlborough*, commanded by David Carcaud, which vessel was commissioned by the Council of Maryland as a Flag of Truce on 15 Oct 1760 to carry French prisoners of war to Port St. Louis on the island of Hispaniola. {Ref: ARMD 31:462-466}

BENFIELD, SAMUEL (Maryland), pvt., Capt. Joshua Beall's Company of MD Troops, Prince George's Co., from 9 Oct 1757 to 31 May 1758 when he reportedly deserted; however, payment to him was recorded in Col. Dagworthy's account book on 8 Mar 1763 for work on Fort Cumberland. {Ref: MHS MS.375; CSOS:83; MHS MS.375.1}

BENFORD, CHARLES (Maryland), pvt., Capt. John Dagworthy's Company of MD Troops, Frederick Co., from 9 Oct 1758 to 8 Nov 1758 (served 31 days). {Ref: MHS MS.375.1; CSOS:75} Payment to him was recorded in Col. Dagworthy's account book on 8 Mar 1763. {Ref: MHS MS.375}

BENNETT, ELIZABETH (Maryland), patriot, Annapolis, Anne Arundel Co., pay account submitted for quartering soldiers in 1757 or 1758, exact dates not given. {Ref: MHM 9:3, p. 260}

BENNETT (BENNET), JOHN (Maryland), pvt., Capt. Richard Pearis' Company of MD Troops, Frederick Co., circa 9 Oct 1757 to 31 May 1758; pvt., Capt. Alexander Beall's Company of MD Troops, Frederick Co., from 9 Oct 1757 to 31 May 1758 when he was discharged. {Ref: MHS MS.375.1; CSOS:80, 90} Payment to him was recorded in Col. Dagworthy's account book on 14 Jul 1762. {Ref: MHS MS.375}

BENNETT (BENNET), JOHN JR. (Maryland), pvt., Capt. Joshua Beall's Company of MD Troops, Prince George's Co., from 1 Jun 1758 to 30 Dec 1758. {Ref: MHS MS.375.1; CSOS:83} Payment to him was recorded in Col. Dagworthy's account book on 12 Jul 1762. {Ref: MHS MS.375}

BENNETT, JOSEPH (Maryland), pvt., Capt. Moses Chapline's Company Muster Roll No. 1, Frederick Co., circa 1757-1758, exact dates not given (served 55 days); bill of credit issued or paid in his behalf to Joseph Chaplin for £2.15.0 on 5 Mar 1767. {Ref: MSA S960 or S752, p. 196; CSOS:113} Pvt., Capt. Moses Chapline's Company Muster Roll No. 3, Frederick Co., circa 1757-1758, exact dates not given (served 6 days); bill of credit issued or paid in his behalf to Joseph Chaplin for £0.6.0 on 5 Mar 1767. {Ref: MSA S960 or S752, p. 198; CSOS:114}

BENNETT, STEPHEN (Delaware), b. c1728, Ipswich, MA (laborer, age 30 in 1758); pvt., enlisted 12 May 1758 "for the campaign in the lower counties" by Capt. John McClughan. {Ref: ARDE I:17; ARPA (2nd Series) 2:570}

BENNETT (BENNET), THOMAS (Delaware), yeoman, m. Elizabeth (N), had children Thomas, Ebenezer, Perry, John, Elizabeth, and Mary, and d. testate in Appoquinimink Hundred by 5 Aug 1779. {Ref: CDSS:14} Ensign in Capt. George Gano's Company, New Castle Co., 1747-1748, during King George's War against Canada; ensign, Appoquinimink Hundred, Lower Regt. of Militia, New Castle Co., 1756. {Ref: ARDE I:12; ARPA (2nd Series) 2:525; HDE I:141}

BENSON, BENJAMIN (Maryland), patriot, Anne Arundel Co., pay account submitted for quartering soldiers in 1757 or 1758, exact dates not given. {Ref: MHM 9:3, p. 262}

BENYAN, PARSLEW (Maryland), pvt., Capt. Richard Pearis' Company of MD Troops, Frederick Co., circa 9 Oct 1757 to 31 May 1758; pvt., Capt. Joshua Beall's Company of MD Troops, Prince George's Co., from 1 Jun 1758 to 30 Dec 1758 when he was discharged; payment to him was recorded in Col. Dagworthy's account book on 15 Jul 1762; name mistakenly transcribed once as "Benjamin Barslaw." {Ref: MHS MS.375; CSOS:83, 90; MHS MS.375.1}

BERGER (BARGAR), PHILIP (Maryland), pvt., Capt. Peter Butler's Company Muster Roll, Frederick Co., circa 1757-1758, exact dates not given (served 34 days); bill of credit or order issued in his behald for £1.14.0 and paid to Casper Shaff on 2 Mar 1767. {Ref: MSA S960 or S752, p. 166; CSOS:96}

BERWICK, EDWARD, see "Edward Barrick," q.v.

BESS, THOMAS (Maryland), indentured servant and soldier who served in the French and Indian War some time between 1756 and 1763 (exact dates not known); his master Thomas Harrison, merchant, requested compensation from the Baltimore County Court due to the loss of use of Bess while in the service. {Ref: MHM 94:4, p. 426, citing Baltimore Co. Court Minutes}

BETTER (BELLER?), CHRISTIAN (Maryland), pvt., Capt. Stephen Rensburg's or Rensburger's Company Muster Roll, Frederick Co., circa 1757-1758, exact dates not given (served 42 days); bill of credit issued or paid in his behalf to Joseph Chaplin for £2.2.0 on 24 Apr 1767. {Ref: MSA S960 or S752, p. 183; CSOS:113}

BETTS, ELIZABETH, see "John Caton," q.v.

BEVIL, ---- (Maryland), cpl., Kent Co., by 1757. {Ref: ARMD 31:207}

BICKLEY, JOSEPH (Delaware), b. c1737, England (laborer, age 21 in 1758); pvt., recruited by Capt. Benjamin Noxon and enlisted on 9 May 1758. {Ref: ARDE I:18; ARPA (2nd Series) 2:566}

BILDERBACK, EPHRAIM (Maryland), pvt., Capt. Joseph Chapline's Company Muster Roll No. 4, Frederick Co., circa 1757-1758, exact dates not given (served 6 days); bill of credit issued or paid in his behalf to Joseph Chaplin for £0.6.0 on 5 Mar 1767. {Ref: MSA S960 or S752, p. 194}

BILLINGSLEY, JAMES, see "Benjamin Shaw," q.v.

BINGELEY, PETER (Maryland), pvt., Capt. Jonathan Hagar's Company Muster Roll, Frederick Co., circa 1757-1758, exact dates not given (served 6 days); bill of credit issued or paid to him for £0.6.0 in 1767, exact date not given. {Ref: MSA S960 or S752, p. 173; CSOS:106}

BIRCHFIELD (BURCHFIELD), AQUILA (Maryland), b. 9 Aug 1738, eldest son of Thomas Burchfield and Sarah Gash. {Ref: BCF:84} Pvt., Capt. Tobias Stansbury's Company Muster Roll, Baltimore Co., circa 1757-1758, exact dates not given; bill of credit issued or paid in his behalf to John Paca for £3.16.0 on 3 Apr 1767. {Ref: MSA S960 or S752, p. 186}

BIRCKHEAD, CHRISTOPHER, see "Pollard Edmondson," q.v.

BIRD, BENJAMIN (Maryland), pvt., Capt. Francis Ware's Company of MD Troops, Charles Co., from 9 Oct 1757 to 8 Nov 1758 (served 396 days); payment to him was recorded in Col. Dagworthy's account book on 12 Jul 1762. {Ref: MHS MS.375.1; CSOS:87; MHS MS.375}

BIRD, EMPSON (Delaware), lieut., Christiana Hundred, Upper Regt. of Militia, Southwest Division, New Castle Co., 1756. {Ref: ARDE I:11; ARPA (2nd Series) 2:526; HDE I:141} Thomas Bird, carpenter, m. Sarah (N), had a son Empson, and d. testate in Christiana Hundred by 10 Dec 1726. {Ref: CDSS:16} Empson Bird was executor of the will of Andrew Gorden of Cecil Co., MD on 2 Jun 1774. {Ref: MCW 15:127}

BIRK, THOMAS (Maryland), patriot, Kent Co., pay account submitted for quartering soldiers in 1757 or 1758, exact dates not given. {Ref: MHM 9:3, p. 261}

BISHOP, HENRY (Maryland), pvt., Capt. Joshua Beall's Company of MD Troops, Prince George's Co., from 9 Oct 1757 to 8 Jun 1758; payment to him was recorded in Col. Dagworthy's account book on 23 Jul 1762. {Ref: MHS MS.375.1; CSOS:83; MHS MS.375}

BISHOP, THOMAS (Maryland), drummer, Capt. Joshua Beall's Company of MD Troops, Prince George's Co., from 29 Oct 1757 to 8 Nov 1758; payment to him was recorded in Col. Dagworthy's account book on 13 Jul 1762. {Ref: M HS MS.375.1; CSOS:83; MHS MS.375}

BLACK, GEORGE (Delaware), b. c1734, Armagh, Ireland (weaver, age 24 in 1758); pvt., enlisted 20 Apr 1758 "for the campaign in the lower counties" by Capt. John McClughan. {Ref: ARDE I:17; ARPA (2nd Series) 2:570}

BLACK, JAMES (Maryland), pvt., Capt. Joseph Chapline's Company Muster Rolls No. 2 and 3, Frederick Co., circa 1757-1758, exact dates not given (served 5 days); militia pay account submitted in 1758, exact date not given. {Ref: MHM 9:4, p. 370; CSOS:104} Bill of credit issued or paid in his behalf to Joseph Chaplin for £0.5.0 on 5 Mar 1767. {Ref: MSA S960 or S752, p. 193} Pvt., Capt. Joseph Chapline's Company Muster Roll No. 4, Frederick Co., circa 1757-1758, exact dates not given (served 6 days); bill of credit issued or paid in his behalf to Joseph Chaplin for £0.6.0 on 5 Mar 1767. {Ref: MSA S960 or S752, p. 194; CSOS:104} He was paid £0.12.0 at Fort Frederick on 15 Jun 1758 for carrying arms for the Western Expedition against Fort Duquesne. {Ref: ARMD 55:773}

BLACK, JOHN (Maryland), pvt., Capt. Joshua Beall's Company of MD Troops, Prince George's Co., from 9 Oct 1757 to 29 Jan 1758 when he was discharged; payment to him was recorded in Col. Dagworthy's account book on 21 Jul 1762. {Ref: MHS MS.375.1; CSOS:83; MHS MS.375}

BLACK, VALENTINE (Maryland), cpl., Capt. Peter Butler's Company Muster Roll, Frederick Co., circa 1757-1758, exact dates not given (served 34 days); bill of credit or order issued in his behald for £2.5.3 and paid to Casper Shaff on 2 Mar 1767. {Ref: MSA S960 or S752, p. 166; CSOS:96}

BLACK, WILLIAM (Maryland), pvt., Capt. John Middaugh's Company Muster Roll, Frederick Co., circa 1757-1758, exact dates not given (served 30 days); bill of credit issued or paid in his behalf to Thomas Beatty, Jr. for £2 on 23 Feb 1767. {Ref: MSA S960 or S752, p. 171; CSOS:100}

BLACKBURN, ROBERT (Maryland), pvt., Capt. Elias Delashmutt's Company Muster Roll, Frederick Co., 13 Aug 1757, exact dates not given (served 52 days); bill of credit issued or paid in his behalf to Joseph Chaplin on 5 Mar 1767 for £2.12.0; name listed once as "Robert Blackbourn." {Ref: MSA S960 or S752, p. 162; CSOS:98} On 6 Aug 1757 he recorded his discharge in Frederick Co. Court, "having got two men to serve in his stead, he has behaved well; signed John Dagworthy." {Ref: FCLR:30} Pvt., Capt. John Wolgomatt's Company of MD Volunteers, Frederick Co., circa 1763-1764; reported on muster roll dated 15 Nov 1764 at Camp at the Forks of Muskingham as "left sick at Fort Cumberland." {Ref: ARMD 32:99}

BLACKBURN, WILLIAM (Delaware), pvt., Capt. Richard McWilliams' Company of Foot, New Castle Co., enlisted 28 Dec 1757. {Ref: ARDE I:14}

BLACKSHARE, MIRIAM, see "Michael Lowber," q.v.

BLACKSHIRE, ROBERT, see "John Rees," q.v.

BLACKWOOD, JOHN (Delaware or Pennsylvania), captain and recruiting officer for PA Troops in the "Three Lower Counties on Delaware" in 1758. {Ref: ARDE I:27}

BLAIDENBURGH, SABINA, see "William Rumsey," q.v.

BLADEN, ANNE, see "Benjamin Tasker, Jr.," q.v.

BLADES, EDMOND (Delaware), b. c1732, MD (carpenter, age 26 in 1758); pvt., recruited by Capt. Benjamin Noxon and enlisted on 2 May 1758. {Ref: ARDE I:18; ARPA (2nd Series) 2:485, 566}

BLAIR, BRICE (Maryland), pvt., Capt. Joseph Chapline's Company Muster Roll No. 4, Frederick Co., circa 1757-1758, exact dates not given (served 6 days); bill of credit issued or paid in his behalf to Joseph Chaplin for £0.6.0 on 5 Mar 1767. {Ref: MSA S960 or S752, p. 194; CSOS:104}

BLAIR, DAVID (Maryland), ensign in Capt. William McClellan's Company of MD Volunteers, Frederick Co., circa 1763-1764; on muster roll dated 15 Nov 1764 at Camp at the Forks of Muskingham. {Ref: ARMD 32:99}

BLAIR, JAMES (Maryland or Pennsylvania), pvt., Capt. Culbertson's Company, was killed in "a recent battle with the Indians" in 1756 (exact date not given) in Cumberland Co., PA, after the burning of McCord's Fort. {Ref: *MD Gazette*, 29 Apr 1756}

BLAIR, JOHN (Maryland), ensign in Capt. John Wolgomatt's Company of MD Volunteers, Frederick Co., circa 1763-1764; on muster roll dated 15 Nov 1764 at Camp at the Forks of Muskingham. {Ref: ARMD 32:99}

BLAIR, JOHN (Maryland or Pennsylvania), pvt., Capt. Hamilton's Company, was killed in "a recent battle with the Indians" in 1756 (exact date not given) in Cumberland Co., PA, after the burning of McCord's Fort. {Ref: *MD Gazette*, 29 Apr 1756}

BLAKE, DOROTHY, see "Charles Carroll, Esq.," q.v.

BLAKE, PHILIP (Maryland), pvt., Capt. Francis Ware's Company of MD Troops, Charles Co., 9 Oct 1757 to 30 Dec 1758; payment to him was recorded in Col. Dagworthy's account book on 7 Mar 1763. {Ref: MHS MS.375.1; CSOS:87; MHS MS.375}

BLAY, CATHERINE, see "John Tilden," q.v.

BLEW, MICHAEL (Delaware), pvt., Capt. Richard McWilliams' Company of Foot, New Castle Co., enlisted 28 Dec 1757. {Ref: ARDE I:14}

BLOIS (BLOYCE), JOHN (Maryland), pvt., Capt. John Dagworthy's Company of MD Troops, Frederick Co., from 9 Oct 1757 to 27 Dec 1758 (served 443 days) and reportedly deserted; however, payment to him was recorded in Col. Dagworthy's account book on 28 Feb 1763. {Ref: MHS MS.375.1; CSOS:75; MHS MS.375}

BLUBOUGH, JACOB (Maryland), pvt., Capt. Thomas Norris' Company, Frederick Co., circa 1757-1758, exact dates not given (served 30 days); bill of credit issued or paid in his behalf to Michael McGuire on 20 Mar 1767 for £1.10.0. {Ref: MSA S960 or S752, p. 176; CSOS:107}

BLUETT, MARTHA, see "Joseph Dashiell," q.v.

BLYTH, BENJAMIN (Maryland or Pennsylvania), pvt., Capt. Culbertson's Company, was wounded in "a recent battle with the Indians" in 1756 (exact date not given) in Cumberland Co., PA, after the burning of McCord's Fort. {Ref: *MD Gazette*, 29 Apr 1756}

BLYZARD, ANN, see "George Fraser (Frazer)," q.v.

BODIGE, BENJAMIN (Maryland), pvt., Capt. John Dagworthy's Company of MD Troops, Frederick Co., from 9 Oct 1757 to 2 Dec 1758 (served 419 days) and reportedly died; however, payment to him was recorded in Col. Dagworthy's account book on 11 Jul 1762 for work on Fort Cumberland. {Ref: MHS MS.375.1; CSOS:75; MHS MS.375}

BOGGS, JAMES (Delaware), pvt., Capt. Richard McWilliams' Company of Foot, New Castle Co., enlisted 28 Dec 1757. {Ref: ARDE I:14}

BOGGS, JOHN (Delaware), m. (N), had a son John Jr., and d. intestate in Kent Co. by 18 Oct 1765 at which time letters of administration were granted to Matthew Boggs, next of kin. {Ref: CDSS:18} Pvt., Kent Co. Militia, Capt. John Caton's Company, 25 Apr 1757 (date of muster roll). {Ref: ARDE I:13}

BOGGS (BOGG), JOHN (Maryland), pvt., Capt. Peregrine Brown's Company Muster Roll, Kent Co., circa 1757-1758, exact dates not given (served 15 days); bill of credit issued or paid in his behalf to Robert Buchanan on 20 Feb 1767 for £0.15.0. {Ref: MSA S960 or S752, p. 180; CSOS:110} Bill of credit issued or paid to him for £0.15.0 in 1767, exact date not given. {Ref: MSA S960 or S752, p. 179}

BOGGS, MATTHEW, see "John Boggs," q.v.

BOGGS, WILLIAM (Maryland), pvt. (age 30 in 1758), resident of Cecil Co., enlisted by Capt. John Singleton for the PA Regt. on 8 May 1758. {Ref: ARPA (2nd Series) 2:474}

BOLTON, JOHN (Maryland), patriot and poss. soldier (rank not specified), Kent Co., militia pay account submitted in 1758, exact date not given. {Ref: MHM 9:4, p. 366}

BOMGARDNER, CHESLEY or CHRISLEY (Maryland), pvt., Capt. Joshua Beall's Company of MD Troops, Prince George's Co., circa 9 Oct 1757 to 30 Dec 1758; pvt., Capt. John Dagworthy's Company of MD Troops, Frederick Co., from 31 Dec 1758 to 26 Apr 1759 (served 117 days) and was discharged; payment to him was recorded in Col. Dagworthy's account book on 8 Jul 1762. {Ref: MHS MS.375; CSOS:75, 83; MHS MS.375}

BOND, ALICE, see "William Johnson," q.v.

BOND, ANN, see "Zachariah Bond" and "Patrick Constantine," q.v.

BOND, GEORGE (Maryland), pvt., Capt. John White's Company Muster Roll, Frederick Co., circa 1757-1758, exact dates not given (served 6 days); bill of credit issued or paid to him for £0.6.0 in 1767, exact date not given. {Ref: MSA S960 or S752, p. 164; CSOS:95}

BOND, JOHN (Delaware), pvt., Capt. French Battell's Company of Lower County Provincials, enlisted 17 May 1758. {Ref: ARDE I:16; ARPA (2nd Series) 2:555}

BOND, JOHN, see "Samuel Bond," q.v.

BOND, MARGARET, see "Zachariah Bond," q.v.

BOND, PETER, see "Samuel Bond," q.v.

BOND, RICHARD, see "Patrick Constantine," q.v.

BOND, SAMUEL (Maryland), pvt., Capt. Tobias Stansbury's Company Muster Roll, Baltimore Co., circa 1757-1758, exact dates not given; bill of credit issued or paid in his behalf to Thomas Bond for £4.8.7½ on 18 May 1767; pvt., Capt. Tobias Stansbury's Company Muster Roll, Baltimore Co., circa 1757-1758, exact dates not given; bill of credit issued or paid to him for £4.8.7½ in 1767, exact date not given; name listed once as "Samuel Bownd." {Ref: MSA S960 or S752, p. 186} *Identification problem:* There were two men with this name who could have served in the war: (1) Samuel Bond, b. 26 Sep 1736, son of Peter Bond and Susanna Butler, m. Charity Clark in 1766; and, (2) Samuel Bond, son of John Bond and Aliceanna Webster, m. Cynthia Richardson. {Ref: BCF:49-52}

BOND, THOMAS, see "Samuel Bond," q.v.

BOND, ZACHARIAH (Maryland), b. by 1716, St. Mary's Company, son of Zachariah Bond and Ann (N), m. Margaret (N). had at least one dau. (N) who m. Henry Greenfield Sothoron, and d. testate by 1 Feb 1776; planter, miller, county justice (1746-1764), member of MD Assembly (1745-1754), captain by 1758 and major by 1760. {Ref: BDML I:143-144; ARMD 56:287; MCW 16:139}

BONNETT (BONNITT), JOHN (Maryland), pvt., Capt. Alexander Beall's Company of Foot, 1756-1757, recorded his discharge in Frederick Co. Court on 22 Nov 1758. Capt. Beall certified that "John Bonnitt served as a private soldier for 15 months and thro sickness is rendered incapable of serving any longer, he is at his own request and by order of his Excellency the Governor hereby discharged, having received his clothing and other necessaries granted to soldiers, also his full pay to 24 Dec, and that the said John Bonnitt has a demand on the said province for 158 days pay at the rate of 9 pence a day from the said 24 Dec to the day of his discharge. Given under my hand at Fort Frederick, 31 May 1758." John Bonnitt made his "B" mark on the receipt which was witnessed by Thomas Ware. {Ref: FCLR:59-60}

BOOKER, BARTHOLOMEW (Maryland), patriot and poss. soldier (rank not specified), Frederick Co., militia pay account submitted in 1758, exact date not given. {Ref: MHM 9:4, p. 370}

BOONE (BOON), JACOB (Maryland), pvt., Capt. Henry Casson's Company Muster Roll, Queen Anne's Co., circa 1757-1758, exact dates not given (served 27 days); bill of credit issued or paid in his behalf to Capt. Casson on 27 Feb 1767 for £1.7.0; name mistakenly listed once as "Jacob Boor." {Ref: MSA S960 or S752, p. 177; CSOS:109}

BOOTH, JAMES (Maryland), pvt., Capt. John Wolgomatt's Company of MD Volunteers, Frederick Co., circa 1763-1764; on muster roll dated 15 Nov 1764 at Camp at the Forks of Muskingham. {Ref: ARMD 32:99}

BOOTH, JAMES (Maryland), pvt., Capt. Moses Chapline's Company Muster Roll No. 1, Frederick Co., circa 1757-1758, exact dates not given (served 55 days); bill of credit issued or paid in his behalf to Joseph Chaplin for £2.15.0 on 13 Jun 1768. {Ref: MSA S960 or S752, p. 196; CSOS:113} Pvt., Capt. Joseph Chapline's Company Muster Roll No. 1, Frederick Co., circa 1757-1758, exact dates not given (served 39 days); bill of credit issued or paid in his behalf to Joseph Chaplin for £1.10.0 on 13 Jun 1768. {Ref: MSA S960 or S752, p. 192; CSOS:102}

BOOTH, JAMES (Maryland), pvt., Capt. Peter Bainbridge's Company Muster Roll, Frederick Co., circa 1757-1758, exact dates not given (served 30 days); bill of credit issued or paid in his behalf to Joseph Chaplin on 13 Jun 1768 for £1.10.0. {Ref: MSA S960 or S752, p. 181; CSOS:111}

BOOTH, JOHN (Maryland), pvt., Capt. Moses Chapline's Company Muster Roll No. 3, Frederick Co., circa 1757-1758, exact dates not given (served 6 days); bill of credit issued or paid in his behalf to Joseph Chapline for £0.6.0 on 8 Jun 1767. {Ref: MSA S960 or S752, p. 198; CSOS:115}

BOOTH, JOHN (Delaware), pvt., Capt. Richard McWilliams' Company of Foot, New Castle Co., enlisted 28 Dec 1757. {Ref: ARDE I:14}

BOOTH, JOSEPH (Delaware), pvt., Capt. French Battell's Company of Lower County Provincials, enlisted 10 May 1758. {Ref: ARDE I:16; ARPA (2nd Series) 2:555}

BORDLEY, JOHN (Maryland), patriot and poss. soldier (rank not specified), Kent Co., militia pay account submitted in 1758, exact date not given. {Ref: MHM 9:4, p. 366}

BORDLEY, STEPHEN (Maryland), b. c1710, Annapolis, son of Thomas Bordley and Ann Miller, d. testate and unmarried on 6 Dec 1764 in Annapolis; patriot, lawyer, member of MD Assembly (1745, 1749-1751, 1754-1756), MD Council (1759-1761), attorney general (1756-1763), naval officer of the Port of Annapolis (1755-1762), mayor of Annapolis (1761, 1764), and commissary general (1762-1764). {Ref: BDML I:146-147; *MD Gazette*, 13 Dec 1764} See "Samuel Gardner," q.v.

BORDLEY, THOMAS, see "Stephen Bordley," q.v.

BOROMAN (BOWMAN?), JOHN (Maryland), pvt., Capt. Jonathan Hagar's Company Muster Roll, Frederick Co., circa 1757-1758, exact dates not given (served 6 days); bill of credit issued or paid in his behalf to Joseph Chaplin for £0.6.0 on 24 Apr 1767. {Ref: MSA S960 or S752, p. 173; CSOS:106}

BOSLEY, JOHN, see "Joseph Finch," q.v.

BOSTIAN (BOSTAIN), GEORGE (Maryland), pvt., Capt. John Middaugh's Company Muster Roll, Frederick Co., circa 1757-1758, exact dates not given (served 30 days); bill of credit issued or paid in his behalf to Thomas Beatty, Jr. for £0.17.0 on 3 Apr 1767. {Ref: MSA S960 or S752, p. 172; CSOS:101}

BOSTON, JOHN (Maryland), pvt., Frederick Co., 1756-1757, recorded his discharge in Frederick Co. Court on 6 Aug 1757. Capt. Alexander Beall certified that he had served 8 months and his pay receipt and clothing were witnessed and signed by Sgt. Robert Lineard and Sgt. George Barrance. {Ref: FCLR:30}

BOSWELL, EDWARD (Maryland), pvt., Capt. Francis Ware's Company of MD Troops, Charles Co., from 9 Oct 1757 to 2 Jul 1758 (served 266 days) when he reportedly deserted; however, payment to him was recorded in Col. Dagworthy's account book on 26 Feb 1762. {Ref: MHS MS.375; MHS MS.375.1}

BOSWELL, SOLVOLITLE, see "Samuel Phillips," q.v.

BOTELER (BOTLER), HENRY (Maryland), lieut., Capt. Peter Bainbridge's Company Muster Roll, Frederick Co., circa 1757-1758, exact dates not given (served 36 days); bill of credit issued or paid in his behalf to Joseph Chaplin on 24 Apr 1767 for £4.4.0. {Ref: MSA S960 or S752, p. 181; CSOS:110} See "Henry Butler," q.v.

BOUCHELLE, SUSANNA, see "Peter Bayard," q.v.

BOUDEN, JAMES (Delaware), pvt., Capt. French Battell's Company of Lower County Provincials, enlisted 13 May 1758. {Ref: ARDE I:16; ARPA (2nd Series) 2:555}

BOUQUET, HENRY (Pennsylvania and Maryland), colonel, PA and MD Forces, circa 1763-1764, which made up part of the 42nd and 60th Royal American Regt., some troops from PA, and two companies of volunteers and riflemen from Frederick Co., MD, under Capt. William McClellan and Capt. John Wolgamott. {Ref: ARMD:99; *The Pennsylvania German in the Settlement of Maryland*, by Daniel W. Nead (1914), pp. 161-162}

BOWELL, WILLIAM (Maryland), pvt., Capt. Moses Chapline's Company Muster Roll No. 1, Frederick Co., circa 1757-1758, exact dates not given (served 55 days); bill of credit issued or paid in his behalf to Joseph Chaplin for £2.15.0 on 5 Mar 1767; name mistakenly transcribed once as "William Bowol." {Ref: MSA S960 or S752, p. 196; CSOS:113} Pvt., Capt. Moses Chapline's Company Muster Roll No. 3, Frederick Co., circa 1757-1758, exact dates not given (served 6 days); bill of credit issued or paid in his behalf to Joseph Chaplin for £0.6.0 on 5 Mar 1767. {Ref: MSA S960 or S752, p. 198; CSOS:114}

BOWEN, GEORGE (Delaware), pvt., Capt. Henry Vanbibber's Company of the Lower Counties on Delaware Troops at New Castle, enlisted on 17 May 1759. {Ref: ARDE I:26; ARPA (2nd Series) 2:594}

BOWEN, JOSIAS (Maryland), b. 22 Dec 1729, son of Benjamin Bowen, Baltimore Co.; never married; d. testate by 2 Mar 1793. {Ref: BCF:62} Lieut. in Capt. Tobias Stansbury's Company, Baltimore Co., circa 1757-1758, exact dates not given; bill of credit issued or paid in his behalf to Thomas Sollars for £4.4.0 on 20 Feb 1767. {Ref: MSA S960 or S752, p. 186; CSOS;117} See "Solomon Butler" and "Henry Stevenson" and "John Long," q.v.

BOWERS, MICHAEL (Maryland), pvt., Capt. Moses Chapline's Company Muster Roll No. 3, Frederick Co., circa 1757-1758, exact dates not given (served 6 days); bill of credit issued or paid in his behalf to James Smith for £0.6.0 on 18 May 1767. {Ref: MSA S960 or S752, p. 198; CSOS:115}

BOWIE, WILLIAM (Maryland), b. 1721, Prince George's Co., son of John Bowie and Mary Mullikin, m. Margaret Sprigg circa 1745, had children Walter, Robert, William, Osborn Sprigg, Elizabeth, Ann, and Margaret Sprigg, and d. by 9 Apr 1791; captain by 1760, county justice (1759-1761), and Revolutionary War patriot (1775-1783). {Ref: BDML I:153-154}

BOWLES, ANDREW (Maryland), pvt., Capt. Peter Bainbridge's Company Muster Roll, Frederick Co., circa 1757-1758, exact dates not given (served 28 days); bill of credit issued or paid in his behalf to Casper Shaff on 4 Mar 1767 for £1.8.0. {Ref: MSA S960 or S752, p. 180; CSOS:111}

BOWLES, JAMES, see "George Plater," q.v.

BOWLES, THOMAS, see "George Shinn" and "George Reed," q.v.

BOWMAN, HANNAH, see "Samuel Robinson," q.v.

BOWMAN, HENRY, see "Nehemiah Davis," q.v.

BOWMAN, JACOB (Maryland), pvt., Capt. John White's Company Muster Roll, Frederick Co., circa 1757-1758, exact dates not given (served 6 days); bill of credit issued or paid to him for £0.6.0 in 1767, exact date not given. {Ref: MSA S960 or S752, p. 164; CSOS:95}

BOWMAN, JOHN, see "John Boroman," q.v.

BOWMAN, MARY, see "Nehemiah Davis," q.v.

BOWMAN, SAMUEL (Maryland), pvt., Capt. William Luckett's Company Muster Roll, Frederick Co., circa 1757-1758, exact dates not given (served 30 days); bill of credit issued or paid in his behalf to William Luckett, Jr. for £1.4.0 on 6 Apr 1767. {Ref: MSA S960 or S752, p. 169; CSOS:100}

BOWMAN, SIMON (Maryland), pvt., Capt. John Middaugh's Company Muster Roll, Frederick Co., circa 1757-1758, exact dates not given (served 30 days). {Ref: CSOS:100}

BOYD, ABRAHAM (Maryland), pvt., Capt. Joshua Beall's Company Muster Roll, Prince George's Co., circa 1757-1758, exact dates not given; bill of credit issued or paid to him for £2.3.0 on 28 Feb 1767. {Ref: MSA S960 or S752, p. 184}

BOYD, JOHN (Delaware), pvt., Capt. Richard McWilliams' Company of Foot, New Castle Co., enlisted 28 Dec 1757. {Ref: ARDE I:15}

BOYD, JOHN (Delaware), pvt., Capt. Henry Vanbibber's Company of the Lower Counties on Delaware Troops at New Castle, enlisted on 14 May 1759. {Ref: ARDE I:26; ARPA (2nd Series) 2:594}

BOYD, WILLIAM (Maryland or Pennsylvania), pvt., Capt. Culbertson's Company, was killed in "a recent battle with the Indians" in 1756 (exact date not given) in Cumberland Co., PA, after the burning of McCord's Fort. {Ref: *MD Gazette*, 29 Apr 1756}

BOYER, JOSEPH (Maryland), pvt., Capt. Jonathan Hagar's Company Muster Roll, Frederick Co., circa 1757-1758, exact dates not given (served 6 days); bill of credit issued or paid to him for £0.6.0 in 1767, exact date not given. {Ref: MSA S960 or S752, p. 173; CSOS:106}

BOZMAN, ELEANOR, see "Joseph Gillis," q.v.

BRADDOCK, GENERAL, see "Horatio Sharpe" and "Christopher Gist" and "Nathaniel Gist" and "John Dagworthy," q.v.

BRADDOCK (BRADOCK), WILLIAM (Maryland), pvt., Capt. Tobias Stansbury's Company Muster Roll, Baltimore Co., circa 1757-1758, exact dates not given; bill of credit issued or paid to him for £1.18.0 in 1767, exact date not given. {Ref: MSA S960 or S752, p. 186}

BRADFORD, THOMAS (Maryland), alias Thomas Radford *[sic]*, pvt., Capt. Elias Delashmutt's Company Muster Roll, Frederick Co., circa 1757-1758, exact dates not given (served 30 days); bill of credit issued or paid in his behalf to Elias Delashmut, Jr. on 16 Mar 1767 for £1.10.0. {Ref: MSA S960 or S752, p. 162; CSOS:94}

BRADMORE, JAMES (Maryland), pvt., Capt. William McClellan's Company of MD Volunteers, Frederick Co., circa 1763-1764; on muster roll dated 15 Nov 1764 at Camp at the Forks of Muskingham. {Ref: ARMD 32:99}

BRAGONER, PETER (Maryland), pvt., Capt. Jonathan Hagar's Company Muster Roll, Frederick Co., circa 1757-1758, exact dates not given (served 6 days); bill of credit issued or paid to him for £0.6.0 in 1767, exact date not given. {Ref: MSA S960 or S752, p. 173; CSOS:106}

BRAKE, PETER (Maryland), alias Peter Praig *[sic]*, pvt., Capt. Peter Butler's Company Muster Roll, Frederick Co., circa 1757-1758, exact dates not given; bill of credit or order issued in his behalf for £1.14.0 to Casper Shaff and paid to David Cumming on 18 Apr 1767. {Ref: MSA S960 or S752, p. 168}

BRAND, JAMES, see "Thomas Perkins," q.v.

BRASHEARS, NACEY or NASIE (Maryland), b. c1730 (exact date not given), son of Samuel Jr. and Elizabeth Brashears, of Queen Anne's P. E. Parish. {Ref: {Ref: PGCR 1:166} Pvt., Capt. Joshua Beall's Company Muster Roll, Prince George's Co., circa 1757-1758, exact dates not given; bill of credit issued or paid in his behalf to David Ross for £2.1.0 on 16 Mar 1767. {Ref: MSA S960 or S752, p. 184}

BRATHET, JOHN (Maryland), pvt., Capt. John White's Company Muster Roll, Frederick Co., circa 1757-1758, exact dates not given (served 6 days); bill of credit issued or paid in his behalf to Joseph Chaplin on 5 Mar 1767 for £0.6.0. {Ref: MSA S960 or S752, p. 164; CSOS:96}

BREHM, LIEUT., see "George Wattwood," q.v.

BRENNER, JOHN (Maryland), pvt., Capt. Stephen Rensburg's or Rensburger's Company Muster Roll, Frederick Co., circa 1757-1758, exact dates not given (served 34 days); bill of credit issued or paid in his behalf to Stephen Rensburg or Rensburger for £1.14.0 on 27 Mar 1767. {Ref: MSA S960 or S752, p. 182; CSOS:112}

BRENNER, JOHN JR. (Maryland), pvt., Capt. Stephen Rensburg's or Rensburger's Company Muster Roll, Frederick Co., circa 1757-1758, exact dates not given (served 42 days); bill of credit issued or paid in his behalf to Stephen Rensburg or Rensburger for £2.2.0 on 27 Mar 1767; name mistakenly transcribed once as "John Bremer, Jr." {Ref: MSA S960 or S752, p. 182; CSOS:112}

BREWER, JOSEPH (Maryland), pvt., Capt. Samuel Chapman's Company Muster Roll, Anne Arundel Co., circa 1757-1758, exact dates not given; bill of credit issued or paid in his behalf to Thomas Gassaway for £1.18.0 on 25 Feb 1767. {Ref: MSA S960 or S752, p. 188}

BREWER, WILLIAM (Maryland), b. 20 Jun 1732, Anne Arundel Co., son of John and Eleanor Brewer, of All Hallow's Parish. {Ref: AACR:50} Pvt., Capt. Samuel Chapman's Company Muster Roll, Anne Arundel Co., circa 1757-1758, exact dates not given; bill of credit issued or paid to him for £1.18.0 on 25 Feb 1767. {Ref: MSA S960 or S752, p. 188}

BRIANT, CHARLES (Maryland), patriot, Annapolis, Anne Arundel Co., pay account submitted for quartering soldiers in 1757 or 1758, exact dates not given. {Ref: MHM 9:3, p. 261}

BRICE, JOHN (Maryland), patriot, Annapolis, Anne Arundel Co., pay account submitted for quartering soldiers in 1757 or 1758, exact dates not given. {Ref: MHM 9:3, p. 261} Served as chief justice of the province, alderman of the City of Annapolis, and one of the judges of the Assize Court for the Western Shore; d. while on the circuit, at the house of Samuel Hanson, in Charles Co. {Ref: *MD Gazette*, 25 Sep 1766}

BRICE, RACHEL, see "Philip Hammond" and "John Hammond," q.v.

BRIDGE, JACOB, see "Jacob Budge," q.v.

BRIGHTWELL, JOHN (Maryland), b. c1737, Prince George's Co. (age about 20 in 1757); pvt., reported as deserted from the MD Forces in July 1757. {Ref: *MD Gazette*, 21 Jul 1757} He subsequently returned to duty as pvt. in Capt. Francis Ware's Company of MD Troops, Charles Co., from 9 Oct 1757 to 8 Nov 1758 (served 396 days); payment to him was recorded in Col. Dagworthy's account book on 22 Feb 1762. {Ref: MHS MS.375.1; CSOS:87; MHS MS.375} John Brightwell, of Prince George's Co., m. (N), had children John (of Frederick Co.), Thomas Coleman, Catherine, Urslee, Pracilla, and Elioner, and d. testate by 24 Nov 1774. {Ref: MCW 16:48}

BRIGHTWELL, THOMAS (Maryland), pvt., Capt. Joshua Beall's Company Muster Roll, Prince George's Co., circa 1757-1758, exact dates not given; bill of credit issued or paid in his behalf to Rezin Beall for £2.3.0 on 20 May 1767. {Ref: MSA S960 or S752, p. 184}

BRIMSTATAR, MATTHIAS (Maryland), pvt., Capt. John White's Company Muster Roll, Frederick Co., circa 1757-1758, exact dates not given (served 6 days); bill of credit issued or paid to him for £0.6.0 in 1767, exact date not given. {Ref: MSA S960 or S752, p. 164; CSOS:96}

BRINCKLE (BRINKLEE, BRINCKLEY), BENJAMIN (Delaware), m. Betty (N), had children Mary, William, Benjamin, Joseph, and Leah, and d. intestate in Kent Co. by 8 Jun 1764. {Ref: CDSS:21} Captain, Lower Part of Mispillion Hundred, Militia of Kent Co. on Delaware, 1756. {Ref: ARDE I:12; ARPA (2nd Series) 2:527-529; HDE I:141; HDE I:141}

BRINCKLE, ELIZABETH, see "Peter Lowber" and "John Clark," q.v.

BRINCKLE (BRINKLEE), JOHN (Delaware), captain, militia, Lower Part of Little Creek Hundred, Kent Co. on Delaware, 1756. {Ref: ARDE I:12; ARPA (2nd Series) 2:527-529; HDE I:141}

BRINCKLE (BRINKLE), JOHN (Delaware), lieut. colonel, Regt. of Militia for Kent Co. on Delaware, 1756. {Ref: ARDE I:12; ARPA (2nd Series) 2:527-529; HDE I:141}

BRINCKLE, JOSEPH (Delaware), pvt., Capt. French Battell's Company of Lower County Provincials, enlisted 24 May 1758. {Ref: ARDE I:16; ARPA (2nd Series) 2:555}

BRIND, ISAAC (Delaware), b. c1724, Wilts, England (shoemaker, age 34 in 1758); pvt., enlisted 1 May 1758 "for the campaign in the lower counties" by Capt. John McClughan; pvt., Capt. Henry Vanbibber's Company of the Lower Counties on Delaware Troops at New Castle, enlisted 7 May 1759. {Ref: ARDE I:17, 26; ARPA (2nd Series) 2:570, 594}

BRINKLEY (BRINKLY), JAMES (Maryland), pvt., Capt. Richard Pearis' Company of MD Troops, Frederick Co., circa 9 Oct 1757 and 31 May 1758;

pvt., Capt. Alexander Beall's Company of MD Troops, Frederick Co., from 1 Jun 1758 to 30 Dec 1758; payment to him was recorded in Col. Dagworthy's account book on 13 Jul 1762. {Ref: MHS MS.375; CSOS:80, 90; MHS MS.375.1}

BRISCOE, ISAAC (Maryland), pvt., Capt. Peregrine Brown's Company Muster Roll, Kent Co., circa 1757-1758, exact dates not given (served 15 days); bill of credit issued or paid in his behalf to Robert Buchanan on 20 May 1767 for £0.15.0. {Ref: MSA S960 or S752, p. 179; CSOS:110}

BRISCOE, JOHN (Maryland), b. 8 Sep 1728, Kent Co., son of John and Hannah Briscoe, of Shrewsbury Parish. {Ref: ESVR} Pvt., Capt. Peregrine Brown's Company Muster Roll, Kent Co., circa 1757-1758, exact dates not given (served 15 days); bill of credit issued or paid in his behalf to Robert Buchanan on 20 Feb 1767 for £0.15.0. {Ref: MSA S960 or S752, p. 180; CSOS:110}

BRISCOE, JOSEPH (Maryland), pvt., Capt. Peregrine Brown's Company, Kent Co., on 19 Feb 1758, by which time he had enlisted, but was unable to march due to health problems. {Ref: ARMD 31:283}

BRISCOE, MARTHA, see "Jonathan Willson," q.v.

BRISCOE, WILLIAM (Maryland), pvt., Capt. Peregrine Brown's Company, Kent Co., on 19 Feb 1758, by which time he had enlisted, but was unable to march due to health problems. {Ref: ARMD 31:283} William Brisco *[sic]* m. Mary Ann Jones on 29 Apr 1739 in Shrewsbury Parish, Kent Co., and their son William was b. 24 Mar 1740/1. {Ref: ESVR}

BROADWAY, JOHN (Maryland), pvt., Capt. Alexander Beall's Company of MD Troops, Frederick Co., from 9 Oct 1757 to 16 Feb 1758 when he was "returned to 35th Rgt. as a deserter from it." However, payment to him was recorded in Col. Dagworthy's account book on 7 Mar 1763. {Ref: MHS MS.375.1; CSOS:80; MHS MS.375}

BROCHSON, JOSEPH (Delaware), b. c1741, Three Runs, DE (planter, age 17 in 1758); pvt., enlisted 19 Apr 1758 "for the campaign in the lower counties" by Capt. John McClughan. {Ref: ARDE I:17; ARPA (2nd Series) 2:570}

BROCK, JOHN (Delaware), pvt., Capt. Richard McWilliams' Company of Foot, New Castle Co., enlisted 28 Dec 1757. {Ref: ARDE I:14}

BROME (BROOME), JOHN (Maryland), b. c1727, Calvert Co., son of John Brome and Anne Gantt, m. Mary Mackall, and d. 1797; lawyer, captain in the militia from 1754 to 1758 (received considerable land in MD and VA for his services in the French and Indian War), and colonel of militia (dates not given); removed to Western Maryland after the peace of 1763 and engaged in the development of his land grants. {Ref: BDML I:167; HCC:122-123}

BROOBACK (BRUBACK), RODY (Maryland), drummer, Capt. Thomas Norris' Company, Frederick Co., circa 1757-1758, exact dates not given (served 30 days); bill of credit issued or paid in his behalf to Charles Englas on 28 Mar 1767 for £2. {Ref: MSA S960 or S752, p. 176; CSOS:107}

BROOKE, BENJAMIN, see "John McNeill," q.v.

BROOKE, ELIZABETH, see "George Beall," q.v.

BROOKE, MARY, see "Bartholomew Ennalls" and "Joseph Sim," q.v.

BROOKE, PRISCILLA, see "Edward Gantt" and "Thomas Gantt," q.v.

BROOKE, REBECCA ISAACS, see "Benjamin Tasker," q.v.
BROOKE, SARAH, see "Arthur Lee" and "Richard Lee," q.v.
BROOKE, THOMAS, see "Arthur Lee" and "Richard Lee;" q.v.
BROOKES, RICHARD, see "John Wilbourn, Jr." and "Robert Richards," q.v.
BROOKS, JAMES, see "John Moale" and "Wamouth Shaw," q.v.

BROOKS, SAMUEL (Delaware), pvt., Kent Co. Militia, Capt. John Caton's Company, 25 Apr 1757 (date of muster roll). {Ref: ARDE I:14}

BROOMBACK, JACOB (Maryland), pvt., Capt. Jonathan Hagar's Company Muster Roll, Frederick Co., circa 1757-1758, exact dates not given (served 6 days); bill of credit issued or paid to him for £0.6.0 in 1767, exact date not given. {Ref: MSA S960 or S752, p. 173; CSOS:107}

BROOMFIELD, FRANCIS (Delaware), b. c1743, Charlestown, MD (tailor, age 16 in 1759); pvt., enlisted by Capt. James Armstrong for the PA Regt. on 29 Apr 1759. {Ref: ARDE I:25; ARPA (2nd Series) 2:502, 585}

BROTHERS, FRANCIS (Maryland), b. c1735, Baltimore Co. (age 21 in 1756), poss. son of Thomas and Hannah Brothers; pvt., Capt. Christopher Gist's Company of VA Militia, 13 Jul 1756, enlisted at Baltimore; still living in 1764. {Ref: BCF:72; MSR I:37}

BROWN, ANN, see "James Brown," q.v.

BROWN, BENJAMIN (Maryland), pvt., Capt. Elias Delashmutt's Company Muster Roll, Frederick Co., 13 Aug 1757, exact dates not given (served 52 days); bill of credit issued or paid in his behalf to Casper Shaff on 2 Mar 1767 for £2.12.0. {Ref: MSA S960 or S752, p. 162; CSOS:98}

BROWN, EDWARD (Maryland), sgt., Capt. Thomas Norris' Company, Frederick Co., circa 1757-1758, exact dates not given (served 30 days); bill of credit issued or paid in his behalf to Michael McGuire on 27 Mar 1767 for £2. {Ref: MSA S960 or S752, p. 176; CSOS:107}

BROWN, GEORGE (Delaware), b. c1732, Derry, Ireland (tanner, age 26 in 1758); cpl., enlisted 25 Apr 1758 "for the campaign in the lower counties" by Capt. John McClughan. {Ref: ARDE I:17; ARPA (2nd Series) 2:570}

BROWN, GEORGE (Maryland), sgt., Capt. Thomas Norris' Company, Frederick Co., circa 1757-1758, exact dates not given (served 30 days); bill of credit issued or paid in his behalf to Michael McGuire on 27 Mar 1767 for £2. {Ref: MSA S960 or S752, p. 176; CSOS:107}

BROWN, GEORGE (Maryland), pvt., Capt. Richard Pearis' Company of MD Troops, Frederick Co., from 9 Oct 1757 to 31 May 1758; payment to him was recorded in Col. Dagworthy's account book on 15 Jul 1762. {Ref: MHS MS.375.1; CSOS:90; MHS MS.375}

BROWN, GEORGE (Maryland), boatman; pvt., Capt. Peregrine Brown's 7th Co. of Foot Militia, Kent Co., on 19 Feb 1758, by which time he had enlisted, but reportedly refused to appear and serve in arms against the enemy; he later stated that he "had been a resident in the county but had followed the sea and going up and down the bay in a shallop for about twelve months before that time, and that the Pressmaster had impressed both himself and his shallop to carry Capt. Browne's men and provisions over the bay, and that he could not do both services and that his vessel was one of those that attempted to carry them over and he was in her during the service he had been impressed to do." {Ref: ARMD 31:283, 286, 288} Militia pay account submitted in 1758, exact date not given. {Ref: MHM 9:4, p. 366}

BROWN, GODFREY (Maryland), pvt., Capt. Peter Butler's Company Muster Roll, Frederick Co., circa 1757-1758, exact dates not given (served 34 days); bill of credit or order issued in his behalf for £1.14.0 and paid to Casper Shaff on 2 Mar 1767. {Ref: MSA S960 or S752, p. 166; CSOS:96}

BROWN, JACOB (Maryland), pvt., Capt. Thomas Norris' Company, Frederick Co., circa 1757-1758, exact dates not given (served 30 days); bill of credit issued or paid in his behalf to Michael McGuire on 27 Mar 1767 for £1.10.0. {Ref: MSA S960 or S752, p. 176; CSOS:107}

BROWN, JAMES (Maryland), m. Ann (N), had children James, Sary, Mary, and Rachel, and d. testate by 19 May 1779. {Ref: WMG 5:3, p. 135} Pvt., Capt. Elias Delashmutt's Company Muster Roll, Frederick Co., 13 Aug 1757, exact dates not given (served 52 days); bill of credit issued or paid in his behalf to Elias Delashmut, Jr. on 16 Mar 1767 for £2.12.0. {Ref: MSA S960 or S752, p. 163; CSOS:98}

BROWN, JAMES (Maryland), b. c1690, Dorchester Co., son of Thomas Brown and Roseannah (N), m. Sarah Clarkson (widow of William Clarkson) by 1713, had children John, Thomas, James, Mary, Sarah, and Margery, and d. testate by 3 May 1770; husbandman, planter, land commissioner in 1728, county justice (1736-1737), member of the MD Assembly (1734-1737), and captain by 1758. {Ref: BDML I:174-175}

BROWN, JAMES (Maryland), b. c1692, d. 1756; captain, Queen Anne's Co., from 1742 to 1756; son Joel Brown (c1735-1787). {Ref: SCWM III:27, 242}

BROWN, JAMES (Maryland), b. 8 Oct 1727, Prince George's Co., son of John and Mary Brown, of Prince George's P. E. Parish. {Ref: PGCR 2:110} Pvt., Capt. Richard Pearis' Company of MD Troops, Frederick Co., from 9 Oct 1757 to 31 May 1758; pvt., Capt. Joshua Beall's Company of MD Troops, Prince George's Co., from 1 Jun 1758 to 30 Dec 1758; payment to him was recorded in Col. Dagworthy's account book on 15 Jul 1762; name listed once as "James Broun." {Ref: MHS MS.375; CSOS:83, 90; MHS MS.375.1}

BROWN, JOEL, see "James Brown," q.v.

BROWN, JOHN (Maryland), pvt., Capt. Joseph Chapline's Company Muster Roll No. 1, Frederick Co., circa 1757-1758, exact dates not given (served 43 days); bill of credit issued or paid in his behalf to Joseph Chaplin for £2.3.0 on 5 Mar 1767. {Ref: MSA S960 or S752, p. 191; CSOS:103} Pvt., Capt. Joseph Chapline's Company Muster Rolls No. 2 and 3, Frederick Co., circa 1757-1758, exact dates not given (served 9 days); bill of credit issued or paid in his behalf to Joseph Chaplin for £0.17.0 on 5 Mar 1767. {Ref: MSA S960 or S752, p. 193; CSOS:104}

BROWN, JOHN (Maryland), cpl., Capt. Moses Chapline's Company Muster Roll No. 2, Frederick Co., circa 1757-1758, exact dates not given (served 14 days); bill of credit issued or paid in his behalf to Joseph Chaplin for £0.18.7½ on 5 Mar 1767. {Ref: MSA S960 or S752, p. 197; CSOS:114}

BROWN, JOHN (Maryland), pvt., Capt. Elias Delashmutt's Company Muster Roll, Frederick Co., 13 Aug 1757, exact dates not given (served 52 days). {Ref: CSOS:98}

BROWN, JOHN, see "James Brown" and "Thomas Brown" and "Timothy McLaulin" and "Peregrine Brown," q.v.

BROWN, MARGERY, see "James Brown," q.v.

BROWN, MARY, see "James Brown," q.v.

BROWN, PEREGRINE (Maryland), b. 1 Oct 1727, Kent Co., son of John and Rachel Brown, of Shrewsbury Parish, m. (N), had children Peregrine and Sophia Charlotte, and d. testate by 19 Aug 1777. {Ref: ESVR; Kent Co. Wills 6:21} Captain, Kent Co., circa 1757-1758, exact dates not given; bill of credit issued or paid in his behalf to Robert Buchanan on 15 Apr 1767 for £2.10.0. {Ref: MSA S960 or S752, p. 179; CSOS:109}

BROWN, RACHEL, see "James Brown" and "Peregrine Brown," q.v.

BROWN, RICHARD (Maryland), pvt., Capt. Richard Pearis' Company of MD Troops, Frederick Co., from 9 Oct 1757 to 31 May 1758; pvt., Capt. John Dagworthy's Company of MD Troops, Frederick Co., from 1 Jun 1758 to 27 Dec 1758 (served 209 days) and was reported as deserted. {Ref: MHS MS.375.1; CSOS:75}

BROWN, SARAH, see "James Brown" and "Thomas Brown," q.v.

BROWN, SOPHIA, see "Peregrine Brown," q.v.

BROWN, THOMAS (Delaware), b. c1735, Ireland (laborer, age 24 in 1759); pvt., enlisted by Capt. James Armstrong for the PA Regt. on 3 May 1759. {Ref: ARDE I:25; ARPA (2nd Series) 2:585}

BROWN, THOMAS (Maryland), b. 1 Jan 1735/6 or 25 Mar 1736 (depending on the calendar used), Baltimore Co., orphan of John Brown in November 1742 "who would be age 7 next New Year's Day." {Ref: BCF:77} Pvt., Capt. Christopher Gist's Company of VA Militia, 13 Jul 1756, enlisted at Baltimore (b. MD, age 20). {Ref: MSR I:37}

BROWN, THOMAS (Maryland), b. c1733, MD (age 23 in 1756); pvt., Capt. Robert McKenzie's Company of VA Militia, enlisted in 1756 in Northumberland, VA. {Ref: MSR I:38} *Identification problem:* There were three men with this name who could have served in the war: (1) Thomas Brown, b. 22 Mar 1735, Baltimore Co., son of Thomas and Sarah Brown, of St. George's P. E. Parish; (2) Thomas Brown, not yet 21 when named in will of Thomas Treadway in July 1749; and, (3) Thomas Brown m. Elizabeth Courtney on 25 Jul 1758, St. George's P. E. Parish. {Ref: BCF:74, 77}

BROWN, WILLIAM (Maryland), sgt., Capt. Thomas Norris' Company, Frederick Co., circa 1757-1758, exact dates not given (served 30 days); bill of credit issued or paid in his behalf to Michael McGuire on 27 Mar 1767 for £2. {Ref: MSA S960 or S752, p. 176; CSOS:107}

BROWN, WILLIAM (Maryland), pvt., Capt. Samuel Chapman's Company Muster Roll, Anne Arundel Co., circa 1757-1758, exact dates not given; bill of credit issued or paid in his behalf to Stephen West for £1.18.0 on 13 Mar 1767. {Ref: MSA S960 or S752, p. 189}

BROWN, WILLIAM (Maryland), pvt., Frederick Co., received £5 bounty money on 16 Aug 1757 for enlisting in the militia. {Ref: ARMD 55:265, 619} Pvt., Capt. Joseph Chapline's Company Muster Roll No. 1, Frederick Co., circa 1757-1758, exact dates not given (served 17 days); bill of credit issued or paid in his behalf to Joseph Chaplin for £0.17.0 on 5 Mar 1767. {Ref: MSA S960 or S752, p. 191} Pvt., Capt. Moses Chapline's Company Muster Roll No. 3, Frederick Co., circa 1757-1758, exact dates not given (served 6 days); bill of credit issued or paid in his behalf to Joseph Chaplin for £0.6.0 on 24 Apr 1767. {Ref: MSA S960 or S752, p. 198; CSOS:115}

BROWN, WILLIAM (Maryland or Virginia), b. c1726 on Patowmack in Northumberland Co., VA (age about 30 in 1756); pvt., Royal American Regt., reported as deserted by Lieut. McBean at Annapolis. {Ref: *MD Gazette*, 16 Dec 1756}

BRUCE, NORMAND, see "Henry Inch," q.v.

BRUMWELL, JACOB (Delaware), pvt., Kent Co. Militia, Capt. John Caton's Company, 25 Apr 1757 (date of muster roll). {Ref: ARDE I:14}

BRUNNER (BRUNER), ELIAS (Maryland), m. Alberdina (N), had sons Peter and Stephen, and d. testate by 14 Oct 1783. {Ref: WMG 6:2, p. 83} Sgt., Capt. Stephen Rensburg's or Rensburger's Company Muster Roll, Frederick Co., circa 1757-1758, exact dates not given (served 42 days); bill of credit issued or paid in his behalf to Stephen Rensburg or Rensburger for £2.16.0 on 27 Mar 1767; name mistakenly transcribed once as "Elias Brimer." {Ref: MSA S960 or S752, p. 182; CSOS:111}

BRUNNER, JOHANNES (Maryland), indentured servant and soldier who served in the French and Indian War some time between 1756 and 1763 (exact dates not known); his master William Parlot, planter, requested compensation from the Baltimore County Court due to the loss of use of Brunner while in the service. {Ref: MHM 94:4, p. 426, citing Baltimore Co. Court Minutes}

BRUNNER (BRUNER), JOHN (Maryland), patriot and poss. soldier (rank not specified), Frederick Co., militia pay account submitted in 1758, exact date not given. {Ref: MHM 9:4, p. 367}

BRUNNER (BRUNER), PETER (Maryland), m. Maria Catherine (N) and d. testate by 27 Apr 1784; no children were named in his will. {Ref: WMG 6:3, p. 123} Pvt., Capt. Peter Bainbridge's Company Muster Roll, Frederick Co., circa 1757-1758, exact dates not given (served 28 days); bill of credit issued or paid in his behalf to Jacob Young on 4 Mar 1767 for £1.8.0. {Ref: MSA S960 or S752, p. 181; CSOS:111}

BRUNTON, ALEXANDER (Maryland), pvt., Capt. Alexander Beall's Company of MD Troops, Frederick Co., from 9 Oct 1757 to 23 Oct 1758 when he reportedly deserted; however, payment to him was recorded in Col. Dagworthy's account book on 12 Jul 1762 for work on Fort Cumberland. {Ref: MHS MS.375; CSOS:80; MHS MS.375.1}

BRYAN, ALEXANDER (Delaware), ensign, St. George's Hundred, Lower Regt. of Militia, New Castle Co., 1756. {Ref: ARDE I:11; ARPA (2nd Series) 2:525; HDE I:141} Alexander Bryan d. testate and unmarried by 15 Dec 1760. {Ref: CDSS:23}

BRYAN, JOHN (Delaware), ensign, New Castle Hundred, Upper Regt. of Militia, South Division, New Castle Co., 1756; 2nd lieut., 22 Apr 1758. {Ref: ARDE I:11, 16; ARPA (2nd Series) 2:526, 580; HDE I:141}

BRYAN, JOHN (Delaware), b. c1738, Ireland (schoolmaster, age 20 in 1758; height 6 ft. ½ in.); pvt., enlisted by Capt. Paul Jackson in New Castle Co. for the PA Troops on 15 May 1758. {Ref: ARDE I:27}

BRYAN (BRIAN), PHILIP (Maryland), pvt., Capt. William Luckett's Company Muster Roll, Frederick Co., circa 1757-1758, exact dates not given (served 30 days); bill of credit issued or paid in his behalf to William Luckett, Jr. for £1.10.0 on 6 Apr 1767. {Ref: MSA S960 or S752, pp. 169-170; CSOS:99}

BRYAN, WILLIAM (Delaware), b. c1724, St. Martin's, MD (planter, age 34 in 1758); pvt., enlisted 3 May 1758 "for the campaign in the lower counties" by Capt. John McClughan (muster roll dated 17 May 1758). {Ref: ARDE I:17; ARPA (2nd Series) 2:489, 570}

BRYAN, WILLIAM (Maryland), b. c1739 (aged about 33 in 1772 deposition); pvt., Capt. Francis Ware's Company of MD Troops, Charles Co., from 9 Oct 1757 to 30 Dec 1758. {Ref: MGSB 33:4, p. 698; MHS MS.375.1; CSOS:87} Payment to him was recorded in Col. Dagworthy's account book on 12 Jul 1762. {Ref: MHS MS.375}

BRYANT, JOHN, see "Henry Hall," q.v.

BRYANT, THOMAS (Maryland), farmer; pvt., Capt. Peregrine Brown's 7th Co. of Foot Militia, Kent Co., on 19 Feb 1758, by which time he had enlisted, but reportedly refused to appear and serve in arms against the enemy; he later stated that he "was constantly troubled with rheumatick pains and always on catching the least cold was laid up in bed, and he was entirely unable to undertake the service and is also a man in years." {Ref: ARMD 31:283, 286, 288}

BRYARLY, ROBERT, see "John Jones" and "Charles Pearce," q.v.

BUCHANAN, ANDREW (Maryland), patriot and merchant, Baltimore Town, m. Susanna Lawson, dau. of Alexander Lawson, in 1760. {Ref: *MD Gazette*, 24 Jul 1760} Pay account submitted for quartering soldiers in 1757 or 1758, exact dates not given. {Ref: MHM 9:3, p. 262}

BUCHANAN, ROBERT, see "Morris Dixon," q.v.

BUCK, CHARLES (Maryland), b. c1720, m. (N), had a son Thomas (1756-1842), and d. 1771; lieut., Frederick Co., in 1751 and prob. served in the French and Indian War in the 1750's. {Ref: SCWM III:28, 242}

BUCKINGHAM, RICHARD (Maryland), pvt., Capt. Francis Ware's Company of MD Troops, Charles Co., from 9 Oct 1757 to 8 Apr 1758 (served 182 days) when he was discharged; payment to him was recorded in Col. Dagworthy's account book on 22 Jul 1762. {Ref: MHS MS.375.1; CSOS:87; MHS MS.375}

BUCKMASTER, WILSON (Delaware), m. Esther or Hester (N), had children John Clifford, George, Wilson, Ann, and Elizabeth, and d. intestate by 31 May 1768; his widow d. testate by 15 Feb 1786. {Ref: CDSS:24} Lieut., Lower Part of Little Creek Hundred, Militia of Kent Co. on Delaware, 1756. {Ref: ARDE I:12; ARPA (2nd Series) 2:527-529; HDE I:141}

BUDD, JOHN (Delaware), pvt., Capt. Henry Vanbibber's Company of the Lower Counties on Delaware Troops at New Castle, enlisted on 13 May 1759. {Ref: ARDE I:26; ARPA (2nd Series) 2:594}

BUDD, THOMAS (Maryland), b. c1730, Dorchester Co. (sawyer, age 27 in 1757); pvt. who reportedly deserted from John Hay on the march to Carlisle Camp. {Ref: *MD Gazette*, 11 Aug 1757}

BUDGE, JACOB (Maryland), pvt., Capt. Moses Chapline's Company Muster Roll No. 1, Frederick Co., circa 1757-1758, exact dates not given (served 55 days); bill of credit issued or paid to him for £0.6.0 in 1767, exact date not given; name transcribed once as "Jacob Bridge." {Ref: MSA S960 or S752, p. 196; CSOS:113} See "Jacob Burge," q.v.

BULL, CONSTANTINE, see "Charles Wallace," q.v.

BULL, JACOB, see "James Munday," q.v.

BULLEN, ---- (Maryland), captain by 1758, was reported as "lately killed by the enemy." {Ref: *MD Gazette*, 14 Sep 1758}

BULLET, BEDY (Delaware), b. c1738, MD (age 21 in 1759); pvt., enlisted in Capt. John Wright's Company and mustered on 11 May 1759. {Ref: ARDE I:25; ARPA (2nd Series) 2:508, 592}

BULLMAN, JOHN (Maryland), b. c1729, MD (age about 28 in 1757); pvt., recruited by Thomas Beall, Prince George's Co. recruiting officer (exact date not given), and subsequently deserted in July 1757. {Ref: *MD Gazette*, 4 Aug 1757}

BULLOCK, GEORGE (Delaware), b. c1732, Ireland (weaver, age 26 in 1758); pvt., recruited by Capt. Benjamin Noxon and enlisted on 15 May 1758. {Ref: ARDE I:18; ARPA (2nd Series) 2:566}

BUMGARDNER (BUMGARNER), JOHN (Maryland), pvt., Capt. John White's Company Muster Roll, Frederick Co., circa 1757-1758, exact dates not given (served 6 days); bill of credit issued or paid to him for £0.6.0 in 1767, exact date not given. {Ref: MSA S960 or S752, p. 164; CSOS:96}

BURGE, JACOB (Maryland), pvt., Capt. Peter Bainbridge's Company Muster Roll, Frederick Co., circa 1757-1758, exact dates not given (served 41 days); bill of credit issued or paid in his behalf to Joseph Chaplin on 13 Jun 1768 for £2.1.0. {Ref: MSA S960 or S752, p. 181; CSOS:111} Pvt., Capt. Moses Chapline's Company Muster Roll No. 1, Frederick Co., circa 1757-1758, exact dates not given (served 55 days); bill of credit issued or paid in his behalf to Joseph Chaplin for £2.15.0 on 13 Jun 1768; name recorded once as "Jacob Budge" and mistakenly transcribed once as "Jacob Bridge." {Ref: MSA S960 or S752, p. 196; CSOS:113}

BURGE, WILLIAM (Maryland), pvt., Capt. Peter Bainbridge's Company Muster Roll, Frederick Co., circa 1757-1758, exact dates not given; bill of credit issued or paid in his behalf to Joseph Chaplin on 5 Mar 1767 for £0.4.0. {Ref: MSA S960 or S752, pp. 180-181}; pvt., Capt. Moses Chapline's Company Muster Roll No. 1, Frederick Co., circa 1757-1758, exact dates not given (served 55 days); bill of credit issued or paid in his behalf to Joseph Chaplin for £2.15.0 on 5 Mar 1767; name transcribed once as "William Birge." {Ref: MSA S960 or S752, p. 196; CSOS:113}

BURGESS, BASIL (Maryland), b. 20 Dec c1735, son of Charles and Martha Burgess, of Queen Anne's P. E. Parish, m. Ann Smith on 8 Feb 1759 and had children Elizabeth, William Frederick Augustus, and Charles. {Ref: PGCR 1:168} Cpl., Capt. Joshua Beall's Company Muster Roll, Prince George's Co., circa 1757-1758, exact dates not given; bill of credit issued or paid to him for £2.12.0 on 28 Feb 1767. {Ref: MSA S960 or S752, p. 184}

BURGESS, CHARLES, see "Basil Burgess," q.v.

BURGESS, JOHN (Maryland), b. c1735, MD (age 21 in 1756); pvt., Capt. Christopher Gist's Company of VA Militia, 13 Jul 1756, enlisted at Baltimore. {Ref: MSR I:37}

BURGESS, MARTHA, see "Basil Burgess," q.v.

BURGESS, RICHARD (Maryland), pvt., Capt. Samuel Chapman's Company Muster Roll, Anne Arundel Co., circa 1757-1758, exact dates not given; bill of credit issued or paid to him for £1.18.0 on 25 Mar 1767. {Ref: MSA S960 or S752, p. 189}

BURGESS, WILLIAM, see William Burge (Burges)," q.v.

BURK, DAVID (Maryland), pvt., Capt. John Middaugh's Company Muster Roll, Frederick Co., circa 1757-1758, exact dates not given (served 30 days); bill of credit issued to him for £1.10.0 in 1767, exact date not given. {Ref: MSA S960 or S752, p. 171; CSOS:100}

BURK, EDWARD (Delaware or Pennsylvania), b. c1741, MD (joiner, age 17 in 1758); pvt., Capt. John Blackwood's Company of the PA Regt., 22 May 1758 (date of muster roll return); pvt., enlisted 4 May 1759 in Capt. Johnstown's Company of the PA Regt. commanded by William Denny, Esq. on 12 May 1759. {Ref: ARPA (2nd Series) 2:487, 503}

BURKHAM, ROGER (Maryland), b. c1698, MD (age 58 *[sic]* in 1756); pvt., Capt. Robert McKenzie's Company of VA Militia, enlisted in 1756 in Hampshire, VA. {Ref: MSR I:38}

BURNALL, RICHARD (Maryland), pvt., Capt. Moses Chapline's Company Muster Roll No. 3, Frederick Co., circa 1757-1758, exact dates not given; bill of credit issued or paid to him for £0.6.0 in 1767, exact date not given; name listed once as "Richard Burrill." {Ref: MSA S960 or S752, p. 198; CSOS:115}

BURNES, PATRICK (Maryland), patriot, Frederick Co., who performed "sundry services at the fort" in 1763 and payment in the amount of £0.4.6 was still owed to him on 25 Nov 1763 (when reported by the Accounts Committee to the MD Assembly). {Ref: ARMD 58:400}

BURNES (BURNS), ROBERT (Maryland), pvt., Capt. Francis Ware's Company of MD Troops, Charles Co., from 9 Oct 1757 to 3 Sep 1758 (served 330 days) when he was discharged. {Ref: MHS MS.375.1} Payment to him was recorded in Col. Dagworthy's account book on 22 Jul 1762. {Ref: MHS MS.375}

BURNS (BURNES), ADAM (Maryland), pvt., Capt. William Luckett's Company Muster Roll, Frederick Co., circa 1757-1758, exact dates not given (served 30 days); militia pay account submitted in 1758, exact date not given. {Ref: MHM 9:4, p. 367} Bill of credit issued or paid in his behalf to William Luckett, Jr. for £1.4.0 on 6 Apr 1767. {Ref: MSA S960 or S752, p. 169; CSOS:100}

BURNS, GEORGE (Maryland), pvt., Capt. Thomas Norris' Company, Frederick Co., circa 1757-1758, exact dates not given (served 30 days); bill of credit issued or paid in his behalf to Valentine Rinehart on 6 May 1767 for £1.10.0. {Ref: MSA S960 or S752, p. 176; CSOS:108}

BURNSTON (BURNSTONE), JOSEPH (Maryland), cpl., Capt. Peter Butler's Company Muster Roll, Frederick Co., circa 1757-1758, exact dates not given (served 34 days); bill of credit or order issued in his behalf for £2.5.3 and paid to Casper Shaff on 2 Mar 1767. {Ref: MSA S960 or S752, p. 166; CSOS:96} Joseph Burnstone m. Ann (N), had children William, Sarah, Thomas, Mary, Anna, Ann, Rebecca, Elizabeth, Joseph, and Isaac, and d. testate by 1 Nov 1774. {Ref: MWG 4:3, p. 120}

BURRILL, RICHARD, see "Richard Burnall," q.v.

BURRIS, JAMES (Maryland), pvt., Capt. William Luckett's Company Muster Roll, Frederick Co., circa 1757-1758, exact dates not given (served 30 days); bill of credit issued or paid in his behalf to William Luckett, Jr. for £1.4.0 on 6 Apr 1767. {Ref: MSA S960 or S752, p. 169; CSOS:100}

BURTON, ARCHIBALD (Maryland), pvt., Capt. Joshua Beall's Company Muster Roll, Prince George's Co., circa 1757-1758, exact dates not given; bill of credit issued or paid to him for £1.19.0 in 1767, exact date not given. {Ref: MSA S960 or S752, p. 184}

BURTON, COMFORT, see "Burton Waples," q.v.

BURTON, JOHN (Delaware), lieut., Southern District of Indian River Hundred, Militia Regt. of Sussex Co., 1756-1758. {Ref: ARDE I:13, 15; ARPA (2nd Series) 2:529, 579; HDE I:141}

BURTON, JOHN (Maryland), pvt., Capt. Joshua Beall's Company Muster Roll, Prince George's Co., circa 1757-1758, exact dates not given; bill of credit issued or paid to him for £1.19.0 in 1767, exact date not given. {Ref: MSA S960 or S752, p. 184}

BURTON, SARAH, see "William Prettyman," q.v.

BURTON, WILLIAM (Maryland), pvt., Capt. Henry Casson's Company Muster Roll, Queen Anne's Co., circa 1757-1758, exact dates not given (served 27 days); bill of credit issued or paid in his behalf to Capt. Casson on 27 Mar 1767 for £1.7.0. {Ref: MSA S960 or S752, p. 178; CSOS:109}

BURTON, WILLIAM, see "William Prettyman," q.v.

BURTON, WOOLSEY, see "William Prettyman," q.v.

BUSH, DAVID (Delaware), New Castle Co., patriot who served as a Justice of the Peace, Justice of the Court of Oyer and Terminer, and Justice of the Court of Common Pleas in 1756. {Ref: GRSD 1:13}

BUSH, JOHN (Delaware), pvt., Kent Co. Militia, Capt. John Caton's Company, 25 Apr 1757 (date of muster roll). {Ref: ARDE I:13}

BUSH, SOLOMON (Maryland), sgt., Capt. Joshua Beall's Company of MD Troops, Prince George's Co., circa 9 Oct 1757 to 30 Dec 1758; payment to him was recorded in Col. Dagworthy's account book on 13 Jul 1762. {Ref: MHS MS.375; CSOS:83; MHS MS.375.1}

BUSHUP (BUSSUP), JOHN (Maryland), pvt., Capt. Thomas Norris' Company, Frederick Co., circa 1757-1758, exact dates not given (served 30 days); bill of credit issued or paid to him for £1.10.0 in 1767, exact date not given. {Ref: MSA S960 or S752, p. 176; CSOS:108}

BUTCHER, NICHOLAS (Maryland), patriot and poss. soldier (rank not specified), Frederick Co., militia pay account submitted in 1758, exact date not given. {Ref: MHM 9:4, p. 367}

BUTLER, EDWARD (Maryland), pvt., Capt. Elias Delashmutt's Company Muster Roll, Frederick Co., 13 Aug 1757, exact dates not given (served 52 days); also served another 30 days, exact dates not given; bill of credit issued or paid in his behalf to Elias Delashmut, Jr. on 16 Mar 1767 for £4.2.0. {Ref: MSA S960 or S752, p. 163; CSOS:94, 98}

BUTLER, HENRY (Maryland), pvt., Capt. Joshua Beall's Company Muster Roll, Prince George's Co., circa 1757-1758, exact dates not given; bill of credit issued or paid in his behalf to Joseph Chaplin for £1.18.0 on 5 Mar 1767. {Ref: MSA S960 or S752, p. 184}

BUTLER, HENRY (Maryland), alias Henry Batcly or Botely *[sic]*, lieut., Capt. Moses Chapline's Company Muster Roll No. 1, Frederick Co., circa 1757-1758, exact dates not given (served 55 days); bill of credit issued or paid in his behalf to Joseph Chaplin for £6.8.3 on 5 Mar 1767. {Ref: MSA S960 or S752, p. 196; CSOS:113} Lieut. in Capt. Moses Chapline's Company (Muster Roll No. 3), Frederick Co., circa 1757-1758, exact dates not given (served 6 days); bill of credit issued or paid in his behalf to Joseph Chaplin for £0.14.0 on 5 Mar 1767. {Ref: MSA S960 or S752, p. 198; CSOS:115} See "Henry Boteler," q.v.

BUTLER, JOHN (Maryland), pvt., Capt. Joshua Beall's Company of MD Troops, Prince George's Co., from 9 Oct 1757 to 16 Feb 1758 when he was discharged; name was mistakenly transcribed once as "John Buller." {Ref: MHS MS.375.1; CSOS:83} Payment to him was recorded in Col. Dagworthy's account book on 23 Jul 1762. {Ref: MHS MS.375}

BUTLER, PETER (Maryland), captain, Frederick Co., circa 1757-1758, exact dates not given; bill of credit or order issued in his behalf for £5.13.3 and paid to his admin. John Darnal on 13 Apr 1767. {Ref: MSA S960 or S752, pp. 166, 168; CSOS:96} "Capt. Peter Butler died lately at Frederick Town, a very useful man in public affairs." {Ref: *MD Gazette*, 19 Jan 1764}

BUTLER, SOLOMON (Maryland), pvt., Capt. Tobias Stansbury's Company Muster Roll, Baltimore Co., circa 1757-1758, exact dates not given; bill of credit issued or paid in his behalf to Josias Bowen for £3.12.0 on 13 Mar 1767. {Ref: MSA S960 or S752, p. 186}

BUTLER, SUSANNA, see "Samuel Bond," q.v.

BUTTEN, JOHN (Maryland), patriot, Annapolis, Anne Arundel Co., pay account submitted for quartering soldiers in 1757 or 1758, exact dates not given. {Ref: MHM 9:3, p. 262}

BUTTERBAUGH, GEORGE (Maryland), pvt., Capt. Jonathan Hagar's Company Muster Roll, Frederick Co., circa 1757-1758, exact dates not given (served 6 days); bill of credit issued or paid to him for £0.6.0 in 1767, exact date not given. {Ref: MSA S960 or S752, p. 173; CSOS:106}

BUTTERFIELD, WILLIAM (Maryland), patriot, Annapolis, Anne Arundel Co., received one drum "for the use of the Town Company" on 24 Sep 1756 and a drum "from the Armourer out of the Magazine" on 6 Feb 1758. {Ref: ARMD 52:614, 55:590} Mrs. Butterfield, wife of William Butterfield, was eating her breakfast on Sun. 15 Mar 1761 "when she was seized with some violent disorder and died before noon." {Ref: *MD Gazette*, 19 Mar 1761}

BUTTRAM, ELIZABETH, see "John Rice," q.v.

BUZZARD, SAMUEL, see "James Woolen," q.v.

BYRUM (BYREM), JAMES (Delaware), pvt., Kent Co. Militia, Capt. John Caton's Company, 25 Apr 1757 (date of muster roll). {Ref: ARDE I:14} James Byrem d. intestate by 25 Nov 1786 at which time Nancy Harden was granted letters of administration. {Ref: CDSS:26}

CADE, MARY, see "John Scarborough," q.v.

CADWALADER, THOMAS (Delaware), New Castle Co., patriot who served as a Justice of the Peace, Justice of the Court of Oyer and Terminer, and Justice of the Court of Common Pleas, 1756-1761. {Ref: GRSD 1:13, 15}

CAECIL, SAMUEL (Maryland), patriot, Frederick Co., was paid £1.4.4 on 16 Oct 1758 "for driving a waggon loaded with arms to Frederick Town" for the Western Expedition against Fort Duquesne. {Ref: ARMD 55:775}

CAGG, NICHOLAS (Maryland), pvt., Capt. John White's Company Muster Roll, Frederick Co., circa 1757-1758, exact dates not given (served 6 days); bill of credit issued or paid to him for £0.6.0 in 1767, exact date not given. {Ref: MSA S960 or S752, p. 164; CSOS:95}

CAHALL, EDWARD (Maryland), pvt., Capt. Henry Casson's Company Muster Roll, Queen Anne's Co., circa 1757-1758, exact dates not given (served 27 days); bill of credit issued or paid in his behalf to Capt. Casson on 27 Feb 1767 for £1.7.0. {Ref: MSA S960 or S752, p. 177; CSOS:109}

CAHALL, JAMES (Maryland), pvt., Capt. Henry Casson's Company Muster Roll, Queen Anne's Co., circa 1757-1758, exact dates not given (served 27 days); bill of credit issued or paid in his behalf to Capt. Casson on 27 Feb 1767 for £1.7.0. {Ref: MSA S960 or S752, p. 177; CSOS:109}

CAHOON, JOHN (Delaware), ensign, militia, Upper Part of Duck Creek Hundred, Kent Co. on Delaware, 1756. {Ref: ARDE I:12; ARPA (2nd Series) 2:527-529; HDE I:141}

CAHOON, SAMUEL (Delaware), pvt., Kent Co. Militia, Capt. John Caton's Company, 25 Apr 1757 (date of muster roll). {Ref: ARDE I:14}

CAHOON, WILLIAM (Delaware), pvt., Kent Co. Militia, Capt. John Caton's Company, 25 Apr 1757 (date of muster roll). {Ref: ARDE I:14}

CAIN, DANIEL (Delaware), son of Francis Cain (d. 1764), prob. m. Leah Shaw, widow of Ephraim Shaw (d. 1771). {Ref: CFD 2:13-14} Pvt., Kent Co. Militia, Capt. John Caton's Company, 25 Apr 1757 (date of muster roll). {Ref: ARDE I:14}

CAIN, FRANCIS (Delaware), son of Francis Cain (d. 1764), prob. m. Rachel (N) and d. by 21 Feb 1797. {Ref: CFD 2:13-14} Pvt., Kent Co. Militia, Capt. John Caton's Company, 25 Apr 1757 (date of muster roll). {Ref: ARDE I:14}

CAIN, LEAH, see "Daniel Cain," q.v.

CAIN, MANNASSEY or MANASSES (Delaware), son of Owen (d. testate by 9 Dec 1741) and Rachel Cain (d. testate by 26 Jul 1760). {Ref: CFD 2:13; CDSS:27} Pvt., Kent Co. Militia, Capt. John Caton's Company, 25 Apr 1757 (date of muster roll). {Ref: ARDE I:13}

CAIN, OWEN (Delaware), son of Owen Cain (d. testate by 9 Dec 1741) and wife Rachel (d. testate by 26 Jul 1760). {Ref: CFD 2:13; CDSS:27} Pvt., Kent Co. Militia, Capt. John Caton's Company, 25 Apr 1757 (date of muster roll). {Ref: ARDE I:13}

CAIN, RACHEL, see "Mannassey Cain" and "Owen Cain," q.v.

CAIN, THOMAS (Delaware), pvt., Kent Co. Militia, Capt. John Caton's Company, 25 Apr 1757 (date of muster roll). {Ref: ARDE I:14} Thomas Cain was a son of Daniel Cain (d. 1748) and his wife Elener (N). {Ref: CFD 2:13}

CAJA, PETER, see "Caja Peter," q.v.

CALDER, JAMES (Maryland), ensign, 44th Regt. of His Majesty's Foot Soldiers, and recruiting officer in Kent County in 1757. {Ref: ARMD 31:205-208}

CALDWELL, ---- (Maryland), sea captain by 1756, was in command of a sloop (name not given) en r oute from Somerset when it was captured by French Privateers. {Ref: *MD Gazette*, 2 Dec 1756}

CALDWELL, ANDREW (Delaware), major, Regt. of Militia for Kent Co. on Delaware, 1756. {Ref: ARDE I:12; ARPA (2nd Series) 2:527-529; HDE I:141}

CALDWELL, ELIZABETH, see "Robert Gordon," q.v.

CALDWELL, JAMES (Delaware), m. Hannah (N) and d. testate by 30 Apr 1783, naming James Caldwell, son of Joseph and Joannah Caldwell, in his will. {Ref: CDSS:28} Ensign, Tidbury Militia, Upper District of Murderkill Hundred, Kent Co. on Delaware, 1756; promoted to lieut. on 29 Mar 1758. {Ref: ARDE I:12, 15; ARPA (2nd Series) 2:527, 577}

CALDWELL, JONATHAN (Delaware), pvt., Kent Co. Militia, Capt. John Caton's Company, 25 Apr 1757 (date of muster roll); ensign, commissioned 23 May 1759. {Ref: ARDE I:13, 20; ARPA (5th Series) 1:300, (2nd Series) 2:583} Commissioned capt., 2nd Co. of Delaware State Troops in Continental Service, 15 Jan 1776. Joseph Caldwell, yeoman, m. Margaret (N), had no children, and d. testate in Murderkill Hundred by 11 Sep 1781. {Ref: CDSS:28}

CALDWELL, JOSEPH (Delaware), yeoman, m. Mary (N) and d. intestate by 10 Mar 1763; children unknown; served as commissioner of Kent Co. in 1759. {Ref: CDSS:28} Lieut., Tidbury Militia, Upper District of Murderkill Hundred, Kent Co. on Delaware, 1756; resigned in March 1758. {Ref: ARDE I:12, 15; ARPA (2nd Series) 2:527, 577; HDE I:14} See "James Caldwell," q.v.

CALLAGER, JOHN (Delaware), pvt., Capt. Henry Vanbibber's Company of the Lower Counties on Delaware Troops at New Castle, enlisted on 9 May 1759. {Ref: ARDE I:26; ARPA (2nd Series) 2:594}

CALLAHAUN, EDWARD (Delaware), pvt., Capt. French Battell's Company of Lower County Provincials, enlisted 22 May 1758. {Ref: ARDE I:16; ARPA (2nd Series) 2:555}

CAMER, LODOWICK (Maryland), pvt., Capt. Jonathan Hagar's Company Muster Roll, Frederick Co., circa 1757-1758, exact dates not given (served 6 days); bill

of credit issued or paid to him for £0.6.0 in 1767, exact date not given. {Ref: MSA S960 or S752, p. 173; CSOS:106}

CAMERON, DANIEL (Delaware), b. c1736, Inverness, Scotland (clerk, age 23 in 1759); pvt., enlisted by Capt. James Armstrong for the PA Regt. on 2 May 1759. {Ref: ARDE I:25; ARPA (2nd Series) 2:585}

CAMHEART, CATHARINE (Maryland), patriot or poss. widow of soldier (unnamed), Frederick Co., pay account submitted in 1758, exact date not given. {Ref: MHM 9:4, p. 367}

CAMPBELL, ANDREW (Maryland), patriot, Frederick Co., was paid on 12 Oct 1758 "for bringing some of the sick militia and their baggage from Fort Cumberland and for carrying arms from Fort Frederick" for the Western Expedition against Fort Duquesne. {Ref: ARMD 55:775}

CAMPBELL, ANN, see "William Campbell," q.v.

CAMPBELL, DAVID (Delaware), pvt., Capt. Richard McWilliams' Company of Foot, New Castle Co., enlisted 28 Dec 1757. {Ref: ARDE I:15}

CAMPBELL, FRANCIS (Maryland or Pennsylvania), pvt., Capt. Culbertson's Company, was wounded in "a recent battle with the Indians" in 1756 (exact date not given) in Cumberland Co., PA, after the burning of McCord's Fort. {Ref: *MD Gazette*, 29 Apr 1756}

CAMPBELL, JOHN (Maryland), patriot, Annapolis, Anne Arundel Co., pay account submitted for quartering soldiers in 1757 or 1758, exact dates not given. {Ref: MHM 9:3, p. 262}

CAMPBELL, ROBERT (Maryland), b. c1737, MD (cooper, age 21 in 1758), pvt., enlisted by Capt. John Singleton for the PA Regt. on 8 May 1758. {Ref: ARPA (2nd Series) 2:474}

CAMPBELL, SARAH, see "John Evans," q.v.

CAMPBELL, WILLIAM (Maryland), b. c1725, m. Ann (N), had children John, Ann, Alexander, and Lizzy, and d. testate by 12 May 1774. {Ref: WMG 4:2, p. 64} Pvt., Capt. John Dagworthy's Company of MD Troops, Frederick Co., from 9 Oct 1757 to 16 Apr 1759 (served 552 days) and reportedly deserted; however, payment to him was recorded in Col. Dagworthy's account book on 26 Feb 1763. {Ref: MHS MS.375.1; CSOS:75; MHS MS.375}

CAMPER (CUMPER), JOHN (Maryland), pvt., Capt. Peter Butler's Company Muster Roll, Frederick Co., circa 1757-1758, exact dates not given (served 34 days); bill of credit or order issued in his behalf for £1.14.0 and paid to Casper Shaff on 2 Mar 1767. {Ref: MSA S960 or S752, p. 166; CSOS:96}

CANDLEMAN, MATTHEW (Maryland or Pennsylvania), German (age not given); pvt. in 1757 who was hanged at Carlisle for desertion. {Ref: *MD Gazette*, 10 Nov 1757}

CANNON, MATTHEW (Delaware), pvt., Capt. Richard McWilliams' Company of Foot, New Castle Co., enlisted 28 Dec 1757. {Ref: ARDE I:14}

CAPROON (CAPEROON), RICHARD (Maryland), pvt., Capt. Joshua Beall's Company of MD Troops, Prince George's Co., from 9 Oct 1757 to 8 Jun 1758. {Ref: MHS MS.375.1; CSOS:83} Payment to him was recorded in Col. Dagworthy's account book on 23 Jul 1762. {Ref: MHS MS.375}

CAPTAIN CHARLES, Indian Chief, see "Evan Shelby," q.v.

CARCAUD, DAVID (Maryland), captain and commander of the brigantine *Duke of Marlborough*, was commissioned by the Council of Maryland as a Flag of Truce on 15 Oct 1760 to carry French prisoners of war to Port St. Louis on the island of Hispaniola. {Ref: ARMD 31:414-415, 458-460}

CARD, BENSON (Maryland), pvt., Capt. Joshua Beall's Company of MD Troops, Prince George's Co., from 9 Oct 1757 to 7 Dec 1757 when he was discharged. {Ref: MHS MS.375.1; CSOS:83} Payment to him was recorded in Col. Dagworthy's account book on 24 Jul 1762. {Ref: MHS MS.375}

CARD, GABRIEL (Maryland), pvt., Capt. Joshua Beall's Company of MD Troops, Prince George's Co., from 9 Oct 1757 to 7 Dec 1757 when he was discharged; payment to him was recorded in Col. Dagworthy's account book on 24 Jul 1762; name listed once as "Gabriel or Sabriet Card." {Ref: MHS MS.375.1; CSOS:83; MHS MS.375}

CARD (CART), VALENTINE (Maryland), alias Felty Card *[sic]*, pvt., Capt. Peter Bainbridge's Company Muster Roll, Frederick Co., circa 1757-1758, exact dates not given (served 30 days); bill of credit issued or paid in his behalf to Casper Shaff on 4 Mar 1767 for £1.8.0; name mistakenly transcribed once as "Folly Card." {Ref: MSA S960 or S752, p. 180; CSOS:111}

CARLIN, JOHN (Delaware), b. c1737, MD (laborer, age 21 in 1758); pvt., recruited by Capt. Benjamin Noxon and enlisted on 3 May 1758. {Ref: ARDE I:18; ARPA (2nd Series) 2:485, 566}

CARLISLE, MARY, see "John Long," q.v.

CARMACK, CORNELIUS (Maryland), son of William Carmack (d. 1776) and Jan (N). {Ref: WMG 5:1, p. 19} Sgt., Capt. John Middaugh's Company Muster Roll, Frederick Co., circa 1757-1758, exact dates not given (served 30 days); bill of credit issued or paid in his behalf to Thomas Beatty, Jr. for £2 on 23 Feb 1767. {Ref: MSA S960 or S752, p. 171; CSOS:100}

CARMACK, WILLIAM (Maryland), son of William Carmack (d. 1776) and Jan (N). {Ref: WMG 5:1, p. 19} Cpl., Capt. John Middaugh's Company Muster Roll, Frederick Co., circa 1757-1758, exact dates not given (served 30 days); bill of credit issued or paid in his behalf to Thomas Beatty, Jr. for £2 on 23 Feb 1767. {Ref: MSA S960 or S752, p. 171; CSOS:100}

CARMICAL (CARMICHAEL), NEAL (Maryland), pvt., Capt. Francis Ware's Company of MD Troops, Charles Co., circa 1757-1758, exact dates not given; pvt., Capt. John Dagworthy's Company of MD Troops, Frederick Co., from 31 Dec 1758 to 26 Apr 1759 (served 119 days) and was discharged. {Ref: MHS MS.375.1; CSOS:76, 87} Payment to him was recorded in Col. Dagworthy's account book on 18 Jul 1762 and an account submitted to the MD Assembly on 25 Nov 1763 indicated he was due £4.12.3 as "granted by the Act for granting a Sum of Money as a present to the Forces, late in the pay and Service of this Province, and taken into his Majesty's Service by Brigadier General Forbes." {Ref: MHS MS.375; ARMD 58:401}

CARN (CARNS, CARNES), BALSUM (Maryland), pvt., Capt. John Dagworthy's Company of MD Troops, Frederick Co., from 9 Oct 1757 to 17 Feb 1758 when promoted to drummer; demoted to pvt. on 9 Jun 1758 and served until 16 Apr 1759 (552 days) when he reportedly deserted; however, payment to him was recorded in Col. Dagworthy's account book on 26 Feb 1763. {Ref: MHS MS.375.1; CSOS:75; MHS MS.375}

CARNAN, JOHN, see "Andrew Ungrie," q.v.

CARNES, JOHN (Delaware), b. c1742, MD (laborer, age 16 in 1758); pvt., recruited by Capt. Benjamin Noxon and enlisted on 3 May 1758. {Ref: ARDE I:18; ARPA (2nd Series) 2:485, 566}

CARPENTER, CHRISTOPHER (Maryland), pvt., Capt. Joseph Chapline's Company Muster Roll No. 4, Frederick Co., circa 1757-1758, exact dates not given (served 7 days); bill of credit issued or paid in his behalf to Joseph Chaplin for £0.7.0 on 5 Mar 1767. {Ref: MSA S960 or S752, p. 194; CSOS:105}

CARPENTER, JOHN (Maryland), b. 6 Mar 1737/8, Baltimore Co., orphan son of John Carpenter (d. by November 1742), court record noting "his son John would be age 6 on 6 Mar 1743." {Ref: BCF:95} Pvt., Capt. Christopher Gist's Company of VA Militia, 13 Jul 1756, enlisted at Baltimore (b. MD, age 19). {Ref: MSR I:37}

CARPENTER, NICHOLAS (Maryland), pvt., Capt. William McClellan's Company of MD Volunteers, Frederick Co., circa 1763-1764; on muster roll dated 15 Nov 1764 at Camp at the Forks of Muskingham. {Ref: ARMD 32:99}

CARR, JOHN (Maryland), pvt., Capt. John White's Company Muster Roll, Frederick Co., circa 1757-1758, exact dates not given (served 6 days); bill of credit issued or paid to him for £0.6.0 in 1767, exact date not given. {Ref: MSA S960 or S752, p. 164; CSOS:95}

CARR, JOHN (Maryland), pvt., Capt. Francis Ware's Company of MD Troops, Charles Co., from 9 Oct 1757 to 14 Sep 1758 (served 340 days) when he was reported as killed; however, payment to him was recorded in Col. Dagworthy's account book on 7 Mar 1763 for work on Fort Cumberland. {Ref: MHS MS.375; CSOS:87; MHS MS.375.1}

CARR, WILLIAM (Delaware), pvt., Capt. Henry Vanbibber's Company of the Lower Counties on Delaware Troops at New Castle, enlisted on 7 May 1759. {Ref: ARDE I:26; ARPA (2nd Series) 2:594}

CARRICK, JOSEPH (Maryland), pvt., Capt. Joshua Beall's Company of MD Troops, Prince George's Co., from 9 Oct 1757 to 7 Apr 1758 when he was discharged; payment to him was recorded in Col. Dagworthy's account book on 16 Jul 1762. {Ref: MHS MS.375; CSOS:83; MHS MS.375.1}

CARRIGAN (CARRIGEN), HUGH (Maryland), pvt., Capt. Alexander Beall's Company of MD Troops, Frederick Co., from 9 Oct 1757 to 14 Sep 1758 when he was reported as killed. {Ref: MHS MS.375.1; CSOS:80} However, such was not the case. On 30 Sep 1760 Hugh Carrigan and Thomas Roles petitioned the MD Assembly "praying some recompence for their past services as soldiers enlisted in the MD Service in 1757 who were taken prisoners by the French and sent to Mississippi and from thence to Old France." {Ref: ARMD 56:339} Payment to him was recorded in Col. Dagworthy's account book on 7 Mar 1763. {Ref: MHS MS.375}

CARROLL, CHARLES (Maryland), b. 22 Mar 1723/4, Annapolis, son of Charles Carroll and Dorothy Blake, m. Margaret Tilghman on 23 Jun 1763, had no surviving children, and d. 23 Mar 1783, Baltimore Co.; patriot, barrister, businessman, member of the MD Assembly (1756-1761), MD Senator (1776-1783), Revolutionary War patriot (Delegate to Continental Congress, 1776-1777, and Council of Safety, 1775-1776). {Ref: BDML I:195-197} Pay account submitted for quartering soldiers in 1757 or 1758, exact dates not given. {Ref: MHM 9:3, p. 262}

CARROLL, CHARLES JR. (Maryland), patriot, Annapolis, Anne Arundel Co., pay account submitted for quartering soldiers in 1757 or 1758, exact dates not given. {Ref: MHM 9:3, p. 262}

CARROLL (CARRILL), JOHN (Maryland), pvt. (county not stated), received £5 bounty money on 25 May 1757 for enlisting in the militia. {Ref: ARMD 55:265, 619}

CARROLL, JULIANA, see "Edward Tilghman," q.v.

CARSON, CHARLES (Delaware), lieut., Appoquinimink Hundred, Lower Regt. of Militia, New Castle Co., 1756 (name listed once as "Charles Casson"). {Ref: ARDE I:11; ARPA (2nd Series) 2:525; HDE I:141}

CARTER, EDMUND (Maryland), merchant; pvt., Capt. Peregrine Brown's 7th Co. of Foot Militia, Kent Co., on 19 Feb 1758, by which time he had enlisted, but reportedly refused to appear and serve in arms against the enemy. {Ref: ARMD 31:283}

CARTER, JOHN (Delaware), pvt., Kent Co. Militia, Capt. John Caton's Company, 25 Apr 1757 (date of muster roll). {Ref: ARDE I:13}

CARTER, JOSEPH (Delaware), b. c1735, MD (age 24 in 1759); pvt., enlisted in Capt. John Wright's Company and mustered on 11 May 1759. {Ref: ARDE I:25; ARPA (2nd Series) 2:508, 592}

CARTER, RICHARD (Maryland), pvt., Capt. Joseph Chapline's Company Muster Roll No. 4, Frederick Co., circa 1757-1758, exact dates not given (served 5 days); bill of credit issued or paid in his behalf to Joseph Chaplin for £0.5.0 on 5 Mar 1767. {Ref: MSA S960 or S752, p. 194; CSOS:104}

CARTER, WILLIAM (Maryland), patriot, Annapolis, Anne Arundel Co., pay account submitted for quartering soldiers in 1757 or 1758, exact dates not given. {Ref: MHM 9:3, p. 261}

CARTER, WILLIAM (Maryland), pvt., Capt. Elias Delashmutt's Company Muster Roll, Frederick Co., circa 1757-1758, exact dates not given (served 30 days); bill of credit issued or paid in his behalf to Elias Delashmut, Jr. on 16 Mar 1767 for £1.10.0. {Ref: MSA S960 or S752, p. 163; CSOS:94}

CARTWRIGHT, JACOB (Delaware), pvt., Capt. Henry Vanbibber's Company of the Lower Counties on Delaware Troops at New Castle, enlisted on 19 May 1759. {Ref: ARDE I:26; ARPA (2nd Series) 2:594}

CARVILL, JOHN (Maryland), patriot and poss. soldier (rank not specified), Kent Co., militia pay account submitted in 1758, exact date not given. {Ref: MHM 9:4, p. 366} John Carvill m. Jane Harris on 25 Nov 1732 and their son John was b. 9 Sep 1733 in Shrewsbury Parish, Kent Co. {Ref: ESVR}

CARY, JAMES (Maryland), patriot and poss. officer, Baltimore Town; when notice was given in 1756 about deserters from the Royal American Regt., it was instructed that if found they should be delivered to Lieut. McBean in Annapolis or James Cary at Baltimore Town. {Ref: *MD Gazette*, 4 Nov 1756}

CARY, JOHN (Maryland), pvt., Capt. Peter Butler's Company Muster Roll, Frederick Co., circa 1757-1758, exact dates not given (served 34 days); bill of credit or order issued in his behalf for £1.14.0 and paid to Robert Couden on 5 Mar 1767. {Ref: MSA S960 or S752, p. 168; CSOS:96} He was paid £53.1.0 on 11 Jul 1758 at Fort Frederick "for 73 blanketts which were sent to Winchester" for the Western Expedition against Fort Duquesne. {Ref: ARMD 55:773}

CARY (CAREY), THOMAS (Maryland), pvt., Capt. Henry Casson's Company Muster Roll, Queen Anne's Co., circa 1757-1758, exact dates not given (served 27 days); bill of credit issued or paid in his behalf to Capt. Casson on 27 Mar 1767 for £1.7.0. {Ref: MSA S960 or S752, p. 178; CSOS:109}

CASE, SIMON (Maryland), pvt., Capt. William Luckett's Company Muster Roll, Frederick Co., circa 1757-1758, exact dates not given (served 30 days); bill of credit issued or paid in his behalf to William Luckett, Jr. for £1.10.0 on 6 Apr 1767. {Ref: MSA S960 or S752, p. 170; CSOS:99}

CASELDINE (CASTLEDINE), JOHN (Maryland), pvt., Capt. Peregrine Brown's Company Muster Roll, Kent Co., circa 1757-1758, exact dates not given (served 15 days); bill of credit issued or paid in his behalf to John Paca on 18 May 1767 for £0.15.0. {Ref: MSA S960 or S752, p. 179; CSOS:110}

CASNER (CASENER), GEORGE (Maryland), pvt., Capt. Jonathan Hagar's Company Muster Roll, Frederick Co., circa 1757-1758, exact dates not given (served 6 days); bill of credit issued or paid in his behalf to Joseph Chaplin for £0.6.0 on 24 Apr 1767. {Ref: MSA S960 or S752, p. 173; CSOS:106}

CASNER, JACOB (Maryland), sgt., Capt. Jonathan Hagar's Company Muster Roll, Frederick Co., circa 1757-1758, exact dates not given (served 6 days); bill of credit issued or paid in his behalf to Joseph Chaplin for £0.8.0 on 24 Apr 1767. {Ref: MSA S960 or S752, p. 173; CSOS:106}

CASNER, JOHN (Maryland), sgt., Capt. Jonathan Hagar's Company Muster Roll, Frederick Co., circa 1757-1758, exact dates not given (served 6 days); bill of credit issued or paid to him for £0.8.0 in 1767, exact date not given. {Ref: MSA S960 or S752, p. 173; CSOS:106}

CASNER, MARTIN (Maryland), lieut., Capt. Jonathan Hagar's Company Muster Roll, Frederick Co., circa 1757-1758, exact dates not given; militia pay account submitted in 1758, exact date not given. {Ref: MHM 9:4, p. 367; CSOS:106} Bill of credit issued or paid in his behalf to Jonathan Hagar for £0.14.0 on 10 Oct 1767. {Ref: MSA S960 or S752, pp. 173-174} On 29 Jul 1758 a payment of £6 was made to Casper Shaaf for Martin Casner at Fort Frederick "for his [Casner] attending the N Carolina Detachments on the New Road with his waggon" and another payment of £2.5.0 "for carrying the N Carolina Troops baggage to Fort Loudoun" for the Western Expedition against Fort Duquesne. {Ref: ARMD 55:774}

CASSON, HENRY (Maryland), captain, Queen Anne's Co., 1757-1758, exact dates not given; a company of militia under his command arrived in Annapolis on 1

Feb 1758 on their way to Fort Frederick. {Ref: CSOS:108; *MD Gazette*, 2 Feb 1758} Pay account submitted in 1758, exact date not given. {Ref: MHM 9:4, p. 367} Pay receipt (signed but not dated): "Received of His Excellency Horatio Sharpe the sum of £22.7.0 currency out of the Subscription Money in his hands towards reimbursing me the money that I was under a necessity of expending in Jany., Feby., and March 1758, when I was marching with my Company of Militia from Queen Anns County to the Frontier of Frederick during my stay there and on my return." {Ref: ARMD 55:777} Capt., Queen Anne's Co. Muster Roll, bill of credit issued or paid to him on 27 Feb 1767 for £4.10.0. {Ref: MSA S960 or S752, p. 177}

CASTLE (CASTEEL), JOHN (Maryland), m. Martha (N), had children John, Deliverance, and Rebecca (all minors in 1778), and d. testate by 3 Oct 1778. {Ref: WMG 5:2, p. 87} Pvt., Capt. Moses Chapline's Company Muster Roll No. 2, Frederick Co., circa 1757-1758, exact dates not given (served 14 days); bill of credit issued or paid in his behalf to Joseph Chaplin for £0.13.0 on 5 Mar 1767. {Ref: MSA S960 or S752, p. 197; CSOS:114} Pvt., Capt. Moses Chapline's Company Muster Roll No. 3, Frederick Co., circa 1757-1758, exact dates not given (served 6 days); bill of credit issued or paid in his behalf to Joseph Chaplin for £0.6.0 on 5 Mar 1767. {Ref: MSA S960 or S752, p. 198; CSOS:114}

CASTLE (CASTEEL), PETER (Maryland), pvt., Capt. Moses Chapline's Company Muster Roll No. 3, Frederick Co., circa 1757-1758, exact dates not given (served 6 days); bill of credit issued or paid in his behalf to Joseph Chaplin for £0.6.0 on 5 Mar 1767. {Ref: MSA S960 or S752, p. 198; CSOS:115} Pvt., Capt. Joseph Chapline's Company Muster Roll No. 1, Frederick Co., circa 1757-1758, exact dates not given (served 33 days); bill of credit issued or paid in his behalf to Joseph Chaplin for £1.13.0 on 5 Mar 1767. {Ref: MSA S960 or S752, pp. 190-191; CSOS:102}

CASTLE (CASTEEL), ZACHARIAH (Maryland), pvt., Capt. Moses Chapline's Company Muster Roll No. 2, Frederick Co., circa 1757-1758, exact dates not given (served 14 days); bill of credit issued or paid in his behalf to Joseph Chaplin for £0.13.0 on 5 Mar 1767. {Ref: MSA S960 or S752, p. 197; CSOS:114} Pvt., Capt. Moses Chapline's Company Muster Roll No. 3, Frederick Co., circa 1757-1758, exact dates not given (served 6 days); bill of credit issued or paid in his behalf to Joseph Chaplin for £0.6.0 on 5 Mar 1767. {Ref: MSA S960 or S752, p. 198; CSOS:115}

CATCHMORE, THOMAS, see "Thomas Ketchmore," q.v.

CATON, BENJAMIN (Delaware), son of John Caton (d. 1744) and Agnes (N), poss. m. Mary (N), had a son James, and prob. d. intestate by 7 Nov 1797. {Ref: CFD 2:16-17; CDSS:34} Pvt., Kent Co. Militia, Capt. John Caton's Company, 25 Apr 1757 (date of muster roll); ensign, 26 Apr 1758; lieut., 3rd PA Regt., commissioned 21 May 1759; name listed once as "Benjamin Catin." {Ref: ARDE I:13, 16, 20; ARPA (2nd Series) 2:580, 582}

CATON, JEANETTE, see "Moses Chapline," q.v.

CATON, JOHN (Delaware), son of John Caton (d. 1744) and Agnes (N), m. Elizabeth Betts (widow of (N) Betts and dau. of John Clark), had no children, and d. testate by 19 Aug 1769. {Ref: CFD 2:14-16; CDSS:34} Captain, Tidbury

Militia, Upper District of Murderkill Hundred, Kent Co. on Delaware, 1756-1758. {Ref: ARDE I:12, 15; ARPA (2nd Series) 2:527, 577; HDE I:141}

CAUFMAN, HENRY (Maryland), pvt., Capt. Peter Butler's Company Muster Roll, Frederick Co., circa 1757-1758, exact dates not given (served 34 days); bill of credit or order issued to him for £1.14.0 in March 1767. {Ref: MSA S960 or S752, p. 167; CSOS:97}

CAVENAUGH (CAVINAUGHT), WILLIAM (Maryland), sgt., Capt. Francis Ware's Company of MD Troops, Charles Co., circa 1757-1758, exact dates not given. {Ref: MHS MS.375.1; CSOS:87} Payment to him was recorded in Col. Dagworthy's account book on 22 Jul 1762. {Ref: MHS MS.375}

CEARSEY, ARCHABALD (Delaware), pvt., Kent Co. Militia, Capt. John Caton's Company, 25 Apr 1757 (date of muster roll). {Ref: ARDE I:13}

CHAILLE, PETER (Maryland), b. c1730, Somerset Co., son of Moses Chaillé and Mary (N), m. 1st to Comfort Houston by 1753 and 2nd to Scarborough Holland (widow of Nehemiah Holland) by 1797, had children Moses, Zachariah, Mary, Henrietta, Margaret, and Comfort, and d. 1802, Worcester Co.; captain by 1762, member of the MD Assembly (1762-1763, 1765-1766, 1771-1780), colonel in the militia in 1776, and county justice (1779-1786). {Ref: BDML I:205}

CHALMERS (CHAILMERS), JAMES (Maryland), patriot, Annapolis, Anne Arundel Co., pay account submitted for quartering soldiers in 1757 or 1758, exact dates not given. {Ref: MHM 9:3, p. 260} Militia pay account submitted in 1758, exact date not given. {Ref: MHM 9:4, p. 366}

CHALMERS (CHAILMERS), JOHN (Maryland), patriot, Annapolis, Anne Arundel Co., pay account submitted for quartering soldiers in 1757 or 1758, exact dates not given. {Ref: MHM 9:3, p. 261}

CHAMBERLAINE, SAMUEL (Maryland), b. 18 May 1698, Cheshire, England, son of Thomas Chamberlaine and Ann Penketh, m. 1st to Mary Ungle in 1721 and 2nd to Henrietta Maria Lloyd in 1729, had children Thomas, James Lloyd, Samuel, Richard, Robert, Henrietta Maria, and Anne, and d. 29 Apr 1773, Talbot Co.; patriot, factor, merchant, member of the MD Assembly and of the MD Council (Lower House, 1728-1732, Upper House, 1739-1768), county justice (1732-1738), and naval officer at Pocomoke (1740-1742) and Oxford (1754-1768). {Ref: BDML I:207-208; *MD Gazette*, 10 Jun 1773}

CHAMBERLAINE, THOMAS (Maryland), b. 1731, Talbot Co., eldest son of Samuel Chamberlaine and Henrietta Maria Lloyd. m. Susanna Robins, had a son (N), and d. 1764 at his father's home near Oxford, MD; colonel (date not given). {Ref: BDML I:207; *MD Gazette*, 17 May 1764}

CHAMBERS (CHAMBESS), JOSEPH (Delaware), b. c1738, MD (laborer, age 20 in 1758); pvt., recruited by Capt. Benjamin Noxon and enlisted on 29 Apr 1758. {Ref: ARDE I:18; ARPA (2nd Series) 2:485, 566}

CHAMBERS, WILLIAM (Maryland or Pennsylvania), pvt., Capt. Culbertson's Company, was killed in "a recent battle with the Indians" in 1756 (exact date not given) in Cumberland Co., PA, after the burning of McCord's Fort. {Ref: *MD Gazette*, 29 Apr 1756}

CHANCE, ALEXANDER (Delaware), yeoman, m. Elizabeth (N), had children Edmund, John, and Mary, and d. testate by 12 Jan 1773. {Ref: CDSS:34-35} Lieut. in Capt. Edward Fitzrandolph's Company, New Castle Co., 1747-1748, during King George's War against Canada; capt., Appoquinimink Hundred, Lower Regt. of Militia, New Castle Co., 1756. {Ref: ARDE I:11; ARPA (2nd Series) 2:525; HDE I:141}

CHANCE, HENRY (Maryland), pvt., Capt. John Middaugh's Company Muster Roll, Frederick Co., circa 1757-1758, exact dates not given (served 30 days). {Ref: CSOS:102}

CHANCY, SARAH, see "Aquila Nelson," q.v.

CHANDLER, DAVID (Delaware), b. c1737, Greenwick, NJ, weaver (age 21 in 1758); pvt., enlisted 24 Apr 1758 "for the campaign in the lower counties" by Capt. John McClughan. {Ref: ARDE I:17; ARPA (2nd Series) 2:570}

CHANDLER, STEPHEN, see "Peter Dent," q.v.

CHANDLER, THOMAS (Maryland), clerk, Capt. Peregrine Brown's Company Muster Roll, Kent Co., circa 1757-1758, exact dates not given (served 15 days); bill of credit issued or paid in his behalf to Thomas Ringgold, Esq. on 20 Feb 1767 for £0.15.0. {Ref: MSA S960 or S752, p. 179; CSOS:110}

CHANDLER, THOMAS JR. (Maryland), b. 19 Oct 1738, Kent Co., son of Thomas and Mary Chandler, of Shrewsbury Parish. {Ref: ESVR} Pvt., Capt. Peregrine Brown's Company Muster Roll, Kent Co., circa 1757-1758, exact dates not given (served 15 days); bill of credit issued or paid in his behalf to Thomas Ringgold, Esq. on 20 Feb 1767 for £0.15.0. {Ref: MSA S960 or S752, p. 179; CSOS:110}

CHANEY, BENJAMIN, see "Richard Chaney," q.v.

CHANEY (CHANY, CHENEY), EZEKIEL (Maryland), b. 25 May 1727, Prince George's Co., son of Charles and Mary Cheeny, of Queen Anne Parish; Ezekiel m. Anne (N), had children Richard, Ezekiel, Nathan, Edward, and others (mentioned, but not named in his will), and d. testate by 20 Aug 1769. {Ref: PGCR 1:169; WMG 3:2, p. 75} Pvt., Frederick Co. militia, 1757; Gov. Horatio Sharpe wrote, in part, to the MD Assembly on 7 Dec 1757: "With regard to the complaint of Ezekiel and Jeremiah Cheney, whose articles and indented servants are said to have run away from them, and to have enlisted into our Provincial Forces, I can only say, that if the case is as they represent it, and they have a right to satisfaction for their servants, the law will give them relief." {Ref: ARMD 55:319-320} Pvt., Capt. Joseph Chapline's Company Muster Rolls No. 2 and 3, Frederick Co., circa 1757-1758, exact dates not given (served 9 days); militia pay account submitted in 1758, exact date not given. {Ref: MHM 9:4, p. 368; CSOS:104} Bill of credit issued or paid in his behalf to Joseph Chaplin for £0.9.0 on 5 Mar 1767. {Ref: MSA S960 or S752, pp. 193-194} Cpl., Capt. Joseph Chapline's Company Muster Roll No. 4, Frederick Co., circa 1757-1758, exact dates not given (served 6 days); bill of credit issued or paid in his behalf to Joseph Chaplin for £0.8.0 on 5 Mar 1767. {Ref: MSA S960 or S752, p. 194; CSOS:104}

CHANEY (CHENEY), GREENBURY or GREENBERRY (Maryland), pvt., Capt. Joseph Chapline's Company Muster Roll No. 1, Frederick Co., circa 1757-1758, exact dates not given (served 55 days); bill of credit issued or paid in his behalf to Joseph Chaplin for £2.15.0 on 5 Mar 1767. {Ref: MSA S960 or S752, p. 191; CSOS:102} Pvt., Capt. Moses Chapline's Company Muster Roll No. 1, Frederick Co., circa 1757-1758, exact dates not given (served 55 days); bill of credit issued or paid in his behalf to Joseph Chaplin for £2.15.0 on 5 Mar 1767. {Ref: MSA S960 or S752, p. 196; CSOS:113} Pvt., Capt. Moses Chapline's Company Muster Roll No. 2, Frederick Co., circa 1757-1758, exact dates not given (served 14 days); bill of credit issued or paid in his behalf to Joseph Chaplin for £0.14.0 on 5 Mar 1767. {Ref: MSA S960 or S752, p. 197; CSOS:114}

CHANEY (CHENEY, CHEENY), JEREMIAH (Maryland), b. 16 Jan 1731/2, Prince George's Co., son of Charles and Mary Cheeny, of Queen Anne Parish. {Ref: PGCR 1:169} Pvt., Frederick Co. militia, 1757; Gov. Horatio Sharpe wrote, in part, to the MD Assembly on 7 Dec 1757: "With regard to the complaint of Ezekiel and Jeremiah Cheney, whose articles and indented servants are said to have run away from them, and to have enlisted into our Provincial Forces, I can only say, that if the case is as they represent it, and they have a right to satisfaction for their servants, the law will give them relief." {Ref: ARMD 55:319-320} Pvt., Capt. Joseph Chapline's Company Muster Roll No. 5, Frederick Co., circa 1757-1758, exact dates not given; bill of credit issued or paid in his behalf to Joseph Chaplin for £0.8.0 on 5 Mar 1767. {Ref: MSA S960 or S752, p. 195}

CHANEY (CHENEY), JOHN (Maryland), alias John Ceny *[sic]*, pvt., Capt. Moses Chapline's Company Muster Roll No. 2, Frederick Co., circa 1757-1758, exact dates not given (served 14 days); bill of credit issued or paid in his behalf to Joseph Chaplin for £0.13.0 on 5 Mar 1767; name mistakenly transcribed once as "John Cerry." {Ref: MSA S960 or S752, p. 197; CSOS:114}

CHANEY (CHENEY, CHANY), JOHN (Maryland), pvt., Capt. Joseph Chapline's Company Muster Rolls No. 2 and 3, Frederick Co., circa 1757-1758, exact dates not given (served 7 days); bill of credit issued or paid in his behalf to Joseph Chaplin for £0.7.0 on 5 Mar 1767. {Ref: MSA S960 or S752, p. 193; CSOS:104} Pvt., Capt. Joseph Chapline's Company Muster Roll No. 4, Frederick Co., circa 1757-1758, exact dates not given (served 5 days); bill of credit issued or paid in his behalf to Joseph Chaplin for £0.5.0 on 5 Mar 1767. {Ref: MSA S960 or S752, p. 194; CSOS:104}

CHANEY (CHENEY), RICHARD (Maryland), b. Nov 1730, Baltimore Co., son of Benjamin and Ruth Chaney, St. John's P. E. Parish. {Ref: BCF:103} Pvt., Capt. Tobias Stansbury's Company Muster Roll, Baltimore Co., circa 1757-1758, exact dates not given; bill of credit issued or paid in his behalf to John Hall, Jr. for £1.19.0 on 1 Apr 1767. {Ref: MSA S960 or S752, p. 186}

CHANEY (CHANY), RICHARD (Maryland), pvt., Capt. Joseph Chapline's Company Muster Roll No. 4, Frederick Co., circa 1757-1758, exact dates not given (served 6 days). {Ref: CSOS:105}

CHANEY (CHANY), SHADRACH (Maryland), pvt., Capt. Moses Chapline's Company Muster Roll No. 1, Frederick Co., circa 1757-1758, exact dates not given (served 55 days); bill of credit issued or paid in his behalf to Joseph Chaplin for £2.15.0 on 5 Mar 1767; name mistakenly transcribed once as

"Shadrick Caney." {Ref: MSA S960 or S752, p. 196; CSOS:113} Pvt., Capt. Moses Chapline's Company Muster Roll No. 2, Frederick Co., circa 1757-1758, exact dates not given (served 13 days); bill of credit issued or paid in his behalf to Joseph Chaplin for £0.13.0 on 5 Mar 1767. {Ref: MSA S960 or S752, p. 197; CSOS:114}

CHANEY (CHENEY), ZACHARIAH (Maryland), pvt., Capt. Joseph Chapline's Company Muster Roll No. 1, Frederick Co., circa 1757-1758, exact dates not given (served 41 days); bill of credit issued or paid in his behalf to Joseph Chaplin for £2.1.0 on 5 Mar 1767. {Ref: MSA S960 or S752, p. 191; CSOS:102}

CHANYWOOLF (CHENEYWOOLF), JOSEPH (Maryland), pvt., Capt. Peter Butler's Company Muster Roll, Frederick Co., circa 1757-1758, exact dates not given (served 34 days); bill of credit or order issued in his behalf to Casper Shaff for £1.14.0 and paid to David Cumming on 18 Apr 1767. {Ref: MSA S960 or S752, p. 168; CSOS:97}

CHAPLINE (CHAPLIN), JOSEPH (Maryland), b. 5 Sep 1707, Prince George's Co., son of William Chapline and Elizabeth Travers, of Queen Anne's P. E. Parish, m. Ruhamah Williams on 22 Oct 1741, had children William Williams, Joseph and Deborah (twins), James, Jeremiah, Ruhamah, Sarah, Jean, and Theodosha (1760-1844), and d. testate by 29 Mar 1769, Frederick Co.; planter, lawyer, businessman, militia captain, county justice (1739-1750), member of the MD Assembly (1749-1768); received over 10,000 acres from Gov. Horatio Sharpe in 1764 in appreciation for financing and supporting the construction of Fort Frederick. {Ref: BDML I:210-211; PGCR 1:169; WMG 3:2, pp. 71-72; ARMD 55:44; MCW 14:88; *MD Gazette*, 12 Jan 1769; SLMH II:62} Capt., Company Muster Roll No. 1, Frederick Co., circa 1757-1758, exact dates not given; militia pay account submitted in 1758, exact date not given. {Ref: MHM 9:4, p. 365; CSOS:102-103} Bill of credit issued or paid to him for £10.6.7½ on 5 Mar 1767. {Ref: MSA S960 or S752, p. 190} Capt., Company Muster Rolls No. 2 and 3, Frederick Co., circa 1757-1758, exact dates not given; bill of credit issued or paid to him for £0.15.0 on 5 Mar 1767. {Ref: MSA S960 or S752, p. 193; CSOS:104} Capt., Company Muster Roll No. 4, Frederick Co., circa 1757-1758, exact dates not given; bill of credit issued or paid to him for £1.16.7½ on 5 Mar 1767. {Ref: MSA S960 or S752, p. 194; CSOS:104-105} Capt., Company Muster Roll No. 5, Frederick Co., circa 1757-1758, exact dates not given; bill of credit issued or paid to him for £1.7.0 on 5 Mar 1767. {Ref: MSA S960 or S752, p. 195}

CHAPLINE (CHAPLIN), MOSES (Maryland), b. 11 Jun 1717, Prince George's Co., son of William Chapline and Elizabeth Travers, m. Janet or Jeanette Caton, had children Josiah, Moses (colonel in Revolutionary War), William, Ruth, Elizabeth, Mary, Agness, Ester, Lydia, and Lovica, and d. testate by 17 Nov 1762, Frederick Co. {Ref: BDML I:210; PGCR 1:169; MCW 12:196} Lieut. in Capt. Joseph Chapline's Company (Muster Roll No. 1), Frederick Co., circa 1757-1758, exact dates not given (served 53 days); militia pay account submitted in 1758, exact date not given. {Ref: MHM 9:4, p. 366; CSOS:102} Bill of credit issued or paid in his behalf to Joseph Chaplin his exec. for £6.3.7½ on 5 Mar 1767. {Ref: MSA S960 or S752, p. 190} Lieut. in Capt. Joseph Chapline's Company (Muster

Rolls No. 2 and 3), Frederick Co., circa 1757-1758, exact dates not given (served 9 days); bill of credit issued or paid in his behalf to Joseph Chaplin for £0.9.0 on 5 Mar 1767. {Ref: MSA S960 or S752, p. 193; CSOS:104} Capt., Company Muster Roll No. 1, Frederick Co., circa 1757-1758, exact dates not given; bill of credit issued or paid in his behalf to Joseph Chaplin his exec. for £10.8.3 on 5 Mar 1767. {Ref: MSA S960 or S752, p. 196} Capt., Company Muster Roll No. 2, Frederick Co., circa 1757-1758, exact dates not given; bill of credit issued or paid in his behalf to Joseph Chaplin his exec. for £2.6.7½ on 5 Mar 1767. {Ref: MSA S960 or S752, p. 197} Capt., Frederick Co., circa 1757-1758, exact dates not given; bill of credit issued or paid in his behalf to Joseph Chaplin his exec. for £1 on 5 Mar 1767. {Ref: MSA S960 or S752, p. 198; CSOS:114-115}

CHAPLINE (CHAPLIN), WILLIAM (Maryland), b. 17 Apr 1726, Prince George's Co., son of William Chapline and Elizabeth Travers, of Queen Anne's P. E. Parish. {Ref: PGCR 1:169} Pvt., Capt. Moses Chapline's Company Muster Roll No. 1, Frederick Co., circa 1757-1758, exact dates not given (served 55 days); bill of credit issued or paid in his behalf to Joseph Chaplin for £2.15.0 on 5 Mar 1767. {Ref: MSA S960 or S752, p. 196; CSOS:113} Pvt., Capt. Joseph Chapline's Company Muster Roll No. 4, Frederick Co., circa 1757-1758, exact dates not given (served 11 days); bill of credit issued or paid in his behalf to Joseph Chaplin for £0.11.0 on 5 Mar 1767. {Ref: MSA S960 or S752, p. 194; CSOS:105}

CHAPMAN, CORNELIUS (Maryland), b. 21 Sep 1734, Anne Arundel Co., son of Thomas and Anna Chapman, of St. Margaret's (Westminster) Parish. {Ref: AACR:116} Pvt., Capt. Christopher Gist's Company of VA Militia, 13 Jul 1756, enlisted at Baltimore, b. MD, age 19 *[sic]*. {Ref: MSR I:37}

CHAPMAN, SAMUEL (Maryland), b. 13 May 1729, Anne Arundel Co., son of William and Rebecca Chapman, of All Hallow's Parish. {Ref: AACR, p. 43} Captain, Anne Arundel Co., circa 1757-1758, exact dates not given; submitted an account on 15 Apr 1757 for payment of £1.8.6 "for expenses of a man servant when ordered out on a Detachment of the Militia." {Ref: ARMD 55:59} Bill of credit issued or paid in his behalf to William Turnor Wootton his exec. for £6.6.7½ on 13 Apr 1767. {Ref: MSA S960 or S752, p. 189}

CHAPPLE, JOHN (Maryland), patriot and poss. soldier (rank not specified), Kent Co., militia pay account submitted in 1758, exact date not given. {Ref: MHM 9:4, p. 366}

CHARLTON, ARTHUR (Maryland), m. Eleanor (N), had children Thomas, Alice, Eleanor, Mary, Usher, Ann, Penn, and Jane, and d. testate by 21 Sep 1771. {Ref: WMG 3:4, p. 147} Pvt., Capt. Peter Butler's Company Muster Roll, Frederick Co., circa 1757-1758, exact dates not given (served 34 days); militia pay account submitted in 1758, exact date not given' bill of credit or order issued his behalf for £1.14.0 and paid to Stewart Richardson on 21 Feb 1767; name listed once as "Arthur Chalten." {Ref: MHM 9:4, p. 367; CSOS:96; MSA S960 or S752, p. 166}

CHARLTON, JOHN (Maryland), m. (N), had a son Thomas, and d. testate by 8 Oct 1766. {Ref: WMG 2:4, pp. 165-166} Pvt., Capt. Peter Butler's Company Muster Roll, Frederick Co., circa 1757-1758, exact dates not given (served 34 days); bill of credit or order issued in his behalf for £1.14.0 and paid to Casper Shaff on 2

Mar 1767; name listed once as "John Chalten." {Ref: MSA S960 or S752, p. 166; CSOS:96}

CHARMIER, DANIEL, see "Andrew Ungrie," q.v.

CHARNAL, NICHOLAS (Maryland), pvt., Capt. John Dagworthy's Company of MD Troops, Frederick Co., from 9 Oct 1757 to 1 Jun 1758 (served 236 days) when reportedly deserted; however, payment to him was recorded in Col. Dagworthy's account book on 8 Mar 1763. {Ref: MHS MS.375.1; CSOS:75; MHS MS.375}

CHENEY, GREENBURY, see "Greenbury Chaney," q.v.

CHENEY, RICHARD, see "Richard Chaney," q.v.

CHERRY, THOMAS (Maryland), patriot, Frederick Co., was paid £2 on 12 Oct 1758 "for pasturing the horses that brought stores to Fort Frederick" for the Western Expedition against Fort Duquesne. {Ref: ARMD 55:775}

CHESLEY, ROBERT (Maryland), b. c1710, m. Ann Waughop by 1735, had children Robert, John, Susannah, Ann, Mary and Elizabeth, and d. testate by 11 Mar 1768, St. Mary's Company; member of the MD Assembly (1742-1744), justice (1739-1747, 1752-1761), sheriff (1748-1751), court justice (1755-c1763), and captain by 1763. {Ref: BDML I:217-218}

CHESQUOTERONE, or YELLOW BIRD, Indian Chief (Maryland), Frederick Co., agreed to join with the English against the French in 1758. {Ref: ARMD 31:266}

CHEW, BENJAMIN (Delaware), New Castle Co., patriot who served as a Justice of the Peace and a Justice of the Court of Oyer and Terminer, 1756-1761. {Ref: GRSD 1:13, 15}

CHEW, ELIZABETH, see "Edward Tilghman," q.v.

CHEW, HENRIETTA MARIA, see "Edward Dorsey," q.v.

CHEW, SAMUEL, see "Walter Dulany," q.v.

CHILD, ELIZABETH, see "Thomas Webb," q.v.

CHILTON, ABEL (Maryland), pvt., Capt. Henry Casson's Company Muster Roll, Queen Anne's Co., circa 1757-1758, exact dates not given (served 27 days); bill of credit issued or paid in his behalf to Capt. Casson on 27 Feb 1767 for £1.7.0. {Ref: MSA S960 or S752, p. 177; CSOS:109}

CHILTON, MATTHIAS (Maryland), pvt., Capt. Henry Casson's Company Muster Roll, Queen Anne's Co., circa 1757-1758, exact dates not given (served 27 days); bill of credit issued to him for £1.7.0 in 1767, exact date not given. {Ref: MSA S960 or S752, p. 177; CSOS:109}

CHILTON (CHELTON, CHELLON), ROBERT (Maryland), pvt., Frederick Co., received £5 bounty money on 15 Sep 1757 for enlisting in the militia. {Ref: ARMD 55:265, 619} Pvt., Capt. John Dagworthy's Company of MD Troops, Frederick Co., from 9 Oct 1757 to 22 Jan 1759 (served 470 days) when he reportedly deserted; however, payment to him was recorded in Col. Dagworthy's account book on 8 Mar 1763 for work on Fort Cumberland. {Ref: MHS MS.375.1; CSOS:75; MHS MS.375}

CHINES, GABRIEL (Maryland), pvt., Capt. Joshua Beall's Company Muster Roll, Prince George's Co., circa 1757-1758, exact dates not given; bill of credit issued or paid to him for £2.1.0 on 25 Feb 1767. {Ref: MSA S960 or S752, p. 184}

CHIPMAN, JAMES (Delaware), lieut., Northern District of Broadkiln Hundred, Militia Regt. of Sussex Co., 1756-1758, and was reported dead in March 1758; name listed once as "James Shipman." {Ref: ARDE I:13, 15; ARPA (2nd Series) 2:529, 579; HDE I:141}

CHIPMAN, PERIS or PARIS (Delaware), blacksmith, m. Judah (N), had children Draper, Paris, Sarah, Betsey, Kezia, Lovey, Milley, and Memory, and d. testate in Sussex Co. by 14 Sep 1781. {Ref: CDSS:35} Pvt., Kent Co. Militia, Capt. John Caton's Company, 25 Apr 1757 (date of muster roll). {Ref: ARDE I:14}

CHITTAM, THOMAS, see "Thomas Simpson," q.v.

CHOCONUNTO, Indian Chief (Maryland), Frederick Co., agreed to join with the English against the French in 1758. {Ref: ARMD 31:266}

CHRIST (CHREST), MICHAEL (Maryland), pvt., Capt. Stephen Rensburg's or Rensburger's Company Muster Roll, Frederick Co., circa 1757-1758, exact dates not given (served 42 days); bill of credit issued or paid in his behalf to Stephen Rensburg or Rensburger for £2.2.0 on 27 Mar 1767. {Ref: MSA S960 or S752, p. 182; CSOS:112}

CILL, ROBERT (Maryland), pvt., Capt. Peregrine Brown's Company, Kent Co., on 19 Feb 1758, by which time he had enlisted, but was unable to march due to health problems. {Ref: ARMD 31:283}

CLAGETT (CLEAGATT), CHARLES JR. (Maryland), pvt., Capt. John Dagworthy's Company of MD Troops, Frederick Co., from 9 Oct 1757 to 7 Dec 1757 (served 60 days) when he was discharged. {Ref: MHS MS.375.1; CSOS:75} Payment to him was recorded in Col. Dagworthy's account book on 22 Jul 1762. {Ref: MHS MS.375}

CLAGETT (CLEAGATT), CHARLES SR. (Maryland), pvt., Capt. John Dagworthy's Company of MD Troops, Frederick Co., from 9 Oct 1757 to 1 Jun 1758 (served 236 days) when he was discharged. {Ref: MHS MS.375.1; CSOS:75} Payment to him was recorded in Col. Dagworthy's account book on 22 Jul 1762. {Ref: MHS MS.375}

CLAGETT, RICHARD, see "William McCulloch," q.v.

CLAMPIT, JONATHAN, see "William Wallace," q.v.

CLANCE, HENRY (Maryland), pvt., Capt. John Middaugh's Company Muster Roll, Frederick Co., circa 1757-1758, exact dates not given (served 30 days); bill of credit issued or paid in his behalf to Thomas Beatty, Jr. for £0.17.0 on 3 Apr 1767. {Ref: MSA S960 or S752, p. 172}

CLANCY, GEORGE (Maryland), b. c1733, MD (age 23 in 1756); pvt., Capt. Robert Stewart's Company of VA Militia, enlisted on 11 May 1756. {Ref: MSR I:38}

CLARK, CHARITY, see "Samuel Bond," q.v.

CLARK, DAVID (Delaware), son of William Clark and Mary Wells, m. Eleanor (N) before 1760. {Ref: CFD 2:28-29} Captain, Upper Part of Duck Creek Hundred,

Militia of Kent Co. on Delaware, 1756. {Ref: ARDE I:12; ARPA (2nd Series) 2:527-529; HDE I:141}

CLARK, ELEANOR, see "David Clark," q.v.

CLARK, ELIZABETH, see "Peter Lowber" and Matthew Clark," q.v.

CLARK, JOHN (Delaware), b. c1729, Ireland (laborer, age 29 in 1758); pvt., recruited by Capt. Benjamin Noxon and enlisted on 24 Apr 1758. {Ref: ARDE I:18; ARPA (2nd Series) 2:566} *Identification problem:* There were five men with this name who could have served in the war: (1) John Clark, son of Thomas Clark and Sarah Luff, m. Elizabeth McNatt, had children Betsy, Caleb, Hugh, Susannah, Priscilla, Henry, and Elizabeth, and d. intestate by 13 Feb 1789; (2) John Clark, son of John Clark and Elizabeth Brinckle, m. Ann (N), had children William, John, Winlock, Clement, Elizabeth, Sarah, and Nancy, and d. testate in 1782; (3) John Clark was brother-in-law and executor of Sarah Gray who d. testate in 1766; (4) John Clark m. widow Mary Price after 1746; and, (5) John Clark, son of John Clark of New Castle Co., m. Elizabeth (N) before 1759. {Ref: CFD 2:23-24, 31-32}

CLARK, JOHN, see "John Caton" and "Peter Lowber," q.v.

CLARK, MARGARET, see "Peter Williams," q.v.

CLARK, MATTHEW (Maryland), m. Elizabeth (N), had a dau. Sarah (and at least one son (N) and other children who were not named in his will), and d. testate by 20 Nov 1772. {Ref: WMG 3:4, p. 153} Pvt., Capt. Moses Chapline's Company Muster Roll No. 3, Frederick Co., circa 1757-1758, exact dates not given (served 6 days); bill of credit or order issued to Casper Shaff and paid to David Cumming for £0.6.0 on 18 Apr 1767. {Ref: MSA S960 or S752, p. 198; CSOS:115}

CLARK (CLARKE), ROBERT (Maryland), pvt., Capt. John Dagworthy's Company of MD Troops, Frederick Co., from 9 Oct 1757 to 17 Apr 1759 (served 555 days) when he reportedly deserted; however, payment to him was recorded in Col. Dagworthy's account book on 8 Mar 1763 for work on Fort Cumberland. {Ref: MHS MS.375.1; CSOS:75; MHS MS.375}

CLARK, SARAH, see "Matthew Clark," q.v.

CLARK, WILLIAM (Delaware), pvt., Capt. Richard McWilliams' Company of Foot, New Castle Co., enlisted 28 Dec 1757. {Ref: ARDE I:14}

CLARK, WILLIAM (Maryland), pvt., Capt. Stephen Rensburg's or Rensburger's Company Muster Roll, Frederick Co., circa 1757-1758, exact dates not given (served 42 days); bill of credit issued or paid in his behalf to Stephen Rensburg or Rensburger for £2.2.0 on 27 Mar 1767. {Ref: MSA S960 or S752, p. 182; CSOS:112}

CLARK, WILLIAM, see "David Clark," q.v.

CLARKE, BRYAN (Maryland), a recruit, Royal American Regt., Baltimore Town, age 27 in 1756, reported as deserted and said to be heading to Conawauga in the company of Cpl. Matthew Jung. {Ref: *MD Gazette*, 4 Nov 1756}

CLARKE (CLARK), THOMAS (Delaware), captain, militia Upper Part of Mispillion Hundred, Kent Co. on Delaware, 1756. {Ref: ARDE I:12; ARPA (2nd Series) 2:527-529; HDE I:141}

CLARKSON, SARAH, see "James Brown," q.v.

CLARKSON, WILLIAM, see "James Brown," q.v.

CLARMAR, LODP. (Maryland), patriot, Frederick Co., who performed "sundry services at the fort" in 1763 and payment in the amount of £6.12.6 was still owed to him on 25 Nov 1763 (when reported by the Accounts Committee to the MD Assembly). {Ref: ARMD 58:399}

CLAWSON, JESPER (Delaware), pvt., Capt. Richard McWilliams' Company of Foot, New Castle Co., enlisted 28 Dec 1757. {Ref: ARDE I:15}

CLAYBAUGH (CLEBEAUGH, CLABOUGH), FREDERICK (Maryland), m. Sarah (N), had children Catherine, Frederick, John, Juddy, Jacob, James, Samuel, and Ann, and d. testate by 10 Jan 1781. {Ref: WMG 5:4, p. 167} Cpl., Capt. John Middaugh's Company Muster Roll, Frederick Co., circa 1757-1758, exact dates not given (served 30 days); bill of credit issued or paid in his behalf to Robert Wood for £2 on 4 Mar 1767. {Ref: MSA S960 or S752, pp. 171-172; CSOS:100}

CLAYLAND, THOMAS (Maryland), patriot and poss. soldier (rank not specified), Frederick Co., militia pay account submitted in 1758, exact date not given. {Ref: MHM 9:4, p. 368}

CLAYPOOLE (CLAYPOOL), GEORGE (Delaware), yeoman, b. 12 Feb 1727/8, eldest son of Jeremiah Claypoole and Sarah Shepherd, d. intestate and unmarried by 3 Sep 1763. {Ref: CFD 3:56-57; CDSS:37} Ensign, Northern District of Broadkiln Hundred, Militia Regt. of Sussex Co., 1756-1758. {Ref: ARDE I:13, 15; ARPA (2nd Series) 2:529, 579; HDE I:141}

CLAYTON, JOHN (Delaware), captain, militia, Town of Dover, Kent Co. on Delaware, 1756. {Ref: ARDE I:12; ARPA (2nd Series) 2:527-529; HDE I:141}

CLEARNTON, SILVESTER (Maryland), pvt., Capt. William Luckett's Company Muster Roll, Frederick Co., circa 1757-1758, exact dates not given (served 30 days); bill of credit issued or paid in his behalf to William Luckett, Jr. for £1.10.0 on 6 Apr 1767. {Ref: MSA S960 or S752, p. 169; CSOS:99}

CLEM, GEORGE (Maryland), patriot and poss. soldier (rank not specified), Frederick Co., militia pay account submitted in 1758, exact date not given. {Ref: MHM 9:4, p. 367}

CLEMENS, JOSEPH (Maryland), pvt., Capt. William McClellan's Company of MD Volunteers, Frederick Co., circa 1763-1764; on muster roll dated 15 Nov 1764 at Camp at the Forks of Muskingham. {Ref: ARMD 32:99}

CLEMENS, THOMAS (Maryland), pvt., Capt. William McClellan's Company of MD Volunteers, Frederick Co., circa 1763-1764; on muster roll dated 15 Nov 1764 at Camp at the Forks of Muskingham. {Ref: ARMD 32:99}

CLEMENTS (CLEMONS), LEONARD (Maryland), pvt., Capt. Stephen Rensburg's or Rensburger's Company Muster Roll, Frederick Co., circa 1757-1758, exact dates not given (served 42 days); bill of credit issued or paid in his behalf to Jacob Young for £2.2.0 on 4 Mar 1767. {Ref: MSA S960 or S752, p. 182; CSOS:112}

CLEMENTS, WILLIAM (Maryland), patriot, Frederick Co., was paid on 10 Jul 1758 at Fort Frederick "for sawing plank to make coffins for the N Carolina and Pensa. soldiers that died at Fort Frederick." {Ref: ARMD 55:773}

CLENDENING, THOMAS, see "Daniel Hamilton," q.v.

CLIFFORD, JOHN (Delaware or Pennsylvania), b. c1741, MD (age 18 in 1759); pvt., enlisted in Capt. Robert Curry's Company of the PA Regt. on 30 Apr 1759 (return of recruits dated June 1759). {Ref: ARPA (2nd Series) 2:500}

CLIFT (CLIFFT), JAMES (Maryland), pvt., Capt. Francis Ware's Company of MD Troops, Charles Co., circa 1757-1758, exact dates not given. {Ref: MHS MS.375.1; CSOS:87} Payment to him was recorded in Col. Dagworthy's account book on 7 Mar 1763 for work on Fort Cumberland. {Ref: MHS MS.375}

CLIMOUR, FRANCIS (Maryland), cpl., Capt. Henry Casson's Company Muster Roll, Queen Anne's Co., circa 1757-1758, exact dates not given (served 4 days as a pvt. and 23 days as a cpl.); bill of credit issued to him for £1.10.7½ as a cpl. and £0.4.0 as a pvt. in 1767, exact dates not given. {Ref: MSA S960 or S752, p. 177; CSOS:109}

CLINE, JACOB (Maryland), pvt., Capt. Peter Bainbridge's Company Muster Roll, Frederick Co., circa 1757-1758, exact dates not given (served 28 days); bill of credit issued or paid in his behalf to Casper Shaff on 4 Mar 1767 for £1.8.0. {Ref: MSA S960 or S752, p. 180; CSOS:111} Pvt., Capt. Moses Chapline's Company Muster Roll No. 1, Frederick Co., circa 1757-1758, exact dates not given (served 55 days); bill of credit issued or paid in his behalf to Joseph Chaplin for £2.15.0 on 5 Mar 1767. {Ref: MSA S960 or S752, p. 196; CSOS:113}

CLINE, JACOB JR. (Maryland), pvt., Capt. Joseph Chapline's Company Muster Roll No. 1, Frederick Co., circa 1757-1758, exact dates not given (served 58 days); bill of credit issued or paid in his behalf to Joseph Chaplin for £2.18.0 on 5 Mar 1767. {Ref: MSA S960 or S752, p. 191; CSOS:102}

CLINE, JOHN (Maryland), patriot, Frederick Co., was paid £3 via Casper Shaaf on 29 Jul 1758 "for carrying baggage to Fort Loudoun" for the Western Expedition against Fort Duquesne. {Ref: ARMD 55:774}

CLOW, CHEANY (Delaware), b. c1734, MD (laborer, age 24 in 1758); pvt., recruited by Capt. Benjamin Noxon and enlisted on 2 May 1758. {Ref: ARDE I:18; ARPA (2nd Series) 2:485, 566}

COATES, ---- (Maryland), sea captain by 1757 who was in command of the ship *Hannah* which was loaded at Patapsco "last year" and captured by a French Privateer on his way from Maryland to London in 1758. {Ref: *MD Gazette*, 16 Feb 1758}

COATS, CHARLES (Maryland), cpl., Capt. William Luckett's Company Muster Roll, Frederick Co., circa 1757-1758, exact dates not given (served 30 days); bill of credit issued or paid in his behalf to William Luckett, Jr. for £2.10.0 on 6 Apr 1767. {Ref: MSA S960 or S752, pp. 169-170; CSOS:99}

COBBIN (COBLIN), PHILIP (Maryland), pvt., Capt. Thomas Norris' Company, Frederick Co., circa 1757-1758, exact dates not given (served 30 days); bill of credit issued or paid in his behalf to Valentine Myres on 10 Apr 1767 for £1.10.0. {Ref: MSA S960 or S752, p. 176; CSOS:107}

COBURN, GEORGE (Maryland), patriot, Frederick Co., 1758; he and several others were called "battomen" when paid on 6 Oct 1758 "for carrying up baggage belonging to the militia that garrisoned Fort Cumberland." {Ref: ARMD 55:775}

COBURN (COBURNE), WILLIAM (Maryland), farmer; pvt., Capt. Peregrine Brown's 7th Co. of Foot Militia, Kent Co., on 19 Feb 1758, by which time he had enlisted, but reportedly refused to appear and serve in arms against the enemy. {Ref: ARMD 31:283, 288}

COCHRAN, ---- (Maryland), captain in Brig. Gen. Stanwix's Battalion of His Majesty's Royal American Regiment of Foot, recruited soldiers in Annapolis at Mr. Inch's in 1759. He also reported deserters in the local newspaper in 1760. {Ref: *MD Gazette* 29 Nov 1759 and 19 Jun 1760}

COCKE, WILLIAM, see "Richard Johnson," q.v.

COCKEY, ELIZABETH, see "James Govane," q.v.

COCKEY, SUSAN, see "John Gist," q.v.

COCKEY, THOMAS, see "Thomas Cockey Deye," q.v.

COCKEY, WILLIAM, see "James Govane," q.v.

COE, WILLIAM (Maryland), pvt., Capt. Joshua Beall's Company of MD Troops, Prince George's Co., from 9 Oct 1757 to 31 May 1758 when he was discharged. {Ref: MHS MS.375.1; CSOS:83} Payment to him was recorded in Col. Dagworthy's account book on 23 Feb 1763. {Ref: MHS MS.375}

COLE, GEORGE (Maryland), pvt., Capt. John White's Company Muster Roll, Frederick Co., circa 1757-1758, exact dates not given (served 6 days); bill of credit issued or paid to him for £0.6.0 in 1767, exact date not given. {Ref: MSA S960 or S752, p. 164; CSOS:96}

COLE, JAMES (Maryland), sea captain by 1757, was in command of the brigantine *Philip and James*, belonging to Maryland, when captured by the French on his way to Maryland from Barbadoes. {Ref: *MD Gazette*, 5 Dec 1757}

COLE, JOHN (Maryland), pvt., Charles Co., received £5 bounty money on 2 Sep 1757 for enlisting in the militia. {Ref: ARMD 55:265, 619} Pvt., Capt. Francis Ware's Company of MD Troops, Charles Co., circa 9 Oct 1757 to 30 Dec 1757. {Ref: MHS MS.375.1; CSOS:87} Payment to him was recorded in Col. Dagworthy's account book on 13 Jul 1762. {Ref: MHS MS.375}

COLE, JOHN (Maryland), sea captain by 1756, was in command of the snow *Eugene* when captured by the French on his way from Bristol to Annapolis. {Ref: *MD Gazette*, 30 Dec 1756}

COLE, PETER (Maryland), pvt., Capt. Peregrine Brown's Company, Kent Co., on 19 Feb 1758, by which time he had enlisted, but was unable to march due to health problems. {Ref: ARMD 31:283}

COLEGATE, JOHN (Delaware), b. c1735, America (cordwainer, age 23 in 1758); pvt., recruited by Capt. Benjamin Noxon and enlisted on 1 May 1758. {Ref: ARDE I:18; ARPA (2nd Series) 2:566}

COLEMAN, JACOB (Maryland), pvt., Capt. Elias Delashmutt's Company Muster Roll, Frederick Co., circa 1757-1758, exact dates not given (served 30 days); bill of credit issued or paid in his behalf to Elias Delashmut, Jr. on 16 Mar 1767 for £1.10.0. {Ref: MSA S960 or S752, p. 162; CSOS:94}

COLESBERY, JACOB (Delaware), pvt., Capt. Richard McWilliams' Company of Foot, New Castle Co., enlisted 28 Dec 1757. {Ref: ARDE I:14}

COLKLEASER, JOHN (Maryland), pvt., Capt. Jonathan Hagar's Company Muster Roll, Frederick Co., circa 1757-1758, exact dates not given (served 6 days); bill of credit issued or paid to him for £0.6.0 in 1767, exact date not given. {Ref: MSA S960 or S752, p. 173; CSOS:107}

COLL, ISAAC (Delaware), b. c1717, London, England (age 42 in 1759); pvt., enlisted in Capt. John Wright's Company and mustered on 11 May 1759. {Ref: ARDE I:25; ARPA (2nd Series) 2:592}

COLLET, JAMES (Maryland), pvt., Capt. Joshua Beall's Company Muster Roll, Prince George's Co., circa 1757-1758, exact dates not given; bill of credit issued or paid to him for £2.3.0 in 1767, exact date not given. {Ref: MSA S960 or S752, p. 184}

COLLET, SARAH, see "Henry Baker" and "Nathan Baker," q.v.

COLLIER, CHARLES (Maryland), pvt., Capt. William Luckett's Company Muster Roll, Frederick Co., circa 1757-1758, exact dates not given (served 30 days); bill of credit issued or paid in his behalf to William Luckett, Jr. for £1.10.0 on 6 Apr 1767. {Ref: MSA S960 or S752, p. 169; CSOS:99}

COLLINGS, BARTHOLOMEW (Maryland or Pennsylvania), Irishman (age not given); pvt. in 1757 who was hanged at Carlisle for desertion. {Ref: *MD Gazette*, 10 Nov 1757}

COLLINGS, WILLIAM (Maryland), pvt., Capt. John Dagworthy's Company of MD Troops, Frederick Co., from 9 Oct 1757 to 2 Mar 1759 (served 509 days) when he reportedly died; however, payment to him was recorded in Col. Dagworthy's account book on 11 Jul 1762 for work on Fort Cumberland. {Ref: MHS MS.375.1; CSOS:75; MHS MS.375}

COLLINS, SIMON (Maryland), patriot, Frederick Co., who performed "sundry services at the fort" in 1763 and payment in the amount of £0.1.9 was still owed to him on 25 Nov 1763 (when reported by the Accounts Committee to the MD Assembly). {Ref: ARMD 58:400}

COLLINS, WILLIAM (Maryland), cpl., Capt. Peregrine Brown's Company Muster Roll, Kent Co., circa 1757-1758, exact dates not given (served 15 days); bill of credit issued or paid in his behalf to Robert Buchanan on 21 Mar 1767 for £1. {Ref: MSA S960 or S752, p. 179; CSOS:110}

COLMORE (COLMURE), GEORGE (Maryland), cpl., Capt. Richard Pearis' Company of MD Troops, Frederick Co., circa 9 Oct 1757 to 31 May 1758); cpl., Capt. Alexander Beall's Company of MD Troops, Frederick Co., from 1 Jun 1758 to 30 Dec 1758 (name listed once as "George Colmine"); payment recorded in Col. Dagworthy's account book on 15 Jul 1762. {Ref: MHS MS.375; CSOS:80, 90; MHS MS.375.1}

COLTER, RICHARD (Maryland), b. c1734, Charles Co. (age about 25 in 1759); pvt., 47th Regt. of Foot, enlisted in Baltimore (date not given) and was reported as a deserter in February 1759. {Ref: *MD Gazette*, 15 Feb 1759}

COLTER, THOMAS (Delaware), b. c1737, Sussex, DE (age 22 in 1759); pvt., enlisted in Capt. John Wright's Company and mustered on 11 May 1759. {Ref: ARDE I:25; ARPA (2nd Series) 2:592}

COLTER, WILLIAM (Delaware), b. c1739, Sussex, DE (age 20 in 1759); pvt., enlisted in Capt. John Wright's Company and mustered on 11 May 1759. {Ref: ARDE I:25; ARPA (2nd Series) 2:592}

COLVILL, JOSEPH (Maryland), pvt., Capt. Richard Pearis' Company of MD Troops, Frederick Co., from 9 Oct 1757 to 23 Nov 1758 when he reportedly deserted; however, payment to him was recorded in Col. Dagworthy's account book on 8 Mar 1763. {Ref: MHS MS.375; MHS MS.375.1}

COLVIN, WILLIAM (Maryland), pvt., Capt. William McClellan's Company of MD Volunteers, Frederick Co., circa 1763-1764; on muster roll dated 15 Nov 1764 at Camp at the Forks of Muskingham. {Ref: ARMD 32:99}

COMBE, ADAM, see "Adam Coomb," q.v.

COMBS, THOMAS (Maryland), b. c1734, MD (age 32 in 1756); pvt., Capt. G. Mercer's Company of VA Militia, enlisted on 2 Aug 1756 in Culpepper, VA. {Ref: MSR I:38}

COMBS, WILLIAM (Delaware), b. c1734, England (mariner, age 24 in 1758); pvt., recruited by Capt. Benjamin Noxon and enlisted on 13 May 1758. {Ref: ARDE I:18; ARPA (2nd Series) 2:566}

CONGLETON, BENJAMIN (Delaware), pvt., Capt. Henry Vanbibber's Company of the Lower Counties on Delaware Troops at New Castle, enlisted on 21 May 1759. {Ref: ARDE I:26; ARPA (2nd Series) 2:594}

CONNANT, ROBERT (Maryland), pvt., Capt. Samuel Chapman's Company Muster Roll, Anne Arundel Co., circa 1757-1758, exact dates not given; bill of credit issued or paid to him for £1.18.0 in 1767, exact date not given. {Ref: MSA S960 or S752, p. 188}

CONNELL, WILLIAM (Delaware), lieut., Capt. John Wright's Company, mustered on 11 May 1759. {Ref: ARDE I:20, 25; ARPA (2nd Series) 2:592}

CONNELLY, BRYAN (Delaware), b. c1738, Monaghan, Ireland (laborer, age 20 in 1758); pvt., enlisted 20 Apr 1758 "for the campaign in the lower counties" by Capt. John McClughan. {Ref: ARDE I:17; ARPA (2nd Series) 2:570}

CONNER, JOHN (Delaware), pvt., Capt. Henry Vanbibber's Company of the Lower Counties on Delaware Troops at New Castle, enlisted on 21 May 1759. {Ref: ARDE I:26; ARPA (2nd Series) 2:594}

CONNER, JONATHAN (Maryland), pvt., Capt. Henry Casson's Company Muster Roll, Queen Anne's Co., circa 1757-1758, exact dates not given (served 27 days); bill of credit issued or paid in his behalf to Capt. Casson on 27 Mar 1767 for £1.7.0. {Ref: MSA S960 or S752, p. 178; CSOS:109}

CONNOLY, JOHN (Maryland), pvt., Capt. John Dagworthy's Company of MD Troops, Frederick Co., from 9 Oct 1757 to 27 Dec 1758 (served 443 days) when he reportedly deserted; however, payment to him was recorded in Col. Dagworthy's account book on 28 Feb 1763. {Ref: MHS.375.1; CSOS:75; MHS MS.375}

CONNOLY (CONNELLY, CONNOLLY), PHILIP (Maryland), b. c1729, St. Mary's Company (age 28 in 1757); soldier reported as deserted by Capt. Joshua Beall at Fort Frederick; he and Aaron Holdsworth were confined to jail by Colmore Beans, Sheriff of Prince George's Co., and they subsequently escaped. {Ref: *MD Gazette*, 3 Mar and 10 Mar 1757} He later returned and was a pvt. in Capt.

Joshua Beall's Company of MD Troops, Prince George's Co., from 10 Sep 1757 to 26 Nov 1757 at which time he was again reported as deserted; however, payment to him was recorded in Col. Dagworthy's account book on 8 Mar 1763. {Ref: MHS MS.375; CSOS:83; MHS MS.375.1}

CONNOWAY, JOHN (Maryland), pvt., Capt. Tobias Stansbury's Company Muster Roll, Baltimore Co., circa 1757-1758, exact dates not given; bill of credit issued or paid to him for £3.10.0 on 6 Mar 1767. {Ref: MSA S960 or S752, p. 186} He may have been the John Conaway who m. Ann Norwood on 14 May 1744 and had children Rachel (b. 1745), Charles (b. 1748), Sarah (b. 1750), Ruth (b. 1753), Ann (b. 1755), John (b. 1757), and Susanna (b. 1760). {Ref: BCF:129} See "Anthony Gott" and "John Oram," q.v.

CONSTANTINE, EDWARD TULLY (Maryland), b. c1737, MD (age 19 in 1756); pvt., Capt. Christopher Gist's Company of VA Militia, 13 Jul 1756, enlisted at Baltimore. {Ref: MSR I:37} Brother of "Patrick Constantine," q.v.

CONSTANTINE, PATRICK (Maryland), b. c1738, MD (age 18 in 1756); pvt., Capt. Christopher Gist's Company of VA Militia, 13 Jul 1756, enlisted at Baltimore. {Ref: MSR I:37} Patrick Constantine m. Ann Bond, dau. of Richard Bond, on 29 Sep 1760 in St. Thomas Parish, Baltimore Co., and had sons Joshua (b. 4 Dec 1760), Daniel (b. 4 Dec 1762), Edward (1763-1817), and Richard (b. 1767). {Ref: Family Records of Howard Constantine (2000); BCF:130}

CONTEE, THOMAS, see "Daniel Page," q.v.

CONWELL, ELIAS (Delaware), b. c1739, Sussex, DE, m. (N), had children Jeremiah, George, Fisher, Elias, David, and Sarah, and d. testate by 14 Aug 1782. {Ref: CDSS:41} Cpl., enlisted in Capt. John Wright's Company and mustered on 11 May 1759 (age 20). {Ref: ARDE I:25; ARPA (2nd Series) 2:592}

CONWELL (CONNELL?), WILLIAM (Delaware), Sussex Co., enrolled 11 May 1759 and commissioned lieut. on 23 May 1759, 3rd Bttn. of PA Regt. {Ref: ARDE I:20; ARPA (2nd Series) 2:582; CDSS:41}

COOCH, THOMAS (Delaware), captain, Pencader Hundred, Lower Regt. of Militia, New Castle Co., 1756; Court Justice, 1761. {Ref: ARDE I:12; ARPA (2nd Series) 2:525; HDE I:141; GRSD 1:15} Thomas Cooch, Jr. m. Sarah (N), had children Thomas, Francis, William, and Elizabeth, and d. testate by 3 Feb 1785. {Ref: CDSS:41}

COODE, MARY, see "John Jordan," q.v.

COOE, JOB (Maryland), cpl., Capt. Thomas Norris' Company, Frederick Co., circa 1757-1758, exact dates not given (served 30 days); bill of credit issued or paid in his behalf to Valentine Myres on 10 Apr 1767 for £2. {Ref: MSA S960 or S752, p. 176; CSOS:107}

COOHEE, MICHAEL (Maryland), pvt., Capt. Thomas Norris' Company, Frederick Co., circa 1757-1758, exact dates not given (served 30 days); bill of credit issued or paid in his behalf to Valentine Myres on 10 Apr 1767 for £1.10.0; name mistakenly listed once as "Michael Cookees." {Ref: MSA S960 or S752, p. 176; CSOS:108}

COOK, FRANCIS (Maryland), pvt., Capt. Peter Butler's Company Muster Roll, Frederick Co., circa 1757-1758, exact dates not given (served 34 days); bill of credit or order issued in his behalf for £1.14.0 and paid to Casper Shaff on 2 Mar 1767. {Ref: MSA S960 or S752, p. 166; CSOS:97}

COOK, JOHN (Delaware), b. c1729, Tyrone, Ireland (laborer, age 30 in 1759); pvt., enlisted by Capt. James Armstrong for the PA Regt. on 28 Apr 1759. {Ref: ARDE I:25; ARPA (2nd Series) 2:585}

COOK, JONEACRE, see "Elias Adgate," q.v.

COOKE, NATHANIEL (Maryland), pvt., Capt. Francis Ware's Company of MD Troops, Charles Co., from 9 Oct 1757 to 25 Dec 1757 (served 77 days) when he reportedly deserted; however, payment to him was recorded in Col. Dagworthy's account book on 7 Mar 1763. {Ref: MHS MS.375; CSOS:87; MHS MS.375.1}

COOKE, NATHANIEL (Delaware), b. c1739, Whitley Creek, DE (farmer, age 19 in 1758); pvt., enlisted 5 May 1758 "for the campaign in the lower counties" by Capt. John McClughan. {Ref: ARDE I:17; ARPA (2nd Series) 2:570}

COOMB (COOMBE, COMBE) ADAM (Maryland), pvt., Capt. Peter Butler's Company Muster Roll, Frederick Co., circa 1757-1758, exact dates not given (served 34 days); bill of credit or order issued in his behalf for £1.14.0 and paid to Casper Shaff on 2 Mar 1767. {Ref: MSA S960 or S752, p. 167; CSOS:97}

COON, GEORGE (Maryland), pvt., Capt. John White's Company Muster Roll, Frederick Co., circa 1757-1758, exact dates not given (served 6 days); bill of credit issued or paid in his behalf to William Good on 5 Jun 1767 for £0.6.0. {Ref: MSA S960 or S752, p. 164; CSOS:95}

COONCE, ADAM (Maryland), pvt., Capt. Alexander Beall's Company of Foot, Frederick Co., 1756-1757, recorded his discharge in Frederick Co. Court on 28 Jul 1757. Capt. Beall certified "he hath served upwards of 8 months and the time of his enlistment has expired." Receipt for clothing and pay was signed by Adam Coonce and witnessed by Sgt. Robert Lineard and Sgt. George Barrance (date and place were not given, but prob. at Fort Frederick circa 10 Feb 1757). {Ref: FCLR:29}

COONCE, HENRY (Maryland), pvt., Capt. Stephen Rensburg's or Rensburger's Company Muster Roll, Frederick Co., circa 1757-1758, exact dates not given (served 34 days); bill of credit issued or paid in his behalf to Casper Shaff for £1.14.0 on 2 Mar 1767. {Ref: MSA S960 or S752, p. 182; CSOS:112}

COONCE, MARY, see "Philip Coonce," q.v.

COONCE (KUNCE), PHILIP (Maryland), cordwainer, m. Mary (N), had no children, and d. testate by 17 Sep 1778. {Ref: WMG 5:2, p. 87} Pvt., Capt. Peter Butler's Company Muster Roll, Frederick Co., circa 1757-1758, exact dates not given (served 34 days); bill of credit or order issued in his behalf for £1.14.0 and paid to Thomas Beatty, Jr. on 23 Feb 1767. {Ref: MSA S960 or S752, p. 166; CSOS:96}

COONCE, WILLIAM (Maryland), pvt., Capt. Stephen Rensburg's or Rensburger's Company Muster Roll, Frederick Co., circa 1757-1758, exact dates not given (served 34 days); bill of credit issued or paid in his behalf to Stephen Rensburg or Rensburger for £1.14.0 on 27 Mar 1767. {Ref: MSA S960 or S752, p. 182; CSOS:112}

COOPER, BENJAMIN (Maryland), pvt., Capt. Henry Casson's Company Muster Roll, Queen Anne's Co., circa 1757-1758, exact dates not given (served 27 days); bill of credit issued or paid in his behalf to Capt. Casson on 27 Mar 1767 for £1.7.0. {Ref: MSA S960 or S752, p. 178; CSOS:109}

COOPER, JAMES (Delaware), b. c1729, Ireland (laborer, age 30 in 1759); pvt., enlisted by Capt. James Armstrong for the PA Regt. on 2 May 1759. {Ref: ARDE I:25; ARPA (2nd Series) 2:585}

COOPER, JAMES (Delaware), pvt., Capt. French Battell's Company of Lower County Provincials, enlisted 12 May 1758. {Ref: ARDE I:16; ARPA (2nd Series) 2:555}

COOPER, RICHARD (Delaware), pvt., Capt. French Battell's Company of Lower County Provincials, enlisted 14 May 1758. {Ref: ARDE I:16; ARPA (2nd Series) 2:555}

COOPER, THOMAS (Maryland), pvt., Capt. Henry Casson's Company Muster Roll, Queen Anne's Co., circa 1757-1758, exact dates not given; bill of credit issued or paid in his behalf to Capt. Casson on 27 Feb 1767 for £1.7.0. {Ref: MSA S960 or S752, p. 177}

COOPER, WILLIAM (Maryland), pvt. (miller, age 27 in 1758), resident of Cecil Co., MD, enlisted by Capt. John Singleton for the PA Regt. on 8 May 1758. {Ref: ARPA (2nd Series) 2:474}

COORMORE, RICHARD (Maryland), pvt., Capt. William McClellan's Company of MD Volunteers, Frederick Co., circa 1763-1764; on muster roll dated 15 Nov 1764 at Camp at the Forks of Muskingham. {Ref: ARMD 32:99}

COPE, ROBERT (Delaware), pvt., Capt. French Battell's Company of Lower County Provincials, enlisted 15 May 1758. {Ref: ARDE I:16; ARPA (2nd Series) 2:555}

CORAFLOW, GEORGE (Maryland), pvt., Capt. John White's Company Muster Roll, Frederick Co., circa 1757-1758, exact dates not given (served 6 days); bill of credit issued or paid to him for £0.6.0 in 1767, exact date not given. {Ref: MSA S960 or S752, p. 164; CSOS:95}

CORAR (CARAR), SAMUEL (Maryland), pvt., Capt. John White's Company Muster Roll, Frederick Co., circa 1757-1758, exact dates not given (served 6 days); bill of credit issued or paid to him for £0.6.0 in 1767, exact date not given. {Ref: MSA S960 or S752, p. 164; CSOS:95}

CORD, JOSEPH (Delaware), b. 1726, DE, son of Joseph Cord (d. 1738) and Ann (N), m. Jane Miers (1733-1787), had children Miers, Isair, William, and Samuel, and d. 17 Jan 1787. {Ref: CFD 3:59-60} Captain, Southern District of Broadkiln Hundred, Militia Regt. of Sussex Co., 1756-1758. {Ref: ARDE I:13, 15; ARPA (2nd Series) 2:529, 579; HDE I:141}

CORKERLIN, JAMES (Delaware), pvt., Capt. French Battell's Company of Lower County Provincials, enlisted 20 May 1758. {Ref: ARDE I:16; ARPA (2nd Series) 2:555}

CORNWELL, SAMUEL (Delaware), b. c1737, VA (age 22 in 1759); pvt., enlisted in Capt. John Wright's Company and mustered on 11 May 1759. {Ref: ARDE I:25; ARPA (2nd Series) 2:592}

COSGRIFT, JOHN (Delaware), b. c1739, Ireland (laborer, age 28 in 1758); pvt., recruited by Capt. Benjamin Noxon and enlisted on 25 Apr 1758. {Ref: ARDE I:18; ARPA (2nd Series) 2:566}

COST, FRANCIS (Maryland), m. (N), had children George, Jacob, and Cathren, and d. testate by 18 Jan 1782. {Ref: WMG 5:4, p. 170} Pvt., Capt. Peter Bainbridge's Company Muster Roll, Frederick Co., circa 1757-1758, exact dates not given (served 30 days); bill of credit issued or paid in his behalf to Casper Shaff on 4 Mar 1767 for £1.8.0. {Ref: MSA S960 or S752, p. 180; CSOS:111}

COTTER, SARAH, see "John Gassaway," q.v.

COTTERAL, ANDREW (Maryland), pvt., Capt. William Luckett's Company Muster Roll, Frederick Co., circa 1757-1758, exact dates not given (served 30 days); bill of credit issued or paid in his behalf to William Luckett, Jr. for £1.10.0 on 6 Apr 1767. {Ref: MSA S960 or S752, p. 169; CSOS:99}

COTTERAL, ANDREW JR. (Maryland), pvt., Capt. William Luckett's Company Muster Roll, Frederick Co., circa 1757-1758, exact dates not given (served 30 days); bill of credit issued or paid in his behalf to William Luckett, Jr. for £1.10.0 on 6 Apr 1767. {Ref: MSA S960 or S752, p. 169; CSOS:99}

COTTERAL, JOHN (Maryland), pvt., Capt. William Luckett's Company Muster Roll, Frederick Co., circa 1757-1758, exact dates not given (served 30 days); bill of credit issued or paid in his behalf to William Luckett, Jr. for £1.10.0 on 6 Apr 1767. {Ref: MSA S960 or S752, p. 170; CSOS:99}

COTTERAL, WILLIAM (Maryland), pvt., Capt. William Luckett's Company Muster Roll, Frederick Co., circa 1757-1758, exact dates not given (served 30 days); bill of credit issued or paid in his behalf to William Luckett, Jr. for £1.10.0 on 6 Apr 1767. {Ref: MSA S960 or S752, p. 169; CSOS:99}

COUDEN, ROBERT (Maryland), patriot, Annapolis, Anne Arundel Co., pay account submitted for quartering soldiers in 1757 or 1758, exact dates not given. {Ref: MHM 9:3, p. 262} See "Carlton Tannihill" and "John Cary" and "Zachariah Evans," q.v.

COUNCILMAN, PETER (Maryland or Pennsylvania), German (age not given); pvt. in 1757 who was hanged at Carlisle for desertion. {Ref: *MD Gazette*, 10 Nov 1757}

COUNTES, HENRY (Maryland), pvt., Capt. Thomas Norris' Company, Frederick Co., circa 1757-1758, exact dates not given (served 30 days); bill of credit issued or paid in his behalf to Charles Englas on 28 Mar 1767 for £1.10.0. {Ref: MSA S960 or S752, p. 176; CSOS:108}

COURSE, TIMOTHY (Maryland), farmer; pvt., Capt. Peregrine Brown's 7th Co. of Foot Militia, Kent Co., on 19 Feb 1758, by which time he had enlisted, but reportedly refused to appear and serve in arms against the enemy. {Ref: ARMD 31:283, 288}

COURSE, WILLIAM (Maryland), pvt., Capt. Peregrine Brown's Company Muster Roll, Kent Co., circa 1757-1758, exact dates not given (served 15 days); bill of credit issued or paid in his behalf to Thomas Ringgold, Esq. on 20 Feb 1767 for £0.15.0. {Ref: MSA S960 or S752, p. 179; CSOS:110}

COURTNEY, ELIZABETH, see "Thomas Brown," q.v.

COURTNEY, WILLIAM (Maryland), pvt., Capt. Alexander Beall's Company of MD Troops, Frederick Co., from 9 Oct 1757 to 16 Feb 1758 when he was discharged. {Ref: MHS MS.375.1} Payment to him was recorded in Col. Dagworthy's account book on 7 Mar 1763. {Ref: MHS MS.375}

COVER, DANIEL (Maryland), m. Eve (N), had a son John Erhart Cover (and other children who were mentioned, but not named in his will), and d. testate by 21 Mar 1770. {Ref: WMG 3:3, p. 108} Pvt., Capt. Thomas Norris' Company, Frederick Co., circa 1757-1758, exact dates not given (served 30 days); bill of credit issued or paid in his behalf to Michael McGuire on 20 Mar 1767 for £1.10.0. {Ref: MSA S960 or S752, p. 176; CSOS:107}

COVINGTON, REBECCA, see "Benjamin Mackall, Jr.," q.v.

COVINGTON, SARAH, see "Edward Lloyd" and "Richard Lloyd," q.v.

COX, EZECHIEL (Maryland), patriot, Frederick Co., 1758; he and several others were called "battomen" when paid on 6 Oct 1758 "for carrying up baggage belonging to the militia that garrisoned Fort Cumberland." {Ref: ARMD 55:775}

CRABB, HENRY WRIGHT (Maryland), b. 16 Jan 1722/3, Prince George's Co., son of Ralph Crabb and Priscilla Sprigg, of Queen Anne's P. E. Parish, m. Ann Snowden by 1759, had children Richard, Ralph, John, Jeremiah, and Elizabeth, and d. testate by 12 Jun 1764, Frederick Co.; captain by 1751, county justice (1750-1754), and member of MD Assembly, 1749-1761 (served on Arms and Ammunition Committee, 1749-1757). {Ref: BDML I:239-240; PGCR 1:171}

CRAGGE (CRAGG), WILLIAM (Maryland), pvt., Capt. Thomas Norris' Company, Frederick Co., circa 1757-1758, exact dates not given (served 30 days); bill of credit issued or paid in his behalf to William Roberts on 13 May 1767 for £1.10.0. {Ref: MSA S960 or S752, pp. 176-177; CSOS:108}

CRAGHEAD, ROBERT (Maryland), b. c1735, MD (age 21 in 1756); pvt., Capt. Christopher Gist's Company of VA Militia, 13 Jul 1756, enlisted at Baltimore. {Ref: MSR I:37}

CRAIG, GEORGE (Maryland), pvt., Capt. Richard Pearis' Company of MD Troops, Frederick Co., from 24 Oct 1757 to 31 May 1758. {Ref: MHS MS.375.1} Payment to him was recorded in Col. Dagworthy's account book on 17 Jul 1762. {Ref: MHS MS.375}

CRAIG, JAMES (Delaware), son of Hugh Craig and Annaleny or Anelena (N); d. testate and unmarried in February 1771. {Ref: CFD 2:40} Pvt., Capt. Richard McWilliams' Company of Foot, New Castle Co., enlisted 28 Dec 1757. {Ref: ARDE I:14}

CRAIG (CRAIGG), JOHN (Maryland), cpl., Capt. Peregrine Brown's Company Muster Roll, Kent Co., circa 1757-1758, exact dates not given (served 15 days); bill of credit issued or paid in his behalf to Robert Buchanan on 21 Mar 1767 for £1. {Ref: MSA S960 or S752, p. 179; CSOS:110}

CRAIG, THOMAS (Delaware), ensign, militia, Lower Part of Murderkill Hundred, Kent Co. on Delaware, 1756. {Ref: ARDE I:12; ARPA (2nd Series) 2:527-529; HDE I:141}

CRAIG (CRAIGE), WILLIAM (Delaware), lieut., Southern District of Broadkiln Hundred, Militia Regt. of Sussex Co., 1756-1758. {Ref: ARDE I:13, 15; ARPA (2nd Series) 2:529, 579; HDE I:141} William Craige was a lieut. in Capt. Joseph Cord's Company on 18 Mar 1758 and was prob. the son of William Craig, yeoman, who d. testate by 5 Feb 1755. {Ref: CDSS:44-45}

CRAM (CRAME), PATRICK (Maryland), b. c1732, a Scotchman (age about 25 in 1757); pvt., Capt. Francis Ware's Company of MD Troops, Charles Co., reported as deserted from his company at Fort Frederick. {Ref: *MD Gazette*, 23 Jun and 1 Sep 1757}

CRAMER, VANDEL (Maryland), pvt., Capt. Peter Bainbridge's Company Muster Roll, Frederick Co., circa 1757-1758, exact dates not given (served 28 days); bill of credit issued or paid to him for £1.8.0 in 1767, exact date not given. {Ref: MSA S960 or S752, p. 180; CSOS:111}

CRAMPHIN, THOMAS JR. (Maryland), b. 26 Jan 1739/40, Prince George's Co., son of Thomas Cramphin and Mary Jackson, of Prince George's P. E. Parish; attended Hungerford Resolves protest meeting in 1774, was an active patriot in Frederick and Montgomery Cos. during the Revolutionary War, and a member of the MD Assembly (1778-1788); d. c1831, Montgomery Co.; never married. {Ref: PGCR 2:112; BDML I:242-243} Cpl., Capt. Elias Delashmutt's Company Muster Roll, Frederick Co., circa 1757-1758, exact dates not given (served 30 days); bill of credit issued or paid in his behalf to Elias Delashmut, Jr. on 16 Mar 1767 for £2.2.3; name mistakenly listed once as "Thomas Crampton." {Ref: MSA S960 or S752, p. 162: CSOS:94}

CRAMPTON, JOHN (Maryland), pvt., Capt. Francis Ware's Company of MD Troops, Charles Co., from 9 Oct 1757 to 8 Nov 1758 (served 396 days). {Ref: MHS MS.375.1; CSOS:87} Payment to him was recorded in Col. Dagworthy's account book on 7 Mar 1763. {Ref: MHS MS.375}

CRANE (CRAIN), DAVID (Maryland), patriot, Kent Co., pay account submitted for quartering soldiers in 1757 or 1758, exact dates not given. {Ref: MHM 9:3, p. 261}

CRANFIELD, HEZEKIAH (Delaware), pvt., Kent Co. Militia, Capt. John Caton's Company, 25 Apr 1757 (date of muster roll). {Ref: ARDE I:14}

CRANOR (CRAYNOR), JOSHUA (Maryland), pvt., Capt. Henry Casson's Company Muster Roll, Queen Anne's Co., circa 1757-1758, exact dates not given (served 27 days); bill of credit issued or paid in his behalf to Capt. Casson on 27 Mar 1767 for £1.7.0. {Ref: MSA S960 or S752, p. 178; CSOS:109} Joshua Craynor (c1735-1800), pvt., Capt. Henry Casson's Company, Eastern Shore of MD Troops in 1757, m. (N), and had dau. Esther Cranor (1759-1824). {Ref: SCWM III:138, 242}

CRAPPER, LEVIN, see "Levin Cropper," q.v.

CRASS (CRAPS?), CASPER (Maryland), pvt., Capt. Jonathan Hagar's Company Muster Roll, Frederick Co., circa 1757-1758, exact dates not given (served 6 days); bill of credit issued or paid to him for £0.6.0 in 1767, exact date not given. {Ref: MSA S960 or S752, p. 173; CSOS:107}

CRAWFORD, CHARLES (Maryland), pvt., Capt. John Dagworthy's Company of MD Troops, Frederick Co., from 27 Dec 1757 to 29 Feb 1759 (served 428 days) when he reportedly deserted; however, payment to him was recorded in Col. Dagworthy's account book on 13 Jul 1762. {Ref: MHS.375.1; CSOS:75; MHS MS.375}

CRAWFORD, ELIZABETH, see "Caesar Rodney," q.v.

CRAWFORD (CRAUFORD), JAMES (Maryland), b. 1 Oct 1732, Prince George's Co., son of James and Mary Crawford, of Queen Anne's P. E. Parish. {Ref: PGCR 1:171} Pvt., Capt. Joshua Beall's Company Muster Roll, Prince George's Co., circa 1757-1758, exact dates not given; bill of credit issued or paid in his behalf to Thomas Ijams for £1.19.0 on 12 Mar 1767. {Ref: MSA S960 or S752, p. 184}

CRAWFORD, JOHN (Delaware), b. c1733, Donegal, Ireland (laborer, age 25 in 1758); pvt., enlisted 29 Apr 1758 "for the campaign in the lower counties" by Capt. John McClughan. {Ref: ARDE I:17; ARPA (2nd Series) 2:570}

CREAGAR, VALENTINE, see "Valentine Cregor," q.v.

CREAGH, PATRICK (Maryland), d. 22 Dec 1760, Anne Arundel Co.; patriot, merchant, and long time inhabitant of Annapolis; pay account submitted by his exec. (unnamed at the time, but the newspaper stated it was Richard Mackubin) for his quartering soldiers in 1757 or 1758, exact dates not given. {Ref: MHM 9:3, p. 261; *MD Gazette*, 24 Dec 1760 and 15 Jan 1761}

CREAGH (CREY, CRAY), WILLIAM (Maryland), pvt., Capt. Joshua Beall's Company of MD Troops, Prince George's Co., from 9 Oct 1757 to 8 May 1758. {Ref: MHS MS.375.1; CSOS:83} Payment to him was recorded in Col. Dagworthy's account book on 8 Mar 1763 for work on Fort Cumberland. {Ref: MHS MS.375}

CREAMER (CREMAR, CRAMER), GEORGE (Maryland), pvt., Capt. John Middaugh's Company Muster Roll, Frederick Co., circa 1757-1758, exact dates not given (served 30 days); bill of credit or order issued to Casper Shaff and paid to David Cumming for £0.17.0 on 18 Apr 1767. {Ref: MSA S960 or S752, pp. 171-172; CSOS:102}

CREAMER (CREMAR, CRAMER), JACOB (Maryland), pvt., Capt. John Middaugh's Company Muster Roll, Frederick Co., circa 1757-1758, exact dates not given (served 30 days); bill of credit or order issued to Casper Shaff and paid to David Cumming for £0.17.0 on 18 Apr 1767. {Ref: MSA S960 or S752, pp. 171-172; CSOS:102}

CREAMER (CREAMORE, CREYMORE), HENRY (Maryland), pvt., Capt. Joseph Chapline's Company Muster Roll No. 1, Frederick Co., circa 1757-1758, exact dates not given (served 45 days); bill of credit issued or paid in his behalf to Joseph Chaplin for £2.5.0 on 5 Mar 1767. {Ref: MSA S960 or S752, p. 191; CSOS:103} Pvt., Capt. Moses Chapline's Company Muster Roll No. 2, Frederick Co., circa 1757-1758, exact dates not given (served 14 days); bill of credit issued or paid to him for £0.14.0 on 10 Oct 1771. {Ref: MSA S960 or S752, p. 197; CSOS:114} Pvt., Capt. Joseph Chapline's Company Muster Rolls No. 2 and 3, Frederick Co., circa 1757-1758, exact dates not given (served 3 days); bill of credit issued or paid in his behalf to Jonathan Hagar for £0.3.0 on 10 Oct 1771. {Ref: MSA S960 or S752, pp. 191, 193; CSOS:104}

CREATH, WILLIAM (Delaware), pvt., Capt. Richard McWilliams' Company of Foot, New Castle Co., enlisted 28 Dec 1757. {Ref: ARDE I:14}

CREGOR (CREAGAR), CONROD (Maryland), pvt., Capt. John Middaugh's Company Muster Roll, Frederick Co., circa 1757-1758, exact dates not given (served 30 days); bill of credit issued or paid in his behalf to Thomas Beatty, Jr. for £1.10.0 on 23 Feb 1767. {Ref: MSA S960 or S752, p. 171; CSOS:101}

CREGOR (CREGAR), ELIAS (Maryland), pvt., Capt. Peter Bainbridge's Company Muster Roll, Frederick Co., circa 1757-1758, exact dates not given (served 28 days); bill of credit issued or paid in his behalf to Henry Snavely on 27 Apr 1767 for £1.8.0. {Ref: MSA S960 or S752, p. 181; CSOS:111}

CREGOR (CREAGAR), VALENTINE (Maryland), pvt., Capt. John Middaugh's Company Muster Roll, Frederick Co., circa 1757-1758, exact dates not given (served 30 days); bill of credit issued or paid in his behalf to Thomas Beatty, Jr. for £1.10.0 on 23 Feb 1767. {Ref: MSA S960 or S752, p. 171; CSOS:100}

CREMER (KREAMER), JACOB (Delaware), b. c1739, Thorlowitz, Germany (laborer, age 19 in 1758); pvt., enlisted 11 May 1758 "for the campaign in the lower counties" by Capt. John McClughan. {Ref: ARDE I:17; ARPA (2nd Series) 2:570}

CREPPELL (CREPPLE), PETER (Maryland), pvt., Capt. John Middaugh's Company Muster Roll, Frederick Co., circa 1757-1758, exact dates not given (served 30 days); bill of credit issued or paid in his behalf to Casper Shaff for £1.10.0 on 2 Mar 1767; name mistakenly listed once as "Peter Cressell." {Ref: MSA S960 or S752, p. 171; CSOS:100}

CRESAP, DANIEL (Maryland), private, Frederick Co., by 1756. "It is said that Thomas and Daniel Cresap (sons of Col. Cresap), with others, dressed as Indians and attacked the women and children at the Indian towns while their warriors were out doing the same to our settlements." {Ref: *MD Gazette*, 29 Apr 1756} Pvt., Capt. Jonathan Hagar's Company Muster Roll, Frederick Co., circa 1757-1758, exact dates not given (served 6 days); bill of credit issued or paid to him for £0.6.0 in 1767, exact date not given. {Ref: MSA S960 or S752, p. 173; CSOS:106} See "Morris Williams," q.v.

CRESAP, MICHAEL, see "Thomas Wiggins, Jr." and "Isaac Lemaster," q.v.

CRESAP, THOMAS (Maryland), b. c1691, Yorkshire, England, m. 1st to Hannah Johnson by 1727 and 2nd to Margaret (N) by 1783, had children Daniel, Thomas Jr. (1732-1756, killed by Indians on St. George's Day), Michael (1741-1775, captain in the Revolutionary War), Elizabeth, and Sarah, and d. testate by 26 Apr 1788, Washington Co. (now Allegany Co.); captain by 1732, fur trader, surveyor, merchant, Indian agent, colonel by 1749, founder of the Ohio Company in 1749, member of the MD Assembly (served on the Arms and Ammunition Committee, 1757-1770). {Ref: BDML I:244-245; *MD Gazette*, 6 May 1756} Col. Thomas Cresap stated he was about 66 years old or thereabouts in a deposition taken on 10 May 1757. {Ref: ARMD 31:252-253} Militia pay account submitted in 1758, exact date not given. {Ref: MHM 9:4, p. 369} See "Henry Wehaun" and "Barnard Keslar" and "Philip Wiggins," q.v.

CRESAP, THOMAS JR. (Maryland), soldier (rank not stated), Frederick Co., by 1756. "Capt. Dagworthy, who came to Annapolis yesterday from Fort Cumberland, says that Thomas Cresap, Jr., his brother and a company of men were in pursuit of the enemy. Mr. Cresap was killed. Cresap, a young widower, left two small children." {Ref: *MD Gazette*, 6 May 1756}

CRESSELL, PETER, see "Peter Creppell," q.v.

CRESWELL, ROBERT (Maryland), b. c1734, MD (age 22 in 1756); pvt., Capt. Christopher Gist's Company of VA Militia, 13 Jul 1756, enlisted at Baltimore. {Ref: MSR I:37}

CRESWELL, THOMAS (Maryland), pvt., Capt. Richard Pearis' Company of MD Troops, Frederick Co., from 9 Oct 1757 to 8 May 1758 when he reportedly deserted; however, payment to him was recorded in Col. Dagworthy's account book on 14 Jul 1763. {Ref: MHS MS.375; MHS MS.375.1}

CREYCROFT (CRAYCROFT), JOSEPH (Maryland), pvt., Capt. Moses Chapline's Company Muster Roll No. 3, Frederick Co., circa 1757-1758, exact dates not given (served 6 days); bill of credit issued or paid in his behalf to Joseph Chapline for £0.6.0 on 13 Jun 1768. {Ref: MSA S960 or S752, p. 198; CSOS:114}

CREYMORE, HENRY, see "Henry Creamer," q.v.

CROCKETT, BENJAMIN (Maryland), doctor and patriot, Baltimore Co., who "agreed to supply the county pensioners in St. George's Parish, also the French Neutrals [i.e., Acadians] belonging to that parish, for the time being, with physick attendance for the ensuing year" in November 1759 and November 1760. {Ref: Baltimore Co. Court Minutes}

CROCKETT, GILBERT, see "Edward Walsh," q.v.

CROMWELL, HANNAH, see "Nicholas Orrick," q.v.

CROMWELL, JOSEPH, see "Edmund Stansbury," q.v.

CROOKHAM, WILLIAM (Delaware), tailor; pvt., Wilmington Township, enlisted by Capt. Samuel Grubb for the PA Regt. in 1759. {Ref: ARDE I:27}

CROPPER, LEVIN (Delaware), m. Betty (N), had children Milton, Levin, Amelia, Leah, and Sarah, and d. testate by 23 Apr 1775. {Ref: CDSS:46} Ensign, Northern District of Cedar Creek Hundred, Militia Regt. of Sussex Co., 1756-1758; ensign in Capt. Benjamin Wynkoop's Company on 18 Mar 1758. {Ref: ARDE I:13, 15; ARPA (2nd Series) 2:529, 579; HDE I:141}

CROSBY, WILLIAM (Maryland), pvt., Capt. John White's Company Muster Roll, Frederick Co., circa 1757-1758, exact dates not given (served 6 days); bill of credit issued or paid to him for £0.6.0 in 1767, exact date not given. {Ref: MSA S960 or S752, p. 164; CSOS:95}

CROSER, BASIL (Maryland), patriot, Anne Arundel or Frederick Co., received two barrels of gunpowder out of the magazine and stores of the City of Annapolis on 5 Jun 1763 to be delivered to Col. Thomas Prather or his order at the mouth of the Conococheague (as reported by the Arms and Ammunition Committee to the MD Assembly). {Ref: ARMD 58:342}

CROSH, PETER (Maryland), pvt., Capt. Peter Butler's Company Muster Roll, Frederick Co., circa 1757-1758, exact dates not given (served 34 days); bill of credit or order issued to him for £1.14.0 and paid in 1767, exact date not given. {Ref: MSA S960 or S752, p. 166; CSOS:96}

CROSS, JOHN (Maryland), b. c1736, MD (age 20 in 1756); pvt., Capt. Christopher Gist's Company of VA Militia, 13 Jul 1756, enlisted at Baltimore. {Ref: MSR I:37} *Identification Problem:* There were two men with this name who could have served in the war: (1) John Cross, son of John Cross and Dinah Wheeler, poss. m. Philizanna Hicks on 28 Aug 1753, d. by 18 Mar 1775; and, (2) John Cross,

b. 10 Dec 1733, son of Joseph Cross and Elizabeth Merryman, m. Edith (N), and noted as "son of Joseph Cross of York Co., dec." in November 1760 deed. {Ref: BCF:149-150}

CROSS (CROSSE), JOHN (Maryland), b. 9 Jan 1732/3, Prince George's Co., son of Robert and Jane Cross, of Queen Anne's P. E. Parish. {Ref: PGCR 1:171} Pvt., Capt. John Middaugh's Company Muster Roll, Frederick Co., circa 1757-1758, exact dates not given (served 30 days); bill of credit issued or paid in his behalf to Thomas Beatty, Jr. for £1.10.0 on 23 Feb 1767. {Ref: MSA S960 or S752, p. 171; CSOS:100}

CROSSLY, PHILIP (Maryland), pvt., Capt. John Dagworthy's Company of MD Troops, Frederick Co., from 9 Oct 1757 to 9 Feb 1759 (served 488 days) when he reportedly died; however, payment to him was recorded in Col. Dagworthy's account book on 22 Jul 1762. {Ref: MHS MS.375.1; CSOS:75; MHS MS.375}

CROUCH, ANNE, see "Richard Lloyd," q.v.

CROWLEY, OWEN (Delaware), b. c1731 (laborer, age 28 in 1759); pvt., enlisted by Capt. James Armstrong for the PA Regt. on 19 May 1759. {Ref: ARDE I:25; ARPA (2nd Series) 2:585}

CROWN, CONROD (Maryland), pvt., Capt. Peter Bainbridge's Company Muster Roll, Frederick Co., circa 1757-1758, exact dates not given (served 28 days); bill of credit issued or paid in his behalf to Jacob Young on 4 Mar 1767 for £1.8.0. {Ref: MSA S960 or S752, p. 181; CSOS:111}

CROZIER, MATTHEW (Delaware), yeoman, of Duck Creek Hundred, m. Rachel (N), had children Matthew, Robert, Mary, Sarah, and Rhoda, and d. intestate by 27 Sep 1773. {Ref: CDSS:47} Ensign, Upper Part of Little Creek Hundred, Militia of Kent Co. on Delaware, 1756. {Ref: ARDE I:12; ARPA (2nd Series) 2:527-529; HDE I:141}

CRUM, GILBERT JR. (Maryland), pvt., Capt. John Middaugh's Company Muster Roll, Frederick Co., circa 1757-1758, exact dates not given (served 30 days); bill of credit or order issued to him for £0.17.0 in 1767, exact date not given. {Ref: MSA S960 or S752, p. 171; MHM 9:3, p. 274; CSOS:102}

CUBE, WILLIAM ANDERSON (Maryland), pvt., Capt. Joseph Chapline's Company Muster Rolls No. 2 and 3, Frederick Co., circa 1757-1758, exact dates not given (served 7 days); bill of credit issued or paid in his behalf to Joseph Chaplin for £0.7.0 on 5 Mar 1767. {Ref: MSA S960 or S752, p. 193; CSOS:104}

CULFORD, PAT. (Maryland), patriot, Frederick Co., who performed "sundry services at the fort" in 1763 and payment in the amount of £1.7.0 was still owed to him on 25 Nov 1763 (when reported by the Accounts Committee to the MD Assembly). {Ref: ARMD 58:400}

CULLEN, WILLIAM (Delaware), m. Sarah (N), had children Ruth, John, William, Mary, James, Thomas, David, Nathan, and Nathaniel, and d. intestate by 2 Dec 1778. {Ref: CDSS:47-48} Pvt., Kent Co. Militia, Capt. John Caton's Company, 25 Apr 1757 (date of muster roll). {Ref: ARDE I:14}

CULLY (KULLEY), JAMES (Maryland), farmer; pvt., Capt. Peregrine Brown's 7th Co. of Foot Militia, Kent Co., on 19 Feb 1758, by which time he had enlisted, but reportedly refused to appear and serve in arms against the enemy. {Ref: ARMD 31:283, 288}

CUMMING, DAVID, see "Henry Hill," q.v.

CUMMING, JOHN (Delaware), b. c1723, Ireland (smith, age 35 in 1758, height 5 ft. 9 in.); pvt., enlisted by Capt. Paul Jackson in New Castle Co. for the PA Troops on 22 May 1758. {Ref: ARDE I:27}

CUMMINS, HANNA, see "George Wells," q.v.

CUMMINS, MARGARET (Maryland), patriot, Annapolis, Anne Arundel Co., pay account submitted for quartering soldiers in 1757 or 1758, exact dates not given. {Ref: MHM 9:3, p. 262}

CUMMINS, ROBERT, see "William Wilson," q.v.

CUMUNTO CHISKYOWE, Indian Chief (Maryland), Frederick Co., agreed to join with the English against the French in 1758. {Ref: ARMD 31:266}

CURRENT, JAMES (Maryland), pvt., Capt. Joshua Beall's Company of MD Troops, Prince George's Co., from 9 Oct 1757 to 29 Jan 1758 when he was discharged. {Ref: MHS MS.375.1; CSOS:83} Payment to him was recorded in Col. Dagworthy's account book on 12 Jul 1762. {Ref: MHS MS.375}

CURRENT, MATHEW (Maryland), pvt., Capt. Joshua Beall's Company of MD Troops, Prince George's Co., from 9 Oct 1757 to 13 Dec 1757 when he was discharged. {Ref: MHS MS.375.1; CSOS:83} Payment to him was recorded in Col. Dagworthy's account book on 24 Jul 1762. {Ref: MHS MS.375}

CURRY, JAMES (Maryland), indentured servant and soldier who served in the French and Indian War some time between 1756 and 1763 (exact dates not known); his master John Martin, farmer, requested compensation from the Baltimore County Court due to the loss of use of Curry while in the service. {Ref: MHM 94:4, p. 426, citing Baltimore Co. Court Minutes}

CURRY, NEIL (Delaware), b. c1723, Scotland (cooper, age 35 in 1758); pvt., recruited by Capt. Benjamin Noxon and enlisted on 22 Apr 1758. {Ref: ARDE I:19; ARPA (2nd Series) 2:566}

CURTIS, DANIEL, see "John Foster," q.v.

CURTS, GEORGE (Maryland), pvt., Capt. Stephen Rensburg's or Rensburger's Company Muster Roll, Frederick Co., circa 1757-1758, exact dates not given (served 34 days); bill of credit issued or paid in his behalf to Stephen Rensburg or Rensburger for £1.14.0 on 27 Mar 1767. {Ref: MSA S960 or S752, p. 182; CSOS:112}

CUSTOGA, Delaware Indian, see "Evan Shelby," q.v.

DAGWORTHY, JOHN (Maryland and Delaware), b. 30 Mar 1721, m. Martha Cadwalader, had a dau. Rachel, and d. testate on 1 May 1784, Sussex Co. On 2 Jun 1732 he was mentioned in a letter to the Duke of New Castle in relation to separate government in New Jersey, as "an honest, bold man, well affected to the government; is of the Church of England; a thriving man and at present high sheriff of the county in which he resides. On 2 Feb 1747 he was again recommended to the Duke of New Castle and was mentioned as Capt. John Dagworthy having in command a company of 85 active men; his services were engaged, for a short time in Canada, from whence he returned to New Jersey.

About 1754 he went to Maryland and served in the French and Indian War under [General] Braddock, sharing in the latter's defeat [in 1755]; for his services he was given a large tract of land in Worcester Co., MD, lying at the head of Pepper's Creek, which later was declared to be in Sussex Co., DE." {Ref: HDE II:1335} Captain, served in Frederick Co. by 1756; was paid £194.13.5½ by the MD Assembly "for the support of the ranging parties on the Western Frontier" from 10 Mar to 16 May 1756; lieut. colonel, MD Troops, Frederick Co., from 9 Oct 1757 to 26 Apr 1759. {Ref: ARMD 31:227, 52:674; MHS MS.375.1} He was mentioned as follows in a letter from Gov. Horatio Sharpe to the MD Assembly on 12 Apr 1757: "I think it proper to inform you, that the Virginia Troops, which have been some time posted at Fort Cumberland, are ordered to leave that place, and to embark for South Carolina, and that Capt. Dagworthy is instructed to march, with a Detachment from the Maryland Forces, to Garrison Fort Cumberland, 'til he shall receive further orders, the Earl of Loudoun having thought that step necessary, and to his Majesty's Service." {Ref: ARMD 55:50} He was referred to as "Lieut. Col. Dagworthy" by the MD Assembly on 22 Dec 1758 and payments to soldiers were recorded in the accont book of "Col. Dagworthy" in 1762 and 1763 at Fort Cumberland. {Ref: ARMD 56:134-135; MHS MS.375} Colonel, Sussex Co. Militia, 1775; brig. general, 1776; justice of the peace, 1777; his service in the Revolutionary War is well documented. {Ref: RPDE:66, HDE II:1335}

DAILEY (DAYLEY), PHILIP (Maryland), pvt., Capt. John Middaugh's Company Muster Roll, Frederick Co., circa 1757-1758, exact dates not given (served 30 days); bill of credit issued or paid in his behalf to Robert Wood for £1.10.0 on 4 Mar 1767. {Ref: MSA S960 or S752, pp. 171-172; CSOS:101}

DAINTY, JOHN (Delaware), b. c1733, Grapner, England (miller, age 25 in 1758); pvt., enlisted 1 May 1758 "for the campaign in the lower counties" by Capt. John McClughan. {Ref: ARDE I:17; ARPA (2nd Series) 2:570}

DALE, GEORGE (Maryland), indentured servant and soldier who served in the French and Indian War some time between 1756 and 1763 (exact dates not known); his master Benjamin Tasker, iron manufacturer, requested compensation from the Baltimore County Court due to the loss of use of Dale while in the service. {Ref: MHM 94:4, p. 426, citing Baltimore Co. Court Minutes}

DALLAM, ELIZABETH, see "William Smith," q.v.

DALLAM, RICHARD, see "William Smith," q.v.

DAMER, ANDREW (Maryland), alias Andrew Tamer *[sic]*, pvt., Capt. Thomas Norris' Company, Frederick Co., circa 1757-1758, exact dates not given (served 30 days); bill of credit issued or paid in his behalf to Michael McGuire on 11 Apr 1767 for £1.10.0; name mistakenly listed once as "Andrew Tanner." {Ref: MSA S960 or S752, p. 176; CSOS:108}

DAMILERY, NICHOLAS (Maryland), indentured servant and soldier who served in the French and Indian War some time between 1756 and 1763 (exact dates not known); his master Brian Philpot, merchant, requested compensation from the Baltimore County Court due to the loss of use of Damilery while in the service. {Ref: MHM 94:4, p. 426, citing Baltimore Co. Court Minutes}

DANIEL, JOHN (Maryland), pvt., Capt. John Middaugh's Company Muster Roll, Frederick Co., circa 1757-1758, exact dates not given (served 30 days); bill of credit issued or paid in his behalf to Thomas Beatty, Jr. for £1.10.0 on 23 Feb 1767. {Ref: MSA S960 or S752, p. 171; CSOS:101}

DANILY (DONELLY), ABNER (Delaware), b. c1739, MD (age 20 in 1759); pvt., enlisted in Capt. John Wright's Company and mustered on 11 May 1759. {Ref: ARDE I:25; ARPA (2nd Series) 2:508, 592}

DARBY, HENRY (Maryland), pvt., Capt. John White's Company Muster Roll, Frederick Co., circa 1757-1758, exact dates not given (served 6 days); bill of credit issued or paid to him for £0.6.0 in 1767, exact date not given. {Ref: MSA S960 or S752, p. 164; CSOS:96}

DARE, JOHN (Maryland), sea captain by 1757, was in command of the ship *Concord* when captured by the French. {Ref: *MD Gazette*, 19 May 1757}

DARE, MARGARET, see "William Allnutt," q.v.

DARNALL, JOHN (Maryland), m. (N), had children John, Henry, Thomas, and Ann, and d. testate by 9 Feb 1768, Frederick Co. {Ref: WMG 3:1, p. 39} Patriot who was paid £50 on 16 Aug 1758 "for 500 bushels of corn sent by sundries to Fort Frederick" for the Western Expedition against Fort Duquesne. {Ref: ARMD 55:774} See "Peter Butler," q.v.

DARRACH, JOHN, see "William White," q.v.

DASHIELL, CLEMENT, see "John Adams," q.v.

DASHIELL, JANE, see "John Handy," q.v.

DASHIELL, JOSEPH (Maryland), b. 1736, Somerset Co., son of George (d. 1748) and Betty (d. 1739) Dashiell, m. 1st to Martha Bluett on 18 May 1757 and 2nd to Susannah (N) by 1774, had children William Pitt, Martha Bluett, and Eleanor Matilda, and d. intestate by February 1787, Worcester Co.; planter, mariner, miller, captain by 1757, member of the MD Assembly (1768-1770, 1775-1776, 1780-1785), lieut. colonel by 1776, colonel by 1777, and court justice (1786-1787). {Ref: BDML I:255}

DAUGHERTY, JAMES (Maryland), lieut., Capt. William McClellan's Company of MD Volunteers, Frederick Co., circa 1763-1764; on muster roll dated 15 Nov 1764 at Camp at the Forks of Muskingham. {Ref: ARMD 32:99}

DAUGHERTY, JOHN (Maryland), pvt., Capt. William McClellan's Company of MD Volunteers, Frederick Co., circa 1763-1764; on muster roll dated 15 Nov 1764 at Camp at the Forks of Muskingham. {Ref: ARMD 32:99}

DAUGHERTY, MARGARET BARKEY, see "Stephen Kimble," q.v.

DAVIDGE, JOHN (Maryland), d. 30 Apr 1764, Anne Arundel Co., of consumption; patriot, deputy commissary, Register of the Prerogative Court, and clerk of the Lower House of the MD Assembly by 24 Sep 1756 at which time he presented a report in behalf of the committee appointed to inspect the arms and ammunition in the City of Annapolis. {Ref: ARMD 52:612-614; *MD Gazette*, 3 May 1764}

DAVIDS, JOHN (Delaware), b. c1723, New Castle Co. (laborer, age 35 in 1758, height 5 ft. 9 in.); pvt., enlisted by Capt. Paul Jackson in New Castle Co. for the PA Troops on 13 May 1758. {Ref: ARDE I:27}

DAVIDSON, JAMES (Maryland), pvt., Capt. Tobias Stansbury's Company Muster Roll, Baltimore Co., circa 1757-1758, exact dates not given; bill of credit issued or paid in his behalf to Thomas Cockey Deye for £1.18.0 on 25 Mar 1767. {Ref: MSA S960 or S752, p. 186}

DAVIDSON, JOHN (Maryland), b. c1732, MD (age 24 in 1756); pvt., Capt. Christopher Gist's Company of VA Militia, 13 Jul 1756, enlisted at Baltimore. {Ref: MSR I:37}

DAVIS, DANIEL (Maryland), pvt., Capt. Elias Delashmutt's Company Muster Roll, Frederick Co., 13 Aug 1757, exact dates not given (served 52 days); bill of credit issued or paid in his behalf to Evan Shelby on 8 May 1767 for £2.12.0. {Ref: MSA S960 or S752, p. 163; CSOS:98}

DAVIS, DANIEL (Maryland), pvt., Capt. Peter Butler's Company Muster Roll, Frederick Co., circa 1757-1758, exact dates not given (served 34 days); bill of credit or order issued in his behalf for £1.14.0 and paid to Peter Grosh on 4 Mar 1767. {Ref: MSA S960 or S752, p. 168; CSOS:97}

DAVIS, DAVID (Maryland), pvt., Capt. Richard Pearis' Company of MD Troops, Frederick Co., circa 9 Oct 1757 to 31 May 1758; militia pay account submitted in 1758, exact date not given. {Ref: CSOS:90; MHM 9:4, p. 367} Pvt., Capt. Joshua Beall's Company of MD Troops, Prince George's Co., from 1 Jun 1758 to 30 Dec 1758; payment to him was recorded in Col. Dagworthy's account book on 12 Jul 1762. {Ref: MHS MS.375; CSOS:84; MHS MS.375.1}

DAVIS, EPHRAIM (Maryland), pvt., Capt. William Luckett's Company Muster Roll, Frederick Co., circa 1757-1758, exact dates not given (served 30 days); bill of credit issued or paid in his behalf to William Luckett, Jr. for £1.10.0 on 6 Apr 1767. {Ref: MSA S960 or S752, p. 169; CSOS:99}

DAVIS, EVEN (Maryland), pvt., Capt. Richard Pearis' Company of MD Troops, Frederick Co., circa 9 Oct 1757 to 31 May 1758. {Ref: MHS MS.375.1; CSOS:90} Payment to him was recorded in Col. Dagworthy's account book on 15 Jul 1762. {Ref: MHS MS.375} See "Owen Davis," q.v.

DAVIS, GEORGE (Maryland), pvt., Capt. Jonathan Hagar's Company Muster Roll, Frederick Co., circa 1757-1758, exact dates not given (served 6 days); bill of credit issued or paid in his behalf to Joseph Chaplin for £0.6.0 on 24 Apr 1767. {Ref: MSA S960 or S752, p. 173; CSOS:107}

DAVIS, GEORGE (Maryland), pvt., Capt. Joseph Chapline's Company Muster Roll No. 1, Frederick Co., circa 1757-1758, exact dates not given (served 26 days); bill of credit issued or paid in his behalf to Joseph Chaplin for £1.16.0 on 24 Apr 1767. {Ref: MSA S960 or S752, p. 192; CSOS:103}

DAVIS, HANOVER (Maryland), pvt., Capt. Moses Chapline's Company Muster Roll No. 1, Frederick Co., circa 1757-1758, exact dates not given (served 55 days); bill of credit issued or paid in his behalf to Jonathan Hagar for £2.15.0 on 10 Oct 1771; name mistakenly transcribed once as "Hanover Deaves." {Ref: MSA S960 or S752, p. 196; CSOS:113} Pvt., Capt. Moses Chapline's Company Muster Roll No. 2, Frederick Co., circa 1757-1758, exact dates not given (served 14 days); bill of credit issued or paid in his behalf to Jonathan Hagar for £0.14.0 on 10 Oct 1771. {Ref: MSA S960 or S752, p. 197; CSOS:114} Pvt., Capt. Moses

Chapline's Company Muster Roll No. 3, Frederick Co., circa 1757-1758, exact dates not given (served 6 days); bill of credit issued or paid in his behalf to Jonathan Hagar for £0.6.0 on 10 Oct 1771. {Ref: MSA S960 or S752, p. 198; CSOS:115}

DAVIS, HONICAL (Maryland), pvt., Capt. Alexander Beall's Company of MD Troops, Frederick Co., from 9 Oct 1757 to 9 Nov 1758. {Ref: MHS MS.375.1; CSOS:80} Payment to him was recorded in Col. Dagworthy's account book on 26 Feb 1763. {Ref: MHS MS.375}

DAVIS, JAMES (Delaware), b. c1739, Down, Ireland (farmer, age 19 in 1758); pvt., enlisted 22 Apr 1758 "for the campaign in the lower counties" by Capt. John McClughan. {Ref: ARDE I:17; ARPA (2nd Series) 2:570}

DAVIS, JOHN (Maryland), b. 10 Mar 1739/40, Kent Co., son of John and Mary Davis, of Shrewsbury Parish. {Ref: ESVR} Pvt., Capt. Peregrine Brown's Company Muster Roll, Kent Co., circa 1757-1758, exact dates not given (served 15 days); bill of credit issued or paid in his behalf to Robert Buchanan for Davis' exec. (unnamed) on 21 Mar 1767 for £0.15.0. {Ref: MSA S960 or S752, p. 179; CSOS:110}

DAVIS, JOHN (Delaware), pvt., Kent Co. Militia, Capt. John Caton's Company, 25 Apr 1757 (date of muster roll). {Ref: ARDE I:13}

DAVIS, JOHN (Maryland), pvt., Capt. Joshua Beall's Company of MD Troops, Prince George's Co., from 9 Oct 1757 to 25 Oct 1758 when he was discharged. {Ref: MHS MS.375.1}

DAVIS, JOSIAH (Maryland), pvt., Capt. William Luckett's Company Muster Roll, Frederick Co., circa 1757-1758, exact dates not given (served 30 days); bill of credit issued or paid in his behalf to William Luckett, Jr. for £1.10.0 on 6 Apr 1767. {Ref: MSA S960 or S752, p. 169; CSOS:99}

DAVIS, LODOWICK (Maryland), Frederick Co., was allowed £2.11.4 3/4 in June Court 1758 "in consideration of his servants-man enlisting in His Majesty's service." {Ref: TWL:178, citing Frederick Co. Judgment Records}

DAVIS, MARK, see "Nehemiah Davis," q.v.

DAVIS, MARY, see "Richard Davis" and "Robert Davis" and "John Davis," q.v.

DAVIS, NATHANIEL, see "Richard Davis" and "Robert Davis," q.v.

DAVIS, NEHEMIAH (Delaware), ensign, Southern District of Cedar Creek Hundred, Militia Regt. of Sussex Co., 1756; ensign, Slaughter Neck District, 1758. {Ref: ARDE I:13, 15; ARPA (2nd Series) 2:529, 579; HDE I:141} *Identification problem:* There were three men with this name who could have served in the war: (1) Nehemiah Davis, Sr., son of Thomas Davis and Mary Bowman (widow of Henry Bowman), m. Susannah (N) and d. testate by 13 Apr 1789; (2) Nehemiah Davis, Jr., son of Nehemiah Davis and Susanna (N), m. 1st to Mary Wattson (widow of Thomas Wattson) and 2nd to Sarah Hill (widow of William Hill); and, (3) Nehemiah Davis, son of Mark Davis and Mary Smith, m. Rachel Atkinson Stringer, and d. testate by 8 Mar 1787. {Ref: CFD 4:40-47; CDSS:51}

DAVIS, OWEN (Maryland), pvt., Frederick Co. militia, pay account submitted in 1758, exact date not given. {Ref: MHM 9:4, p. 370} Pvt., Capt. John Dagworthy's Company of MD Troops, Frederick Co., from 1 Jun 1758 to 9 Dec 1758 (served

191 days) and reportedly deserted on 9 Dec 1758. {Ref: MHS MS.375.1; CSOS:76} See "Even Davis," q.v.

DAVIS, RICHARD (Maryland), b. 1 Apr 1734, Baltimore Co., son of Nathaniel and Mary Davis, St. Paul's P. E. Parish; poss. m. Margaret (N). {Ref: BCF:160} Pvt., Capt. Christopher Gist's Company of VA Militia, 13 Jul 1756, enlisted at Baltimore (b. MD, age 22). {Ref: MSR I:37}

DAVIS, ROBERT (Maryland), b. 7 Jun 1739, Baltimore Co., son of Nathaniel and Mary Davis, St. Paul's P. E. Parish. {Ref: BCF:160} Pvt., Capt. Tobias Stansbury's Company Muster Roll, Baltimore Co., circa 1757-1758, exact dates not given; bill of credit issued or paid in his behalf to Robert Adair for £3.18.0 on 22 May 1767. {Ref: MSA S960 or S752, p. 187}

DAVIS, THOMAS, see "Henry Hall" and "Nehemiah Davis," q.v.

DAVIS, THOMAS (Maryland), pvt., Capt. John Wolgomatt's Company of MD Volunteers, Frederick Co., circa 1763-1764; on muster roll dated 15 Nov 1764 at Camp at the Forks of Muskingham. {Ref: ARMD 32:99}

DAVIS, ZACHARIAH (Maryland), pvt., Capt. William Luckett's Company Muster Roll, Frederick Co., circa 1757-1758, exact dates not given (served 30 days); bill of credit issued or paid in his behalf to William Luckett, Jr. for £1.10.0 on 6 Apr 1767. {Ref: MSA S960 or S752, p. 170; CSOS:99}

DAVYER, WILLIAM (Delaware or Pennsylvania), b. c1737, MD (laborer, age 21 in 1758); pvt., Capt. John Bull's Company of the PA Regt., 1 Jun 1758 (date of muster roll return). {Ref: ARPA (2nd Series) 2:491}

DAWKINS, REBECCA, see "Alexander Somervell," q.v.

DAWSON, ELIZABETH, see "Woolman Gibson," q.v.

DAWSON, WILLIAM (Maryland), pvt., Capt. Joseph Chapline's Company Muster Roll No. 4, Frederick Co., circa 1757-1758, exact dates not given; bill of credit issued or paid in his behalf to Joseph Chaplin for £0.5.0 on 24 Apr 1767. {Ref: MSA S960 or S752, p. 195} See "William Dorson," q.v.

DAWTON, THOMAS (Maryland), pvt., Capt. Joseph Hanson Harrison's Company Muster Roll, Charles Co., circa 1757-1758, exact dates not given; bill of credit issued or paid in his behalf to Capt. Joseph Hanson Harrison for £2.12.0 on 9 Nov 1770. {Ref: MSA S960 or S752, p. 189}

DAY, JOHN (Maryland), pvt., Prince George's Co., received £5 bounty money on 23 Jul 1757 for enlisting in the militia. {Ref: ARMD 55:265, 619} Pvt., Capt. Joshua Beall's Company of MD Troops, Prince George's Co., from 9 Oct 1757 to 12 Oct 1758 (promoted to cpl. on 29 Jan 1758). {Ref: MHS MS.375.1; CSOS:83} Payment to him was recorded in Col. Dagworthy's account book on 26 Feb 1763. {Ref: MHS MS.375}

DAY, LEONARD (Maryland), pvt., Capt. John Dagworthy's Company of MD Troops, Frederick Co., from 9 Oct 1757 to 22 Jan 1759 (served 470 days) when he reportedly deserted; however, payment to him was recorded in Col. Dagworthy's account book on 11 Jul 1762 for work on Fort Cumberland. {Ref: MHS MS.375.1; CSOS:76; MHS MS.375}

DAY, RICHARD (Maryland), lieut., Capt. Robert Sollers' Militia Co. in the lower part of Calvert Co., circa 1756-1758 (exact dates not given). {Ref: HCC:121}

DEAKINS, RICHARD (Maryland), pvt., Capt. Joshua Beall's Company Muster Roll, Prince George's Co., circa 1757-1758, exact dates not given; bill of credit issued or paid to him for £1.6.0 in 1767, exact date not given. {Ref: MSA S960 or S752, p. 184}

DEAL (DEALE), JOHN (Maryland), farmer; b. 25 Jun 1733, Kent Co., son of Nathaniel and Martha Deal, of Shrewsbury Parish. {Ref: ESVR} Pvt., Capt. Peregrine Brown's 7th Co. of Foot Militia, Kent Co., on 19 Feb 1758, by which time he had enlisted, but reportedly refused to appear and serve in arms against the enemy. {Ref: ARMD 31:283}

DEAN, JOHN (Maryland), pvt., Capt. William McClellan's Company of MD Volunteers, Frederick Co., circa 1763-1764; on muster roll dated 15 Nov 1764 at Camp at the Forks of Muskingham. {Ref: ARMD 32:99}

DEAN (DEANE), RICHARD (Maryland), pvt., Capt. Joseph Chapline's Company Muster Roll No. 2, Frederick Co., circa 1757-1758, exact dates not given (served 7 days); bill of credit issued or paid in his behalf to Joseph Chaplin for £0.7.0 on 5 Mar 1767. {Ref: MSA S960 or S752, p. 193; CSOS:104} Pvt., Capt. Moses Chapline's Company Muster Roll No. 3, Frederick Co., circa 1757-1758, exact dates not given (served 6 days); bill of credit issued or paid in his behalf to Joseph Chaplin for £0.6.0 on 5 Mar 1767. {Ref: MSA S960 or S752, p. 198; CSOS:115}

DEAN, SAMUEL (Maryland), pvt., Capt. Francis Ware's Company of MD Troops, Charles Co., circa 9 Oct 1757 to 30 Dec 1758. {Ref: MHS MS.375.1; CSOS:87} Payment to him was recorded in Col. Dagworthy's account book on 7 Mar 1763 for work on Fort Cumberland. {Ref: MHS MS.375}

DEAN (DEANE), THOMAS (Maryland), pvt., Capt. Joseph Chapline's Company Muster Roll No. 1, Frederick Co., circa 1757-1758, exact dates not given (served 39 days); bill of credit issued or paid in his behalf to Joseph Chaplin for £1.19.0 on 5 Mar 1767. {Ref: MSA S960 or S752, p. 191; CSOS:103}

DEAN (DEANE), WILLIAM (Maryland), pvt., Capt. Joseph Chapline's Company Muster Roll No. 1, Frederick Co., circa 1757-1758, exact dates not given (served 58 days); bill of credit issued or paid in his behalf to Joseph Chaplin for £2.18.0 on 5 Mar 1767. {Ref: MSA S960 or S752, p. 190; CSOS:102}

DEAVER (DEAVES), HANNOVER (Maryland), pvt., Capt. Moses Chapline's Company Muster Roll No. 1, Frederick Co., circa 1757-1758, exact dates not given; bill of credit issued or paid to him for £0.6.0 in 1767, exact date not given. {Ref: MSA S960 or S752, p. 196; CSOS:113} See "Hannover Davis," q.v.

DEAVERBOUGH, CHRISTOPHER (Maryland), pvt., Capt. Tobias Stansbury's Company Muster Roll, Baltimore Co., circa 1757-1758, exact dates not given; bill of credit issued or paid to him for £1.18.0 in 1767, exact date not given. {Ref: MSA S960 or S752, p. 186}

DECHEIZER, MR., see "Robert Power," q.v.

DELANAWAY, PHILLOMAN (Delaware), pvt., Kent Co. Militia, Capt. John Caton's Company, 25 Apr 1757 (date of muster roll). {Ref: ARDE I:14}

DELASHMUTT (DELASHMUT), ELIAS (Maryland), prob. son of Peter De La Chaumette of Gloucester Co., NJ, settled in Frederick Co., MD, m. Elizabeth Nelson, had children Elias, Jr., Elizabeth, Rachel, Basil, Ann, Lindsey, and another dau. (N), and d. testate by 18 Apr 1778. {Ref: WMG 5:1, pp. 3-13} Capt., Frederick Co., circa 1757-1758, exact dates not given; bill of credit issued or paid in his behalf to Elias Delashmut, Jr. on 16 Mar 1767 for £13.13.3. {Ref: MSA S960 or S752, p. 162; CSOS:94, 98}

DELASHMUTT (DELASHMUT), ELIAS JR. (Maryland), son of Elias Delashmutt and Elizabeth Nelson, m. Catherine Waugh and had children William Waugh, Peter, Sarah Ann, Elias N., and Elizabeth. {Ref: WMG 5:1, p. 10} Pvt., Capt. Elias Delashmutt's Company Muster Roll, Frederick Co., 13 Aug 1757, exact dates not given (served 52 days); also served another 30 days, exact dates not given; bill of credit issued or paid to him on 16 Mar 1767 for £4.2.0. {Ref: MSA S960 or S752, p. 162; CSOS:94, 98}

DELATER, LAWRENCE (Maryland), pvt., Capt. Peter Bainbridge's Company Muster Roll, Frederick Co., circa 1757-1758, exact dates not given (served 41 days); bill of credit issued or paid in his behalf to John Grosnickle on 9 Jun 1767 for £2.1.0. {Ref: MSA S960 or S752, p. 181; CSOS:111}

DELFORD, JOHN (Maryland), patriot and poss. soldier (rank not specified), Frederick Co., militia pay account submitted in 1758, exact date not given. {Ref: MHM 9:4, p. 368}

DELLINGER (DENTLINGER), ANTHONY (Maryland), pvt., Capt. Thomas Norris' Company, Frederick Co., circa 1757-1758, exact dates not given (served 30 days); bill of credit issued or paid in his behalf to Valentine Myres on 10 Apr 1767 for £1.10.0. {Ref: MSA S960 or S752, p. 176; CSOS:108}

DELONEY, WILLIAM, see "William Withers," q.v.

DELOTTA, GEORGE (Maryland), patriot, Frederick Co., who performed "sundry services at the fort" in 1763 and payment in the amount of £0.16.6 was still owed to him on 25 Nov 1763 (when reported by the Accounts Committee to the MD Assembly). {Ref: ARMD 58:400}

DENBEE, ROBERT (Maryland), pvt., Capt. Tobias Stansbury's Company Muster Roll, Baltimore Co., circa 1757-1758, exact dates not given; bill of credit issued or paid in his behalf to Abraham Jarrett for £1.18.0 on 23 Apr 1770. {Ref: MSA S960 or S752, p. 187}

DENNIS, JOHN (Maryland), pvt., Capt. Richard Pearis' Company of MD Troops, Frederick Co., from 9 Oct 1757 to 23 Nov 1757 when he reportedly deserted; however, payment to him was recorded in Col. Dagworthy's account book on 8 Mar 1763. {Ref: MHS MS.375; MHS MS.375.1}

DENNIS, JOHN JR. (Maryland), b. c1724, Somerset Co., son of John Dennis and Mary Purnell, m. Anna Maria (N), had sons John and Robert, and d. testate by 6 Jun 1782, Worcester Co.; planter, miller, member of MD Assembly (1754-1755), county justice (1751-1755, 1764-1782), sheriff (1755-1758), captain by 1758, colonel by 1759, court justice (1777-1782), and Continental Loan Office subscription officer in 1779. {Ref: BDML I:261; ARMD 31:316}

DENNY, WILLIAM (Delaware), New Castle Co., lieut. governor in 1756 and acting governor in 1757; William Denny, Esq., commanded a PA Regt. on 12 May 1759. {Ref: GRSD 1:13; HDE II:942; ARPA (2nd Series) 2:487, 503}

DENNY, WILLIAM (Delaware or Pennsylvania), pvt., Capt. Culbertson's Company, was killed in "a recent battle with the Indians" in 1756 (exact date not given) in Cumberland Co., PA, after the burning of McCord's Fort. {Ref: *MD Gazette*, 29 Apr 1756}

DENT, ELEANOR, see "John Jordan," q.v.

DENT, GEORGE (Maryland), b. c1725, Charles Co., son of George Dent and Anne Harbert, m. Eleanor Hawkins circa 1748, had children Henry, George, Eleanor, Joanna, Jane, and Anne, and d. by 31 Dec 1785; sheriff (1753-1756), captain by 1757, member of the MD Assembly, 1757-1763 (served on the Arms and Ammunition Committee, 1757-1761), county justice (1757-1774), and Judge of the Court of Appeals in 1778. {Ref: BDML I:262-263} See "Richard Harrison," q.v.

DENT, GEORGE (Maryland), pvt., Capt. Peregrine Brown's Company, Kent Co., on 19 Feb 1758, by which time he had enlisted, but was unable to march due to health problems. {Ref: ARMD 31:283}

DENT, PETER (Maryland), b. c1736 near Cool Springs, St. Mary's Company; soldier who was reported as a deserter from the 1st Bttn. of the Royal American Regt. at Frederick Town in February 1760, age about 24. A notice placed in Annapolis newspaper by Ensign James Gorrell indicated Dent had left clothes at Stephen Chandler's house in Charles County where he had formerly kept school. {Ref: *MD Gazette*, 28 Feb 1760} A subsequent notice indicated Thomas Simpson left on Ensign Gorrell's horse (date not given) and said he was going to look for the deserter Peter Dent, but Simpson may have deserted as well. {Ref: *MD Gazette*, 5 Jun 1760}

DENT, WILLIAM, see "Arthur Lee" and "Richard Lee," q.v.

DENWOOD, BETTY, see "George Gale," q.v.

DERHAM, RICHARD (Delaware), pvt., Capt. Richard McWilliams' Company of Foot, New Castle Co., enlisted 28 Dec 1757. {Ref: ARDE I:14}

DERRY, WILLIAM (Delaware), b. c1735, DE (cooper, age 23 in 1758); pvt., recruited by Capt. Benjamin Noxon and enlisted on 24 Apr 1758. {Ref: ARDE I:19; ARPA (2nd Series) 2:566}

DESERT, BENJAMIN (Delaware), b. c1742, Cumberland, PA (cordwainer, age 17 in 1759); pvt., enlisted by Capt. James Armstrong for the PA Regt. on 5 May 1759. {Ref: ARDE I:25; ARPA (2nd Series) 2:585}

DEVILBISS, GEORGE, see "Conrod Whetstone," q.v.

DEVINING, CORNELIUS (Delaware), pvt., Capt. Richard McWilliams' Company of Foot, New Castle Co., enlisted 28 Dec 1757. {Ref: ARDE I:15}

DEYE, THOMAS COCKEY (Maryland), b. 27 Jan c1728, Baltimore Co., prob. son of Thomas Cockey and Penelope Deye; d. 7 May 1807, Baltimore Co., without progeny; patriot, gentleman, and member of the MD Assembly, 1757-1792 (served on the Arms and Ammunition Committee, 1758-1761, 1773-1774; Speaker, 1781-1792). {Ref: BDML I:268} See "James Davidson" and "John Henderson" and "Aquila Nelson" and "Daniel Shaw" and "Henry Wise" and "Edmund Stansbury," q.v.

DICK, GEORGE PETER (Maryland), pvt., Capt. Stephen Rensburg's or Rensburger's Company Muster Roll, Frederick Co., circa 1757-1758, exact dates not given (served 42 days); bill of credit issued or paid in his behalf to Stephen Rensburg or Rensburger for £2.2.0 on 27 Mar 1767. {Ref: MSA S960 or S752, p. 182; CSOS:112}

DICK, JAMES (Maryland), pvt., Capt. Samuel Chapman's Company Muster Roll, Anne Arundel Co., circa 1757-1758, exact dates not given; bill of credit issued or paid in his behalf to Thomas Richardson for £1.18.0 on 21 Feb 1767. {Ref: MSA S960 or S752, p. 188} Patriot in Annapolis, Anne Arundel Co., pay account submitted for quartering soldiers in 1757 or 1758, exact dates not given. {Ref: MHM 9:3, p. 261} James Dick, merchant, of Edinburgh, Scotland, son of Thomas Dick, came to MD on 1 Jun 1734 and settled in London Town on South River. In 1740 he returned to Edinburgh and came back to MD in 1741, bringing his wife Margaret and dau. Mary (b. 20 Nov 1732, Edinburgh); children born in MD were Jean (b. 14 Mar 1742, m. Anthony Stewart on 15 Mar 1764), Alexander (b. 4 Dec 1747), and Margaret (b. 23 Jul 1750, d. 12 Nov 1762). Margaret Dick, wife of James, d. 23 Oct 1766, All Hallow's Parish. {Ref: AACR:57-58} See "Nicholas Pearce," q.v.

DICKEY, JAMES (Delaware), b. c1735, Octararo, PA (smith, age 23 in 1758); pvt., enlisted 24 Apr 1758 "for the campaign in the lower counties" by Capt. John McClughan. {Ref: ARDE I:17; ARPA (2nd Series) 2:570}

DICKINSON, RACHEL, see "Pollard Edmondson," q.v.

DICKSON, ---- (Maryland), patriot (county not stated) who was paid £41.3.7½ by the MD Assembly in 1756 "for blanketts for Capt. Beall's party and for sundries" for the support of the ranging parties on the Western Frontier. {Ref: ARMD 52:674}

DICKSON, MORRIS (Maryland), b. c1734 near the Forks of Patuxent (age 23 in 1757); soldier who was reported by Lieut. Greenfield, at Annapolis, as deserted from a recruiting party at Joppa, in Baltimore County, commanded by Maj. Gen. Abercrombie. {Ref: *MD Gazette*, 3 Mar 1757}

DIEUS, WILLIAM (Delaware), pvt., Capt. Henry Vanbibber's Company of the Lower Counties on Delaware Troops at New Castle, enlisted on 15 May 1759. {Ref: ARDE I:26; ARPA (2nd Series) 2:594}

DIGGES, ANNE, see "George Steuart," q.v.

DIGGES, CHARLES (Maryland), patriot, Annapolis, Anne Arundel Co., pay account submitted for quartering soldiers in 1757 or 1758, exact dates not given. {Ref: MHM 9:3, p. 262}

DIXON, JANE, see "Edmund Stansbury," q.v.

DIXON, MORRIS (Maryland), pvt., Capt. Tobias Stansbury's Company Muster Roll, Baltimore Co., circa 1757-1758, exact dates not given; bill of credit or order issued and assigned to Luke Griffith paid to Robert Buchanan for £1.19.0 on 24 Mar 1767. {Ref: MSA S960 or S752, p. 186}

DIXSON, WILLIAM (Delaware), b. c1733, New Castle, DE (farmer, age 25 in 1758); pvt., enlisted 2 Apr 1758 "for the campaign in the lower counties" by Capt. John McClughan. {Ref: ARDE I:17; ARPA (2nd Series) 2:570}

DOBSON, ANN, see "Cord Hazzard," q.v.

DOCKERY, SARAH, see "William Hopper," q.v.

DOCKRAY, MATTHEW (Maryland), patriot and poss. soldier (rank not specified), Queen Anne's Co., militia pay account submitted in 1758, exact date not given. {Ref: MHM 9:4, p. 366} See "William Hopper," q.v.

DODD, MORRIS (Maryland), pvt., Capt. Alexander Beall's Company of MD Troops, Frederick Co., from 9 Oct 1757 to 8 Apr 1758. {Ref: MHS MS.375.1; CSOS:80} Payment to him was recorded in Col. Dagworthy's account book on 7 Mar 1763. {Ref: MHS MS.375}

DOGAN, WILLIAM (Maryland), pvt., Capt. Alexander Beall's Company of MD Troops, Frederick Co., from 9 Oct 1757 to 14 Sep 1758 when he was reported as killed; however, payment to him was recorded in Col. Dagworthy's account book on 26 Feb 1763. {Ref: MHS MS.375; CSOS:80; MHS MS.375.1}

DOMER, GEORGE (Maryland), pvt., Capt. Stephen Rensburg's or Rensburger's Company Muster Roll, Frederick Co., circa 1757-1758, exact dates not given (served 42 days); bill of credit issued or paid in his behalf to Stephen Rensburg or Rensburger for £1.14.0 on 27 Mar 1767. {Ref: MSA S960 or S752, p. 182; CSOS:112}

DONALDSON, JOHN (Maryland), pvt., Capt. Moses Chapline's Company Muster Roll No. 3, Frederick Co., circa 1757-1758, exact dates not given (served 6 days); bill of credit issued or paid in his behalf to Joseph Chaplin for £0.6.0 on 5 Mar 1767. {Ref: MSA S960 or S752, p. 198; CSOS:115}

DONELLY, ABNER, see "Abner Danily," q.v.

DONNALON, LAUGHLIN (Maryland), mariner on the brigantine *Duke of Marlborough*, commanded by David Carcaud, which vessel was commissioned by the Council of Maryland as a Flag of Truce on 15 Oct 1760 to carry French prisoners of war to Port St. Louis on the island of Hispaniola. {Ref: ARMD 31:458-460}

DORNEY (DOURNEY), JOHN (Maryland), pvt., Capt. Peter Butler's Company Muster Roll, Frederick Co., circa 1757-1758, exact dates not given (served 34 days); bill of credit or order issued in his behalf for £1.14.0 and paid to Casper Shaff on 2 Mar 1767. {Ref: MSA S960 or S752, p. 167; CSOS:97}

DORR, PETER (Maryland), pvt., Capt. John Middaugh's Company Muster Roll, Frederick Co., circa 1757-1758, exact dates not given (served 30 days); bill of credit issued or paid in his behalf to Thomas Beatty, Jr. for £0.17.0 on 3 Apr 1767. {Ref: MSA S960 or S752, p. 172; CSOS:102}

DORRETT, JOHN (Maryland), pvt., Capt. Francis Ware's Company of MD Troops, Charles Co., from 9 Oct 1757 to 16 Feb 1758 (served 131 days) when he was discharged. {Ref: MHS MS.375.1; CSOS:87} Payment to him was recorded in Col. Dagworthy's account book on 7 Mar 1763. {Ref: MHS MS.375}

DORRETT, WILLIAM GARNET (Maryland), drummer, Capt. Alexander Beall's Company of MD Troops, Frederick Co., from 9 Oct 1757 to 18 Oct 1758 when he reportedly deserted (name listed once as "Wm. Garnet Dosset"); however, payment to him was recorded in Col. Dagworthy's account book on 22 Feb 1763. {Ref: MHS MS.375; CSOS:80; MHS MS.375.1}

DORSEY, ACHSAH, see "Henry Woodward," q.v.

DORSEY, ARIANNA, see "Thomas Sollers," q.v.

DORSEY, CHARLES (Maryland), son of Edward Dorsey and Sarah Todd, m. cousin Lydia Dorsey (dau. of Nicholas Dorsey and Sarah Griffith) and removed from Baltimore Co., MD to Nelson Co., KY by 1796. {Ref: Dorsey & Nimmo's *The Dorsey Family*, pp. 64, 145} Pvt., MD Forces (company not stated), received £5 bounty money on 23 Aug 1757 for enlisting in the militia. {Ref: ARMD 55:265, 619}

DORSEY, COMFORT, see "John Hammond Dorsey," q.v.

DORSEY, DEBORAH, see "Charles Ridgely," q.v.

DORSEY, EDWARD (Maryland), b. 1718, Anne Arundel Co., son of Caleb Dorsey and Elinor Warfield; bapt. 31 Oct 1718, St. Anne's Parish, m. Henrietta Maria Chew on 18 Feb 1748, had daus. Henrietta Maria and Elinor (both d. young), and d. 27 Mar 1760, Newport, RI (while returning home to MD after a trip north for his health); lawyer, businessman, and member of the MD Assembly (1757-1760). {Ref: BDML I:274-275} Pay account submitted by his exec. (unnamed at the time, but the newspaper stated it was his wife; she d. 17 May 1762 in her 32nd year) for his quartering soldiers in 1757 or 1758, exact dates not given. {Ref: MHM 9:3, p. 261; *MD Gazette*, 9 Oct 1760, 25 Jun 1761 and 20 May 1762; AACR:83}

DORSEY, JOHN HAMMOND (Maryland), b. 1724, Baltimore Co., son of John Dorsey and Comfort Stimson or Stimpson, m. Frances Watkins on 16 Feb 1743/4 and had children John Hammond (b. 12 Feb 1744/5, d. young), Stephen (1747-1749), Mary Hammond (b. 21 Feb 1749), Rebecca (b. 22 Mar 1752), John Hammond (b. 14 Feb 1754), Frances (b. 19 Apr 1756), and Stephen (b. 7 Mar 1758); d. intestate in 1774. {Ref: BCF:181} Planter, merchant, county justice (1753), captain by 1756, and member of the MD Assembly, 1757-1763 (served on the Arms and Ammunition Committee, 1757-1761). {Ref: BDML I:277}

DORSEY, LYDIA, see "Charles Dorsey," q.v.

DORSEY, MARY, see "John Ridgely," q.v.

DORSEY, NICHOLAS, see "Charles Dorsey," q.v.

DORSEY, REBECCA, see "Charles Ridgely," q.v.

DORSEY, RICHARD (Maryland), b. 10 Jun 1714, Anne Arundel Co., son of Caleb and Elenor Dorsey, of St. Anne's Parish, m. Elizabeth Beale (widow of William Nicholson) by 1736, had children Caleb, Ann, Elizabeth, Elinor, and Mary, and d. 2 Sep 1760 at his plantation "of the gout in his stomach, head and bowels." He was a patriot, magistrate, and clerk of the Paper Currency Office for about 20 years. {Ref: Dorsey & Nimmo's *The Dorsey Family*, pp. 162-164; BDML I:274; *MD Gazette*, 11 Sep 1760; AACR:71} Pay account submitted for quartering soldiers in 1757 or 1758, exact dates not given. {Ref: MHM 9:3, p. 260}

DORSON, EDWARD (Maryland), pvt., Capt. Joseph Chapline's Company Muster Roll No. 1, Frederick Co., circa 1757-1758, exact dates not given (served 7 days); bill of credit issued or paid in his behalf to Joseph Chaplin for £0.7.0 on 5 Mar 1767. {Ref: MSA S960 or S752, p. 191; CSOS:103} Pvt., Capt. Moses Chapline's Company Muster Roll No. 2, Frederick Co., circa 1757-1758, exact dates not given (served 13 days); bill of credit issued or paid in his behalf to Joseph

Chaplin for £0.13.0 on 5 Mar 1767. {Ref: MSA S960 or S752, p. 197; CSOS:114} Pvt., Capt. Joseph Chapline's Company Muster Roll No. 4, Frederick Co., circa 1757-1758, exact dates not given (served 5 days); bill of credit issued or paid in his behalf to Joseph Chaplin for £0.5.0 on 5 Mar 1767. {Ref: MSA S960 or S752, p. 194; CSOS:105}

DORSON, HALLAM (Maryland), pvt., Capt. Joseph Chapline's Company Muster Roll No. 1, Frederick Co., circa 1757-1758, exact dates not given (served 25 days); bill of credit issued or paid in his behalf to Joseph Chaplin for £1.5.0 on 5 Mar 1767. {Ref: MSA S960 or S752, p. 191; CSOS:103} Pvt., Capt. Joseph Chapline's Company Muster Rolls No. 2 and 3, Frederick Co., circa 1757-1758, exact dates not given (served 8 days); bill of credit issued or paid in his behalf to Joseph Chaplin for £0.8.0 on 5 Mar 1767; name listed once as "Hallan Dorson." {Ref: MSA S960 or S752, p. 193; CSOS:104} Pvt., Capt. Joseph Chapline's Company Muster Roll No. 4, Frederick Co., circa 1757-1758, exact dates not given (served 7 days); bill of credit issued or paid in his behalf to Joseph Chaplin for £0.7.0 on 5 Mar 1767; name listed once as "Hallam Dason." {Ref: MSA S960 or S752, p. 194; CSOS:105}

DORSON, JAMES (Maryland), quartermaster, Capt. Joseph Chapline's Company Muster Roll No. 4, Frederick Co., circa 1757-1758, exact dates not given (served 5 days); bill of credit issued or paid in his behalf to Joseph Chaplin for £0.12.0 on 5 Mar 1767. {Ref: MSA S960 or S752, p. 194; CSOS:104}

DORSON, WILLIAM (Maryland), pvt., Capt. Joseph Chapline's Company Muster Roll No. 4, Frederick Co., circa 1757-1758, exact dates not given (served 5 days). {Ref: CSOS:105} See "William Dawson," q.v.

DOUGHADAY, JOHN, see "John Howard," q.v.

DOUGHERTY, CHARLES (Delaware), b. c1729, Donegal, Ireland (farmer, age 29 in 1758); sgt., enlisted 22 Apr 1758 "for the campaign in the lower counties" by Capt. John McClughan. {Ref: ARDE I:17; ARPA (2nd Series) 2:570}

DOUGHERTY, JOHN (Delaware), b. c1741, Donegal, Ireland (farmer, age 17 in 1758); pvt., enlisted 5 May 1758 "for the campaign in the lower counties" by Capt. John McClughan. {Ref: ARDE I:17; ARPA (2nd Series) 2:570}

DOUGHERTY, OWEN (Delaware), b. c1725, Donegal, Ireland (laborer, age 33 in 1758); pvt., enlisted 26 Apr 1758 "for the campaign in the lower counties" by Capt. John McClughan. {Ref: ARDE I:17; ARPA (2nd Series) 2:570}

DOUGHERTY, PATRICK (Delaware), b. c1734, Donegal, Ireland (laborer, age 24 in 1758); pvt., enlisted 23 Apr 1758 "for the campaign in the lower counties" by Capt. John McClughan; a Patrick Dougherty was also a pvt. in the Upper District of Pencader Hundred in 1779-1780. {Ref: ARDE I:17; ARPA (2nd Series) 2:570; RPDE:78}

DOUGHLAND, JOHN (Maryland), pvt., Capt. William McClellan's Company of MD Volunteers, Frederick Co., circa 1763-1764; on muster roll dated 15 Nov 1764 at Camp at the Forks of Muskingham. {Ref: ARMD 32:99}

DOUGLASS (DUGLAS), WILLIAM (Maryland), pvt., Capt. John White's Company Muster Roll, Frederick Co., circa 1757-1758, exact dates not given (served 6 days); bill of credit issued or paid to him for £0.6.0 in 1767, exact date not given. {Ref: MSA S960 or S752, p. 164; CSOS:96}

DOWAL, JOHN (Delaware), pvt., Capt. Richard McWilliams' Company of Foot, New Castle Co., enlisted 28 Dec 1757. {Ref: ARDE I:14}

DOWDEN, JOHN (Maryland), m. Mary (N), had children John, Rebecca, and Martha, and d. testate by 21 May 1772. {Ref: WMG 3:4, p. 151} Sgt., Capt. William Luckett's Company Muster Roll, Frederick Co., circa 1757-1758, exact dates not given (served 30 days); bill of credit issued or paid in his behalf to William Luckett, Jr. for £2.10.0 on 6 Apr 1767. {Ref: MSA S960 or S752, p. 170; CSOS:99}

DOWDEN, MICHAEL A. (Maryland), pvt., Capt. William Luckett's Company Muster Roll, Frederick Co., circa 1757-1758, exact dates not given (served 30 days); bill of credit issued or paid in his behalf to William Luckett, Jr. for £1.10.0 on 6 Apr 1767. {Ref: MSA S960 or S752, p. 170; CSOS:99}

DOWDEN, NATHANIEL (Maryland), pvt., Capt. William Luckett's Company Muster Roll, Frederick Co., circa 1757-1758, exact dates not given (served 30 days); bill of credit issued or paid in his behalf to William Luckett, Jr. for £1.10.0 on 6 Apr 1767. {Ref: MSA S960 or S752, p. 169; CSOS:99}

DOWDEN, RACHEL (Maryland), patriot or poss. widow of soldier (unnamed), Frederick Co., pay account submitted in 1758, exact date not given. {Ref: MHM 9:4, p. 367}

DOWNES (DOWNS), NATHAN (Maryland), cpl., Capt. Henry Casson's Company Muster Roll, Queen Anne's Co., circa 1757-1758, exact dates not given (served 27 days); bill of credit issued or paid in his behalf to Capt. Casson on 27 Mar 1767 for £1.16.0. {Ref: MSA S960 or S752, p. 178; CSOS:109}

DOWNES (DOWNS), SOLOMON (Maryland), cpl., Capt. Henry Casson's Company Muster Roll, Queen Anne's Co., circa 1757-1758, exact dates not given (27 days); bill of credit issued or paid in his behalf to Capt. Casson for Downes' exec. (unnamed) on 27 Mar 1767 for £1.16.0. {Ref: MSA S960 or S752, p. 178; CSOS:108} Solomon Downes m. Nancy Baning on 29 Oct 1754 in St. John's Parish, Queen Anne's Co. {Ref: MGSB 16:2, p. 74}

DOWNEY, WILLIAM (Maryland), patriot and poss. soldier (rank not specified), Frederick Co., militia pay account submitted in 1758, exact date not given. {Ref: MHM 9:4, p. 370}

DOWNHAM, RICHARD (Delaware), m. (N) prob. Powell, had children Isaac, Richard, Ruth, Mary, Sarah, Elizabeth, and Rachel, and d. testate by 18 Jun 1773. {Ref: CDSS:56} Pvt., Kent Co. Militia, Capt. John Caton's Company, 25 Apr 1757 (date of muster roll). {Ref: ARDE I:13}

DOWNING, TIMOTHY (Maryland), pvt., Capt. Joseph Chapline's Company Muster Roll No. 4, Frederick Co., circa 1757-1758, exact dates not given (served 3 days); bill of credit issued or paid in his behalf to Joseph Chaplin for £0.3.0 on 5 Mar 1767. {Ref: MSA S960 or S752, p. 194; CSOS:105}

DOWNING, WILLIAM (Maryland), pvt., Capt. Joseph Chapline's Company Muster Roll No. 4, Frederick Co., circa 1757-1758, exact dates not given (served 6 days); bill of credit issued or paid in his behalf to Joseph Chaplin for £0.6.0 on 5 Mar 1767. {Ref: MSA S960 or S752, p. 195; CSOS:105}

DOWNS, JOSEPH (Delaware), b. c1729, London, England (laborer, age 30 in 1759); pvt., enlisted by Capt. James Armstrong for the PA Regt. on 1 May 1759. {Ref: ARDE I:25; ARPA (2nd Series) 2:585}

DOWNS, THOMAS (Delaware), b. c1738, England (glassblower, age 20 in 1758); pvt., recruited by Capt. Benjamin Noxon and enlisted on 29 Apr 1758. {Ref: ARDE I:19; ARPA (2nd Series) 2:566}

DOWNS, THOMAS (Delaware), b. c1738, MD (laborer, age 20 in 1758); pvt., recruited by Capt. Benjamin Noxon and enlisted on 29 Apr 1758. {Ref: ARDE I:19; ARPA (2nd Series) 2:485, 566}

DOWTHET (DOUTHIT), JOHN (Maryland), pvt., Capt. Stephen Rensburg's or Rensburger's Company Muster Roll, Frederick Co., circa 1757-1758, exact dates not given (served 42 days); bill of credit issued or paid in his behalf to Stephen Rensburg or Rensburger for £2.2.0 on 27 Mar 1767. {Ref: MSA S960 or S752, p. 182; CSOS:112}

DOYLE, JOHN (Maryland), pvt., Capt. Joshua Beall's Company of MD Troops, Prince George's Co., from 9 Oct 1757 to 25 Oct 1757 when he was discharged; payment to him was recorded in Col. Dagworthy's account book on 24 Jul 1762. {Ref: MHS MS.375; CSOS:84; MHS MS.375.1}

DRAPIER (DRAPER), JOHN (Maryland), pvt., Capt. William Luckett's Company Muster Roll, Frederick Co., circa 1757-1758, exact dates not given (served 30 days); bill of credit issued or paid in his behalf to William Luckett, Jr. for £1.10.0 on 6 Apr 1767. {Ref: MSA S960 or S752, pp. 169-170; CSOS:99}

DRUGAN, EDWARD (Maryland), patriot and boatman, Kent Co., who was impressed in 1758 to carry the troops of Capt. Peregrine Brown's Company {Ref: ARMD 31:287} See "Thomas Honour" and "James Poole," q.v.

DRUM, JAMES HEROIT (Delaware), b. c1740, New Castle, DE (laborer, age 19 in 1759); pvt., enlisted by Capt. James Armstrong for the PA Regt. on 3 May 1759. {Ref: ARDE I:26; ARPA (2nd Series) 2:585}

DRUMMOND, ANNE, see "John Selby," q.v.

DUCKERY, THOMAS (Maryland), patriot and poss. soldier (rank not specified), Frederick Co., militia pay account submitted in 1758, exact date not given. {Ref: MHM 9:4, p. 368}

DUCKETT, JOHN (Maryland), patriot, Frederick Co., was paid on 12 Oct 1758 "for bringing some of the sick militia and their baggage from Fort Cumberland and for carrying arms from Fort Frederick" for the Western Expedition against Fort Duquesne. {Ref: ARMD 55:775}

DUFF, THOMAS (Delaware), ensign, Christiana Hundred, Upper Regt. of Militia, Southwest Division, New Castle Co., 1756; major, 1775; colonel, 1st Militia Regt., 1778; member of the General Assembly, 1781; and, justice of the peace, 1783. {Ref: ARDE I:11; ARPA (2nd Series) 2:526; HDE I:141; RPDE:80}

DUFLER, GEORGE (Maryland), pvt., Capt. Stephen Rensburg's or Rensburger's Company Muster Roll, Frederick Co., circa 1757-1758, exact dates not given (served 34 days); bill of credit or order issued to Casper Shaff and paid to David Cumming for £1.14.0 on 18 Apr 1767. {Ref: MSA S960 or S752, p. 183; CSOS:112}

DUFLER, PETER (Maryland), pvt., Capt. Stephen Rensburg's or Rensburger's Company Muster Roll, Frederick Co., circa 1757-1758, exact dates not given (served 42 days); bill of credit issued or paid in his behalf to Thomas Schley for £2.2.0 on 23 Mar 1767; name listed once as "Peter Tufler." {Ref: MSA S960 or S752, p. 182; CSOS:112}

DUGMORE, EDWARD (Maryland), pvt., Capt. Francis Ware's Company of MD Troops, Charles Co., from 9 Oct 1757 to 14 Sep 1758 (served 340 days) when he was reported as killed; however, payment to him was recorded in Col. Dagworthy's account book on 7 Mar 1763. {Ref: MHS MS.375; CSOS:87; MHS MS.375.1}

DUHASAN, ELINOR, see "Hanse Jorg Rochnor," q.v.

DUKE, BASIL (Maryland), pvt., Capt. Joshua Beall's Company of MD Troops, Prince George's Co., from 9 Oct 1757 to 7 Dec 1757 when he was discharged; payment to him was recorded in Col. Dagworthy's account book on 24 Jul 1762. {Ref: MHS MS.375; CSOS:84; MHS MS.375.1}

DULANY, DANIEL JR. (Maryland), b. 28 Jun 1722, Annapolis, Anne Arundel Co., son of Daniel Dulany and Rebecca Smith, bapt. 29 Jul 1722, St. Anne's Parish, m. Rebecca Tasker on 16 Sep 1749, had children Daniel, Benjamin Tasker, and Ann, and d. 17 Mar 1797, Baltimore City, buried in St. Paul's Cemetery; patriot, lawyer, businessman, member of the MD Assembly (1749-1774), commissary general (1754-1756, 1759-1761), mayor of Annapolis (1764-1765), member of the MD Council (1757-1776), Secretary of Maryland (1761-1776). {Ref: BDML I:286-287; AACR:89-90} Pay account submitted for quartering soldiers in 1757 or 1758, exact dates not given. {Ref: MHM 9:3, p. 262} See "Benjamin Young," q.v.

DULANY, HENRIETTA MARIA, neé Lloyd (Maryland), patriot, Annapolis, Anne Arundel Co., d. 1766, widow of both Daniel Dulany (1685-1753) and Samuel Chew (1704-1736); pay account submitted for quartering soldiers in 1757 or 1758, exact dates not given. {Ref: BDML I:218, 286; MHM 9:3, p. 261}

DULANY, JAMES (Maryland), pvt., Capt. John Wolgomatt's Company of MD Volunteers, Frederick Co., circa 1763-1764; on muster roll dated 15 Nov 1764 at Camp at the Forks of Muskingham. {Ref: ARMD 32:99}

DULANY, MARY, see "Benjamin Young," q.v.

DULANY, WALTER (Maryland), b. c1724, Annapolis, Anne Arundel Co., son of Daniel Dulany and Rebecca Smith, m. circa 1745 to Mary Grafton (1727-1801, dau. of Richard Grafton of New Castle, DE), had children Daniel, Walter Jr., Grafton, Rebecca, Mary, Margaret, and Catherine, and d. 20 Sep 1773, Annapolis; patriot, merchant, investor, businessman, member of MD Assembly (1745-1765), deputy commissary (1749-1754), councilman (1756-1764) and mayor of Annapolis (1764-1766), naval officer at Patuxent (1765-1767), commissary general (1767-1773), and member of the MD Council (1767-1773). {Ref: BDML I:287-289; *MD Gazette*, 23 Sep 1773 and 17 Sep 1801} Pay account submitted for quartering soldiers in 1757 or 1758, exact dates not given. {Ref: MHM 9:3, p. 262}

DULE, JOHN (Maryland), indentured servant and soldier who served in the French and Indian War some time between 1756 and 1763 (exact dates not known); his master Renaldo Monk, planter, requested compensation from the Baltimore County Court due to the loss of use of Dule while in the service. {Ref: MHM 94:4, p. 426, citing Baltimore Co. Court Minutes}

DUNBAR, JOHN (Delaware), b. c1733, Ireland (laborer, age 26 in 1759); pvt., enlisted by Capt. James Armstrong for the PA Regt. on 8 May 1759. {Ref: ARDE I:26; ARPA (2nd Series) 2:585}

DUNBAR, JOHN (Delaware), b. c1734, Tyrone, Ireland (weaver, age 24 in 1758); pvt., enlisted 25 Apr 1758 "for the campaign in the lower counties" by Capt. John McClughan. {Ref: ARDE I:17; ARPA (2nd Series) 2:570}

DUNCAN, JOHN (Maryland), pvt., Capt. Joshua Beall's Company of MD Troops, Prince George's Co., from 9 Oct 1757 to 14 Sep 1758 when he was reported as killed; however, payment to him was recorded in Col. Dagworthy's account book on 13 Jul 1762. {Ref: MHS MS.375; CSOS:83; MHS MS.375.1}

DUNFEE, MICHAEL (Delaware), b. c1736, Wexford, Ireland (laborer, age 22 in 1758); pvt., enlisted 2 May 1758 "for the campaign in the lower counties" by Capt. John McClughan. {Ref: ARDE I:17; ARPA (2nd Series) 2:570}

DUNFIELD, FREDERICK (Maryland), patriot, Frederick Co., was paid £3.2.6 on 30 Aug 1758 "for carrying some people who had the smallpox from Fort Frederick and fetching ammunition thither" for the Western Expedition against Fort Duquesne. {Ref: ARMD 55:774}

DUNLAP, ALLEN (Delaware), pvt., Kent Co. Militia, Capt. John Caton's Company, 25 Apr 1757 (date of muster roll). {Ref: ARDE I:14}

DUNLAP, JOHN (Delaware), pvt., Kent Co. Militia, Capt. John Caton's Company, 25 Apr 1757 (date of muster roll). {Ref: ARDE I:14}

DUNLAP, JOHN (Delaware), b. Ireland, laborer, age 28 in 1758; pvt., enlisted 6 May 1758 "for the campaign in the lower counties" by Capt. John McClughan. {Ref: ARDE I:17; ARPA (2nd Series) 2:570}

DUNLAP, PETER (Delaware), pvt., Kent Co. Militia, Capt. John Caton's Company, 25 Apr 1757 (date of muster roll). {Ref: ARDE I:14}

DUNN, THOMAS (Delaware), lieut., White Clay Hundred, Upper Regt. of Militia, East Division, New Castle Co., 1756; elected sheriff in 1760. {Ref: ARDE I:11; ARPA (2nd Series) 2:526; HDE I:141, 143}

DUNSTILL, CHARLES (Maryland), pvt., Capt. Joshua Beall's Company of MD Troops, Prince George's Co., from 9 Oct 1757 to 11 Nov 1758. {Ref: MHS MS.375.1; CSOS:84} Payment to him was recorded in Col. Dagworthy's account book on 8 Mar 1763 for work on Fort Cumberland. {Ref: MHS MS.375}

DUNWIDIE, WILLIAM (Maryland), pvt., Capt. John Wolgomatt's Company of MD Volunteers, Frederick Co., circa 1763-1764; on muster roll dated 15 Nov 1764 at Camp at the Forks of Muskingham. {Ref: ARMD 32:99}

DURBIN, WILLIAM (Maryland), cpl., Capt. Thomas Norris' Company, Frederick Co., circa 1757-1758, exact dates not given (served 30 days); bill of credit issued or paid in his behalf to Michael McGuire on 11 Apr 1767 for £2. {Ref: MSA S960 or S752, p. 176; CSOS:107}

DURBORROW, ISAAC (Delaware), pvt., Capt. French Battell's Company of Lower County Provincials, enlisted 28 May 1758. {Ref: ARDE I:16; ARPA (2nd Series) 2:555}

DURHAM, MORDECAI (Maryland), b. 1 Feb 1734/5, Baltimore Co., son of Samuel Durham and Eleanor Smithson, St. John's P. E. Parish. {Ref: Ella Rowe's *Clark, Rigdon, Wilson and Durham Families of Harford County, MD*, pp. 61, 66} Pvt., Capt. Tobias Stansbury's Company Muster Roll, Baltimore Co., circa 1757-1758, exact dates not given; bill of credit issued or paid in his behalf to John Paca for £1.18.0 on 1 Oct 1771. {Ref: MSA S960 or S752, p. 187} Mordecai Durham subsequently served as a private in the militia in 1775, was a signer of the Association of Freemen in 1776, and d. testate and unmarried by 7 Feb 1778. {Ref: Henry C. Peden, Jr.'s *Revolutionary Patriots of Harford County, 1775-1783*, p. 71}

DURN, WILLIAM (Maryland), patriot and poss. soldier (rank not specified), Frederick Co., militia pay account submitted in 1758, exact date not given. {Ref: MHM 9:4, p. 368}

DUSHANE, JEROME (Delaware), yeoman, of Red Lion Hundred, m. Hannah (N), had children Jesse, Anthony, Thomas, Hannah, Mary, Katharine, Elizabeth, Margaret, Jaminia, and Francina, and d. testate by 29 Mar 1775. {Ref: CDSS:58} Lieut. in Capt. David Stewart's Company, New Castle Co., 1747-1748, during King George's War against Canada; lieut., St. George's Hundred, Lower Regt. of Militia, Capt. John Jones' Company, 1756. {Ref: ARDE I:7, 11; ARPA (2nd Series) 2:525; HDE I:141}

DUTZ, SAMUEL (Delaware), pvt., Capt. Richard McWilliams' Company of Foot, New Castle Co., enlisted 28 Dec 1757. {Ref: ARDE I:15}

DUVAL, COMFORT, see "Philip Hammond," q.v.

DWIGGINS, JOHN JR. (Maryland), pvt., Capt. Henry Casson's Company Muster Roll, Queen Anne's Co., circa 1757-1758, exact dates not given (served 27 days); bill of credit issued or paid in his behalf to Capt. Casson on 27 Mar 1767 for £1.7.0. {Ref: MSA S960 or S752, p. 178; CSOS:109}

DWIGGINS, JOHN SR. (Maryland), pvt., Capt. Henry Casson's Company Muster Roll, Queen Anne's Co., circa 1757-1758, exact dates not given (served 27 days); bill of credit issued or paid in his behalf to Capt. Casson on 27 Mar 1767 for £1.7.0. {Ref: MSA S960 or S752, p. 178; CSOS:109}

DWIGGINS, JOSEPH (Maryland), pvt., Capt. Henry Casson's Company Muster Roll, Queen Anne's Co., circa 1757-1758, exact dates not given (served 27 days); bill of credit issued or paid in his behalf to Capt. Casson on 27 Mar 1767 for £1.7.0. {Ref: MSA S960 or S752, p. 178; CSOS:109}

DYER, ---- (Maryland), sea captain by 1757, was in command of a ship (not named) when captured by the French. {Ref: *MD Gazette*, 26 May 1757}

DYER, JAMES (Delaware), pvt., Capt. Richard McWilliams' Company of Foot, New Castle Co., enlisted 28 Dec 1757. {Ref: ARDE I:15}

EADES (EDDES), SAMUEL (Maryland), pvt., Capt. Alexander Beall's Company of MD Troops, Frederick Co., circa 9 Oct 1757 to 30 Dec 1758. {Ref: MHS MS.375.1; CSOS:80} Payment to him was recorded in Col. Dagworthy's account book on 12 Jul 1762. {Ref: MHS MS.375}

EAGERTON (EAGINTON), GABRIEL (Maryland), pvt., Capt. Francis Ware's Company of MD Troops, Charles Co., from 9 Oct 1757 to 8 Nov 1758 (served 396 days); payment to him was recorded in Col. Dagworthy's account book on 13 Jul 1762; name listed once as "Gabriel or Sabriet Eaginton." {Ref: MHS MS.375.1; CSOS:87; MHS MS.375}

EAGLESTON (EGLESTON), ABRAHAM or ABRAM (Maryland), b. 20 Dec 1734, Baltimore Co., son of Abraham Eagleston and Charity Johns, St. Paul's P. E. Parish, m. (N), had children Jonathan, Benjamin, Mary, Elizabeth, Ann, Charity, Henry, and Thomas, and d. testate by 25 Oct 1783. {Ref: Baltimore Co. Wills 3:494-495; BCF:195; SCWM III:150, 249} Pvt., Capt. Tobias Stansbury's Company Muster Roll, Baltimore Co., circa 1757-1758, exact dates not given; pvt., Capt. Richard Pearis' Company of MD Troops in Frederick Co. circa 9 Oct 1757 to 31 May 1758); pvt., Capt. John Dagworthy's Company of MD Troops in Frederick Co. from 1 Jul 1758 to 14 Sep 1758 (the date was mistakenly transcribed once as 14 Sep 1738) and he was reportedly killed. {Ref: MHS MS.375; CSOS:76, 90; MS.375.1} However, such was not the case. A payment to him was recorded in Col. Dagworthy's account book on 12 Jul 1762 and another account submitted to the MD Assembly on 25 Nov 1763 indicated he was due £4.12.3 as "granted by the Act for Granting a Sum of Money as a Present to the Forces, late in the Pay and Service of this Province, and taken into his Majesty's Service by Brigadier General Forbes." {Ref: ARMD 58:401} A bill of credit or order was issued in his behalf for £1.19.0, assigned to William Lux, and paid to Robert Adair on 1 Apr 1767. {Ref: MSA S960 or S752, p. 186}

EAGLETON (EGLETON), JOHN (Maryland), pvt., Capt. John Middaugh's Company Muster Roll, Frederick Co., circa 1757-1758, exact dates not given (served 30 days); bill of credit issued or paid in his behalf to Thomas Beatty, Jr. for £1.10.0 on 23 Feb 1767. {Ref: MSA S960 or S752, p. 171; CSOS:101}

EARL, JOHN (Maryland), lieut., Capt. William McClellan's Company of MD Volunteers, Frederick Co., circa 1763-1764; on muster roll dated 15 Nov 1764 at Camp at the Forks of Muskingham. {Ref: ARMD 32:99}

EARLE, ANNA MARIA, see "Thomas Ringgold," q.v.

EARLE, HENRIETTA MARIA, see "William Hemsley," q.v.

EARLY (EARLEY), FRANCIS (Maryland), pvt., Capt. Joshua Beall's Company of MD Troops, Prince George's Co., from 9 Oct 1757 to 30 Dec 1758 (promoted to cpl. on 13 Oct 1758). {Ref: MHS MS.375.1; CSOS:84} Payment to him was recorded in Col. Dagworthy's account book on 12 Jul 1762 for work on Fort Cumberland. {Ref: MHS MS.375}

EASON, JOHN (Maryland), pvt., Capt. Elias Delashmutt's Company Muster Roll, Frederick Co., circa 1757-1758, exact dates not given (served 30 days); bill of credit issued or paid in his behalf to Elias Delashmut, Jr. on 16 Mar 1767 for £1.10.0. {Ref: MSA S960 or S752, p. 162; CSOS:94}

EATRY, JACOB (Maryland), pvt., Capt. Joshua Beall's Company of MD Troops, Prince George's Co., from 9 Oct 1757 to 14 Feb 1758 when he was discharged. {Ref: MHS MS.375.1; CSOS:84} Payment to him was recorded in Col. Dagworthy's account book on 12 Jul 1762. {Ref: MHS MS.375}

EDELIN (EDELEN), CHRISTOPHER (Maryland), pvt., Capt. Peter Butler's Company Muster Roll, Frederick Co., circa 1757-1758, exact dates not given (served 34 days); militia pay account submitted in 1758, exact date not given. {Ref: MHM 9:4, p. 366; CSOS:97} Bill of credit or order issued in his behalf for £1.14.0 and paid to Casper Shaff on 2 Mar 1767. {Ref: MSA S960 or S752, p. 166}

EDEN, ROBERT, see "Horatio Sharpe," q.v.

EDGIN (EDGEN), BENJAMIN (Delaware), b. c1734, MD (age 24 in 1759); pvt., enlisted in Capt. John Wright's Company and mustered on 11 May 1759. {Ref: ARDE I:25; ARPA (2nd Series) 2:508 592}

EDINGTON, THOMAS (Maryland), pvt., Capt. William McClellan's Company of MD Volunteers, Frederick Co., circa 1763-1764; on muster roll dated 15 Nov 1764 at Camp at the Forks of Muskingham. {Ref: ARMD 32:99}

EDLEMAN, ADAM (Maryland), pvt., Capt. Jonathan Hagar's Company Muster Roll, Frederick Co., circa 1757-1758, exact dates not given (served 6 days); bill of credit issued or paid to him for £0.6.0 in 1767, exact date not given. {Ref: MSA S960 or S752, p. 173; CSOS:106}

EDMONDSON, POLLARD (Maryland), b. c1718, Talbot Co., son of John Edmondson and Margaret Pollard. m. 1st to Mary Dickinson on 5 Mar 1738 and 2nd to Rachel McManus (widow of Philip McManus and dau. of Christopher Birckhead) circa 1765, had children James, Pollard, Horatio, John, Lucretia, Ann, and Mary, and d. by 28 Oct 1794, Talbot Co.; colonel of a troop of horse in 1748 and member of the MD Assembly, 1751-1776 (served on the Arms and Ammunition Committee). {Ref: BDML I:302}

EDMONDSON, ROBERT (Maryland), pvt., Capt. Joseph Chapline's Company Muster Roll No. 1, Frederick Co., circa 1757-1758, exact dates not given (served 25 days); bill of credit issued or paid to him for £1.6.0 in 1767, exact date not given. {Ref: MSA S960 or S752, p. 191; CSOS:103}

EDMONSON, JOHN (Maryland), farmer; pvt., Capt. Peregrine Brown's 7th Co. of Foot Militia, Kent Co., on 19 Feb 1758, by which time he had enlisted, but reportedly refused to appear and serve in arms against the enemy; he later stated that he "is constantly affected with the rheumatism and was quite unable from his state of health to undertake the service and is a man in years." {Ref: ARMD 31:283, 288}

EDMONSTON, JOHN (Maryland), captain by 1757, Frederick Co. {Ref: FCLR:79}

EDWARDS, IGNATIUS (Maryland), b. c1732, MD (age 24 in 1756); pvt., Capt. G. Mercer's Company of VA Militia, enlisted on 2 Aug 1756 in Stafford, VA. {Ref: MSR I:38}

EDWARDS, JOSIAH (Delaware), b. c1737, Wales (tailor, age 21 in 1758); pvt., recruited by Capt. Benjamin Noxon and enlisted on 22 Apr 1758. {Ref: ARDE I:19; ARPA (2nd Series) 2:566}

EDWARDS, WILLIAM (Maryland), pvt., Capt. John Dagworthy's Company of MD Troops, Frederick Co., from 9 Oct 1757 to 12 Jun 1758 (served 246 days) when he reportedly died; however, payment to him was recorded in Col. Dagworthy's account book on 8 Mar 1763. {Ref: MHS MS.375.1; CSOS:76; MHS MS.375}

EGLE, WILLIAM (Maryland), pvt., Capt. Tobias Stansbury's Company Muster Roll, Baltimore Co., circa 1757-1758, exact dates not given; bill of credit issued or paid in his behalf to Andrew Stigar (Stigars) for £2.12.0 on 27 Feb 1767. {Ref: MSA S960 or S752, p. 186}

ELIOT, MARGARET, see "Henry Waggaman," q.v.

ELLIOTT (ELLIOT), JOHN (Delaware), ensign, Brandywine Hundred, Upper Regt. of Militia, Southwest Division, New Castle Co., 1756. {Ref: ARDE I:11; ARPA (2nd Series) 2:526; HDE I:141}

ELLIS, SAMUEL (Maryland), sgt., Capt. William Luckett's Company Muster Roll, Frederick Co., circa 1757-1758, exact dates not given (served 30 days); bill of credit issued or paid in his behalf to William Luckett, Jr. for £2.10.0 on 6 Apr 1767. {Ref: MSA S960 or S752, p. 170; CSOS:99}

ELLIS, WILLIAM (Maryland), pvt., Capt. William Luckett's Company Muster Roll, Frederick Co., circa 1757-1758, exact dates not given (served 30 days); bill of credit issued or paid in his behalf to William Luckett, Jr. for £1.10.0 on 6 Apr 1767. {Ref: MSA S960 or S752, p. 169; CSOS:99}

ELLIS, ZACHARIAH (Maryland), pvt., Capt. William Luckett's Company Muster Roll, Frederick Co., circa 1757-1758, exact dates not given (served 30 days); bill of credit issued or paid in his behalf to William Luckett, Jr. for £1.13.0 on 6 Apr 1767. {Ref: MSA S960 or S752, p. 170; CSOS:99}

ELMS, CHRISTOPHER (Delaware), b. c1743, Conococheague, PA (laborer, age 15 in 1758); drummer, enlisted 6 May 1758 "for the campaign in the lower counties" by Capt. John McClughan. {Ref: ARDE I:17; ARPA (2nd Series) 2:570}

ELSON, RICHARD (Maryland), pvt., Capt. Joshua Beall's Company Muster Roll, Prince George's Co., circa 1757-1758, exact dates not given; bill of credit issued or paid to him for £2.1.0 on 8 Apr 1767. {Ref: MSA S960 or S752, p. 184}

ELTINGE (ELTING), RUDOLPH or RUDOLPHUS (Maryland), pvt., Capt. William Luckett's Company Muster Roll, Frederick Co., circa 1757-1758, exact dates not given (served 30 days); militia pay account submitted in 1758, exact date not given. {Ref: MHM 9:4, p. 366; CSOS:100} Bill of credit issued or paid in his behalf to William Luckett for £0.15.0 on 1 Dec 1769. {Ref: MSA S960 or S752, p. 170} He was paid £17.15.0 at Fort Frederick on 12 Aug 1758 for carrying artillery stores to Fort Cumberland for the Western Expedition against Fort Duquesne. {Ref: ARMD 55:774}

EMERSON, CATHERINE, see "Tobias Stansbury," q.v.

EMMERY, WILLIAM (Delaware), b. c1734, Talbot Co., MD (laborer, age 25 in 1759); pvt., recruited by Capt. John Martin and enlisted on 26 May 1759 (list of recruits dated 15 Jun 1759). {Ref: ARPA (2nd Series) 2:504}

EMMETT ---- (Maryland), captain, Frederick Co., who performed "sundry services at the fort" in 1763 and payment in the amount of £3 was still owed to him on 25 Nov 1763 (when reported by the Accounts Committee to the MD Assembly). {Ref: ARMD 58:399}

EMMETT, ABRAHAM (Maryland), patriot and poss. soldier (rank not specified), Cecil Co., militia pay account submitted in 1758, exact date not given. {Ref: MHM 9:4, p. 368}

EMORY, ANN, see "Emory Sudler," q.v.

EMPSON, WILLIAM (Delaware), captain, Brandywine Hundred, Upper Regt. of Militia, Southwest Division, New Castle Co., 1756. {Ref: ARDE I:11; ARPA (2nd Series) 2:526; HDE I:141}

ENDLESS, JOHN (Delaware), b. c 1724, Gregory Strohe, England (age 34 in 1758); pvt., enlisted 24 Apr 1758 "for the campaign in the lower counties" by Capt. John McClughan. {Ref: ARDE I:17; ARPA (2nd Series) 2:570}

ENGLAS (ENGLAR), PETER (Maryland), pvt., Capt. Peter Butler's Company Muster Roll, Frederick Co., circa 1757-1758, exact dates not given (served 34 days); bill of credit or order issued in his behalf for £1.14.0 and paid to Casper Shaff on 2 Mar 1767. {Ref: MSA S960 or S752, pp. 166-167; CSOS:97}

ENNALLS, ANNE, see "Henry Hooper, Jr.," q.v.

ENNALLS, BARTHOLOMEW (Maryland), b. c 1700, Dorchester Co., son of Joseph Ennalls and Mary Brooke, m. 1st to Mary Smith by 1725 and 2nd to Elizabeth Taylor (widow of William Taylor and dau. of Henry Trippe) by 1735, had children Joseph, Henry, William, Bartholomew, Mary, Sarah, Elizabeth, Ann, and Leah, and d. 1783; gentleman, planter, mariner, captain by 1730, major by 1748, and styled colonel in 1776; county justice (1734-1743), member of MD Assembly (1738-1748), sheriff (1749-1752), deputy commissary (1753-1755). {Ref: BDML I:306-307}

ENNALLS, MARY, see "Henry Hooper, Jr.," q.v.

ENNIS, ROBERT (Delaware), b. c1736, Scotland (weaver, age 22 in 1758); pvt., recruited by Capt. Benjamin Noxon and enlisted on 3 May 1758. {Ref: ARDE I:19; ARPA (2nd Series) 2:566}

ENNISS, WALTER (Maryland), pvt., Capt. Alexander Beall's Company of MD Troops, Frederick Co., from 9 Oct 1757 to 8 Nov 1758. {Ref: MHS MS.375.1; CSOS:80} Payment to him was recorded in Col. Dagworthy's account book on 7 Mar 1763. {Ref: MHS MS.375}

ENOCHS (ENOCKS, ENOCH), ABRAHAM (Maryland), pvt., Capt. Joseph Chapline's Company Muster Roll No. 1, Frederick Co., circa 1757-1758, exact dates not given (served 52 days); bill of credit issued or paid in his behalf to Joseph Chaplin for £2.12.0 on 24 Apr 1767. {Ref: MSA S960 or S752, p. 192; CSOS:103} Pvt., Capt. Joseph Chapline's Company Muster Rolls No. 2 and 3, Frederick Co., circa 1757-1758, exact dates not given (served 8 days); bill of credit issued or paid in his behalf to Joseph Chaplin for £0.8.0 on 24 Apr 1767. {Ref: MSA S960 or S752, p. 193; CSOS:104} Pvt., Capt. Jonathan Hagar's Company Muster Roll, Frederick Co., circa 1757-1758, exact dates not given (served 6 days); bill of credit issued or paid in his behalf to Joseph Chaplin for £0.6.0 on 24 Apr 1767. {Ref: MSA S960 or S752, p. 173; CSOS:106} Pvt., Capt. John Wolgomatt's Company of MD Volunteers, Frederick Co., circa 1763-1764; reported on muster roll dated 15 Nov 1764 at Camp at the Forks of Muskingham as "left sick at Fort Cumberland." {Ref: ARMD 32:99}

ENOCHS (ENOCKS, ENOCH), ENOCH (Maryland), pvt., Capt. Joseph Chapline's Company Muster Rolls No. 2 and 3, Frederick Co., circa 1757-1758, exact dates not given (served 52 days and 8 days); bill of credit issued or paid in his behalf to Joseph Chaplin for £0.8.0 on 24 Apr 1767. {Ref: MSA S960 or S752, p. 193; CSOS:103-104}

ENOCHS (ENOCKS, ENOCH), JOHN (Maryland), pvt., Capt. Joseph Chapline's Company Muster Roll No. 1, Frederick Co., circa 1757-1758, exact dates not given (served 51 days); bill of credit issued or paid in his behalf to Joseph Chaplin for £2.11.0 on 24 Apr 1767. {Ref: MSA S960 or S752, p. 192; CSOS:103} Pvt., Capt. Joseph Chapline's Company Muster Rolls No. 2 and 3, Frederick Co., circa 1757-1758, exact dates not given (served 8 days); bill of credit issued or paid in his behalf to Joseph Chaplin for £0.8.0 on 24 Apr 1767. {Ref: MSA S960 or S752, p. 193; CSOS:104} Pvt., Capt. Jonathan Hagar's Company Muster Roll, Frederick Co., circa 1757-1758, exact dates not given; bill of credit issued or paid in his behalf to Joseph Chaplin for £0.6.0 on 24 Apr 1767. {Ref: MSA S960 or S752, p. 173}

ENOS, JOSEPH (Delaware), pvt., Capt. Richard McWilliams' Company of Foot, New Castle Co., enlisted 28 Dec 1757. {Ref: ARDE I:14}

ENOS, RICHARD (Delaware), pvt., Capt. Richard McWilliams' Company of Foot, New Castle Co., enlisted 28 Dec 1757. {Ref: ARDE I:14}

ENOS, STEPHEN (Delaware), pvt., Capt. Richard McWilliams' Company of Foot, New Castle Co., enlisted 28 Dec 1757. {Ref: ARDE I:14}

ENSOR, GEORGE, see "Thomas Mash," q.v.

ENSOR, JOSEPH, see "William Jones," q.v.

ERTTEWINE (ERLLEWINE), ADAM (Maryland), cpl., Capt. John White's Company Muster Roll, Frederick Co., circa 1757-1758, exact dates not given (served 6 days); bill of credit issued or paid to him for £0.8.0 in 1767, exact date not given. {Ref: MSA S960 or S752, p. 164; CSOS:95}

ESLER, GEORGE (Maryland), pvt., Capt. Elias Delashmutt's Company Muster Roll, Frederick Co., circa 1757-1758, exact dates not given; bill of credit issued or paid to him in March 1767 for £1.10.0; name mistakenly listed once as "George Easter." {Ref: MSA S960 or S752, p. 162; CSOS:94}

EVANS, DANIEL (Delaware), pvt., Capt. French Battell's Company of Lower County Provincials, enlisted 28 May 1758. {Ref: ARDE I:16; ARPA (2nd Series) 2:555}

EVANS (EVENS, EVINS), EVAN or EVEN (Maryland), pvt., Capt. Francis Ware's Company of MD Troops, Charles Co., circa 9 Oct 1757 to 30 Dec 1758. {Ref: MHS MS.375.1; CSOS:87} Payment to him was recorded in Col. Dagworthy's account book on 23 Feb 1763. {Ref: MHS MS.375}

EVANS, ISAAC (Maryland), pvt., Capt. Tobias Stansbury's Company Muster Roll, Baltimore Co., circa 1757-1758, exact dates not given; bill of credit issued or paid to him for £1.18.0 in 1767, exact date not given. {Ref: MSA S960 or S752, p. 186}

EVANS (EVENS), JAMES (Maryland), pvt., Capt. Joseph Chapline's Company Muster Roll No. 4, Frederick Co., circa 1757-1758, exact dates not given (served 7 days); bill of credit issued or paid in his behalf to Joseph Chaplin for £0.7.0 on 5 Mar 1767. {Ref: MSA S960 or S752, p. 194; CSOS:105}

EVANS, JEREMIAH (Maryland), cpl., Capt. Joshua Beall's Company Muster Roll, Prince George's Co., circa 1757-1758, exact dates not given; bill of credit issued or paid to him for £2.17.4½ in 1767, exact date not given. {Ref: MSA S960 or S752, p. 184}

EVANS, JOHN (Delaware), New Castle Co., patriot and court justice in 1761. {Ref: GRSD 1:15}

EVANS, JOHN (Delaware), b. c1740, MD (age 19 in 1759); pvt., enlisted in Capt. John Wright's Company and mustered on 11 May 1759. {Ref: ARDE I:25; ARPA (2nd Series) 2:508, 592}

EVANS, JOHN (Maryland), b. c1705, Somerset Co., MD, or poss. VA, son of John Evans, m. Sarah Campbell circa 1727, had children Elisha, John, Ebenezer, Edward, David, Elizabeth, Sophia, and poss. Isaac, and d. testate by 19 May 1768, Worcester Co.; captain by 1753, major by 1756, member of the MD Assembly (1751-1754), and county justice (1754-1768). {Ref: BDML I:313-314}

EVANS, JOHN (Maryland), b. c1735 (aged about 37 in 1772 deposition); cpl., Capt. Joseph Hanson Harrison's Company Muster Roll, Charles Co., circa 1757-1758, exact dates not given; bill of credit issued or paid in his behalf to Capt. Joseph Hanson Harrison for £4.1.9 on 11 Jun 1768. {Ref: MGSB 33:4, p. 707; MSA S960 or S752, p. 189}

EVANS (EVENS, EVINS), THOMAS (Maryland), cpl., Capt. Francis Ware's Company of MD Troops, Charles Co., from 9 Oct 1757 to 8 Nov 1758 (promoted 18 Feb 1758, reduced again 2 Sep 1758). {Ref: MHS MS.375.1; CSOS:87} Payment to him was recorded in Col. Dagworthy's account book on 26 Feb 1763. {Ref: MHS MS.375}

EVANS (EVENS, EVINS), WILLIAM (Maryland), pvt., Capt. Richard Pearis' Company of MD Troops, Frederick Co., circa 9 Oct 1757 and 31 May 1758; pvt., Capt. Joshua Beall's Company of MD Troops, Prince George's Co., from 1 Jun 1758 to 4 Jul 1758 when he reportedly deserted; however, payment to him was recorded in Col. Dagworthy's account book on 14 Jul 1762. {Ref: MHS MS.375; CSOS:84, 90; MHS MS.375.1}

EVANS, WILLIAM (Maryland), pvt., Capt. Henry Casson's Company Muster Roll, Queen Anne's Co., circa 1757-1758, exact dates not given (served 27 days); bill of credit issued or paid in his behalf to Capt. Casson on 27 Feb 1767 for £1.7.0. {Ref: MSA S960 or S752, p. 177; CSOS:109} William Evans m, Mary Knotts on 11 Oct 1754 in St. John's Parish, Queen Anne's Co. {Ref: MGSB 16:2, p. 74}

EVANS, ZACHARIAH (Maryland), pvt., Capt. Joshua Beall's Company Muster Roll, Prince George's Co., circa 1757-1758, exact dates not given; bill of credit issued and ordered his assignment to Christopher Lowndes to Robert Couden for £1.17.6 on 20 May 1767. {Ref: MSA S960 or S752, p. 184}

EVARTT, ADAM, see "Adam Avart," q.v.

EVERETT, JOHN (Maryland), pvt., Capt. Peregrine Brown's Company Muster Roll, Kent Co., circa 1757-1758, exact dates not given (served 15 days); bill of credit issued or paid in his behalf to Robert Buchanan on 20 Feb 1767 for £0.15.0. {Ref: MSA S960 or S752, p. 180; CSOS:110}

EVERLY, ADAM (Maryland), pvt., Capt. Peter Bainbridge's Company Muster Roll, Frederick Co., circa 1757-1758, exact dates not given (served 28 days);

bill of credit issued or paid in his behalf to Jacob Young on 4 Mar 1767 for £1.8.0. {Ref: MSA S960 or S752, p. 181; CSOS:111}

EVERLY, CASPER (Maryland), patriot, Frederick Co., was paid on 7 Aug 1758 "for working on the new road to Fort Frederick" for the Western Expedition against Fort Duquesne. {Ref: ARMD 55:774}

EVERLY, LEONARD (Maryland), pvt., Capt. Peter Bainbridge's Company Muster Roll, Frederick Co., circa 1757-1758, exact dates not given (served 28 days); bill of credit issued or paid in his behalf to Jacob Young on 4 Mar 1767 for £1.8.0. {Ref: MSA S960 or S752, p. 181; CSOS:111}

EVERLY, MICHAEL (Maryland), pvt., Capt. Peter Bainbridge's Company Muster Roll, Frederick Co., circa 1757-1758, exact dates not given (served 30 days); bill of credit issued or paid in his behalf to Casper Shaff on 4 Mar 1767 for £1.8.0. {Ref: MSA S960 or S752, p. 180; CSOS:111}

EVERSOLE (EVERSOAL), CHRISTIAN (Maryland), pvt., Capt. Joseph Chapline's Company Muster Roll No. 4, Frederick Co., circa 1757-1758, exact dates not given (served 6 days); militia pay account submitted in 1758, exact date not given; name mistakenly transcribed once as "Christian Everyone." {Ref: MHM 9:4, p. 367; CSOS:105} Bill of credit issued or paid in his behalf to Joseph Chaplin for £0.6.0 on 5 Mar 1767. {Ref: MSA S960 or S752, p. 194}

EVES, JAMES (Delaware), pvt., Capt. Richard McWilliams' Company of Foot, New Castle Co., enlisted 28 Dec 1757. {Ref: ARDE I:14}

EVES, JOHN (Delaware), pvt., Capt. Richard McWilliams' Company of Foot, New Castle Co., enlisted 28 Dec 1757. {Ref: ARDE I:15}

EVETTS, MATTHEW (Maryland), cpl., Capt. Stephen Rensburg's or Rensburger's Company Muster Roll, Frederick Co., circa 1757-1758, exact dates not given (served 42 days); bill of credit issued or paid in his behalf to Stephen Rensburg or Rensburger for £2.16.0 on 27 Mar 1767. {Ref: MSA S960 or S752, p. 182; CSOS:112}

EVITT, JOHN (Maryland), patriot, Annapolis, Anne Arundel Co., pay account submitted for quartering soldiers in 1757 or 1758, exact dates not given. {Ref: MHM 9:3, p. 261}

EVITT, JOSEPH (Maryland), patriot, Annapolis, Anne Arundel Co., pay account submitted for quartering soldiers in 1757 or 1758, exact dates not given. {Ref: MHM 9:3, p. 261}

EYRE, THOMAS (Maryland), lieut., 44th Regt. of Foot, was in Annapolis in January 1759 and reported the names of two deserters in the local newspaper. {Ref: *MD Gazette*, 12 Jan 1759}

FACT, GEORGE ADAM (Maryland), pvt., Capt. Jonathan Hagar's Company Muster Roll, Frederick Co., circa 1757-1758, exact dates not given; bill of credit issued or paid to him for £0.6.0 in 1767, exact date not given. {Ref: MSA S960 or S752, p. 174}

FAHEE, THOMAS (Maryland), pvt., Capt. Francis Ware's Company of MD Troops, Charles Co., circa 9 Oct 1757 to 30 Dec 1758. {Ref: MHS MS.375.1; CSOS:87} Payment to him was recorded in Col. Dagworthy's account book on 7 Mar 1763. {Ref: MHS MS.375}

FALSEY, ABRAHAM (Maryland), alias Abraham Tansey or Fransey *[sic]*, pvt., Capt. Elias Delashmutt's Company Muster Roll, Frederick Co., circa 1757-1758, exact dates not given (served 52 days); bill of credit issued or paid in his behalf to Elias Delashmut, Jr. on 16 Mar 1767 for £4.2.0. {Ref: MSA S960 or S752, p. 162; CSOS:98}

FALSEY, EDWARD (Maryland), alias Edward Tansey or Fransey *[sic]*, pvt., Capt. Elias Delashmutt's Company Muster Roll, Frederick Co., circa 1757-1758, exact dates not given (served 52 days); bill of credit issued or paid in his behalf to Casper Shaff on 2 Mar 1767 for £2.12.0. {Ref: MSA S960 or S752, p. 162; SS:98}

FAMING, FRANCIS (Maryland), pvt., Capt. Tobias Stansbury's Company Muster Roll, Baltimore Co., circa 1757-1758, exact dates not given; bill of credit issued or paid to him for £1.19.0 in 1767, exact date not given. {Ref: MSA S960 or S752, p. 186}

FANCHIL (FRANCHIL), ANDREW (Maryland), alias Andrew Tannihil *[sic]*, pvt., Capt. Elias Delashmutt's Company Muster Roll, Frederick Co., 13 Aug 1757, exact dates not given (served 52 days); bill of credit issued or paid in his behalf to Elias Delashmut, Jr. on 16 Mar 1767 for £2.12.0. {Ref: MSA S960 or S752, p. 163; CSOS:98}

FARMER, HANNAH, see "Samuel Wilson," q.v.

FARRELL, JAMES (Delaware), b. c1727, MD (laborer, age 31 in 1758); pvt., recruited by Capt. Benjamin Noxon and enlisted on 15 Apr 1758; pvt., Capt. John McClughan's Company, 17 May 1758. {Ref: ARDE I:18, 19; ARPA (2nd Series) 2:485, 489, 566, 570}

FARRELL (FARREL), THOMAS (Maryland), pvt., Capt. Francis Ware's Company of MD Troops, Charles Co., circa 9 Oct 1757 to 30 Dec 1758. {Ref: MHS MS.375.1; CSOS:88} Payment to him was recorded in Col. Dagworthy's account book on 7 Mar 1763. {Ref: MHS MS.375}

FAULKNER, DANIEL (Maryland), pvt., Capt. Henry Casson's Company Muster Roll, Queen Anne's Co., circa 1757-1758, exact dates not given (served 27 days); bill of credit issued or paid in his behalf to Capt. Casson on 27 Feb 1767 for £1.7.0. {Ref: MSA S960 or S752, p. 177; CSOS:109}

FAULKNER (FOLKNER), JOHN (Maryland), pvt., Capt. Joshua Beall's Company of MD Troops, Prince George's Co., from 9 Oct 1757 to 8 Nov 1758. {Ref: MHS MS.375.1; CSOS:84} Payment to him was recorded in Col. Dagworthy's account book on 26 Feb 1763. {Ref: MHS MS.375}

FEE, THOMAS (Maryland), pvt., Capt. Peter Bainbridge's Company Muster Roll, Frederick Co., circa 1757-1758, exact dates not given (served 28 days); bill of credit issued or paid in his behalf to Casper Shaff on 4 Mar 1767 for £1.8.0; name mistakenly transcribed once as "Thomas Lee." {Ref: MSA S960 or S752, p. 180; CSOS:111}

FELL, JOHN (Maryland), sgt., Capt. John Dagworthy's Company of MD Troops, Frederick Co., from 9 Oct 1757 to 22 Jan 1759 (served 470 days) when he reportedly deserted; however, payment to him was recorded in Col. Dagworthy's account book on 22 Feb 1763. {Ref: MHS.375.1; CSOS:76; MHS MS.375}

FELTY, THOMAS, or FELTY THOMAS (Maryland), pvt., Capt. Elias Delashmutt's Company Muster Roll, Frederick Co., circa 1757-1758, exact dates not given; bill of credit issued or paid in his behalf to Elias Delashmut, Jr. on 16 Mar 1767 for £1.10.0. {Ref: MSA S960 or S752, p. 163}

FERGUSON (FURGUSON), JOHN (Maryland), cpl. or sgt., Capt. Peter Butler's Company Muster Roll, Frederick Co., circa 1757-1758, exact dates not given (served 34 days); bill of credit or order issued in his behalf for £2.5.3 and paid to Casper Shaff on 2 Mar 1767. {Ref: MSA S960 or S752, p. 166; CSOS:96}

FERGUSON, ROBERT (Maryland), captain and commander of the ship *Rainbow* of the Province of Maryland, was commissioned by the Council as a Flag of Truce on 13 Jun 1759 to carry French prisoners of war to the island of Hispaniola. {Ref: ARMD 31:358-360}

FERRELL, JOHN (Maryland), drummer, Capt. Joseph Hanson Harrison's Company Muster Roll, Charles Co., circa 1757-1758, exact dates not given; bill of credit issued or paid in his behalf to Capt. Joseph Hanson Harrison for £4.1.9 on 11 Jun 1768. {Ref: MSA S960 or S752, p. 189}

FERRELL, JOHN (Maryland), pvt., Capt. Elias Delashmutt's Company Muster Roll, Frederick Co., circa 1757-1758, exact dates not given (served 30 days); bill of credit issued or paid in his behalf to Casper Shaff on 18 Apr 1767 for £4.2.0. {Ref: MSA S960 or S752, p. 163; CSOS:94}

FIELD, AGNES, see "Peter Marsh," q.v.

FIELD, MATHEW (Maryland), pvt., Capt. Richard Pearis' Company of MD Troops, Frederick Co., circa 9 Oct 1757 to 31 May 1758; pvt., Capt. John Dagworthy's Company of MD Troops, Frederick Co., from 1 Jun 1758 to 28 Dec 1758 (served 210 days) and reportedly deserted; however, payment to him was recorded in Col. Dagworthy's account book on 11 Jul 1762 for work on Fort Cumberland. {Ref: MHS MS.375.1; CSOS:76, 90; MHS MS.375}

FIELD, NEHEMIAH, see "Peter Marsh," q.v.

FIELDING, JOHN (Maryland), pvt., Capt. Joshua Beall's Company of MD Troops, Prince George's Co., circa 9 Oct 1757 to 30 Dec 1758 {Ref: MHS MS.375.1; CSOS:84} Payment to him was recorded in Col. Dagworthy's account book on 7 Mar 1763 for work on Fort Cumberland. {Ref: MHS MS.375}

FIELDS, HENRY (Maryland), sgt., Capt. Alexander Beall's Company of MD Troops, Frederick Co., circa 9 Oct 1757 to 30 Dec 1758. {Ref: MHS MS.375.1; CSOS:80} He was paid £1 on 7 Nov 1758 "for apprehending and bringing to Fort Frederick five deserters from the Carolina troops" during the Western Expedition against Fort Duquesne. {Ref: ARMD 55:776} Another payment to him was recorded in Col. Dagworthy's account book on 26 Feb 1763. {Ref: MHS MS.375}

FIFE, WILLIAM (Maryland), pvt., Capt. John Wolgomatt's Company of MD Volunteers, Frederick Co., circa 1763-1764; on muster roll dated 15 Nov 1764 at Camp at the Forks of Muskingham. {Ref: ARMD 32:99}

FINCH, JOSEPH (Maryland), indentured servant and soldier who served in the French and Indian War some time between 1756 and 1763 (exact dates not known); his master John Bosley, planter, requested compensation from the

Baltimore County Court due to the loss of use of Finch while in the service. {Ref: MHM 94:4, p. 426, citing Baltimore Co. Court Minutes}

FINDLY (FINDLEY), PATRICK (Maryland), pvt., Capt. John Dagworthy's Company of MD Troops, Frederick Co., from 9 Oct 1757 to 16 Apr 1759 (served 554 days) when he reportedly deserted; however, payment to him was recorded in Col. Dagworthy's account book on 11 Jul 1762. {Ref: MHS MS.375.1; CSOS:76; MHS MS.375}

FINNEY, ARCHIBALD (Delaware), ensign, New Castle Co., 24 Apr 1758; promoted to 2nd lieut. on 16 Jun 1758 and served to at least 22 May 1759; name mistakenly transcribed once as "Arch. Finig." {Ref: ARDE I:16, 20; ARPA (2nd Series) 2:579}

FINNEY, DAVID (Delaware), attorney; pvt., Capt. Richard McWilliams' Company of Foot, New Castle Co., enlisted 28 Dec 1757; court justice in 1761; subscribed to the Oath of Fidelity and Allegiance in 1778. {Ref: ARDE 1:15; GRSD 1:15; RDPE:91}

FINNEY, JOHN (Delaware), lieut. colonel, Upper Regt. of Militia, New Castle Co., 1756. {Ref: ARDE I:11; ARPA (2nd Series) 2:526; HDE I:141} Patriot who served as a Justice of the Peace, Justice of the Court of Oyer and Terminer, and Justice of the Court of Common Pleas in 1756. {Ref: GRSD 1:13}

FISHER, ESTHER, see "Benjamin Wynkoop," q.v.

FISHER, PETER (Maryland), pvt., Capt. Jonathan Hagar's Company Muster Roll, Frederick Co., circa 1757-1758, exact dates not given (served 6 days); bill of credit issued or paid to him for £0.6.0 in 1767, exact date not given. {Ref: MSA S960 or S752, p. 174; CSOS:107}

FITZGERALD, JOHN (Delaware), b. c1743, Queen Anne's Co., MD (smith, age 15 in 1758); drummer, enlisted 2 May 1758 "for the campaign in the lower counties" by Capt. John McClughan (muster roll dated 17 May 1758). {Ref: ARDE I:17; ARPA (2nd Series) 2:489, 570}

FITZGERALD, JOHN (Maryland), pvt., Capt. Alexander Beall's Company of MD Troops, Frederick Co., from 9 Oct 1757 to 8 Jul 1758. {Ref: MHS MS.375.1; CSOS:80} Payment to him was recorded in Col. Dagworthy's account book on 7 Mar 1763 for work on Fort Cumberland. {Ref: MHS MS.375}

FITZGERALD, MORRIS (Maryland), pvt., Capt. Alexander Beall's Company of MD Troops, Frederick Co., circa 9 Oct 1757 to 30 Dec 1758. {Ref: MHS MS.375.1; CSOS:80} Payment to him was recorded in Col. Dagworthy's account book on 23 Feb 1763. {Ref: MHS MS.375}

FITZHUGH, WILLIAM (Maryland), b. c1722, VA, son of George Fitzhugh and Mary Mason; resided in Calvert Co. from 1752 to 1793, m. 1st to (N) (widow of George Turberville and dau. of Richard Lee, of London, England) and m. 2nd to Ann Rousby (widow of John Rousby and dau. of Peregrine Frisby) in January 1752, had children George, John, and Peregrine, and d. 10 Feb 1798, Washington Co., MD; gentleman, planter, miller, distiller, horse racer, and close friend of George Washington; colonel by 1752, fought in the French and Indian War, participated in the West Indian expedition, and in the Revolutionary War; county justice (1752-1769); member of the MD Assembly (1754-1783, served on the Arms and Ammunition Committee, 1754-1761), member of the MD Council (1769-1774), Treasurer of the Western Shore (1773-1774), commissary general (1773), and recruiting officer (1780). {Ref: BDML I:321-322}

FITZIMMONS, JOHN (Delaware), b. c1730, Ireland (laborer, age 28 in 1758, height 5 ft. 4 in.); pvt., enlisted by Capt. Paul Jackson in New Castle Co. for the PA Troops on 11 May 1758. {Ref: ARDE I:27}

FITZJEFFERY, JAMES (Maryland), b. c1731, Boston, MA (seaman, age 26 in 1757); soldier who reportedly deserted from John Hay on the march to Carlisle Camp and "probably gone to Point Look Out as his wife and friends live there." {Ref: *MD Gazette*, 11 Aug 1757}

FITZPATRICK, THOMAS (Maryland), pvt., Capt. Richard Pearis' Company of MD Troops, Frederick Co., circa 9 Oct 1757 to 31 May 1758; pvt., Capt. Alexander Beall's Company of MD Troops, Frederick Co., from 9 Oct 1757 to 30 Dec 1758. {Ref: MHS MS.375.1; CSOS:80, 90} Payment to him was recorded in Col. Dagworthy's account book on 12 Jul 1762 for work on Fort Cumberland. {Ref: MHS MS.375}

FITZSIMMONS, JOHN (Delaware), b. c1731, Dublin, Ireland (laborer, age 27 in 1758); pvt., enlisted 11 May 1758 "for the campaign in the lower counties" by Capt. John McClughan. {Ref: ARDE I:17; ARPA (2nd Series) 2:570} See "John Fitzimmons," q.v.

FITZWATER, LEVIN (Maryland), pvt., Capt. John Dagworthy's Company of MD Troops, Frederick Co., from 9 Oct 1757 to 14 Sep 1758 (served 341 days) when he was reportedly killed; however, payment to him was recorded in Col. Dagworthy's account book on 8 Mar 1763. {Ref: MHS MS.375; CSOS:76; MHS MS.375.1} An account submitted to the MD Assembly on 25 Nov 1763 also indicated "Levin Fishwater" was due £4.12.3 as "granted by the Act for Granting a Sum of Money as a Present to the Forces, late in the Pay and Service of this Province, and taken into his Majesty's Service by Brigadier General Forbes." {Ref: ARMD 58:401}

FLANNEGAN (FLANNENGEN), RICHARD (Maryland), pvt., Capt. Francis Ware's Company of MD Troops, Charles Co., from 9 Oct 1757 to 14 Jun 1758 (served 248 days) when he was reported as killed; however, payment to him was recorded in Col. Dagworthy's account book on 7 Mar 1763. {Ref: MHS MS.375; CSOS:88; MHS MS.375.1}

FLEMING (FLEMMING), ARCHIBALD (Delaware), son of Alexander Fleming (d. 1770) and Isabel McKnitt, m. Esther (N), had children Joseph, Samuel, George, Andrew, Alexander, Sarah, Barbary, and Isabel, and d. testate by 26 Apr 1783. {Ref: CFD 2:73; CDSS:66} Lieut., Middle Part of Mispillion Hundred, Militia of Kent Co. on Delaware, 1756. {Ref: ARDE I:12; ARPA (2nd Series) 2:527-529; HDE I:141}

FLEMMING, ROBERT (Maryland), pvt., Capt. Tobias Stansbury's Company Muster Roll, Baltimore Co., circa 1757-1758, exact dates not given; bill of credit issued or paid to him for £1.18.0 in 1767, exact date not given. {Ref: MSA S960 or S752, p. 186}

FLENNER, JOHN (Maryland), pvt., Capt. Jonathan Hagar's Company Muster Roll, Frederick Co., circa 1757-1758, exact dates not given (served 6 days); bill of credit issued or paid to him for £0.6.0 in 1767, exact date not given. {Ref: MSA S960 or S752, p. 174; CSOS:106}

FLETCHER, JOHN (Maryland), ensign in Capt. William Luckett's Company Muster Roll, Frederick Co., circa 1757-1758, exact dates not given (served 30 days); bill of credit issued or paid in his behalf to William Luckett, Jr. for £3 on 6 Apr 1767; name transcribed once as "John Fletchall." {Ref: MSA S960 or S752, p. 169; CSOS:99}

FLICK, JOSEPH (Maryland), pvt., Capt. Peter Bainbridge's Company Muster Roll, Frederick Co., circa 1757-1758, exact dates not given; bill of credit issued or paid to him on 4 Mar 1767 for £1.8.0. {Ref: MSA S960 or S752, p. 180}

FLICK, MICHAEL (Maryland), pvt., Capt. John Middaugh's Company Muster Roll, Frederick Co., circa 1757-1758, exact dates not given (served 30 days); bill of credit issued or paid in his behalf to Casper Shaff for £1.10.0 on 2 Mar 1767. {Ref: MSA S960 or S752, p. 171; CSOS:100}

FLINN, JOHN (Maryland), pvt., Kent County, by 1757. {Ref: ARMD 31:208}

FLINT, DAVID (Maryland), pvt., Capt. Joseph Hanson Harrison's Company Muster Roll, Charles Co., circa 1757-1758, exact dates not given; bill of credit issued or paid in his behalf to Josias Beall, Jr. for £2.9.0 on 25 Mar 1767. {Ref: MSA S960 or S752, p. 189}

FLINTHAM, WILLIAM (Maryland), pvt., Capt. Henry Sneavely's Company Muster Roll, Frederick Co., circa 1757-1758, exact dates not given; bill of credit issued or paid to him for £0.8.0 in 1767, exact date not given. {Ref: MSA S960 or S752, p. 190}

FLINTON (FLINTOM), WILLIAM (Maryland), pvt., Capt. John White's Company Muster Roll, Frederick Co., circa 1757-1758, exact dates not given (served 6 days); bill of credit issued or paid to him for £0.6.0 in 1767, exact date not given. {Ref: MSA S960 or S752, p. 164; CSOS:95}

FLORA, ISAAC (Maryland), pvt., Capt. William McClellan's Company of MD Volunteers, Frederick Co., circa 1763-1764; on muster roll dated 15 Nov 1764 at Camp at the Forks of Muskingham. {Ref: ARMD 32:99}

FLORA, WILLIAM (Maryland), pvt., Capt. William McClellan's Company of MD Volunteers, Frederick Co., circa 1763-1764; on muster roll dated 15 Nov 1764 at Camp at the Forks of Muskingham. {Ref: ARMD 32:99}

FLOYD, JAMES (Maryland), pvt., Capt. Joshua Beall's Company of MD Troops, Prince George's Co., from 9 Oct 1757 to 7 Dec 1757 when he was discharged. {Ref: MHS MS.375.1; CSOS:84} Payment to him was recorded in Col. Dagworthy's account book on 24 Jul 1762. {Ref: MHS MS.375}

FLUCK, JACOB (Maryland), pvt., Capt. Peter Bainbridge's Company Muster Roll, Frederick Co., circa 1757-1758, exact dates not given (served 28 days); bill of credit issued or paid to him on 4 Mar 1767 for £1.8.0. {Ref: MSA S960 or S752, p. 181; CSOS:111}

FOARD (FORD), CHARLES (Maryland), b. 24 Aug 1739, Kent Co., son of Charles and Ann Ford, of Shrewsbury Parish. {Ref: ESVR} Pvt., Capt. Peregrine

Brown's Company Muster Roll, Kent Co., circa 1757-1758, exact dates not given (served 15 days); bill of credit issued or paid in his behalf to Robert Buchanan on 21 Mar 1767 for £0.15.0. {Ref: MSA S960 or S752, p. 179; CSOS:110}

FOARD (FORD), ROBERT JR. (Maryland), b. 15 Sep 1738, Kent Co., son of Charles and Ann Ford, of Shrewsbury Parish. {Ref: ESVR} Pvt., Capt. Peregrine Brown's Company Muster Roll, Kent Co., circa 1757-1758, exact dates not given (served 15 days); bill of credit issued or paid in his behalf to Robert Buchanan on 21 Mar 1767 for £0.15.0. {Ref: MSA S960 or S752, p. 179; CSOS:110}

FOARD (FORD), WILLIAM (Maryland), pvt., Capt. Peregrine Brown's Company Muster Roll, Kent Co., circa 1757-1758, exact dates not given (served 15 days); bill of credit issued or paid in his behalf to Robert Buchanan on 21 Mar 1767 for £0.15.0. {Ref: MSA S960 or S752, p. 179; CSOS:110} William Ford, of Kent Co., m. (N), had children Moses, William, Joseph, Robert, and Sarah, and d. testate by 16 Nov 1781. {Ref: Kent Co. Wills 7:1}

FOGELER, ANTHONY (Maryland), pvt., Capt. Stephen Rensburg's or Rensburger's Company Muster Roll, Frederick Co., circa 1757-1758, exact dates not given (served 4 days); bill of credit or order issued to Casper Shaff and paid to David Cumming for £2.2.0 on 18 Apr 1767. {Ref: MSA S960 or S752, p. 183; CSOS:112}

FORBES, GENERAL, see "John Harwood" and "James Havens," q.v.

FORD, ANN, see "Charles Foard (Ford)," q.v.

FORD, BENJAMIN JR. (Delaware), lieut., Brandywine Hundred, Upper Regt. of Militia, Northeast Division, New Castle Co., 1756. {Ref: ARDE I:11; ARPA (2nd Series) 2:526; HDE I:141}

FORD, CHARLES, see "Charles Foard (Ford)," q.v.

FORD, EDWARD (Maryland), pvt., Capt. Francis Ware's Company of MD Troops, Charles Co., from 9 Oct 1757 to 2 Apr 1758 (served 175 days) and reportedly deserted; however, payment to him was recorded in Col. Dagworthy's account book on 7 Mar 1763. {Ref: MHS MS.375; CSOS:87; MHS MS.375.1}

FORD, JACOB (Delaware), pvt., Kent Co. Militia, Capt. John Caton's Company, 25 Apr 1757 (date of muster roll). {Ref: ARDE I:14}

FORD, JEHOSEPHAT (Delaware), pvt., Kent Co. Militia, Capt. John Caton's Company, 25 Apr 1757 (date of muster roll). {Ref: ARDE I:14}

FORD, JOHN (Delaware), pvt., Kent Co. Militia, Capt. John Caton's Company, 25 Apr 1757 (date of muster roll). {Ref: ARDE I:14}

FORD, JOSEPH (Maryland), pvt., Capt. Alexander Beall's Company of MD Troops, Frederick Co., from 9 Oct 1757 to 18 Oct 1758 when he reportedly deserted; however, payment to him was recorded in Col. Dagworthy's account book on 16 Jul 1762. {Ref: MHS MS.375; CSOS:80; MHS MS.375.1}

FORD, PETER (Maryland), pvt., Capt. John Wolgomatt's Company of MD Volunteers, Frederick Co., circa 1763-1764; on muster roll dated 15 Nov 1764 at Camp at the Forks of Muskingham. {Ref: ARMD 32:99}

FORD, ROBERT (Maryland), pvt., Capt. William McClellan's Company of MD Volunteers, Frederick Co., circa 1763-1764; on muster roll dated 15 Nov 1764 at Camp at the Forks of Muskingham. {Ref: ARMD 32:99}

FORD, ROBERT JR., see "Robert Foard," q.v.

FORD, WILLIAM, see "William Foard," q.v.

FOREMAN, BENJAMIN (Maryland), drummer, Capt. Peregrine Brown's Company Muster Roll, Kent Co., circa 1757-1758, exact dates not given (served 15 days); bill of credit issued or paid in his behalf to Thomas Ringgold, Esq. on 20 Feb 1767 for £1. {Ref: MSA S960 or S752, p. 179; CSOS:110}

FORENOR, EDWARD (Maryland), patriot and poss. soldier (rank not specified), Kent Co., militia pay account submitted in 1758, exact date not given. {Ref: MHM 9:4, p. 368}

FORKCUM, JOHN (Delaware), pvt., Kent Co. Militia, Capt. John Caton's Company, 25 Apr 1757 (date of muster roll). {Ref: ARDE I:13} "John Forcum" d. intestate by 29 Oct 1791 at which time Joshua Forcum was granted letters of administration. {Ref: CDSS:68}

FORKCUM, RENN (Delaware), pvt., Kent Co. Militia, Capt. John Caton's Company, 25 Apr 1757 (date of muster roll). {Ref: ARDE I:13} "Renn Forkham" m. Hannah Rash (dau. of John Rash, d. 1760). "Wren Forkham" lived in Murderkill Hundred in 1756. {Ref: CDSS:68-69}

FORRESTER, ROBERT (Maryland), b. c1721, Rhode Island; recruit, Royal American Regt., Baltimore Town (age 35 in 1756); reported as deserted in Baltimore, noting that he served as an indentured servant for 5 years with Mr. Lisby of South River, Anne Arundel Co. {Ref: *MD Gazette*, 4 Nov 1756}

FORSHE, JOHN (Maryland), pvt., Capt. Joseph Chapline's Company Muster Roll No. 1, Frederick Co., circa 1757-1758, exact dates not given (served 55 days); bill of credit issued or paid in his behalf to Joseph Chaplin for £2.15.0 on 5 Mar 1767. {Ref: MSA S960 or S752, p. 191; CSOS:103}

FORSHE, OBEDIAH (Maryland), alias Obediah Fowler *[sic]*, pvt., Capt. Moses Chapline's Company Muster Roll No. 3, Frederick Co., circa 1757-1758, exact dates not given (served 6 days); bill of credit issued or paid in his behalf to Joseph Chaplin for £0.6.0 on 5 Mar 1767; name mistakenly transcribed once as "Obediah Forster." {Ref: MSA S960 or S752, p. 198; CSOS:115}

FOSTER (FORSTER), ADAM (Maryland), pvt., Capt. John Dagworthy's Company of MD Troops, Frederick Co., from 9 Oct 1757 to 21 Apr 1758 (served 341 days) when he reportedly died; however, payment to him was recorded in Col. Dagworthy's account book on 8 Mar 1763 for work on Fort Cumberland. {Ref: MHS MS.375.1; CSOS:76; MHS MS.375}

FOSTER, BEZALEEL, see "John Foster," q.v.

FOSTER, ELEANOR, see "John Foster," q.v.

FOSTER, FUCHER (Delaware), b. c1730, Rehoboth, DE (planter, age 28 in 1758); pvt., enlisted 20 Apr 1758 "for the campaign in the lower counties" by Capt. John McClughan. {Ref: ARDE I:17; ARPA (2nd Series) 2:570}

FOSTER, JOHN (Maryland), b. 3 or 4 Nov 1737, Baltimore Co., son of Bezaleel Foster and Mary Meed, St. John's P. E. Parish, and m. Eleanor (N), children not known. {Ref: BCF:225} Pvt., Capt. Tobias Stansbury's Company Muster Roll, Baltimore Co., circa 1757-1758, exact dates not given; bill of credit issued or paid in his behalf to Daniel Curtis for £1.18.0 on 15 Jan 1771. {Ref: MSA S960 or S752, p. 187}

FOSTER (FORSTER), NATHANIEL (Maryland), pvt., Capt. Joseph Chapline's Company Muster Roll No. 1, Frederick Co., circa 1757-1758, exact dates not given (served 29 days); militia pay account submitted in 1758, exact date not given. {Ref: MHM 9:4, p. 368} Bill of credit issued or paid in his behalf to Joseph Chaplin for £1.9.0 on 5 Mar 1767. {Ref: MSA S960 or S752, p. 191; CSOS:102}

FOSTER, WILLIAM (Delaware), b. c1731, MD (age 28 in 1759); pvt., enlisted in Capt. John Wright's Company and mustered on 11 May 1759. {Ref: ARDE I:25; ARPA (2nd Series) 2:508, 592}

FOUT (FOUTS), BALSER (Maryland), pvt., Capt. Stephen Rensburg's or Rensburger's Company Muster Roll, Frederick Co., circa 1757-1758, exact dates not given (served 42 days); bill of credit issued or paid in his behalf to Casper Shaff for £1.14.0 on 2 Mar 1767; name mistakenly transcribed once as "Balser Trouts." {Ref: MSA S960 or S752, p. 182; CSOS:112}

FOUT, HENRY (Maryland), pvt., Capt. Stephen Rensburg's or Rensburger's Company Muster Roll, Frederick Co., circa 1757-1758, exact dates not given; bill of credit issued or paid in his behalf to Stephen Rensburg or Rensburger for £2.2.0 on 27 Mar 1767; name mistakenly transcribed once as "Henry Trout." {Ref: MSA S960 or S752, p. 182; CSOS:113}

FOUT, JACOB (Maryland), pvt., Capt. Stephen Rensburg's or Rensburger's Company Muster Roll, Frederick Co., circa 1757-1758, exact dates not given (served 34 days); bill of credit issued or paid to him for £2.2.0 on 27 Mar 1767; name mistakenly transcribed once as "Jacob Trout." {Ref: MSA S960 or S752, p. 182}

FOWLER, MATTHEW (Maryland), b. c1736, MD (age 20 in 1756); pvt., Capt. Christopher Gist's Company of VA Militia, 13 Jul 1756, enlisted at Baltimore. {Ref: MSR I:37}

FOWLER, OBEDIAH, see "Obediah Forshe," q.v.

FOWLER, THOMAS (Maryland or Pennsylvania), b. c1737, Wiltshire, England (weaver, age 22 in 1759); soldier reported as deserted in 1759 by Capt. Richard Pearis, of the PA Provincials, who was then recruiting in Annapolis. {Ref: *MD Gazette*, 15 Mar 1759}

FOWLER, WILLIAM (Maryland), b. 9 Apr 1730, Prince George's Co., son of William and Elizabeth Fowler, of Queen Anne's P. E. Parish. {Ref: PGCR 1:177} Pvt., Capt. Joshua Beall's Company Muster Roll, Prince George's Co., circa 1757-1758, exact dates not given; bill of credit issued or paid to him for £0.5.0 in 1767, exact date not given. {Ref: MSA S960 or S752, p. 184}

FOX, GEORGE (Maryland), pvt., Capt. Peter Butler's Company Muster Roll, Frederick Co., circa 1757-1758, exact dates not given (served 34 days); bill of credit or order issued in his behalf to Casper Shaff for £1.14.0 and paid to David Cumming on 18 Apr 1767. {Ref: MSA S960 or S752, p. 168; CSOS:97}

FOX, JAMES (Maryland), pvt., Capt. John Wolgomatt's Company of MD Volunteers, Frederick Co., circa 1763-1764; reported as deserted on muster roll dated 15 Nov 1764 at Camp at the Forks of Muskingham. {Ref: ARMD 32:99}

FRANCIS, HENRY (Maryland), b. c1734, MD (age 22 in 1756); pvt., Capt. Christopher Gist's Company of VA Militia, 13 Jul 1756, enlisted at Baltimore. {Ref: MSR I:37}

FRANCIS, JOHN (Maryland), b. c1721, MD (age 35 in 1756); pvt., Capt. J. Lewis' Company of VA Militia, enlisted in 1756 in Frederick, VA. {Ref: MSR I:38}

FRANCIS, JOSEPH (Maryland), pvt., Capt. Francis Ware's Company of MD Troops, Charles Co., from 9 Oct 1757 to 3 Dec 1757 (served 423 days) when he reportedly deserted; he returned (date not given) and deserted again on 28 Dec 1757. {Ref: MHS MS.375.1; CSOS:87}

FRANKLIN, THOMAS (Maryland), b. c1706, England, immigrated to MD by 1728, m. 1st to Ruth (N) by 1730 and 2nd to Ruth Ingram (widow of Peasley Ingram and dau. of Charles Hammond) by 1744, had children Thomas Heath, Benjamin, James, Sarah, and Elizabeth, and d. by 27 Apr 1787, Baltimore Co.; captain by 1747, major by 1754, colonel by 1771; member of MD Assembly (1751-1752), court justice (1750-1751, 1753, 1758-1763), sheriff (1752). {Ref: BDML I:328-329; ARMD 56:288; Baltimore Co. Court Minutes, 1758}

FRASER (FRAZER), GEORGE (Maryland), b. c1709, Charles Co. or Prince George's Co., son of Rev. John Fraser and Ann Blyzard, of VA and MD; d. December 1764, Prince George's Co., unmarried; patriot, planter, county justice (1741-1757), member of the MD Assembly (1752-1761, served on the Arms and Ammunition Committee), and styled captain by 1757. {Ref: BDML I:329; ARMD 55:67}

FRAUBERG(?), ANDREW (Delaware), captain, Christiana Hundred, Upper Regt., New Castle Co., 1756. {Ref: ARDE I:11; ARPA (2nd Series) 2:526}

FRAZIER, PETER (Maryland), pvt., Capt. Joshua Beall's Company of MD Troops, Prince George's Co., from 9 Oct 1757 to 7 Dec 1757 when he was discharged. {Ref: MHS MS.375.1; CSOS:84} Payment to him was recorded in Col. Dagworthy's account book on 24 Jul 1762 and in March 1763 for work on Fort Cumberland. {Ref: MHS MS.375}

FREDERICK, JOHN (Maryland), pvt., Capt. John Middaugh's Company Muster Roll, Frederick Co., circa 1757-1758, exact dates not given; bill of credit issued or paid in his behalf to Charles Beatty for £1.10.0 on 9 Oct 1770. {Ref: MSA S960 or S752, p. 172}

FREDERICK, SAMUEL (Maryland), pvt., Capt. William Luckett's Company Muster Roll, Frederick Co., circa 1757-1758, exact dates not given (served 30 days); bill of credit issued or paid in his behalf to William Luckett, Jr. for £1.10.0 on 6 Apr 1767. {Ref: MSA S960 or S752, p. 170; CSOS:100}

FREEBORN, MARY, see "Walter Tolley," q.v.

FREELAND, JOHN (Delaware), pvt., Capt. French Battell's Company of Lower County Provincials, enlisted 13 May 1758. {Ref: ARDE I:16; ARPA (2nd Series) 2:555}

FREEMAN, AARON (Maryland), pvt., Capt. Joshua Beall's Company of MD Troops, Prince George's Co., from 9 Oct 1757 to 16 Oct 1758 when he was discharged; one undated account indicated "Calvert County." {Ref: MHS MS.375.1; CSOS:84, 116} Bill of credit issued or paid to him for £1.3.0 in 1767, exact date not given. {Ref: MSA S960 or S752, p. 184} Payment to him was recorded in Col. Dagworthy's account book on 12 Jul 1762. {Ref: MHS MS.375}

FREEMAN, BENJAMIN (Maryland), pvt., Capt. Francis Ware's Company of MD Troops, Charles Co., by 12 Oct 1758 (served 96 days) and was mistakenly reported as killed; pvt., Capt. John Dagworthy's Company of MD Troops, Frederick Co., from 31 Dec 1758 to 26 Apr 1759 (served 117 days); payment to him was recorded in Col. Dagworthy's account book on 13 Jul 1762. {Ref: MHS MS.375.1; CSOS:76, 87; MHS MS.375}

FREEMAN, ESSAIS or ESIAS (Maryland), pvt., Capt. Francis Ware's Company of MD Troops, Charles Co., circa 9 Oct 1757 to 30 Dec 1758. {Ref: MHS MS.375.1; CSOS:87} Payment to him was recorded in Col. Dagworthy's account book on 12 Jul 1762 for work on Fort Cumberland. {Ref: MHS MS.375}

FREEMAN, FERGUSON, see "Furguson Truman," q.v.

FREEMAN, JAMES (Maryland), pvt., Capt. Joshua Beall's Company Muster Roll, Prince George's Co., circa 1757-1758, exact dates not given; bill of credit issued or paid to him for £1.7.0 in 1767, exact date not given; one undated account indicated "Calvert County." {Ref: MSA S960 or S752, p. 184; CSOS:116}

FREEMAN, JOHN (Maryland), sgt., Capt. Henry Casson's Company Muster Roll, Queen Anne's Co., circa 1757-1758, exact dates not given (served 27 days); bill of credit issued or paid in his behalf to Capt. Casson on 27 Mar 1767 for £1.16.0. {Ref: MSA S960 or S752, p. 178; CSOS:109}

FREEMAN, NATHANIEL (Maryland), b. c1733 (aged about 42 in 1775 deposition); pvt., Capt. Francis Ware's Company of MD Troops, Charles Co., from 9 Oct 1757 to 12 Oct 1758 when he was wounded. {Ref: MGSB 33:4, p. 708; MHS MS.375.1; CSOS:88}

FREEMAN, PENELOPE, see "Owen Irons," q.v.

FREEMAN, RICHARD (Maryland), pvt., Capt. Richard Pearis' Company of MD Troops, Frederick Co., circa 9 Oct 1757 to 31 May 1758; pvt., Capt. John Dagworthy's Company of MD Troops, Frederick Co., from 1 Jun 1758 to 26 Dec 1758 (served 208 days), having transferred from Capt. Richard Pearis' Company where he was mistakenly reported as deserted; payment to him was recorded in Col. Dagworthy's account book on 11 Jul 1762 for work on Fort Cumberland. {Ref: MHS MS.375.1; CSOS:76, 90; MHS MS.375}

FREEMAN, SAMUEL (Maryland), pvt., Capt. Alexander Beall's Company of MD Troops, Frederick Co., circa 9 Oct 1757 to 30 Dec 1758; pvt., Capt. John Dagworthy's Company of MD Troops, Frederick Co., from 31 Dec 1758 to 18 Apr 1759 (served 108 days), having transferred from Capt. Alexander Beall's Company where he was mistakenly reported as deserted; however, payment to him was recorded in Col. Dagworthy's account book on 12 Jul 1762. {Ref: MHS MS.375.1; CSOS:76, 80; MHS MS.375}

FREEMAN, THOMAS (Maryland), sgt., Capt. John Dagworthy's Company of MD Troops, Frederick Co., circa 9 Oct 1757 to 26 Apr 1759, exact dates not given. {Ref: MHS MS.375.1; CSOS:76} Payment to him was recorded in Col. Dagworthy's account book on 14 Jul 1762. {Ref: MHS MS.375}

FRENCH, JACOB (Maryland), pvt., Capt. John White's Company Muster Roll, Frederick Co., circa 1757-1758, exact dates not given (served 6 day); bill of credit issued or paid to him for £0.6.0 in 1767, exact date not given. {Ref: MSA S960 or S752, p. 164; CSOS:95}

FRENCH, PETER (Maryland), pvt., Capt. John White's Company Muster Roll, Frederick Co., circa 1757-1758, exact dates not given (served 6 days); bill of credit issued or paid to him for £0.6.0 in 1767, exact date not given. {Ref: MSA S960 or S752, p. 164; CSOS:95}

FRENCH, SAMUEL (Maryland), b. c1729, MD (age 27 in 1756); cpl., Capt. G. Mercer's Company of VA Militia, enlisted on 2 Aug 1756 in Fairfax, VA. {Ref: MSR I:38}

FRIDAY, JOHN AUGUSTUS (Delaware), b. c1739, Hanover, Germany (laborer, age 19 in 1758); pvt., enlisted 23 Apr 1758 "for the campaign in the lower counties" by Capt. John McClughan. {Ref: ARDE I:17; ARPA (2nd Series) 2:570}

FRIEND, GABRIEL (Maryland), pvt., Capt. Joseph Chapline's Company Muster Roll No. 1, Frederick Co., circa 1757-1758, exact dates not given (served 4 days); bill of credit issued or paid in his behalf to Joseph Chaplin for £0.4.0 on 13 Jun 1768. {Ref: MSA S960 or S752, p. 192; CSOS:103} Pvt., Capt. Jonathan Hagar's Company Muster Roll, Frederick Co., circa 1757-1758, exact dates not given (served 6 days); bill of credit issued or paid to him for £0.6.0 in 1767, exact date not given. {Ref: MSA S960 or S752, p. 174; CSOS:107}

FRIEND, JACOB (Maryland), pvt., Capt. Jonathan Hagar's Company Muster Roll, Frederick Co., circa 1757-1758, exact dates not given (served 6 days); bill of credit issued or paid to him for £0.6.0 in 1767, exact date not given. {Ref: MSA S960 or S752, p. 174; CSOS:106}

FRISBY, PEREGRINE, see "William Fitzhugh," q.v.

FRUGATE (TRUGATE?), PETER (Maryland), pvt., Capt. John White's Company Muster Roll, Frederick Co., circa 1757-1758, exact dates not given (served 6 days); bill of credit issued or paid to him for £0.6.0 in 1767, exact date not given. {Ref: MSA S960 or S752, p. 164; CSOS:96}

FRUSH, VANDEL or VANDLE (Maryland), pvt., Capt. John Middaugh's Company Muster Roll, Frederick Co., circa 1757-1758, exact dates not given (served 30 days); bill of credit issued or paid in his behalf to Casper Shaff for £1.10.0 on 2 Mar 1767. {Ref: MSA S960 or S752, p. 171; CSOS:101}

FRY, HENRY (Maryland), pvt., Capt. John White's Company Muster Roll, Frederick Co., circa 1757-1758, exact dates not given (served 34 days); bill of credit issued or paid to him for £0.6.0 in 1767, exact date not given. {Ref: MSA S960 or S752, p. 164; CSOS:96}

FRYER, WILLIAM (Maryland), pvt., Capt. Richard Pearis' Company of MD Troops, Frederick Co., circa 9 Oct 1757 to 31 May 1758; pvt., Capt. Francis Ware's Company of MD Troops, Charles Co., from 1 Jun 1758 to 7 Nov 1758 (served 396 days altogether); payment to him was recorded in Col. Dagworthy's account book on 15 Jul 1762. {Ref: MHS MS.375; CSOS:88, 90; MHS MS.375.1}

FUDAR (TUDAR?), JOHN (Maryland), pvt., Capt. Elias Delashmutt's Company Muster Roll, Frederick Co., 13 Aug 1757, exact dates not given (served 52 days); bill of credit issued or paid in his behalf to Elias Delashmut, Jr. on 16 Mar 1767 for £2.12.0. {Ref: MSA S960 or S752, p. 163; CSOS:98}

FULDWEDER (FULWEDER), HENRY (Maryland), pvt., Capt. Stephen Rensburg's or Rensburger's Company Muster Roll, Frederick Co., circa 1757-1758, exact dates not given (served 34 days); bill of credit issued or paid in his behalf to Stephen Rensburg or Rensburger for £1.14.0 on 27 Mar 1767. {Ref: MSA S960 or S752, p. 182; CSOS:113}

FULLER, ESTHER, see "William Standiford," q.v.

FUNK, HENRY (Maryland), b. 1724, d. 1784; pvt., Capt. Stephen Rensburg's or Rensburger's Company Muster Roll, Frederick Co., circa 1757-1758, exact dates not given (served 42 days); bill of credit issued or paid in his behalf to Stephen Rensburg or Rensburger for £1.14.0 on 27 Mar 1767; name mistakenly transcribed once as "Henry Trunk." {Ref: MSA S960 or S752, p. 182; CSOS:112} Coroner's Inquest, 31 Dec 1784: "Henry Funk (age 60) had been in the woods alone cutting firewood and a tree appears to have fallen on him." {Ref: WMG 1:1, p. 41}

FURBEE (FURBE), CALEB (Delaware), ensign, Murderkill Hundred, Kent Co. on Delaware, 29 Mar 1758. {Ref: ARDE I:15; ARPA (2nd Series) 2:577} Served on a jury that was empowered to try cases of treason in Kent Co. in 1783; d. intestate by 9 May 1796 at which time Sarah Furbee was granted letters of administration. {Ref: RPDE:96; CDSS:71}

FURNANTZ, ANTHONY (Delaware), b. c1727, Maderia, Portugal (laborer, age 31 in 1758); pvt., enlisted 1 May 1758 "for the campaign in the lower counties" by Capt. John McClughan. {Ref: ARDE I:17; ARPA (2nd Series) 2:570}

FURNISS, ROBERT (Delaware), pvt., Capt. Richard McWilliams' Company of Foot, New Castle Co., enlisted 28 Dec 1757. {Ref: ARDE I:15}

FUTNEY (FATNEY), HENRY (Maryland), pvt., Capt. Elias Delashmutt's Company Muster Roll, Frederick Co., circa 1757-1758, exact dates not given (served 30 days); bill of credit issued or paid in his behalf to Elias Delashmut, Jr. on 16 Mar 1767 for £1.10.0. {Ref: MSA S960 or S752, p. 162; CSOS:94}

FYFE, JAMES (Maryland), alias James Tryfe *[sic]*, pvt., Capt. William Luckett's Company Muster Roll, Frederick Co., circa 1757-1758, exact dates not given (served 30 days); bill of credit issued or paid in his behalf to William Luckett, Jr. for £1.10.0 on 6 Apr 1767; name mistakenly transcribed once as "James Fyse." {Ref: MSA S960 or S752, p. 169; CSOS:99}

GADAY, JOHN (Maryland), pvt., Capt. Joseph Hanson Harrison's Company Muster Roll, Charles Co., circa 1757-1758, exact dates not given; bill of credit issued or paid to him for £2.12.0 in 1767, exact date not given. {Ref: MSA S960 or S752, p. 189}

GAIL, JOHN (Maryland), indentured servant and soldier who served in the French and Indian War some time between 1756 and 1763 (exact dates not known); his master Joshua Hall, joiner, requested compensation from the Baltimore County Court due to the loss of use of Gail while in the service. {Ref: MHM 94:4, p. 426, citing Baltimore Co. Court Minutes}

GAITHER, SAMUEL (Maryland), son of John and (N) Gaither, bapt. 7 Apr 1717, All Hallow's Parish. {Ref: AACR:32} Patriot, Annapolis, Anne Arundel Co., pay account submitted for quartering soldiers in 1757 or 1758, exact dates not given. {Ref: MHM 9:3, p. 261}

GALE, GEORGE (Maryland), b. c1705, Somerset Co., son of George Gale and Betty Denwood, m. Elizabeth (N) by 1736 and d. testate by 11 Jan 1772, no surviving children; planter, merchant, gentleman, colonel by 1744, member of the MD Assembly (1742-1744), and court justice (1757-1762). {Ref: BDML I:335}

GALE, JOHN JR. (Maryland), pvt., Capt. Peregrine Brown's Company, Kent Co., on 19 Feb 1758, by which time he had enlisted, but was unable to march due to health problems. {Ref: ARMD 31:283} John Gale m. Bersheba (N), had children John, Malachi, James, Mary, Cathrine, and Rosamond, and d. testate by 30 Jan 1776. One of the witnesses to his will on 4 Dec 1775 was Macall Medford, a fellow soldier. {Ref: MCW 16:125}

GALE, RASIN (Maryland), sgt., Capt. Peregrine Brown's Company Muster Roll, Kent Co., circa 1757-1758, exact dates not given (served 15 days); bill of credit issued or paid in his behalf to Thomas Ringgold, Esq. on 20 Feb 1767 for £1. {Ref: MSA S960 or S752, p. 179; CSOS:109} Rasin Gale, of Kent Co., m. Rebecca (N), had children George, Rasin Jr., Thomas, John, Rachel, Mary, Elizabeth, Mary, and another dau. (N) who pre-deceased him, and d. testate by 29 Nov 1797. {Ref: Kent Co. Wills 7:589}

GALFORD, WILLIAM (Maryland), cpl., Capt. William Luckett's Company Muster Roll, Frederick Co., circa 1757-1758, exact dates not given (served 30 days); militia pay account submitted in 1758, exact date not given. {Ref: MHM 9:4, p. 367; CSOS:99} Bill of credit issued or paid in his behalf to William Luckett, Jr. for £2.12.0 on 6 Apr 1767. {Ref: MSA S960 or S752, p. 170}

GALLAWAY, RICHARD (Delaware), m. Lydia (N), had children Henrietta, Elizabeth, Samuel, and Joseph, and d. intestate by 6 Jun 1761. {Ref: CDSS:72} Pvt., Kent Co. Militia, Capt. John Caton's Company, 25 Apr 1757 (date of muster roll). {Ref: ARDE I:13}

GANO, DANIEL (Delaware), b. c1729, DE (laborer, age 29 in 1758); pvt., recruited by Capt. Benjamin Noxon and enlisted on 29 Apr 1758. {Ref: ARDE I:19; ARPA (2nd Series) 2:566}

GANO, GEORGE (Delaware), captain, Appoquinimink Hundred, Lower Regt. of Militia, New Castle Co., 1756 (name mistakenly listed once as "George Ganz"). {Ref: ARDE I:12; ARPA (2nd Series) 2:525; HDE I:141}

GANSHORN, MATTHIAS (Maryland or Pennsylvania), pvt., Capt. Hamilton's Company, was wounded in "a recent battle with the Indians" in 1756 (exact date not given) in Cumberland Co., PA, after the burning of McCord's Fort. {Ref: *MD Gazette*, 29 Apr 1756}

GANTT, ANNE, see "John Brome (Broome)," q.v.

GANTT, EDWARD (Maryland), b. c1725, Prince George's Co., son of Thomas Gantt and Priscilla Brooke, m. Elizabeth Wheeler by 1749, had children Thomas, Edward, and Mary, and d. by 1783, Calvert Co.; planter, gentleman, captain by 1751, and member of the MD Assembly (1751-1776, served on the

Arms and Ammunition Committee, 1751-1754). {Ref: BDML I:339-340} Captain and commander of the Calvert Co. militia in Lyon's Creek Hundred circa 1756-1758 (exact dates not given). {Ref: HCC:120}

GANTT (GAUNT), THOMAS (Maryland), b. c1710, Prince George's Co., son of Thomas Gantt and Priscilla Brooke, m. 1st to Rachel Smith by 1734 and 2nd to Eleanor Hillary by 1754, had children Thomas Jr., Edward, John, Levi, Rachel, Elizabeth, Priscilla, Ann, and Sarah. and d. testate by 28 Mar 1785; planter, gentleman, captain by 1743, county justice (1738-1740, 1748-1751), and member of the MD Assembly (1757-1758). {Ref: BDML I:342-343}

GANTT (GHENT), THOMAS (Maryland), cpl., Capt. Joshua Beall's Company Muster Roll, Prince George's Co., circa 1757-1758, exact dates not given; bill of credit issued or paid to him for £2.17.4½ on 27 Feb 1767. {Ref: MSA S960 or S752, p. 184}

GARDINHOVER, JACOB (Maryland), pvt., Capt. Peter Butler's Company Muster Roll, Frederick Co., circa 1757-1758, exact dates not given (served 34 days); bill of credit or order issued in his behalf for £1.14.0 and paid to Peter Grosh on 4 Mar 1767. {Ref: MSA S960 or S752, p. 168; CSOS:97}

GARDNER, SAMUEL (Maryland), captain, 47th Regt., Baltimore. On 15 Aug 1756 Capt. Gardner reported to the Governor of MD that in July his recruiting sgt. (unnamed) was attacked by Charles Ridgely and other who forcibly took away six recruits from him; Joseph Watkins and others rescued another recruit from said sgt. on his way from Joppa to Baltimore Town; he (the captain) applied to Stephen Bordley, attorney general, for redress, but got no satisfaction. {Ref: CMSP-The Black Books:133; ARMD 6:461} See "Capt. Orrick" and "Sabrit Sellers, Jr." q.v.

GARNER, FRANCIS (Maryland), pvt., Capt. Joshua Beall's Company of MD Troops, Prince George's Co., from 9 Oct 1757 to 7 Dec 1757 (served 60 days) when he was discharged. {Ref: MHS MS.375.1; CSOS:84}

GARNETT, JOHN (Maryland), pvt., Capt. Tobias Stansbury's Company Muster Roll, Baltimore Co., circa 1757-1758, exact dates not given; bill of credit issued or paid in his behalf to Thomas Johnson, Jr. for £1.19.0 on 9 Mar 1767; name listed once as "John Garrett or Garnett." {Ref: MSA S960 or S752, p. 186}

GARNETT, THOMAS (Maryland), patriot, Annapolis, Anne Arundel Co., pay account submitted for quartering soldiers in 1757 or 1758, exact dates not given. {Ref: MHM 9:3, p. 262}

GARRATSON, CORNUS (Delaware), pvt., Capt. Richard McWilliams' Company of Foot, New Castle Co., enlisted 28 Dec 1757. {Ref: ARDE I:14}

GARRETT, AMOS, see "Joseph Lewis," q.v.

GARRETT, ELIZABETH, see "James Matthews," q.v.

GARRETT, JAMES, see "James Gorrell," q.v.

GARRETT, JOHN (Delaware), b. c1735, MD (laborer, age 23 in 1758); pvt., recruited by Capt. Benjamin Noxon and enlisted on 4 Apr or 24 Apr 1758. {Ref: ARDE I:19; ARPA (2nd Series) 2:485, 566}

GARRETT, RICHARD (Delaware), b. c1738, MD (laborer, age 20 in 1758); pvt., recruited by Capt. Benjamin Noxon and enlisted on 1 May 1758; a Richard

Garrett served in the Revolutionary War as a pvt. in the 8th Co. of Foot, DE Regt., in 1778 and reportedly died some time during that year. {Ref: ARDE I:19; ARPA (2nd Series) 2:485, 566: RPDE:98}

GARRETT (GARRET), RICHARD (Maryland), pvt., Capt. Francis Ware's Company of MD Troops, Charles Co., circa 9 Oct 1757 to 30 Dec 1758. {Ref: MHS MS.375.1; CSOS:88} Payment to him was recorded in Col. Dagworthy's account book on 17 Jul 1762. {Ref: MHS MS.375}

GARRETTSON, CORNELIUS (Maryland), patriot, Annapolis, Anne Arundel Co., pay account submitted for quartering soldiers in 1757 or 1758, exact dates not given. {Ref: MHM 9:3, p. 261}

GARRETTSON, MARY, see "Walter Tolley," q.v.

GARRISON, BENJAMIN (Delaware), b. c1737, New Castle, DE (laborer, age 22 in 1759); pvt., enlisted by Capt. James Armstrong for the PA Regt. on 25 Apr 1759. {Ref: ARDE I:26; ARPA (2nd Series) 2:585}

GARRISON, FREDERICK (Maryland), patriot and poss. soldier (rank not specified), Frederick Co., militia pay account submitted in 1758, exact date not given. {Ref: MHM 9:4, p. 370}

GARRISON, JOHN (Delaware), b. c1740, New Castle, DE (laborer, age 19 in 1759); pvt., enlisted by Capt. James Armstrong for the PA Regt. on 20 May 1759. {Ref: ARDE I:26; ARPA (2nd Series) 2:585} He may have been the John Garrison, b. 23 Feb 1741/2, who m. Mary Griest, served as a pvt. in the Whig Bttn. in 1777, and d. 15 Dec 1810. {Ref: RPDE:98}

GARSNELL, MORDICAI, see "Mordecai Gosnell," q.v.

GARY, CLARE, see "Thomas MacKeele," q.v.

GASH, SARAH, see "Aquila Birchfield," q.v.

GASSAWAY, JOHN (Maryland), b. 16 Sep 1707, Anne Arundel Co., son of Thomas Gassaway and Susanna Hanslap, bapt. 12 Mar 1707/8, All Hallow's Parish, m. his first cousin Sarah Cotter on 5 Dec 1727, had children Thomas, William, Nicholas, Henry, Isaac, and Anne, and d. 10 Jun 1762 on his plantation at South River; captain by 1754, county justice (1742-1747, 1757-1758), sheriff (1748-1751), and member of the MD Assembly (1753-1761); captain of the South River Co. in 1756. {Ref: BDML I:346-347; ARMD 52:614, 55:44; *MD Gazette*, 17 Jun 1762; AACR:26}

GASSAWAY, THOMAS, see "Joseph Brewer," q.v.

GASSETT (GASSET), JOHN (Maryland), pvt., Capt. Francis Ware's Company of MD Troops, Charles Co., from 9 Oct 1757 to 8 Nov 1758 (served 395 days) when he reportedly deserted; however, payment to him was recorded in Col. Dagworthy's account book on 7 Mar 1763; name mistakenly listed once as "John Gassell." {Ref: MHS MS.375; CSOS:88; MHS MS.375.1}

GATSINDANER, GABRIEL (Maryland), cpl., Capt. Stephen Rensburg's or Rensburger's Company Muster Roll, Frederick Co., circa 1757-1758, exact dates not given (served 42 days); bill of credit issued or paid in his behalf to Stephen Rensburger for £2.16.0 on 27 Mar 1767. {Ref: MSA S960 or S752, pp. 182-183; CSOS:112}

GATTON, JAMES (Maryland), pvt., Capt. William Luckett's Company Muster Roll, Frederick Co., circa 1757-1758, exact dates not given (served 30 days); bill of credit issued or paid in his behalf to William Luckett, Jr. for £1.10.0 on 6 Apr 1767. {Ref: MSA S960 or S752, p. 170; CSOS:99}

GELSTRAP (GILSTRAP), WILLIAM (Maryland), pvt., Capt. Richard Pearis' Company of MD Troops, Frederick Co., circa 9 Oct 1757 to 31 May 1758; pvt., Capt. Joshua Beall's Company of MD Troops, Prince George's Co., from 9 Oct 1757 to 16 Jun 1758 when he reportedly died; however, payment to him was recorded in Col. Dagworthy's account book on 17 Jul 1762. {Ref: MHS MS.375; CSOS:84, 90; MHS MS.375.1}

GENATER (GENNETER, JENATOR), JOHN (Maryland), b. c1737, London, England (glazier and painter, age about 20 in 1757); pvt., enlisted in Charles Co. (date not given) and reportedly deserted from the MD Forces in July 1757. {Ref: *MD Gazette*, 21 Jul 1757} He subsequently returned to duty as a pvt. in Capt. Richard Pearis' Company (date not given), transferred to Capt. Alexander Beall's Company of MD Troops, Frederick Co., and served from 1 Jun 1758 to 14 Sep 1758 when he was reported as killed; name mistakenly transcribed once as "John Genates." {Ref: MHS MS.375; CSOS:80; MHS MS.375.1} However, payment to him was recorded in Col. Dagworthy's account book on 14 Jul 1762 and an account submitted to the MD Assembly on 25 Nov 1763 indicated "John Jenator" was due £4.12.3 as "granted by the Act for Granting a Sum of Money as a Present to the Forces, late in the Pay and Service of this Province, and taken into his Majesty's Service by Brigadier General Forbes." {Ref: ARMD 58:401}

GENSLER (GENALER?), JOHN (Maryland), pvt., Capt. Richard Pearis' Company of MD Troops, Frederick Co., circa 9 Oct 1757 to 31 May 1758. {Ref: MHS MS.375.1; CSOS:90}

GEORGE, JOHN (Maryland), patriot, Frederick Co., who performed "sundry services at the fort" in 1763 and payment in the amount of £0.4.6 was still owed to him on 25 Nov 1763 (when reported by the Accounts Committee to the MD Assembly). {Ref: ARMD 58:400}

GEORGE, JOHN (Maryland), pvt., Capt. Joseph Chapline's Company Muster Roll No. 1, Frederick Co., circa 1757-1758, exact dates not given (served 30 days); bill of credit issued or paid in his behalf to Joseph Chaplin for £1.10.0 on 24 Apr 1767. {Ref: MSA S960 or S752, p. 192; CSOS:102} Pvt., Capt. Moses Chapline's Company Muster Roll No. 1, Frederick Co., circa 1757-1758, exact dates not given (served 55 days); bill of credit issued or paid in his behalf to Joseph Chaplin for £2.15.0 on 24 Apr 1767. {Ref: MSA S960 or S752, p. 196; CSOS:113} Pvt., Capt. Moses Chapline's Company Muster Roll No. 2, Frederick Co., circa 1757-1758, exact dates not given (served 14 days); bill of credit issued or paid in his behalf to Joseph Chaplin for £0.14.0 on 24 Apr 1767. {Ref: MSA S960 or S752, p. 197; CSOS:114} Pvt., Capt. Moses Chapline's Company Muster Roll No. 3, Frederick Co., circa 1757-1758, exact dates not given (served 6 days); bill of credit issued or paid in his behalf to Joseph Chaplin for £0.6.0 on 24 Apr 1767. {Ref: MSA S960 or S752, p. 198; CSOS:114}

GEORGE, JOSEPH (Maryland), pvt., Capt. Peter Butler's Company Muster Roll, Frederick Co., circa 1757-1758, exact dates not given (served 34 days); bill of credit or order issued in his behalf for £1.14.0 and paid to Casper Shaff on 2 Mar 1767. {Ref: MSA S960 or S752, p. 166; CSOS:97}

GEORGE, JOSHUA (Maryland), pvt., Capt. Peregrine Brown's Company Muster Roll, Kent Co., circa 1757-1758, exact dates not given (served 15 days); bill of credit issued or paid to him on 23 Oct 1771 for £0.15.0. {Ref: MSA S960 or S752, p. 180; CSOS:110}

GIBBIN, DANIEL (Delaware), b. c1737, Ireland (laborer, age 21 in 1758); pvt., recruited by Capt. Benjamin Noxon and enlisted on 3 May 1758. {Ref: ARDE I:19; ARPA (2nd Series) 2:566}

GIBBINS (GIBBONS), JOHN (Maryland), b. 7 Apr 1736, Baltimore Co., son of Thomas and Mary Gibbons, St. John's P. E. Parish. {Ref: BCF:24} Pvt., Capt. Tobias Stansbury's Company Muster Roll, Baltimore Co., circa 1757-1758, exact dates not given; bill of credit issued or paid to him for £1.18.0 on 13 Mar 1767. {Ref: MSA S960 or S752, p. 186}

GIBBONS, JOHN (Delaware), b. c1730, Devon, England (laborer, age 28 in 1758); pvt., enlisted 26 Apr 1758 "for the campaign in the lower counties" by Capt. John McClughan. {Ref: ARDE I:17; ARPA (2nd Series) 2:570}

GIBBS, JOHN (Maryland), pvt., Capt. Joshua Beall's Company Muster Roll, Prince George's Co., circa 1757-1758, exact dates not given; bill of credit issued or paid to him for £1.10.6 in 1767, exact date not given. {Ref: MSA S960 or S752, p. 184}

GIBSON, WILLIAM (Delaware), b. c1729, Ireland (laborer, age 30 in 1759); pvt., enlisted by Capt. James Armstrong for the PA Regt. on 27 Apr 1759. {Ref: ARDE I:26; ARPA (2nd Series) 2:585}

GIBSON, WOOLMAN (Maryland), b. c1725, Talbot Co., son of Woolman Gibson and Elizabeth Dawson, m. Rachel (N), had children John, Jonathan, Woolman, Jacob, and Mary, and d. by 12 May 1786; lieut. in 1748, captain by 1759, member of the MD Assembly (1758-1761, 1765-1766), and sheriff (1761-1764). {Ref: BDML I:351-352}

GILLIS (GILLISS), JOSEPH (Maryland), b. c1706, Somerset Co., son of John Gillis and Mary (N), m. Eleanor Bozman by 1735, had sons George and William, and d. after 1783; captain by 1755, member of the MD Assembly (1751-1754), and county justice (1754-1774). {Ref: BDML I:353}

GILLIS, THOMAS (Maryland), captain, Somerset Co., by 1760. {Ref: ARMD 56:288}

GILMOR, WILLIAM (Delaware), b. c1741, Kent, DE (tailor, age 17 in 1758); pvt., enlisted by Capt. John Hasslet on 10 May 1758. {Ref: ARDE I:27}

GILPIN, HANNAH, see "John Grubb," q.v.

GIST, CHRISTOPHER (Maryland), b. c1705, Baltimore Co., son of Richard Gist and Zipporah Murray, m. Sarah Howard, had children Richard (b. 2 Sep 1729, killed at the Battle of King's Mountain, SC in 1780), Violetta (b. 4 Jul 1731), Nathaniel (b. 15 Oct 1733), Anne (or Nancy), and Thomas (c1736-1785), and d. in the summer of 1759 in South Carolina or Georgia; merchant and coroner in Baltimore Co. in 1743-1745; by 1750 he was living on the Yadkin River in

North Carolina; explored and surveyed parts of Ohio and Kentucky for the Ohio Company in 1750-1751, and was guide and companion of George Washington on his journey to Lake Erie in 1753; served as a guide and scout in General Braddock's expedition (with sons Nathaniel and Thomas) and the defeat in 1755; commissioned lieut. in the VA Forces on 1 Oct 1755 and was at Fort Cumberland, MD by June 1756; captain of a company of scouts or rangers in the VA militia on 13 Jul 1756; went to the Carolinas to enlist Cherokee Indians for the English service and for a time he served as Indian Agent before he died of smallpox in 1759. {Ref: BCF:258; MSR I:37; *MD Gazette*, 10 Jun 1756; MDG I:507-508' SLMH II:106}

GIST, JOHN (Maryland), b. 22 Nov 1738, son of Thomas Gist and Susan Cockey, d. 1800. {Ref: BCF:258; MDG I:409} Pvt., Capt. Tobias Stansbury's Company Muster Roll, Baltimore Co., circa 1757-1758, exact dates not given; bill of credit issued or paid in his behalf to Thomas Gist for £3.10.0 on 18 Mar 1767. {Ref: MSA S960 or S752, p. 186}

GIST, NATHANIEL (Maryland), b. 15 Oct 1733, son of Christopher Gist and Sarah Howard, m. Judith Cary Bell, had children Henry Cary, Thomas Cecil, Sarah Howard, Judith Cary, Anne Cary, Eliza Violet, and Maria Cecil, and d. after 1800 in Kentucky; served with his father and brother Thomas at General Braddock's defeat on the Monongahela in 1755 and later served in the Revolutionary War; commissioned colonel of the Extra Regiment in the Continental Army on 11 Jan 1777, was taken prisoner at Charleston on 12 May 1780, and retired from service on 1 Jan 1781. {Ref: MDG I:509-510}

GIST, RICHARD, see "Christopher Gist," q.v.

GIST, THOMAS, see "John Gist," q.v.

GIST, WILLIAM, see "Charles Howard," q.v.

GLASSFORD, JOHN (Maryland), farmer; pvt., Capt. Peregrine Brown's 7th Co. of Foot Militia, Kent Co., on 19 Feb 1758, by which time he had enlisted, but reportedly refused to appear and serve in arms against the enemy. {Ref: ARMD 31:283, 288}

GLAZIER, FREDERICK (Maryland), sgt., Capt. John Dagworthy's Company of MD Troops, Frederick Co., from 9 Oct 1757 to 9 Nov 1758 (at which time he was demoted to cpl.) and served until 16 Mar 1759 when he reportedly deserted; however, payment to him was recorded in Col. Dagworthy's account book on 8 Mar 1763. {Ref: MHS MS.375.1; CSOS:76; MHS MS.375}

GLEBRA (GLIBRA), JOHN (Maryland), pvt., Capt. Francis Ware's Company of MD Troops, Charles Co., circa 9 Oct 1757 to 30 Dec 1758. {Ref: MHS MS.375.1; CSOS:88} Payment to him was recorded in Col. Dagworthy's account book on 7 Mar 1763. {Ref: MHS MS.375}

GLEGHORN, MATTHEW (Delaware), b. c1724, Ireland (laborer, age 34 in 1758); pvt., recruited by Capt. Benjamin Noxon and enlisted on 8 May 1758. {Ref: ARDE I:19; ARPA (2nd Series) 2:566}

GODSON, JAMES (Maryland), pvt., Capt. John Dagworthy's Company of MD Troops, Frederick Co., from 1 Jun 1758 to 28 Jul 1758 (served 58 days), having transferred from Capt. Richard Pearis' Company, and was discharged (mistakenly reported as deserted); payment to him was recorded in Col. Dagworthy's account book on 17 Jul 1762. {Ref: MHS MS.375.1; CSOS:76; MHS MS.375}

GOLDEN, ELEAZER (Delaware), b. c1724, Cape May, NJ (sailor, age 34 in 1758); pvt., enlisted 25 Apr 1758 "for the campaign in the lower counties" by Capt. John McClughan. {Ref: ARDE I:17; ARPA (2nd Series) 2:570}

GOLDER, JOHN (Maryland), patriot, Annapolis, Anne Arundel Co., pay account submitted for quartering soldiers in 1757 or 1758, exact dates not given. {Ref: MHM 9:3, p. 261}

GOLDSBARRY, ROBERT (Maryland), b. c1738, MD (age 19 in 1757); pvt., 2nd Co. of VA Rangers under Capt. John Ashby on 21 Oct 1757. {Ref: MSR I:37}

GOLDSBARRY, WILLIAM (Maryland), b. c1736, MD (age 21 in 1757); pvt., 2nd Co. of VA Rangers under Capt. John Ashby on 21 Oct 1757. {Ref: MSR I:37}

GOLDSBOROUGH, CHARLES (Maryland), b. 26 Jun 1707, Talbot Co., son of Robert Goldsborough and Elizabeth Greenberry, m. 1st to Elizabeth Ennalls on 18 Jul 1730 and 2nd to Elizabeth Dickinson on 2 Aug 1739, had children Robert (1733-1788), Charles (1740-1769), and Elizabeth Greenberry (1731-1820), and d. testate on 14 Jul 1767 "of a dropsy" in Dorchester Co.; clerk of the court (1728-1738), patriot, lawyer, gentleman, member of the Lower House of the MD Assembly (1751-1762), member of the MD Council (1762-1767), and commissary general (1761-1767). {Ref: BDML I:356-358; SCWM III:113, 251; MDG II:9-14}

GOLDSBOROUGH, JOHN (Maryland), b. 12 Oct 1711, Talbot Co., son of Robert Goldsborough and Elizabeth Greenberry, m. 1st to Anne Turbutt (dau. of Foster Turbutt) on 31 Oct 1733 and m. 2nd to Mary Skinner (dau. of Richard Skinner and widow of Jacob Lookerman) by 1774, had children Robert, John, Charles, William, Elizabeth, Anne, Henrietta Maria, Mary, and Anna Maria, and d. 18 Jan 1778, Talbot Co.; patriot, planter, sheriff (1736-1739), justice (1741-1777), member of the Lower House of the MD Assembly (1742-1770), and "member of the Stamp Act Court that adjourned in 1765 rather than enforce the act." {Ref: BDML I:359-360; MDG II:19-21}

GOLDSBOROUGH, WILLIAM (Maryland), b. 6 Jul 1709, Talbot Co., son of Robert Goldsborough and Elizabeth Greenberry, m. 1st to Elizabeth Robins (sister of George Robins) on 23 Jan 1734/5 and m. 2nd to Henrietta Maria Robins (widow of George Robins and dau. of Richard Tilghman) on 2 Sep 1747, had children Greenbury, William, Henrietta Maria, and Elizabeth H. (all d. young), and d. 21 Sep 1760; lawyer, gentleman, justice of the Provincial Court (1754-1757), colonel by 1755, member of MD Assembly (1755-1760), member of MD Council (1755-1760), and Judge of the Court of Vice Admiralty (appointed 1756). In 1760 Gov. Horatio Sharpe remarked that "No person in the country had a better character than this gentleman ... nor have I been disappointed in my expectations concerning him." {Ref: BDML I:364-366; *MD Gazette*, 25 Sep 1760; MDG II:14-18}

GOOD, JACOB (Maryland), of Taney Town, m. Eleanor (N), had a dau. Mary, and d. testate by 12 Apr 1783. {Ref: WMG 6:1, p. 33} Pvt., Capt. Moses Chapline's

Company Muster Roll No. 3, Frederick Co., circa 1757-1758, exact dates not given; bill of credit issued or paid in his behalf to Joseph Chaplin for £0.6.0 on 5 Mar 1767. {Ref: MSA S960 or S752, p. 198}

GOOD, RICHARD, see "John McNeill," q.v.

GOOD, WILLIAM (Maryland), pvt., Capt. Joseph Chapline's Company Muster Roll No. 5, Frederick Co., circa 1757-1758, exact dates not given; bill of credit issued or paid in his behalf to Joseph Chaplin for £0.8.0 on 5 Mar 1767. {Ref: MSA S960 or S752, p. 195} See "George Coon" and "Jacob Rise," q.v.

GOODING, ISAAC (Delaware), ensign, St. George's Hundred, Lower Regt. of Militia, New Castle Co., 1756; subscribed to the Oath of Fidelity and Allegiance in 1778. {Ref: ARDE I:11; ARPA (2nd Series) 2:525; HDE I:1411 RPDE:102}

GOODING, JACOB (Delaware), captain, Red Lion Hundred, Lower Regt. of Militia, New Castle Co., 1756. {Ref: ARDE I:12; ARPA (2nd Series) 2:525; HDE I:141} Patriot who served as a Justice of the Peace, Justice of the Court of Oyer and Terminer, Justice of the Court of Common Pleas in 1756, and rendered material aid to the military during the Revolutionary War in 1776. {Ref: GRSD 1:13; RPDE:102}

GOODING, JACOB JR. (Delaware), 1st lieut., New Castle Co., 18 Apr 1758, and promoted to capt. on 13 Jun 1758. {Ref: ARDE I:16; ARPA (2nd Series) 2:579-580}

GOODING, JOHN (Delaware), pvt., Kent Co. Militia, Capt. John Caton's Company, 25 Apr 1757 (date of muster roll). {Ref: ARDE I:14}

GOODSON, THOMAS (Maryland), sgt., Capt. Thomas Norris' Company, Frederick Co., circa 1757-1758, exact dates not given (served 30 days); bill of credit issued or paid to him for £2 in 1767, exact date not given. {Ref: MSA S960 or S752, p. 176; CSOS:107}

GOODWIN, MATHEW (Maryland), pvt., Capt. Richard Pearis' Company of MD Troops, Frederick Co., circa 9 Oct 1757 to 31 May 1758; pvt., Capt. John Dagworthy's Company of MD Troops, Frederick Co., from 1 Jun 1758 to 2 Jan 1759 (served 215 days) and reportedly deserted; however, payment to him was recorded in Col. Dagworthy's account book on 14 Jul 1762. {Ref: MHS MS.375.1; CSOS:76, 90; MHS MS.375}

GOODWIN, PLEASANCE, see "John Smith," q.v.

GOODWIN, RACHEL, see "Jesse Hollingsworth," q.v.

GOODWIN, WILLIAM, see "Nathaniel Owings," q.v.

GORDEN, ANDREW, see "Empson Bird," q.v.

GORDON, JOHN, see "Robert Gordon," q.v.

GORDON, ROBERT (Delaware), son of John Gordon and Elizabeth Caldwell, m. Filles or Philis (N), had sons John and Robert, and d. testate by 15 Feb 1759. {Ref: CFD 2:89} Pvt., Kent Co. Militia, Capt. John Caton's Company, 25 Apr 1757 (date of muster roll). {Ref: ARDE I:13}

GORDON, WILLIAM (Maryland), pvt., Capt. Elias Delashmutt's Company Muster Roll, Frederick Co., 13 Aug 1757, exact dates not given (served 52 days); bill of credit issued or paid to him in March 1767 for £1.10.0; name mistakenly transcribed once as "William Groddu." {Ref: MSA S960 or S752, p. 162; CSOS:98}

GORE, CLEMENT (Maryland), pvt., Capt. William Luckett's Company Muster Roll, Frederick Co., circa 1757-1758, exact dates not given (served 30 days); bill of credit issued or paid in his behalf to William Luckett, Jr. for £1.10.0 on 6 Apr 1767. {Ref: MSA S960 or S752, p. 169; CSOS:99}

GORE, JAMES (Maryland), cpl., Capt. William Luckett's Company Muster Roll, Frederick Co., circa 1757-1758, exact dates not given (served 30 days); bill of credit issued or paid in his behalf to William Luckett, Jr. for £2 on 6 Apr 1767. {Ref: MSA S960 or S752, p. 169; CSOS:99}

GORE, JAMES MANNEN (Maryland), pvt., Capt. William Luckett's Company Muster Roll, Frederick Co., circa 1757-1758, exact dates not given (served 30 days); bill of credit issued or paid in his behalf to William Luckett, Jr. for £1.10.0 on 6 Apr 1767. {Ref: MSA S960 or S752, p. 170; CSOS:99} James Manning Gore m. (N) and "in consideration of the natural love and affection he has for his son James Gore" he conveyed land to him on 20 Mar 1759. {Ref: FCLR:69}

GORE, THOMAS (Maryland), pvt., Capt. William Luckett's Company Muster Roll, Frederick Co., circa 1757-1758, exact dates not given (served 30 days); bill of credit issued or paid in his behalf to William Luckett, Jr. for £1.4.0 on 6 Apr 1767. {Ref: MSA S960 or S752, p. 169; CSOS:100}

GORMAN, JOHN (Maryland), pvt., Capt. John Dagworthy's Company of MD Troops, Frederick Co., circa 9 Oct 1757 to 26 Apr 1759; payment to him was recorded in Col. Dagworthy's account book on 22 Feb 1763. {Ref: MHS MS.375.1; CSOS:76; MHS MS.375}

GORRELL, JAMES (Maryland), ensign in Capt. Joshua Beall's Company of MD Troops, Prince George's Co., from 9 Oct 1757 to 28 Jun 1758; ensign in Capt. John Dagworthy's Company of MD Troops, Frederick Co., from 29 Jun 1758 to 8 Nov 1758 (served 133 days); promoted to 2nd lieut. and served from 9 Nov 1758 to 26 Apr 1759 (169 days); name mistakenly transcribed twice as "James Garrett." {Ref: MHS MS.375.1; CSOS:75, 83} Ensign, Royal American Regt. of Foot, commissioned 30 May 1759; ensign, 1st Bttn., Royal American Regt., at Frederick Town, by February 1760; lieut., commissioned 2 Mar 1762; payment recorded in Col. Dagworthy's account book on 19 Jul 1762; granted 2,000 acres in Albany Co., NY (date not given). {Ref: MHS MS.375; *MD Gazette*, 28 Feb 1760; MHS Filing Case A} See "Peter Dent" and "Thomas Simpson," q.v.

GOSE, GEORGE (Maryland), alias George Yose or Yost *[sic]*, pvt., Capt. John Middaugh's Company Muster Roll, Frederick Co., circa 1757-1758, exact dates not given (served 30 days); bill of credit issued or paid in his behalf to Casper Shaff for £1.10.0 on 2 Mar 1767. {Ref: MSA S960 or S752, p. 171; CSOS:101}

GOSLING, EZEKIEL (Maryland), sgt., Capt. William Luckett's Company Muster Roll, Frederick Co., circa 1757-1758, exact dates not given (served 30 days); bill of credit issued or paid in his behalf to William Luckett, Jr. for £2.12.0 on 6 Apr 1767; name mistakenly transcribed once as "Ezekiel Cosling." {Ref: MSA S960 or S752, p. 170; CSOS:99}

GOSNELL, CHARLES (Maryland), b. c1736, Baltimore Co., son of Peter and Anne Gosnell, of Soldier's Delight Hundred. {Ref: BCF:269-270}. Pvt., Capt. Tobias Stansbury's Company Muster Roll, Baltimore Co., circa 1757-1758, exact dates not given; bill of credit issued or paid in his behalf to Alexander Wells for £1.15.0 on 27 Mar 1767. {Ref: MSA S960 or S752, p. 186}

GOSNELL (GARSNELL), MORDICAI (Maryland), b. MD, age 27 [transcribed as 22] in 1756; pvt., Capt. Christopher Gist's Company of VA Militia, 13 Jul 1756, enlisted at Baltimore. {Ref: MSR I:37} Mordecai Gosnell, b. 16 Jan 1729/30, son of Peter and Anne Gosnell, of Soldier's Delight Hundred, Baltimore Co. {Ref: BCF:269}

GOSTWICK, ELIZABETH, see "Samuel Sergeant," q.v.

GOSTWICK, KEZIAH, see "Edmund Stansbury," q.v.

GOTT, ANTHONY (Maryland), b. 19 Mar 1731/2, Baltimore Co., son of Richard and Sarah Gott. {Ref: BCF:272} Pvt., Capt. Tobias Stansbury's Company Muster Roll, Baltimore Co., circa 1757-1758, exact dates not given; bill of credit issued or paid in his behalf to John Connoway for £1.18.0 on 6 Mar 1767. {Ref: MSA S960 or S752, p. 186}

GOVANE, WILLIAM (Maryland), b. 4 Feb 1716/7, Anne Arundel Co., son of James Govane and Elizabeth Cockey (widow of William Hammond and dau. of William Cockey), of St. Anne's Parish, m. Anne Homewood (widow of Thomas Homewood and dau. of Charles Hammond) circa 1740, had no children, divorced by court decree in 1750, moved to Baltimore Co., lived with Mary Salisbury, had two natural children James Govane and Mary Govane, and d. September 1768, Baltimore Co.; merchant, gentleman, constable in 1749, captain by 1754, and member of the MD Assembly, 1751-1761 (served on the Arms and Ammunition Committee, 1754-1757). {Ref: BDML I:368-369; ARMD 52:605; AACR:79} See "John McDaniel" and "---- Riordan," q.v.

GOWEN, ZADOCK (Maryland), b. c1732, MD (age 24 in 1756); pvt., Capt. Christopher Gist's Company of VA Militia, 13 Jul 1756, enlisted at Baltimore. {Ref: MSR I:37}

GRABLE (GRABBLE), JOSEPH (Maryland), pvt., Capt. Jonathan Hagar's Company Muster Roll, Frederick Co., circa 1757-1758, exact dates not given (served 6 days); bill of credit issued or paid to him for £0.6.0 in 1767, exact date not given. {Ref: MSA S960 or S752, p. 174; CSOS:106}

GRAFTON, MARY, see "Daniel Dulany," q.v.

GRAFTON, RICHARD, see "Daniel Dulany," q.v.

GRAHAM, FRANCIS (Delaware), b. c1725, Ireland (laborer, age 33 in 1758); pvt., "formerly with Sir Wm. Pepperal," recruited by Capt. Benjamin Noxon and enlisted on 26 Apr 1758. {Ref: ARDE I:19; ARPA (2nd Series) 2:566}

GRAHAM, JOHN (Delaware), b. c1737, Slator Neck, DE (laborer, age 21 in 1758); pvt., enlisted 24 Apr 1758 "for the campaign in the lower counties" by Capt. John McClughan. {Ref: ARDE I:17; ARPA (2nd Series) 2:570}

GRAHAM, JOHN (Maryland), sgt. and clerk, Capt. Henry Casson's Company Muster Roll, Queen Anne's Co., circa 1757-1758, exact dates not given (served 27 days); bill of credit issued or paid in his behalf to Robert Loyd on 26 Feb 1767 for £1.16.0. {Ref: MSA S960 or S752, pp. 177-178: CSOS:108}

GRAHAM (GRAHAME), ROBERT (Maryland), pvt., Capt. Alexander Beall's Company of MD Troops, Frederick Co., from 9 Oct 1757 to 8 Apr 1758. {Ref:

MHS MS.375.1; CSOS:80} Payment to him was recorded in Col. Dagworthy's account book on 26 Feb 1763. {Ref: MHS MS.375}

GRANTLET, JOHN (Delaware), b. c1735, MD (laborer, age 23 in 1758); pvt., recruited by Capt. Benjamin Noxon and enlisted on 29 Apr 1758. {Ref: ARDE I:19; ARPA (2nd Series) 2:485, 566}

GRAVES, JAMES (Maryland), pvt., Capt. Joshua Beall's Company of MD Troops, Prince George's Co., circa 9 Oct 1757 to 30 Dec 1758; pvt., Capt. John Dagworthy's Company of MD Troops, Frederick Co., from 31 Dec 1758 to 16 Apr 1759, having transferred from Capt. Joshua Beall's Company where he had been reported as deserted; payment to him was recorded in Col. Dagworthy's account book on 26 Feb 1763. {Ref: MHS MS.375; CSOS:76, 84; MHS MS.375.1}

GRAY, ADAM (Maryland), patriot and poss. soldier (rank not specified), Kent Co., militia pay account submitted in 1758, exact date not given. {Ref: MHM 9:4, p. 369}

GRAY, BENJAMIN (Delaware), b. c1741, New Castle, DE (miller, age 18 in 1759); pvt., enlisted by Capt. James Armstrong for the PA Regt. on 7 May 1759. {Ref: ARDE I:26; ARPA (2nd Series) 2:585}

GRAY, JOSEPH COX (Maryland), b. c1720, son of Joseph and Elizabeth Gray, m. 1st to Sarah Lookerman by 1741 and 2nd to Rosannah Lookerman (widow of Jacob Lookerman and dau. of James Woolford) by 1745, had children James, Joseph, John, Sarah, and Rosalinda, and d. before 24 May 1764, Dorchester Co.; county justice (1754-1764), member of the MD Assembly (1753-1763), and captain by 1764. {Ref: BDML I:371-372; MD Admin. Accts. 12:673; *MD Gazette*, 24 May 1764}

GRAY, PATRICK (Maryland), patriot, Frederick Co., who performed "sundry services at the fort" in 1763 and payment in the amount of £0.4.6 was still owed to him on 25 Nov 1763 (when reported by the Accounts Committee to the MD Assembly). {Ref: ARMD 58:400}

GRAY, SARAH, see "John Clark," q.v.

GRAY, THOMAS (Delaware), captain, Mill Creek Hundred, Upper Regt. of Militia, South Division, New Castle Co., 1756. {Ref: ARDE I:11; ARPA (2nd Series) 2:526; HDE I:141}

GRAYBILL, HENRY (Maryland), sgt., Capt. William McClellan's Company of MD Volunteers, Frederick Co., circa 1763-1764; on muster roll dated 15 Nov 1764 at Camp at the Forks of Muskingham. {Ref: ARMD 32:99}

GREATHOUSE (GRATEHOUSE), HARMAN (Maryland), pvt., Capt. Joseph Chapline's Company Muster Roll No. 4, Frederick Co., circa 1757-1758, exact dates not given (served 5 days); bill of credit issued or paid in his behalf to Joseph Chaplin for £0.5.0 on 5 Mar 1767. {Ref: MSA S960 or S752, p. 194; CSOS:105}

GREAVES (GRAVES), WILLIAM (Maryland), pvt., Capt. Elias Delashmutt's Company Muster Roll, Frederick Co., circa 1757-1758, exact dates not given (served 30 days); bill of credit issued or paid in his behalf to Elias Delashmut, Jr. on 16 Mar 1767 for £1.10.0. {Ref: MSA S960 or S752, p. 162; CSOS:94}

GREEN, ANN CATHERINE, see "Jonas Green," q.v.

GREEN, ELISHA, see "Benjamin Hall," q.v.

GREEN, JAMES (Maryland), pvt., Capt. William Luckett's Company Muster Roll, Frederick Co., circa 1757-1758, exact dates not given (served 30 days); bill of credit issued or paid in his behalf to William Luckett, Jr. for £1.10.0 on 6 Apr 1767. {Ref: MSA S960 or S752, p. 169; CSOS:99}

GREEN, JOHN (Maryland), pvt., Capt. Tobias Stansbury's Company Muster Roll, Baltimore Co., circa 1757-1758, exact dates not given; bill of credit issued or paid to him for £1.18.0 in 1767, exact date not given. {Ref: MSA S960 or S752, p. 186} *Identification problem:* There were four men with this name who could have served in the war: (1) John Green, b. 16 Aug 1720, son of Robert Green and Susanna Haile; (2) John Green m. Mary Sampson in December 1720; (3) John Green m. Anna Hardesty on 8 Mar 1753; and, (4) John Green m. Catherine Todd on 27 Mar 1757. {Ref: BCF:276-278}

GREEN, JONAS (Maryland), patriot and printer, Annapolis, Anne Arundel Co., m. Ann Catherine (N) by 1738, St. Anne's Parish; had children John (1738-1739), Rebecca (b. 22 Sep 1740), Catherine (1743-1744), Mary (b. 9 Jan 1745/6), William (b. 21 Dec 1746), Anne Catherine (1748-1753), Frederick (b. 20 Jan 1750/1), Elizabeth (1753-1755), Jonas (1755-1756), Samuel (b. 27 Apr 1757), and Augusta (b. 4 Apr 1760); pay account submitted for quartering soldiers in 1757 or 1758, exact dates not given. {Ref: MHM 9:3, p. 261; AACR:98-104}

GREEN, ROBERT, see "John Green," q.v.

GREEN, VALENTINE (Maryland), sgt., Capt. Henry Casson's Company Muster Roll, Queen Anne's Co., circa 1757-1758, exact dates not given (served 27 days); bill of credit issued or paid in his behalf to Capt. Casson for Green's exec. (unnamed) on 27 Feb 1767 for £1.16.0. {Ref: MSA S960 or S752, p. 177; CSOS:108}

GREEN, WILLIAM (Delaware), b. c1737, Sussex, DE (carpenter, age 22 in 1759); sgt., enlisted in Capt. John Wright's Company and mustered on 11 May 1759. {Ref: ARDE I:25; ARPA (2nd Series) 2:592}

GREENBERRY, ELIZABETH, see "John Goldsborough" and "Charles Goldsborough" and "William Goldsborough," q.v.

GREENFIELD, ELIZABETH, see "Micajah Greenfield" and "Thomas Greenfield," q.v.

GREENFIELD, ELEANOR SMITH, see "Joshua Beall," q.v.

GREENFIELD, LIEUT., see "Morris Dickson," q.v.

GREENFIELD, MICAJAH (Maryland), b. 24 Jul 1733, Baltimore Co., son of William and Elizabeth Greenfield. {Ref: BCF:279} Pvt., Capt. Tobias Stansbury's Company Muster Roll, Baltimore Co., circa 1757-1758, exact dates not given; bill of credit issued or paid in his behalf to John Hall, Jr. for £3.16.0 on 30 Apr 1767; name listed once as "Micajah Greendfield." {Ref: MSA S960 or S752, p. 186}

GREENFIELD, THOMAS (Maryland), b. c1715, St. Mary's Company, son of Maj. Trueman Greenfield and Elizabeth (N), m. Dorothy Barber, had children Trueman, Thomas, Rebecca, and Dorothy, and d. testate by 15 Apr 1774; planter, miller, inspector, captain by 1749, and county justice (1755-1773). {Ref: BDML I:374-375}

GREENFIELD, THOMAS SMITH (Maryland), cpl., Capt. Joshua Beall's Company Muster Roll, Prince George's Co., circa 1757-1758, exact dates not given; bill of credit issued or paid in his behalf to John Harrison for £2.17.4½ on 11 Mar 1767. {Ref: MSA S960 or S752, p. 184}

GREENFIELD, TRUEMAN, see "Thomas Greenfield," q.v.

GREENFIELD, WALTER SMITH (Maryland), sgt., Capt. Joshua Beall's Company Muster Roll, Prince George's Co., circa 1757-1758, exact dates not given; bill of credit issued or paid to him for £2.17.4½ on 30 Mar 1767. {Ref: MSA S960 or S752, p. 184}

GREENFIELD, WILLIAM, see "Micajah Greenfield," q.v.

GREENWOOD, BENJAMIN (Maryland), farmer; pvt., Capt. Peregrine Brown's 7th Co. of Foot Militia, Kent Co., on 19 Feb 1758, by which time he had enlisted, but reportedly refused to appear and serve in arms against the enemy; he later stated that he was "a minor under age as was his brother, and both the sons of a poor old distressed widow who had nobody else but these sons for her whole support, to get her firewood, feed her stock, and take care of her affairs, that she consented one of her sons should go with Capt. Browne but laid her commands on the other to stay with her or she must perish as well as her stock if they both went and left her, on which the other son went and Benjamin stayed with his mother." {Ref: ARMD 31:283, 286, 288}

GREENWOOD, CALEB (Maryland), pvt., Capt. Elias Delashmutt's Company Muster Roll, Frederick Co., circa 1757-1758, exact dates not given (served 30 days); bill of credit issued or paid in his behalf to Casper Shaff on 2 Mar 1767 for £1.10.0. {Ref: MSA S960 or S752, p. 162; CSOS:94}

GREENWOOD, JAMES (Maryland), b. c1725, m. Rebecca Stavely on 10 Feb 1749/50 in Shrewsbury Parish, Kent Co., and their son James was b. 20 Aug 1750. {Ref: ESVR} Pvt., Capt. Peregrine Brown's Company Muster Roll, Kent Co., circa 1757-1758, exact dates not given (served 15 days); bill of credit issued or paid in his behalf to Robert Buchanan for Greenwood's admin. (unnamed) on 20 Feb 1767 for £0.15.0. {Ref: MSA S960 or S752, p. 179; CSOS:119}

GREENWOOD, JOSEPH (Delaware), pvt., Capt. French Battell's Company of Lower County Provincials, enlisted 18 May 1758. {Ref: ARDE I:16; ARPA (2nd Series) 2:555}

GREENWOOD, JOSEPH (Maryland), pvt., Capt. Peregrine Brown's Company Muster Roll, Kent Co., circa 1757-1758, exact dates not given (served 15 days); bill of credit issued or paid in his behalf to Robert Buchanan on 21 Mar 1767 for £0.15.0. {Ref: MSA S960 or S752, p. 179; CSOS:110}

GREENWOOD, SARAH, see "Jonathan Turner," q.v.

GREENWOOD, WILLIAM (Maryland), b. c1736, Prince George's Co. (age 21 in 1757); soldier who was reported by Lieut. Greenfield, at Annapolis, as deserted from a recruiting party at Joppa, in Baltimore County, commanded by Maj. Gen. Abercrombie. {Ref: *MD Gazette*, 3 Mar 1757}

GREGORY, JAMES (Maryland), b. 9 Sep 1734, Baltimore Co., son of John and Elizabeth Gregory. {Ref: BCF:282} Pvt., Capt. Tobias Stansbury's Company Muster Roll, Baltimore Co., circa 1757-1758, exact dates not given; bill of credit issued or paid in his behalf to Thomas Sollars for £1.19.0 on 20 Feb 1767. {Ref: MSA S960 or S752, p. 186}

GREWELL, JOHN (Delaware), pvt., Kent Co. Militia, Capt. John Caton's Company, 25 Apr 1757 (date of muster roll). {Ref: ARDE I:13}

GREY, GABRIEL (Maryland), pvt., Capt. Francis Ware's Company of MD Troops, Charles Co., circa 9 Oct 1757 to 30 Dec 1758; payment to him was recorded in Col. Dagworthy's account book on 7 Mar 1763; name listed once as "Gabriel or Sabriet Grey." {Ref: MHS MS.375.1; CSOS:88; MHS MS.375}

GREY, JAMES (Maryland), pvt., Capt. Richard Pearis' Company of MD Troops, Frederick Co., from 9 Oct 1757 to 31 May 1758. {Ref: MHS MS.375.1} Payment to him was recorded in Col. Dagworthy's account book on 17 Jul 1762. {Ref: MHS MS.375}

GRIBBIN, JAMES (Delaware), b. c1731, MD (laborer, age 27 in 1758); pvt., recruited by Capt. Benjamin Noxon and enlisted on 29 Apr 1758. {Ref: ARDE I:19; ARPA (2nd Series) 2:485, 566}

GRIEST, MARY, see "John Garrison," q.v.

GRIFFIN, BENJAMIN (Maryland), pvt., Capt. John Dagworthy's Company of MD Troops, Frederick Co., cicra 9 Oct 1757 to 26 Apr 1759. {Ref: MHS MS.375.1; CSOS:76} Payment to him was recorded in Col. Dagworthy's account book on 13 Jul 1762. {Ref: MHS MS.375} An account submitted to the MD Assembly on 25 Nov 1763 indicated he was due £4.12.3 as "granted by the Act for Granting a Sum of Money as a Present to the Forces, late in the Pay and Service of this Province, and taken into his Majesty's Service by Brigadier General Forbes." {Ref: ARMD 58:401}

GRIFFIN, EDWARD (Maryland), sgt., Calvert Co., Capt. Edward Gantt's Militia Co., Lyon's Creek Hundred circa 1756-1757 (exact dates not given). {Ref: HCC:120}

GRIFFITH, LUKE, see "Morris Dixon," q.v.

GRIFFITH, SARAH, see "Charles Dorsey," q.v.

GRILL, ANDREW (Maryland), indentured servant and soldier who served in the French and Indian War some time between 1756 and 1763 (exact dates not known); his master, Dr. William Lyon, requested compensation from the Baltimore County Court due to the loss of use of Grill while in the service. {Ref: MHM 94:4, p. 426, citing Baltimore Co. Court Minutes}

GRIM, ANDREW (Maryland), cpl., Capt. John White's Company Muster Roll, Frederick Co., circa 1757-1758, exact dates not given (served 6 days); bill of credit issued or paid to him for £0.8.0 in 1767, exact date not given. {Ref: MSA S960 or S752, p. 164; CSOS:95}

GRIMES, EDWARD (Maryland), pvt., Capt. Peter Bainbridge's Company Muster Roll, Frederick Co., circa 1757-1758, exact dates not given (served 41 days); bill of credit issued or paid in his behalf to Joseph Chaplin on 5 Mar 1767 for £2.1.0. {Ref: MSA S960 or S752, p. 181; CSOS:111}

GRIMES, HUGH (Maryland), pvt., Capt. Alexander Beall's Company of MD Troops, Frederick Co., circa 9 Oct 1757 to 30 Dec 1758. {Ref: MHS MS.375.1; CSOS:80} Payment to him was recorded in Col. Dagworthy's account book on 26 Feb 1763. {Ref: MHS MS.375}

GRIMES, MARTIN (Maryland), pvt., Capt. John Middaugh's Company Muster Roll, Frederick Co., circa 1757-1758, exact dates not given (served 30 days); bill of credit issued or paid in his behalf to Robert Wood for £1.10.0 on 4 Mar 1767. {Ref: MSA S960 or S752, p. 172; CSOS:101}

GRISSAL, WILLIAM (Delaware), b. c1726, Stroud, England (scribler, age 32 in 1758); pvt., enlisted 12 May 1758 "for the campaign in the lower counties" by Capt. John McClughan. {Ref: ARDE I:17; ARPA (2nd Series) 2:570}

GROOME, SAMUEL (Maryland), pvt., Capt. Peregrine Brown's Company Muster Roll, Kent Co., circa 1757-1758, exact dates not given (served 15 days); bill of credit issued or paid in his behalf to Thomas Ringgold, Esq. on 20 Feb 1767 for £1.15.0. {Ref: MSA S960 or S752, p. 179; CSOS:110}

GROSH, CONRAD (Maryland), ensign in Capt. Peter Butler's Company Muster Roll, Frederick Co., circa 1757-1758, exact dates not given (served 34 days). {Ref: CSOS:96} Militia pay account submitted in 1758, exact date not given. {Ref: MHM 9:4, p. 369} Bill of credit or order issued in his behalf for £3.8.0 and paid to Peter Grosh on 4 Mar 1767. {Ref: MSA S960 or S752, p. 168} He was paid £9 at Fort Frederick on 19 Jul 1758 for carrying 3 loads of corn to Fort Frederick for the Western Expedition against Fort Duquesne. {Ref: ARMD 55:774}

GROSH, PETER (Maryland), pvt., Capt. Peter Butler's Company Muster Roll, Frederick Co., circa 1757-1758, exact dates not given; bill of credit or order issued to him for £1.14.0 on 4 Mar 1767. {Ref: MSA S960 or S752, p. 168} See "Henry Sneavely," q.v.

GROSNICKLE, JOHN, see "Lawrence Delater," q.v.

GROVE, GEORGE (Maryland), pvt., Capt. Tobias Stansbury's Company Muster Roll, Baltimore Co., circa 1757-1758, exact dates not given; bill of credit issued or paid in his behalf to his admin. (unnamed) for £2.12.0 on 11 Sep 1771. {Ref: MSA S960 or S752, p. 187} He may have been the George Groves (brother of William Groves, and sons of George and Dorothy Groves) who m. Johanna Rigbie on 26 Aug 1752. {Ref: BCF:285}

GROVE, VALENTINE (Maryland), patriot and poss. soldier (rank not specified), Frederick Co., militia pay account submitted in 1758, exact date not given. {Ref: MHM 9:4, p. 366}

GROVE, WILLIAM (Maryland), pvt., Capt. Tobias Stansbury's Company Muster Roll, Baltimore Co., circa 1757-1758, exact dates not given; bill of credit issued or paid to him for £1.10.0 on 11 Sep 1771. {Ref: MSA S960 or S752, p. 187} He may have been the William Groves who was the brother of George Groves (sons of George and Dorothy Groves). {Ref: BCF:285}

GROVES, JONATHAN (Delaware), b. c1738, New Castle, DE (laborer, age 20 in 1758); pvt., enlisted 24 Apr 1758 "for the campaign in the lower counties" by Capt. John McClughan. {Ref: ARDE I:17; ARPA (2nd Series) 2:570}

GROVES, JOSEPH (Maryland), pvt., Capt. William Luckett's Company Muster Roll, Frederick Co., circa 1757-1758, exact dates not given (served 30 days); bill of credit issued or paid in his behalf to William Luckett, Jr. for £1.10.0 on 6 Apr 1767. {Ref: MSA S960 or S752, p. 169; CSOS:99}

GROWDEN, LAWRENCE (Delaware), New Castle Co., patriot who served as a Justice of the Peace and a Justice of the Court of Oyer and Terminer, 1756-1761. {Ref: GRSD 1:13, 15}

GRUBB, EMANUEL JR. (Delaware), son of Emanuel Grubb (d. 1767) and Anne Hedge Koch, m. Anne (N), had children Benjamin, Peter, James, Nicholas, and William Ford; served in the French and Indian War in 1756 and also in the Revolutionary War in 1775; d. testate by 17 Aug 1799. {Ref: CFD 5:83; CDSS:79; RPDE:109} Captain, Brandywine Hundred, Upper Regt. of Militia, Northeast Division, New Castle Co., 1756. {Ref: ARDE I:11; ARPA (2nd Series) 2:526; HDE I:141}

GRUBB, JOHN (Delaware), b. c1732, prob. son of William Grubb and Lydia Hewes, m. Hannah Gilpin in 1769, served in the French and Indian War in 1758 and in the Revolutionary War in 1778, and d. testate in 1796. {Ref: CFD 5:88; RPDE:109} Pvt., enlisted 11 May 1758 "for the campaign in the lower counties" by Capt. John McClughan; b. Brandywine Hundred, DE (tanner, age 26 in 1758). {Ref: ARDE I:17; ARPA (2nd Series) 2:570}

GRUBB, SAMUEL (Delaware or Pennsylvania), captain and recruiting officer for PA Troops in Wilmington Township in 1758. {Ref: ARDE I:27}

GRUBB, WILLIAM, see "John Grubb," q.v.

GRUNDY, THOMAS (Delaware), b. c1725, Liverpool, England (bricklayer, age 33 in 1758); pvt., enlisted 27 Apr 1758 "for the campaign in the lower counties" by Capt. John McClughan. {Ref: ARDE I:17; ARPA (2nd Series) 2:570}

GRUNNET, CHRISTOPHER (Delaware), b. c1729, Germany (saddler, age 30 in 1759); pvt., enlisted by Capt. James Armstrong for the PA Regt. on 1 May 1759. {Ref: ARDE I:26; ARPA (2nd Series) 2:585}

GUMRY, SAMUEL (Delaware), b. c1738, England (weaver, age 20 in 1758); pvt., recruited by Capt. Benjamin Noxon and enlisted on 2 May 1758. {Ref: ARDE I:19; ARPA (2nd Series) 2:566}

GUNDY, ROBERT (Maryland), pvt., Capt. John Dagworthy's Company of MD Troops, Frederick Co., circa 9 Oct 1757 to 26 Apr 1759. {Ref: MHS MS.375.1; CSOS:76} Payment to him was recorded in Col. Dagworthy's account book on 11 Jul 1762 for work on Fort Cumberland. {Ref: MHS MS.375}

GUTTRIDGE (GUTRIDGE), JAMES (Maryland), pvt., Capt. Elias Delashmutt's Company Muster Roll, Frederick Co., 1757, exact dates not given (served 30 days); pvt., Capt. Alexander Beall's Company of MD Troops, Frederick Co., from 9 Oct 1757 to 31 May 1758 when he was discharged. {Ref: MHS MS.375.1; CSOS:80, 94} He recorded his discharge in Frederick Co. Court on 20 Nov 1759. Capt. Beall certified that "James Gutridge served as a private soldier for 14 months, who is unfit for the campaign, he is at his own request and by order of his Excellency the Governor hereby discharged, having received his clothing and other necessaries granted soldiers, and also full pay to 4 Jan last, inclusive. And I do further certify that he has a demand on the said Province for 148 days pay at the rate of 9 pence a day from the said 4 Jan to his discharge. Signed at Fort Frederick, 31 May 1758." {Ref: FCLR:86} Payment to him was recorded in Col. Dagworthy's account book on 11 Jul 1762. {Ref: MHS MS.375} Bill of credit issued or paid in his behalf to Elias Delashmut, Jr. on 16 Mar 1767 for £1.10.0. {Ref: MSA S960 or S752, p. 162}

GUY, NICHOLAS (Delaware), b. c1738, VA (age 21 in 1759); pvt., enlisted in Capt. John Wright's Company and mustered on 11 May 1759. {Ref: ARDE I:25; ARPA (2nd Series) 2:592}

GUYTON, SAMUEL (Maryland), b. 6 Nov 1727, Baltimore Co., son of John and Mary Guyton. {Ref: BCF:287} Pvt., Capt. Tobias Stansbury's Company Muster Roll, Baltimore Co., circa 1757-1758, exact dates not given; bill of credit issued or paid to him for £2.10.7½ in 1767, exact date not given. {Ref: MSA S960 or S752, p. 186}

GWIN, MARY, see "John Hall," q.v.

GWINN, JOHN, see "Arthur Lee," q.v.

HACK, JOHN (Maryland), pvt., Capt. Francis Ware's Company of MD Troops, Charles Co., circa 9 Oct 1757 to 30 Dec 1758. {Ref: MHS MS.375.1; CSOS:88} Payment to him was recorded in Col. Dagworthy's account book on 12 Jul 1762. {Ref: MHS MS.375}

HACKADORN (HICKADORN), JACOB (Maryland), pvt., Capt. Stephen Rensburg's or Rensburger's Company Muster Roll, Frederick Co., circa 1757-1758, exact dates not given (served 34 days); bill of credit or order issued to Casper Shaff and paid to David Cumming for £1.14.0 on 18 Apr 1767. {Ref: MSA S960 or S752, p. 183; CSOS:112}

HACKET (HACKETT), PETER (Maryland), pvt., Capt. Elias Delashmutt's Company Muster Roll, Frederick Co., 13 Aug 1757, exact dates not given (served 52 days); bill of credit issued or paid in his behalf to Elias Delashmut, Jr. on 16 Mar 1767 for £2.12.0. {Ref: MSA S960 or S752, p. 163; CSOS:98}

HAGAR (HAGER), JONATHAN (Maryland), b. c1715-1720, Germany, immigrated to MD circa 1730, m. Elizabeth Kirshner in 1740, had children Jonathan Jr. and Rosina, and was killed in an accident at his sawmill on 6 Nov 1775; miller, founder of Elizabeth Town (now Hagerstown), captain by 1757, and member of MD Assembly (1771-1773). {Ref: BDML I:379-380} Captain, Frederick Co., circa 1757-1758, exact dates not given; militia pay account submitted in 1758, exact date not given. {Ref: MHM 9:4, p. 367; CSOS:106} Bill of credit issued or paid in his behalf to James Smith for £1 on 18 May 1767. {Ref: MSA S 960 or S 752, p. 173} See "Nicholas Pearce" and "Henry Creamore" and "Hannover Davis," q.v.

HAGARD, WILLIAM (Delaware), b. c1739, Ulster, Ireland (cordwainer, age 20 in 1759); pvt., enlisted by Capt. James Armstrong for the PA Regt. on 29 Apr 1759. {Ref: ARDE I:26; ARPA (2nd Series) 2:585}

HAILE, SUSANNA, see "John Green," q.v.

HAILS (HALES), ROGER (Maryland), pvt., Capt. Peregrine Brown's Company, Kent Co., on 19 Feb 1758, by which time he had enlisted, but was unable to march due to health problems. {Ref: ARMD 31:283} Roger Hales, of Kent Co., farmer, m. Mary (N), had no children, and d. testate by 18 Feb 1779. {Ref: Kent Co. Wills 6:110}

HAINES, JACOBUS JR. (Delaware), pvt., Capt. Richard McWilliams' Company of Foot, New Castle Co., enlisted 28 Dec 1757; pvt., Capt. Isaac Grantham's Company, 1778 (noted as being above 50 years of age). {Ref: ARDE I:14; RPDE:110}

HAINES, MOSES (Maryland), indentured servant and soldier who served in the French and Indian War some time between 1756 and 1763 (exact dates not known); his master Thomas Harrison, merchant, requested compensation from the Baltimore County Court due to the loss of use of Haines while in the service. {Ref: MHM 94:4, p. 426, citing Baltimore Co. Court Minutes}

HAIZMAN, HENRY (Maryland), pvt., Capt. Tobias Stansbury's Company Muster Roll, Baltimore Co., circa 1757-1758, exact dates not given; bill of credit issued or paid to him for £1.19.0 in 1767, exact date not given. {Ref: MSA S960 or S752, p. 186}

HALDIMAND, COLONEL (Maryland), by 1757, was "in command of the 2nd Battn. of Royal Americans, living at Annapolis for the winter, helped celebrate the birthday of the Princess Dowager of Wales yesterday." {Ref: *MD Gazette*, 1 Dec 1757}

HALL, ANNE, see "Henry Hall," q.v.

HALL, AQUILA (Maryland), b. 10 Jan 1727/8, Baltimore Co., son of Aquila Hall and Johanna (Kemp) Phillips (widow of James Phillips), m. his cousin Sophia White (dau. of Col. Thomas White and Sophia Hall) on 14 Feb 1750, had children Thomas, James White, Aquila, William, John, Edward, Benedict, Charlotte, Mary, Sophia, Martha, and Elizabeth, and d. testate by 10 Apr 1779, Harford Co.; planter, merchant, miller, esquire, gentleman justice (1757-1762, 1769-1779), sheriff (1762-1763), member of the Lower House of the MD Assembly at times between 1770-1778, served on the Committee of Observation in 1774-1775 at the beginning of the Revolutionary War (one undocumented statement indicated he served on a Committee of Observation in 1761, which would have been during the French and Indian War), captain of a militia co. in 1775, county lieutenant (Harford Co.) in 1777, colonel of militia (1776-1779), and signer of the Bush Declaration on 22 Mar 1775. {Ref: St. George's P. E. Parish Register; BDML I:380; Henry C. Peden, Jr.'s *Revolutionary Patriots of Harford County, MD, 1775-1783*, pp. 98-99}

HALL, BENJAMIN (Maryland), b. 25 Jul 1732, Prince George's Co., son of Henry and Martha Hall, of Queen Anne's P. E. Parish. {Ref: PGCR 1:178} Cpl., Capt. Joshua Beall's Company Muster Roll, Prince George's Co., circa 1757-1758, exact dates not given; bill of credit issued or paid in his behalf to Elisha Green for £2.17.4½ on 13 May 1767. {Ref: MSA S960 or S752, p. 184}

HALL, DAVID (Delaware), son of Nathaniel Hall (d. 1734) and Jane (N), m. Mary Manlove circa 1745. {Ref: CFD 4:77} Captain, Northern District of Lewes and Rehoboth Hundred, Militia Regt. of Sussex Co., 1756-1758; county commissioner in 1759. {Ref: ARDE I:13, 15; ARPA (2nd Series) 2:529, 579; HDE I:141}

HALL, ELIZA, see "John Hall," q.v.

HALL, ELIZABETH, see "Henry Hall," q.v.

HALL, ESTHER, see "Moses Hall," q.v.

HALL, GEORGE (Delaware), b. c1736, Milford Hundred, DE (cooper, age 22 in 1758); pvt., enlisted 10 May 1758 "for the campaign in the lower counties" by Capt. John McClughan. {Ref: ARDE I:17; ARPA (2nd Series) 2:570}

HALL, HENRY, see "John Hall" and "Benjamin Hall," q.v.

HALL, HENRY (Maryland), b. 27 May 1727, Anne Arundel Co. (bapt. 2 Aug 1727, All Hallow's Parish), son of Henry Hall and Martha Bateman, m. Elizabeth Watkins in 1748, had children Henry, Nicholas, William, John Stephen or Stevens, Martha, Mary, Margaret, Anne, and Elizabeth, and d. testate on 11 Jan 1770; gentleman, merchant, land speculator, member of the MD Assembly (1762-1766), county justice (1752-1770), and styled major at the time of his death (dates of service not indicated). {Ref: BDML I:385; *MD Gazette*, 18 Jan 1770; AACR:42; MCW 14:116; SLMH II:114-115} Lieut. in Capt. Samuel Chapman's Company, Anne Arundel Co., circa 1757-1758, exact dates not given; bill of credit issued or paid to him for £4.8.7½ on 25 Feb 1767; also £3.16.0 was paid to him as admin. of John Watkins, £1.18.0 was paid by assignment from John Bryant, and £1.18.0 was paid by assignment from Thomas Davis. {Ref: MSA S960 or S752, p. 188}

HALL, ISAAC (Delaware), ensign, Lower Part of Mispillion Hundred, Militia of Kent Co. on Delaware, 1756. {Ref: ARDE I:12; ARPA (2nd Series) 2:527-529; HDE I:141}

HALL, JAMES, see "James Hull," q.v.

HALL, JAMES (Delaware), pvt., Kent Co. Militia, Capt. John Caton's Company, 25 Apr 1757 (date of muster roll). {Ref: ARDE I:13}

HALL, JANE, see "David Hall," q.v.

HALL, JOHN (Delaware), ensign, Northern District of Lewes and Rehoboth Hundred, Militia Regt. of Sussex Co., 1756-1758, and was reported dead in March 1758. {Ref: ARDE I:13, 15; ARPA (2nd Series) 2:529, 579; HDE I:141}

HALL, JOHN (Maryland), b. c1739, MD (age 17 in 1756); pvt., Capt. Christopher Gist's Company of VA Militia, 13 Jul 1756, enlisted at Baltimore. {Ref: MSR I:37} *Identification problem:* There were five men with this name who could have served in the war: (1) John Hall, b. 8 Oct 1737, son of John Hall and Hannah Johns, of St. George's P. E. Parish; (2) John Hall, son of Henry and Eliza Hall, of Patapsco Hundred; (3) John Hall, son of Joshua Hall and Dinah Spicer, m. 1st to Mary Price on 14 Aug 1747 and 2nd to Elizabeth Williamson; (4) John Hall, son of William Hall and Mary Gwin, who was a minor when his father died in October 1750; and, (5) John Hall, b. 31 Jul 1735, son of William Hall and Mary Merryman, of St. Paul's P. E. Parish. {Ref: BCF:293-295}

HALL, JOHN, see "John Wood" and "Richard Cheney" and "Micajah Greenfield" and "Henry Hall" and "Belcher Michael," q.v.

HALL, JOSHUA, see "John Gail" and "John Hall," q.v.

HALL, MARGARET, see "Henry Hall," q.v.

HALL, MARTHA, see "Walter Tolley" and "Henry Hall" and "Benjamin Hall," q.v.

HALL, MARY, see "Henry Hall," q.v.

HALL, MOSES (Delaware), b. c1731, MD (age 28 in 1759), m. Esther (N), and d. intestate in 1784, Sussex Co.; pvt., enlisted in Capt. John Wright's Company and mustered on 11 May 1759; subscribed to the Oath of Fidelity and Allegiance in 1779. {Ref: ARDE I:25; ARPA (2nd Series) 2:508, 592; RPDE:112}

HALL, NATHANIEL, see "David Hall," q.v.

HALL, NICHOLAS, see "Henry Hall," q.v.

HALL, PHILIP (Maryland), pvt., Capt. Samuel Chapman's Company Muster Roll, Anne Arundel Co., circa 1757-1758, exact dates not given; bill of credit issued or paid to him for £0.9.0 on 27 Feb 1767. {Ref: MSA S960 or S752, p. 188}

HALL, SOPHIA, see "Aquila Hall," q.v.

HALL, THOMAS (Delaware), pvt., Capt. French Battell's Company of Lower County Provincials, enlisted 20 May 1758. {Ref: ARDE I:16; ARPA (2nd Series) 2:555}

HALL, WILLIAM (Delaware), pvt., Kent Co. Militia, Capt. John Caton's Company, 25 Apr 1757 (date of muster roll). {Ref: ARDE I:13}

HALL, WILLIAM (Delaware), pvt., Capt. Henry Vanbibber's Company of the Lower Counties on Delaware Troops at New Castle, enlisted on 21 May 1759. {Ref: ARDE I:26; ARPA (2nd Series) 2:594}

HALL, WILLIAM (Maryland), patriot and poss. soldier (rank not specified), Elk Ridge, Anne Arundel Co., militia pay account submitted in 1758, exact date not given. {Ref: MHM 9:4, p. 367} See "Henry Hall," q.v.

HALL, WILLIAM (Maryland), pvt., Capt. John White's Company Muster Roll, Frederick Co., circa 1757-1758, exact dates not given (served 6 days); bill of credit issued or paid to him for £0.6.0 in 1767, exact date not given. {Ref: MSA S960 or S752, p. 164; CSOS:96}

HALL, WILLIAM, see "John Hall," q.v.

HALTZ (HALTS), JACOB (Maryland), pvt., Capt. John Middaugh's Company Muster Roll, Frederick Co., circa 1757-1758, exact dates not given (served 30 days); bill of credit issued or paid to him for £0.17.0 in 1767, exact date not given. {Ref: MSA S960 or S752, p. 171; CSOS:101}

HAMILTON, DANIEL (Maryland), indentured servant and soldier who served in the French and Indian War some time between 1756 and 1763 (exact dates not known); his master Thomas Clendening, merchant and innkeeper, requested compensation from the Baltimore County Court due to the loss of use of Hamilton while in the service. {Ref: MHM 94:4, p. 426, citing Baltimore Co. Court Minutes}

HAMILTON, HANSE (Maryland or Pennsylvania), captain, by 1757, who went in pursuit of the Indians who had killed settlers near Conococheague, including John Campbell and James Hamilton, and had taken away some of their children, in Cumberland Co., PA. {Ref: *MD Gazette*, 7 Apr 1757}

HAMILTON, JAMES (Delaware), b. c1737, PA (hunter, age 21 in 1758); pvt., recruited by Capt. Benjamin Noxon and enlisted on 2 May 1758. {Ref: ARDE I:19; ARPA (2nd Series) 2:566}

HAMILTON, JAMES (Delaware), New Castle Co., patriot who served as a Justice of the Peace and Justice of the Court of Oyer and Terminer in 1756, Lieut. Governor (1756-1759) and Governor of Delaware from November 1759 to 1763. {Ref: GRSD 1:13-14; HDE I:123, 140, 143; HDE II:1037}

HAMILTON, JAMES (Maryland), pvt., Capt. Richard Pearis' Company of MD Troops, Frederick Co., circa 9 Oct 1757 and 31 May 1758; pvt., Capt. Joshua Beall's Company of MD Troops, Prince George's Co., from 1 Jun 1758 to 30 Dec 1758. {Ref: MHS MS.375.1; CSOS:84, 90} Payment to him was recorded in Col. Dagworthy's account book on 12 Jul 1762. {Ref: MHS MS.375}

HAMILTON, JOHN (Maryland), pvt., Capt. Richard Pearis' Company of MD Troops, Frederick Co., circa 9 Oct 1757 and 31 May 1758; pvt., Capt. Joshua Beall's Company of MD Troops, Prince George's Co., from 1 Jun 1758 to 30 Dec 1758. {Ref: MHS MS.375.1; CSOS:84, 90} Payment to him was recorded in Col. Dagworthy's account book on 12 Jul 1762. {Ref: MHS MS.375}

HAMILTON, WILLIAM (Maryland), pvt., Capt. Joshua Beall's Company of MD Troops, Prince George's Co., from 9 Oct 1757 to 12 Jan 1758 when he was discharged. {Ref: MHS MS.375.1; CSOS:84} Payment to him was recorded in Col. Dagworthy's account book on 23 Jul 1762; bill of credit issued or paid in his behalf to Thomas Gant, Jr. for £1.10.6 on 27 Feb 1767. {Ref: MHS MS.375; MSA S960 or S752, p. 184}

HAMMOND, CHARLES (Maryland), major, Anne Arundel Co., by 24 Sep 1756 when he received supplies for his company at the Head of Severn by order of Col. Charles Hammond. {Ref: ARMD 52:614} See "Philip Hammond" and "Thomas Franklin" and "William Govane," q.v.

HAMMOND, HENRY (Maryland), sea captain by 1756, was in command of the schooner *Sea Horse* when captured by the French on his way from Maryland to Barbadoes. {Ref: *MD Gazette*, 2 Dec 1756}

HAMMOND, JOHN (Maryland), son of Thomas John Hammond; patriot, Annapolis, Anne Arundel Co., pay account submitted for quartering soldiers in 1757 or 1758, exact dates not given. {Ref: MHM 9:3, p. 260}

HAMMOND, JOHN (Maryland), b. 1735, Anne Arundel Co., son of Philip Hammond and Rachel Brice, m. Ann (N) by 1772, had children William, Thomas, Sarah, Mary, Elizabeth, and Henrietta, and d. by 21 Feb 1784; patriot, lawyer, and member of the MD Assembly (1760-1771). {Ref: BDML I:394} Pay account submitted for quartering soldiers in 1757 or 1758, exact dates not given. {Ref: MHM 9:3, p. 260}

HAMMOND, LAWRENCE (Delaware), pvt., Capt. French Battell's Company of Lower County Provincials, enlisted 19 May 1758. {Ref: ARDE I:16; ARPA (2nd Series) 2:555}

HAMMOND, LAWRENCE, see "Thomas Hammond," q.v.

HAMMOND, MARY, see "Tobias Stansbury," q.v.

HAMMOND, NATHAN JR., see "Ann Rait," q.v.

HAMMOND, PHILIP (Maryland), b. 1697, Anne Arundel Co., son of Charles Hammond and Hannah Howard, m. 1st to Comfort Duval and 2nd to Rachel Brice, had children Joshua, Charles, John, Philip, Denton, Matthias, Rezin, and Anne, and d. 3 May 1760; patriot, planter, merchant, gentleman, clerk of the Prerogative Court (1718-1721), and member of the MD Assembly (1732-1760). {Ref: BDML I:397-398} Pay account submitted for his exec. (unnamed) for his quartering soldiers in 1757 or 1758, exact dates not given. {Ref: MHM 9:3, p. 262} See "John Hammond," q.v.

HAMMOND, RACHEL, see "John Moale," q.v.

HAMMOND, SUSANNA, see "Nicholas Orrick," q.v.

HAMMOND, THOMAS (Maryland), b. 12 Mar 1737/8, Baltimore Co., son of Lawrence Hammond and Avarilla Simkins, of St. Paul's P. E. Parish. {Ref: BCF:298} Pvt., Capt. Christopher Gist's Company of VA Militia, 13 Jul 1756, enlisted at Baltimore (b. MD, age about 19). {Ref: MSR I:37}

HAMMOND, THOMAS (Maryland), captain, Baltimore Co., d. before June 1761 at which time "Mrs. Hammond, widow of Capt. Thomas Hammond, was granted a license to keep an ordinary" [tavern]. {Ref: Baltimore Co. Court Minutes, June 1761} He was poss. the son of Thomas Hammond (d. 1724) and his 1st wife Rebecca Lightfoot (widow of Thomas Lightfoot and poss. dau. of John Larkin). {Ref: BCF:298}

HAMMOND, THOMAS, see "John Hammond" and "Tobias Stansbury," q.v.

HAMMOND, WILLIAM, see "James Govane," q.v.

HAN, JOHN (Maryland), pvt., Capt. Moses Chapline's Company Muster Roll No. 3, Frederick Co., circa 1757-1758, exact dates not given (served 6 days); bill of credit issued or paid in his behalf to Joseph Chaplin for £0.6.0 on 5 Mar 1767; one source listed the name as "John Horn." {Ref: MSA S960 or S752, p. 198; CSOS:114}

HANDCOCK, THOMAS (Maryland), indentured servant and soldier who served in the French and Indian War some time between 1756 and 1763 (exact dates not known); his master Alexander Lawson, iron manufacturer, requested compensation from the Baltimore County Court due to the loss of use of Handcock while in the service. {Ref: MHM 94:4, p. 426, citing Baltimore Co. Court Minutes}

HANDS, THOMAS BEDINGFIELD (Maryland), b. c1720, prob. Kent Co., m. Sarah McGahon (1721-1754), had children Thomas Bedingfield, Margaret, and Elizabeth, and d. testate by 2 Dec 1769, giving his name and residence as "Thos. Bedingfield Hands, Cecil Co., of Chester, Maryland" in his will; patriot, gentleman, Treasurer of the Eastern Shore, and a Justice of the Provincial Court; pay account submitted for quartering soldiers in 1757 or 1758, exact dates not given. {Ref: MHM 9:3, p. 261; MCW 14:105; BDML I:401; *MD Gazette*, 28 Sep 1769} On 25 Aug 1756 "Bedingfield Hands" reported to the Governor of MD that "the papers sent herewith were taken from a Frenchman traveling through the country without a pass; he had passed from place to place where the neutral French reside; he owns having impersonated a priest; he either is, or well impersonates a lunatic with lucid intervals; the Governor is asked whether he thinks it proper to detain him." {Ref: CSMP-The Black Books:133} The letter also stated "on examination he appears by his own confession to be a native Frenchman and a papist of the Province of Gascoign, he talks Latin pretty well, says he came from Havre de Grace to Quebeck, thence to Montreal to Albany, York, Boston, Philadelphia, has been at Annapolis, has passed from place to place where the neutral French reside." {Ref: ARMD 31:156}

HANDY, AMELIA, see "John Handy," q.v.

HANDY, BENJAMIN (Maryland), b. c1720, Somerset Co., son of Ebenezer Handy and Betty (N), m. 1st to his first cousin Priscilla Handy and 2nd to Elizabeth (N) by 1756, had a son John, and died "soon after 25 Apr 1763" in Worcester Co.; planter, miller, gentleman, county justice (1747-1763), tax collector (1758-1759), sheriff (1758-1761), member of the MD Assembly (1756-1758, served on the Arms and Ammunition Committee), captain by 1756 and major by 1758. {Ref: BDML I:401-402; *MD Gazette*, 1 Feb 1759}

HANDY, EBENEZER, see "Benjamin Handy," q.v.

HANDY, ELIZABETH, see "Benjamin Handy," q.v.

HANDY, JOHN (Maryland), b. c1724, Somerset Co., son of John Handy and Jane Dashiell, m. Ann Nutter on 25 Dec 1748, had children Thomas, Levin, Amelia, and Priscilla, and d. 6 Nov 1756 "of a nervous fever" in Somerset Co.; merchant, gentleman, magistrate, captain by 1752, and member of the MD Assembly (1751-1756). {Ref: BDML I:403; ARMD 55:45; *MD Gazette*, 2 Dec 1756}

HANDY, JOHN (Maryland), pvt., Capt. William Luckett's Company Muster Roll, Frederick Co., circa 1757-1758, exact dates not given (served 30 days); bill of credit issued or paid in his behalf to Josiah Beall, Jr. for £1.10.0 on 11 Jun 1768. {Ref: MSA S960 or S752, p. 170; CSOS:99}

HANDY, LEVIN, see "John Handy," q.v.

HANDY, PRISCILLA, see "Benjamin Handy" and "John Handy," q.v.

HANDY, THOMAS (Maryland), captain, Worcester Co., by 1760. {Ref: ARMD 56:288} See "John Handy," q.v.

HANEY (HANCY), PETER (Maryland), pvt., Capt. Jonathan Hagar's Company Muster Roll, Frederick Co., circa 1757-1758, exact dates not given (served 6 days); bill of credit issued or paid to him for £0.6.0 in 1767, exact date not given. {Ref: MSA S960 or S752, p. 174; CSOS:107}

HANNIEL, WILLIAM (Maryland), pvt., Capt. William McClellan's Company of MD Volunteers, Frederick Co., circa 1763-1764; on muster roll dated 15 Nov 1764 at Camp at the Forks of Muskingham. {Ref: ARMD 32:99}

HANRICK, ---- (Maryland), sea captain by 1756, was in command of a snow (name not given) belonging to Mr. Galloway, of West River, when it was captured by a French Privateer on his way from Maryland to Barbadoes. {Ref: *MD Gazette*, 23 Dec 1756}

HANSLAP, SUSANNA, see "John Gassaway," q.v.

HANSON, CHARITY, see "Arthur Lee," q.v.

HANSON, DOROTHY, see "Richard Harrison," q.v.

HANSON, EDWARD (Maryland), b. 7 Jan 1731/2, Baltimore Co., son of Jacob Hanson and Rebecca Miles. {Ref: BCF:301} Pvt., Capt. Tobias Stansbury's Company Muster Roll, Baltimore Co., circa 1757-1758, exact dates not given; bill of credit issued or paid to him for £3.16.0 on 3 Apr 1767. {Ref: MSA S960 or S752, p. 186}

HANSON, JACOB, see "Edward Hanson," q.v.

HANSON, JANE, see "William Luckett," q.v.

HANSON, ROBERT (Maryland), lieut., Capt. Joseph Hanson Harrison's Company Muster Roll, Charles Co., circa 1757-1758, exact dates not given; bill of credit issued or paid in his behalf to John Hanson, Jr. for £7.17.6 on 23 Feb 1767. {Ref: MSA S960 or S752, p. 189} See "Oswald Addams," q.v.

HANSON, THOMAS, see "Arthur Lee," q.v.

HANZER, SAMUEL (Delaware), b. c1735, Sussex, DE (age 24 in 1759); pvt., enlisted in Capt. John Wright's Company and mustered on 11 May 1759. {Ref: ARDE I:25; ARPA (2nd Series) 2:592}

HANZER, THOMAS (Delaware), b. c1740, Sussex, DE (age 19 in 1759); pvt., enlisted in Capt. John Wright's Company and mustered on 11 May 1759. {Ref: ARDE I:25; ARPA (2nd Series) 2:592}

HARBADGE, EDWARD (Delaware), b. c1734, London, England (brushmaker, age 24 in 1758); pvt., enlisted 26 Apr 1758 "for the campaign in the lower counties" by Capt. John McClughan. {Ref: ARDE I:17; ARPA (2nd Series) 2:570}

HARBERT, ANNE, see "George Dent," q.v.

HARBIN (HARBEN), ANTHONY (Maryland), pvt., Capt. Richard Pearis' Company of MD Troops, Frederick Co., from 9 Oct 1757 to 31 May 1758. {Ref: MHS MS.375.1} Payment to him was recorded in Col. Dagworthy's account book on 15 Jul 1762 which was paid to Thomas Harbin on 22 Feb 1763. {Ref: MHS MS.375}

HARBIN, WILLIAM (Maryland), pvt., Capt. Joshua Beall's Company Muster Roll, Prince George's Co., circa 1757-1758, exact dates not given; bill of credit issued or paid to him for £1.8.0 in 1767, exact date not given. {Ref: MSA S960 or S752, p. 184}

HARBOUCK, LODWICK or LODOWICK (Maryland), pvt., Capt. Peter Bainbridge's Company Muster Roll, Frederick Co., circa 1757-1758, exact dates not given (served 28 days); bill of credit issued or paid in his behalf to Henry Snavely on 27 Apr 1767 for £1.8.0. {Ref: MSA S960 or S752, p. 181; CSOS:111}

HARDCASTLE, ANN, see "William Beall," q.v.

HARDCASTLE, ROBERT JR. (Maryland), pvt., Capt. Henry Casson's Company Muster Roll, Queen Anne's Co., circa 1757-1758, exact dates not given (served 27 days); bill of credit issued to him for £1.7.0 in 1767, exact date not given. {Ref: MSA S960 or S752, p. 178; CSOS:109}

HARDEN, NANCY, see "James Byrum," q.v.

HARDESTY, ANNA, see "John Green," q.v.

HARDIKER, RICHARD (Maryland), pvt., Capt. Joshua Beall's Company of MD Troops, Prince George's Co., circa 9 Oct 1757 to 30 Dec 1758. {Ref: MHS MS.375.1; CSOS:84} Payment to him was recorded in Col. Dagworthy's account book on 13 Jul 1762. {Ref: MHS MS.375}

HARDMAN, JOSEPH (Maryland), pvt., Capt. Peter Butler's Company Muster Roll, Frederick Co., circa 1757-1758, exact dates not given (served 34 days); bill of credit or order issued in his behalf for £1.14.0 and paid to Casper Shaff on 2 Mar 1767; name listed once as "Joseph Hardman, Jr." {Ref: MSA S960 or S752, p. 166; CSOS:97}

HARIGAN (HARAGON), CORNELIUS (Delaware), b. c1730, Ireland (laborer, age 28 in 1758); pvt., recruited by Capt. Benjamin Noxon and enlisted on 25 Apr 1758. {Ref: ARDE I:19; ARPA (2nd Series) 2:566}

HARLIN (HARLINS), ISAAC (Maryland), cpl., Capt. John Middaugh's Company Muster Roll, Frederick Co., circa 1757-1758, exact dates not given (served 30 days); bill of credit issued or paid to him for £2 on 4 Mar 1767. {Ref: MSA S960 or S752, pp. 171-172; CSOS:100}

HARLIN, JACOB (Maryland), pvt., Capt. John Middaugh's Company Muster Roll, Frederick Co., circa 1757-1758, exact dates not given (served 30 days); bill of credit issued or paid in his behalf to Thomas Owings for £1.10.0 on 15 May 1767. {Ref: MSA S960 or S752, p. 172; CSOS:101}

HARLIN, JOHN (Maryland), pvt., Capt. Alexander Beall's Company, Frederick Co., 1756-1757, recorded his discharge in Frederick Co. Court on 16 Aug 1757. Capt. Beall certified his service of 7 months on 10 Feb 1757 and his receipt for clothing and pay was signed by Sgt. Robert Lineard and Sgt. George Barrance. John Harlin made his "X" mark. {Ref: FCLR:30}

HARMAN, MICHAEL (Maryland), patriot and poss. soldier (rank not specified), Frederick Co., militia pay account submitted in 1758, exact date not given. {Ref: MHM 9:4, p. 366}

HARMAN, NICHOLAS (Maryland), pvt., Capt. Jonathan Hagar's Company Muster Roll, Frederick Co., circa 1757-1758, exact dates not given (served 6 days); bill of credit issued or paid in his behalf to Joseph Chaplin for £0.6.0 on 24 Apr 1767. {Ref: MSA S960 or S752, pp. 173-174; CSOS:106}

HARMASON (HARMISON), JOHN (Maryland), patriot, Frederick Co., paid on 7 Aug 1758 "for working on the new road to Fort Frederick" for the Western Expedition against Fort Duquesne; he and several others were called "battomen" when paid on 6 Oct 1758 "for carrying up baggage belonging to the militia that garrisoned Fort Cumberland." {Ref: ARMD 55:774, 775}

HARPER, MARK (Delaware), pvt., Kent Co. Militia, Capt. John Caton's Company, 25 Apr 1757 (date of muster roll). {Ref: ARDE I:14}

HARRAGAN, CORNELIUS (Delaware), pvt., Capt. Henry Vanbibber's Company of the Lower Counties on Delaware Troops at New Castle, enlisted on 9 May 1759. {Ref: ARDE I:26; ARPA (2nd Series) 2:594}

HARRIS, BENJAMIN (Maryland), pvt., Capt. William Luckett's Company Muster Roll, Frederick Co., circa 1757-1758, exact dates not given (served 30 days); bill of credit issued or paid in his behalf to William Luckett, Jr. for £1.10.0 on 6 Apr 1767. {Ref: MSA S960 or S752, p. 170; CSOS:99}

HARRIS, BENTON (Maryland), b. c1716, Somerset Co., prob. son of John Harris, m. Betty Whittington (widow of both William Whittington and Hampton Hopkins, and dau. of Robert Martin) by 1753, had no children, and d. testate by September 1777, Worcester Co.; captain by 1745, sheriff (1745-1746), county justice (1762-1777), member of the MD Assembly (1757-1766), member of the Committee of Observation in 1776, and appointed Register of Wills in 1777. {Ref: BDML I:412}

HARRIS, JANE, see "John Carvill," q.v.

HARRIS, JOHN, see "Benton Harris," q.v.

HARRIS, JOHN (Delaware), pvt., Capt. Richard McWilliams' Company of Foot, New Castle Co., enlisted 28 Dec 1757. {Ref: ARDE I:15}

HARRIS (HARRISS), JOSEPH (Maryland), pvt., Capt. Francis Ware's Company of MD Troops, Charles Co., circa 9 Oct 1757 to 8 Apr 1758 when he was discharged; payment to him was recorded in Col. Dagworthy's account book on 7 Mar 1763 for work on Fort Cumberland. {Ref: MHS MS.375; CSOS:88; MHS MS.375.1}

HARRIS, MARGARET, see "William Hynson," q.v.

HARRIS (HARRISS, HAZARD?), MICHAEL (Maryland), pvt., Capt. Francis Ware's Company of MD Troops, Charles Co., from 1 Jun 1758 to 7 Nov 1758 (transferred from Capt. Richard Pearis' Company; served 161 days altogether); name listed once as "Michael Hazard." {Ref: MHS MS.375.1; CSOS:90} Payment to him was recorded in Col. Dagworthy's account book on 13 Jul 1762 (name strangely entered as "Michael Harriss Say Hazard"). {Ref: MHS MS.375}

HARRIS, WILLIAM (Delaware), pvt., Kent Co. Militia, Capt. John Caton's Company, 25 Apr 1757 (date of muster roll). {Ref: ARDE I:14}

HARRISON, BURR (Maryland), ensign in Capt. Alexander Beall's Company of MD Troops, Frederick Co., from 9 Oct 1757 to 9 Nov 1758; 2nd lieut., Capt. Alexander Beall's Company of MD Troops, Frederick Co., from 9 Nov 1758 to 30 Dec 1758; name mistakenly transcribed once as "Ben: Harrison." {Ref: MHS MS.375.1; CSOS:79} Payment recorded in Col. Dagworthy's account book on 11 Jul 1762. {Ref: MHS MS.375}

HARRISON, DOROTHY, see "Joseph Hanson Harrison," q.v.

HARRISON, HENRY (Maryland), cpl., Calvert Co., Capt. Edward Gantt's Militia Co., Lyon's Creek Hundred circa 1756-1757 (exact dates not given). {Ref: HCC:120} See "Will Parks" and "Thomas Seal" and "Will Wilson," q.v.

HARRISON, JOHN (Maryland), pvt., Capt. Joseph Chapline's Company Muster Roll No. 4, Frederick Co., circa 1757-1758, exact dates not given (served 7 days); bill of credit issued or paid to him for £0.7.0 in 1767, exact date not given. {Ref: MSA S960 or S752, p. 194; CSOS:105} See "Thomas Smith Greenfield," q.v.

HARRISON, JOHN (Maryland), indentured servant and soldier who served in the French and Indian War some time between 1756 and 1763 (exact dates not known); his master Brian Philpot, merchant, requested compensation from the Baltimore County Court due to the loss of use of Harrison while in the service. {Ref: MHM 94:4, p. 426, citing Baltimore Co. Court Minutes}

HARRISON, JOSEPH, see "Joseph Hanson Harrison" and "Richard Harrison," q.v.

HARRISON, JOSEPH HANSON (Maryland), b. c1722, Charles Co. (aged about 41 in 1763 deposition and aged about 50 in 1772 deposition), son of Joseph Harrison and Verlinda Stone, m. Mary (N) before 1763, had children Joseph White, Richard, Dorothy, and Mary, and d. testate by 28 May 1785; planter, gentleman, county justice (1759-1773), member of the MD Assembly (1768-1780), captain by 1757, and elected to the Committee of Observation in 1774-1775. {Ref: BDML I:417; MGSB 34:1, p. 10} Captain in Charles Co. militia circa

1757-1758 (exact dates not given); militia pay account submitted in 1758, exact date not given. {Ref: MHM 9:4, p. 368} Bill of credit issued or paid in his behalf to John McPherson for £16.6.9 on 25 Mar 1767. {Ref: MSA S960 or S752, p. 189}

HARRISON, MARY, see "Joseph Hanson Harrison," q.v.

HARRISON, RICHARD (Maryland), pvt., Capt. Joseph Chapline's Company Muster Roll No. 4, Frederick Co., circa 1757-1758, exact dates not given (served 6 days); bill of credit issued or paid in his behalf to Joseph Chaplin for £0.6.0 on 13 Jun 1768. {Ref: MSA S960 or S752, p. 195; CSOS:105} See "Joseph Hanson Harrison," q.v.

HARRISON, RICHARD (Maryland), b. c1716, Charles Co. (aged about 41 in 1757 deposition), son of Joseph Harrison and Verlinda Stone, m. 1st to Dorothy Hanson by 1746 and 2nd to Elizabeth Penn (widow of William Penn and dau. of George Dent), had sons Robert Hanson, William, and Walter Hanson, and d. testate by 16 Sep 1780; planter, gentleman, county justice (1741-1769), captain by 1747, member of the MD Assembly (1742-1748, 1751-1754), and colonel by 1754. {Ref: BDML I:417-418; MGSB 34:1, p. 10}

HARRISON, ROBERT (Maryland), pvt., Capt. Moses Chapline's Company Muster Roll No. 2, Frederick Co., circa 1757-1758, exact dates not given (served 13 days); bill of credit issued or paid in his behalf to Joseph Chaplin for £0.13.0 on 24 Apr 1767. {Ref: MSA S960 or S752, p. 197; CSOS:114}

HARRISON, ROBERT HANSON, see "Richard Harrison," q.v.

HARRISON, THOMAS, see "Moses Haines" and "Thomas Bess," q.v.

HARRISON, WALTER, see "Richard Harrison," q.v.

HARRISON, WILLIAM, see "Richard Harrison," q.v.

HARROD, JAMES (Maryland), b. c1733, Norwich, England (about age 26 in 1759); pvt. who was reported by Lieut. Harrington Baudin, 58th [American] Regt., at Annapolis, as deserted after being persuaded to do so by his late master Nicholas Orrick (q.v.), living near Baltimore Town. {Ref: *MD Gazette*, 15 Mar 1759}

HARROD, JOHN (Maryland), pvt., Capt. Joseph Chapline's Company Muster Roll No. 1, Frederick Co., circa 1757-1758, exact dates not given; bill of credit issued or paid in his behalf to Joseph Chaplin for £3.18.7½ on 5 Mar 1767. {Ref: MSA S960 or S752, p. 190} Cpl., Capt. Joseph Chapline's Company Muster Rolls No. 2 and 3, Frederick Co., circa 1757-1758, exact dates not given (served 8 days); bill of credit issued or paid in his behalf to Joseph Chaplin for £0.8.0 on 5 Mar 1767. {Ref: MSA S960 or S752, p. 193; CSOS:104}

HARROD, JOHN JR. (Maryland), cpl., Capt. Henry Sneavely's Company Muster Roll, Frederick Co., circa 1757-1758, exact dates not given; bill of credit issued or paid in his behalf to Joseph Chaplin for £0.8.0 on 24 Apr 1767; name listed once without the "Jr." {Ref: MSA S960 or S752, pp. 190, 193}

HARSEY, WILLIAM (Maryland), pvt., Capt. Joshua Beall's Company Muster Roll, Prince George's Co., circa 1757-1758, exact dates not given; bill of credit issued or paid to him for £2.2.0 in 1767, exact date not given. {Ref: MSA S960 or S752, p. 184}

HART, THOMAS (Maryland), b. 9 Jan 1738/9, Kent Co., son of Richard and Rachel Hart, of Shrewsbury Parish. {Ref: ESVR} Pvt., Capt. Peregrine Brown's

Company Muster Roll, Kent Co., circa 1757-1758, exact dates not given (served 15 days); bill of credit issued or paid in his behalf to Robert Buchanan on 20 May 1767 for £0.15.0. {Ref: MSA S960 or S752, p. 179; CSOS:110}

HARTLEY, GEORGE (Maryland), m. (N), had several sons and daus. (who were mentioned, but not named in his will), and d. testate by 20 Oct 1776. {Ref: WMG 5:1, p. 20} Pvt., Capt. John White's Company Muster Roll, Frederick Co., circa 1757-1758, exact dates not given (served 6 days); bill of credit issued or paid to him for £0.6.0 in 1767, exact date not given. {Ref: MSA S960 or S752, p. 164; CSOS:96}

HARTSMAN, HENRY (Maryland), pvt., Capt. Jonathan Hagar's Company Muster Roll, Frederick Co., circa 1757-1758, exact dates not given (served 6 days); bill of credit issued or paid to him for £0.6.0 in 1767, exact date not given. {Ref: MSA S960 or S752, p. 174; CSOS:107}

HARTSOCK, GEORGE (Maryland), pvt., Capt. John Middaugh's Company Muster Roll, Frederick Co., circa 1757-1758, exact dates not given (served 30 days); bill of credit issued or paid in his behalf to Robert Wood for £0.17.0 on 4 Mar 1767. {Ref: MSA S960 or S752, p. 171; CSOS:102}

HARTSOCK, NICHOLAS (Maryland), pvt., Capt. John Middaugh's Company Muster Roll, Frederick Co., circa 1757-1758, exact dates not given (served 30 days); bill of credit issued or paid in his behalf to Robert Wood for £0.17.0 on 4 Mar 1767. {Ref: MSA S960 or S752, p. 172; CSOS:102}

HARVEY, NEWMAN (Maryland), cpl., Calvert Co., Capt. Edward Gantt's Militia Co., Lyon's Creek Hundred circa 1756-1757 (exact dates not given). {Ref: HCC:120}

HARWOOD (HEARWOOD), JOHN (Maryland), pvt., Capt. Moses Chapline's Company Muster Roll No. 1, Frederick Co., circa 1757-1758, exact dates not given (served 25 days); bill of credit issued or paid in his behalf to Joseph Chaplin for £1.5.0 on 24 Apr 1767. {Ref: MSA S960 or S752, p. 196; CSOS:113}

HARWOOD, JOHN (Maryland), sgt., Capt. Joseph Chapline's Company Muster Roll No. 1, Frederick Co., circa 1757-1758, exact dates not given (served 59 days); bill of credit issued or paid to him for £3.18.7½ in 1767, exact date not given. {Ref: MSA S960 or S752, p. 191; CSOS:102} Previously paid £1.2.6 on 2 Nov 1758 at Fort Frederick "for bringing a letter from Winchester from Gen. Forbes" regarding the Western Expedition against Fort Duquesne. {Ref: ARMD 55:775}

HARWOOD, JOHN (Maryland), pvt., Capt. Francis Ware's Company of MD Troops, Charles Co., from 9 Oct 1757 to 8 Apr 1758 (served 182 days) when he was discharged. {Ref: MHS MS.375.1; CSOS:88} Payment to him was recorded in Col. Dagworthy's account book on 22 Jul 1762. {Ref: MHS MS.375}

HARWOOD, RICHARD (Maryland), pvt., Capt. Samuel Chapman's Company Muster Roll, Anne Arundel Co., circa 1757-1758, exact dates not given; bill of credit issued or paid to him for £1.18.0 on 13 Mar 1767. {Ref: MSA S960 or S752, p. 189}

HARWOOD (HOWARD), RICHARD (Maryland), pvt., Capt. Alexander Beall's Company of MD Troops, Frederick Co., from 1 Jun 1758 to 30 Dec 1758; transferred from Capt. Richard Pearis' Company {Ref: MHS MS.375.1; CSOS:81}

Payment to him was recorded in Col. Dagworthy's account book on 12 Jul 1762. {Ref: MHS MS.375}

HARWOOD, SAMUEL (Maryland), cpl., Capt. Alexander Beall's Company of MD Troops, Frederick Co., circa 9 Oct 1757 to 30 Dec 1758. {Ref: MHS MS.375.1; CSOS:80} Payment to him was recorded in Col. Dagworthy's account book on 23 Feb 1763. {Ref: MHS MS.375}

HARWOOD, THOMAS (Maryland), cpl., Capt. Alexander Beall's Company of MD Troops, Frederick Co., circa 9 Oct 1757 to 30 Dec 1758 (promoted to cpl. on 9 Nov 1757). {Ref: MHS MS.375.1; CSOS:80} Payment to him was recorded in Col. Dagworthy's account book on 112 Jul 1762. {Ref: MHS MS.375}

HARWOOD (HEARWOOD), WILLIAM (Maryland), pvt., Capt. Moses Chapline's Company Muster Roll No. 1, Frederick Co., circa 1757-1758, exact dates not given (served 31 days); bill of credit issued or paid in his behalf to Joseph Chaplin for £1.11.0 on 24 Apr 1767. {Ref: MSA S960 or S752, p. 196; CSOS:113}

HASLET (HASSLET, HAZLET), JOHN (Delaware), b. c1735 in Ireland, immigrated to Dover, DE, m. Jemima (N), had children Joseph, John, Mary, Ann, and Jemima, and d. 3 Jan 1777; captain, New Castle Co., and recruiting officer for PA Troops in the "Three Lower Counties on Delaware" in 1758; colonel, Delaware Bttn. of Continental Troops, on 19 Jan 1776; killed at the Battle of Princeton on 3 Jan 1777, initially buried at Dover, and reinterred in the First Presbyterian Church Cem. at Philadelphia in 1841. {Ref: CDSS:88; ARDE I:23, 27, 35; RPDE:118}

HASTY, PETER (Maryland), pvt., Capt. Francis Ware's Company of MD Troops, Charles Co., from 9 Oct 1757 to 12 Oct 1758 (served 368 days) when he was reported as killed; however, payment to him was recorded in Col. Dagworthy's account book on 7 Mar 1763 for work on Fort Cumberland. {Ref: MHS MS.375; CSOS:88; MHS MS.375.1}

HATFIELD, JOHN JR. (Delaware), pvt., Kent Co. Militia, Capt. John Caton's Company, 25 Apr 1757 (date of muster roll). {Ref: ARDE I:13}

HATFIELD, MARY, see "Whitly Hatfield," q.v.

HATFIELD, THOMAS (Delaware), pvt., Kent Co. Militia, Capt. John Caton's Company, 25 Apr 1757 (date of muster roll). {Ref: ARDE I:13}

HATFIELD, WHITLY or WHEATLY (Delaware), b. c1741, MD (age 18 in 1759); pvt., enlisted in Capt. John Wright's Company and mustered on 11 May 1759. {Ref: ARDE I:25; ARPA (2nd Series) 2:508, 592} "Wheatly Hatfield" was the son of William Hatfield (d. 1797) and Mary (N); in 1783 he was admin. of the estate of Cottingham Hatfield (a schooner captain during the Revolutionary War) in Sussex Co. {Ref: CDSS:88; RPDE:118}

HATFIELD, WILLIAM (Delaware), pvt., Kent Co. Militia, Capt. John Caton's Company, 25 Apr 1757 (date of muster roll). {Ref: ARDE I:13}

HATTON, BARTHOLOMEW (Maryland), pvt., Capt. Jonathan Hagar's Company Muster Roll, Frederick Co., circa 1757-1758, exact dates not given (served 6 days); bill of credit issued or paid to him for £0.6.0 in 1767, exact date not given. {Ref: MSA S960 or S752, p. 174; CSOS:107}

HAUSMAN, CATHERINE, see "Henry Sneavely (Schnebely)," q.v.

HAVEN, BARTHOLOMEW (Maryland), farmer; pvt., Capt. Peregrine Brown's 7th Co. of Foot Militia, Kent Co., on 19 Feb 1758, by which time he had enlisted, but reportedly refused to appear and serve in arms against the enemy. {Ref: ARMD 31:283, 288}

HAVENER (HAVENOR), FREDERICK (Maryland), pvt., Capt. Stephen Rensburg's or Rensburger's Company Muster Roll, Frederick Co., circa 1757-1758, exact dates not given (served 42 days); militia pay account submitted in 1758, exact date not given. {Ref: MHM 9:4, p. 367} Bill of credit issued or paid to him for £1.14.0 on 27 Mar 1767. {Ref: MSA S960 or S752, p. 182; CSOS:112}

HAVENER (HAVENOR), MICHAEL (Maryland), pvt., Capt. Stephen Rensburg's or Rensburger's Company Muster Roll, Frederick Co., circa 1757-1758, exact dates not given (served 34 days); militia pay account submitted in 1758, exact date not given. {Ref: MHM 9:4, p. 367} Bill of credit issued or paid in his behalf to Casper Shaff for £2.2.0 on 2 Mar 1767. {Ref: MSA S960 or S752, p. 182; CSOS:112}

HAVENS, FARWELL or FAREWELL (Maryland), drummer, Capt. Francis Ware's Company of MD Troops, Charles Co., circa 9 Oct 1757 to 30 Dec 1758. {Ref: MHS MS.375.1; CSOS:88} Payment to him was recorded in Col. Dagworthy's account book on 7 Mar 1763. {Ref: MHS MS.375}

HAVENS, JAMES (Maryland), patriot, Frederick Co., was paid £10.10.0 on 29 Jul 1758 "for his waggon attending the Detachments on the road, etc." for the Western Expedition against Fort Duquesne; was paid £0.15.0 "for carrying a letter of Gen. Forbes from Fort Frederick to Winchester" on 21 Aug 1758. {Ref: ARMD 55:774}

HAVERLOE (HAVELOE), JOHN (Delaware), captain, Northern District of Broadkiln Hundred, Militia Regt. of Sussex Co., 1756. {Ref: ARDE I:13; ARPA (2nd Series) 2:529; HDE I:141}

HAWKINS, EDWARD (Maryland), pvt., Capt. Alexander Beall's Company of MD Troops, Frederick Co., circa 1757-1758, exact dates not given; pvt., Capt. John Dagworthy's Company of MD Troops, Frederick Co., from 31 Dec 1758 to 16 Apr 1759, having transferred from Capt. Alexander Beall's Company where he had been reported as deserted. {Ref: MHS MS.375.1; CSOS:77} However, payment to him was recorded in Col. Dagworthy's account book on 14 Jul 1762. {Ref: MHS MS.375}

HAWKINS, ELEANOR, see "George Dent," q.v.

HAWKINS, JOHN (Maryland), Englishman, b. c1727; soldier in Frederick Co. in 1756 (about age 29) who had been a servant for some time with the Widow Swaford between North and South Mountain in Frederick Co., was reported by Capt. Dagworthy as being a deserter from the MD Forces at Fort Frederick. {Ref: *MD Gazette*, 5 Aug 1756}

HAWKINS, THOMAS (Maryland), ensign in Capt. Elias Delashmutt's Company Muster Roll, Frederick Co., circa 1757-1758, exact dates not given; bill of credit issued or paid in his behalf to Elias Delashmut, Jr. on 16 Mar 1767 for £9.1.3. {Ref: MSA S960 or S752, p. 162; CSOS:94, 98}

HAY, JOHN (Maryland), officer (rank not stated) by 1757; a notice appeared in the Annapolis newspaper that two men had deserted from John Hay on their march to Carlisle Camp. {Ref: *MD Gazette*, 11 Aug 1757}

HAY, WILLIAM (Delaware), lieut., Christiana Hundred, Upper Regt. of Militia, Southeast Division, New Castle Co., 1756. {Ref: ARDE I:11; ARPA (2nd Series) 2:526; HDE I:141}

HAYS, CHARLES (Maryland), pvt., Capt. Joshua Beall's Company of MD Troops, Prince George's Co., circa 9 Oct 1757 to 30 Dec 1758. {Ref: MHS MS.375.1; CSOS:84} Payment to him was recorded in Col. Dagworthy's account book on 21 Jul 1762. {Ref: MHS MS.375} Pvt., Capt. William McClellan's Company of MD Volunteers, Frederick Co., circa 1763-1764; reported as deserted on muster roll dated 15 Nov 1764 at Camp at the Forks of Muskingham. {Ref: ARMD 32:99}

HAYS, JEREMIAH (Maryland), patriot and poss. soldier (rank not specified), Frederick Co., militia pay account submitted in 1758, exact date not given. {Ref: MHM 9:4, p. 367}

HAZARD, MICHAEL (Maryland), pvt., Capt. Richard Pearis' Company of MD Troops, Frederick Co., circa 9 Oct 1757 to 31 May 1758. {Ref: MHS MS.375.1; CSOS:90} See "Michael Harris," q.v.

HAZZARD, CORD (Delaware), son of Cord Hazzard (d. by 11 Jan 1771) and Rachel (N), m. Ann Dobson, had a dau. Elizabeth (b. 1749), and d. before 31 Jan 1766 (at which time his father had written his will). {Ref: CFD 3:81, 84; CDSS:89} Captain, Northern District of Indian River Hundred, Militia Regt. of Sussex Co., 1756; Captain, Angola District, 1758, "but would not take the qualifications." {Ref: ARDE I:13, 15; ARPA (2nd Series) 2:529, 579; HDE I:141}

HEABARD, PRISCILLA, see "William Smallwood," q.v.

HEARD, STEPHEN (Maryland), patriot, Frederick Co., who performed "sundry services at the fort" in 1763 and payment in the amount of £2.5.6 was still owed to him on 25 Nov 1763 (when reported by the Accounts Committee to the MD Assembly). {Ref: ARMD 58:400}

HEATON, JOHN (Maryland), pvt., Capt. Joshua Beall's Company Muster Roll, Prince George's Co., circa 1757-1758, exact dates not given; bill of credit issued or paid to him for £2.3.0 in 1767, exact date not given. {Ref: MSA S960 or S752, p. 184}

HEBBITS, WILLIAM (Delaware), pvt., Kent Co. Militia, Capt. John Caton's Company, 25 Apr 1757 (date of muster roll). {Ref: ARDE I:13}

HEDGE (HEDGES), CHARLES (Maryland), ensign in Capt. Stephen Rensburg's or Rensburger's Company Muster Roll, Frederick Co., circa 1757-1758, exact dates not given (served 42 days); bill of credit issued or paid in his behalf to Stephen Rensburger for £4 on 27 Mar 1767. {Ref: MSA S960 or S752, p. 183; CSOS:111}

HEDGE (HEDGES), MOSES (Maryland), pvt., Capt. Stephen Rensburg's or Rensburger's Company Muster Roll, Frederick Co., circa 1757-1758, exact dates not given (served 42 days); bill of credit issued or paid in his behalf to Stephen Rensburg or Rensburger for £2.2.0 on 27 Mar 1767. {Ref: MSA S960 or S752, p. 182; CSOS:113}

HEDGE (HEDGES), NICHOLAS (Maryland), pvt., Capt. Henry Sneavely's Company Muster Roll, Frederick Co., circa 1757-1758, exact dates not given; bill of credit issued or paid to him for £0.8.0 in 1767, exact date not given. {Ref: MSA S960 or S752, p. 190}

HEINES, CORNELIUS (Delaware), pvt., Capt. Richard McWilliams' Company of Foot, New Castle Co., enlisted 28 Dec 1757. {Ref: ARDE I:15}

HEINZMAN, HENRY, see "Henry Hunzman," q.v.

HEISLER (HESILER), NICHOLAS (Maryland), cpl., Capt. Peter Butler's Company Muster Roll, Frederick Co., circa 1757-1758, exact dates not given (served 34 days); bill of credit or order issued in his behalf for £1.14.0 and paid to Casper Shaff on 2 Mar 1767. {Ref: MSA S960 or S752, p. 166; CSOS:96}

HELDPRUND, ERANMUS or ERASMUS (Maryland), pvt., Capt. Elias Delashmutt's Company Muster Roll, Frederick Co., circa 1757-1758, exact dates not given; bill of credit issued or paid in his behalf to Peter Grosh on 4 Mar 1767 for £1.10.0. {Ref: MSA S960 or S752, p. 162; CSOS:94}

HELLEN, DAVID, see "David Hillen (Hellen)," q.v.

HELMS, JOSEPH (Maryland), pvt., Capt. Joseph Chapline's Company Muster Roll No. 5, Frederick Co., circa 1757-1758, exact dates not given; bill of credit issued or paid in his behalf to Joseph Chaplin for £0.8.0 on 5 Mar 1767. {Ref: MSA S960 or S752, p. 195}

HEMMINS (HEMINGS), JAMES (Delaware), b. c1742, Sussex, DE (age 17 in 1759); pvt., enlisted in Capt. John Wright's Company and mustered on 11 May 1759; subscribed to the Oath of Fidelity and Allegiance in 1778. {Ref: ARDE I:25; ARPA (2nd Series) 2:592; RPDE:122}

HEMMINS (HEMMONS), JOHN (Delaware), b. c1737, Sussex, DE (age 22 in 1759), m. Elizabeth (N), had children Thomas, William Leather, Mary, and Elizabeth, and d. testate by 8 Dec 1789. {Ref: CDSS:90} Pvt., enlisted in Capt. John Wright's Company and mustered on 11 May 1759. {Ref: ARDE I:25; ARPA (2nd Series) 2:592}

HEMSLEY, WILLIAM (Maryland), b. 23 Jan 1736/7, Queen Anne's Co., son of William Hemsley and Anna Maria Tilghman, m. 1st to first cousin Henrietta Maria Earle on 3 Apr 1758, m. 2nd to Sarah Williamson after 1767, m. 3rd to his first cousin Anna Maria Tilghman after 1794, had children William, Philemon, Thomas, Alexander, James, Mary, Charlotte, Sarah, Henrietta Maria, Anna Maria, and Juliana, and d. 5 Jun 1812; planter, miller, gentleman, major by 1760, Treasurer of the Eastern Shore (1769, 1773), colonel (20th Bttn.) in 1777, senator (1776-1781, 1786-1788), member of the Council of Safety (1776-1777), county lieutenant in 1777, county justice in 1777, purchasing agent in 1779, and Judge of the Court of Appeals in 1786. {Ref: BDML I:432-434}

HENDERSON, DANIEL (Maryland), pvt., Capt. John Dagworthy's Company of MD Troops, Frederick Co., from 9 Oct 1757 to 8 May 1758. {Ref: MHS MS.375.1; CSOS:76} Payment to him was recorded in Col. Dagworthy's account book on 28 Feb 1763 for work on Fort Cumberland. {Ref: MHS MS.375}

HENDERSON, JAMES (Delaware), b. c1728, Antrim, Ireland (laborer, age 30 in 1758); pvt., enlisted 8 May 1758 "for the campaign in the lower counties" by Capt. John McClughan. {Ref: ARDE I:17; ARPA (2nd Series) 2:570}

HENDERSON, JOHN (Maryland), pvt., Capt. Tobias Stansbury's Company Muster Roll, Baltimore Co., circa 1757-1758, exact dates not given; bill of credit issued or paid in his behalf to Thomas Cockey Deye for £3.16.0 on 13 Jun 1768. {Ref: MSA S960 or S752, p. 187}

HENDERSON, WILLIAM (Maryland), pvt., Capt. Joseph Hanson Harrison's Company Muster Roll, Charles Co., circa 1757-1758, exact dates not given; bill of credit issued or paid to him for £2.9.0 in 1767, exact date not given. {Ref: MSA S960 or S752, p. 189}

HENDERSON, WILLIAM (Maryland), cpl., Capt. Francis Ware's Company of MD Troops, Charles Co., from 9 Oct 1757 (promoted to sgt. on 19 Feb 1758) to 30 Dec 1758. {Ref: MHS MS.375.1; CSOS:88}

HENDLEY, JOHN (Maryland), pvt., Capt. Francis Ware's Company of MD Troops, Charles Co., from 9 Oct 1757 to 17 Oct 1758 when he reportedly deserted; however, payment to him was recorded in Col. Dagworthy's account book on 7 Mar 1763. {Ref: MHS MS.375; MHS MS.375.1}

HENDRICK, JOHN (Maryland), pvt., Capt. John Middaugh's Company Muster Roll, Frederick Co., circa 1757-1758, exact dates not given (served 30 days); bill of credit issued or paid to him for £1.10.0 in 1767, exact date not given. {Ref: MSA S960 or S752, p. 171; CSOS:101}

HENDRICKSON, JOHN (Delaware), b. 1732, d. 1804, buried in Old Swedes Cem. at Wilmington; ensign, Christiana Hundred, Upper Regt. of Militia, North Division, New Castle Co., 1756; 1st lieut., 16 Sep 1775 to at least 1778. {Ref: ARDE I:11; ARPA (2nd Series) 2:526; HDE I:141; RPDE:123}

HENLEY, DARBY (Maryland), b. 4 May 1733, son of Darby Henley (or Hernley) who had leased 100 acres of Gunpowder Manor in 1736 for the lifetime of three of his children, all of whom had "gone to Carolina" by 1763. {Ref: BCF:322} Pvt., Capt. Tobias Stansbury's Company Muster Roll, Baltimore Co., circa 1757-1758, exact dates not given; bill of credit issued or paid in his behalf to Robert Adair for £2.10.0 on 22 May 1767. {Ref: MSA S960 or S752, p. 187}

HENRY, JOHN (Maryland), b. c1714, Somerset Co., son of Rev. John Henry and Mary Jenkins, m. Dorothy Rider (b. 1725, d. before 1781), had children Charles Rider, Rider, Francis Jenkins, John Jr., Robert, Charlotte, Niturah (Keturah?), Dorothy, Nancy, and Sally, and d. testate by 13 Sep 1781, Worcester Co.; merchant, colonel by 1749, and member of the MD Assembly (1744-1758, 1766). {Ref: BDML I:435-436; ARMD 55:44}

HENRY, JOHN (Maryland), Baltimore Co., prob. m. Mary Copeland (widow) on 10 Feb 1757; d. testate in 1770; no children. {Ref: BCF:321} Pvt., Capt. Tobias Stansbury's Company Muster Roll, Baltimore Co., circa 1757-1758, exact dates not given; bill of credit issued or paid to him for £1.18.0 on 18 Mar 1767. {Ref: MSA S960 or S752, p. 186} See "James Matthews" and "John Peacock," q.v.

HENRY, MATTHEW (Delaware), pvt., Kent Co. Militia, Capt. John Caton's Company, 25 Apr 1757 (date of muster roll). {Ref: ARDE I:13}

HENRY, ROBERT JENKINS (Maryland), b. c1712, Somerset Co., son of Rev. John Henry and Mary Jenkins, m. Gertrude Rousby in 1746, had children Robert Jenkins, Edward, Mary King, Ann, Elizabeth, and Gertrude, and d. October 1766 of the gout (at his brother's home in Dorchester Co.); planter, merchant, captain by 1735, member of the MD Assembly (1738-1741, 1747-1766), justice of the Provincial Court (1746-1756), justice of the Assize Court (1747-1766), major by 1745, colonel by 1752, member of the MD Council (1756-1766), and naval officer at Pocomoke (1762-1766). {Ref: BDML I:437-438; ARMD 55:200; *MD Gazette*, 23 Oct 1766}

HENTHORN, ADAM (Maryland), pvt., Capt. Joseph Chapline's Company Muster Roll No. 1, Frederick Co., circa 1757-1758, exact dates not given (served 47 days); bill of credit issued or paid in his behalf to Joseph Chaplin for £2.7.0 on 5 Mar 1767. {Ref: MSA S960 or S752, p. 190; CSOS:102} Pvt., Capt. Joseph Chapline's Company Muster Rolls No. 2 and 3, Frederick Co., circa 1757-1758, exact dates not given (served 6 days); bill of credit issued or paid in his behalf to Joseph Chaplin for £0.8.0 on 5 Mar 1767. {Ref: MSA S960 or S752, p. 193; CSOS:104} Pvt., Capt. Joseph Chapline's Company Muster Roll No. 4, Frederick Co., circa 1757-1758, exact dates not given (served 14 days); bill of credit issued or paid in his behalf to Joseph Chaplin for £0.8.0 on 5 Mar 1767. {Ref: MSA S960 or S752, p. 194; CSOS:104} Pvt., Capt. Moses Chapline's Company Muster Roll No. 2, Frederick Co., circa 1757-1758, exact dates not given (served 13 days); bill of credit issued or paid in his behalf to Joseph Chaplin for £0.13.0 on 5 Mar 1767. {Ref: MSA S960 or S752, p. 197; CSOS:114}

HENTHORN, JAMES (Maryland), pvt., Capt. Joseph Chapline's Company Muster Roll No. 4, Frederick Co., circa 1757-1758, exact dates not given (served 6 days); bill of credit issued or paid in his behalf to Joseph Chaplin for £0.6.0 on 5 Mar 1767. {Ref: MSA S960 or S752, p. 194; CSOS:105}

HENTHORN, JOHN (Maryland), patriot and poss. soldier (rank not specified), Frederick Co., militia pay account submitted in 1758, exact date not given. {Ref: MHM 9:4, p. 366}

HEPBURN, JOHN JR., see "Francis Piles," q.v.

HEPBURN (HEPBORN), THOMAS (Maryland), pvt., Capt. Peregrine Brown's Company Muster Roll, Kent Co., circa 1757-1758, exact dates not given (served 15 days); bill of credit issued or paid in his behalf to Robert Buchanan on 20 Feb 1767 for £0.15.0. {Ref: MSA S960 or S752, p. 180; CSOS:110} Thomas Hepborn m. Ann (N), had children John, Thomas, Joseph, Sarah, and Ann, and d. testate by 8 Apr 1786. {Ref: Kent Co. Wills 7:138}

HERRING, SARAH, see "William Prettyman," q.v.

HERSMAN, ANDREW (Maryland), pvt., Capt. John White's Company Muster Roll, Frederick Co., circa 1757-1758, exact dates not given (served 6 days); bill of credit issued or paid to him for £0.6.0 in 1767, exact date not given. {Ref: MSA S960 or S752, p. 164; CSOS:95}

HERSMAN, MATTHIAS (Maryland), pvt., Capt. John White's Company Muster Roll, Frederick Co., circa 1757-1758, exact dates not given; bill of credit issued or paid to him for £0.6.0 in 1767, exact date not given. {Ref: MSA S960 or S752, p.

164} Matthias Hersman was prob. son of this noteworthy gentleman: "Matthias Hersman, died 18th ult., at Patterson's Creek in Hampshire Co., VA; the deceased was a native of Germany, aged by the most accurate accounts, 125 years old; he had three wives in Germany and one in this country; Baltimore, May 13." {Ref: *MD Gazette*, 21 May 1801}

HERVILL, JOHN (Delaware), pvt., Capt. French Battell's Company of Lower County Provincials, enlisted 16 May 1758. {Ref: ARDE I:16; ARPA (2nd Series) 2:555}

HESHON, VENOL (Maryland), pvt., Capt. Thomas Norris' Company, Frederick Co., circa 1757-1758, exact dates not given (served 30 days); bill of credit issued or paid in his behalf to Michael McGuire on 11 Apr 1767 for £1.10.0; name listed once as "William or Venil Heshon." {Ref: MSA S960 or S752, p. 176; CSOS:108}

HEWES, LYDIA, see "John Grubb," q.v.

HICKLE, LUDERICK, see "Ludwick Huckle," q.v.

HICKMAN, CONRAD (Maryland), pvt., Capt. Stephen Rensburg's or Rensburger's Company Muster Roll, Frederick Co., circa 1757-1758, exact dates not given (served 34 days); bill of credit or order issued to Casper Shaff and paid to David Cumming for £1.14.0 on 18 Apr 1767; name mistakenly transcribed once as "Conrad Kickman." {Ref: MSA S960 or S752, p. 183; CSOS:112}

HICKMAN, DAVID (Maryland), pvt., Capt. William Luckett's Company Muster Roll, Frederick Co., circa 1757-1758, exact dates not given (served 30 days); bill of credit issued or paid in his behalf to William Luckett, Jr. for £1.10.0 on 6 Apr 1767. {Ref: MSA S960 or S752, p. 170; CSOS:99}

HICKMAN, HENRY (Maryland), sgt., Capt. William Luckett's Company Muster Roll, Frederick Co., circa 1757-1758, exact dates not given (served 30 days); militia pay account submitted in 1758, exact date not given. {Ref: MHM 9:4, p. 367} Bill of credit issued or paid in his behalf to William Luckett, Jr. for £2.10.0 on 6 Apr 1767. {Ref: MSA S960 or S752, p. 170; CSOS:99}

HICKMAN, JOHN (Maryland), lieut., Capt. William Luckett's Company Muster Roll, Frederick Co., circa 1757-1758, exact dates not given; bill of credit issued or paid in his behalf to William Luckett, Jr. for £3.10.0 on 6 Apr 1767. {Ref: MSA S960 or S752, p. 170}

HICKMAN, JOSHUA (Maryland), lieut., Capt. William Luckett's Company Muster Roll, Frederick Co., circa 1757-1758, exact dates not given (served 30 days); militia pay account submitted in 1758, exact date not given. {Ref: MHM 9:4, p. 367; CSOS:99}

HICKMAN, JOSHUA JR. (Maryland), pvt., Capt. William Luckett's Company Muster Roll, Frederick Co., circa 1757-1758, exact dates not given (served 30 days); bill of credit issued or paid in his behalf to William Luckett, Jr. for £1.10.0 on 6 Apr 1767. {Ref: MSA S960 or S752, p. 170; CSOS:100}

HICKMAN, SOLOMON (Maryland), pvt., Capt. William Luckett's Company Muster Roll, Frederick Co., circa 1757-1758, exact dates not given (served 30 days); bill of credit issued or paid in his behalf to William Luckett, Jr. for £1.4.0 on 6 Apr 1767. {Ref: MSA S960 or S752, p. 170; CSOS:100}

HICKMAN, STEPHEN (Maryland), son of William, m. (N), had children William, Stephen, Richard, and Ann, and d. testate by 12 Feb 1776. {Ref: WMG 4:4, p. 84} Pvt., Capt. William Luckett's Company Muster Roll, Frederick Co., circa 1757-1758, exact dates not given (served 30 days); bill of credit issued or paid in his behalf to William Luckett, Jr. for £1.10.0 on 6 Apr 1767. {Ref: MSA S960 or S752, p. 169; CSOS:100}

HICKMAN, WILLIAM (Maryland), m. (N), had children Stephen, Elizabeth, Betty, Ann, and prob. others not named in his will, and d. testate by 17 Dec 1766. {Ref: WMG 2:4, p. 167} Patriot and poss. soldier (rank not specified), Frederick Co., militia pay account submitted in 1758, exact date not given. {Ref: MHM 9:4, p. 367}

HICKS, ANN, see "Henry Travers," q.v.

HICKS, JOHN (Maryland), pvt., Capt. Peregrine Brown's Company Muster Roll, Kent Co., circa 1757-1758, exact dates not given (served 15 days); bill of credit issued or paid in his behalf to Robert Buchanan on 20 Feb 1767 for £0.15.0. {Ref: MSA S960 or S752, p. 179; CSOS:110}

HICKS, JOHN JR. (Maryland), farmer; b. 8 Nov 1731, Kent Co., son of John and Sarah Hicks, of Shrewsbury Parish; pvt., Capt. Peregrine Brown's 7th Co. of Foot Militia, Kent Co., on 19 Feb 1758, by which time he had enlisted, but reportedly refused to appear and serve in arms against the enemy. {Ref: ESVR; ARMD 31:283, 288}

HICKS, PHILIZANNA, see "John Cross," q.v.

HICKSON, FREDERICK (Maryland), pvt., Capt. Joseph Chapline's Company Muster Roll No. 1, Frederick Co., circa 1757-1758, exact dates not given (served 37 days); bill of credit issued or paid in his behalf to Joseph Chaplin for £1.17.0 on 5 Mar 1767. {Ref: MSA S960 or S752, p. 191; CSOS:103}

HIET, EZEKIEL (Maryland), pvt., Capt. Moses Chapline's Company Muster Roll No. 2, Frederick Co., circa 1757-1758, exact dates not given (served 13 days); bill of credit issued or paid in his behalf to Joseph Chaplin for £0.13.0 on 13 Jun 1767. {Ref: MSA S960 or S752, p. 197; CSOS:114}

HIGGS, JOHN (Maryland), pvt., Capt. Richard Pearis' Company of MD Troops, Frederick Co., from 9 Oct 1757 to 31 May 1758. {Ref: MHS MS.375.1} Payment to him was recorded in Col. Dagworthy's account book on 15 Jul 1762. {Ref: MHS MS.375}

HILDERBRAND (HILDEBRAND), HERONIMUS (Maryland), pvt., Capt. John Middaugh's Company Muster Roll, Frederick Co., circa 1757-1758, exact dates not given (served 30 days); bill of credit or order issued to Casper Shaff and paid to David Cumming for £1.10.0 on 18 Apr 1767. {Ref: MSA S960 or S752, p. 172; CSOS:100}

HILL, ARTHUR (Delaware), pvt., Capt. French Battell's Company of Lower County Provincials, enlisted 17 May 1758. {Ref: ARDE I:16; ARPA (2nd Series) 2:555}

HILL, HENRY (Maryland), m. (N), had children Robert, Joseph, Henry Truman, Philip, Thomas, John, Elizabeth, Catharine, and Ann, and d. testate by 24 Mar 1773. {Ref: WMG 3:4, p. 154} Pvt., Capt. Elias Delashmutt's Company Muster Roll, Frederick Co., circa 1757-1758, exact dates not given (served 30 days); bill of credit or order issued to Casper Shaff and paid to David Cumming on 18 Apr 1767 for £1.10.0. {Ref: MSA S960 or S752, p. 163; CSOS:94}

HILL, HENRY (Maryland), drummer, Capt. John Dagworthy's Company of MD Troops, Frederick Co., from 9 Oct 1757 to 16 Feb 1758 when he was discharged. {Ref: MHS MS.375.1; CSOS:76} Payment to him was recorded in Col. Dagworthy's account book on 22 Jul 1762. {Ref: MHS MS.375}

HILL, JAMES (Maryland), pvt., Capt. Francis Ware's Company of MD Troops, Charles Co., from 9 Oct 1757 to 14 Sep 1758 (served 340 days) when he was reported as killed; however, payment to him was recorded in Col. Dagworthy's account book on 21 Jul 1762. {Ref: MHS MS.375; CSOS:88; MHS MS.375.1}

HILL, JOHN (Delaware), pvt., Kent Co. Militia, Capt. John Caton's Company, 25 Apr 1757 (date of muster roll). {Ref: ARDE I:14}

HILL, JOHN (Maryland), pvt., Capt. Elias Delashmutt's Company Muster Roll, Frederick Co., 13 Aug 1757, exact dates not given (served 52 days); also served another 30 days, exact dates not given; bill of credit issued or paid in his behalf to Elias Delashmut, Jr. on 16 Mar 1767 for £4.2.0. {Ref: MSA S960 or S752, p. 163; CSOS:94, 98}

HILL, JONATHAN (Delaware), b. c1741, Sussex, DE (age 18 in 1759); pvt., enlisted in Capt. John Wright's Company and mustered on 11 May 1759. {Ref: ARDE I:25; ARPA (2nd Series) 2:592}

HILL, JONATHAN (Maryland), pvt., Capt. Alexander Beall's Company of MD Troops, Frederick Co., from 9 Oct 1757 to 8 Nov 1758. {Ref: MHS MS.375.1; CSOS:80} Payment to him was recorded in Col. Dagworthy's account book on 12 Jul 1762. {Ref: MHS MS.375}

HILL, ROBERT (Maryland), pvt., Capt. Elias Delashmutt's Company Muster Roll, Frederick Co., circa 1757-1758, exact dates not given (served 30 days); bill of credit issued or paid in his behalf to Elias Delashmut, Jr. on 16 Mar 1767 for £1.10.0. {Ref: MSA S960 or S752, p. 162; CSOS:94}

HILL, SARAH, see "Nehemiah Davis," q.v.

HILL, SILVESTER (Maryland), pvt., Capt. Richard Pearis' Company of MD Troops, Frederick Co., circa 9 Oct 1757 to 31 May 1758; pvt., Capt. Alexander Beall's Company of MD Troops, Frederick Co., from 1 Jun 1758 to 26 Sep 1758 when he reportedly deserted; however, payment to him was recorded in Col. Dagworthy's account book on 17 Jul 1762. {Ref: MHS MS.375.1; CSOS:81, 90; MHS MS.375}

HILL, THOMAS, see "Thomas Till" and "Thomas Beall," q.v.

HILL, THOMAS (Maryland), pvt., Capt. Henry Casson's Company Muster Roll, Queen Anne's Co., circa 1757-1758, exact dates not given (served 27 days); bill of credit issued or paid in his behalf to Capt. Casson for Hill's widow (unnamed) on 27 Mar 1767 for £1.7.0. {Ref: MSA S960 or S752, p. 178; CSOS:109} Thomas Hill m. Elizabeth Roe on 19 Feb 1757 in St. John's Parish, Queen Anne's Co. {Ref: MGSB 16:2, p. 74}

HILL, THOMAS (Maryland), b. c1722, chairmaker (age about 35 in 1757); pvt., enlisted by Thomas Beall, Prince George's Co. recruiting officer (exact date not given); reportedly deserted in July 1757. {Ref: *MD Gazette*, 4 Aug 1757} However,

Gov. Horatio Sharpe wrote, in part, to the MD Assembly on 7 Dec 1757: "One Thomas Beall, a young fellow of Prince George's Co. (who was empowered by me to enlist men for his Majesty's Service, in consequence of several Acts of Assembly lately passed in this province) is accused of having pretended to enlist the said [Edward] Seares, [Thomas] Hill and [David] Mackelfish, of treating them afterwards as deserters, of compelling Seares to pay £10 for a discharged, which he could not give, and of endeavouring to oblige the other two to purchase their discharges likewise. Mr. Beall is not present to hear what is alleged against him, yet I don't think it would be right to condemn him unheard; he is no officer that I know of, neither is he in the least dependent on me; and if the complainants can prove that he has acted illegally, I hope they may redress themselves without applying to any branch of the Legislature; but if it should, on farther enquiry, appear that they were duly enlisted, you will not, I am persuaded, take it amiss if they are apprehended and delivered up to one of his Majesty's Officers." {Ref: ARMD 55:320}

HILL, WILLIAM (Maryland), pvt., Capt. William Luckett's Company Muster Roll, Frederick Co., circa 1757-1758, exact dates not given (served 30 days); bill of credit issued or paid in his behalf to William Luckett, Jr. for £1.10.0 on 6 Apr 1767. {Ref: MSA S960 or S752, p. 169; CSOS:100}

HILL, WILLIAM, see "Nehemiah Davis," q.v.

HILLARY, ELEANOR, see "Thomas Gantt," q.v.

HILLEN (HELLEN), DAVID (Maryland), pvt., Capt. Joshua Beall's Company of MD Troops, Prince George's Co., from 9 Oct 1757 to 7 Dec 1757 when he was discharged. {Ref: MHS MS.375.1; CSOS:84} Payment to him was recorded in Col. Dagworthy's account book on 24 Jul 1762. {Ref: MHS MS.375}

HILLEN (HELLEN), JACOB (Maryland), pvt., Capt. Richard Pearis' Company of MD Troops, Frederick Co., circa 9 Oct 1757 to 31 May 1758; pvt., Capt. Joshua Beall's Company of MD Troops, Prince George's Co., from 1 Jun 1758 to 8 Nov 1758. {Ref: MHS MS.375.1; CSOS:84, 90} Payment to him was recorded in Col. Dagworthy's account book on 12 Jul 1762 for work on Fort Cumberland. {Ref: MHS MS.375}

HILLEN (HELLEN), JOHN (Maryland), pvt., Capt. Joshua Beall's Company of MD Troops, Prince George's Co., from 9 Oct 1757 to 29 Jan 1758 when he was discharged; payment to him was recorded in Col. Dagworthy's account book on 12 Jul 1762 for work on Fort Cumberland. {Ref: MHS MS.375; CSOS:84; MHS MS.375.1}

HILLEN (HELLEN), THOMAS (Maryland), pvt., Capt. Francis Ware's Company of MD Troops, Charles Co., circa 1757-1758, exact dates not given; pvt., Capt. John Dagworthy's Company of MD Troops, Frederick Co., from 31 Dec 1758 to 26 Apr 1759 (served 117 days). {Ref: MHS MS.375.1; CSOS:76} Payment to him was recorded in Col. Dagworthy's account book on 21 Jul 1762. {Ref: MHS MS.375}

HILLIARD, ANN, see "William White," q.v.

HILLYARD, CHARLES (Delaware), lieut., militia, Murderkill Hundred, Kent Co. on Delaware, 1756; resigned in March 1758. {Ref: ARDE I:12, 15; ARPA (2nd Series) 2:527, 577; HDE I:141}

HILLYARD, CHARLES (Delaware), captain, militia, Lower Part of Duck Creek Hundred, Kent Co. on Delaware, 1756. {Ref: ARDE I:12; ARPA (2nd Series) 2:527-529; HDE I:141}

HINCKLE (HINCLE), GEORGE (Maryland), pvt., Capt. John Middaugh's Company Muster Roll, Frederick Co., circa 1757-1758, exact dates not given; bill of credit issued or paid to him for £0.17.0 in 1767, exact date not given. {Ref: MSA S960 or S752, p. 171}

HINCKLE, JOHN (Delaware or Pennsylvania), b. c1737, MD (smith, age 21 in 1758); pvt., Capt. John Bull's Company of the PA Regt., by 1 Jun 1758 (date of muster roll return). {Ref: ARPA (2nd Series) 2:491}

HINDMAN, JACOB (Maryland), b. c1710, Queen Anne's Co., son of Rev. James Hindman and Mary Lookerman, m. Mary Trippe on 29 Jan 1738/9, had children James, William, Jacob Henderson, Edward, John, Mary, Elizabeth, and Sarah, and d. 9 Sep 1766, Talbot Co.; patriot, planter, gentleman, captain by 1741, member of the MD Assembly (Dorchester Co. representative, 1741-1744, and sheriff, 1737-1740; Talbot Co. representative, 1745-1748, 1755-1758, and justice, 1749-1766), and refused to meet to carry out the provisions of the Stamp Act in 1765. {Ref: BDML I:442-443; *MD Gazette*, 11 Sep 1766}

HINDSLEY, AMOS (Delaware), yeoman, of Murderkill Hundred, m. Pations (N), had children James, John, Amos, Daniel, Meriam, Hannah, and Pations, and d. testate by 4 Feb 1796. {Ref: CDSS:94} Pvt., Kent Co. Militia, Capt. John Caton's Company, 25 Apr 1757 (date of muster roll). {Ref: ARDE I:14}

HINMAN (HENMAN), BENJAMIN (Maryland), pvt., Capt. Alexander Beall's Company of MD Troops, Frederick Co., from 9 Oct 1757 to 8 Nov 1758. {Ref: MHS MS.375.1; CSOS:81} Payment to him was recorded in Col. Dagworthy's account book on 22 Feb 1763. {Ref: MHS MS.375}

HISER, GASPER (Maryland), patriot and prob. soldier, Frederick Co., petitioned the court in June 1758, stating "that whereas the Court Martial hath fined your petitioner in the sum of 400 lbs. of tobacco for not mustering as the law directs, your petitioner being unacquainted with the said law and likewise being near the age of 57 years, and troubled with a violent pain in his back which disabled him for many days together ... being but a foreigner hath no English etc. Likewise the Court Martial hath fined John Hiser the son of your petitioner four fines though your petitioner's said son was not of age of 16 years until the 28th day of April last." He asked that the fines be remitted, but the Court rejected his plea and it was recorded in the judgment records. {Ref: TWL:178, citing Frederick Co. Judgment Records}

HISSEL, SAMUEL (Maryland), pvt., Capt. Joseph Chapline's Company Muster Roll No. 4, Frederick Co., circa 1757-1758, exact dates not given (served 6 days); bill of credit issued or paid to him for £0.6.0 in 1767, exact date not given. {Ref: MSA S960 or S752, p. 194; CSOS:105}

HITE, JOHN (Maryland), pvt., Capt. Peter Butler's Company Muster Roll, Frederick Co., circa 1757-1758, exact dates not given (served 34 days); bill of credit or order issued to him for £1.14.0 in March 1767. {Ref: MSA S960 or S752, p. 167; CSOS:97}

HOBSON, THOMAS (Maryland), pvt., Capt. Richard Pearis' Company of MD Troops, Frederick Co., from 9 Oct 1757 to 4 Apr 1758 when he reportedly deserted; however, payment to him was recorded in Col. Dagworthy's account book on 8 Mar 1763. {Ref: MHS MS.375; CSOS:90; MHS MS.375.1}

HODGENS (HODGINS), ROBERT (Maryland), pvt., Capt. Francis Ware's Company of MD Troops, Charles Co., from 1 Jun 1758 to 8 Nov 1758 (transferred from Capt. Richard Pearis' Company; exact dates of service not given; served 161 days altogether). {Ref: MHS MS.375.1; CSOS:88, 90} Payment to him was recorded in Col. Dagworthy's account book on 15 Jul 1762. {Ref: MHS MS.375}

HODGES, JOHN (Maryland), pvt., Capt. John Dagworthy's Company of MD Troops, Frederick Co., from 9 Oct 1757 to 16 Apr 1759 when he reportedly deserted; however, payment to him was recorded in Col. Dagworthy's account book on 26 Feb 1763. {Ref: MHS MS.375; CSOS:76; MHS MS.375.1} See "Jane Morgan," q.v.

HODGINS, ROBERT (Maryland), pvt., Capt. Richard Pearis' Company of MD Troops, Frederick Co., circa 9 Oct 1757 to 31 May 1758. {Ref: MHS MS.375.1; CSOS:90}

HODGSON, ROBERT (Delaware), pvt., Kent Co. Militia, Capt. John Caton's Company, 25 Apr 1757 (date of muster roll); 2nd lieut., 23 Apr 1758. {Ref: ARDE I:14, 16; ARPA (2nd Series) 2:580}

HODGSON (HODGSDON), THOMAS JR. (Maryland), pvt., Capt. Thomas Norris' Company, Frederick Co., circa 1757-1758, exact dates not given (served 30 days); bill of credit issued or paid to him for £1.10.0 in 1767, exact date not given. {Ref: MSA S960 or S752, p. 176; CSOS:108}

HODGSON, WILLIAM (Delaware), pvt., Kent Co. Militia, Capt. John Caton's Company, 25 Apr 1757 (date of muster roll). {Ref: ARDE I:13}

HOGG, JAMES (Maryland or Pennsylvania), lieut., Capt. Hamilton's Company, killed during Col. Armstrong's attack on Kittanning in 1756. {Ref: *MD Gazette*, 30 Sep 1756}

HOLDSWORTH (HOLSWORTH), AARON (Maryland), b. c1737 in England, came to America and served his time at Snowden's Iron Works in MD; soldier who was reported as deserted by Capt. Joshua Beall at Fort Frederick (age 20 in 1757); he and Philip Connolly were confined to jail by Colmore Beans, Sheriff of Prince George's Co., and subsequently escaped. {Ref: *MD Gazette*, 3 Mar and 10 Mar 1757}

HOLDSWORTH, THOMAS, see "Benjamin Mackall, Jr.," q.v.

HOLLAND, NEHEMIAH, see "Peter Chaillé," q.v.

HOLLAND, SCARBOROUGH, see "Peter Chaillé," q.v.

HOLLAND, WILLIAM (Maryland), patriot, Annapolis, Anne Arundel Co., pay account submitted for quartering soldiers in 1757 or 1758, exact dates not given. {Ref: MHM 9:3, p. 260}

HOLLIDAY, CLEMENT (Maryland), pvt., Capt. Joshua Beall's Company Muster Roll, Prince George's Co., circa 1757-1758, exact dates not given; bill of credit issued or paid to him for £2.3.0 on 22 Oct 1771. {Ref: MSA S960 or S752, p. 185}

HOLLINGSWORTH, JESSE (Maryland), b. 12 Mar 1732/3, Cecil Co., son of Zebulon Hollingsworth and Ann Mauldin, m. 1st to Sinai Ricketts circa 1758 and 2nd to Rachel Lyde Goodwin in 1790, had children Zebulon, Francis, John, Ann, and Mary, and d. testate by 6 Oct 1810, Baltimore City; merchant, privateer, gentleman, commissioner (to make roads leading to Baltimore) in 1774, activist in organizing the Methodist Society in Baltimore in 1775, arranger for the transport of troops and supplies (agent for the state) during the Revolutionary War, and member of the MD Assembly (1786-1787). {Ref: BDML I:448-449} Captain of a militia company that departed Head of Elk in Cecil Co. on 16 Aug 1758 and marched to Fort Frederick. {Ref: *MD Gazette*, 7 Sep 1758} Militia pay account submitted in 1758, exact date not given; name listed as "Jesse Hollandsworth." {Ref: MHM 9:4, p. 365}

HOLM, MICHAEL (Maryland), pvt., Capt. Jonathan Hagar's Company Muster Roll, Frederick Co., circa 1757-1758, exact dates not given (served 6 days); bill of credit issued or paid to him for £0.6.0 in 1767, exact date not given. {Ref: MSA S960 or S752, p. 174; CSOS:106}

HOLMES, WILLIAM (Maryland), patriot and merchant, Baltimore Co., petitioned the MD Assembly on 20 Oct 1757 "praying an allowance may be made him for twenty one fusils and some other articles furnished the militia under the command of Capt. Stansbury in the year 1756." {Ref: ARMD 55:159}

HOLSTON, WILLIAM (Delaware), b. c1736, Pocomock, MD (shoemaker, age 22 in 1758); pvt., enlisted 10 May 1758 "for the campaign in the lower counties" by Capt. John McClughan (muster roll dated 17 May 1758). {Ref: ARDE I:17; ARPA (2nd Series) 2:489, 570}

HOLT (HOLTS), BENJAMIN (Maryland), pvt., Capt. Stephen Rensburg's or Rensburger's Company Muster Roll, Frederick Co., circa 1757-1758, exact dates not given (served 42 days); bill of credit issued or paid in his behalf to Casper Shaff for £2.2.0 on 2 Mar 1767. {Ref: MSA S960 or S752, p. 182; CSOS:112}

HOLT, PHILIP (Maryland), pvt., Capt. John Dagworthy's Company of MD Troops, Frederick Co., from 9 Oct 1757 to 13 Jan 1758 when he was discharged; payment to him was recorded in Col. Dagworthy's account book on 8 Mar 1763 for work on Fort Cumberland. {Ref: MHS MS.375; CSOS:76; MHS MS.375.1}

HOLT, RYVES or RIVES (Delaware), Esq., m. Catharine (N), had children (N), and d. intestate by 8 Aug 1771. {Ref: CDSS:96} Lieut. Colonel, Militia Regt. of Sussex Co., 1756-1758; Justice of the Peace and Justice of the Supreme Court, 1756-1760. {Ref: GRSD 1:14; ARDE I:13, 15; ARPA (2nd Series) 2:529, 579; HDE I:141}

HOLT, RYVES JR. (Delaware), ensign in Capt. John Wright's Company, mustered on 11 May 1759; commissioned 23 May 1759 and served in 3rd Bttn. of PA Regt. {Ref: ARDE I:25; ARPA (2nd Series) 2:583, 592}

HOLTON, MARGARET, see "Thomas Richardson Roe," q.v.

HOLTZ, JACOB (Maryland), pvt., Capt. John Middaugh's Company Muster Roll, Frederick Co., circa 1757-1758, exact dates not given; bill of credit issued or paid in his behalf to Casper Shaff for £1.10.0 on 2 Mar 1767. {Ref: MSA S960 or S752, p. 171}

HOMEWOOD, ANNE, see "William Govane," q.v.

HOMEWOOD, THOMAS, see "William Govane," q.v.

HOMSTEAD, JOHN (Delaware), pvt., Kent Co. Militia, Capt. John Caton's Company, 25 Apr 1757 (date of muster roll). {Ref: ARDE I:13}

HONOUR, THOMAS (Maryland), farmer; pvt., Capt. Peregrine Brown's 7th Co. of Foot Militia, Kent Co., on 19 Feb 1758, by which time he had enlisted, but reportedly refused to appear and serve in arms against the enemy; he later stated that he "was a very ailing person with rheumatick pains which he is subject to upon every cold he catches, but that before the company marched he got something better, and resolved tho' he risqued his life, he would endeavour to go with the rest, and accordingly went with his baggage on board Edward Drugan's vessel which was impressed to carry him, and staid some time there waiting and ready to go 'till he heard they the rest were all gone in the other vessels." {Ref: ARMD 31:283, 286-288} See "James Poole," q.v.

HOOD, BENNETT (Maryland), pvt., Capt. Samuel Chapman's Company Muster Roll, Anne Arundel Co., circa 1757-1758, exact dates not given; bill of credit issued or paid to him for £1.18.0 on 25 Feb 1767. {Ref: MSA S960 or S752, p. 188}

HOOFER (HOOVER), JAC or JOE (Maryland), pvt., Capt. Moses Chapline's Company Muster Roll No. 3, Frederick Co., circa 1757-1758, exact dates not given (served 6 days); bill of credit issued or paid to him for £0.6.0 in 1767, exact date not given. {Ref: MSA S960 or S752, p. 198; CSOS:115}

HOOFER (HOOVER), JACOB (Maryland), pvt., Capt. Moses Chapline's Company Muster Roll No. 3, Frederick Co., circa 1757-1758, exact dates not given (served 6 days); bill of credit issued or paid to him for £0.6.0 in 1767, exact date not given. {Ref: MSA S960 or S752, p. 198; CSOS:115}

HOOFER (HOOVER), JOHN (Maryland), pvt., Capt. Moses Chapline's Company Muster Roll No. 3, Frederick Co., circa 1757-1758, exact dates not given (served 6 days); bill of credit issued or paid to him for £0.6.0 in 1767, exact date not given. {Ref: MSA S960 or S752, p. 198; CSOS:115}

HOOFMAN (HOOPMAN), ADAM (Maryland), pvt., Capt. Joseph Chapline's Company Muster Roll No. 1, Frederick Co., circa 1757-1758, exact dates not given (served 36 days); bill of credit issued or paid in his behalf to Joseph Chaplin for £1.16.0 on 24 Apr 1767. {Ref: MSA S960 or S752, p. 192; CSOS:103}

HOOK, ADAM (Maryland), pvt., Capt. Joseph Chapline's Company Muster Roll No. 1, Frederick Co., circa 1757-1758, exact dates not given (served 21 days); bill of credit issued or paid in his behalf to Joseph Chaplin for £1.1.0 on 24 Apr 1767. {Ref: MSA S960 or S752, p. 192; CSOS:103}

HOOK, BRICE (Maryland), pvt., Capt. Joseph Chapline's Company Muster Roll No. 1, Frederick Co., circa 1757-1758, exact dates not given (served 25 days);

bill of credit issued or paid in his behalf to Joseph Chaplin for £1.1.0 on 8 Jun 1767. {Ref: MSA S960 or S752, p. 192; CSOS:103}

HOOKS, FREDERICK (Maryland), pvt., Capt. John White's Company Muster Roll, Frederick Co., circa 1757-1758, exact dates not given (served 6 days); bill of credit issued or paid to him for £0.6.0 in 1767, exact date not given. {Ref: MSA S960 or S752, p. 164; CSOS:95}

HOOPER, HENRY JR. (Maryland), b. c1727, Dorchester Co., son of Henry Hooper and Mary Ennalls, m. his first cousin Ann Ennalls by 1746, had children William Ennalls, Henry, John, Mary, Sarah, and Anne, and d. by December 1790; captain by 1751, deputy commissary (1748-1750), county justice (1754-1769), colonel by 1772, member of the MD Assembly (1768-1780), member of the Council of Safety in 1775, county lieutenant in 1777, and brigadier general of the lower Eastern Shore (1776-1783). {Ref: BDML I:457-458}

HOOPER, THOMAS (Maryland), pvt., Capt. Joshua Beall's Company Muster Roll, Prince George's Co., circa 1757-1758, exact dates not given; bill of credit issued and ordered his assignment to Stephen West for £1.10.6 on 11 Mar 1767. {Ref: MSA S960 or S752, p. 184}

HOOVER, ADAM (Maryland), pvt., Capt. John Middaugh's Company Muster Roll, Frederick Co., circa 1757-1758, exact dates not given (served 30 days); bill of credit issued or paid to him for £1.10.0 in 1767, exact date not given. {Ref: MSA S960 or S752, p. 171; CSOS:101}

HOOVER, JACOB (Maryland), tailor; pvt., Capt. Peter Butler's Company Muster Roll, Frederick Co., circa 1757-1758, exact dates not given (served 34 days); bill of credit or order issued in his behalf for £1.14.0 and paid to Casper Shaff on 2 Mar 1767. {Ref: MSA S960 or S752, p. 166; CSOS:97}

HOOVER, JACOB (Maryland), carpenter; pvt., Capt. Peter Butler's Company Muster Roll, Frederick Co., circa 1757-1758, exact dates not given (served 34 days); bill of credit or order issued in his behalf for £1.14.0 and paid to Casper Shaff on 2 Mar 1767. {Ref: MSA S960 or S752, p. 166; CSOS:97}

HOOVER, JOHN, see "John Hoofer," q.v.

HOOVER, PETER (Maryland), pvt., Capt. John Middaugh's Company Muster Roll, Frederick Co., circa 1757-1758, exact dates not given (served 30 days); bill of credit issued or paid to him for £1.10.0 in 1767, exact date not given. {Ref: MSA S960 or S752, p. 171; CSOS:101}

HOPE, HENRY (Maryland), pvt., Capt. Richard Pearis' Company of MD Troops, Frederick Co., circa 9 Oct 1757 to 31 May 1758; pvt., Capt. Alexander Beall's Company of MD Troops, Frederick Co., from 1 Jun 1758 to 30 Dec 1758. {Ref: MHS MS.375.1; CSOS:81, 90} Payment to him was recorded in Col. Dagworthy's account book on 15 Jul 1762. {Ref: MHS MS.375}

HOPEWELL, ANN, see "Thomas Aisquith," q.v.

HOPEWELL, HUGH, see "Thomas Aisquith," q.v.

HOPEWELL, JOSEPH (Maryland), sgt., Capt. William McClellan's Company of MD Volunteers, Frederick Co., circa 1763-1764; on muster roll dated 15 Nov 1764 at Camp at the Forks of Muskingham. {Ref: ARMD 32:99}

HOPHAM, GEORGE (Maryland), b. c1734, Baltimore Co., son of William and Jane Hopham. {Ref: BCF:339} Pvt., Capt. Tobias Stansbury's Company Muster Roll, Baltimore Co., circa 1757-1758, exact dates not given; bill of credit issued or paid to him for £1.19.0 in 1767, exact date not given; name mistakenly transcribed once as "George Hopson." {Ref: MSA S960 or S752, p. 186; CSOS:118}

HOPKINS, HAMPTON, see "Benton Harris," q.v.

HOPPER, ELIZABETH, see "Joseph Nicholson," q.v.

HOPPER, MARY, see "Joseph Nicholson," q.v.

HOPPER, WILLIAM (Maryland), b. 11 Jul 1707, Queen Anne's Co., son of William Hopper and (N), m. 1st to Esther Sweatnam by 1739, m. 2nd to Mary Anne Wright on 21 May 1741, m. 3rd to Sarah Dockery (widow of Matthew Dockery) in 1763, had children William (1743-1806), Mary, Elizabeth, Henrietta, Mary Ann, Sally, and Dorothy, and d. 16 Apr 1772; carpenter in 1729, counter of tobacco plants in 1730, merchant by 1737, captain by 1746 (Light Horse Co., 1751), member of the MD Assembly (1745-1754, 1758-1761, 1770, and served on the Arms and Ammunition Committee, 1751-1754), sheriff (1754-1757), tax collector by 1756, colonel by 1758, and county justice (1743-1772). {Ref: BDML I:460-461; SCWM III:102, 255} Militia pay account submitted in 1758, exact date not given. {Ref: MHM 9:4, p. 367; *MD Gazette*, 28 Sep 1758 and 16 Apr 1772}

HOPSON, GEORGE, see "George Hopham," q.v.

HORAN, HENRY (Delaware), pvt., Capt. Richard McWilliams' Company of Foot, New Castle Co., enlisted 28 Dec 1757. {Ref: ARDE I:15}

HORINE (HOREIN), TOBIAS (Maryland), son of Adam Horein (of Flyne, Germany), m. Elizabeth (N), had children Adam, Tobias, Samuel, Magdalen, Susanna, Catharine, Judith, Mary, and Elizabeth, and d. testate by 30 Oct 1773 at Mill Creek, Frederick Co. {Ref: WMG 4:1, p. 11} Pvt., Capt. Peter Bainbridge's Company Muster Roll, Frederick Co., circa 1757-1758, exact dates not given (served 28 days); bill of credit issued or paid in his behalf to Casper Shaff on 4 Mar 1767 for £1.8.0; name mistakenly transcribed once as "Tobias Houme." {Ref: MSA S960 or S752, p. 180; CSOS:111}

HORN, JOHN, see "John Han," q.v.

HORNER, JAMES (Maryland), pvt., Capt. Joshua Beall's Company of MD Troops, Prince George's Co., from 9 Oct 1757 to 31 May 1758 when he reportedly deserted; however, payment to him was recorded in Col. Dagworthy's account book on 26 Feb 1763. {Ref: MHS MS.375; CSOS:84; MHS MS.375.1}

HORSEY, SARAH, see "John Adams" and "William Adams," q.v.

HOSKINSON (HOCKINSON), CHARLES (Maryland), pvt., Capt. William Luckett's Company Muster Roll, Frederick Co., circa 1757-1758, exact dates not given (served 30 days); bill of credit issued or paid in his behalf to William Luckett, Jr. for £1.10.0 on 6 Apr 1767; name mistakenly transcribed once as "Charles Horkinson." {Ref: MSA S960 or S752, p. 170; CSOS:99}

HOUGH (HOFF), JACOB (Maryland), pvt., Capt. Stephen Rensburg's or Rensburger's Company Muster Roll, Frederick Co., circa 1757-1758, exact dates not given (served 42 days); militia pay account submitted in 1758, exact date not given. {Ref: MHM 9:4, p. 367} Bill of credit issued or paid in his behalf to Casper Shaff for £1.14.0 on 2 Mar 1767. {Ref: MSA S960 or S752, p. 182; CSOS:112}

HOUSE, GEORGE (Maryland), pvt., Capt. Moses Chapline's Company Muster Roll No. 3, Frederick Co., circa 1757-1758, exact dates not given (served 6 days); bill of credit issued or paid in his behalf to Joseph Chapline for £0.6.0 on 8 Jun 1767. {Ref: MSA S960 or S752, p. 198; CSOS:115}

HOUSE, WILLIAM (Maryland), pvt., Capt. Peter Butler's Company Muster Roll, Frederick Co., circa 1757-1758, exact dates not given (served 34 days); bill of credit or order issued in his behalf for £1.14.0 and paid to Casper Shaff on 2 Mar 1767. {Ref: MSA S960 or S752, p. 166; CSOS:97}

HOUSTON (HUSTON), ALEXANDER (Delaware), b. c1733, Toboyne, Ireland (laborer, age 25 in 1758); pvt., enlisted 1 May 1758 "for the campaign in the lower counties" by Capt. John McClughan. "Alexander Houston" was a pvt. in the militia in 1777 and "Alexander Huston, of Murderkill Hundred" m. Ann (N), had children John, Samuel, and Ann, and d. testate in Kent Co. in 1785. {Ref: ARDE I:17; ARPA (2nd Series) 2:570; RPDE:130}

HOUSTON (HUSTON), ROBERT (Delaware), b. c1728, Ireland (cordwainer, age 30 in 1758); pvt., recruited by Capt. Benjamin Noxon and enlisted on 22 Apr 1758. {Ref: ARDE I:19; ARPA (2nd Series) 2:566} On 5 Jul 1776 he was among those who requested that the Council of Safety form militia companies; served as a justice of the peace in 1778. {Ref: RPDE:130}

HOUSTON, COMFORT, see "Peter Chaillé," q.v.

HOVER, ANDREW (Maryland), pvt., Capt. John White's Company Muster Roll, Frederick Co., circa 1757-1758, exact dates not given (served 6 days); bill of credit issued or paid to him for £0.6.0 in 1767, exact date not given. {Ref: MSA S960 or S752, p. 164; CSOS:96}

HOWARD, CHARLES (Maryland), b. c1737, Baltimore Co., son of Edmund and Ruth Howard. {Ref: BCF:343} Pvt., Capt. Tobias Stansbury's Company Muster Roll, Baltimore Co., circa 1757-1758, exact dates not given; bill of credit issued or paid in his behalf to William Gist for £3.6.0 on 6 Mar 1767. {Ref: MSA S960 or S752, p. 186}

HOWARD, CORNELIUS (Maryland), pvt., Capt. William Luckett's Company Muster Roll, Frederick Co., circa 1757-1758, exact dates not given (served 30 days); bill of credit issued or paid in his behalf to William Luckett, Jr. for £1.10.0 on 6 Apr 1767. {Ref: MSA S960 or S752, p. 169; CSOS:99}

HOWARD, EDMUND, see "Charles Howard," q.v.

HOWARD, HANNAH, see "Philip Hammond," q.v.

HOWARD, JOHN (Maryland), pvt., Capt. Tobias Stansbury's Company Muster Roll, Baltimore Co., circa 1757-1758, exact dates not given; bill of credit issued or paid in his behalf to John Doughaday for £1.18.0 on 13 May 1767. {Ref: MSA S960 or S752, p. 186} See "Arthur Lee," q.v.

HOWARD, RACHEL, see "Charles Ridgely" and "John Ridgely," q.v.

HOWARD, REZIN or REASIN (Maryland), pvt., Capt. William Luckett's Company Muster Roll, Frederick Co., circa 1757-1758, exact dates not given (served 30 days); bill of credit issued or paid in his behalf to William Luckett, Jr. for £1.10.0 on 6 Apr 1767. {Ref: MSA S960 or S752, p. 169; CSOS:99}

HOWARD, RICHARD (Maryland), pvt., Capt. Richard Pearis' Company of MD Troops, Frederick Co., circa 9 Oct 1757 to 31 May 1758. {Ref: MHS MS.375.1; CSOS:90}

HOWARD, RUTH, see "Charles Howard," q.v.

HOWARD, SAMUEL (Maryland), patriot, Annapolis, Anne Arundel Co., pay account submitted for quartering soldiers in 1757 or 1758, exact dates not given. {Ref: MHM 9:3, p. 260}

HOWARD, SARAH, see "Christopher Gist" and "Nathaniel Gist," q.v.

HOWE, SARAH, see "Alexander Somervell," q.v.

HOWELL, DAVID (Delaware), b. c1730, m. Sarah (N), had children David, Thomas, Oliver, Samuel, Dinah, and Nancy, and d. testate in Pencader Hundred in 1792. {Ref: RPDE:130} Ensign, Red Lion Hundred, Lower Regt. of Militia, New Castle Co., 1756. {Ref: ARDE I:12; ARPA (2nd Series) 2:525; HDE I:141} Lieut. in the militia in 1777; subscribed to the Oath of Fidelity and Allegiance in 1778. {Ref: RPDE:130}

HOWELL, ELIAS (Delaware), pvt., Kent Co. Militia, Capt. John Caton's Company, 25 Apr 1757 (date of muster roll). {Ref: ARDE I:14}

HOWELL, JOS. JR. (Delaware), pvt., Kent Co. Militia, Capt. John Caton's Company, 25 Apr 1757 (date of muster roll). {Ref: ARDE I:14}

HOWELL, MARY, see "William Reynolds," q.v.

HOWELL, SAMUEL (Delaware), pvt., Kent Co. Militia, Capt. John Caton's Company, 25 Apr 1757 (date of muster roll). {Ref: ARDE I:14}

HOWELL, SARAH, see "David Howell," q.v.

HOZIER, JOSHUA (Maryland), pvt., Capt. John Dagworthy's Company of MD Troops, Frederick Co., circa 9 Oct 1757 to 26 Apr 1759. {Ref: MHS MS.375.1; CSOS:76} Payment to him was recorded in Col. Dagworthy's account book on 11 Jul 1762. {Ref: MHS MS.375}

HUBBART (HUBBARD), EDWARD (Maryland), pvt., Capt. Joseph Hanson Harrison's Company Muster Roll, Charles Co., circa 1757-1758, exact dates not given; bill of credit issued or paid in his behalf to Francis Ware for £2.9.0 on 20 Feb 1767. {Ref: MSA S960 or S752, p. 189}

HUCKLE (HUKLE), LUDWICK (Maryland), pvt., Capt. Stephen Rensburg's or Rensburger's Company Muster Roll, Frederick Co., circa 1757-1758, exact dates not given (served 34 days); bill of credit or order issued to Casper Shaff and paid to David Cumming for £1.14.0 on 18 Apr 1767; name transcribed once as "Luderick Hickle." {Ref: MSA S960 or S752, p. 183; CSOS:113}

HUDSON, JEREMIAH (Maryland), pvt., Capt. Francis Ware's Company of MD Troops, Charles Co., from 9 Oct 1757 to 2 Nov 1758 (served 24 days) when he was reported as dead; however, payment to him was recorded in Col. Dagworthy's account book on 7 Mar 1763. {Ref: MHS MS.375; CSOS:88; MHS MS.375.1}

HUDSON, JOHN (Delaware), shallopman; pvt., Kent Co. Militia, Capt. John Caton's Company, 25 Apr 1757 (date of muster roll). {Ref: ARDE I:13}

HUET, JEAN, see "Samuel Bevens Turner," q.v.

HUFF, ABRAHAM (Maryland), pvt., Capt. John Middaugh's Company Muster Roll, Frederick Co., circa 1757-1758, exact dates not given (served 30 days); bill of credit issued or paid in his behalf to Peter Grosh for £1.10.0 on 4 Mar 1767. {Ref: MSA S960 or S752, p. 172; CSOS:101}

HUFF, JOHN (Maryland), b. c1728, MD; pvt., Capt. Robert Stewart's Company of VA Militia, enlisted on 2 Aug 1756 (age 28). {Ref: MSR I:38}

HUFF, LAWRENCE (Maryland), pvt., Capt. John Middaugh's Company Muster Roll, Frederick Co., circa 1757-1758, exact dates not given (served 30 days); bill of credit issued or paid in his behalf to Peter Grosh for £1.10.0 on 4 Mar 1767. {Ref: MSA S960 or S752, p. 172; CSOS:101}

HUFF, MICHAEL (Maryland), pvt., Capt. Thomas Norris' Company, Frederick Co., circa 1757-1758, exact dates not given (served 30 days); bill of credit issued or paid in his behalf to Thomas Owings on 15 May 1767 for £1.10.0. {Ref: MSA S960 or S752, p. 177; CSOS:108}

HUFFMAN, GEORGE (Maryland), pvt., Capt. Peter Butler's Company Muster Roll, Frederick Co., circa 1757-1758, exact dates not given (served 34 days); bill of credit or order issued in his behalf for £1.14.0 and paid to Peter Grosh on 4 Mar 1767. {Ref: MSA S960 or S752, p. 168; CSOS:97}

HUFFMAN, JACOB (Maryland), pvt., Capt. Peter Butler's Company Muster Roll, Frederick Co., circa 1757-1758, exact dates not given (served 34 days); bill of credit or order issued in his behalf for £1.14.0 and paid to Thomas Beatty, Jr. on 3 Apr 1767. {Ref: MSA S960 or S752, p. 168; CSOS:97}

HUGHES, ANDREW, see "Thomas Hughes," q.v.

HUGHES, BARNABAS (Maryland), b. c1718, MD (laborer, age 40 in 1758); pvt., enlisted by Lieut. McClay for Capt. Montgomery in the PA Regt. on 12 Jun 1758. {Ref: ARPA (2nd Series) 2:484}

HUGHES, JOSEPH (Maryland), pvt., Capt. Alexander Beall's Company of Foot, Frederick Co., 1756-1757, recorded his discharge in Frederick Co. Court on 25 Jul 1757. Capt. Beall certified "he hath served upwards of 7 months and the time of his enlistment has expired. Given under my hand at Fort Frederick, MD, 10 Feb 1757." Receipt for clothing and pay was signed by Joseph Hughes and witnessed by Sgt. Robert Lineard and Sgt. George Barrance. {Ref: FCLR:29}

HUGHES, PATRICK (Delaware), pvt., Capt. Richard McWilliams' Company of Foot, New Castle Co., enlisted 28 Dec 1757. {Ref: ARDE I:14}

HUGHES (HUGHS), THOMAS (Maryland), pvt., Capt. Francis Ware's Company of MD Troops, Charles Co., from 9 Oct 1757 to 17 Oct 1758 when he reportedly deserted; however, payment to him was recorded in Col. Dagworthy's account book on 22 Jul 1762; payment was also made to Thomas Hughes for his brother Andrew Hughes. {Ref: MHS MS.375; CSOS:88; MHS MS.375.1}

HUGHES, WILLIAM (Maryland or Pennsylvania), Welshman (age not given); pvt. in 1757 who was hanged at Carlisle for desertion. {Ref: *MD Gazette*, 10 Nov 1757}

HUGONS, JOHN (Delaware or Pennsylvania), b. c1734, Cecil Co., MD (weaver, age 25 in 1759); pvt., recruited by Capt. John Haslet and enlisted on 11 May

1759 (name appeared on a list of recruits dated 20 May 1759). {Ref: ARPA (2nd Series) 2:506}

HULL, DAVID (Maryland), cpl., Capt. Peregrine Brown's Company Muster Roll, Kent Co., circa 1757-1758, exact dates not given (served 15 days); bill of credit issued in his behalf to Thomas Ringgold, Esq. and paid to Hull's exec. (unnamed) on 21 Feb 1767 for £1. {Ref: MSA S960 or S752, pp. 179-180; CSOS:110}

HULL, JAMES (Maryland), farmer; b. 3 Jun 1740, Kent Co., son of Joseph and Margret Hull, of Shrewsbury Parish; pvt., Capt. Peregrine Brown's 7th Co. of Foot Militia, Kent Co., on 19 Feb 1758, by which time he had enlisted, but reportedly refused to appear and serve in arms against the enemy; he later stated that he "was at the time in a very ill state of health and had the ague and fever very bad so that he was not able to go and do service in such a state of health, even in a mild season of the year." [Note: His name was given as James Kull, James Hull and James Hall in various parts of this record]. {Ref: ESVR; ARMD 31:283-288}

HULL, JOSEPH (Maryland), pvt., Capt. Peregrine Brown's Company Muster Roll, Kent Co., circa 1757-1758, exact dates not given; bill of credit issued or paid in his behalf to Robert Buchanan on 20 Feb 1767 for £0.15.0. {Ref: MSA S960 or S752, p. 180} See "James Hull," q.v.

HUMES, JOHN (Delaware), pvt., Capt. Richard McWilliams' Company of Foot, New Castle Co., enlisted 28 Dec 1757. {Ref: ARDE I:14}

HUMES, WILLIAM (Delaware), pvt., Capt. Richard McWilliams' Company of Foot, New Castle Co., enlisted 28 Dec 1757. {Ref: ARDE I:14}

HUMPHREYS, WILLIAM (Delaware), b. c1733, MD (laborer, age 25 in 1758); pvt., recruited by Capt. Benjamin Noxon and enlisted on 2 May 1758. {Ref: ARDE I:19; ARPA (2nd Series) 2:485, 566}

HUNN, MARY, see "Caleb Sipple," q.v.

HUNT, JOHN (Maryland), pvt., Capt. John Dagworthy's Company of MD Troops, Frederick Co., from 9 Oct 1757 to 27 Dec 1758 when he reportedly deserted; however, payment to him was recorded in Col. Dagworthy's account book on 1 Mar 1763. {Ref: MHS MS.375; CSOS:76; MHS MS.375.1}

HUNT, WILLIAM (Delaware), pvt., Capt. Richard McWilliams' Company of Foot, New Castle Co., enlisted 28 Dec 1757. {Ref: ARDE I:14}

HUNTER, WILLIAM (Delaware), b. c1736, England (laborer, age 22 in 1758); pvt., recruited by Capt. Benjamin Noxon and enlisted on 8 May 1758. {Ref: ARDE I:19; ARPA (2nd Series) 2:566}

HUNTER, WILLIAM (Maryland), pvt., Capt. Joshua Beall's Company of MD Troops, Prince George's Co., from 9 Oct 1757 to 7 Dec 1757; payment to him was recorded in Col. Dagworthy's account book on 24 Jul 1762. {Ref: MHS MS.375; CSOS:84; MHS MS.375.1}

HUNTER, WILLIAM (Maryland or Pennsylvania), pvt., Capt. Hamilton's Company, was wounded in "a recent battle with the Indians" in 1756 (exact date not given) in Cumberland Co., PA, after the burning of McCord's Fort. {Ref: *MD Gazette*, 29 Apr 1756}

HUNZMAN (HEINZMAN), HENRY (Maryland), doctor in Capt. Alexander Beall's Company of MD Troops, Frederick Co., from 9 Oct 1757 to 30 Dec 1758 when he was promoted to surgeon; taken to King's Hospital on 29 Jul 1758 and continued on rolls. {Ref: MHS MS.375.1; CSOS:79} Payment to him was recorded in Col. Dagworthy's account book on 15 Jul 1762. {Ref: MHS MS.375}

HURLEY, EDMOND (Maryland), pvt., Capt. Alexander Beall's Company of MD Troops, Frederick Co., from 9 Oct 1757 to 10 Mar 1758. {Ref: MHS MS.375.1; CSOS:80} Payment to him was recorded in Col. Dagworthy's account book on 11 Jul 1762. {Ref: MHS MS.375}

HURLEY, ZACHARIAH (Maryland), pvt., Capt. Joseph Chapline's Company Muster Roll No. 1, Frederick Co., circa 1757-1758, exact dates not given (served 29 days); bill of credit issued or paid in his behalf to Joseph Chaplin for £1.9.0 on 13 Jun 1768. {Ref: MSA S960 or S752, p. 192; CSOS:103}

HURST, JACOB (Maryland), pvt., Capt. Alexander Beall's Company of MD Troops, Frederick Co., from 9 Oct 1757 to 8 Nov 1758. {Ref: MHS MS.375.1; CSOS:81} Payment to him was recorded in Col. Dagworthy's account book on 16 Jul 1762. {Ref: MHS MS.375}

HUTCHENSON, WILLIAM (Maryland), pvt., Capt. Alexander Beall's Company of MD Troops, Frederick Co., from 9 Oct 1757 to 23 Oct 1758 when he reportedly deserted; however, payment to him was recorded in Col. Dagworthy's account book on 11 Jul 1762. {Ref: MHS MS.375; CSOS:80; MHS MS.375.1}

HUTCHINGS, THOMAS ELLIOT (Maryland), patriot and poss. soldier (rank not specified), Queen Anne's Co., militia pay account submitted in 1758, exact date not given. {Ref: MHM 9:4, p. 367}

HUTCHINS, JAMES (Maryland), patriot and poss. soldier (rank not specified), Baltimore or Frederick Co., militia pay account submitted in 1758, exact date not given. {Ref: MHM 9:4, p. 369}

HUTCHINSON (HUTCHESON), JOSEPH (Delaware), lieut., Lower Part of Murderkill Hundred, Kent Co. on Delaware, 1756. {Ref: ARDE I:12; ARPA (2nd Series) 2:527-529; HDE I:141}

HUTSETT (HUTSELL?), GEORGE (Maryland), pvt., Capt. Stephen Rensburg's or Rensburger's Company Muster Roll, Frederick Co., circa 1757-1758, exact dates not given (served 34 days); bill of credit or order issued to Casper Shaff and paid to David Cumming for £1.14.0 on 18 Apr 1767. {Ref: MSA S960 or S752, p. 183; CSOS:112}

HYDE, PHILIP (Maryland), pvt., Capt. John Dagworthy's Company of MD Troops, Frederick Co., from 9 Oct 1757 to 26 Dec 1758 when he reportedly deserted; however, payment to him was recorded in Col. Dagworthy's account book on 28 Feb 1763. {Ref: MHS MS.375; CSOS:76; MHS MS.375.1}

HYDE, THOMAS (Maryland), patriot, Annapolis, Anne Arundel Co., pay account submitted for quartering soldiers in 1757 or 1758, exact dates not given. {Ref: MHM 9:3, p. 262}

HYLAND, JOHN (Maryland), b. 1716, Cecil Co., son of Nicholas Hyland and Millicent (N), m. Martha Tilden on 29 Apr 1739, had children Nicholas,

Stephen, John, Charles, Lambert, Rebecca, and Millicent and styled captain at time of his death in 1756. {Ref: BDML I:474}

HYLAND, NICHOLAS (Maryland), b. c1714, Cecil Co., son of Nicholas Hyland and Millicent (N), m. Elizabeth (N), had children John, Nicholas, Isaac and Jacob (twins), Samson, Michael, and Millicent, and d. by 27 Apr 1774; yeoman, gentleman, captain by 1742, county justice (1742-1774), member of the MD Assembly (1742-1766, served on the Arms and Ammunition Committee, 1754-1758), major by 1757, and colonel by 1758. {Ref: BDML I:474; ARMD 55:44} Militia pay account submitted in 1758, exact date not given. {Ref: MHM 9:4, p. 370}

HYNSON, JOHN (Maryland), patriot, d. 1761, Kent Co.; pay account submitted for quartering soldiers in 1757 or 1758, exact dates not given. {Ref: MHM 9:3, p. 261} "John Hynson died owning 150 acres on Eastern Neck Island, Kent Co.; Frances Hynson is the executrix." {Ref: *MD Gazette*, 17 Sep 1761}

HYNSON, JOHN JR. (Maryland), patriot, Kent Co., pay account submitted for quartering soldiers in 1757 or 1758, exact dates not given. {Ref: MHM 9:3, p. 261}

HYNSON, WILLIAM (Maryland), b. 23 Dec 1708, Kent Co., son of Charles Hynson and Margaret Harris, m. Martha Wickes and d. by 17 Oct 1767, prob. without issue; planter, gentleman, county justice (1748-1759), member of the MD Assembly (1754-1766), and major by 1756. {Ref: BDML I:477; ARMD 52:564, 55:44; *MD Gazette*, 28 Sep 1758}

IGO (IGOE), WILLIAM (Maryland), b. 22 Aug 1729, Baltimore Co., son of Lewis and Mary Igo, m. Elizabeth (N), had children Mary, Elizabeth, Rachel, Joshua (b. 1760, served in Revolutionary War in PA), Ephraim (b. 1768), Peter, Jacob, Thomas, and Susannah, and d. by 1798. {Ref: BCF:351} Pvt., Capt. Tobias Stansbury's Company Muster Roll, Baltimore Co., circa 1757-1758, exact dates not given; bill of credit issued or paid in his behalf to Alexander Wells for £1.15.0 on 27 Mar 1767. {Ref: MSA S960 or S752, p. 186}

IJAMS, ANN, see "Lewis Stockett," q.v.

IJAMS, THOMAS, see "James Crauford" and "Joseph Williams," q.v.

IJAMS, WILLIAM (Maryland), b. 22 Nov 1721, Anne Arundel Co., son of William and Elizabeth Ijams, of All Hallow's Parish. {Ref: AACR:40} Pvt., Capt. Samuel Chapman's Company Muster Roll, Anne Arundel Co., circa 1757-1758, exact dates not given; bill of credit issued or paid in his behalf to Henry Hall for £1.18.0 on 25 Feb 1767. {Ref: MSA S960 or S752, p. 188}

INCH, HENRY (Maryland), pvt., Capt. Thomas Norris' Company, Frederick Co., circa 1757-1758, exact dates not given (served 30 days); bill of credit issued or paid in his behalf to Normand Bruce on 20 May 1767 for £1.10.0. {Ref: MSA S960 or S752, p. 177; CSOS:108}

INCH, JOHN (Maryland), b. 1721, m. Jane Reynolds on 6 Jul 1745, Anne Arundel Co., St. Anne's Parish, had a dau. Elizabeth (b. 11 Sep 1746), and d. 14 Mar 1763; patriot, merchant and goldsmith in Annapolis; pay account submitted for his exec. (unnamed) for his quartering soldiers in 1757 or 1758, exact dates not given. {Ref: MHM 9:3, p. 262; AACR:100-101} "John Inch, age 42, a goldsmith of Annapolis, died 14 Mar 1763 and his funeral was attended by a procession of the Brethren of the Lodge. His widow Jane Inch and son-in-law Baruch

Maybury were his administrators." {Ref: *MD Gazette*, 17 Mar 1763 and 24 Mar 1763} See "Capt. ---- Cochran" and "John McNeill," q.v.

INGRAM (INGRIM), JOHN (Maryland), pvt., Capt. Moses Chapline's Company Muster Roll No. 3, Frederick Co., circa 1757-1758, exact dates not given (served 6 days); bill of credit or order issued to Casper Shaff and paid to David Cumming for £0.6.0 on 5 Mar 1767. {Ref: MSA S960 or S752, p. 198; CSOS:115}

INGRUM, DANIEL (Delaware), pvt., Kent Co. Militia, Capt. John Caton's Company, 25 Apr 1757 (date of muster roll). {Ref: ARDE I:14}

INNIS, TIMOTHY (Delaware), b. c1728, Kildare, Ireland (tailor, age 30 in 1758); pvt., enlisted 9 May 1758 "for the campaign in the lower counties" by Capt. John McClughan. {Ref: ARDE I:17; ARPA (2nd Series) 2:570}

IRELAND, HANCE (Maryland), pvt., Capt. Tobias Stansbury's Company Muster Roll, Baltimore Co., circa 1757-1758, exact dates not given; bill of credit issued or paid to him for £0.2.7½ in 1767, exact date not given. {Ref: MSA S960 or S752, p. 187}

IRONS, OWEN (Delaware), son of Timothy Irons (d. 1740) and Catherine (N), m. Penelope Freeman; prob. the Owen Irons, yeoman, of the forest of Murtherkill Hundred in 1767. {Ref: CFD 1:115-117} Pvt., Kent Co. Militia, Capt. John Caton's Company, 25 Apr 1757 (date of muster roll). {Ref: ARDE I:14}

ISAAC, SUTTON (Maryland), captain and commander of the Calvert Co. militia in Upper Hundred of the Cliffs; sent to the Western Frontier to help defend against the Indians circa 1756-1757 (exact dates not given). {Ref: HCC:121-122}

ISENPECK, GEORGE (Maryland), pvt., Capt. Peter Butler's Company Muster Roll, Frederick Co., circa 1757-1758, exact dates not given (served 34 days); bill of credit or order issued in his behalf for £1.14.0 and paid to Casper Shaff on 2 Mar 1767. {Ref: MSA S960 or S752, p. 167; CSOS:97}

ISRAELS, EDWARD (Maryland), pvt., Capt. Tobias Stansbury's Company Muster Roll, Baltimore Co., circa 1757-1758, exact dates not given; bill of credit issued or paid to him for £1.15.0 in 1767, exact date not given. {Ref: MSA S960 or S752, p. 187}

IVES, WILLIAM (Maryland), pvt., Capt. John Dagworthy's Company of MD Troops, Frederick Co., from 9 Oct 1757 to 11 Jul 1758 when he reportedly deserted; however, payment to him was recorded in Col. Dagworthy's account book on 8 Mar 1763. {Ref: MHS MS.375; CSOS:77; MHS MS.375.1}

IVORY, THOMAS (Maryland), indentured servant and soldier who served in the French and Indian War some time between 1756 and 1763 (exact dates not known); his master Benjamin Tasker, iron manufacturer, requested compensation from the Baltimore County Court due to the loss of use of Ivory while in the service. {Ref: MHM 94:4, p. 426, citing Baltimore Co. Court Minutes}

JACK (JACKE), JOHN (Maryland), pvt., Capt. Joshua Beall's Company Muster Roll, Prince George's Co., circa 1757-1758, exact dates not given; bill of credit issued or paid in his behalf to his exec. (unnamed) for £2.1.10½ in 1767, exact date not given. {Ref: MSA S960 or S752, p. 184}

JACK, JAMES (Maryland), pvt., Capt. Joshua Beall's Company Muster Roll, Prince George's Co., circa 1757-1758, exact dates not given; bill of credit issued or paid to him for £1.1.10½ in 1767, exact date not given. {Ref: MSA S960 or S752, p. 184}

JACKSON, ----, see "William Ringgold," q.v.

JACKSON, BENJAMIN (Delaware), pvt., Capt. French Battell's Company of Lower County Provincials, enlisted 23 May 1758. {Ref: ARDE I:16; ARPA (2nd Series) 2:555}

JACKSON, BENNETT (Maryland), pvt., Capt. Joseph Hanson Harrison's Company Muster Roll, Charles Co., circa 1757-1758, exact dates not given; bill of credit issued or paid in his behalf to Francis Ware for £2.9.0 on 20 Feb 1767. {Ref: MSA S960 or S752, p. 189}

JACKSON, GEORGE (Delaware), b. c1731, MD (age 28 in 1759); pvt., enlisted in Capt. John Wright's Company and mustered on 11 May 1759. {Ref: ARDE I:25; ARPA (2nd Series) 2:508, 592}

JACKSON, HANNAH, see "Stephen Kimble," q.v.

JACKSON, HUGH (Maryland), pvt., Capt. Joseph Chapline's Company Muster Roll No. 4, Frederick Co., circa 1757-1758, exact dates not given (served 6 days); bill of credit issued or paid in his behalf to Joseph Chaplin for £0.6.0 on 5 Mar 1767. {Ref: MSA S960 or S752, p. 194; CSOS:105}

JACKSON, JAMES (Maryland), farmer; pvt., Capt. Peregrine Brown's 7th Co. of Foot Militia, Kent Co., on 19 Feb 1758, by which time he had enlisted, but reportedly refused to appear and serve in arms against the enemy; he later stated that he "was very sickly and ailing at the time" and the justice, William Ringgold, also stated "from my own view of him I can certifie that he was a weakly dimunitive creature, very unfit for such a service, and has a very bad scald head, which I myself viewed and found in a most miserable condition, I think quite unfit for such a service, besides such a person must have been very offensive to the other men." {Ref: ARMD 31:283, 286, 288}

JACKSON, JOSEPH (Delaware), pvt., Kent Co. Militia, Capt. John Caton's Company, 25 Apr 1757 (date of muster roll). {Ref: ARDE I:14}

JACKSON, MARY, see "Thomas Cramphin, Jr.," q.v.

JACKSON, PAUL (Delaware or Pennsylvania), captain and recruiting officer for PA Troops in the "Three Lower Counties on Delaware" in 1758. {Ref: ARDE I:27}

JACKSON, ROBERT (Maryland), pvt., Capt. Joseph Chapline's Company Muster Roll No. 4, Frederick Co., circa 1757-1758, exact dates not given (served 5 days); bill of credit issued or paid in his behalf to Joseph Chaplin for £0.5.0 on 5 Mar 1767. {Ref: MSA S960 or S752, p. 194; CSOS:105}

JACKSON, SOUTHEY (Delaware), b. c1738, Indian River, MD (shoemaker, age 20 in 1758); pvt., enlisted 19 Apr 1758 "for the campaign in the lower counties" by Capt. John McClughan. {Ref: ARDE I:17; ARPA (2nd Series) 2:570}

JACKSON, THOMAS (Delaware), pvt., Kent Co. Militia, Capt. John Caton's Company, 25 Apr 1757 (date of muster roll). {Ref: ARDE I:14}

JACKSON, WILLIAM (Delaware), pvt., Kent Co. Militia, Capt. John Caton's Company, 25 Apr 1757 (date of muster roll). {Ref: ARDE I:14}

JACOBS, MARTIN (Maryland), pvt., Capt. John White's Company Muster Roll, Frederick Co., circa 1757-1758, exact dates not given (served 6 days); bill of credit issued or paid to him for £0.6.0 in 1767, exact date not given. {Ref: MSA S960 or S752, p. 164; CSOS:96}

JACOBS, SAMUEL (Maryland), cpl., Capt. Francis Ware's Company of MD Troops, Charles Co., circa 9 Oct 1757 to 30 Dec 1758. {Ref: MHS MS.375.1; CSOS:88} Payment to him was recorded in Col. Dagworthy's account book on 7 Mar 1763. {Ref: MHS MS.375}

JACOBS, THOMAS (Maryland), pvt., Capt. John Dagworthy's Company of MD Troops, Frederick Co., from 9 Oct 1757 to 16 Apr 1759 when he reportedly deserted; however, payment to him was recorded in Col. Dagworthy's account book on 8 Mar 1763. {Ref: MHS MS.375; CSOS:77; MHS MS.375.1}

JACQUES, LANCELOTT (Maryland), patriot, Annapolis, Anne Arundel Co., pay account submitted for quartering soldiers in 1757 or 1758, exact dates not given. {Ref: MHM 9:3, p. 262}

JACQUET, THOMAS (Delaware), pvt., Capt. Richard McWilliams' Company of Foot, New Castle Co., enlisted 28 Dec 1757. {Ref: ARDE I:15}

JAKE, ROBERT (Delaware), pvt., Capt. Henry Vanbibber's Company of the Lower Counties on Delaware Troops at New Castle, enlisted on 23 May 1759. {Ref: ARDE I:26; ARPA (2nd Series) 2:594}

JAKES, JAMES (Maryland), pvt., Capt. Henry Casson's Company Muster Roll, Queen Anne's Co., circa 1757-1758, exact dates not given (served 27 days); bill of credit issued or paid in his behalf to Capt. Casson on 27 Mar 1767 for £1.7.0. {Ref: MSA S960 or S752, p. 178; CSOS:109}

JAMES, DANIEL (Delaware), captain, Murderkill Hundred, Kent Co. on Delaware, 29 Mar 1758. {Ref: ARDE I:15; ARPA (2nd Series) 2:577}

JAMES, GEORGE (Delaware), pvt., Capt. Richard McWilliams' Company of Foot, New Castle Co., enlisted 28 Dec 1757. {Ref: ARDE I:15}

JAMES, THOMAS (Delaware), major, Lower Regt. of Militia, New Castle Co., 1756. {Ref: ARDE I:11; ARPA (2nd Series) 2:525; HDE I:141} Patriot who served as a Justice of the peace, Justice of the Court of Oyer and Terminer, and Justice of the Court of Common Pleas, 1756-1761. {Ref: GRSD 1:13, 15}

JAMIESON, ---- (Maryland or Pennsylvania), ensign in Capt. Hamilton's Company, was wounded in "a recent battle with the Indians" in 1756 (exact date not given) in Cumberland Co., PA, after the burning of McCord's Fort. {Ref: *MD Gazette*, 29 Apr 1756}

JANUARY, BENJAMIN (Delaware), b. c1716, New Castle, DE (shoemaker, age 43 in 1759); pvt., Capt. Johnston's Company, enlisted in PA Regt. on 24 Apr 1759. {Ref: ARDE I:27}

JANVIER, ISAAC (Delaware), pvt., Capt. Richard McWilliams' Company of Foot, New Castle Co., enlisted 28 Dec 1757 [Note: This name appeared twice on the enlistment roll]. {Ref: ARDE I:14}

JANVIER, JACOB (Delaware), pvt., Capt. Richard McWilliams' Company of Foot, New Castle Co., enlisted 28 Dec 1757. {Ref: ARDE I:14}

JANVIER, PHILIP (Delaware), pvt., Capt. Richard McWilliams' Company of Foot, New Castle Co., enlisted 28 Dec 1757. {Ref: ARDE I:14}

JANVIER, RICHARD (Delaware), pvt., Capt. Richard McWilliams' Company of Foot, New Castle Co., enlisted 28 Dec 1757. {Ref: ARDE I:15}

JANVIER, SAMUEL (Delaware), pvt., Capt. Richard McWilliams' Company of Foot, New Castle Co., enlisted 28 Dec 1757. {Ref: ARDE I:14}

JAQUET, JOHN (Delaware), pvt., Capt. Richard McWilliams' Company of Foot, New Castle Co., enlisted 28 Dec 1757. {Ref: ARDE I:14}

JAQUET, JOSEPH (Delaware), pvt., Capt. Richard McWilliams' Company of Foot, New Castle Co., enlisted 28 Dec 1757. {Ref: ARDE I:14}

JAQUET, PETER (Delaware), pvt., Capt. Richard McWilliams' Company of Foot, New Castle Co., enlisted 28 Dec 1757 [Note: This name appeared twice on the enlistment roll]. {Ref: ARDE I:14}

JARRETT, ABRAHAM, see "William Rhoe" and "Robert Denbee" and "Isaac Whitacre," q.v.

JEFFERSON, HENRY (Maryland), b. c1734, MD (age 22 in 1756); pvt., Capt. Christopher Gist's Company of VA Militia, 13 Jul 1756, enlisted at Baltimore. {Ref: MSR I:37}

JEFFERSON, JOHN (Maryland), pvt., Capt. Joshua Beall's Company of MD Troops, Prince George's Co., from 9 Oct 1757 to 13 Dec 1758 when he was discharged. {Ref: MHS MS.375.1; CSOS:84} Payment to him was recorded in Col. Dagworthy's account book on 24 Jul 1762. {Ref: MHS MS.375}

JEFFREYS, MICHAEL (Maryland), pvt., Capt. Joshua Beall's Company Muster Roll, Prince George's Co., circa 1757-1758, exact dates not given; bill of credit issued or paid to him for £2.3.0 in 1767, exact date not given. {Ref: MSA S960 or S752, p. 184}

JENATOR, JOHN see "John Genater," q.v.

JENIFER, DANIEL OF ST. THOMAS (Maryland), b. 1723, Charles Co., son of Dr. Daniel Jenifer and Elizabeth Mason (widow of John Rogers and dau. of Robert Mason); never married; d. 16 Nov 1790, Annapolis; planter, merchant, gentleman, captain by 1756 and styled major by 1765; member of the MD Assembly (1756-1757, 1771-1774), lottery manager in 1763, Justice of the Provincial Court (1766-1773), Rent Roll Keeper of the Western Shore (appointed 1768), MD Council (1771-1776), Council of Safety (1775-1777), President of MD Senate (1777-1781), Delegate to Continental Congress (1779-1780), and held other offices; unsuccessful candidate for Governor of MD in 1785. {Ref: BDML II:485-486; ARMD 52:364, 55:44; *MD Gazette*, 18 Nov 1790}

JENKINS, ASHMEL or ASHMET (Maryland), pvt., Capt. Elias Delashmutt's Company Muster Roll, Frederick Co., 13 Aug 1757, exact dates not given (served 52 days); also served another 30 days, exact dates not given; bill of credit issued or paid in his behalf to Elias Delashmut, Jr. on 16 Mar 1767 for £4.2.0; name also listed as "Ashmet Jinkins" and "Ashman Jenkins." {Ref: MSA S960 or S752, p. 163; CSOS:94, 98}

JENKINS, ISAAC (Maryland), pvt., Capt. Joseph Hanson Harrison's Company Muster Roll, Charles Co., circa 1757-1758, exact dates not given; bill of credit issued or paid to him for £2.9.0 in 1767, exact date not given. {Ref: MSA S960 or S752, p. 189}

JENKINS, MARY, see "John Henry" and "Robert Jenkins Henry," q.v.
JENKINS, WILLIAM, see "John Jones," q.v.

JENNINGS, CATHERINE (Maryland), patriot, Annapolis, Anne Arundel Co., pay account submitted for quartering soldiers in 1757 or 1758, exact dates not given. {Ref: MHM 9:3, p. 262}

JENNINGS, REBECCA, see "Thomas Jennings," q.v.

JENNINGS, THOMAS (Maryland), d. 26 Apr 1759, patriot, Annapolis, Anne Arundel Co.; pay account submitted for his exec. (unnamed) for his quartering soldiers in 1757 or 1758, exact dates not given. {Ref: MHM 9:3, p. 261} "Mr. Thomas Jennings died last Sunday here; Chief Clerk of the Land Office and for a great many years, in the commission of the Peace for Anne Arundel Co." Rebecca Jennings was his administratrix. {Ref: *MD Gazette*, 30 Aug 1759 and 8 Nov 1759}

JENNINGS, WILLIAM (Maryland), pvt., Frederick Co., received £5 bounty money on 4 Sep 1757 for enlisting in the militia. {Ref: ARMD 55:265, 619} Pvt., Capt. Alexander Beall's Company of MD Troops, Frederick Co., from 9 Oct 1757 to 8 Nov 1758. {Ref: MHS MS.375.1; CSOS:81} Payment to him was recorded in Col. Dagworthy's account book on 7 Mar 1763. {Ref: MHS MS.375}

JESSERANG, MICHAEL (Maryland), pvt., Capt. Peter Butler's Company Muster Roll, Frederick Co., circa 1757-1758, exact dates not given (served 34 days); bill of credit or order issued in his behalf for £1.14.0 and paid to Casper Shaff on 2 Mar 1767. {Ref: MSA S960 or S752, p. 166; CSOS:97}

JESTER, JOHN (Delaware), pvt., Capt. French Battell's Company of Lower County Provincials, enlisted 16 May 1758. {Ref: ARDE I:16; ARPA (2nd Series) 2:555}

JOHN, DANIEL (Delaware), b. c1731, Pencader, DE (laborer, age 27 in 1758); pvt., enlisted 8 May 1758 "for the campaign in the lower counties" by Capt. John McClughan. {Ref: ARDE I:17; ARPA (2nd Series) 2:570}

JOHNS, HANNAH, see "John Hall," q.v.

JOHNSON (JOHNSTOWN), ANDREW (Maryland), cpl., Capt. Richard Pearis' Company of MD Troops, Frederick Co., from 9 Oct 1757 to 26 Nov 1757 (reduced to pvt. on 18 Nov 1757) and reportedly deserted; however, payment to him was recorded in Col. Dagworthy's account book on 8 Mar 1763. {Ref: MHS MS.375; MHS MS.375.1}

JOHNSON (JOHNSTOWN), ARTHUR (Maryland), sgt., Capt. John Dagworthy's Company of MD Troops, Frederick Co., circa 9 Oct 1757 to 26 Apr 1759. {Ref: MHS MS.375.1; CSOS:77} Payment to him was recorded in Col. Dagworthy's account book on 8 Mar 1763. {Ref: MHS MS.375}

JOHNSON, BATRIX (Maryland), patriot and poss. soldier (rank not specified), Kent Co., militia pay account submitted in 1758, exact date not given. {Ref: MHM 9:4, p. 368}

JOHNSON, DAVID (Maryland), pvt., Capt. John Wolgomatt's Company of MD Volunteers, Frederick Co., circa 1763-1764; on muster roll dated 15 Nov 1764 at Camp at the Forks of Muskingham. {Ref: ARMD 32:99}

JOHNSON, DUNCAN (Maryland), pvt., Capt. Alexander Beall's Company of MD Troops, Frederick Co., circa 1757-1758, exact dates not given; pvt., Capt. John

Dagworthy's Company of MD Troops, Frederick Co., from 31 Dec 1758 to 22 Feb 1759 and reportedly deserted; however, payment to him was recorded in Col. Dagworthy's account book on 11 Jul 1762 for work on Fort Cumberland. {Ref: MHS MS.375; CSOS:77, 81; MHS MS.375.1}

JOHNSON, EDWARD (Maryland), pvt., Capt. Peter Bainbridge's Company Muster Roll, Frederick Co., circa 1757-1758, exact dates not given (served 41 days); bill of credit issued or paid in his behalf to Casper Shaff on 4 Mar 1767 for £2.1.0. {Ref: MSA S960 or S752, p. 180; CSOS:111}

JOHNSON, ELEANOR, see "William Johnson," q.v.

JOHNSON, GEORGE (Maryland), patriot, Annapolis, Anne Arundel Co., pay account submitted for his exec. (unnamed) for his quartering soldiers in 1757 or 1758, exact dates not given. {Ref: MHM 9:3, p. 261}

JOHNSON, GRIFFITH (Maryland), pvt., Frederick Co., MD Forces, by 1757. In early February 1758 he and Samuel Lane were out scouting on the Potomac and found Indian tracks leading to George's Creek near Savage River. Lane had been taken prisoner by the Indians last November. {Ref: *MD Gazette*, 16 Feb 1758}

JOHNSON, HANNAH, see "Thomas Cresap," q.v.

JOHNSON, JAMES (Maryland), patriot, Annapolis, Anne Arundel Co., was authorized money by the MD Assembly on 24 Nov 1757 "as a present provision for the quartering of his Majesty's Forces as are expected to come to the City of Annapolis for quarters." {Ref: ARMD 55:173} Pay account submitted by Johnson's exec. (unnamed) for his quartering soldiers in 1757 or 1758, exact dates not given. {Ref: MHM 9:3, p. 262}

JOHNSON, JOHN (Maryland), pvt., Capt. Joseph Chapline's Company Muster Roll No. 1, Frederick Co., circa 1757-1758, exact dates not given (served 25 days); bill of credit issued or paid in his behalf to Joseph Chaplin for £1.5.0 on 5 Mar 1767. {Ref: MSA S960 or S752, p. 191; CSOS:102} Pvt., Capt. Moses Chapline's Company Muster Roll No. 3, Frederick Co., circa 1757-1758, exact dates not given (served 6 days); bill of credit issued or paid in his behalf to Joseph Chaplin for £0.6.0 on 5 Mar 1767. {Ref: MSA S960 or S752, p. 198; CSOS:114}

JOHNSON, JOHN (Maryland), pvt., Capt. Elias Delashmutt's Company Muster Roll, Frederick Co., circa 1757-1758, exact dates not given (served 30 days); bill of credit issued or paid in his behalf to Elias Delashmut, Jr. on 16 Mar 1767 for £1.10.0; bill of credit issued or paid in his behalf to Casper Shaff on 18 Apr 1767 for £2.12.0. {Ref: MSA S960 or S752, pp. 162-163; CSOS:94}

JOHNSON, JOHN (Maryland), pvt., Capt. Peter Bainbridge's Company Muster Roll, Frederick Co., circa 1757-1758, exact dates not given (served 36 days); bill of credit issued or paid in his behalf to Joseph Chaplin on 5 Mar 1767 for £1.16.0. {Ref: MSA S960 or S752, p. 181; CSOS:111}

JOHNSON, JOHN, of Monocacy (Maryland), pvt., Capt. Peter Bainbridge's Company Muster Roll, Frederick Co., circa 1757-1758, exact dates not given (served 30 days); bill of credit or order issued to Casper Shaff and paid to David Cumming on 18 Apr 1767 for £1.10.0. {Ref: MSA S960 or S752, p. 181; CSOS:111}

JOHNSON, JOHN JR. (Maryland), pvt., Capt. Elias Delashmutt's Company Muster Roll, Frederick Co., 13 Aug 1757, exact dates not given (served 52 days). {Ref: CSOS:98}

JOHNSON, JOSEPH (Maryland), pvt., Capt. Joseph Chapline's Company Muster Roll No. 1, Frederick Co., circa 1757-1758, exact dates not given (served 28 days); bill of credit issued or paid in his behalf to Joseph Chaplin for £1.8.0 on 5 Mar 1767. {Ref: MSA S960 or S752, p. 191; CSOS:103} Pvt., Capt. Moses Chapline's Company Muster Roll No. 1, Frederick Co., circa 1757-1758, exact dates not given (served 55 days); bill of credit issued or paid in his behalf to Joseph Chaplin for £2.15.0 on 5 Mar 1767. {Ref: MSA S960 or S752, p. 196; CSOS:113}

JOHNSON, LYDIA, see "William Johnson," q.v.

JOHNSON, MARTHA, see "William Johnson," q.v.

JOHNSON, MARTIN GILL (Delaware), pvt., Capt. Henry Vanbibber's Company of the Lower Counties on Delaware Troops at New Castle, enlisted on 15 May 1759. {Ref: ARDE I:26; ARPA (2nd Series) 2:594}

JOHNSON, RICHARD (Maryland), b. c1731, MD (age 24 in 1755); pvt. in a company of VA Rangers under Capt. William Cocke on 21 Oct 1755 (and prob. in 1756-1757). {Ref: MSR I:37}

JOHNSON, RICHARD (Maryland), Englishman; pvt. by 1758 in Capt. Prince's Company, 2nd Bttn. of Royal Americans, when he was committed to jail in Anne Arundel Co. for desertion and subsequently escaped. {Ref: *MD Gazette*, 9 Mar 1758}

JOHNSON, SAMUEL (Delaware), pvt., Kent Co. Militia, Capt. John Caton's Company, 25 Apr 1757 (date of muster roll). {Ref: ARDE I:14}

JOHNSON, SARAH, see "William Johnson" and "William Ringgold," q.v.

JOHNSON, THOMAS, see "William Johnson," q.v.

JOHNSON, THOMAS (Maryland), sgt., Capt. Peter Bainbridge's Company Muster Roll, Frederick Co., circa 1757-1758, exact dates not given (served 36 days); bill of credit issued or paid in his behalf to Joseph Chaplin on 13 Jun 1768 for £2.8.0. {Ref: MSA S960 or S752, p. 181; CSOS:110} *Identification problem:* There were three men with this name who died in Frederick County between 1767 and 1783: (1) Thomas Johnson, Sr., m. Sarah (N), had children Bazell, Thomas, John, and Mary, and d. testate by 10 Aug 1767. {Ref: WMG 3:1, p. 36} (2) Thomas Johnson m. (N), had children John, Thomas, William, and Richard, and d. testate by 17 Oct 1778. {Ref: WMG 5:2, p. 88} (3) Thomas Johnson m. Mary (N), had children John, Thomas, Joseph, Mary, Martha, Henry, and Robert, and d. testate by 17 Mar 1783. {Ref: WMG 5:2, pp. 82-83}

JOHNSON, THOMAS (Maryland), cpl., Capt. Joseph Chapline's Company Muster Roll No. 1, Frederick Co., circa 1757-1758, exact dates not given (served 25 days); bill of credit issued or paid in his behalf to Joseph Chaplin for £1.13.4½ on 5 Mar 1767. {Ref: MSA S960 or S752, pp. 190-191; CSOS:102} Cpl., Capt. Moses Chapline's Company Muster Roll No. 3, Frederick Co., circa 1757-1758, exact dates not given (served 6 days); bill of credit issued or paid in his behalf to Joseph Chaplin for £0.8.0 on 5 Mar 1767. {Ref: MSA S960 or S752, p. 198; CSOS:114} See the other men named Thomas Johnson as noted above.

JOHNSON, THOMAS JR., see "John Garnett," q.v.

JOHNSON, WILLIAM (Maryland), pvt., Capt. Tobias Stansbury's Company Muster Roll, Baltimore Co., circa 1757-1758, exact dates not given; bill of credit issued or paid in his behalf to Thomas Sollars for £3.16.0 on 20 Feb 1767. {Ref: MSA S960 or S752, p. 186} *Identification problem:* There were six men with this name who could have served in the war: (1) William Johnson, b. 9 Sep 1729, son of Thomas Johnson and Alice Bond; (2) William Johnson, b. 18 Dec 1733, son of William and Sarah Johnson, m. Eleanor (N); (3) William Johnson, son of Amos and Lydia Johnson, was in Colleton Co., SC by 1773; (4) William Johnson, b. 31 Dec 1731, son of Joseph and Martha Johnson; (5) William Johnson m. Mary Ann Poaling on 22 Sep 1733; and, (6) William Johnson, alias Thomas Martin, b. c1741, England (age about 15 in 1756), was a runaway from Thomas Harvey, of Garrison Ridge, in June 1756. {Ref: BCF:366-370}

JOHNSTON, JOHN (Delaware), b. c1736, Ulster, Ireland (laborer, age 23 in 1759); pvt., enlisted by Capt. James Armstrong for the PA Regt. on 2 May 1759. {Ref: ARDE I:26; ARPA (2nd Series) 2:585}

JOHNSTOWN, ARTHUR, see "Arthur Johnson," q.v.

JONAS, JOHN (Maryland), pvt., Capt. John White's Company Muster Roll, Frederick Co., circa 1757-1758, exact dates not given (served 6 days); bill of credit issued or paid to him for £0.6.0 in 1767, exact date not given. {Ref: MSA S960 or S752, p. 164; CSOS:96}

JONES, ABEL (Delaware), b. c1730 (joiner, age 29 in 1759); pvt., enlisted by Capt. James Armstrong for the PA Regt. on 1 May 1759. {Ref: ARDE I:26; ARPA (2nd Series) 2:585}

JONES, ABRAHAM (Maryland or Pennsylvania), pvt., Capt. Culbertson's Company, was wounded in "a recent battle with the Indians" in 1756 (exact date not given) in Cumberland Co., PA, after the burning of McCord's Fort. {Ref: *MD Gazette*, 29 Apr 1756}

JONES, CHRISTOPHER (Delaware), b. c1733, West Meath, Ireland (miller, age 25 in 1758); pvt., enlisted 26 Apr 1758 "for the campaign in the lower counties" by Capt. John McClughan. {Ref: ARDE I:17; ARPA (2nd Series) 2:570}

JONES, DAVID (Maryland), pvt., Capt. Elias Delashmutt's Company Muster Roll, Frederick Co., 13 Aug 1757, exact dates not given (served 52 days). {Ref: CSOS:98} Militia pay account submitted in 1758, exact date not given. {Ref: MHM 9:4, p. 370} Bill of credit issued or paid in his behalf to Peter Grosh on 4 Mar 1767 for £2.12.0. {Ref: MSA S960 or S752, p. 162}

JONES, DAVID JR. (Maryland), sgt., Capt. Jonathan Hagar's Company Muster Roll, Frederick Co., circa 1757-1758, exact dates not given (served 6 days); militia pay account submitted in 1758, exact date not given. {Ref: MHM 9:4, p. 370; CSOS:106} Bill of credit issued or paid in his behalf to Joseph Chaplin for £0.8.0 on 5 Mar 1767. {Ref: MSA S960 or S752, pp. 173-174}

JONES, HENRY (Maryland), pvt., Capt. Samuel Chapman's Company Muster Roll, Anne Arundel Co., circa 1757-1758, exact dates not given; bill of credit issued or paid in his behalf to Henry Hall for £1.18.0 on 25 Feb 1767. {Ref: MSA S960 or S752, p. 188}

JONES, HENRY (Maryland or Pennsylvania), pvt., Capt. Hamilton's Company, was killed in "a recent battle with the Indians" in 1756 (exact date not given) in Cumberland Co., PA, after the burning of McCord's Fort. {Ref: *MD Gazette*, 29 Apr 1756}

JONES, JACOB (Maryland), pvt., Capt. Samuel Chapman's Company Muster Roll, Anne Arundel Co., circa 1757-1758, exact dates not given; bill of credit issued or paid in his behalf to Henry Hall for £1.18.0 on 25 Feb 1767. {Ref: MSA S960 or S752, p. 188}

JONES, JACOB (Maryland or Pennsylvania), pvt., Capt. Culbertson's Company, was killed in "a recent battle with the Indians" in 1756 (exact date not given) in Cumberland Co., PA, after the burning of McCord's Fort. {Ref: *MD Gazette*, 29 Apr 1756}

JONES, JOHN (Delaware), captain, St. George's Hundred, Lower Regt. of Militia, New Castle Co., 1756. {Ref: ARDE I:11; ARPA (2nd Series) 2:525; HDE I:141} Patriot who served as a Justice of the peace, Justice of the Court of Oyer and Terminer, and Justice of the Court of Common Pleas, 1756-1761. {Ref: GRSD 1:13, 15}

JONES, JOHN (Delaware), b. c1738, Philadelphia, PA (barber, age 20 in 1758); sgt., enlisted 19 Apr 1758 "for the campaign in the lower counties" by Capt. John McClughan. {Ref: ARDE I:17; ARPA (2nd Series) 2:570}

JONES, JOHN (Delaware), b. c1733, Wales (laborer, age 25 in 1758); pvt., recruited by Capt. Benjamin Noxon and enlisted on 15 Apr 1758. {Ref: ARDE I:19; ARPA (2nd Series) 2:566}

JONES, JOHN (Maryland), pvt., Capt. Francis Ware's Company of MD Troops, Charles Co., from 9 Oct 1757 to 8 Nov 1758 (served 396 days). {Ref: MHS MS.375.1; CSOS:88} Payment to him was recorded in Col. Dagworthy's account book on 12 Jul 1762. {Ref: MHS MS.375}

JONES, JOHN (Maryland), pvt., Capt. Tobias Stansbury's Company Muster Roll, Baltimore Co., circa 1757-1758, exact dates not given; bill of credit issued or paid in his behalf to John Ridgley for £1.18.0 on 3 Apr 1767. {Ref: MSA S960 or S752, p. 186} *Identification problem:* There were eight men with this name who could have served in the war: (1) John Jones, b. 17 Apr 1721, son of Benjamin Jones and Elizabeth Pickett; (2) John Jones, b. 9 Apr 1737, St. John's P. E. Parish, son of John Jones and Hannah Wooley, m. Esther (N), served in the Third Regt. of the Baltimore County Militia in 1775, and had children Ann, John, Sophia, Eleanor, Elisha, Joshua, Caleb, and Enoch; d. testate in 1785; (3) John Jones, b. c1740, son of Thomas and Mary Jones; (4) John Jones, son of Philip Jones and Ann Rattenbury; (5) John Jones, son of William Jones, owned land by 1745; (6) John Jones m. Mary (N) and between 1753 and 1768 had children Solomon, Mary, Gay, Margaret, Cloe, and Comfort; (7) John Jones m. Sarah (N) and owned land between 1745 and 1771; (8) John Jones, an Irishman, was a runaway convict servant from William Jenkins in October 1754; and, (9) indentured servant and soldier who served in the French and Indian War some time between 1756 and 1763 (exact dates not known); his master Robert Bryarly, planter, requested compensation from the Baltimore County Court due to the loss of use of Jones while in the service. {Ref: BCF:371-377; MHM 94:4, p. 426, citing Baltimore Co. Court Minutes}

JONES, JOHN (Maryland), patriot and poss. soldier (rank not specified), Frederick Co., militia pay account submitted in 1758, exact date not given. {Ref: MHM 9:4, p. 370} He was paid £3 at Fort Frederick on 26 Jun 1758 "for carrying arms" for the Western Expedition against Fort Duquesne. {Ref: ARMD 55:773}

JONES, JOHN (Maryland), sea captain by 1757, in command "of the sloop *Unity*, belonging to Baltimore Town, was taken by the French on last December 29th and taken to Cape Tiberon. Capt. Jones was so ill-used by his captors that he died. He had worked over 12 years here." {Ref: *MD Gazette*, 4 May 1758}

JONES, JOSEPH (Delaware), b. c1738, Wales (joiner, age 20 in 1758); pvt., recruited by Capt. Benjamin Noxon and enlisted on 24 Apr 1758. {Ref: ARDE I:19; ARPA (2nd Series) 2:566}

JONES, JOSEPH (Maryland), pvt., Frederick Co., received £5 bounty money on 30 May 1757 for enlisting in the militia. {Ref: ARMD 55:265, 619} Pvt., Capt. William Luckett's Company Muster Roll, Frederick Co., circa 1757-1758, exact dates not given (served 30 days); bill of credit issued or paid in his behalf to to William Luckett, Jr. for £1.10.0 on 6 Apr 1767. {Ref: MSA S960 or S752, p. 169; CSOS:99}

JONES, JOSEPH (Maryland), pvt., Capt. John Dagworthy's Company of MD Troops, Frederick Co., from 1 Jun 1758 (transferred from Capt. Richard Pearis' Company where he had been a drummer) to 9 Jun 1758 when he was promoted again to drummer and served until 16 Apr 1759 when he reportedly deserted; however, payment to him was recorded in Col. Dagworthy's account book on 11 Jul 1762. {Ref: MHS MS.375; CSOS:77, 90; MHS MS.375.1}

JONES, LAYTON, see "William Wallace," q.v.

JONES, MARY ANN, see "William Briscoe," q.v.

JONES, NEHEMIAH (Maryland), pvt., Capt. Richard Pearis' Company of MD Troops, Frederick Co., from 9 Oct 1757 to 31 May 1758. {Ref: MHS MS.375.1} Payment to him was recorded in Col. Dagworthy's account book on 15 Jul 1762, {Ref: MHS MS.375}

JONES, REES (Delaware), captain, White Clay Hundred, Upper Regt. of Militia, West Division, New Castle Co., 1756. {Ref: ARDE I:11; ARPA (2nd Series) 2:526; HDE I:141}

JONES, RICHARD MARIOT (Delaware), b. c1724, Kent Co. (laborer, age 35 in 1759, long visaged, brown hair, brown complexion, slender limbed, height 5 ft. 11 in.); pvt. enlisted by Capt. Samuel Neilson in Philadelphia for the PA Regt. on 12 May 1759. {Ref: ARDE I:28}

JONES, SARAH, see "William Ringgold," q.v.

JONES, THOMAS (Delaware), b. c1736, Wales (laborer, age 22 in 1758); pvt., recruited by Capt. Benjamin Noxon and enlisted on 24 Apr 1758. {Ref: ARDE I:19; ARPA (2nd Series) 2:566}

JONES, THOMAS (Maryland), pvt., Capt. Francis Ware's Company of MD Troops, Charles Co., circa 9 Oct 1757 to 30 Dec 1758. {Ref: MHS MS.375.1;

CSOS:88} Payment to him was recorded in Col. Dagworthy's account book on 7 Mar 1763. {Ref: MHS MS.375}

JONES, WILLIAM (Maryland), pvt., Capt. Tobias Stansbury's Company Muster Roll, Baltimore Co., circa 1757-1758, exact dates not given; bill of credit issued or paid in his behalf to Joseph Ensor for £1.18.0 on 22 May 1767. {Ref: MSA S960 or S752, p. 187}

JONES, WILLIAM (Maryland), b. c1727, Prince William Co., VA (carpenter, age about 30 in 1757); soldier who was reported as deserted from the MD Forces in July 1757. {Ref: *MD Gazette*, 21 Jul 1757} Subsequently returned to duty as pvt. in Capt. Francis Ware's Company of MD Troops, Charles Co., from 4 Jun 1758 to 8 Jun 1758 (served 5 days). {Ref: MHS MS.375.1; CSOS:88} Payment to him was recorded in Col. Dagworthy's account book on 8 Mar 1763. {Ref: MHS MS.375}

JORDAN, JOHN (Maryland), b. c1725, St. Mary's Company, prob. son of Justinian Jordan and Mary Coode, m. Eleanor Dent, had children William, John, and Anne, and d. 29 May 1763, Charles Co.; planter, merchant, captain by 1754, and member of the MD Assembly (1754-1757, served on the Arms and Ammunition Committee). {Ref: BDML II:500; ARMD 55:44}

JORDON, WILLIAM (Maryland), pvt., Capt. Joshua Beall's Company of MD Troops, Prince George's Co., from 20 Sep 1757 to 31 May 1758 when he reportedly deserted; however, payment to him was recorded in Col. Dagworthy's account book on 8 Mar 1763. {Ref: MHS MS.375; CSOS:84; MHS MS.375.1}

JUDY (JUDEY), WINEBART (Maryland), pvt., Capt. Stephen Rensburg's or Rensburger's Company Muster Roll, Frederick Co., circa 1757-1758, exact dates not given (served 42 days); bill of credit issued or paid in his behalf to Casper Shaff for £2.2.0 on 2 Mar 1767. {Ref: MSA S960 or S752, p. 182; CSOS:112}

JUDY, JACOB (Maryland), pvt., Capt. John White's Company Muster Roll, Frederick Co., circa 1757-1758, exact dates not given (served 6 days); bill of credit issued or paid to him for £0.6.0 in 1767, exact date not given. {Ref: MSA S960 or S752, p. 164; CSOS:95}

JULIAN, STEPHEN (Maryland), pvt., Capt. Stephen Rensburg's or Rensburger's Company Muster Roll, Frederick Co., circa 1757-1758, exact dates not given; bill of credit issued or paid in his behalf to Stephen Rensburger for £2.2.0 on 27 Mar 1767. {Ref: MSA S960 or S752, p. 183}

JUMP (JUMPE), NATHAN (Maryland), pvt., Capt. Henry Casson's Company Muster Roll, Queen Anne's Co., circa 1757-1758, exact dates not given (served 27 days); bill of credit issued or paid in his behalf to Capt. Casson on 27 Mar 1767 for £1.7.0. {Ref: MSA S960 or S752, p. 178; CSOS:109}

JUMP (JUMPE), PETER (Maryland), sgt., Capt. Henry Casson's Company Muster Roll, Queen Anne's Co., circa 1757-1758, exact dates not given (served 4 days as a pvt. and 23 days as a cpl.); bill of credit issued or paid in his behalf to Capt. Casson on 27 Mar 1767 for £1.10.7½ as a sgt. and £0.5.3 as a cpl. {Ref: MSA S960 or S752, p. 178; CSOS:108}

JUMP (JUMPE), SOLLO. or SOLOMON (Maryland), pvt., Capt. Henry Casson's Company Muster Roll, Queen Anne's Co., circa 1757-1758, exact dates not given (served 27 days). {Ref: CSOS:109}

JUMP (JUMPE), VAUGHAN (Maryland), pvt., Capt. Henry Casson's Company Muster Roll, Queen Anne's Co., circa 1757-1758, exact dates not given (served 27 days); bill of credit issued or paid in his behalf to Capt. Casson on 27 Mar 1767 for £1.7.0. {Ref: MSA S960 or S752, p. 178; CSOS:109}

JUNG, MATTHEW (Maryland), cpl., Royal American Regt., Baltimore Town, German born (age not given), reported as deserted in 1756; "formerly kept a school at Conawauga and was seen with his wife and child on the way to that place." {Ref: *MD Gazette*, 4 Nov 1756} See "Bryan Clarke," q.v.

JUSTICE, WILLIAM (Maryland), pvt., Capt. Francis Ware's Company of MD Troops, Charles Co., from 9 Oct 1757 to 20 Apr 1758 (served 193 days) when he was reported as dead; however, payment to him was recorded in Col. Dagworthy's account book on 8 Mar 1763. {Ref: MHS MS.375; CSOS:88; MHS MS.375.1}

KAIN, DANIEL (Delaware), b. c1729, Antrim, Ireland (shoemaker, age 29 in 1758); pvt., enlisted 20 Apr 1758 "for the campaign in the lower counties" by Capt. John McClughan. {Ref: ARDE I:17; ARPA (2nd Series) 2:570}

KANHART (KERNHART), HENRY (Maryland), pvt., Capt. Stephen Rensburg's or Rensburger's Company Muster Roll, Frederick Co., circa 1757-1758, exact dates not given (served 42 days); bill of credit issued or paid in his behalf to Stephen Rensburger for £2.2.0 on 27 Mar 1767. {Ref: MSA S960 or S752, p. 183; CSOS:113}

KAYLE, THOMAS (Delaware), b. c1728 (carpenter, age 30 in 1758); pvt., enlisted 12 May 1758 "for the campaign in the lower counties" by Capt. John McClughan. {Ref: ARDE I:17; ARPA (2nd Series) 2:570}

KEALHUINECAY, or BLACK DOG, Indian Chief (Maryland), Frederick Co., agreed to join with the English against the French in 1758. {Ref: ARMD 31:266}

KEECH, JOHN (Maryland), cpl., Capt. Francis Ware's Company of MD Troops, Charles Co., from 9 Oct 1757 to 30 Dec 1758 (promoted 13 Oct 1758). {Ref: MHS MS.375.1; CSOS:88} Payment to him was recorded in Col. Dagworthy's account book on 7 Mar 1763. {Ref: MHS MS.375}

KEEDEE, HENRY (Maryland), pvt., Capt. Moses Chapline's Company Muster Roll, Frederick Co., circa 1757-1758, exact dates not given (served 6 days). {Ref: CSOS:115}

KEENE, BENJAMIN, see "Thomas MacKeele," q.v.

KEES, JOHN (Maryland), pvt., Capt. Thomas Norris' Company, Frederick Co., circa 1757-1758, exact dates not given (served 30 days); bill of credit issued or paid in his behalf to Michael McGuire on 27 Mar 1767 for £1.10.0. {Ref: MSA S960 or S752, p. 176; CSOS:108}

KEITH, CHARLES (Delaware), pvt., Capt. Henry Vanbibber's Company of the Lower Counties on Delaware Troops at New Castle, enlisted on 28 May 1759. {Ref: ARDE I:26; ARPA (2nd Series) 2:594}

KEITH, GEORGE (Delaware or Pennsylvania), b. c1736, MD (cooper, age 23 in 1759); pvt., enlisted 8 Mar 1759 by Capt. Richardson of the 3rd Bttn., PA Regt. commanded by William Denny, Esq. {Ref: ARPA (2nd Series) 2:507}

KELER, GEORGE (Maryland), cpl., Capt. John White's Company Muster Roll, Frederick Co., circa 1757-1758, exact dates not given (served 6 days); bill of credit issued or paid to him for £0.8.0 in 1767, exact date not given. {Ref: MSA S960 or S752, p. 164; CSOS:95}

KELLAM, BENJAMIN (Delaware), m. Mary (N), had no children, and d. testate by 3 Feb 1775. {Ref: CDSS:112} Ensign, Brandywine Hundred, Upper Regt. of Militia, Northeast Division, New Castle Co., 1756. {Ref: ARDE I:11; ARPA (2nd Series) 2:526; HDE I:141}

KELLER, CHRISTOPHER (Maryland), pvt., Capt. Jonathan Hagar's Company Muster Roll, Frederick Co., circa 1757-1758, exact dates not given (served 6 days); bill of credit issued or paid to him for £0.6.0 in 1767, exact date not given. {Ref: MSA S960 or S752, p. 174; CSOS:106}

KELLER, JACOB (Maryland), pvt., Capt. John Middaugh's Company Muster Roll, Frederick Co., circa 1757-1758, exact dates not given (served 30 says); bill of credit issued or paid in his behalf to Thomas Beatty, Jr. for £1.10.0 on 3 Apr 1767. {Ref: MSA S960 or S752, p. 172; CSOS:101}

KELLEY, SAMUEL (Maryland), pvt., Capt. Joseph Chapline's Company Muster Roll No. 5, Frederick Co., circa 1757-1758, exact dates not given; bill of credit issued or paid in his behalf to Joseph Chaplin for £0.8.0 on 5 Mar 1767. {Ref: MSA S960 or S752, p. 195}

KELLY, DANIEL (Maryland), pvt., Capt. William Luckett's Company Muster Roll, Frederick Co., circa 1757-1758, exact dates not given (served 30 days); bill of credit issued or paid in his behalf to William Luckett, Jr. for £1.10.0 on 6 Apr 1767. {Ref: MSA S960 or S752, p. 170; CSOS:99}

KELLY, DANIEL (Maryland), pvt., Capt. Joseph Chapline's Company Muster Roll No. 5, Frederick Co., circa 1757-1758, exact dates not given; bill of credit issued or paid in his behalf to Joseph Chaplin for £0.8.0 on 8 Jun 1767. {Ref: MSA S960 or S752, p. 195} Pvt., Capt. Moses Chapline's Company Muster Roll No. 3, Frederick Co., circa 1757-1758, exact dates not given (served 6 days); bill of credit issued or paid in his behalf to Joseph Chapline for £0.6.0 on 8 Jun 1767. {Ref: MSA S960 or S752, p. 198; CSOS:114}

KELLY (KULLEY), JAMES (Maryland), farmer; pvt., Capt. Peregrine Brown's Company, Kent Co., on 19 Feb 1758, by which time he had enlisted, but was unable to march due to health problems. {Ref: ARMD 31:283, 288}

KELLY, JOHN (Delaware), b. c1730, Down, Ireland (laborer, age 28 in 1758); pvt., enlisted 20 Apr 1758 "for the campaign in the lower counties" by Capt. John McClughan. {Ref: ARDE I:18; ARPA (2nd Series) 2:570}

KELLY, JOHN (Maryland or Pennsylvania), pvt., Capt. Hamilton's Company, was killed in "a recent battle with the Indians" in 1756 (exact date not given) in Cumberland Co., PA, after the burning of McCord's Fort. {Ref: *MD Gazette*, 29 Apr 1756}

KELLY, MATTHEW (Delaware), b. c1733, Ireland (laborer, age 25 in 1758); pvt., recruited by Capt. Benjamin Noxon and enlisted on 24 Apr 1758. {Ref: ARDE I:19; ARPA (2nd Series) 2:566}

KELLY, THOMAS (Maryland), pvt., Capt. Joseph Chapline's Company Muster Rolls No. 2 and 3, Frederick Co., circa 1757-1758, exact dates not given; militia pay account submitted in 1758, exact date not given. {Ref: MHM 9:4, p. 370} Bill of credit issued or paid in his behalf to Joseph Chaplin for £0.9.0 on 5 Mar 1767. {Ref: MSA S960 or S752, p. 193} Pvt., Capt. Joseph Chapline's Company Muster Roll No. 4, Frederick Co., circa 1757-1758, exact dates not given (served 6 days); bill of credit issued or paid in his behalf to Joseph Chaplin for £0.6.0 on 5 Mar 1767; name listed once as "Thomas Kiley." {Ref: MSA S960 or S752, p. 194; CSOS:105}

KELLY, URATH, see "Nathaniel Owings," q.v.

KELLY, WILLIAM (Maryland), pvt., Capt. Thomas Norris' Company, Frederick Co., circa 1757-1758, exact dates not given (served 30 days); bill of credit issued or paid to him for £1.10.0 in 1767, exact date not given. {Ref: MSA S960 or S752, p. 176; CSOS:108}

KELLY, WILLIAM, see "Nathaniel Owings," q.v.

KELLY, WILLIAM G. (Maryland), pvt., Capt. Henry Sneavely's Company Muster Roll, Frederick Co., circa 1757-1758, exact dates not given; bill of credit issued or paid to him for £0.8.0 in 1767, exact date not given. {Ref: MSA S960 or S752, p. 190}

KELSE, RICHARD (Delaware), pvt., Capt. Henry Vanbibber's Company of the Lower Counties on Delaware Troops at New Castle, enlisted on 21 May 1759. {Ref: ARDE I:26; ARPA (2nd Series) 2:594}

KEMMEY, JOHN (Delaware), pvt., Capt. French Battell's Company of Lower County Provincials, enlisted 22 May 1758. {Ref: ARDE I:16; ARPA (2nd Series) 2:555}

KEMP, FREDERICK (Maryland), pvt., Capt. Stephen Rensburger's Company Muster Roll, Frederick Co., circa 1757-1758, exact dates not given (served 34 days). {Ref: CSOS:113}

KEMP, GILBERT (Maryland), pvt., Capt. Stephen Rensburg's or Rensburger's Company Muster Roll, Frederick Co., circa 1757-1758, exact dates not given (served 34 days); bill of credit issued or paid in his behalf to Casper Shaff for £1.14.0 on 2 Mar 1767. {Ref: MSA S960 or S752, p. 182; CSOS:113}

KEMP, JOHANNA, see "Aquila Hall," q.v.

KEMP, JOHN (Maryland), pvt., Capt. Thomas Norris' Company, Frederick Co., circa 1757-1758, exact dates not given (served 30 days); bill of credit issued in his behalf to Alexander Wells and paid to Kemp's exec. (unnamed) on 27 Mar 1767 for £1.10.0. {Ref: MSA S960 or S752, p. 176; CSOS:108}

KEMP, LEWIS (Maryland), pvt., Capt. Elias Delashmutt's Company Muster Roll, Frederick Co., 13 Aug 1757, exact dates not given (served 52 days); bill of credit issued or paid in his behalf to Casper Shaff on 2 Mar 1767 for £2.12.0. {Ref: MSA S960 or S752, p. 162; CSOS:98}

KEMP, PETER (Maryland), pvt., Capt. Stephen Rensburg's or Rensburger's Company Muster Roll, Frederick Co., circa 1757-1758, exact dates not given (served 34 days); bill of credit issued or paid in his behalf to Casper Shaff for £1.14.0 on 2 Mar 1767. {Ref: MSA S960 or S752, p. 182; CSOS:112}

KEMPTON (KIMPTON), THOMAS (Maryland), pvt., Capt. Joshua Beall's Company of MD Troops, Prince George's Co., from 9 Oct 1757 to 1 Nov 1758 when he reportedly deserted; however, payment to him was recorded in Col. Dagworthy's account book on 7 Mar 1763 for work on Fort Cumberland. {Ref: MHS MS.375; CSOS:84; MHS MS.375.1}

KENIGH (KEIOUGH?), WILLIAM (Maryland), sgt., Kent County, by 1757. {Ref: ARMD 31:208}

KENNAN, JAMES (Maryland), indentured servant and soldier who served in the French and Indian War some time between 1756 and 1763 (exact dates not known); his master Robert Mills, farmer, requested compensation from the Baltimore County Court due to the loss of use of Kennan while in the service. {Ref: MHM 94:4, p. 426, citing Baltimore Co. Court Minutes}

KENNARD, THOMAS (Maryland), farmer; pvt., Capt. Peregrine Brown's 7th Co. of Foot Militia, Kent Co., on 19 Feb 1758, by which time he had enlisted, but reportedly refused to appear and serve in arms against the enemy. {Ref: ARMD 31:283, 288}

KENNEDY (KANEDY), JAMES (Delaware), b. c1736 (laborer, age 23 in 1759); pvt., enlisted by Capt. James Armstrong for the PA Regt. on 6 May 1759. {Ref: ARDE I:26; ARPA (2nd Series) 2:585}

KENNETT, JOSEPH (Maryland), sgt., Capt. Moses Chapline's Company Muster Roll No. 1, Frederick Co., circa 1757-1758, exact dates not given (served 55 days); bill of credit issued or paid in his behalf to Joseph Chaplin for £2.15.0 on 5 Mar 1767. {Ref: MSA S960 or S752, p. 196; CSOS:113} Sgt., Capt. Moses Chapline's Company Muster Roll No. 3, Frederick Co., circa 1757-1758, exact dates not given (served 6 days); bill of credit issued or paid in his behalf to Joseph Chaplin for £0.8.0 on 5 Mar 1767. {Ref: MSA S960 or S752, p. 198; CSOS:115}

KEPHART, ANDREW (Maryland), pvt., Capt. John White's Company Muster Roll, Frederick Co., circa 1757-1758, exact dates not given (served 6 days); bill of credit issued or paid to him for £0.6.0 in 1767 (exact date not given); name listed once as "Andrew Keptrart." {Ref: MSA S960 or S752, p. 164; CSOS:96}

KERNHART, HENRY, see "Henry Kanhart," q.v.

KERR, ROBERT (Maryland or Pennsylvania), pvt., Capt. Culbertson's Company, was killed in "a recent battle with the Indians" in 1756 (exact date not given) in Cumberland Co., PA, after the burning of McCord's Fort. {Ref: *MD Gazette*, 29 Apr 1756}

KERR, WILLIAM (Maryland or Pennsylvania), pvt., Capt. Culbertson's Company, was killed in "a recent battle with the Indians" in 1756 (exact date not given) in Cumberland Co., PA, after the burning of McCord's Fort. {Ref: *MD Gazette*, 29 Apr 1756}

KESLAR, BARNARD (Maryland), pvt., Capt. Peter Butler's Company Muster Roll, Frederick Co., circa 1757-1758, exact dates not given (served 34 days); bill of credit or order issued in his behalf for £1.14.0 and paid to Thomas Cresap on 2 Mar 1767. {Ref: MSA S960 or S752, p. 168; CSOS:97}

KETCHERSIDE, JAMES (Maryland), pvt., Capt. Alexander Beall's Company of MD Troops, Frederick Co., circa 9 Oct 1757 to 30 Dec 1758. {Ref: MHS MS.375.1;

CSOS:81} Payment to him was recorded in Col. Dagworthy's account book on 11 Jul 1762. {Ref: MHS MS.375}

KETCHINDANER, BALSER (Maryland), pvt., Capt. Stephen Rensburg's or Rensburger's Company Muster Roll, Frederick Co., circa 1757-1758, exact dates not given (served 42 days); bill of credit issued or paid in his behalf to Stephen Rensburger for £2.2.0 on 27 Mar 1767. {Ref: MSA S960 or S752, p. 183; CSOS:112}

KETCHINDANER, JACOB (Maryland), pvt., Capt. Stephen Rensburg's or Rensburger's Company Muster Roll, Frederick Co., circa 1757-1758, exact dates not given (served 34 days); bill of credit issued or paid in his behalf to Stephen Rensburger for £1.14.0 on 27 Mar 1767. {Ref: MSA S960 or S752, p. 183; CSOS:112}

KETCHMORE (CATCHMORE), THOMAS (Delaware), b. c1736, England (blacksmith, age 22 in 1758); pvt., recruited by Capt. Benjamin Noxon and enlisted on 19 Apr 1758. {Ref: ARDE I:19; ARPA (2nd Series) 2:566} Pvt., Capt. Henry Vanbibber's Company of the Lower Counties on Delaware Troops at New Castle, enlisted on 13 May 1759. {Ref: ARDE I:26; ARPA (2nd Series) 2:594}

KEY, JOHN (Maryland), pvt., Capt. Moses Chapline's Company Muster Roll No. 3, Frederick Co., circa 1757-1758, exact dates not given (served 6 days); bill of credit issued or paid in his behalf to Joseph Chaplin for £0.6.0 on 5 Mar 1767. {Ref: MSA S960 or S752, p. 198; CSOS:115}

KEYHEARKE, Indian Chief (Maryland), Frederick Co., agreed to join with the English against the French in 1758. {Ref: ARMD 31:266}

KEYMAN, ALEXANDER (Maryland), pvt., Capt. Joseph Hanson Harrison's Company Muster Roll, Charles Co., circa 1757-1758, exact dates not given; bill of credit issued or paid to him for £2.12.0 in 1767, exact date not given. {Ref: MSA S960 or S752, p. 189}

KEYS, ELIZABETH, see "Benjamin Nearn," q.v.

KEYS, WILLIAM (Delaware), pvt., Capt. French Battell's Company of Lower County Provincials, enlisted 17 May 1758. {Ref: ARDE I:16; ARPA (2nd Series) 2:555}

KIDD, JOHN (Maryland), ensign in Capt. John Dagworthy's Company of MD Troops, Frederick Co., by 26 Sep 1756 at which time he was paid £2.5.0 by the MD Assembly for enlisting two men; ensign on company muster roll from 9 Oct 1757 to 29 Jun 1758 at which time he resigned (served 264 days); account paid 4 Mar 1763. {Ref: MHS MS.375; ARMD 52:608; MS.375.1; CSOS:75}

KILEY, THOMAS (Maryland), pvt., Capt. Joseph Chapline's Company Muster Roll No. 3, Frederick Co., circa 1757-1758, exact dates not given (served 9 days); bill of credit issued or paid to him for £0.9.0 in 1767, exact date not given. {Ref: MSA S960 or S752, p. 193; CSOS:104} See "Thomas Kelly," q.v.

KILLEN, ROBERT (Delaware), Esq., m. Mary (N), had children Robert, William, Adam, Henry, John, and Mark, and d. testate by 18 Jan 1771. {Ref: CDSS:114} Captain, Middle Part of Mispillion Hundred, Militia of Kent Co. on Delaware, 1756. {Ref: ARDE I:12; ARPA (2nd Series) 2:527-529; HDE I:141}

KILPATRICK, PATRICK (Delaware), b. c1734, Faughboyne, Ireland (weaver, age 24 in 1758); pvt., enlisted 24 Apr 1758 "for the campaign in the lower counties" by Capt. John McClughan. {Ref: ARDE I:18; ARPA (2nd Series) 2:570}

KILTY (KILTEY), WILLIAM (Maryland), pvt., Capt. John White's Company Muster Roll, Frederick Co., circa 1757-1758, exact dates not given (served 6 days); bill of credit issued or paid to him for £0.6.0 in 1767, exact date not given; name mistakenly listed once as "William Killey." {Ref: MSA S960 or S752, p. 164; MHM 9:3, p. 265; CSOS:95}

KIMBELL (KIMBOLL, KIMBALL), JOHN (Maryland), m. Lettice (N), had son William and dau. (N), and d. testate by 13 Feb 1770. {Ref: WMG 5:2, p. 82} Lieut. in Capt. John Middaugh's Company, Frederick Co., circa 1757-1758 (served 30 days), exact dates not given; militia pay account submitted in 1758, exact date not given. {Ref: MHM 9:4, pp. 366, 368; CSOS:100} Bill of credit issued or paid to him for £3.10.0 on 23 Feb 1767. {Ref: MSA S960 or S752, p. 171}

KIMBLE (KIMBOLD), STEPHEN (Maryland), b. 13 Sep 1738, Baltimore Co., son of Rowland Kimble and Hannah Jackson, m. Mrs. Margaret Barkey Daugherty on 22 Mar 1758, had children Mary, George, James [#1], James [#2], Frances, and Eleanor, and d. testate in 1782 (will probated in June 1784); pvt., Capt. Tobias Stansbury's Company Muster Roll, Baltimore Co., circa 1757-1758, exact dates not given; bill of credit issued or paid in his behalf to John Paca for £3.16.0 on 18 May 1767. {Ref: BCF:386; MSA S960 or S752, pp. 186-187} Pvt., Capt. Dorsey's Militia Co. in Harford Co., 1775, and signed the Association of Freemen in 1776. {Ref: Henry C. Peden, Jr.'s *Revolutionary Patriots of Harford County, MD, 1775-1783*, p. 134}

KIMBLE, WILLIAM (Maryland), drummer, Capt. Peter Butler's Company Muster Roll, Frederick Co., circa 1757-1758, exact dates not given (served 34 days); bill of credit or order issued in his behalf for £2.5.3 and paid to Casper Shaff on 2 Mar 1767. {Ref: MSA S960 or S752, p. 167; CSOS:96}

KIMBOLL, WILLIAM (Maryland), pvt., Capt. Alexander Beall's Company of Foot, 1756-1757, recorded his discharge in Frederick Co. Court on 22 Nov 1758. Capt. Beall certified that "Will Kimboll hath served for 8 months and the time of his enlistment being expired is hereby discharged." Receipt for pay and clothing, and all other demands as a soldier in Capt. Beall's Company, signed 10 Feb 1757 by William Kimboll and witnessed by Sgt. Robert Linard and Sgt. George Barrance. {Ref: FCLR:59}

KIMMEY, JOHLN (Delaware), pvt., Kent Co. Militia, Capt. John Caton's Company, 25 Apr 1757 (date of muster roll). {Ref: ARDE I:14}

KING, CHARLES (Maryland), pvt., Capt. Joseph Hanson Harrison's Company Muster Roll, Charles Co., circa 1757-1758, exact dates not given; bill of credit issued or paid in his behalf to Josias Beall for £2.9.0 on 1 Dec 1769. {Ref: MSA S960 or S752, p. 189}

KING, FRANCIS (Maryland), pvt., Capt. John Dagworthy's Company of MD Troops, Frederick Co., from 9 Oct 1757 to 9 Nov 1758 when he was promoted to cpl. and served until 28 Jun 1759 when he was reported as dead; however, payment to him was recorded in Col. Dagworthy's account book on 28 Feb 1763. {Ref: MHS MS.375; CSOS:77; MHS MS.375.1}

KING, JOSEPH (Maryland), pvt., Capt. Peregrine Brown's Company Muster Roll, Kent Co., circa 1757-1758, exact dates not given (served 15 days); bill of credit issued or paid in his behalf to Robert Buchanan on 20 Feb 1767 for £0.15.0. {Ref: MSA S960 or S752, p. 179; CSOS:110}

KING, MARY ELIZABETH, see "Abraham Barnes," q.v.

KING, REBECCA, see "Thomas Price," q.v.

KING, ROBERT (Maryland), pvt., Capt. John Dagworthy's Company of MD Troops, Frederick Co., from 9 Oct 1757 to 24 Dec 1757 when he was discharged. {Ref: MHS MS.375.1; CSOS:77} Payment to him was recorded in Col. Dagworthy's account book on 8 Mar 1763. {Ref: MHS MS.375} This may or may not be the same man: "Robert King accidentally drowned at George Town, Frederick Co., on Tues. last week, a man who had a wife and six children." {Ref: *MD Gazette*, 28 Jun 1764}

KING, WILLIAM (Maryland), pvt., Capt. Alexander Beall's Company of MD Troops, Frederick Co., from 1 Jun 1758 to 30 Dec 1758 (transferred from Capt. Richard Pearis' Company; exact dates of service not given). {Ref: MHS MS.375.1; CSOS:81, 90} Payment to him was recorded in Col. Dagworthy's account book on 12 Jul 1762. {Ref: MHS MS.375}

KINK, JOHN (Delaware), pvt., Capt. Richard McWilliams' Company of Foot, New Castle Co., enlisted 28 Dec 1757. {Ref: ARDE I:15}

KINKERLY (KINKLEY), FREDERICK (Maryland), carpenter, m. Anna Barbara (N), had children George, Frederick, Philip Jacob, and Jacob, and d. testate by 26 Feb 1780. {Ref: WMG 5:4, p. 165} Pvt., Capt. Peter Butler's Company Muster Roll, Frederick Co., circa 1757-1758, exact dates not given (served 34 days); bill of credit or order issued in his behalf for £1.14.0 and paid to Casper Shaff on 2 Mar 1767. {Ref: MSA S960 or S752, p. 167: CSOS:97}

KINNEY, DANIEL (Delaware), pvt., Kent Co. Militia, Capt. John Caton's Company, 25 Apr 1757 (date of muster roll). {Ref: ARDE I:13}

KINSEL (KINSELL), ADAM (Maryland), pvt., Capt. Peter Butler's Company Muster Roll, Frederick Co., circa 1757-1758, exact dates not given (served 34 days); bill of credit or order issued to him for £1.14.0 in March 1767. {Ref: MSA S960 or S752, p. 167: CSOS:97}

KIPP (KIPPS), ABRAHAM (Maryland), pvt., Capt. Peter Butler's Company Muster Roll, Frederick Co., circa 1757-1758, exact dates not given; bill of credit or order issued in his behalf for £1.14.0 and paid to Peter Grosh on 4 Mar 1767. {Ref: MSA S960 or S752, p. 168}

KIPPART, GEORGE (Maryland), patriot, Frederick Co., who performed "sundry services at the fort" in 1763 and payment in the amount of £1.15.2 was still owed to him on 25 Nov 1763 (when reported by the Accounts Committee to the MD Assembly). {Ref: ARMD 58:400}

KIRKPATRICK, DAVID (Delaware), 2nd lieut., New Castle Co., on 25 Apr 1758, and subsequently reported as dead (exact date not given). {Ref: ARDE I:16; ARPA (2nd Series) 2:580}

KIRKPATRICK, JOHN (Delaware), b. c1733, Ireland (laborer, age 25 in 1758); pvt., recruited by Capt. Benjamin Noxon and enlisted on 23 May 1758. {Ref: ARDE I:19; ARPA (2nd Series) 2:566}

KIRKPATRICK, JOHN (Maryland), patriot, Annapolis, Anne Arundel Co., pay account submitted for quartering soldiers in 1757 or 1758, exact dates not given. {Ref: MHM 9:3, p. 260}

KIRKPATRICK, MICHAEL (Maryland), pvt., Capt. Henry Sneavely's Company Muster Roll, Frederick Co., circa 1757-1758, exact dates not given; bill of credit issued or paid to him for £0.8.0 in 1767, exact date not given. {Ref: MSA S960 or S752, p. 190}

KIRSHAW, JAMES (Maryland), lieut., Capt. Robert Sollers' Militia Co. in the lower part of Calvert Co. circa 1756-1757 (exact dates not given). {Ref: HCC:121}

KIRSHNER, ELIZABETH, see "Jonathan Hagar," q.v.

KISNER, CONROD (Maryland), pvt., Capt. Joseph Chapline's Company Muster Roll No. 1, Frederick Co., circa 1757-1758, exact dates not given (served 26 days); bill of credit issued or paid in his behalf to Joseph Chaplin for £1.16.0 on 24 Apr 1767. {Ref: MSA S960 or S752, p. 192; CSOS:103}

KISNER, GEORGE (Maryland), pvt., Capt. Joseph Chapline's Company Muster Roll No. 1, Frederick Co., circa 1757-1758, exact dates not given; bill of credit issued or paid in his behalf to Joseph Chaplin for £2 on 5 Mar 1767. {Ref: MSA S960 or S752, p. 191}

KISSINGER, GEORGE (Maryland), pvt., Capt. John White's Company Muster Roll, Frederick Co., circa 1757-1758, exact dates not given (served 6 days); bill of credit issued or paid to him for £0.6.0 in 1767, exact date not given. {Ref: MSA S960 or S752, p. 164; CSOS:95}

KISSINGER, JOHN (Maryland), pvt., Capt. Joseph Chapline's Company Muster Roll No. 4, Frederick Co., circa 1757-1758, exact dates not given (served 7 days); bill of credit issued or paid in his behalf to Joseph Chaplin for £0.7.0 on 5 Mar 1767. {Ref: MSA S960 or S752, p. 194; CSOS:105}

KITEMAN, CHRISTOPHER (Maryland), pvt., Capt. John Middaugh's Company Muster Roll, Frederick Co., circa 1757-1758, exact dates not given (served 30 days); bill of credit issued or paid in his behalf to Thomas Beatty, Jr. for £1.10.0 on 3 Apr 1767. {Ref: MSA S960 or S752, p. 172; CSOS:102}

KITSINGER, GEORGE (Maryland), pvt., Capt. Henry Sneavely's Company Muster Roll, Frederick Co., circa 1757-1758, exact dates not given; bill of credit issued or paid to him for £0.8.0 in 1767, exact date not given. {Ref: MSA S960 or S752, p. 190}

KITSON, THOMAS (Delaware), b. c1724, Worcester, England (laborer, age 34 in 1758); pvt., enlisted 24 Apr 1758 "for the campaign in the lower counties" by Capt. John McClughan. {Ref: ARDE I:18; ARPA (2nd Series) 2:570}

KITTLE, MAGNUS (Delaware), pvt., Capt. Richard McWilliams' Company of Foot, New Castle Co., enlisted 28 Dec 1757. {Ref: ARDE I:14}

KNAVE, JACOB (Maryland), patriot and poss. soldier (rank not specified), Frederick Co., militia pay account submitted in 1758, exact date not given. {Ref: MHM 9:4, p. 370}

KNOPP, JAMES (Maryland), soldier (rank not specified) who was committed to jail in Prince George's Co. (exact date not given) by Dr. David Ross on suspicion of being a deserter from Fort Cumberland; he subsequently escaped from jail in July 1757. {Ref: *MD Gazette*, 28 Jul 1757}

KNOTTS, MARY, see "William Evans," q.v.

KOCH, ANNE HEDGE, see "Emanuel Grubb," q.v.

KOLLOCK, COMFORT, see "William Prettyman," q.v.

KOLLOCK, JACOB (Delaware), son of Jacob Kollock, Esq., of Lewes, DE, and wife Mary (N), m. Margaret (N), had children Phillip, Jacob Jr., Hester, Mary, Catherine, Hannah, Magdalen, Jane, and Susanna, and d. testate by 21 Feb 1772. {Ref: CFD 2:109-110; CDSS:116} Colonel, Militia Regt. of Sussex Co., 1756-1758. {Ref: ARDE I:13, 15; ARPA (2nd Series) 2:529, 579; HDE I:141}

KOLLOCK, JACOB JR. (Delaware), gent., m. Mary (N), had children Cornelius, John Leech, Phillip, Jacob, Rebecca, Mary, Alice, and Hester, and d. testate by 4 Nov 1790. {Ref: CDSS:116} Lieut., Northern District of Lewes and Rehoboth Hundred, Militia Regt. of Sussex Co., 1756-1758. {Ref: ARDE I:13, 15; ARPA (2nd Series) 2:529, 579; HDE I:141}

KOLLOCK, MARY, see "Jacob Kollock" and Jacob Kollock, Jr.," q.v.

KULL, JAMES, see "James Hull," q.v.

KULLEY, JAMES, see "James Kelly," q.v.

KUNCE, PHILIP, see "Philip Coonce," q.v.

LABORN, GEORGE (Maryland), patriot, Kent Co., pay account submitted for quartering soldiers in 1757 or 1758, exact dates not given. {Ref: MHM 9:3, p. 261}

LABROUSE, BENJAMIN (Maryland), pvt., Capt. Joshua Beall's Company of MD Troops, Prince George's Co., from 9 Oct 1757 to 8 Jun 1758; payment to him was recorded in Col. Dagworthy's account book on 23 Jul 1762. {Ref: MHS MS.375.1; CSOS:85; MHS MS.375}

LAINEY (LANY), MATTHEW (Maryland), sgt., Capt. Stephen Rensburg's or Rensburger's Company Muster Roll, Frederick Co., circa 1757-1758, exact dates not given (served 42 days); bill of credit issued or paid in his behalf to Robert Wood for £2.16.0 on 4 Mar 1767. {Ref: MSA S960 or S752, p. 182; CSOS:112}

LAKE, JOHN (Delaware), b. c1728, Great Hornet, England (butcher, age 30 in 1758); pvt., enlisted 6 May 1758 "for the campaign in the lower counties" by Capt. John McClughan. {Ref: ARDE I:18; ARPA (2nd Series) 2:570}

LAKINS (LEKINS), ABRAHAM (Maryland), pvt., Capt. Peter Bainbridge's Company Muster Roll, Frederick Co., circa 1757-1758, exact dates not given (served 28 days); bill of credit issued or paid in his behalf to Casper Shaff on 4 Mar 1767 for £1.8.0. {Ref: MSA S960 or S752, pp. 180-181; CSOS:111}

LAMBERT, JOHN (Maryland), pvt., Capt. John White's Company Muster Roll, Frederick Co., circa 1757-1758, exact dates not given (served 6 days); bill of credit issued or paid to him for £0.6.0 in 1767, exact date not given. {Ref: MSA S960 or S752, p. 165; CSOS:96}

LANCASTER, HENRY (Delaware), b. c1735, MD (laborer, age 23 in 1758); pvt., recruited by Capt. Benjamin Noxon and enlisted on 29 Apr 1758. {Ref: ARDE I:19; ARPA (2nd Series) 2:485, 566}

LANCASTER, SINCLAIR (Delaware), b. c1737, MD (cordwainer, age 21 in 1758); pvt., recruited by Capt. Benjamin Noxon and enlisted on 25 Apt 1758. {Ref: ARDE I:19; ARPA (2nd Series) 2:485, 566}

LANCOUNT, ANTHONY (Maryland), pvt., Capt. Tobias Stansbury's Company Muster Roll, Baltimore Co., circa 1757-1758, exact dates not given; bill of credit issued or paid to him for £2.12.0 in 1767, exact date not given. {Ref: MSA S960 or S752, p. 187}

LANDOUZ, JOSEPH (Maryland or Pennsylvania), German (age not given); pvt. in 1757 who was hanged at Carlisle for desertion (exact date not given). {Ref: *MD Gazette*, 10 Nov 1757}

LANE, GEORGE (Maryland), patriot, Frederick Co., who performed "sundry services at the fort" in 1763 and payment in the amount of £3.12.0 was still owed to him on 25 Nov 1763 (when reported by the Accounts Committee to the MD Assembly). {Ref: ARMD 58:400}

LANE, JOHN (Maryland), pvt., Capt. Elias Delashmutt's Company Muster Roll, Frederick Co., circa 1757-1758, exact dates not given (served 30 days). {Ref: CSOS:94} In early February 1758 he and Griffith Johnson were out scouting on the Potomac and found Indian tracks leading to George's Creek near Savage River. Lane had been taken prisoner by the Indians last November. {Ref: *MD Gazette*, 16 Feb 1758} Bill of credit issued or paid in his behalf to Elias Delashmut, Jr. for him on 16 Mar 1767 for £1.10.0. {Ref: MSA S960 or S752, p. 162}

LANE (LAINE), THOMAS (Maryland), pvt., Capt. Moses Chapline's Company Muster Roll No. 3, Frederick Co., circa 1757-1758, exact dates not given (served 6 days); bill of credit issued or paid in his behalf to Joseph Chaplin for £0.6.0 on 5 Mar 1767. {Ref: MSA S960 or S752, pp. 198-199; CSOS:115}

LARDINER (LARDNER), LINFORD (Delaware), New Castle Co., patriot who served as a Justice of the Peace and a Justice of the Court of Oyer and Terminer, 1756-1761. {Ref: GRSD 1:13, 15}

LARIMORE, HUGH (Delaware), b. c1723, Ireland (weaver, age 35 in 1758); pvt., recruited by Capt. Benjamin Noxon and enlisted on 3 May 1758. {Ref: ARDE I:19; ARPA (2nd Series) 2:566}

LARKIN, JOHN, see "Thomas Hammond," q.v.

LARKINS, JOHN (Delaware), pvt., Capt. French Battell's Company of Lower County Provincials, enlisted 22 May 1758. {Ref: ARDE I:16; ARPA (2nd Series) 2:555}

LASCELLES, GENERAL, see "Sabrit Sellers, Jr." q.v.

LATIMER, JAMES (Delaware), captain, Christiana Hundred, Upper Regt. of Militia, Southwest Division, New Castle Co., 1756; court justice, 1761. {Ref: GRSD 1:15; ARDE I:11; ARPA (2nd Series) 2:526; HDE I:141} Lieut. Colonel, New Castle Co. Militia, 1775; member of the Council of Safety, 1776; Justice of the Court of Common Pleas and Orphans Court, 1777; subscribed to the Oath of Fidelity and Allegiance in 1778. {Ref: RPDE:153}

LAVEL, DAVID (Delaware), b. c1744, New Castle, DE (laborer, age 15 in 1759); pvt., enlisted by Capt. John Haslet on 7 May 1759. {Ref: ARDE I:27}

LAWRENCE, JOHN (Maryland), m. Martha (N), had children John Stephen, Upton, Ann West, Susannah, Rachel, Elizabeth, and Peggy, and d. testate by 6

May 1782. {Ref: WMG 6:1, p. 27-28} Pvt., Capt. Joseph Chapline's Company Muster Roll No. 1, Frederick Co., circa 1757-1758, exact dates not given (served 58 days); bill of credit issued or paid in his behalf to Joseph Chaplin for £1.1.0 on 5 Jun 1767. {Ref: MSA S960 or S752, p. 192; CSOS:102} Pvt., Capt. Moses Chapline's Company Muster Roll No. 2, Frederick Co., circa 1757-1758, exact dates not given (served 13 days); bill of credit issued or paid in his behalf to Joseph Chaplin for £0.13.0 on 5 Jun 1767. {Ref: MSA S960 or S752, p. 197; CSOS:114}

LAWRENCE, JONATHAN, see "John Stevenson," q.v.

LAWS, GEORGE (Maryland), pvt. (county not stated), received £5 bounty money on 14 Jul 1757 for enlisting in the militia. {Ref: ARMD 55:265, 619}

LAWSON, ALEXANDER (Maryland), patriot and poss. soldier (rank not specified), Baltimore Co., militia pay account submitted in 1758, exact date not given. {Ref: MHM 9:4, p. 366} "Mr. Alexander Lawson died last week [in October 1760] at his house in Baltimore Town, after a long and tedious indisposition of the gout." {Ref: *MD Gazette*, 23 Oct 1760} See "Andrew Buchanan" and "Richard Bacchus" and "Thomas Handcock" and "Jacob Nusser" and "Christopher Weaner" and "John Wolfe," q.v.

LAWSON, JOHN (Maryland), pvt., Capt. Richard Pearis' Company of MD Troops, Frederick Co., circa 9 Oct 1757 to 31 May 1758; pvt., Capt. Alexander Beall's Company of MD Troops, Frederick Co., from 1 Jun 1758 to 30 Dec 1758. {Ref: MHS MS.375.1; CSOS:81, 90} Payment to him was recorded in Col. Dagworthy's account book on 15 Jul 1762. {Ref: MHS MS.375}

LAWSON, SUSANNA, see "Andrew Buchanan," q.v.

LAY, GEORGE (Maryland), patriot and poss. soldier (rank not specified), Frederick Co., militia pay account submitted in 1758, exact date not given. {Ref: MHM 9:4, p. 367}

LAY, WILLIAM (Maryland), pvt. (county not stated, poss. Frederick Co.), received £5 bounty money on 4 Aug 1757 for enlisting in the militia. {Ref: ARMD 55:265, 619}

LAYMAN (LAMAN), PHILIP JACOB (Maryland), m. (N), had children Jacob, Salome, Susannah, and Clora, and d. testate by 17 Dec 1782. {Ref: WMG 6:1, p. 28}Ppvt., Capt. Stephen Rensburg's or Rensburger's Company Muster Roll, Frederick Co., circa 1757-1758, exact dates not given (served 34 days); bill of credit issued or paid in his behalf to Stephen Rensburger for £1.14.0 on 27 Mar 1767. {Ref: MSA S960 or S752, p. 183; CSOS:112}

LAYSON, JOHN (Maryland or Pennsylvania), pvt., Capt. Culbertson's Company, was killed in "a recent battle with the Indians" in 1756 (exact date not given) in Cumberland Co., PA, after the burning of McCord's Fort. {Ref: *MD Gazette*, 29 Apr 1756}

LAZARUS, HENRY (Maryland), d. testate and unmarried by 1 Mar 1779. {Ref: WMG 5:3, p. 133} Pvt., Capt. Peter Butler's Company Muster Roll, Frederick Co., circa 1757-1758, exact dates not given (served 34 days); militia pay account submitted in 1758, exact date not given; bill of credit or order issued in his behalf for £1.14.0 and paid to Casper Shaff on 2 Mar 1767; name listed once as "Henry Lazures." {Ref: MHM 9:4, p. 368; CSOS:97; MSA S960 or S752, p. 167}

LAZARUS, SAMSON (Maryland), pvt., Capt. Peter Butler's Company Muster Roll, Frederick Co., circa 1757-1758, exact dates not given; bill of credit or order issued in his behalf for £1.14.0 and paid to Casper Shaff on 2 Mar 1767. {Ref: MSA S960 or S752, p. 167}

LAZER (LAZEAR), JOSEPH (Maryland), pvt., Capt. Peter Bainbridge's Company Muster Roll, Frederick Co., circa 1757-1758, exact dates not given (served 41 days); bill of credit issued or paid in his behalf for £2.1.0 and paid to Joseph Chaplin on 5 Mar 1767. {Ref: MSA S960 or S752, p. 181; CSOS:111}

LAZER, MATTHIAS (Maryland), pvt., Capt. John White's Company Muster Roll, Frederick Co., circa 1757-1758, exact dates not given (served 6 days); bill of credit issued or paid to him for £0.6.0 in 1767, exact date not given. {Ref: MSA S960 or S752, p. 165; CSOS:95}

LEACH, PHILIP (Maryland), pvt., Capt. Tobias Stansbury's Company Muster Roll, Baltimore Co., circa 1757-1758, exact dates not given; bill of credit issued or paid to him for £1.19.0 in 1767, exact date not given. {Ref: MSA S960 or S752, p. 187}

LEADERMAN (LEDERMAN), CHRISTIAN (Maryland), sgt., Capt. Peter Bainbridge's Company Muster Roll, Frederick Co., circa 1757-1758, exact dates not given (served 41 days); bill of credit issued or paid in his behalf to Casper Shaff on 2 Mar 1767 for £2.14.7½. {Ref: MSA S960 or S752, pp. 180-181; CSOS:110}

LEAMON, GEORGE (Maryland), pvt., Capt. Thomas Norris' Company, Frederick Co., circa 1757-1758, exact dates not given (served 30 days); bill of credit issued or paid in his behalf to Michael McGuire on 11 Apr 1767 for £1.10.0; name listed once as "George Leamon, son of John." {Ref: MSA S960 or S752, p. 176; CSOS:108}

LEAMON, JOHN (Maryland), pvt., Capt. Thomas Norris' Company, Frederick Co., circa 1757-1758, exact dates not given (served 30 days); bill of credit issued or paid in his behalf to Charles Englas on 28 Mar 1767 for £1.10.0; name listed once as "John Leamon, Jr." {Ref: MSA S960 or S752, p. 176; CSOS:108}

LEASON, JOSEPH (Maryland), pvt., Capt. Tobias Stansbury's Company Muster Roll, Baltimore Co., circa 1757-1758, exact dates not given; bill of credit issued or paid to him for £1.18.0 in 1767, exact date not given. {Ref: MSA S960 or S752, p. 187}

LEASON, SAMUEL (Maryland), pvt., Capt. Joshua Beall's Company of MD Troops, Prince George's Co., from 9 Oct 1757 to 7 Dec 1757. {Ref: MHS MS.375.1; CSOS:84} Payment to him was recorded in Col. Dagworthy's account book on 24 Jul 1762. {Ref: MHS MS.375}

LEASURE (LEIZURE), JOSEPH (Maryland), pvt., Capt. Joseph Chapline's Company Muster Roll No. 1, Frederick Co., circa 1757-1758, exact dates not given (served 9 days); bill of credit issued or paid in his behalf to Joseph Chaplin for £0.9.0 on 5 Mar 1767. {Ref: MSA S960 or S752, p. 191; CSOS:103}

LEATHER, JOHN (Maryland), pvt., Capt. Stephen Rensburg's or Rensburger's Company Muster Roll, Frederick Co., circa 1757-1758, exact dates not given (served 34 days); bill of credit issued or paid in his behalf to Stephen Rensburger for £1.14.0 on 27 Mar 1767. {Ref: MSA S960 or S752, p. 183; CSOS:112}

LEATHERBURY, COMFORT, see "William Prettyman," q.v.

LEATHERBURY, JONATHAN (Maryland), patriot and poss. soldier (rank not specified), Kent Co., militia pay account submitted in 1758, exact date not given. {Ref: MHM 9:4, p. 366}

LECOCK, THOMAS (Maryland), pvt., Capt. Tobias Stansbury's Company Muster Roll, Baltimore Co., circa 1757-1758, exact dates not given; bill of credit issued or paid to him for £1.18.0 in 1767, exact date not given. {Ref: MSA S960 or S752, p. 187}

LECOMPT, PETER (Delaware), pvt., Capt. French Battell's Company of Lower County Provincials, enlisted 24 May 1758. {Ref: ARDE I:16; ARPA (2nd Series) 2:555}

LEE, ARON (Maryland), pvt., Capt. Alexander Beall's Company, Frederick Co., 1756-1757, recorded his discharge in Frederick Co. Court on 9 Aug 1757. Capt. Beall certified "he hath served 8 months" and the receipt for clothing and pay was signed by Sgt. Robert Leonard and Sgt. George Barrance. Aron Lee made his "X" mark. {Ref: FCLR:30}

LEE, ARTHUR (Maryland), b. c1715-1720, Charles Co., son of Philip Lee (descended from the Lees of Virginia) and Sarah Brooke (widow of William Dent and dau. of Thomas Brooke), m. 1st to Ann Gwinn (widow of Robert Yates and dau. of John Gwinn) in 1744, m. 2nd to Charity Hanson (widow of John Howard and dau. of Samuel Hanson), had children Arthur and Sarah Eleanor Ann, and d. 13 Jul 1760; planter, justice (1745-1760), captain by 1748, and member of the MD Assembly (1749-1754, 1757-1760). {Ref: BDML II:522-523; ARMD 55:199; *MD Gazette*, 17 Jul 1760} See "Richard Lee," q.v.

LEE, DANIEL (Maryland), pvt., Capt. Francis Ware's Company of MD Troops, Charles Co., from 9 Oct 1757 to 16 Jan 1758 (served 100 days). {Ref: MHS MS.375.1; CSOS:88} Payment to him was recorded in Col. Dagworthy's account book on 21 Jul 1762. {Ref: MHS MS.375}

LEE, HANNAH, see "George Plater," q.v.

LEE, JOHN (Maryland), pvt., Capt. Richard Pearis' Company of MD Troops, Frederick Co., circa 9 Oct 1757 to 31 May 1758; pvt., Capt. Joshua Beall's Company of MD Troops, Prince George's Co., from 1 Jun 1758 to 14 Sep 1758 when he was reported as killed; however, payment to him was recorded in Col. Dagworthy's account book on 11 Jul 1762 for work on Fort Cumberland. {Ref: MHS MS.375; CSOS:85, 90; MHS MS.375.1}

LEE, PHILIP, see "Arthur Lee" and "Richard Lee" and "Joseph Sim (Simm)," q.v.

LEE, RICHARD (Maryland), b. c1707, Prince George's Co., son of Philip Lee (descended from the Lees of Virginia) and Sarah Brooke (widow of William Dent and dau. of Thomas Brooke), m. Grace Ashton, of Westmoreland Co., VA, had children Richard Jr., Philip Thomas, Sarah Lettice, Hannah, Alice, and Eleanor Ann, and d. 26 Jan 1787, Charles Co.; planter, lawyer, gentleman, sheriff (1728-1730, 1734-1737), justice (1730-1733), captain by 1734, naval officer of the Potomac (1744-1774), member of the MD Assembly (1745-1771), MD Council (1745-1776), colonel by 1756, and Acting Governor of MD for brief periods in 1774 and 1776. {Ref: BDML II:528-529; ARMD 52:564}

LEE, RICHARD, see "William Fitzhugh," q.v.

LEE, THOMAS (Maryland), pvt., Capt. Francis Ware's Company of MD Troops, Charles Co., from 9 Nov 1757 to 8 Nov 1757. {Ref: MHS MS.375.1} Payment to him was recorded in Col. Dagworthy's account book on 7 Mar 1763 for work at Fort Cumberland. {Ref: MHS MS.375}

LEE, Thomas, see "Thomas Fee," q.v.

LEECH, JAMES (Delaware), b. c1740, MD (laborer, age 18 in 1758); pvt., recruited by Capt. Benjamin Noxon and enlisted on 9 May 1758. {Ref: ARDE I:19; ARPA (2nd Series) 2:485, 566}

LEECH, JAMES (Delaware), pvt., Capt. French Battell's Company of Lower County Provincials, enlisted 28 May 1758. {Ref: ARDE I:16; ARPA (2nd Series) 2:555}

LEFEVER, JAMES (Delaware), pvt., Capt. Richard McWilliams' Company of Foot, New Castle Co., enlisted 28 Dec 1757. {Ref: ARDE I:14}

LEGO (LEEGO), CHARLES (Maryland), pvt., Capt. Richard Pearis' Company of MD Troops, Frederick Co., circa 9 Oct 1757 to 31 May 1758; pvt., Capt. Joshua Beall's Company of MD Troops, Prince George's Co., from 1 Jun 1758 to 1 Nov 1758 when he reportedly deserted; however, payment to him was recorded in Col. Dagworthy's account book on 13 Jul 1762. {Ref: MHS MS.375; CSOS:84, 90; MHS. MS.375.1}

LELAND, JOHN (Maryland), captain and recruiting officer at Annapolis in 1759. {Ref: *MD Gazette*, 15 Mar 1759} See "Harrington Baudin," q.v.

LEMASTER, ISAAC (Maryland), pvt., Capt. Joseph Chapline's Company Muster Roll No. 4, circa 1757-1758, exact dates not given (served 6 days); bill of credit issued or paid in his behalf to Michael Cresap for £0.6.0 on 20 Apr 1767. {Ref: MSA S960 or S752, p. 195; CSOS:105}

LEMASTER (LAMASTER), JACOB (Maryland), pvt., Capt. Alexander Beall's Company of MD Troops, Frederick Co., circa 9 Oct 1757 to 30 Dec 1758. {Ref: MHS MS.375.1; CSOS:81} Payment to him was recorded in Col. Dagworthy's account book on 26 Feb 1763. {Ref: MHS MS.375}

LENDRUM, ANDREW, see "Peter Sullivan," q.v.

LEONARD, ROBERT (Maryland), sgt., Capt. Alexander Beall's Company of MD Troops, Frederick Co., from 9 Oct 1757 to 8 Nov 1758 when he was discharged. {Ref: MHS MS.375.1; FCLR:30, 37, 70} Payment to him was recorded in Col. Dagworthy's account book on 7 Mar 1763. {Ref: MHS MS.375} See "Robert Lineard," q.v.

LESTER, SARAH, see "Robert McGaw," q.v.

LESTON, EBENEZER (Delaware), b. c1733, DE (laborer, age 25 in 1758); pvt., recruited by Capt. Benjamin Noxon and enlisted on 3 May 1758. {Ref: ARDE I:19; ARPA (2nd Series) 2:566}

LETRO (LETROE), JOHN (Maryland), pvt., Capt. Alexander Beall's Company of MD Troops, Frederick Co., circa 9 Oct 1757 to 30 Dec 1758. {Ref: MHS MS.375.1; CSOS:81} Payment to him was recorded in Col. Dagworthy's account book on 26 Feb 1763. {Ref: MHS MS.375}

LETSINGER, MICHAEL (Maryland), pvt., Capt. John White's Company Muster Roll, Frederick Co., circa 1757-1758, exact dates not given (served 6 days); bill

of credit issued or paid to him for £0.6.0 in 1767, exact date not given. {Ref: MSA S960 or S752, p. 165; CSOS:96}

LETTINGER, PHILIP (Maryland), pvt., Capt. John White's Company Muster Roll, Frederick Co., circa 1757-1758, exact dates not given (served 6 days); bill of credit issued or paid to him for £0.6.0 in 1767, exact date not given. {Ref: MSA S960 or S752, p. 165; CSOS:95}

LEVAR (LAVAR), JOHN (Maryland), pvt., Capt. Francis Ware's Company of MD Troops, Charles Co., from 9 Oct 1757 to 24 Dec 1757 when he was reported as dead; however, payment to him was recorded in Col. Dagworthy's account book on 7 Mar 1763. {Ref: MHS MS.375; CSOS:88; MHS MS.375.1}

LEVERSTON, JOHN (Maryland), pvt., Capt. Joseph Chapline's Company Muster Roll No. 1, Frederick Co., circa 1757-1758, exact dates not given (served 58 days); bill of credit issued or paid in his behalf to Joseph Chaplin for £2.18.0 on 5 Mar 1767. {Ref: MSA S960 or S752, p. 191; CSOS:102}

LEVERTON, JOHN (Maryland), cpl., Capt. Henry Casson's Company Muster Roll, Queen Anne's Co., circa 1757-1758, exact dates not given (served 4 days as a pvt. and 23 days as a cpl.); bill of credit issued or paid in his behalf to Capt. Casson on 27 Mar 1767 for £1.10.7½ as a cpl. and £0.4.0 as a pvt. {Ref: MSA S960 or S752, p. 178; CSOS:109}

LEWER (LOWER), HARMAN (Maryland), pvt., Capt. Thomas Norris' Company, Frederick Co., circa 1757-1758, exact dates not given (served 30 days); bill of credit issued or paid in his behalf to Valentine Myres on 10 Apr 1767 for £1.10.0. {Ref: MSA S960 or S752, p. 176; CSOS:108}

LEWIS, ANDREW, see "John Ponty," q.v.

LEWIS, EVAN or EVEN (Delaware), m. Sarah (N), had children Abraham, Robert, Evan, Ruth, Miriam, and Elizabeth, and d. testate by 13 Mar 1786. {Ref: CDSS:121} Pvt., Kent Co. Militia, Capt. John Caton's Company, 25 Apr 1757 (date of muster roll); ensign, Upper District of Mother Kill Hundred, Kent Co. on Delaware, commissioned 29 Mar 1758. {Ref: ARDE I:14, 15; ARPA (2nd Series) 2:577}

LEWIS, J., see "John Francis" and "John Loakey," q.v.

LEWIS, JOHN (Maryland), pvt., Capt. Thomas Norris' Company, Frederick Co., circa 1757-1758, exact dates not given (served 30 days); bill of credit issued or paid in his behalf to Valentine Rinehart on 6 May 1767 for £1.10.0. {Ref: MSA S960 or S752, p. 176; CSOS:108}

LEWIS, JOHN (Maryland), pvt., recruited by Thomas Beall, Prince George's Co. recruiting officer in 1757 (age and exact date not given); subsequently deserted in July 1757. {Ref: *MD Gazette*, 4 Aug 1757}

LEWIS, JOSEPH (Maryland), pvt., Capt. Tobias Stansbury's Company Muster Roll, Baltimore Co., circa 1757-1758, exact dates not given; bill of credit issued or paid in his behalf to Amos Garrett for £1.19.0 on 28 Apr 1773. {Ref: MSA S960 or S752, p. 187}

LEWIS, SARAH, see "Evan Lewis," q.v.

LEWIS, THOMAS (Delaware), pvt., Kent Co. Militia, Capt. John Caton's Company, 25 Apr 1757 (date of muster roll). {Ref: ARDE I:14}

LEWIS, WILLIAM (Delaware), b. c1719, Chester, PA (laborer, age 40 in 1759); pvt., enlisted by Capt. James Armstrong for the PA Regt. on 10 May 1759. {Ref: ARDE I:26; ARPA (2nd Series) 2:585}

LIDAY, ADAM (Maryland), pvt., Capt. Peter Bainbridge's Company Muster Roll, Frederick Co., circa 1757-1758, exact dates not given (served 28 days); bill of credit issued or paid in his behalf to Casper Shaff on 2 Mar 1767 for £1.8.0. {Ref: MSA S960 or S752, p. 180; CSOS:111}

LIGHTER (LITER), MELCHOR or MELKER (Maryland), pvt., Capt. Peter Bainbridge's Company Muster Roll, Frederick Co., circa 1757-1758, exact dates not given (served 28 days); bill of credit issued or paid in his behalf to Jacob Young on 4 Mar 1767 for £1.8.0. {Ref: MSA S960 or S752, p. 181; CSOS:111}

LIGHTFOOT, REBECCA, see "Thomas Hammond," q.v.

LIGHTFOOT, THOMAS, see "Thomas Hammond," q.v.

LINDSEY, GEORGE (Delaware), pvt., Capt. French Battell's Company of Lower County Provincials, enlisted 24 May 1758. {Ref: ARDE I:16; ARPA (2nd Series) 2:555}

LINEARD (LINARD, LEONARD), ROBERT (Maryland), sgt., Capt. Alexander Beall's Company of Foot, Frederick Co., by August 1757 at which time he was stationed at Fort Frederick. {Ref: FCLR: 30} See "John Boston" and "Adam Coonce" and "John Harlin" and "Joseph Hughes" and "William Kimboll" and "Aron Lee" and "Benjamin Martin" and "Henry Pitnar" and "William Smith" and "Henry Yea," q.v.

LINEGAR, WILLIAM (Delaware), b. c1736 (age 23 in 1759); pvt., enlisted in Capt. John Wright's Company and mustered on 11 May 1759. {Ref: ARDE I:25; ARPA (2nd Series) 2:592}

LINGAN, THOMAS (Maryland), doctor and patriot, Baltimore Co., who "agreed to supply the county pensioners in St. John's Parish, also the French Neutrals [i.e., Acadians] belonging to that parish, for the time being, with physick attendance for the ensuing year" in November 1759 and November 1760. {Ref: Baltimore Co. Court Minutes}

LINGENFELTER, ABRAHAM (Maryland), pvt., Capt. Peter Butler's Company Muster Roll, Frederick Co., circa 1757-1758, exact dates not given (served 34 days); bill of credit or order issued to him for £1.14.0 and paid to Casper Shaff on 2 Mar 1767. {Ref: MSA S960 or S752, p. 167; CSOS:97}

LINGENFELTER, BARTON or BARNETT (Maryland), pvt., Capt. John Middaugh's Company Muster Roll, Frederick Co., circa 1757-1758, exact dates not given (served 30 days); bill of credit issued or paid in his behalf to Thomas Beatty, Jr. for £1.10.0 on 23 Feb 1767. {Ref: MSA S960 or S752, p. 171; CSOS:101}

LINGENFELTER, JOHN (Maryland), pvt., Capt. Peter Butler's Company Muster Roll, Frederick Co., circa 1757-1758, exact dates not given (served 34 days); bill of credit or order issued in his behalf for £1.14.0 and paid to Casper Shaff on 2 Mar 1767. {Ref: MSA S960 or S752, p. 167; CSOS:97}

LINGO, ARCHIBALD (Delaware), b. c1742, VA (age 17 in 1759); pvt., enlisted in Capt. John Wright's Company and mustered on 11 May 1759 (his name was transcribed once as "Archibald Lings"). {Ref: ARDE I:25; ARPA (2nd Series) 2:592}

LINN, ANDREW (Maryland), pvt., Capt. John White's Company Muster Roll, Frederick Co., circa 1757-1758, exact dates not given (served 6 days); bill of credit issued or paid to him for £0.6.0 in 1767, exact date not given; name mistakenly transcribed once as "Andrew Link." {Ref: MSA S960 or S752, p. 165; CSOS:95} On 10 Jul 1758 he was paid "for sawing plank to make coffins for the N Carolina and Pensa. soldiers that died at Fort Frederick." {Ref: ARMD 55:773}

LINN, DANIEL (Maryland), patriot, Frederick Co., was paid on 10 Jul 1758 at Fort Frederick "for sawing plank to make coffins for the N Carolina and Pensa. soldiers that died at Fort Frederick." {Ref: ARMD 55:773}

LINN, WILLIAM (Maryland), 1st lieut., Capt. John Dagworthy's Company of MD Troops, Frederick Co., from 9 Oct 1757 to 26 Apr 1759. {Ref: MHS MS.375.1; CSOS:75} Account paid 12 Jul 1762. {Ref: MHS MS.375}

LINTON, JAMES (Maryland), pvt., Capt. Francis Ware's Company of MD Troops, Charles Co., circa 9 Oct 1757 to 30 Dec 1758. {Ref: MHS MS.375.1; CSOS:88} Payment to him was recorded in Col. Dagworthy's account book on 13 Jul 1762. {Ref: MHS MS.375}

LINTON, JOHN (Maryland), pvt., Capt. John Dagworthy's Company of MD Troops, Frederick Co., from 9 Oct 1757 to 26 Dec 1758 when he reportedly deserted; however, payment to him was recorded in Col. Dagworthy's account book on 8 Mar 1763 for work on Fort Cumberland. {Ref: MHS MS.375; CSOS:77; MHS MS.375.1}

LIPPART, JOHN (Maryland), indentured servant and soldier who served in the French and Indian War some time between 1756 and 1763 (exact dates not known); his master, William Miser, requested compensation from the Baltimore County Court due to the loss of use of Lippart while in the service. {Ref: MHM 94:4, p. 426, citing Baltimore Co. Court Minutes}

LISBY, MR., see "Robert Forrester," q.v.

LITTLE (LITTELL), ABSALOM (Delaware), ensign, Southern District of Broadkiln Hundred, Militia Regt. of Sussex Co., 1756-1758. {Ref: ARDE I:13, 15; ARPA (2nd Series) 2:529, 579; HDE I:141}

LITTLE, HEZEKIAH (Maryland), pvt., Capt. Joshua Beall's Company Muster Roll, Prince George's Co., circa 1757-1758, exact dates not given; bill of credit issued or paid to him for £1.10.6 on 27 Apr 1767. {Ref: MSA S960 or S752, p. 184}

LITTLE, RICHARD (Delaware), b. c1732, Ireland (schoolmaster, age 26 in 1758); pvt., enlisted 21 Apr 1758 "for the campaign in the lower counties" by Capt. John McClughan. {Ref: ARDE I:18; ARPA (2nd Series) 2:570}

LIVINGSTON (LEVENSTAN), JOHN (Maryland), pvt., Capt. Jonathan Hagar's Company Muster Roll, Frederick Co., circa 1757-1758, exact dates not given (served 6 days); bill of credit issued or paid to him for £0.6.0 in 1767, exact date not given. {Ref: MSA S960 or S752, p. 174; CSOS:107}

LIVINGSTON, MARY, see "Thomas Ogle, Jr.," q.v.

LLOYD, ANNA MARIA, see "Edward Tilghman" and "Matthew Tilghman" and "William Tilghman," q.v.

LLOYD, ANNE, see "Matthew Tilghman," q.v.

LLOYD, EDWARD (Maryland), b. 8 May 1711, Talbot Co., son of Edward Lloyd and Sarah Covington, m. Anne Rousby on 26 Mar 1739, had children Elizabeth, Edward, Henrietta Maria, and Richard Bennett, and d. testate on 27 Jan 1770; colonel, esquire, and Treasurer of the Eastern Shore by 1757. {Ref: MDG II:175-176; ARMD 55:99; MCW 14:114} "Col. Edward Lloyd, Esq., died at his seat on Wye River in Talbot Co.; formerly one of His Lordship's Council of State, and Agent and Receiver General for this Province." {Ref: *MD Gazette*, 8 Feb 1770}

LLOYD, HENRIETTA MARIA, see "Samuel Chamberlaine" and "Walter Dulany," q.v.

LLOYD, MARGARET, see "William Tilghman," q.v.

LLOYD, RICHARD (Maryland), b. 19 Mar 1717/8, Talbot Co., son of Edward Lloyd and Sarah Covington, m. 1st to Anne Crouch by 1745 and 2nd to Elizabeth (N) by 1770, had children James, Ann (or Anna Maria), and Charles, and d. testate by 14 Nov 1786, Kent Co.; planter, merchant, businessman, county justice (1744-1751), member of the MD Assembly (1749-1751, served on the Arms and Ammunition Committee, and 1762-1766), justice of the Provincial Court in 1754, served on the Committee of Correspondence in 1774 and the Council of Safety in 1775, and appointed Judge of the Court of Appeals in 1778. {Ref: BDML II:542-543; MDG II:173-176} Colonel in the militia; pay account submitted in 1758, exact dates not given. {Ref: MHM 9:4, pp. 368-369}

LOAKEY, JOHN (Maryland), b. c1733, MD (age 23 in 1756); pvt., Capt. J. Lewis' Company of VA Militia, enlisted in 1756 in Accomack, VA. {Ref: MSR I:38} It is interesting to note that a John Lockey, son of John and Mary Lockey, of Childrey near Wantage, Berkshire, England, was bapt. on 3 Sep 1732 and by 1756 was an indentured servant with one more year to serve in Baltimore County. {Ref: BCF:406-407, Addendum}

LOCKER, BUTLER (Maryland), pvt., Capt. Joshua Beall's Company Muster Roll, Prince George's Co., circa 1757-1758, exact dates not given; bill of credit issued or paid to him for £1.17.0 in 1767, exact date not given. {Ref: MSA S960 or S752, p. 184}

LOCKER, JOSEPH (Maryland), pvt., Capt. William Luckett's Company Muster Roll, Frederick Co., circa 1757-1758, exact dates not given (served 30 days); bill of credit issued or paid in his behalf to William Luckett, Jr. for £1.10.0 on 6 Apr 1767. {Ref: MSA S960 or S752, p. 170; CSOS:100}

LOCKER, THOMAS (Maryland), pvt., Capt. Richard Pearis' Company of MD Troops, Frederick Co., from 9 Oct 1757 to 4 Apr 1758 when he reportedly deserted; however, payment to him was recorded in Col. Dagworthy's account book on 17 Jul 1762. {Ref: MHS MS.375; MHS MS.375.1}

LOCKERMAN, J., see "Basil Warren," q.v.

LOCKEY, JOHN, see "John Loakey," q.v.

LOCKHEAD, WILLIAM (Maryland), pvt., Capt. William McClellan's Company of MD Volunteers, Frederick Co., circa 1763-1764; on muster roll dated 15 Nov 1764 at Camp at the Forks of Muskingham. {Ref: ARMD 32:99}

LOCKWOOD, ARMWELL (Delaware), b. 28 Apr 1738, Kent Co., m. Gertrude Muncy (1743-1818) on 8 Jan 1761, had children Thomas, Isaac, Richard,

Armwell Jr. (d. 1795), Mary, Levi, John, Eunity, James, Gertrude, and Margaret, and d. 30 Jan 1806. {Ref: CDSS:123-124} Pvt., Capt. John Caton's Company, by 25 Apr 1757 (date of muster roll); promoted to ensign (date not given); ensign, 8th Militia Regt. at Dover during the Revolutionary War, 1779-1780; later referred to as captain. {Ref: ARDE I:14; CDSS:123; RPDE:159}

LOFFLIN, JOSEPH (Maryland), pvt., Capt. Francis Ware's Company of MD Troops, Charles Co., circa 9 Oct 1757 to 30 Dec 1758. {Ref: MHS MS.375.1; CSOS:88} Payment to him was recorded in Col. Dagworthy's account book on 13 Jul 1762. {Ref: MHS MS.375}

LOGAN, WILLIAM (Delaware), New Castle Co., patriot who served as a Justice of the Peace and a Justice of the Court of Oyer and Terminer, 1756-1761. {Ref: GRSD 1:13, 15}

LOGSDON, EDWARD (Maryland), pvt., Capt. Thomas Norris' Company, Frederick Co., circa 1757-1758, exact dates not given (served 30 days); bill of credit issued or paid in his behalf to Thomas Owings on 15 May 1767 for £1.10.0. {Ref: MSA S960 or S752, p. 177; CSOS:108}

LOGSDON (LODGSDON), JOHN (Maryland), pvt., Capt. Thomas Norris' Company, Frederick Co., circa 1757-1758, exact dates not given (served 30 days); bill of credit issued or paid in his behalf to Michael McGuire on 27 Mar 1767 for £1.10.0. {Ref: MSA S960 or S752, p. 176; CSOS:108}

LOGSDON (LODGSDON), THOMAS JR. (Maryland), pvt., Capt. Thomas Norris' Company, Frederick Co., circa 1757-1758, exact dates not given (served 30 days); bill of credit issued or paid in his behalf to Michael McGuire on 11 Apr 1767 for £1.10.0. {Ref: MSA S960 or S752, p. 176; CSOS:108}

LONG, BAKER (Maryland), pvt., Capt. Joshua Beall's Company of MD Troops, Prince George's Co., from 9 Oct 1757 to 17 Nov 1757 when he was discharged. {Ref: MHS MS.375.1; CSOS:85} Payment to him was recorded in Col. Dagworthy's account book on 22 Jul 1762. {Ref: MHS MS.375}

LONG, DAVID (Maryland), cpl., Capt. Jonathan Hagar's Company Muster Roll, Frederick Co., circa 1757-1758, exact dates not given (served 6 days); militia pay account submitted in 1758, exact date not given. {Ref: MHM 9:4, p. 370; CSOS:106} Bill of credit issued or paid to him for £0.8.0 in 1767, exact date not given. {Ref: MSA S960 or S752, p. 174}

LONG, FREDERICK (Maryland), pvt., Capt. Jonathan Hagar's Company Muster Roll, Frederick Co., circa 1757-1758, exact dates not given (served 6 days); bill of credit issued or paid to him for £0.6.0 in 1767, exact date not given. {Ref: MSA S960 or S752, p. 174; CSOS:107}

LONG, JAMES (Maryland), patriot and poss. soldier (rank not specified), Frederick Co., militia pay account submitted in 1758, exact date not given. {Ref: MHM 9:4, p. 367} He was paid £16.10.0 at Fort Frederick on 30 Aug 1758 "for carrying a load of arms to Winchester, his waggon's attending afterwards on the new road and fetching a load of corn" and was also paid £6 "for going as Wagon Master with a brigade to Winchester from Conegocheague and riding about to engage waggons to carry stores to Fort Cumberland" for the Western Expedition against Fort Duquesne. {Ref: ARMD 55:775}

LONG, JOHN (Maryland), pvt., Capt. Tobias Stansbury's Company Muster Roll, Baltimore Co., circa 1757-1758, exact dates not given; bill of credit or order issued to his exec. (unnamed) and paid to Josias Bowen for £4.8.7½ on 20 May 1767. {Ref: MSA S960 or S752, p. 186} *Identification problem:* There were five men with this name who could have served in the war: (1) John Long, son of Thomas Long, conveyed land in 1745; (2) John Long, son of Thomas Long (d. 1721) and Susanna Mead, m. Eleanor Owings in 1735 and d. in 1759; (3) John Long m. Blanch Whitaker on 31 Jan 1748; (4) John Long owned land in Baltimore Co. by 1750; and, (5) John Long m. Mary Carlisle by 1753. {Ref: BCF:410}

LONG, SOLOMON (Delaware), b. c1728, Ireland (laborer, age 30 in 1758); pvt., "formerly with ye Royal Americans," recruited by Capt. Benjamin Noxon and enlisted on 15 Apr 1758. {Ref: ARDE I:19; ARPA (2nd Series) 2:566}

LONG, THOMAS, see "John Long," q.v.

LONGBOTTOM, JUDAH (Maryland), pvt., Capt. Peter Butler's Company Muster Roll, Frederick Co., circa 1757-1758, exact dates not given (served 34 days); bill of credit or order issued in his behalf for £1.14.0 and paid to Casper Shaff on 2 Mar 1767. {Ref: MSA S960 or S752, p. 167; CSOS:97}

LONGWILL, JAMES (Delaware), b. c1736, St. Johnson, Ireland (laborer, age 22 in 1758); pvt., enlisted 27 Apr 1758 "for the campaign in the lower counties" by Capt. John McClughan. {Ref: ARDE I:18; ARPA (2nd Series) 2:570}

LOOKERMAN, JACOB, see "Joseph Cox Gray," q.v.

LOOKERMAN, JOHN, see "John Goldsborough," q.v.

LOOKERMAN, MARY, see "James Hindman," q.v.

LOOKERMAN, ROSANNAH, see "Joseph Cox Gray," q.v.

LORD, JOHN (Maryland), pvt., Capt. Joshua Beall's Company Muster Roll, Prince George's Co., circa 1757-1758, exact dates not given; bill of credit issued or paid in his behalf to James Marshall for £2.3.0 on 22 May 1767. {Ref: MSA S960 or S752, p. 184}

LOVE, AARON (Maryland), pvt., Capt. Richard Pearis' Company of MD Troops, Frederick Co., circa 9 Oct 1757 to 31 May 1758; pvt., Capt. Alexander Beall's Company of MD Troops, Frederick Co., from 1 Jun 1758 to 30 Dec 1758. {Ref: MHS MS.375.1; CSOS:81, 90} Payment to him was recorded in Col. Dagworthy's account book on 12 Jul 1762 for work on Fort Cumberland. {Ref: MHS MS.375}

LOVE, PHILIP (Maryland), cpl., Capt. Joseph Hanson Harrison's Company Muster Roll, Charles Co., circa 1757, exact dates not given; bill of credit issued or paid to him for £4.1.9 in 1767, exact date not given. {Ref: MSA S960 or S752, p. 189} Sgt., Capt. Alexander Beall's Company of MD Troops, Frederick Co., from 9 Oct 1757 to 8 Nov 1758; entered as a cadet 9 Feb 1758; ensign in Capt. John Dagworthy's Company of MD Troops, Frederick Co., from 9 Nov 1758 to 26 Apr 1759 (served 169 days); payment recorded in Col. Dagworthy's account book on 26 Feb 1763. {Ref: MHS MS.375.1; CSOS:75; MHS MS.375}

LOVE, ROBERT (Delaware), b. c1738 (a bold looking Scotchman, age 20 in 1758); pvt., enlisted New Castle Co. by Capt. John Singleton in May 1758. {Ref: ARDE I:27}

LOWBER, GRACE, see "John Reynolds" and "Michael Reynolds," q.v.

LOWBER, MATTHEW (Delaware), son of Michael and Unity Lowber, m. Hannah Robinson (widow of Samuel Robinson), and d. testate in 1772, leaving children Matthew, Peter, Jonathan, Susanna, Elizabeth and Meriam. {Ref: CFD 1:133-134} Pvt., Kent Co. Militia, Capt. John Caton's Company, 25 Apr 1757 (date of muster roll). {Ref: ARDE I:13}

LOWBER, MICHAEL or MICHIEL (Delaware), eldest son of Michael and Unity Lowber. {Ref: CFD 1:134} Pvt., Kent Co. Militia, Capt. John Caton's Company, 25 Apr 1757 (date of muster roll). {Ref: ARDE I:14}

LOWBER, PETER JR. (Delaware), pvt., Kent Co. Militia, Capt. John Caton's Company, 25 Apr 1757 (date of muster roll). {Ref: ARDE I:14} *Identification problem:* There were perhaps three or four men with this name who could have served in the war: (1) Peter Lowber, prob. son of Michael and Unity Lowber; (2) Peter Lowber m. (N) before 1767 and had a dau. Catrine; (3) Peter Lowber m. Elizabeth Brinckle before 1766: and, (4) Peter Lowber m. Elizabeth Clark (widow of John Clark) after 1755. {Ref: CFD 1:134-136; CDSS:125}

LOWBER, UNITY, see "Matthew Lowber," q.v.

LOWDER, JAMES (Maryland or Pennsylvania), ensign in Capt. Hamilton's Company, was wounded in "a recent battle with the Indians" in 1756 (exact date not given) in Cumberland Co., PA, after the burning of McCord's Fort, and subsequently died. {Ref: *MD Gazette*, 29 Apr 1756}

LOWEBEAN, JOHN (Maryland), pvt., Capt. Joshua Beall's Company Muster Roll, Prince George's Co., circa 1757-1758, exact dates not given; bill of credit issued and ordered his assignment to John Tolson for £2.3.0 on 13 Apr 1767. {Ref: MSA S960 or S752, p. 184}

LOWES, HENRY (Maryland), b. c1710, prob. immigrated to MD circa 1736, resided in Somerset Co., m. Esther Waters, had sons Henry and Tubman, and d. testate by 15 May 1767; mariner by 1736, merchant (1736-1767), captain of a brigantine in 1747, gentleman and member of the MD Assembly (1757-1758). {Ref: BDML II:551-552; ARMD 55:239}

LOWNDES, CHRISTOPHER (Maryland), patriot, Frederick or Prince George's Co., pay account submitted for 90 lbs. of biscuit supplied for the use of the militia in 1758, exact date not given. {Ref: MHM 9:4, p. 370} See "Zachariah Evans," q.v.

LOWNDES, FRANCIS (Maryland), sea captain by 1758, was headed for Maryland with a French prize on 25 Nov 1758 and it was thought he may have in turn been taken by the French, but he subsequently arrived safely in Maryland in January 1759. {Ref: *MD Gazette*, 4 Jan and 12 Jan 1759}

LOY, GEORGE (Maryland), pvt., Capt. Stephen Rensburg's or Rensburger's Company Muster Roll, Frederick Co., circa 1757-1758, exact dates not given (served 34 days); bill of credit issued or paid in his behalf to Stephen Rensburger for Loy's exec. (unnamed) for £1.14.0 on 27 Mar 1767. {Ref: MSA S960 or S752, p. 183; CSOS:112}

LOYD, JOHN (Maryland), pvt., Capt. John Middaugh's Company Muster Roll, Frederick Co., circa 1757-1758, exact dates not given (served 30 days); bill of credit issued or paid to him for £1.10.0 in 1767, exact date not given. {Ref: MSA S960 or S752, p. 172; CSOS:101}

LUCAS, BARTON (Maryland), b. 29 Jan 1729/30, Prince George's Co., son of Thomas and Ann Lucas, of Prince George's P. E. Parish. {Ref: PGCR 2:117} Sgt., Capt. Joshua Beall's Company Muster Roll, Prince George's Co., circa 1757, exact dates not given; bill of credit issued or paid to him for £2.14.9 on 20 Feb 1767. {Ref: MSA S960 or S752, p. 184} Cadet, Capt. Joshua Beall's Company of MD Troops, Prince George's Co., from 17 Nov 1757 to 9 Nov 1758; promoted to ensign on 10 Nov 1758; ensign in Capt. Alexander Beall's Company of MD Troops, Frederick Co., from 9 Nov 1758 to 30 Dec 1758. {Ref: MHS MS.375.1; CSOS:79, 85} Payment to him was recorded in Col. Dagworthy's account book on 15 Jul 1762. {Ref: MHS MS.375} Also received £40 from the MD Assembly in December 1765 for his services and expenses during the French and Indian War. {Ref: ARMD 59:196, 251}

LUCAS, JOHN (Maryland), patriot, Frederick Co., who performed "sundry services at the fort" in 1763 and payment in the amount of £1.1.0 was still owed to him on 25 Nov 1763 (when reported by the Accounts Committee to the MD Assembly). {Ref: ARMD 58:400}

LUCAS, RICHARD (Maryland), pvt., Capt. Joseph Chapline's Company Muster Roll No. 4, Frederick Co., circa 1757-1758, exact dates not given (served 5 days); bill of credit issued or paid in his behalf to Joseph Chaplin for £0.5.0 on 5 Mar 1767. {Ref: MSA S960 or S752, p. 194; CSOS:105}

LUCAS, ROBINSON (Maryland), pvt., Capt. Joseph Chapline's Company Muster Roll No. 1, Frederick Co., circa 1757-1758, exact dates not given (served 30 days); bill of credit issued or paid in his behalf to Joseph Chaplin for £1.10.0 on 5 Mar 1767. {Ref: MSA S960 or S752, p. 190; CSOS:102} Pvt., Capt. Moses Chapline's Company Muster Roll No. 3, Frederick Co., circa 1757-1758, exact dates not given (served 6 days); bill of credit issued or paid in his behalf to Joseph Chaplin for £0.6.0 on 5 Mar 1767. {Ref: MSA S960 or S752, p. 198; CSOS:115}

LUCAS, SAMUEL (Maryland), pvt., Capt. Joseph Chapline's Company Muster Roll No. 4, Frederick Co., circa 1757-1758, exact dates not given (served 5 days). {Ref: CSOS:105}

LUCAS, THOMAS, see "Barton Lucas," q.v.

LUCKETT, ---- (Maryland), patriot, Frederick Co., "Mr. Luckett died in a powder magazine explosion at Fort Cumberland." {Ref: *MD Gazette*, 19 Oct 1758}

LUCKETT, IGNATIUS, see "William Luckett," q.v.

LUCKETT, SAMUEL (Maryland), b. c1740, son of William Luckett and Charity Middleton, and d. 9 Jun 1777 without progeny. {Ref: BDML II:553} Company Clerk, Capt. William Luckett's Company Muster Roll, Frederick Co., circa 1757-1758, exact dates not given (served 30 days); bill of credit issued or paid in his behalf to William Luckett, Jr. for £1.10.0 on 6 Apr 1767. {Ref: MSA S960 or S752, p. 170; CSOS:99}

LUCKETT, WILLIAM (Maryland), b. 1711, Charles Co., son of Ignatius Luckett and Jane Hanson, m. Charity Middleton by 1739, had children William, John, Thomas Hussey, Leven, Samuel, Verlinda, Susanna, Ann, Elizabeth, and Mary, and d. testate by 17 Jan 1783, Montgomery Co.; planter, ferryman, captain by 1757, justice (Frederick Co., 1757-1759, 1763, 1768-1775), member of the MD Assembly (1768-1770), and capt. in militia (34th Bttn.) in 1776. {Ref: BDML II:553} Capt., Frederick Co., circa 1757-1758, exact dates not given; bill of credit issued or paid in his behalf to William Luckett, Jr. for £5 on 6 Apr 1767. {Ref: MSA S960 or S752, p. 169; CSOS:99} See "John Wilcoxon," q.v.

LUCKETT, WILLIAM JR. (Maryland), b. c1737, son of William Luckett, m. Sarah Nelson and d. c1817, Frederick Co.; pvt., Capt. William Luckett's Company Muster Roll, Frederick Co., circa 1757-1758, exact dates not given (served 30 days); bill of credit issued or paid in his behalf to William Luckett, Jr. for £1.10.0 on 6 Apr 1767; served as a county justice (1777-1780) and an officer in the Continental Loan Office in 1779. {Ref: BDML II:553; MSA S960 or S752, p. 170; CSOS:99}

LUFF, CALEB (Delaware), prob. son of Nathaniel (d. 1760) and Deborah Luff, d. intestate by 19 Mar 1783. {Ref: CDSS:125-126} Ensign, Dover Hundred, Militia of Kent Co. on Delaware, 1756. {Ref: ARDE I:12; ARPA (2nd Series) 2:527-529; HDE I:141}

LUFF, SARAH, see "John Clark," q.v.

LUTS, JONAS (Maryland), pvt., Capt. John Middaugh's Company Muster Roll, Frederick Co., circa 1757-1758, exact dates not given (served 30 days); bill of credit issued or paid to him for £1.10.0 in 1767, exact date not given. {Ref: MSA S960 or S752, p. 172; CSOS:101}

LUTZ, JACOB (Maryland), pvt., Capt. John Middaugh's Company Muster Roll, Frederick Co., circa 1757-1758, exact dates not given; bill of credit issued or paid in his behalf to Casper Shaff for £1.10.0 on 2 Mar 1767. {Ref: MSA S960 or S752, p. 171}

LUX, WILLIAM (Maryland), b. c1725, son of Darby Lux and Ann Sanders, bapt. 18 Feb 1730/1, All Hallow's Parish, Anne Arundel Co., m. Agnes Walker on 16 Jul 1752, had sons George and William, and d. 10 May 1778, Baltimore Town; patriot, merchant, businessman, ship owner, town clerk (1746-1756), county justice (1752-1754, 1756, 1777), an organizer of the Baltimore Sons of Liberty in 1766, served on the Committees of Observation and Correspondence (1774-1776), and continental purchasing agent (1776-1778). "A man of major political importance in Baltimore." {Ref: BDML II:556-557; AACR:45} Patriot and poss. soldier (rank not specified), militia pay account submitted in 1758, exact date not given. {Ref: MHM 9:4, p. 369} See "Edward Baxter" and "Abraham Egleston" and "William Rowles" and "Henry Tarr" and "Abram Upham" and "Philip Wilkinson," q.v.

LUXENBURGER, JOSEPH (Maryland), pvt., Capt. Peter Butler's Company Muster Roll, Frederick Co., circa 1757-1758, exact dates not given (served 34 days); bill of credit or order issued in his behalf for £1.14.0 and paid in March 1767. {Ref: MSA S960 or S752, p. 167; CSOS:97}

LYLE, SABRET (Maryland), sgt., Calvert Co., Capt. Sutton Isaac's Militia Co. in the Upper Hundred of the Cliffs; sent to the Western Frontier to help defend against the Indians circa 1756-1757 (exact dates not given). {Ref: HCC:121-122}

LYLE, WILLIAM (Maryland), sgt., Calvert Co., Capt. Sutton Isaac's Militia Co. in the Upper Hundred of the Cliffs; sent to the Western Frontier to help defend against the Indians circa 1756-1757 (exact dates not given). {Ref: HCC:121-122}

LYNCH, BARTHOLOMEW (Maryland), sea captain by 1756, was in command of the sloop *Charming Patty* when captured by the French on his way from Maryland to Antigua. {Ref: *MD Gazette*, 2 Dec 1756}

LYNCH (LINCH), JETHRO (Maryland), pvt., Capt. Tobias Stansbury's Company Muster Roll, Baltimore Co., circa 1757-1758, exact dates not given; bill of credit or order issued to his admin. (not named) and paid to Charles Ridgley, Jr. for £3.16.0 on 25 Apr 1767. {Ref: MSA S960 or S752, p. 186}

LYNCH (LINCH), THOMAS (Maryland), pvt., Capt. John Dagworthy's Company of MD Troops, Frederick Co., circa 9 Oct 1757 to 26 Apr 1758. {Ref: MHS MS.375.1; CSOS:77} Payment to him was recorded in Col. Dagworthy's account book on 8 Mar 1763 for work on Fort Cumberland. {Ref: MHS MS.375}

LYNN, AARON (Maryland), sea captain by 1756, late of Somerset Co., was reported to have taken several French prizes before he was captured. {Ref: *MD Gazette*, 2 Dec 1756}

LYNN, WILLIAM (Maryland), pvt., Capt. Joseph Chapline's Company Muster Roll No. 1, Frederick Co., circa 1757-1758, exact dates not given (served 12 days); bill of credit issued or paid in his behalf to Joseph Chaplin for £0.12.0 on 5 Mar 1767. {Ref: MSA S960 or S752, p. 191; CSOS:103} Received £60 from the MD Assembly in December 1765 for his services and expenses during the French and Indian War. {Ref: ARMD 59:252}

LYON, JAMES (Maryland), pvt., Capt. Joshua Beall's Company of MD Troops, Prince George's Co., from 9 Oct 1757 to 8 Jun 1758. {Ref: MHS MS.375.1; CSOS:84} Payment to him was recorded in Col. Dagworthy's account book on 23 Jul 1762. {Ref: MHS MS.375}

LYON, MARTIN (Maryland), pvt., Capt. Moses Chapline's Company Muster Roll No. 3, Frederick Co., circa 1757-1758, exact dates not given (served 6 days); bill of credit issued or paid in his behalf to Joseph Chaplin for £0.6.0 on 5 Mar 1767. {Ref: MSA S960 or S752, p. 198; CSOS:115}

LYON, WILLIAM (Maryland), doctor and patriot, Baltimore Co., who "agreed to supply the county pensioners in St. Thomas and St. Paul's Parishes, also the French Neutrals [i.e., Acadians] belonging to those parishes, for the time being, with physick attendance for the ensuing year" in November 1759 and November 1760. {Ref: Baltimore Co. Court Minutes} See "Andrew Grill," q.v.

LYTTLE, WILLIAM (Maryland), pvt., Capt. Tobias Stansbury's Company Muster Roll, Baltimore Co., circa 1757-1758, exact dates not given; bill of credit issued or paid in his behalf to his admin. (unnamed) for £3.16.0 on 31 Oct 1770. {Ref: MSA S960 or S752, p. 187}

MACCRORY, DANIEL (Maryland), pvt., Capt. Peter Butler's Company Muster Roll, Frederick Co., circa 1757-1758, exact dates not given (served 34 days); bill of credit or order issued in his behalf for £1.14.0 and paid to Casper Shaff on 2 Mar 1767. {Ref: MSA S960 or S752, p. 167; CSOS:97}

MACCUBBIN (McCUBBIN), JAMES (Maryland), patriot, Annapolis, Anne Arundel Co., was authorized money by the MD Assembly on 24 Nov 1757 "as a present provision for the quartering of his Majesty's Forces as are expected to come to the City of Annapolis for quarters." {Ref: ARMD 55:173} Pay account submitted for quartering soldiers in 1757 or 1758, exact dates not given. {Ref: MHM 9:3, p. 262}

MACCUBBIN (McCUBBIN), NICHOLAS (Maryland), patriot, Annapolis, Anne Arundel Co., pay account submitted for quartering soldiers in 1757 or 1758, exact dates not given. {Ref: MHM 9:3, p. 262}

MACCUBBIN (McCUBBIN), RICHARD (Maryland), patriot, Annapolis, Anne Arundel Co., pay account submitted for quartering soldiers in 1757 or 1758, exact dates not given. {Ref: MHM 9:3, p. 262} See "Patrick Creagh," q.v.

MACDONALD, JOHN (Maryland), pvt., Capt. Tobias Stansbury's Company Muster Roll, Baltimore Co., circa 1757-1758, exact dates not given; bill of credit issued or paid to him for £1.19.0 in 1767, exact date not given. {Ref: MSA S960 or S752, p. 187}

MACEVER (McEVEER), ANDREW (Maryland), pvt., Capt. Jonathan Hagar's Company Muster Roll, Frederick Co., circa 1757-1758, exact dates not given (served 6 days); bill of credit issued or paid to him for £0.6.0 in 1767, exact date not given. {Ref: MSA S960 or S752, p. 174; CSOS:106}

MACKALL, BENJAMIN JR. (Maryland), b. c1723, Calvert Co., only son of Benjamin Mackall and Barbara Smith (widow of Thomas Holdsworth and dau. of Capt. Richard Smith), m. Rebecca Covington on 24 Apr 1756, had children Benjamin, Levin Covington, Leonard, Walter, Richard, Barbara, and Rebecca Covington, and d. April 1795; patriot, planter, merchant, gentleman, member of the MD Assembly (1749-1766, served on the Arms and Ammunition Committee), justice (1766, 1769, 1773), and attended the convention in 1776 (home plantation burned by the British in February 1783). {Ref: BDML II:560-561}

MACKALL, JAMES (Maryland), pvt., Capt. William Luckett's Company Muster Roll, Frederick Co., circa 1757-1758, exact dates not given (served 30 days); bill of credit issued or paid in his behalf to William Luckett, Jr. for £1.10.0 on 6 Apr 1767. {Ref: MSA S960 or S752, p. 169; CSOS:99}

MACKALL, MARY, see "John Brome (Broome)," q.v.

MACKANING, WILLIAM (Delaware), b. c1738, MD (age 21 in 1759); pvt., enlisted in Capt. John Wright's Company and mustered on 11 May 1759. {Ref: ARDE I:25; ARPA (2nd Series) 2:508, 592}

MACKEELE (MacKEEL, McKEEL), THOMAS (Maryland), b. c1710, Dorchester Co., son of Thomas MacKeele and Clare Gary, m. Mary Stevens (who later m. Benjamin Keene), had children John, Thomas, and Mary, and d. testate by 28 Jan 1762; soldier, churchman, influential landowner; appointed county coroner, 1741; captain of a Troop of Horse in 1748 [and likely participated in the French and Indian War in the 1750's]. {Ref: MDG II:193-194; MCW 12:113-114}

MACKEY, BENJAMIN (Maryland), pvt., Capt. Joseph Hanson Harrison's Company Muster Roll, Charles Co., circa 1757-1758, exact dates not given; bill of credit issued or paid in his behalf to Capt. Joseph Hanson Harrison for £2.9.0 on 18 Jun 1768. {Ref: MSA S960 or S752, p. 189}

MACKLAND, MATTHEW (Maryland), pvt., Capt. Elias Delashmutt's Company Muster Roll, Frederick Co., circa 1757-1758, exact dates not given (served 30 days); bill of credit issued or paid in his behalf to Casper Shaff on 2 Mar 1767 for £1.10.0. {Ref: MSA S960 or S752, p. 162; CSOS:94}

MACKLEFISH (MACKELFISH), DAVID (Maryland), planter; b. c 1730 (age about 27 in 1757); pvt., recruited by Thomas Beall, Prince George's Co. recruiting officer (exact date not given), and reportedly deserted in July 1757. {Ref: *MD Gazette*, 4 Aug 1757} However, Gov. Horatio Sharpe wrote, in part, to the MD Assembly on 7 Dec 1757: "One Thomas Beall, a young fellow of Prince George's Co. (who was empowered by me to enlist men for his Majesty's Service, in consequence of several Acts of Assembly lately passed in this province) is accused of having pretended to enlist the said [Edward] Seares, [Thomas] Hill and [David] Mackelfish, of treating them afterwards as deserters, of compelling Seares to pay £10 for a discharged, which he could not give, and of endeavouring to oblige the other two to purchase their discharges likewise. Mr. Beall is not present to hear what is alleged against him, yet I don't think it would be right to condemn him unheard; he is no officer that I know of, neither is he in the least dependent on me; and if the complainants can prove that he has acted illegally, I hope they may redress themselves without applying to any branch of the Legislature; but if it should, on farther enquiry, appear that they were duly enlisted, you will not, I am persuaded, take it amiss if they are apprehended and delivered up to one of his Majesty's Officers." {Ref: ARMD 55:320}

MACKLEFISH (MACCLEFISH), RICHARD (Maryland), pvt., Capt. Moses Chapline's Company Muster Roll No. 3, Frederick Co., circa 1757-1758, exact dates not given (served 6 days); bill of credit issued or paid in his behalf to Joseph Chaplin for £0.6.0 on 5 Mar 1767. {Ref: MSA S960 or S752, pp. 198-199; CSOS:115}

MACKLERAINE, CHARLES (Maryland), waggoner, Frederick Co., was shot by Indians near Fort Frederick in 1757. {Ref: *MD Gazette*, 21 Apr 1757}

MACNEAL, JAMES, see "James McNiel," q.v.

MADDEN (MADDING), MORDECAI (Maryland), cpl., Capt. Alexander Beall's Company of MD Troops, Frederick Co., from 9 Oct 1757 to 30 Dec 1758; transferred from Capt. Richard Pearis' Company (exact dates of service not given). {Ref: MHS MS.375.1; CSOS:81} On 10 Jul 1758 George Ross was paid £9.10.0 at Fort Frederick "for a horse that was shot yesterday by Indians [from] under Corporal Madden as he was going to Carlyle with a letter to Sir John St. Clair" for the Western Expedition against Fort Duquesne. {Ref: ARMD 55:773,776} Payment to him was recorded in Col. Dagworthy's account book on 11 Jul 1762. {Ref: MHS MS.375}

MADDEN (MADDING), FRANCIS (Maryland), pvt., Capt. Francis Ware's Company of MD Troops, Charles Co., circa 9 Oct 1757 to 30 Dec 1758. {Ref:

MHS MS.375.1; CSOS:88} Payment to him was recorded in Col. Dagworthy's account book on 11 Jul 1762 for work on Fort Cumberland. {Ref: MHS MS.375}

MAGRUDER, NATHAN (Maryland), b. c1718, Prince George's Co., son of John Magruder and Susanna Smith, m. his first cousin Rebecca Beall by 1742, had children Nathan, Isaac, John Beall, Jeffry, Susannah, Elizabeth, Rebecca, Sarah, and Verlinda, and d. testate by 25 Apr 1786, Montgomery Co.; planter, justice (Frederick Co., 1749-1754), soldier in 1748 and captain by 1759, member of the MD Assembly (1751-1754, 1761-1763, 1774), and served on the Committee of Observation in 1775. {Ref: BDML II:569-570; SLMH II:179}

MAGRUDER, VERLINDA, see "Samuel Beall," q.v.

MAHAN, THOMAS (Delaware), b. c1731, Ireland (chairmaker, age 27 in 1758); pvt., recruited by Capt. Benjamin Noxon and enlisted on 2 May 1758. {Ref: ARDE I:19; ARPA (2nd Series) 2:566}

MAHONE (MAHON, MAYHON), ANTHONY (Maryland), pvt., Capt. Joseph Chapline's Company Muster Roll No. 1, Frederick Co., circa 1757-1758, exact dates not given (served 30 days); bill of credit issued or paid in his behalf to Joseph Chaplin for £1.10.0 on 5 Mar 1767. {Ref: MSA S960 or S752, p. 190; CSOS:102} Pvt., Capt. Moses Chapline's Company Muster Roll No. 2, Frederick Co., circa 1757-1758, exact dates not given (served 14 days); bill of credit issued or paid in his behalf to Joseph Chaplin for £0.14.0 on 5 Mar 1767. {Ref: MSA S960 or S752, p. 197; CSOS:114} Pvt., Capt. Moses Chapline's Company Muster Roll No. 3, Frederick Co., circa 1757-1758, exact dates not given (served 6 days); bill of credit issued or paid in his behalf to Joseph Chaplin for £0.6.0 on 5 Mar 1767. {Ref: MSA S960 or S752, p. 198; CSOS:115} Pvt., Capt. Joseph Chapline's Company Muster Roll No. 5, Frederick Co., circa 1757-1758, exact dates not given; bill of credit issued or paid in his behalf to Joseph Chaplin for £0.8.0 on 5 Mar 1767. {Ref: MSA S960 or S752, p. 195}

MAHONE (MAYHONE), WILLIAM (Maryland), pvt., Capt. Tobias Stansbury's Company Muster Roll, Baltimore Co., circa 1757-1758, exact dates not given; bill of credit issued or paid in his behalf to John Paca for £1.18.0 on 3 Apr 1767. {Ref: MSA S960 or S752, p. 186; CSOS:113}

MAHOOD, JOHN (Delaware), b. c1737, DE (carpenter, age 21 in 1758); pvt., recruited by Capt. Benjamin Noxon and enlisted on 20 May 1758. {Ref: ARDE I:19; ARPA (2nd Series) 2:566}

MAINS, THOMAS (Maryland), patriot, Frederick Co., paid £5.12.6 on 17 Jul 1758 at Fort Frederick "for his waggon's attending the Pensilvania Detachments under the command of Major Wells on the New Road" for the Western Expedition against Fort Duquesne. {Ref: ARMD 55:773}

MAIR, ELIAS (Maryland), pvt., Capt. Peter Bainbridge's Company Muster Roll, Frederick Co., circa 1757-1758, exact dates not given (served 30 days); bill of credit issued or paid in his behalf to Henry Snavely on 27 Apr 1767 for £1.10.0; name transcribed once as "Elias Man." {Ref: MSA S960 or S752, p. 181; CSOS:111}

MAKEL, JOHN (Delaware), pvt., Capt. Richard McWilliams' Company of Foot, New Castle Co., enlisted 28 Dec 1757. {Ref: ARDE I:14}

MAKEN (MAKIN), JOHN (Maryland), pvt., Capt. Richard Pearis' Company of MD Troops, Frederick Co., circa 9 Oct 1757 to 31 May 1758; pvt., Capt. John Dagworthy's Company of MD Troops, Frederick Co., from 1 Jun 1758 to 26 Apr 1759. {Ref: MHS MS.375.1; CSOS:77, 91} Payment to him was recorded in Col. Dagworthy's account book on 12 Jul 1762 for work on Fort Cumberland. {Ref: MHS MS.375}

MALONE, JOHN (Maryland), pvt., Capt. Thomas Norris' Company, Frederick Co., circa 1757-1758, exact dates not given (served 30 days); bill of credit issued or paid to him for £1.10.0 in 1767, exact date not given. {Ref: MSA S960 or S752, p. 176; CSOS:110}

MAN, WILLIAM (Delaware), b. c1737, Sussex, DE (age 22 in 1759); pvt., enlisted in Capt. John Wright's Company and mustered on 11 May 1759. {Ref: ARDE I:25; ARPA (2nd Series) 2:592}

MANCE, CASPER (Maryland), pvt., Capt. Peter Butler's Company Muster Roll, Frederick Co., circa 1757-1758, exact dates not given (served 34 days); bill of credit or order issued in his behalf for £1.14.0 and paid to Casper Shaff on 2 Mar 1767. {Ref: MSA S960 or S752, p. 167; CSOS:97}

MANCE, PETER (Maryland), pvt., Capt. Peter Butler's Company Muster Roll, Frederick Co., circa 1757-1758, exact dates not given (served 34 days); bill of credit or order issued in his behalf to Casper Shaff for £1.14.0 and paid to David Cumming on 18 Apr 1767. {Ref: MSA S960 or S752, p. 168; CSOS:97}

MANERY, SAMUEL (Maryland), pvt., Capt. Francis Ware's Company of MD Troops, Charles Co., from 9 Oct 1757 to 3 Nov 1757 (served 25 days) when he was reported as dead; however, payment to him was recorded in Col. Dagworthy's account book on 7 Mar 1763. {Ref: MHS MS.375; CSOS:89; MHS MS.375.1}

MANLOVE, CHRISTOPHER (Maryland), pvt. and drummer, Capt. Henry Casson's Company Muster Roll, Queen Anne's Co., circa 1757-1758, exact dates not given (served 27 days); bill of credit issued to him for £0.4.0 in 1767, exact date not given. {Ref: MSA S960 or S752, p. 178: CSOS:109}

MANLOVE, MARY, see "David Hall," q.v.

MANLOVE, WILLIAM (Delaware), m. Alse (N), had children Mary, Sarah and a son (N) poss. William, and d. testate by 24 Mar 1761. {Ref: CDSS:127} Pvt., Kent Co. Militia, Capt. John Caton's Company, 25 Apr 1757 (date of muster roll). {Ref: ARDE I:14}

MANN, WILLIAM (Delaware), b. c1741, Angola Hundred, DE (farmer, age 17 in 1758); pvt., enlisted 22 Apr 1758 "for the campaign in the lower counties" by Capt. John McClughan. {Ref: ARDE I:18; ARPA (2nd Series) 2:570}

MANNERLY, WILLIAM (Delaware), pvt., Capt. French Battell's Company of Lower County Provincials, enlisted 17 May 1758. {Ref: ARDE I:16; ARPA (2nd Series) 2:555}

MANWARING (MAINWARING), RICHARD (Delaware), m. Susannah (N), had children Charles, Thomas, Richard, Hannah, Sarah, Margaret, Ann, and Elizabeth, and d. testate by 5 Dec 1794. {Ref: CDSS:128} Pvt., Kent Co. Militia, Capt. John Caton's Company, 25 Apr 1757 (date of muster roll). {Ref: ARDE I:13}

MARA, PATRICK (Maryland), indentured servant and soldier who served in the French and Indian War some time between 1756 and 1763 (exact dates not known); his master Thomas Archer, iron manufacturer, requested compensation from the Baltimore County Court due to the loss of use of Mara while in the service. {Ref: MHM 94:4, p. 426, citing Baltimore Co. Court Minutes}

MARBLE, JOHN (Maryland), pvt., Capt. Thomas Norris' Company, Frederick Co., circa 1757-1758, exact dates not given; bill of credit issued or paid in his behalf to Michael McGuire on 20 Mar 1767 for £1.10.0. {Ref: MSA S960 or S752, p. 176}

MARKER, FREDERICK (Delaware), pvt., Kent Co. Militia, Capt. John Caton's Company, 25 Apr 1757 (date of muster roll). {Ref: ARDE I:14}

MARR (MASS?), JOHN BAPTIST (Maryland), pvt., Capt. Richard Pearis' Company of MD Troops, Frederick Co., circa 9 Oct 1757 to 31 May 1758; pvt., Capt. Joshua Beall's Company of MD Troops, Prince George's Co., from 1 Jun 1758 to 30 Dec 1758. {Ref: MHS MS.375.1; CSOS:85, 91} Payment to him was recorded in Col. Dagworthy's account book on 15 Jul 1762. {Ref: MHS MS.375}

MARRAT, JOSEPH (Delaware), m. (N), had children John, Samuel, Martha, Easter Ann, and prob. other daus., and d. testate by 21 Oct 1795. {Ref: CDSS:128} Ensign, Upper Part of Mispillion Hundred, Militia of Kent Co. on Delaware, 1756. {Ref: ARDE I:12; ARPA (2nd Series) 2:527-529; HDE I:141}

MARSH, PETER (Delaware), b. c1712, England, son of Peter Marsh (d. 1725), m. 1st to Esther Purnell by 1740 (of Worcester Co., MD, d. 1757), m. 2nd to Agnes Field (widow of Nehemiah Field and dau. of John Rhoades) by 1761, had children Peter, Joseph, Mary, John, Philip, and Thomas Purnell by 1st wife and Hester and Sarah by 2nd wife, and d. testate by 13 Jul 1769, age 57. {Ref: CFD 3:124-125; CDSS:129} Ensign, Southern District of Lewes and Rehoboth Hundred, Militia Regt. of Sussex Co., 1756-1758; name listed once as "Peter March." {Ref: ARDE I:13, 15; ARPA (2nd Series) 2:529, 579; HDE I:141}

MARSHALL, JAMES (Maryland), pvt., Capt. Francis Ware's Company of MD Troops, Charles Co., circa 9 Oct 1757 to 30 Dec 1758. {Ref: MHS MS.375.1; CSOS:88} Payment to him was recorded in Col. Dagworthy's account book on 12 Jul 1762. {Ref: MHS MS.375} See "John Lord," q.v.

MARSHALL, JOHN (Maryland), pvt., Capt. Joseph Chapline's Company Muster Roll No. 1, Frederick Co., circa 1757-1758, exact dates not given (served 30 days); bill of credit issued or paid in his behalf to Joseph Chaplin for £1.10.0 on 5 Mar 1767. {Ref: MSA S960 or S752, p. 190; CSOS:102} Pvt., Capt. Joseph Chapline's Company Muster Rolls No. 2 and 3, Frederick Co., circa 1757-1758, exact dates not given (served 7 days); bill of credit issued or paid in his behalf to Joseph Chaplin for £0.7.0 on 5 Mar 1767. {Ref: MSA S960 or S752, p. 193; CSOS:104}

MARSHALL, JOHN (Maryland), pvt., Capt. Moses Chapline's Company Muster Roll No. 1, Frederick Co., circa 1757-1758, exact dates not given (served 55 days); bill of credit issued or paid in his behalf to Joseph Chaplin for £2.15.0 on 5 Mar 1767. {Ref: MSA S960 or S752, p. 196; CSOS:113} Pvt., Capt. Moses Chapline's Company Muster Roll No. 3, Frederick Co., circa 1757-1758, exact dates not given (served 6 days); bill of credit issued or paid in his behalf to Joseph Chaplin for £0.6.0 on 5 Mar 1767. {Ref: MSA S960 or S752, p. 198; CSOS:114}

MARSHALL, THOMAS (Maryland), pvt., Capt. Joshua Beall's Company of MD Troops, Prince George's Co., from 19 Oct 1757 to 10 Oct 1758 when he reportedly deserted; however, payment to him was recorded in Col. Dagworthy's account book on 8 Mar 1763 for work on Fort Cumberland. {Ref: MHS MS.375; CSOS:85; MHS MS.375.1}

MARSHALL, WILLIAM (Maryland), cpl., Capt. Elias Delashmutt's Company Muster Roll, Frederick Co., circa 1757-1758, exact dates not given (served 30 days); bill of credit issued or paid in his behalf to Elias Delashmut, Jr. on 16 Mar 1767 for £2.13.3. {Ref: MSA S960 or S752, p. 162: CSOS:94}

MARSHALL, WILLIAM (Maryland), pvt., Capt. John Wolgomatt's Company of MD Volunteers, Frederick Co., circa 1763-1764; reported as deserted on muster roll dated 15 Nov 1764 at Camp at the Forks of Muskingham. {Ref: ARMD 32:99}

MARTIN, BENJAMIN (Maryland), sgt., Capt. John Middaugh's Company Muster Roll, Frederick Co., 1756-1757, exact dates not given; bill of credit issued or paid to him for £2 in 1767, exact date not given. {Ref: MSA S960 or S752, p. 172} He recorded his discharge in Frederick Co. Court on 4 Aug 1757. "Capt. Alexander Beall, commander of one of the MD Company's of Foot, certified that Benjamin Martin has served 3 months and his enlistment is up 10 Feb 1757. Receipt and clothing witnessed by Sgt. Robert Lineard and Sgt. George Barrance." {Ref: FCLR:30}

MARTIN, ELIZABETH, see "William Smith," q.v.

MARTIN, GEORGE, see "James Tybout," q.v.

MARTIN, HUGH (Delaware), b. c1728, Tyrone, Ireland (weaver, age 30 in 1758); pvt., enlisted 29 Apr 1758 "for the campaign in the lower counties" by Capt. John McClughan. {Ref: ARDE I:18; ARPA (2nd Series) 2:570}

MARTIN, JAMES (Maryland), pvt., Capt. Joseph Chapline's Company Muster Roll No. 1, Frederick Co., circa 1757-1758, exact dates not given (served 57 days); bill of credit issued or paid in his behalf to Joseph Chaplin for £2.17.0 on 5 Mar 1767. {Ref: MSA S960 or S752, p. 191; CSOS:102}

MARTIN, JOHN, see "James Curry," q.v.

MARTIN, RACHEL, see "James Tybout," q.v.

MARTIN, ROBERT (Maryland), cpl., Capt. Joseph Hanson Harrison's Company Muster Roll, Charles Co., circa 1757-1758, exact dates not given; bill of credit issued or paid in his behalf to John Hanson, Jr. for £4.1.9 on 23 Feb 1767. {Ref: MSA S960 or S752, p. 189} See "Benton Harris," q.v.

MARTIN, THOMAS, see "William Johnson," q.v.

MARTIN (MARTEN), THOMAS (Maryland), pvt., Capt. Richard Pearis' Company of MD Troops, Frederick Co., from 9 Oct 1757 to 25 Apr 1758 when he was reported as dead; however, payment to him was recorded in Col. Dagworthy's account book on 17 Jul 1762. {Ref: MHS MS.375; CSOS:90; MHS MS.375.1}

MARTIN, WILLIAM, see "William Smith," q.v.

MARTINDALL (MARTINDALE), THOMAS (Maryland), cpl., Capt. Henry Casson's Company Muster Roll, Queen Anne's Co., circa 1757-1758, exact dates not given (served 2 days); bill of credit issued in his behalf to Capt.

Casson and paid to Martindall's brother (unnamed) on 27 Mar 1767 for £0.2.7½. {Ref: MSA S960 or S752, p. 178; CSOS:109}

MARTZ, THEOBOLD (Maryland), pvt., Capt. Peter Butler's Company Muster Roll, Frederick Co., circa 1757-1758, exact dates not given (served 34 days); bill of credit or order issued in his behalf for £1.14.0 and paid to Casper Shaff on 2 Mar 1767. {Ref: MSA S960 or S752, p. 167; CSOS:97}

MASH, THOMAS (Maryland), indentured servant and soldier who served in the French and Indian War some time between 1756 and 1763 (exact dates not known); his master George Ensor, planter, requested compensation from the Baltimore County Court due to the loss of use of Mash while in the service. {Ref: MHM 94:4, p. 426, citing Baltimore Co. Court Minutes}

MASON, EDWARD (Maryland), pvt., Capt. Richard Pearis' Company of MD Troops, Frederick Co., circa 9 Oct 1757 to 31 May 1758; pvt., Capt. Alexander Beall's Company of MD Troops, Frederick Co., from 1 Jun 1758 to 8 Nov 1758. {Ref: MHS MS.375.1; CSOS:81, 91} Payment to him was recorded in Col. Dagworthy's account book on 15 Jul 1763. {Ref: MHS MS.375}

MASON, ELIAS (Delaware), b. c1740, Kent, DE (age 19 in 1759); pvt., enlisted in Capt. John Wright's Company and mustered on 11 May 1759. {Ref: ARDE I:25; ARPA (2nd Series) 2:592} He served on a jury in Sussex Co. that was empowered to try cases of treason in 1781; also a soldier from Sussex Co. who died of his wounds in September 1781. {Ref: RPDE:166}

MASON, ELIJAH (Maryland), pvt., Capt. Joseph Chapline's Company Muster Roll No. 1, Frederick Co., circa 1757-1758, exact dates not given (served 52 days); bill of credit issued or paid in his behalf to Joseph Chaplin for £2.12.0 on 5 Mar 1767. {Ref: MSA S960 or S752, p. 191; CSOS:103}

MASON, ELIZABETH, see "Daniel of St. Thomas Jenifer," q.v.

MASON, HENRY (Maryland), patriot and poss. soldier (rank not specified), Frederick Co., militia pay account submitted in 1758, exact date not given. {Ref: MHM 9:4, p. 368}

MASON, MARY, see "William Fitzhugh," q.v.

MASON, ROBERT, see "Daniel of St. Thomas Jenifer," q.v.

MASON, WILLIAM (Maryland), b. c1736, MD (age 20 in 1756); pvt., Capt. Christopher Gist's Company of VA Militia, 13 Jul 1756, enlisted at Baltimore. {Ref: MSR I:37}

MASON, WILLIAM (Maryland), pvt., Capt. Richard Pearis' Company of MD Troops, Frederick Co., circa 9 Oct 1757 to 31 May 1758; pvt., Capt. John Dagworthy's Company of MD Troops, Frederick Co., from 1 Jun 1758 until 14 Jun 1758 and was discharged. {Ref: MHS MS.375.1; CSOS:77, 91} Payment to him was recorded in Col. Dagworthy's account book on 17 Jul 1762. {Ref: M HS MS.375}

MASS, JOHN BAPTIST, see "John Baptist Marr," q.v.

MASTERS, JOHN (Maryland), pvt., Capt. William McClellan's Company of MD Volunteers, Frederick Co., circa 1763-1764; on muster roll dated 15 Nov 1764 at Camp at the Forks of Muskingham. {Ref: ARMD 32:99}

MASTERS, ROBERT (Maryland), pvt., Capt. William Luckett's Company Muster Roll, Frederick Co., circa 1757-1758, exact dates not given (served 30 days); bill of credit issued or paid in his behalf to William Luckett, Jr. for £1.10.0 on 6 Apr 1767. {Ref: MSA S960 or S752, p. 169; CSOS:100}

MASTERSON, HUGH (Maryland), pvt., Capt. Alexander Beall's Company of MD Troops, Frederick Co., from 9 Oct 1757 to 9 Jan 1758 and then he joined the Royal Americans Regt. {Ref: MHS MS.375.1; CSOS:81} Payment to him was recorded in Col. Dagworthy's account book on 7 Mar 1763. {Ref: MHS MS.375}

MATTESON, SAMUEL (Delaware), pvt., Kent Co. Militia, Capt. John Caton's Company, 25 Apr 1757 (date of muster roll). {Ref: ARDE I:14}

MATTHEWS, JAMES (Maryland), b. 7 Sep 1727, Baltimore Co., son of Roger Matthews and Elizabeth Garrett; never married; wrote his will on 13 May 1759 and d. by 5 Mar 1760 (date of probate). {Ref: BCF:428} Pvt., Capt. Tobias Stansbury's Company Muster Roll, Baltimore Co., circa 1757-1758, exact dates not given; bill of credit or order issued to his exec. (not named) and paid to John Henry for £4.8.9 on 18 Mar 1767. {Ref: MSA S960 or S752, p. 186}

MATTHEWS, JOHN (Maryland), cpl., Capt. John Middaugh's Company Muster Roll, Frederick Co., circa 1757-1758, exact dates not given (served 30 days); bill of credit issued or paid in his behalf to Robert Wood for £2 on 4 Mar 1767. {Ref: MSA S960 or S752, p. 171; CSOS:100}

MATTHEWS, ROGER, see "James Matthews," q.v.

MATTHEWS, SAMUEL (Maryland), m. Sarah (N), had a son Chidley, another son (N), and three daus. (N) who were mentioned, but not named in his will; d. testate 11 May 1770. {Ref: WMG 3:3, p. 108} Pvt., Capt. John Middaugh's Company Muster Roll, Frederick Co., circa 1757-1758, exact dates not given (served 30 days); bill of credit issued or paid in his behalf to Robert Wood for £1.10.0 on 4 Mar 1767. {Ref: MSA S960 or S752, p. 171; CSOS:101}

MATTHEWS, THOMAS (Maryland), lieut., Capt. Joshua Beall's Company Muster Roll, Prince George's Co., circa 1757-1758, exact dates not given. {Ref: MSA S960 or S752, p. 184; CSOS:116} Payment to him was recorded in Col. Dagworthy's account book on 25 Feb 1763. {Ref: MHS MS.375} Another account submitted to the MD Assembly on 25 Nov 1763 indicated "Lieut. Thomas Mathews was due £4.12.3 as granted by the Act for Granting a Sum of Money as a Present to the Forces, late in the Pay and Service of this Province, and taken into his Majesty's Service by Brigadier General Forbes." {Ref: ARMD 58:401} Bill of credit issued or paid to him for £5.0.4½ in 1767, exact date not given. {Ref: MSA S960 or S752, p. 184}

MATTHEWS, THOMAS (Maryland), 2nd lieut., Capt. Alexander Beall's Company of MD Troops, Frederick Co. (transferred from Capt. Richard Pearis' Company, exact date not given) and served from 1 Jun 1758 to 12 Oct 1758 when he was reported as killed. {Ref: MHS MS.375.1; CSOS:79} A newspaper indicated "Lieut. Matthews was killed in the late battle" (date not given). {Ref: *MD Gazette*, 2 Nov 1758}

MATTHEWS, TOWNSEND (Delaware), pvt., Capt. Richard McWilliams' Company of Foot, New Castle Co., enlisted 28 Dec 1757. {Ref: ARDE I:15}

MATTHEWS, WILLIAM (Maryland), pvt., Capt. Alexander Beall's Company of MD Troops, Frederick Co., circa 9 Oct 1757 to 30 Dec 1758. {Ref: MHS MS.375.1; CSOS:81} Payment to him was recorded in Col. Dagworthy's account book on 12 Jul 1762. {Ref: MHS MS.375}

MATTHIAS, STEPHEN (Maryland), pvt., Capt. Thomas Norris' Company, Frederick Co., circa 1757-1758, exact dates not given (served 30 days); bill of credit issued or paid in his behalf to Michael McGuire on 27 Mar 1767 for £1.10.0. {Ref: MSA S960 or S752, p. 176; CSOS:108}

MATTISON, GEORGE (Maryland), pvt., Capt. William McClellan's Company of MD Volunteers, Frederick Co., circa 1763-1764; on muster roll dated 15 Nov 1764 at Camp at the Forks of Muskingham. {Ref: ARMD 32:99}

MAULDIN, ANN, see "Jesse Hollingsworth," q.v.

MAXELL (MAXWELL), ANDREW (Maryland), pvt., Capt. John Middaugh's Company Muster Roll, Frederick Co., circa 1757-1758, exact dates not given (served 30 days); bill of credit issued or paid in his behalf to Thomas Beatty, Jr. for £1.10.0 on 23 Feb 1767. {Ref: MSA S960 or S752, pp. 171-172; CSOS:101}

MAXWELL, JOHN (Maryland), cpl., Capt. Alexander Beall's Company of MD Troops, Frederick Co., from 9 Oct 1757 to 30 Dec 1758 (reduced to a pvt. on 14 Oct 1757). {Ref: MHS MS.375.1; CSOS:81} Payment to him was recorded in Col. Dagworthy's account book on 28 Feb 1763. {Ref: MHS MS.375}

MAXWELL, THOMAS (Delaware), pvt., Kent Co. Militia, Capt. John Caton's Company, 25 Apr 1757 (date of muster roll). {Ref: ARDE I:14}

MAY, EDWARD (Maryland), pvt., Capt. Richard Pearis' Company of MD Troops, Frederick Co., circa 9 Oct 1757 to 31 May 1758; pvt., Capt. Joshua Beall's Company of MD Troops, Prince George's Co., from 1 Jun 1758 to 24 Oct 1758. {Ref: MHS MS.375.1; CSOS:85, 91} Payment to him was recorded in Col. Dagworthy's account book on 17 Jul 1762. {Ref: MHS MS.375}

MAYBURY, BARUCH, see "John Inch," q.v.

MAYER, SAMUEL (Maryland), patriot and poss. soldier (rank not specified), Frederick Co., militia pay account submitted in 1758, exact date not given. {Ref: MHM 9:4, p. 367}

MAYHEW, JOSEPH (Maryland), sgt., Capt. Stephen Rensburg's or Rensburger's Company Muster Roll, Frederick Co., circa 1757-1758, exact dates not given (served 42 days); bill of credit or order issued to Casper Shaff and paid to David Cumming for Mayhew's exec. (unnamed) for £2.16.0 on 18 Apr 1767. {Ref: MSA S960 or S752, p. 183; CSOS:111} One Joseph Mayhew was appointed Pressmaster for Frederick County in 1758, but he petitioned the court in November 1758, stating that he "thinks himself uncapable, being an old man and much troubled with the sceatick pains" and asked that he be relieved. The court appointed John Kimboll in his place and it was recorded in the judgment records. {Ref: TWL:186, citing Frederick Co. Judgment Records}

MAYHEW, THOMAS (Maryland), pvt., Capt. Samuel Chapman's Company Muster Roll, Anne Arundel Co., circa 1757-1758, exact dates not given; bill of credit issued or paid to him for £1.18.0 on 11 Mar 1767. {Ref: MSA S960 or S752, p. 188}

McADOW, JOHN (Maryland), indentured servant and soldier who served in the French and Indian War some time between 1756 and 1763 (exact dates not known); his master Joseph Smith, iron manufacturer, requested compensation from the Baltimore County Court due to the loss of use of McAdow while in the service. {Ref: MHM 94:4, p. 426, citing Baltimore Co. Court Minutes}

McAFFEE, JOHN (Delaware), b. c1734, Long Island, NY (age 25 in 1759); pvt., enlisted in Capt. John Wright's Company and mustered on 11 May 1759. {Ref: ARDE I:25; ARPA (2nd Series) 2:592}

McANULTY, JOHN (Delaware), b. c1730, Derry, Ireland (farmer, age 28 in 1758); pvt., enlisted 22 Apr 1758 "for the campaign in the lower counties" by Capt. John McClughan. {Ref: ARDE I:18; ARPA (2nd Series) 2:570}

McARTHUR, THOMAS (Maryland), 2nd lieut., Capt. Richard Pearis' Company of MD Troops, Frederick Co., circa 9 Oct 1757 to 31 May 1758. {Ref: MHS MS.375.1; CSOS:90}

McBEAN, ALEXANDER (Maryland), lieut., Royal American Regt., stationed at Baltimore Town and Annapolis in 1756. {Ref: *MD Gazette*, 4 Nov and 25 Nov 1756}

McCARTY, ---- (Maryland), an officer (rank not stated) by 7 Dec 1757 at which time Gov. Horatio Sharpe wrote to the MD Assembly, stating in part: "What became of Lake and Smith they know not, but have heard that Smith was a waiter on one Mr. McCarty, an officer, and who Mr. McCarty is, or where he is to be met with, they do not say." {Ref: ARMD 55:320}

McCARTY, ADAM (Maryland), patriot, Frederick Co., was paid £1.10.0 at Fort Frederick on 29 Jun 1758 "for assisting Capt. Shelby in laying out a new road to Fort Cumberland" for the Western Expedition against Fort Duquesne. {Ref: ARMD 55:773}

McCARTY, JOHN (Maryland or Pennsylvania), pvt., Capt. Hamilton's Company, was killed in "a recent battle with the Indians" in 1756 (exact date not given) in Cumberland Co., PA, after the burning of McCord's Fort. {Ref: *MD Gazette*, 29 Apr 1756}

McCASTLE, WILLIAM (Delaware), b. c1733, Antrim, Ireland (laborer, age 26 in 1759); pvt., enlisted by Capt. James Armstrong for the PA Regt. on 30 Apr 1759. {Ref: ARDE I:26; ARPA (2nd Series) 2:585}

McCAU (MCAU), WILLIAM (Maryland), indentured servant and soldier who served in the French and Indian War some time between 1756 and 1763 (exact dates not known); his master Joseph Smith, iron manufacturer, requested compensation from the Baltimore County Court due to the loss of use of McCau while in the service. {Ref: MHM 94:4, p. 426, citing Baltimore Co. Court Minutes}

McCLAY, LIEUT., see "Barnabas Hughes," q.v.

McCLEARN, JAMES (Delaware), b. c1731, Londonderry, Ireland (laborer, age 27 in 1758); pvt., enlisted 1 May 1758 "for the campaign in the lower counties" by Capt. John McClughan. {Ref: ARDE I:18; ARPA (2nd Series) 2:570}

McCLELLAN, JAMES (Delaware), b. c1729, Antrim, Ireland (laborer, age 29 in 1758); pvt., enlisted 29 Apr 1758 "for the campaign in the lower counties" by Capt. John McClughan. {Ref: ARDE I:18; ARPA (2nd Series) 2:570}

McCLELLAN, WILLIAM (Maryland), captain, MD Volunteers, Frederick Co., circa 1763-1764; on muster roll dated 15 Nov 1764 at Camp at the Forks of Muskingham. {Ref: ARMD 32:99} See "Henry Bouquet," q.v.

McCLOUD, JOHN (Delaware), pvt., Capt. French Battell's Company of Lower County Provincials, enlisted 18 May 1758. {Ref: ARDE I:16; ARPA (2nd Series) 2:555}

McCLUGHAN, JOHN (Delaware), captain, New Castle Co., 16 Apr 1758; in a letter written to Richard Peters on 15 May 1759, Capt. John Haslet stated "tis in favour of Capt. McClughan, a gentleman who served last year to ye westward, but thro' the misrepresentation of some to his Honour, ye Governor, has been neglected this year; were he only an honest man be assured, sir, I would not imploy your time w't this, but that he was also a good officer I can get attested by all impartial officers of his acquaintance ... he merits the place he held last year." McClughan was commissioned on 21 May 1759, but the commission was subsequently revoked (reason not stated). {Ref: ARDE I:16, 20, 23; ARPA (2nd Series) 2:580, 582, 725}

McCLUGHAN, JOHN (Delaware), pvt., Capt. Richard McWilliams' Company of Foot, New Castle Co., enlisted 28 Dec 1757. {Ref: ARDE I:14}

McCLUNE, THOMAS, see "James McMurry," q.v.

McCLURE, SAMUEL (Delaware), b. c1733, Ulster, Ireland (laborer, age 26 in 1759); pvt., enlisted by Capt. James Armstrong for the PA Regt. on 30 Apr 1759. {Ref: ARDE I:26; ARPA (2nd Series) 2:585}

McCOOMBS, PATRICK (Maryland), pvt., Capt. John Dagworthy's Company of MD Troops, Frederick Co., from 9 Oct 1757 to 10 Dec 1758 when he reportedly deserted; however, payment to him was recorded in Col. Dagworthy's account book on 8 Mar 1763 for work on Fort Cumberland. {Ref: MHS MS.375; CSOS:77; MHS MS.375.1}

McCORD, SAMUEL (Maryland), pvt., Capt. John Wolgomatt's Company of MD Volunteers, Frederick Co., circa 1763-1764; on muster roll dated 15 Nov 1764 at Camp at the Forks of Muskingham. {Ref: ARMD 32:99}

McCORMICK, DAVID (Delaware), pvt., Capt. Henry Vanbibber's Company of the Lower Counties on Delaware Troops at New Castle, enlisted on 28 May 1759. {Ref: ARDE I:26; ARPA (2nd Series) 2:594}

McCOY (MacCOY), ARCHIBALD (Maryland), cpl., Capt. John White's Company Muster Roll, Frederick Co., circa 1757-1758, exact dates not given (served 6 days); bill of credit issued or paid in his behalf to Joseph Chaplin on 5 Mar 1767 for £0.8.0. {Ref: MSA S960 or S752, pp. 164-165; CSOS:95}

McCOY (MacCOY), DANIEL (Maryland), pvt., Capt. John White's Company Muster Roll, Frederick Co., circa 1757-1758, exact dates not given (served 6 days); bill of credit issued or paid to him for £0.6.0 in 1767, exact date not given. {Ref: MSA S960 or S752, p. 165; CSOS:95}

McCOY, DANIEL (Maryland or Pennsylvania), pvt., Capt. Hamilton's Company, was killed in "a recent battle with the Indians" in 1756 (exact date not given) in Cumberland Co., PA, after the burning of McCord's Fort. {Ref: *MD Gazette*, 29 Apr 1756}

McCOY (McKOY), JAMES (Maryland), pvt., Capt. Alexander Beall's Company of MD Troops, Frederick Co., from 9 Oct 1757 to 14 Sep 1758 when he was reported as killed; however, payment to him was recorded in Col. Dagworthy's account book on 14 Jul 1762. {Ref: MHS MS.375; CSOS:81; MHS MS.375.1}

McCRORY, DANIEL (Maryland), pvt., Capt. John Dagworthy's Company of Foot, Frederick Co., 1756-1757, recorded his discharge in Frederick Co. Court on 2 Jul 1757. Capt. Dagworthy certified "he has served upwards of 6 months and the time of his enlistment has expired this 10 Feb 1757." {Ref: FCLR:28}

McCUBBIN (McCUBBINS), WILLIAM (Maryland), pvt., Capt. Richard Pearis' Company of MD Troops, Frederick Co., from 9 Oct 1757 to 31 May 1758. {Ref: MHS MS.375.1} Payment to him was recorded in Col. Dagworthy's account book on 14 Jul 1762. {Ref: MHS MS.375}

McCULLOCH, WILLIAM (Maryland), pvt., Capt. Joseph Hanson Harrison's Company Muster Roll, Charles Co., circa 1757-1758, exact dates not given; bill of credit issued or paid in his behalf to Richard Clagett for £2.12.0 on 21 May 1767. {Ref: MSA S960 or S752, p. 189}

McCULLUM, JOHN (Maryland), pvt., Capt. Richard Pearis' Company, Frederick Co. (age about 18 in 1757), reported as deserted from the MD Forces in July 1757. {Ref: *MD Gazette*, 21 Jul 1757}

McCULLY, HUGH (Delaware), b. c1733, Monaghan, Ireland (cordwainer, age 26 in 1759); pvt., enlisted by Capt. James Armstrong for the PA Regt. on 25 Apr 1759. {Ref: ARDE I:26; ARPA (2nd Series) 2:585}

McCULLY, SAMUEL (Delaware), b. c1737, Ireland (laborer, age 21 in 1758); pvt., recruited by Capt. Benjamin Noxon and enlisted on 23 May 1758. {Ref: ARDE I:19; ARPA (2nd Series) 2:566}

McCUTCHEN, JOHN (Maryland), b. c1738 (age 20 in 1758), resident of Cecil Co., MD in 1758; pvt., enlisted by Capt. John Singleton for the PA Regt. on 8 May 1758. {Ref: ARPA (2nd Series) 2:474}

McDANIEL, HUGH (Maryland), patriot and poss. soldier, Frederick Co., petitioned the court in March 1761, stating that he "was on the 17th day of last July taken up and put into goal on suspicion of being a deserter and there has been continued until this time which is eight months and as nothing of the kind has appeared, I hope Your Worships will be pleased to order that I may be disposed of in some manner to discharge my fees and free me from gaol." It was ordered in the judgment records that he be freed upon paying all fees due. {Ref: TWL:220, citing Frederick Co. Judgment Records}

McDANIEL, JOHN (Maryland), indentured servant and soldier who served in the French and Indian War some time between 1756 and 1763 (exact dates not known); his master William Govane, merchant, requested compensation from the Baltimore County Court due to the loss of use of McDaniel while in the service. {Ref: MHM 94:4, p. 426, citing Baltimore Co. Court Minutes}

McDANIEL, MICHAEL (Maryland), indentured servant and soldier who served in the French and Indian War some time between 1756 and 1763 (exact dates not known); his master Samuel Webb, tanner, requested compensation from the

Baltimore County Court due to the loss of use of McDaniel while in the service. {Ref: MHM 94:4, p. 426, citing Baltimore Co. Court Minutes}

McDARMOTT, SARAH (Maryland), patriot or poss. widow of a soldier (unnamed), Kent Co., pay account submitted in 1758, exact date not given. {Ref: MHM 9:4, p. 369}

McDAVID, NEILL (Delaware), b. c1729 (shoemaker, age 30 in 1759); pvt., enlisted by Capt. James Armstrong for the PA Regt. on 1 May 1759. {Ref: ARDE I:26; ARPA (2nd Series) 2:585}

McDONALD, JOHN (Maryland or Pennsylvania), pvt., Capt. Culbertson's Company, was wounded in "a recent battle with the Indians" in 1756 (exact date not given) in Cumberland Co., PA, after the burning of McCord's Fort. {Ref: *MD Gazette*, 29 Apr 1756}

McDONALD, JONATHAN (Maryland), pvt., Capt. Joshua Beall's Company of MD Troops, Prince George's Co., from 9 Oct 1757 to 9 May 1758. {Ref: MHS MS.375.1; CSOS:85} Payment to him was recorded in Col. Dagworthy's account book on 8 Mar 1763 for work on Fort Cumberland. {Ref: MHS MS.375}

McDONNELL, JOHN (Delaware), b. c1719, Ulster, Ireland (laborer, age 40 in 1759); pvt., enlisted by Capt. James Armstrong for the PA Regt. on 26 Apr 1759. {Ref: ARDE I:26; ARPA (2nd Series) 2:585}

McDOWELL, ISAAC (Delaware), pvt., Capt. Richard McWilliams' Company of Foot, New Castle Co., enlisted 28 Dec 1757. {Ref: ARDE I:14}

McFADDIN (McFADEN), JOHN (Maryland), pvt., Capt. Joseph Chapline's Company Muster Roll No. 1, Frederick Co., circa 1757-1758, exact dates not given (served 6 days); militia pay account submitted in 1758, exact date not given. {Ref: MHM 9:4, p. 368; CSOS:105}

McFADDIN (McFADEN), WILLIAM (Maryland), pvt., Capt. Joseph Chapline's Company Muster Roll No. 1, Frederick Co., circa 1757-1758, exact dates not given (served 53 days); bill of credit issued or paid in his behalf to Joseph Chaplin for £2.13.0 on 5 Mar 1767. {Ref: MSA S960 or S752, p. 191; CSOS:102} Pvt., Capt. Joseph Chapline's Company Muster Roll No. 4, Frederick Co., circa 1757-1758, exact dates not given (served 5 days); bill of credit issued or paid in his behalf to Joseph Chaplin for £0.5.0 on 5 Mar 1767. {Ref: MSA S960 or S752, p. 194; CSOS:105}

McFARLAND, JOHN (Delaware), pvt., Capt. Richard McWilliams' Company of Foot, New Castle Co., enlisted 28 Dec 1757. {Ref: ARDE I:15}

McGAFFERTY (McGAFFERTHY), CORNELIUS (Maryland), pvt., Capt. Alexander Beall's Company of MD Troops, Frederick Co., from 9 Oct 1757 to 8 Nov 1758 when he reportedly deserted; however, payment to him was recorded in Col. Dagworthy's account book on 11 Jul 1762. {Ref: MHS MS.375; CSOS:81; MHS MS.375.1}

McGAHON, SARAH, see "Thomas Bedingfield Hands," q.v.

McGARVIN, JAMES (Delaware), b. c1724, Ireland (laborer, age 34 in 1758); pvt., recruited by Capt. Benjamin Noxon and enlisted on 23 May 1758. {Ref: ARDE I:19; ARPA (2nd Series) 2:566}

McGAW (MEGAW, McGAUGH, McGAY), ROBERT (Maryland), b. c1735, m. Sarah Lester on 2 Feb 1758, Baltimore Co., St. George's P. E. Parish, had children George (b. 28 Jan 1759), John (b. 7 Aug 1761), Robert (b. 2 Mar 1763), William (b. 20 Jun 1765), Hugh (b. 21 Feb 1767), and James (b. 11 Feb 1770), and d. intestate by 1 May 1783, Harford Co. {Ref: BCF:438; Henry C. Peden, Jr.'s *Heirs and Legatees of Harford Co., MD, 1774-1802*, pp. 18, 30, 34} Pvt., Capt. Tobias Stansbury's Company Muster Roll, Baltimore Co., circa 1757-1758, exact dates not given; bill of credit issued or paid in his behalf to Nathaniel Nicholson for £1.18.0 on 23 Apr 1770. {Ref: MSA S960 or S752, p. 187}

McGEE, JOHN (Maryland or Pennsylvania), Irishman (age not given); pvt. in 1757 who was hanged at Carlisle for desertion. {Ref: *MD Gazette*, 10 Nov 1757}

McGENNIS, DANIEL (Delaware), pvt., Capt. Richard McWilliams' Company of Foot, New Castle Co., enlisted 28 Dec 1757. {Ref: ARDE I:14}

McGILL, ANDREW (Delaware), b. c1735, MD ("Indian," age 24 in 1759); pvt., enlisted in Capt. John Wright's Company and mustered on 11 May 1759. {Ref: ARDE I:25; ARPA (2nd Series) 2:508, 592}

McGILL, PATRICK (Delaware), b. c1729, Armagh, Ireland (laborer, age 30 in 1759); pvt., enlisted by Capt. James Armstrong for the PA Regt. on 25 Apr 1759. {Ref: ARDE I:26; ARPA (2nd Series) 2:585}

McGILL, PATRICK (Delaware), b. c1732, Kilmore, Ireland (weaver, age 26 in 1758); pvt., enlisted 30 Apr 1758 "for the campaign in the lower counties" by Capt. John McClughan. {Ref: ARDE I:18; ARPA (2nd Series) 2:570}

McGILL, ROWLAND (Maryland), pvt., Capt. Joshua Beall's Company of MD Troops, Prince George's Co., circa 9 Oct 1757 to 30 Dec 1758. {Ref: MHS MS.375.1; CSOS:85} He was reported as a deserter from the 44th Regt. of Foot in January 1759, noting he was born in Ireland, had previously belonged to the MD Forces, and had a furlough from Capt. Joshua Beall. {Ref: *MD Gazette*, 12 Jan 1759} Payment to him was recorded in Col. Dagworthy's account book on 21 Jul 1762. {Ref: MHS MS.375}

McGINTA (McGINTO), JOHN (Maryland), pvt., Capt. Francis Ware's Company of MD Troops, Charles Co., circa 9 Oct 1757 to 30 Dec 1758. {Ref: MHS MS.375.1; CSOS:88} Payment to him was recorded in Col. Dagworthy's account book on 28 Feb 1763. {Ref: MHS MS.375}

McGOWEN, JAMES (Maryland), pvt., Capt. Alexander Beall's Company of MD Troops, Frederick Co., circa 9 Oct 1757 to 30 Dec 1758. {Ref: MHS MS.375.1; CSOS:81} Payment to him was recorded in Col. Dagworthy's account book on 26 Feb 1763. {Ref: MHS MS.375}

McGRAW, JAMES (Delaware), b. c1738, MD (tailor, age 21 in 1759); pvt., enlisted in Capt. John Wright's Company and mustered on 11 May 1759. {Ref: ARDE I:25; ARPA (2nd Series) 2:508, 592}

McGRAY, GEORGE (Delaware), b. c1737, Sussex, DE (age 22 in 1759); pvt., enlisted in Capt. John Wright's Company and mustered on 11 May 1759. {Ref: ARDE I:25; ARPA (2nd Series) 2:592}

McGUIRE, BARTHOLOMEW (Delaware), b. c1728, Ireland (laborer, age 30 in 1758, height 5 ft. 8 in.); pvt., enlisted by Capt. Paul Jackson in New Castle Co. for the PA Troops on 15 May 1758. {Ref: ARDE I:27}

McGUIRE, JOHN (Maryland), sgt., Capt. Peregrine Brown's Company Muster Roll, Kent Co., circa 1757-1758, exact dates not given (served 15 days); bill of credit issued or paid in his behalf to Robert Buchanan on 20 Feb 1767 for £1. {Ref: MSA S960 or S752, p. 179; CSOS:110}

McHUGH, JOSEPH (Maryland), b. c1732 in lower part of Prince George's Co. near Patuxent (age about 25 in 1757); soldier in the MD Forces who was reported as deserted in June 1757. It was noted that when found he should be delivered to Capt. Richard Pearis or Lieut. McRae. {Ref: *MD Gazette*, 23 Jun 1757}

McINTIRE, JOHN (Maryland), sgt., Capt. Moses Chapline's Company Muster Roll No. 3, Frederick Co., circa 1757-1758, exact dates not given (served 6 days); bill of credit issued or paid in his behalf to Joseph Chaplin for £0.8.0 on 5 Mar 1767. {Ref: MSA S960 or S752, p. 198; CSOS:114}

McINTOSH, HUGH (Delaware), b. c1723, Perth, Scotland (laborer, age 35 in 1758); pvt., enlisted 8 May 1758 "for the campaign in the lower counties" by Capt. John McClughan. {Ref: ARDE I:18; ARPA (2nd Series) 2:570}

McINTOSH, JOHN (Delaware), b. c1739, Indian River, DE (laborer, age 19 in 1758); pvt., enlisted 9 May 1758 "for the campaign in the lower counties" by Capt. John McClughan. {Ref: ARDE I:18; ARPA (2nd Series) 2:570}

McKEAN, DANIEL (Delaware), b. c1729, Antrim, Ireland (laborer, age 30 in 1759); pvt., enlisted by Capt. James Armstrong for the PA Regt. on 24 Apr 1759. {Ref: ARDE I:26; ARPA (2nd Series) 2:585}

McKEAN, THOMAS (Delaware), attorney; pvt., Capt. Richard McWilliams' Company of Foot, New Castle Co., enlisted 28 Dec 1757. {Ref: ARDE I:14}

McKENNESS (McKINNISS), JOHN (Maryland), pvt., Capt. Joshua Beall's Company of MD Troops, Prince George's Co., from 9 Oct 1757 to 13 Jan 1758 when he was discharged. {Ref: MHS MS.375.1; CSOS:85} Payment to him was recorded in Col. Dagworthy's account book on 23 Jul 1762. {Ref: MHS MS.375}

McKENNEY, AMOS (Delaware), pvt., Capt. French Battell's Company of Lower County Provincials, enlisted 20 May 1758. {Ref: ARDE I:16; ARPA (2nd Series) 2:555}

McKENNY, CHARLES (Delaware), b. c1738, Ireland (cooper, age 20 in 1758); pvt., recruited by Capt. Benjamin Noxon and enlisted on 1 May 1758. {Ref: ARDE I:19; ARPA (2nd Series) 2:566}

McKENZIE, ROBERT, see "Thomas Brown" and "Roger Burkham" and "James Munday," q.v.

McKEY, GEORGE (Maryland), pvt., Capt. John Dagworthy's Company of MD Troops, Frederick Co., from 9 Oct 1757 to 16 Apr 1759 when he reportedly deserted; however, payment to him was recorded in Col. Dagworthy's account book on 21 Jul 1762. {Ref: MHS MS.375; CSOS:77; MHS MS.375.1}

McKIM, JAMES (Delaware), New Castle Co., patriot and court justice in 1761. {Ref: GRSD 1:15}

McKIM, THOMAS (Delaware), m. Agnes (N), had children Jean, John, Robert, Alexander, and Elizabeth, and d. testate by 22 Sep 1784. {Ref: CDSS:140} Lieut.,

Brandywine Hundred, Upper Regt. of Militia, Southwest Division, New Castle Co., 1756. {Ref: ARDE I:11; ARPA (2nd Series) 2:526; HDE I:141}

McKINLEY, JOHN (Delaware), b. 21 Feb 1721/2, m. Jane (N), prob. had no children, and d. testate 31 Aug 1796; major, Upper Regt. of Militia, New Castle Co., 1756; brig. general, New Castle Co. Militia and President of the Council of Safety on 8 Jan 1776; later became Speaker of the House of Assembly and Commander in Chief of the State of Delaware. {Ref: ARDE I:11; ARPA (2nd Series) 2:526; HDE I:141; RPDE:181}

McKINNEY (McKENNEY), JOHN (Maryland), pvt., Capt. Francis Ware's Company of MD Troops, Charles Co., circa 9 Oct 1757 to 30 Dec 1758. {Ref: MHS MS.375.1; CSOS:88} Payment to him was recorded in Col. Dagworthy's account book on 7 Mar 1763. {Ref: MHS MS.375}

McKNITT, EZEBELL, see "Archibald Flemming," q.v.

McLACHLAN (McLALAND), JAMES (Maryland), pvt., Capt. Joshua Beall's Company of MD Troops, Prince George's Co., from 9 Oct 1757 to 30 Dec 1758; name mistakenly transcribed once as "James McLatano." {Ref: MHS MS.375.1; CSOS:85} Payment to him was recorded in Col. Dagworthy's account book on 8 Mar 1763 for work on Fort Cumberland. {Ref: MHS MS.375}

McLAUGHLAN, JOHN, see "Daniel Smith," q.v.

McLAULIN, TIMOTHY (Maryland), indentured servant and soldier who served in the French and Indian War some time between 1756 and 1763 (exact dates not known); his master John Brown, saddler, requested compensation from the Baltimore County Court due to the loss of use of McLaulin while in the service. {Ref: MHM 94:4, p. 426, citing Baltimore Co. Court Minutes}

McLEAN, CATHERINE, see "Norman Stinchcomb," q.v.

McLOY, JOHN (Delaware), b. c1732, Ireland (weaver, age 26 in 1758); pvt., recruited by Capt. Benjamin Noxon and enlisted on 8 May 1758. {Ref: ARDE I:19; ARPA (2nd Series) 2:566}

McMANAMON (MACMANNAN), HUGH (Maryland), pvt., Capt. Alexander Beall's Company of MD Troops, Frederick Co., from 9 Oct 1757 to 2 Apr 1758 when he reportedly deserted; however, payment to him was recorded in Col. Dagworthy's account book on 7 Mar 1763. {Ref: MHS MS.375; CSOS:81; MHS MS.375.1}

McMANN, ROBERT (Delaware), pvt., Capt. Richard McWilliams' Company of Foot, New Castle Co., enlisted 28 Dec 1757. {Ref: ARDE I:14}

McMANUS, PHILIP, see "Pollard Edmondson," q.v.

McMANUS, RACHEL, see "Pollard Edmondson," q.v.

McMEDUN (McMIDAN), JAMES (Delaware), New Castle Co., patriot who served as a Justice of the Peace, Justice of the Court of Oyer and Terminer, and Justice of the Court of Common Pleas, 1756. {Ref: GRSD 1:13}

McMECHAN, WILLIAM (Delaware), ensign, New Castle Co., commissioned 21 May 1759. {Ref: ARDE I:20; ARPA (5th Series) 1:301, (2nd Series) 2:582}

McMECHAN (McMACHON, McMEEHAN), WILLIAM (Delaware), lieut., Mill Creek Hundred, Upper Regt. of Militia, South Division, New Castle Co., 1756; surgeon, 20 Apr 1758; 2nd lieut., 3 Oct 1758; surgeon, 3rd Bttn. of PA Regt.,

23 May 1759. {Ref: ARDE I:11, 16, 20; ARPA (2nd Series) 2:526, 579-580, (5th Series) 1:301; HDE I:141}

McMURPHY, ARCHIBALD (Delaware), b. c1731, Scotland (laborer, age 27 in 1758); pvt., recruited by Capt. Benjamin Noxon and enlisted on 22 Apr 1758; subscribed to the Oath of Fidelity and Allegiance in 1778. {Ref: ARDE I:19; ARPA (2nd Series) 2:566; RPDE:184}

McMURRY, JAMES (Maryland), pvt., Capt. Thomas Norris' Company, Frederick Co., circa 1757-1758, exact dates not given (served 30 days); bill of credit issued or paid in his behalf to Thomas McClune on 27 May 1767 for £1.10.0; name mistakenly listed once as "James McMunay." {Ref: MSA S960 or S752, pp. 176-177; CSOS:108}

McNAMARA (MACNAMARRA), MICHAEL (Maryland), indentured servant and soldier who served in the French and Indian War some time between 1756 and 1763 (exact dates not known); his master John Seely, planter, requested compensation from the Baltimore County Court due to the loss of use of McNamara while in the service. {Ref: MHM 94:4, p. 426, citing Baltimore Co. Court Minutes}

McNAMARA, PETER (Delaware), pvt., enlisted 9 May 1758 "for the campaign in the lower counties" by Capt. John McClughan. {Ref: ARDE I:18; ARPA (2nd Series) 2:570}

McNAMIE, JOHN (Delaware), pvt., Capt. Richard McWilliams' Company of Foot, New Castle Co., enlisted 28 Dec 1757. {Ref: ARDE I:14}

McNATT, ELIZABETH, see "John Clark," q.v.

McNEAL, JOHN (Maryland), pvt., Capt. Tobias Stansbury's Company Muster Roll, Baltimore Co., circa 1757-1758, exact dates not given; bill of credit issued or paid to him for £1.19.0 in 1767, exact date not given. {Ref: MSA S960 or S752, p. 187}

McNEES (MACNEES), GEORGE (Maryland), pvt., Capt. Henry Casson's Company Muster Roll, Queen Anne's Co., circa 1757-1758, exact dates not given (served 27 days); bill of credit issued or paid in his behalf to Capt. Casson on 27 Mar 1767 for £1.7.0. {Ref: MSA S960 or S752, p. 178; CSOS:109}

McNEIL, HECTOR (Delaware), pvt., Capt. Richard McWilliams' Company of Foot, New Castle Co., enlisted 28 Dec 1757. {Ref: ARDE I:15}

McNEIL (McNIEL, MACNEAL), JAMES (Maryland), pvt., Charles Co., received £5 bounty money on 15 Sep 1757 for enlisting in the militia. {Ref: ARMD 55:265, 619} Pvt., Capt. Francis Ware's Company of MD Troops, Charles Co., circa 9 Oct 1757 to 30 Dec 1758. {Ref: MHS MS.375.1; CSOS:88} Payment to him was recorded in Col. Dagworthy's account book on 21 Jul 1762. {Ref: MHS MS.375}

McNEILL, JOHN (Maryland or Virginia), captain in a VA Regt., recruiting in MD in 1761, placed a notice in Annapolis newspaper for interested men to apply to John Inch in Annapolis, or Benjamin Brooke in Upper Marlborough, or Sgt. Richard Good in Port Tobacco. {Ref: *MD Gazette*, 14 May 1761} See "Solomon Phillips," q.v.

McNULLAN, JAMES (Delaware), pvt., Capt. Richard McWilliams' Company of Foot, New Castle Co., enlisted 28 Dec 1757. {Ref: ARDE I:15}

McPHERSON, DANIEL (Maryland), patriot, Frederick Co., was paid £56.4.0 on 29 Jul 1758 "for liquor dld. to the parties that worked on the New Road between Fort Frederick and Fort Cumberland" for the Western Expedition against Fort Duquesne. {Ref: ARMD 55:774}

McPHERSON, JOHN, see "Joseph Hanson Harrison" and "Hines Roby," q.v.

McRAE, DUNCAN (Maryland), 1st lieut., Capt. Alexander Beall's Company of MD Troops, Frederick Co. (transferred from Capt. Richard Pearis' Company, exact date not given) and served from 1 Jun 1758 to 14 Sep 1758 when he was reported as killed. {Ref: MHS MS.375.1; CSOS:79, 90} A jailed runaway slave named James was mentioned in the newspaper in 1759 as "formerly belonged to Lieut. Duncan McRae, late in the Maryland Service." {Ref: *MD Gazette*, 3 May 1759} Payment due him was recorded in Col. Dagworthy's account book on 4 Mar 1763 and another account submitted to the MD Assembly on 25 Nov 1763 indicated Lieut. Drucan *[sic]* McRae was due £4.12.3 as "granted by the Act for Granting a Sum of Money as a Present to the Forces, late in the Pay and Service of this Province, and taken into his Majesty's Service by Brigadier General Forbes." {Ref: MHS MS.375; ARMD 58:400-401}

McSWAIN, GEORGE (Maryland), pvt. and/or cadet, Capt. Joshua Beall's Company of MD Troops, Prince George's Co., from 9 Oct 1757 to 17 Jun 1758 when he was reported as killed; however, payment was recorded in Col. Dagworthy's account book on 22 Jul 1762. {Ref: MHS MS.375; CSOS:85; MHS MS.375.1} He may have been the "Mr. McSwaine" who was a guide for Col. John Armstrong on his march on the Indians at Kittatinning in 1756. {Ref: *MD Gazette*, 23 Sep 1756}

McWILLIAMS, RICHARD (Delaware), m. Rebecca (N), had children Ann, Sarah, Rebecca, Louisa, and Hester, and d. testate by 19 May 1786. {Ref: CDSS:143} Captain, New Castle Hundred, Upper Regt. of Militia, North Division, New Castle Co., 1756. {Ref: ARDE I:11; ARPA (2nd Series) 2:526; HDE I:141} Patriot who served as a Justice of the Peace, Justice of the Court of Oyer and Terminer, and Justice of the Court of Common Pleas, 1756-1763; Recorder of Deeds, Clerk of the Orphans Court, and Register of Wills, 1777; and, was a justice who administered the Oath of Fidelity and Allegiance in 1778. {Ref: GRSD 1:13; RPDE:185}

MEAD, SUSANNA, see "John Long," q.v.

MEARNS, SAMUEL (Maryland), doctor and pvt. in Capt. John Dagworthy's Company of MD Troops, Frederick Co., from 9 Oct 1757 to 26 Apr 1759. {Ref: MHS MS.375.1; CSOS:77} Payment to him was recorded in Col. Dagworthy's account book on 14 Jul 1762. {Ref: MHS MS.375}

MEARS, SARAH, see "William Allnutt," q.v.

MEDAH, JOHN (Maryland), patriot and poss. soldier (rank not specified), Frederick Co., militia pay account submitted in 1758, exact date not given. {Ref: MHM 9:4, p. 369}

MEDFORD, MACALL or McCALL (Maryland), cpl., Capt. Peregrine Brown's Company Muster Roll, Kent Co., circa 1757-1758, exact dates not given (served 15 days); bill of credit issued or paid in his behalf to Thomas Ringgold, Esq. on

20 Feb 1767 for £1. {Ref: MSA S960 or S752, p. 179; CSOS:110} Macall Medford, of Kent Co., m. Susannah (N), had children Macall, Unit, Manlove, Mary, Susannah, and Sarah, and d. testate by 6 May 1781. {Ref: Kent Co. Wills 6:168} See "John Gale, Jr.," q.v.

MEED, MARY, see "John Foster," q.v.

MEEKS, WILLIAM (Maryland), pvt., Capt. Alexander Beall's Company of MD Troops, Frederick Co., from 17 Feb 1758 to 8 Nov 1758. {Ref: MHS MS.375.1; CSOS:81} Payment to him was recorded in Col. Dagworthy's account book on 26 Feb 1763. {Ref: MHS MS.375}

MEIR, CASPER (Maryland), patriot and poss. soldier (rank not specified), Frederick Co., militia pay account submitted in 1758, exact date not given. {Ref: MHM 9:4, p. 367}

MELOTT, PETER (Maryland), pvt., Capt. Joseph Chapline's Company Muster Roll No. 4, Frederick Co., circa 1757-1758, exact dates not given (served 6 days); bill of credit issued or paid in his behalf to Joseph Chaplin for £0.6.0 on 5 Mar 1767. {Ref: MSA S960 or S752, p. 195; CSOS:105}

MERCER, G., see "Thomas Combs" and "Ignatius Edwards" and "Samuel French," q.v.

MERCER, HUGH, see "James Young," q.v.

MERCH, PASTIAN (Maryland), pvt., Capt. John White's Company Muster Roll, Frederick Co., circa 1757-1758, exact dates not given (served 6 days); bill of credit issued or paid to him for £0.6.0 in 1767, exact date not given. {Ref: MSA S960 or S752, p. 165; CSOS:96}

MERIDETH, JOB or JOBE (Delaware), pvt., Kent Co. Militia, Capt. John Caton's Company, 25 Apr 1757 (date of muster roll). {Ref: ARDE I:14} Job Merydith d. intestate by 17 Mar 1762. {Ref: CDSS:144}

MERIDETH, JOB or JOBE (Delaware), pvt., Kent Co. Militia, Capt. John Caton's Company, 25 Apr 1757 (date of muster roll). {Ref: ARDE I:13} Job Meredith or Merydith, poss. son of Robert Merydith who m. Rachel (N) and d. 1767, m. (N), had children Lydia, David, Peter, Job, Obedi, Henry, Stephen, James, David, Abner, Benjamin, Rachel, and Elizabeth, d. intestate by 17 Oct 1793. {Ref: CDSS:144}

MERIDETH, JOHN (Maryland), patriot and poss. soldier (rank not specified), Frederick Co., militia pay account submitted in 1758, exact date not given. {Ref: MHM 9:4, p. 368}

MERIDETH, JOHN (Delaware), pvt., Kent Co. Militia, Capt. John Caton's Company, 25 Apr 1757 (date of muster roll). {Ref: ARDE I:13} John Meridith m. Sophia (N) and d. intestate by 11 Nov 1767. {Ref: CDSS:144}

MERIDETH, JOSEPH (Delaware), pvt., Kent Co. Militia, Capt. John Caton's Company, 25 Apr 1757 (date of muster roll). {Ref: ARDE I:13} *Identification problem:* There were two men with this name who could have served in the war: (1) Joseph Meredith d. intestate by 14 Apr 1795 at which time letters of administration were granted to William Meredith, next of kin; and, (2) Joseph Meridith m. (N), had children Samuel, Jacob, Martha, Elizabeth, and Ann, d.

intestate by 4 Jan 1796 at which time letters of administration were granted to Samuel Meridith. {Ref: CDSS:144}

MERIDETH, JOSHUA (Delaware), pvt., Kent Co. Militia, Capt. John Caton's Company, 25 Apr 1757 (date of muster roll). {Ref: ARDE I:13} Joshua Meridith, yeoman, d. intestate in Murderkill Hundred by 28 Dec 1775 at which time letters of administration were granted to Ruth Meridith and Luff Meridith. {Ref: CDSS:145}

MERIDETH, ROBERT JR. (Delaware), pvt., Kent Co. Militia, Capt. John Caton's Company, 25 Apr 1757 (date of muster roll). {Ref: ARDE I:14} He may have been the Robert Merydith who m. Rachel (N), had a son Job, and d. testate by 7 Oct 1767. {Ref: CDSS:145}

MERIDETH, WHELOR (Delaware), pvt., Kent Co. Militia, Capt. John Caton's Company, 25 Apr 1757 (date of muster roll). {Ref: ARDE I:13} Wheelor Meridith m. Susannah (N) and d. intestate by 15 Nov 1773. {Ref: CDSS:145}

MERIDETH, WILLIAM (Delaware), pvt., Kent Co. Militia, Capt. John Caton's Company, 25 Apr 1757 (date of muster roll). {Ref: ARDE I:13} William Meredith m. Margaret (N) and d. intestate by 28 Dec 1797. {Ref: CDSS:145}

MERRICK, GRIFFITH (Maryland), pvt., Capt. William Luckett's Company Muster Roll, Frederick Co., circa 1757-1758, exact dates not given (served 30 days); bill of credit issued or paid in his behalf to William Luckett, Jr. for £1.4.0 on 6 Apr 1767. {Ref: MSA S960 or S752, p. 170; CSOS:100}

MERRYMAN, ELIZABETH, see "John Cross," q.v.

MERRYMAN, JEMIMA, see "Henry Stevenson," q.v.

MERRYMAN, MARY, see "John Hall," q.v.

MESSER, JOHN (Maryland), pvt., Capt. Tobias Stansbury's Company Muster Roll, Baltimore Co., circa 1757-1758, exact dates not given; bill of credit issued or paid to him for £0.2.7½ in 1767, exact date not given. {Ref: MSA S960 or S752, p. 187}

MICHAEL, BALSHER or BALTSHER (Maryland), poss. Georg Balthasar Michel, b. 21 Dec 1729 in Pfalz, Germany, son of Johann Jacob Michel and Mary Philippina Stab; immigrated to Baltimore Co. by 1754 (poss. the Geo. Michel who arrived in Philadelphia on 26 Oct 1754). Baltsher, as George Michael, m. 1st to Barbary Rissard (prob. Barbara Reichard) on 2 Aug 1755 in St. George's Parish, Baltimore (now Harford) Co., and had sons John and James; m. 2nd to Ann Osborn (1748-1834) circa 1766 and had children Bennett, Jacob, Susannah, Daniel, William, Josias, George, Martha, Aquila, Elizabeth, and Henry; and, d. 14 Feb 1795, buried at Hall's Cross Roads (now Aberdeen), Harford Co. {Ref: "Baltsher Michael of Harford County, Maryland," by Jon Harlan Livezey, MGSB 39:1, pp. 96-115; Henry C. Peden, Jr.'s *Heirs and Legatees of Harford County, MD, 1774-1802*, p. 45;} Pvt., Capt. Tobias Stansbury's Company Muster Roll, Baltimore Co., circa 1757-1758 (exact dates not given); bill of credit issued or paid in his behalf to John Hall, Jr. for £1.18.0 on 30 Apr 1767 (name listed once as "Belcher Michael"); pvt., Capt. Rodgers' Militia Co., Harford Co., in 1775; signer of the Association of Freemen in 1776 (signed name as "Belser Mical"); and, subscribed to the Oath of Fidelity and Allegiance in 1778. {Ref: Henry C.

Peden, Jr.'s *Revolutionary Patriots of Harford County, MD, 1775-1783*, p. 158; MSA S960 or S752, pp. 186-187}

MICHAEL, DANIEL (Maryland), pvt., Capt. John Middaugh's Company Muster Roll, Frederick Co., circa 1757-1758, exact dates not given (served 30 days); bill of credit issued or paid in his behalf to Thomas Beatty, Jr. for £1.10.0 on 3 Apr 1767. {Ref: MSA S960 or S752, p. 172; CSOS:101}

MIDDAUGH (MIDDAGH), JOHN (Maryland), m. Mary (N), had a son John Gaites Middagh (a minor in 1778), and d. testate in 1778. {Ref: WMG 5:2, p. 87} Pvt., Capt. Tobias Stansbury's Company Muster Roll, Baltimore Co., circa 1757-1758, exact dates not given; bill of credit issued or paid to him for £0.18.9 in 1767, exact date not given. {Ref: MSA S960 or S752, p. 187} Coroner's Inquest, 1 Aug 1778: "On the 30th this instant John Middaugh, who was insane, wandered to a field owned by Obed Pierpont and was there found dead. No marks of violence appearing on his body, it was determined that he came to his death by the Act of God." {Ref: WMG 1:1, p. 36}

MIDDAUGH, JOHN (Maryland), captain, Frederick Co., circa 1757-1758, exact dates not given; bill of credit issued or paid in his behalf to Thomas Beatty, Jr. for £5 on 23 Feb 1767. {Ref: MSA S960 or S752, p. 171; CSOS:100} In November Court 1755 he was appointed one of the pressmasters of Frederick County for the ensuing year. {Ref: TWL:176, citing Frederick Co. Judgment Records}

MIDDAUGH, JOHN JR. (Maryland), pvt., Capt. John Middaugh's Company Muster Roll, Frederick Co., circa 1757-1758, exact dates not given (served 30 days); bill of credit issued or paid in his behalf to Thomas Beatty, Jr. for £1.10.0 on 23 Feb 1767. {Ref: MSA S960 or S752, p. 171; CSOS:100}

MIDDLETON, CHARITY, see "William Luckett," q.v.

MIDDLETON, LUKE (Maryland), pvt., Capt. Peregrine Brown's Company Muster Roll, Kent Co., circa 1757-1758, exact dates not given (served 15 days); bill of credit issued or paid in his behalf to Robert Buchanan on 21 Mar 1767 for £0.15.0. {Ref: MSA S960 or S752, p. 179; CSOS:110}

MIDDLETON, SAMUEL (Maryland), patriot, Annapolis, Anne Arundel Co., pay account submitted for quartering soldiers in 1757 or 1758, exact dates not given. {Ref: MHM 9:3, p. 261}

MIERS, JANE, see "Joseph Cord," q.v.

MIFLIN, JOHN (Delaware), New Castle Co., patriot who served as a Justice of the Peace, Justice of the Court of Oyer and Terminer, and Justice of the Court of Common Pleas, 1756. {Ref: GRSD 1:13}

MILES, REBECCA, see "Edward Hanson," q.v.

MILLER, ANN, see "Stephen Bordley," q.v.

MILLER, CONROD (Maryland), pvt., Capt. Jonathan Hagar's Company Muster Roll, Frederick Co., circa 1757-1758, exact dates not given (served 6 days); bill of credit issued or paid to him for £0.6.0 in 1767, exact date not given. {Ref: MSA S960 or S752, p. 174; CSOS:106}

MILLER, FRANCIS (Maryland), pvt., Capt. John White's Company Muster Roll, Frederick Co., 13 Aug 1757, exact dates not given (served 52 days); bills of credit issued or paid in his behalf to James Smith on 18 May 1767 for £0.6.0

and £2.12.0. {Ref: MSA S960 or S752, pp. 163-164; CSOS:98} Pvt., Capt. Henry Sneavely's Company Muster Roll, Frederick Co., circa 1757-1758, exact dates not given; bill of credit issued or paid in his behalf to James Smith for £0.8.0 on 18 May 1767. {Ref: MSA S960 or S752, p. 190}

MILLER, FREDERICK (Maryland), patriot and poss. soldier (rank not specified), Frederick Co., militia pay account submitted in 1758, exact date not given. {Ref: MHM 9:4, p. 368}

MILLER, ISAAC (Maryland or Pennsylvania), pvt., Capt. Culbertson's Company, was wounded in "a recent battle with the Indians" in 1756 (exact date not given) in Cumberland Co., PA, after the burning of McCord's Fort. {Ref: *MD Gazette*, 29 Apr 1756}

MILLER, JACOB (Maryland), pvt., Capt. John White's Company Muster Roll, Frederick Co., circa 1757-1758, exact dates not given (served 6 days); bill of credit issued or paid to him for £0.6.0 in 1767, exact date not given. {Ref: MSA S960 or S752, p. 165; CSOS:96}

MILLER, JACOB (Maryland), pvt., Capt. Jonathan Hagar's Company Muster Roll, Frederick Co., circa 1757-1758, exact dates not given (served 6 days); bill of credit issued or paid to him for £0.6.0 in 1767, exact date not given. {Ref: MSA S960 or S752, p. 174; CSOS:106}

MILLER, JACOB (Maryland), son of Conrod Miller; pvt., Capt. Jonathan Hagar's Company Muster Roll, Frederick Co., circa 1757-1758, exact dates not given (served 6 days); bill of credit issued or paid to him for £0.6.0 in 1767, exact date not given. {Ref: MSA S960 or S752, p. 174; CSOS:107}

MILLER, JACOB JR. (Maryland), pvt., Capt. Jonathan Hagar's Company Muster Roll, Frederick Co., circa 1757-1758, exact dates not given (served 6 days); bill of credit issued or paid to him for £0.6.0 in 1767, exact date not given. {Ref: MSA S960 or S752, p. 174; CSOS:106}

MILLER, JOHN (Delaware), b. c1740, Ulster, Ireland (laborer, age 19 in 1759); pvt., enlisted by Capt. James Armstrong for the PA Regt. on 1 May 1759. {Ref: ARDE I:26; ARPA (2nd Series) 2:585}

MILLER (MILER), JOHN (Maryland), b. c1734, prob. Charles Co. (aged about 32 in 1766 deposition); pvt., Capt. Francis Ware's Company of MD Troops, Charles Co., from 9 Oct 1757 to 18 Nov 1757 (served 40 days) when he reportedly deserted; however, payment to him was recorded in Col. Dagworthy's account book on 7 Mar 1763. {Ref: MGSB 34:1, p. 19; MHS MS.375; CSOS:88; MHS MS.375.1}

MILLER, JOHN (Maryland), pvt., Capt. Jonathan Hagar's Company Muster Roll, Frederick Co., circa 1757-1758, exact dates not given (served 6 days); bill of credit issued or paid to him for £0.6.0 in 1767, exact date not given. {Ref: MSA S960 or S752, p. 174; CSOS:106} John Miller m. Magdalena (N), had children John, Michael, Catharine, Henry, Jacob, George, Martin, Christian, Abalona, and Barbara, and d. testate by 5 May 1774. {Ref: MWG 4:2, p. 64}

MILLER, JOHN JR. (Maryland), pvt., Capt. Jonathan Hagar's Company Muster Roll, Frederick Co., circa 1757-1758, exact dates not given (served 6 days); bill

of credit issued or paid to him for £0.6.0 in 1767, exact date not given. {Ref: MSA S960 or S752, p. 174; CSOS:106}

MILLER, JOSEPH (Maryland), b. c1725, m. Mary Oursler on 11 Sep 1759, Baltimore Co., St. Thomas' P. E. Parish, and had children Ely (b. 27 Oct 1760), Rachel (b. 5 Aug 1762), George (b. 25 Sep 1764), Ruth (b. 31 Aug 1765), and Elijah (b. 7 Apr 1768). {Ref: BCF:450} Pvt., Capt. Tobias Stansbury's Company Muster Roll, Baltimore Co., circa 1757-1758, exact dates not given; bill of credit issued or paid in his behalf to James Rogers for £3.10.0 on 11 Apr 1767. {Ref: MSA S960 or S752, p. 186}

MILLER, MICHAEL (Maryland), pvt., Capt. John White's Company Muster Roll, Frederick Co., circa 1757-1758, exact dates not given (served 6 days); bill of credit issued or paid to him for £0.6.0 in 1767, exact date not given. {Ref: MSA S960 or S752, p. 165; CSOS:95}

MILLER, PETER (Maryland), pvt., Capt. Stephen Rensburg's or Rensburger's Company Muster Roll, Frederick Co., circa 1757-1758, exact dates not given (served 34 days); bill of credit issued or paid in his behalf to Stephen Rensburger for £1.14.0 on 27 Mar 1767. {Ref: MSA S960 or S752, p. 183; CSOS:112}

MILLER, PHILIP JACOB (Maryland), pvt., Capt. Jonathan Hagar's Company Muster Roll, Frederick Co., circa 1757-1758, exact dates not given (served 6 days); bill of credit issued or paid to him for £0.6.0 in 1767, exact date not given. {Ref: MSA S960 or S752, p. 174; CSOS:107}

MILLER, WILLIAM (Maryland), pvt., Capt. John Dagworthy's Company of MD Troops, Frederick Co., from 9 Oct 1757 to 12 Nov 1758 when he reportedly died; however, payment to him was recorded in Col. Dagworthy's account book on 8 Mar 1763 for work on Fort Cumberland. Another account submitted to the MD Assembly on 25 Nov 1763 indicated he was due £4.12.3 as "granted by the Act for Granting a Sum of Money as a Present to the Forces, late in the Pay and Service of this Province, and taken into his Majesty's Service by Brigadier General Forbes." {Ref: MHS MS.375; CSOS:77; MHS MS.375.1; ARMD 58:401}

MILLER, ZACHARIAH (Maryland), pvt., Capt. Jonathan Hagar's Company Muster Roll, Frederick Co., circa 1757-1758, exact dates not given (served 6 days); bill of credit issued or paid to him for £0.6.0 in 1767, exact date not given. {Ref: MSA S960 or S752, p. 174; CSOS:107}

MILLS, ANDREW (Maryland), patriot, Talbot Co., pay account submitted for quartering soldiers in 1757 or 1758, exact dates not given. {Ref: MHM 9:3, p. 262}

MILLS, LEVY (Maryland), pvt., Capt. Moses Chapline's Company Muster Roll No. 3, Frederick Co., circa 1757-1758, exact dates not given (served 6 days); bill of credit issued or paid in his behalf to Joseph Chapline for £0.6.0 on 8 Jun 1767. {Ref: MSA S960 or S752, p. 198; CSOS:115}

MILLS, ROBERT, see "James Kennan," q.v.

MILLS, WILLIAM (Maryland), pvt., Capt. Richard Pearis' Company of MD Troops, Frederick Co., circa 9 Oct 1757 to 31 May 1758; pvt., Capt. Francis Ware's Company of MD Troops, Charles Co., from 1 Jun 1758 to 30 Dec 1758 (served 213 days). {Ref: MHS MS.375.1; CSOS:89, 91} Payment to him was recorded in Col. Dagworthy's account book on 15 Jul 1762. {Ref: MHS MS.375}

MINCHEE, JACOB (Maryland), pvt., Capt. Joseph Hanson Harrison's Company Muster Roll, Charles Co., circa 1757-1758, exact dates not given; bill of credit issued or paid to him for £1.11.0 in 1767, exact date not given. {Ref: MSA S960 or S752, p. 189}

MINSKEY, NICHOLAS (Maryland), patriot, Annapolis, Anne Arundel Co., pay account submitted for quartering soldiers in 1757 or 1758, exact dates not given. {Ref: MHM 9:3, p. 260}

MIRCRIP, JOHN (Delaware), b. c1734, New Castle, DE (laborer, age 25 in 1759); pvt., enlisted by Capt. James Armstrong for the PA Regt. on 30 Apr 1759. {Ref: ARDE I:26; ARPA (2nd Series) 2:585}

MISER, WILLIAM, see "John Lippart," q.v.

MISSEL, FREDERICK (Maryland), pvt., Capt. Peter Butler's Company Muster Roll, Frederick Co., circa 1757-1758, exact dates not given (served 34 days); bill of credit or order issued in his behalf for £1.14.0 and paid to Casper Shaff on 2 Mar 1767. {Ref: MSA S960 or S752, p. 167; CSOS:97}

MITCHELL, EDWARD (Maryland), patriot and poss. soldier (rank not specified), Cecil Co., militia pay account submitted in 1758, exact date not given; pay account submitted for quartering His Majesty's Independent Co. at Charles Town in March 1758. {Ref: MHM 9:4, pp. 369-370}

MITCHELL, JOHN (Maryland), pvt., Capt. Peregrine Brown's Company Muster Roll, Kent Co., circa 1757-1758, exact dates not given (served 15 days); bill of credit issued or paid in his behalf to Robert Buchanan on 20 Feb 1767 for £0.15.0. {Ref: MSA S960 or S752, p. 180; CSOS:110}

MITCHELL, JOSEPH (Delaware), b. c1738, Down, Ireland (cooper, age 20 in 1758); pvt., enlisted 12 May 1758 "for the campaign in the lower counties" by Capt. John McClughan. {Ref: ARDE I:18; ARPA (2nd Series) 2:570}

MITCHELL (MITCHEL), WILLIAM (Delaware), ensign, Pencader Hundred, Lower Regt. of Militia, New Castle Co., 1756. {Ref: ARDE I:12; ARPA (2nd Series) 2:525; HDE I:141}

MITRE (METRE), NICHOLAS (Maryland), pvt., Capt. John Dagworthy's Company of MD Troops, Frederick Co., from 9 Oct 1757 to 1 Jun 1758 when he was discharged. {Ref: MHS MS.375.1; CSOS:77} Payment to him was recorded in Col. Dagworthy's account book on 8 Mar 1763. {Ref: MHS MS.375}

MOALE, JOHN (Maryland), b. 2 Jan 1731/2, Baltimore Co., son of John Moale and Rachel Hammond, St. Paul's P. E. Parish, m. Ellin North on 25 May 1758, had children Elizabeth (b. 8 Sep 1759), John (b. 17 May 1761), Rebecca (b. 17 Mar 1763), Richard Hatton (b. 25 Jan 1765), Thomas (b. 22 Sep 1766), William North (1768-1769), Robert (1769-1769), Robert North (b. 22 Jan 1771), Samuel (b. 4 Jan 1773), Rachel (1775-1776), Frances (1777-1781), William (1779-1779), George Washington (b. 1780, d. young), Randle Hulse (b. 26 Jan 1782), and Mary North (1783-1787), and d. 5 Jul 1798, Baltimore City; patriot, planter, merchant, land developer, gentleman, Baltimore Town commissioner by 1768, member of the MD Assembly (1768-1769), lieut. colonel (1776-1777), colonel (1777-1780), county justice (1769-1775, 1777-1789, 1791-1797), served on the Committee of Observation by 1776, Orphans Court justice (1777,

1781-1790), tax commissioner (1777-1783), and Criminal Court justice (1788-1790, 1793). {Ref: BCF:452; BDML II:600-602} Pvt., Capt. Tobias Stansbury's Company Muster Roll, Baltimore Co., circa 1757-1758, exact dates not given; bill of credit issued or paid in his behalf to James Brooks for £0.7.0 on 12 Dec 1769. {Ref: MSA S960 or S752, p. 187} See "Wamouth Shaw," q.v.

MOFFET, ROBERT (Delaware), b. c1737, New Castle, DE (laborer, age 22 in 1759); pvt., enlisted by Capt. James Armstrong for the PA Regt. on 26 Apr 1759. {Ref: ARDE I:26; ARPA (2nd Series) 2:585}

MOLATT (MOLLATT), BENJAMIN (Maryland), pvt., Capt. Jonathan Hagar's Company Muster Roll, Frederick Co., circa 1757-1758, exact dates not given (served 6 days); bill of credit issued or paid to him for £0.6.0 in 1767, exact date not given. {Ref: MSA S960 or S752, p. 174; CSOS:107}

MOLLESTON (MOLLISTON), JOHN (Delaware), prob. son of Henry Molleston and wife Jemima (d. 1760). {Ref: CDSS:148} Lieut., Lower Part of Mispillion Hundred, Militia of Kent Co. on Delaware, 1756. {Ref: ARDE I:12; ARPA (2nd Series) 2:527-529; HDE I:141}

MOLTON, WILLIAM (Maryland), pvt., Capt. William Luckett's Company Muster Roll, Frederick Co., circa 1757-1758, exact dates not given (served 30 days); bill of credit issued or paid in his behalf to William Luckett, Jr. for £1.10.0 on 6 Apr 1767. {Ref: MSA S960 or S752, p. 169; CSOS:99}

MONEY, ROBERT (Delaware), b. c1724, MD (carpenter, age 34 in 1758); pvt., recruited by Capt. Benjamin Noxon and enlisted on 28 Apr 1758. {Ref: ARDE I:19; ARPA (2nd Series) 2:485, 566}

MONG, ADAM (Maryland), sgt., Capt. Peter Butler's Company Muster Roll, Frederick Co., circa 1757-1758, exact dates not given (served 34 days); bill of credit or order issued in his behalf for £2.5.3 and paid to Casper Shaff on 2 Mar 1767. {Ref: MSA S960 or S752, p. 167; CDD:96}

MONG, GEORGE (Maryland), pvt., Capt. John White's Company Muster Roll, Frederick Co., circa 1757-1758, exact dates not given (served 6 days); bill of credit issued or paid to him for £0.6.0 in 1767, exact date not given. {Ref: MSA S960 or S752, p. 165; CSOS:95}

MONK, RENALDO, see "John Dule," q.v.

MONLOTT, CATHERINE (Maryland), patriot or poss. widow of soldier (unnamed), Frederick Co., pay account submitted in 1758, exact date not given. {Ref: MHM 9:4, p. 366}

MONROE, ALEXANDER (Maryland), sgt., Capt. Richard Pearis' Company of MD Troops, Frederick Co., circa 9 Oct 1757 to 31 May 1758; sgt., Capt. Alexander Beall's Company of MD Troops, Frederick Co., from 1 Jun 1758 to 30 Dec 1758. {Ref: MHS MS.375.1; CSOS:81, 90} Payment to him was recorded in Col. Dagworthy's account book on 11 Jul 1762. {Ref: MHS MS.375}

MONROE (MUNROE), ROBERT (Maryland), pvt., Fort Frederick, paid £2 on 29 Jun 1758 "for going express from Fort Frederick to Carlyle" for the Western Expedition against Fort Duquesne. {Ref: ARMD 55:773} Pvt., Capt. John Dagworthy's Company of MD Troops, Frederick Co., from 9 Oct 1757 to 14 Sep 1758 when he was reported as killed; however, payment to him was recorded in Col. Dagworthy's account book on 8 Mar 1763 for work on Fort Cumberland. {Ref: MHS MS.375; CSOS:77; MHS MS.375.1} Another account submitted to the MD Assembly on 25 Nov 1763 indicated he was due £4.12.3 as "granted by the Act for Granting a Sum of Money as a Present to the Forces, late in the Pay and Service of this Province, and taken into his Majesty's Service by Brigadier General Forbes." {Ref: ARMD 58:401}

MONTGOMERY, ALEXANDER (Delaware), ensign, Mill Creek Hundred, Upper Regt. of Militia, South Division, New Castle Co., 1756. {Ref: ARDE I:11; ARPA (2nd Series) 2:526; HDE I:141}

MOODEY, JOHN (Delaware), pvt., Capt. Richard McWilliams' Company of Foot, New Castle Co., enlisted 28 Dec 1757. {Ref: ARDE I:14}

MOODIE, HUGH or HENRY HUGH (Maryland), cpl., Capt. Richard Pearis' Company of MD Troops, Frederick Co., circa 9 Oct 1757 to 31 May 1758). {Ref: MHS MS.375.1; CSOS:90} Pvt., Capt. Alexander Beall's Company of MD Troops, Frederick Co., from 1 Jun 1758 to 7 Nov 1758, having transferred from Capt. Richard Pearis' Company {Ref: MHS MS.375.1; CSOS:81} Payment to him was recorded in Col. Dagworthy's account book on 12 Jul 1762. {Ref: MHS MS.375}

MOODIE, HUGH (Maryland),

MOODY, JAMES (Delaware), b. c1731, Ireland (tailor, age 27 in 1758); pvt., recruited by Capt. Benjamin Noxon and enlisted on 22 Apr 1758. {Ref: ARDE I:19; ARPA (2nd Series) 2:566}

MOOR, JOHN (Delaware), pvt., Capt. French Battell's Company of Lower County Provincials, enlisted 22 May 1758. {Ref: ARDE I:16; ARPA (2nd Series) 2:555}

MOORE, AARON (Maryland), pvt., Capt. Joseph Chapline's Company Muster Roll No. 4, Frederick Co., circa 1757-1758, exact dates not given (served 11 days); bill of credit issued or paid in his behalf to Joseph Chaplin for £0.11.0 on 5 Mar 1767. {Ref: MSA S960 or S752, p. 194; CSOS:105}

MOORE, CHARLES (Delaware), pvt., Kent Co. Militia, Capt. John Caton's Company, 25 Apr 1757 (date of muster roll). {Ref: ARDE I:14}

MOORE, DANIEL (Maryland), pvt., Capt. Moses Chapline's Company Muster Roll No. 3, Frederick Co., circa 1757-1758, exact dates not given (served 6 days); bill of credit issued or paid in his behalf to Joseph Chapline for £0.6.0 on 8 Jun 1767. {Ref: MSA S960 or S752, p. 198; CSOS:114}

MOORE, EZEKIEL (Maryland), pvt., Capt. Joseph Chapline's Company Muster Roll No. 4, Frederick Co., circa 1757-1758, exact dates not given (served 5 days); bill of credit issued or paid in his behalf to Joseph Chaplin for £0.5.0 on 5 Mar 1767. {Ref: MSA S960 or S752, p. 194; CSOS:105}

MOORE, GEORGE (Maryland), pvt., Capt. Moses Chapline's Company Muster Roll No. 3, Frederick Co., circa 1757-1758, exact dates not given (served 6 days); bill of credit issued or paid in his behalf to Joseph Chaplin for £0.6.0 on 5 Mar 1767. {Ref: MSA S960 or S752, p. 198; CSOS:115}

MOORE, GEORGE JR. (Maryland), pvt., Capt. Joseph Chapline's Company Muster Roll No. 4, Frederick Co., circa 1757-1758, exact dates not given (served 11 days); bill of credit issued or paid in his behalf to Joseph Chaplin for £0.11.0 on 5 Mar 1767. {Ref: MSA S960 or S752, p. 194; CSOS:105}

MOORE, JOHN (Delaware), b. c1734, Wales (cordwainer, age 24 in 1758); pvt., prob. in Capt. John McClughan's Company, 15 Apr 1758. {Ref: ARDE I:18; ARPA (2nd Series) 2:570}

MOORE, JOHN (Delaware), b. c1734, MD (laborer, age 24 in 1758); pvt., recruited by Capt. Benjamin Noxon and enlisted on 15 Apr 1758. {Ref: ARDE I:19; ARPA (2nd Series) 2:485, 566}

MOORE, JOHN 3RD (Maryland), pvt., Capt. Joseph Chapline's Company Muster Roll No. 4, Frederick Co., circa 1757-1758, exact dates not given (served 11 days); bill of credit issued or paid in his behalf to Joseph Chaplin for £0.11.0 on 5 Mar 1767. {Ref: MSA S960 or S752, p. 194; CSOS:105}

MOORE, JOSHUA (Delaware), pvt., Kent Co. Militia, Capt. John Caton's Company, 25 Apr 1757 (date of muster roll). {Ref: ARDE I:13}

MOORE, MICHAEL (Maryland), Baltimore Co., m. Keziah Shipton on 20 Apr 1758, St. John's P. E. Parish. {Ref: BCF:455} Pvt., Capt. Tobias Stansbury's Company Muster Roll, Baltimore Co., circa 1757-1758, exact dates not given; bill of credit issued or paid to him for £1.19.0 in 1767, exact date not given. {Ref: MSA S960 or S752, p. 187}

MOORE, RUTH, see "George Beall," q.v.

MOORE, SIMON or SIMION (Maryland), pvt., Capt. Joseph Chapline's Company Muster Roll No. 4, Frederick Co., circa 1757-1758, exact dates not given (served 11 days); bill of credit issued or paid in his behalf to Joseph Chaplin for £0.11.0 on 5 Mar 1767. {Ref: MSA S960 or S752, p. 194; CSOS:105}

MOORE, THOMAS (Delaware), pvt., Kent Co. Militia, Capt. John Caton's Company, 25 Apr 1757 (date of muster roll). {Ref: ARDE I:13}

MOORE, WILLIAM (Delaware), pvt., Kent Co. Militia, Capt. John Caton's Company, 25 Apr 1757 (date of muster roll). {Ref: ARDE I:14}

MOORE, WILLIAM (Delaware), b. c1742, Chester, PA (hatter, age 17 in 1759); pvt., enlisted by Capt. James Armstrong for the PA Regt. on 9 May 1759. {Ref: ARDE I:26; ARPA (2nd Series) 2:585}

MOORE, ZEBULON (Maryland), pvt., Capt. Joseph Chapline's Company Muster Roll No. 1, Frederick Co., circa 1757-1758, exact dates not given (served 16 days); bill of credit issued or paid in his behalf to Joseph Chaplin for £0.16.0 on 5 Mar 1767. {Ref: MSA S960 or S752, p. 191; CSOS:102}

MORAN, EDMUND (Maryland), ensign in Capt. William McClellan's Company of MD Volunteers, Frederick Co., circa 1763-1764; on muster roll dated 15 Nov 1764 at Camp at the Forks of Muskingham. {Ref: ARMD 32:99}

MORAN, JOHN (Maryland), ensign in Capt. William McClellan's Company of MD Volunteers, Frederick Co., circa 1763-1764; on muster roll dated 15 Nov 1764 at Camp at the Forks of Muskingham. {Ref: ARMD 32:99}

MORAN, JOHN (Delaware), pvt., Capt. Henry Vanbibber's Company of the Lower Counties on Delaware Troops at New Castle, enlisted on 15 May 1759. {Ref: ARDE I:26; ARPA (2nd Series) 2:594}

MOREHEAD, MATTHEW (Delaware), b. c1730, Ireland (weaver, age 28 in 1758); pvt., recruited by Capt. Benjamin Noxon and enlisted on 29 May 1758. {Ref: ARDE I:19; ARPA (2nd Series) 2:566}

MOREN (MORAN), JOHN (Delaware), b. c1737, DE (laborer, age 21 in 1758); pvt., recruited by Capt. Benjamin Noxon and enlisted on 26 Apr 1758. {Ref: ARDE I:19; ARPA (2nd Series) 2:566}

MORGAN, BENNETT (Maryland), pvt., Capt. Henry Casson's Company Muster Roll, Queen Anne's Co., circa 1757-1758, exact dates not given (served 27 days); bill of credit issued or paid in his behalf to Capt. Casson on 27 Mar 1767 for £1.7.0. {Ref: MSA S960 or S752, p. 178; CSOS:109}

MORGAN, JANE (Maryland), patriot, Frederick Co.; account book of Col. Dagworthy indicated the following under the name of John Hodges: "26 Feb 1763, paid David Ross £0.8.6 for the use of Jane Morgan." {Ref: MHS MS.375}

MORGAN, RICHARD (Maryland), mariner (age 22 when deposed on 14 Mar 1761) on the brigantine *Duke of Marlborough*, commanded by David Carcaud, which vessel was commissioned by the Council of Maryland as a Flag of Truce on 15 Oct 1760 to carry French prisoners of war to Port St. Louis on the island of Hispaniola. {Ref: ARMD 31:460-462}

MORRIS, ELIJAH (Delaware), lieut., militia, Upper Part of Mispillion Hundred, Kent Co. on Delaware, 1756; elected to the Committee of Correspondence in Kent Co. on 14 Aug 1775. {Ref: ARDE I:12; ARPA (2nd Series) 2:527-529; HDE I:141; RPDE:195}

MORRIS, THOMAS (Delaware), pvt., Kent Co. Militia, Capt. John Caton's Company, 25 Apr 1757 (date of muster roll). {Ref: ARDE I:14}

MORRISS, WILLIAM (Maryland), pvt., Capt. Joseph Hanson Harrison's Company Muster Roll, Charles Co., circa 1757-1758, exact dates not given; bill of credit issued or paid in his behalf to John Hanson, Jr. for £2.9.0 on 21 Feb 1767. {Ref: MSA S960 or S752, p. 189}

MORTON, PETER (Delaware), pvt., Capt. Richard McWilliams' Company of Foot, New Castle Co., enlisted 28 Dec 1757. {Ref: ARDE I:15}

MOSELEY (MOZELEY), CHARLES (Maryland), pvt., Capt. Francis Ware's Company of MD Troops, Charles Co., circa 9 Oct 1757 to 30 Dec 1758. {Ref: MHS MS.375.1; CSOS:88} Payment to him was recorded in Col. Dagworthy's account book on 23 Feb 1763. {Ref: MHS MS.375}

MOUNSEY, NATHANIEL (Delaware), pvt., Kent Co. Militia, Capt. John Caton's Company, 25 Apr 1757 (date of muster roll). {Ref: ARDE I:14}

MOUNSEY, THOMAS (Delaware), pvt., Kent Co. Militia, Capt. John Caton's Company, 25 Apr 1757 (date of muster roll). {Ref: ARDE I:13}

MOUNTS, PROVIDENCE (Maryland), pvt., Capt. Joseph Chapline's Company Muster Roll No. 4, Frederick Co., circa 1757-1758, exact dates not given (served 6 days); bill of credit issued or paid to him for £0.6.0 in 1767, exact date not given. {Ref: MSA S960 or S752, p. 194; CSOS:105}

MUDD, GEORGE (Maryland), pvt., Capt. Joseph Hanson Harrison's Company Muster Roll, Charles Co., circa 1757-1758, exact dates not given; bill of credit issued or paid in his behalf to Capt. Joseph Hanson Harrison for £1.4.0 on 9 Nov 1770. {Ref: MSA S960 or S752, p. 189}

MUDD, GEORGE (Maryland), pvt., Capt. Alexander Beall's Company of MD Troops, Frederick Co., from 9 Oct 1757 to 8 May 1758. {Ref: MHS MS.375.1;

CSOS:81} Payment to him was recorded in Col. Dagworthy's account book on 11 Jul 1762. {Ref: MHS MS.375}

MULLAN, DANIEL (Delaware), b. c1740, Dunluce, Ireland (miller, age 18 in 1758); pvt., enlisted 29 Apr 1758 "for the campaign in the lower counties" by Capt. John McClughan. {Ref: ARDE I:18; ARPA (2nd Series) 2:570}

MULLIKIN, BASIL (Maryland), pvt., Capt. Joshua Beall's Company Muster Roll, Prince George's Co., circa 1757-1758, exact dates not given; bill of credit issued or paid to him for £2.1.0 on 4 Mar 1767. {Ref: MSA S960 or S752, p. 184}

MULLIKIN, MARY, see "William Bowie," q.v.

MULLIKIN, THOMAS JR. (Maryland), pvt., Capt. Joshua Beall's Company Muster Roll, Prince George's Co., circa 1757-1758, exact dates not given; bill of credit issued or paid to him for £2.1.0 in 1767, exact date not given. {Ref: MSA S960 or S752, p. 185}

MUNCY, GERTRUDE, see "Armwell Lockwood," q.v.

MUNDAY, JAMES (Maryland), b. c1740, MD (age about 16 in 1756); pvt., Capt. Robert McKenzie's Company of VA Militia, enlisted in 1756 in Baltimore. {Ref: MSR I:38} James Munday, b. 2 Mar 1738/9, orphan son of Henry Munday and Susanna Temple, was bound out to Jacob Bull (admin. of Henry Munday, dec.) in June 1740. {Ref: BCF:461}

MUNFORD, WILLIAM (Maryland), pvt., Capt. Moses Chapline's Company Muster Roll No. 3, Frederick Co., circa 1757-1758, exact dates not given (served 6 days); bill of credit issued or paid in his behalf to Joseph Chaplin for £0.6.0 on 24 Apr 1767. {Ref: MSA S960 or S752, p. 198; CSOS:115}

MUNROW, DANIEL (Maryland), pvt., Capt. Joseph Hanson Harrison's Company Muster Roll, Charles Co., circa 1757-1758, exact dates not given; bill of credit issued or paid in his behalf to John Hanson, Jr. for £2.9.0 on 21 Feb 1767. {Ref: MSA S960 or S752, p. 189}

MURDOCK, CATHERINE, see "Joseph Sim (Simm)," q.v.

MURDOCK, WILLIAM (Maryland), pvt., Capt. John Dagworthy's Company of MD Troops, Frederick Co., from 9 Oct 1757 to 8 Nov 1758 when he was promoted to cpl.; prob. served until 26 Apr 1759, but exact date not given. {Ref: MHS MS.375.1; CSOS:77} Payment to him was recorded in Col. Dagworthy's account book on 8 Mar 1763 for work on Fort Cumberland. {Ref: MHS MS.375} William Murdock was prob. the son of Rev. George Murdock (d. 1761) and Eleanor Sprigg, of Prince George's Parish. {Ref: MDG II:247}

MURPHEE (MURPHEW), WILLIAM (Maryland), pvt., Capt. John Dagworthy's Company of MD Troops, Frederick Co., from 2 Dec 1757 to 26 Apr 1759 (served 511 days). {Ref: MHS MS.375.1; CSOS:77} Payment to him was recorded in Col. Dagworthy's account book on 11 Jul 1762 for work on Fort Cumberland. {Ref: MHS MS.375}

MURPHEW (MURPHIE), WILLIAM (Maryland), cpl., Capt. Francis Ware's Company of MD Troops, Charles Co., from 9 Oct 1757 to 12 Oct 1758 (served 368 days) when he was reported as killed; however, payment to him was recorded in Col. Dagworthy's account book on 13 Jul 1762. {Ref: MHS MS.375; CSOS:88; MHS MS.375.1}

MURPHEY, THOMAS (Delaware), pvt., Kent Co. Militia, Capt. John Caton's Company, 25 Apr 1757 (date of muster roll). {Ref: ARDE I:13}

MURPHY, ---- (Maryland), cpl., Frederick Co., paid £0.15.0 on 7 Nov 1758 "for going to Winchester from Fort Frederick with a packet from the General" during the Western Expedition against Fort Duquesne. {Ref: ARMD 55:776}

MURPHY, BRYAN (Delaware), b. c1743, Tyrone, Ireland (laborer, age 16 in 1759); pvt., enlisted by Capt. James Armstrong for the PA Regt. on 1 May 1759. {Ref: ARDE I:26; ARPA (2nd Series) 2:585}

MURPHY, JAMES (Delaware), b. c1737, Ireland (schoolmaster, age 21 in 1758); pvt., recruited by Capt. Benjamin Noxon and enlisted on 2 May 1758. {Ref: ARDE I:19; ARPA (2nd Series) 2:566}

MURRAIN, JOHN (Delaware), b. c1730, Dublin, Ireland (laborer, age 28 in 1758); pvt., enlisted 7 May 1758 "for the campaign in the lower counties" by Capt. John McClughan. {Ref: ARDE I:18; ARPA (2nd Series) 2:570}

MURRAY, JOHN (Maryland), pvt., Capt. William McClellan's Company of MD Volunteers, Frederick Co., circa 1763-1764; reported as deserted on muster roll dated 15 Nov 1764 at Camp at the Forks of Muskingham. {Ref: ARMD 32:99}

MURRAY, NATHANIEL (Maryland), b. c1735, m. Rachel Bailey on 24 Jan 1760, Baltimore Co., St. John's P. E. Parish. {Ref: BCF:464} Pvt., Capt. Tobias Stansbury's Company Muster Roll, Baltimore Co., circa 1757-1758, exact dates not given; bill of credit issued or paid to him for £1.18.0 in 1767, exact date not given. {Ref: MSA S960 or S752, p. 187}

MURRAY, ZIPPORAH, see "Christopher Gist," q.v.

MUSGROVE, BENJAMIN (Maryland), cpl., Capt. Alexander Beall's Company of MD Troops, Frederick Co., circa 9 Oct 1757 (exact date not given); transferred to Capt. Francis Ware's Company, Charles Co., was promoted to sgt. on 4 Nov 1757 and was reported as killed on 12 Oct 1758; however, payment to him was recorded in Col. Dagworthy's account book on 22 Feb 1763. {Ref: MHS MS.375; CSOS:88; MHS MS.375.1}

MUSGROVE, BENJAMIN JR. (Maryland), pvt., Capt. Joshua Beall's Company Muster Roll, Prince George's Co., circa 1757-1758, exact dates not given; bill of credit issued or paid in his behalf to his admin. (unnamed) for £1.8.0 on 25 Feb 1767. {Ref: MSA S960 or S752, p. 184}

MYER, CASPER (Maryland), m. Barbara (N), had a son Henry and other children (who were mentioned, but not named in his will), and d. testate by 12 Jul 1773. {Ref: WMG 4:1, p. 10} Pvt., Capt. Stephen Rensburg's or Rensburger's Company Muster Roll, Frederick Co., circa 1757-1758, exact dates not given (served 42 days); bill of credit issued or paid in his behalf to Casper Shaff for £2.2.0 on 2 Mar 1767; name listed once as "Casper Mire." {Ref: MSA S960 or S752, p. 182; CSOS:112}

MYER, GEORGE, see "Daniel Sehr," q.v.

MYER (MYRE), SIMON (Maryland), pvt., Capt. Jonathan Hagar's Company Muster Roll, Frederick Co., circa 1757-1758, exact dates not given (served 6 days); bill of credit issued or paid in his behalf to Jonathan Hagar for £0.6.0 on 10 Oct 1767. {Ref: MSA S960 or S752, p. 174; CSOS:107}

MYERS, HENRY (Maryland), pvt., Capt. Tobias Stansbury's Company Muster Roll, Baltimore Co., circa 1757-1758, exact dates not given; bill of credit issued or paid to him for £1.18.0 in 1767, exact date not given. {Ref: MSA S960 or S752, p. 187}

MYERS (MYRES), JAMES (Maryland), pvt., Capt. John Wolgomatt's Company of MD Volunteers, Frederick Co., circa 1763-1764; reported on muster roll dated 15 Nov 1764 at Camp at the Forks of Muskingham as "left sick at Fort Pitt." {Ref: ARMD 32:99}

MYERS, JESSE (Maryland), pvt., Capt. Joshua Beall's Company Muster Roll, Prince George's Co., circa 1757-1758, exact dates not given; bill of credit issued or paid to him for £1.12.0 in 1767, exact date not given. {Ref: MSA S960 or S752, p. 185}

MYERS (MYRES), VALENTINE (Maryland), patriot and poss. soldier (rank not specified), Frederick Co., militia pay account submitted in 1758, exact date not given. {Ref: MHM 9:4, p. 366} See "Philip Cobbin," q.v.

NARRIER, DANIEL (Delaware), b. c1741, Tyrone, Ireland (laborer, age 18 in 1759); pvt., enlisted by Capt. James Armstrong for the PA Regt. on 3 May 1759. {Ref: ARDE I:26; ARPA (2nd Series) 2:585}

NASH, THOMAS (Maryland), pvt., Capt. John Dagworthy's Company of MD Troops, Frederick Co., circa 9 Oct 1757 to 26 Apr 1759. {Ref: MHS MS.375.1; CSOS:77} Payment to him was recorded in Col. Dagworthy's account book on 15 Jul 1762. {Ref: MHS MS.375}

NAWOOD, DANIEL (Delaware), b. c1739, Angola Hundred, DE (farmer, age 19 in 1758); pvt., enlisted 19 Apr 1758 "for the campaign in the lower counties" by Capt. John McClughan. {Ref: ARDE I:18; ARPA (2nd Series) 2:570}

NAWOOD, NATHAN (Delaware), b. c1735, Indian River, DE (planter, age 23 in 1758); pvt., enlisted 19 Apr 1758 "for the campaign in the lower counties" by Capt. John McClughan. {Ref: ARDE I:18; ARPA (2nd Series) 2:570}

NAYLOR, BENJAMIN (Maryland), sgt., Capt. John Dagworthy's Company of MD Troops, Frederick Co., from 1 Jun 1758 (transferred from Capt Richard Pearis' Company) until 12 Jun 1758 when he reportedly died (having served 10 days); however, payment to him was recorded in Col. Dagworthy's account book on 14 Jul 1762. {Ref: MHS MS.375; CSOS:77; MHS MS.375.1}

NAYLOR (NAYLER), GEORGE (Maryland), cpl., Capt. Francis Ware's Company of MD Troops, Charles Co., from 9 Oct 1757 to 30 Dec 1758 (promoted 3 Sep 1758); payment to him was recorded in Col. Dagworthy's account book on 12 Jul 1762. {Ref: MHS MS.375.1; CSOS:89; MHS MS.375}

NAYLOR (NAYLER), JOSHUA (Maryland), sgt., Capt. Joshua Beall's Company of MD Troops, Prince George's Co. (transferred from Capt. Richard Pearis' Company) from 1 Jun 1758 to 30 Dec 1758; payment to him was recorded in Col. Dagworthy's account book on 12 Jul 1762 for work on Fort Cumberland. {Ref: MHS MS.375.1; CSOS:85; MHS MS.375}

NEAL, JOHN (Delaware), pvt., New Castle Co. (age 20 in 1758; pvt., enlisted by Capt. John Singleton in May 1758. {Ref: ARDE I:27}

NEALE, EDWARD (Maryland), patriot and poss. soldier (rank not specified), Queen Anne's Co., d. by 1758; militia pay account submitted by exec. (unnamed) in 1758, exact date not given. {Ref: MHM 9:4, p. 367}

NEALE (NEAL), JAMES (Maryland), pvt., Capt. Alexander Beall's Company of MD Troops, Frederick Co., 9 Oct 1757 to 30 Dec 1758; payment to him was recorded in Col. Dagworthy's account book on 7 Mar 1763 for work on Fort Cumberland. {Ref: MHS MS.375.1; CSOS:81; MHS MS.375}

NEALL (NEAL), WILLIAM (Maryland), pvt., Capt. John Dagworthy's Company of MD Troops, Frederick Co., from 9 Oct 1757 to 8 Apr 1758 when he was discharged; payment to him was recorded in Col. Dagworthy's account book on 8 Mar 1763. {Ref: MHS MS.375.1; CSOS:77; MHS MS.375}

NEBB (NEVO?), JOHN (Maryland), pvt., Capt. Alexander Beall's Company of MD Troops, Frederick Co., from 9 Oct 1757 to 4 Jul 1758 when he reportedly deserted; however, payment to him was recorded in Col. Dagworthy's account book on 7 Mar 1763. {Ref: MHS MS.375; MHS MS.375.1}

NEED, MATTHIAS (Maryland), pvt., Capt. Jonathan Hagar's Company Muster Roll, Frederick Co., circa 1757-1758, exact dates not given (served 6 days); bill of credit issued or paid to him for £0.6.0 in 1767, exact date not given. {Ref: MSA S960 or S752, p. 174; CSOS:106}

NEEDLES, THOMAS (Delaware), m. Sarah (N), had children William, Mary, Nancy, and Sarah, and d. testate by 10 Dec 1791. {Ref: CDSS:155} Pvt., Kent Co. Militia, Capt. John Caton's Company, 25 Apr 1757 (date of muster roll). {Ref: ARDE I:14}

NEFF, JACOB (Maryland), patriot and poss. soldier (rank not specified), Frederick Co., militia pay account submitted in 1758, exact date not given. {Ref: MHM 9:4, p. 368}

NEIGHBOUR (NEIGHBOURS), NATHAN (Maryland), pvt., Capt. William Luckett's Company Muster Roll, Frederick Co., circa 1757-1758, exact dates not given (served 30 days); bill of credit issued or paid in his behalf to William Luckett, Jr. for £1.10.0 on 6 Apr 1767. {Ref: MSA S960 or S752, p. 169; CSOS:99}

NEILSON, WILLIAM (Maryland), pvt., Capt. Francis Ware's Company of MD Troops, Charles Co., circa 9 Oct 1757 to 30 Dec 1758. {Ref: MHS MS.375.1; CSOS:89} Payment to him was recorded in Col. Dagworthy's account book on 12 Jul 1762. {Ref: MHS MS.375}

NELSON (NEILSON), AQUILA (Maryland), b. c1731, Baltimore Co., son of John Nelson and Frances Rhodes, m. Sarah Chancey on 20 Jan 1757, and had a son John (b. 19 Nov 1757), St. George's P. E. Parish. {Ref: BCF:466} Pvt., Capt. Tobias Stansbury's Company Muster Roll, Baltimore Co., circa 1757-1758, exact dates not given; bill of credit issued or paid in his behalf to Thomas Cockey Deye for £3.16.0 on 13 Jun 1768. {Ref: MSA S960 or S752, p. 187}

NELSON, ARTHUR (Maryland), clerk, Capt. Elias Delashmutt's Company Muster Roll, Frederick Co., circa 1757-1758, exact dates not given (served 30 days); bill of credit issued or paid in his behalf to Elias Delashmut, Jr. on 16 Mar 1767 for £1.10.0. {Ref: MSA S960 or S752, p. 162; CSOS:94}

NELSON, ELIZABETH, see "Elias Delashmut," q.v.

NELSON, JOHN, see "Aquila Nelson," q.v.

NELSON, SARAH, see "William Luckett, Jr.," q.v

NESBIT, WILLIAM (Delaware), pvt., Capt. Richard McWilliams' Company of Foot, New Castle Co., enlisted 28 Dec 1757. {Ref: ARDE I:15}

NESBITT, CHARLES (Maryland), pvt., Capt. William Luckett's Company Muster Roll, Frederick Co., circa 1757-1758, exact dates not given (served 30 days); bill of credit issued or paid in his behalf to William Luckett, Jr. for £1.10.0 on 6 Apr 1767. {Ref: MSA S960 or S752, p. 170; CSOS:99}

NETTIWELL, JOHN (Maryland), ensign, Frederick Town, by 1757; a letter addressed to him was left at the post office in Annapolis in 1757. {Ref: *MD Gazette*, 28 Apr 1757}

NEARN (NAIRN, NEURN), BENJAMIN (Maryland), b. 22 Dec 1732, Baltimore Co., son of Robert Nearn and Ann Tarman, St. John's P. E. Parish, m. Elizabeth Keys on 11 Feb 1752. {Ref: BCF:465} Cpl., Capt. Thomas Norris' Company, Frederick Co., circa 1757-1758, exact dates not given (served 30 days); bill of credit issued or paid in his behalf to Michael McGuire on 27 Mar 1767 for £2. {Ref: MSA S960 or S752, p. 176; CSOS:107}

NEVILL, JAMES (Maryland), b. 1735 at Turkey Point Neck in Cecil Co., age 21 in 1756; cpl., Royal American Regt., was reported as deserted by Lieut. McBean at Annapolis in 1756. {Ref: *MD Gazette*, 16 Dec 1756}

NEVO, JOHN, see "John Nebb," q.v.

NEWBOLD, JOHN (Delaware), b. c1737, MD (carpenter, age 22 in 1759); sgt., enlisted in Capt. John Wright's Company and mustered on 11 May 1759. {Ref: ARDE I:25; ARPA (2nd Series) 2:508, 592}

NEWBOLD, JOHN (Delaware), b. c1736, Somerset, MD (farmer, age 22 in 1758); pvt., enlisted 5 May 1758 "for the campaign in the lower counties" by Capt. John McClughan (muster roll dated 17 May 1758). {Ref: ARDE I:18; ARPA (2nd Series) 2:489, 570}

NEWBOLD, JOHN (Delaware), captain, Southern District of Lewes and Rehoboth Hundred, Militia Regt. of Sussex Co., 1756-1758. {Ref: ARDE I:13, 15; ARPA (2nd Series) 2:529, 579; HDE I:141}

NEWCOMB, BAPTIST (Delaware), b. c1736, son of Thomas Newcomb and Hester Smith (d. 1757), m. Comfort (N) by 1763. {Ref: CFD 3:134} Pvt., enlisted in Capt. John Wright's Company and mustered on 11 May 1759 (b. Sussex Co.; age 23 in 1759). {Ref: ARDE I:25; ARPA (2nd Series) 2:592}

NEWCOMB, JOHN, see "John Newcomer," q.v.

NEWCOMB, THOMAS (Delaware), b. c1740, son of Thomas Newcomb and Hester Smith (d. 1757), m. Elizabeth (N) by 1763. {Ref: CFD 3:134} Pvt., enlisted in Capt. John Wright's Company and mustered on 11 May 1759 (b. Sussex, DE; age 19 in 1759). {Ref: ARDE I:25; ARPA (2nd Series) 2:592}

NEWCOMER, JOHN (Maryland), pvt., Capt. Jonathan Hagar's Company Muster Roll, Frederick Co., circa 1757-1758, exact dates not given (served 6 days); bill of credit issued or paid to him for £0.6.0 in 1767, exact date not given; name listed once as "John Newcomb." {Ref: MSA S960 or S752, p. 174; CSOS:107}

NEWMAN, NATHANIEL (Delaware), pvt., Capt. French Battell's Company of Lower County Provincials, enlisted 28 May 1758. {Ref: ARDE I:16; ARPA (2nd Series) 2:555}

NEWTON, JOHN (Delaware), b. c1740, MD (age 19 in 1759); pvt., enlisted in Capt. John Wright's Company and mustered on 11 May 1759. {Ref: ARDE I:25; ARPA (2nd Series) 2:508, 592}

NICHOLAS, JOHN (Maryland), pvt., Capt. Moses Chapline's Company Muster Roll No. 1, Frederick Co., circa 1757-1758, exact dates not given (served 55 days); bill of credit issued or paid in his behalf to Joseph Chaplin for £2.15.0 on 5 Mar 1767. {Ref: MSA S960 or S752, p. 196; CSOS:113}

NICHOLAS, MATTHIAS (Maryland), pvt., Capt. Joseph Chapline's Company Muster Roll No. 3, Frederick Co., circa 1757-1758, exact dates not given (served 9 days); lieut., Capt. John Wolgomatt's Company of MD Volunteers, Frederick Co., circa 1763-1764; on muster roll dated 15 Nov 1764 at Camp at the Forks of Muskingham. {Ref: CSOS:104; ARMD 32:99}

NICHOLLS, ---- (Maryland), sea captain by 1756, was in command of a schooner (name not given) when it was captured by the French. {Ref: *MD Gazette*, 2 Dec 1756}

NICHOLS (NICHOLLS), AMOS (Maryland), pvt., Capt. Joseph Chapline's Company Muster Roll No. 1, Frederick Co., circa 1757-1758, exact dates not given (served 40 days); bill of credit issued or paid in his behalf to Joseph Chaplin for £2 on 5 Mar 1767. {Ref: MSA S960 or S752, p. 191; CSOS:103} Pvt., Capt. Joseph Chapline's Company Muster Rolls No. 2 and 3, Frederick Co., circa 1757-1758, exact dates not given (served 8 days); bill of credit issued or paid in his behalf to Joseph Chaplin for £0.8.0 on 5 Mar 1767. {Ref: MSA S960 or S752, p. 193; CSOS:104}

NICHOL (NICHOLLS), HENRY (Maryland), pvt., Capt. Francis Ware's Company of MD Troops, Charles Co., from 9 Oct 1757 to 5 Nov 1757 (served 28 days) when he reportedly died; however, payment to him was recorded in Col. Dagworthy's account book on 7 Mar 1763. {Ref: MHS MS.375; CSOS:89; MHS MS.375.1}

NICHOLS, JAMES (Maryland), cpl., Capt. Jonathan Hagar's Company Muster Roll, Frederick Co., circa 1757-1758, exact dates not given (served 6 days); bill of credit issued or paid to him for £0.8.0 in 1767, exact date not given. {Ref: MSA S960 or S752, p. 174; CSOS:106}

NICHOLS (NICHOLLS), JOHN (Maryland), pvt., Capt. Joseph Chapline's Company Muster Rolls No. 2 and 3, Frederick Co., circa 1757-1758, exact dates not given (served 7 days); bill of credit issued or paid in his behalf to Joseph Chaplin for £0.7.0 on 5 Mar 1767. {Ref: MSA S960 or S752, p. 193} Sgt., Capt. Moses Chapline's Company Muster Roll No. 3, Frederick Co., circa 1757-1758, exact dates not given (served 6 days); bill of credit issued or paid in his behalf to Joseph Chaplin for £0.8.0 on 5 Mar 1767. {Ref: MSA S960 or S752, pp. 198-199; CSOS:115}

NICHOLS (NICHOLLS), MATTHIAS (Maryland), pvt., Capt. Moses Chapline's Company Muster Roll No. 1, Frederick Co., circa 1757-1758, exact dates not given (served 55 days); bill of credit issued or paid in his behalf to Joseph

Chaplin for £2.15.0 on 5 Mar 1767; name transcribed once as "Mathias Nicholas." {Ref: MSA S960 or S752, p. 196; CSOS:113} Pvt., Capt. Joseph Chapline's Company Muster Roll No. 1, Frederick Co., circa 1757-1758, exact dates not given (served 4 days); bill of credit i ssued or paid in his behalf to Joseph Chaplin for £0.4.0 on 5 Mar 1767. {Ref: MSA S960 or S752, p. 191; CSOS:103} Pvt., Capt. Joseph Chapline's Company Muster Rolls No. 2 and 3, Frederick Co., circa 1757-1758, exact dates not given; bill of credit issued or paid in his behalf to Joseph Chaplin for £0.17.0 on 25 Apr 1767. {Ref: MSA S960 or S752, p. 193} Pvt., Capt. Jonathan Hagar's Company Muster Roll, Frederick Co., circa 1757-1758, exact dates not given (served 6 days); bill of credit issued or paid in his behalf to Joseph Chaplin for £0.6.0 on 24 Apr 1767. {Ref: MSA S960 or S752, pp. 173-174; CSOS:107}

NICHOLSON, JOHN (Maryland), pvt., Capt. Elias Delashmutt's Company Muster Roll, Frederick Co., circa 1757-1758, exact dates not given (served 30 days); bill of credit issued or paid in his behalf to Elias Delashmut, Jr. on 16 Mar 1767 for £1.10.0; name listed once as "John Nichols or Nicholson." {Ref: MSA S960 or S752, p. 162; CSOS:94}

NICHOLSON, JOSEPH (Maryland), b. 1709, Anne Arrundel Co., son of William and Elizabeth Nicholson, m. 1st to Hannah Smith and 2nd to Mary Hopper by 1772, had children Joseph Jr., Henrietta, James, and Elizabeth, and d. testate by 5 Feb 1787 in Chestertown. Joseph Nicholson, Sr., a merchant, served as high sheriff of Kent Co., as deputy commissary, and was a colonel of the militia for many years (dates not given). Joseph Nicholson, Jr., a lawyer, m. Elizabeth Hopper and served as county justice, sheriff, member of the convention of 1775, and member of the MD Senate and Council of Safety during the Revolutionary War. {Ref: SLMH II:187; BDML II:614; Kent Co. Wills 7:173}

NICHOLSON, NATHANIEL, see "Robert McGaw," q.v.

NICHOLSON, WILLIAM, see "Joseph Nicholson" and "Richard Dorsey," q.v.

NICKELL, JOHN (Delaware), b. c1728, Bedony, Ireland (laborer, age 30 in 1758); pvt., enlisted 26 Apr 1758 "for the campaign in the lower counties" by Capt. John McClughan. {Ref: ARDE I:18; ARPA (2nd Series) 2:570}

NIGHT, GEORGE (Maryland), pvt., Capt. Francis Ware's Company of MD Troops, Charles Co., circa 9 Oct 1757 to 30 Dec 1758. {Ref: MHS MS.375.1; CSOS:89} Payment to him was recorded in Col. Dagworthy's account book on 22 Feb 1763. {Ref: MHS MS.375}

NIGHT, SAMUEL (Maryland), pvt., Capt. John Dagworthy's Company of MD Troops, Frederick Co., from 9 Oct 1757 to 12 Jan 1759 (served 460 days) when he reportedly deserted; however, payment to him was recorded in Col. Dagworthy's a ccount b ook o n 1 8 Ju l 1 762. {Ref: MHS MS.375; CSOS:77; MHS MS.375.1}

NOBLE, JAMES (Maryland), pvt., Capt. Peregrine Brown's Company, Kent Co., on 19 Feb 1758, by which time he had enlisted, but was unable to march due to health problems. {Ref: ARMD 31:283}

NOBLE, MARK (Maryland), pvt., Capt. Peregrine Brown's Company Muster Roll, Kent Co., circa 1757-1758, exact dates not given (serve 15 days); bill of credit issued or paid in his behalf to Robert Buchanan on 20 Feb 1767 for £0.15.0. {Ref: MSA S960 or S752, p. 180; CSOS:110}

NOBLE, WILLIAM (Delaware), b. c1727, England (laborer, age 31 in 1758); pvt., recruited by Capt. Benjamin Noxon and enlisted on 19 Apr 1758. {Ref: ARDE I:19; ARPA (2nd Series) 2:566}

NOLEMAN, RICHARD (Delaware), b. c1738, MD (carpenter, age 20 in 1758); pvt., recruited by Capt. Benjamin Noxon and enlisted on 29 Apr 1758. {Ref: ARDE I:19; ARPA (2nd Series) 2:485, 566}

NORFOLK, JOHN (Maryland), cpl., Calvert Co., Capt. Edward Gantt's Militia Co., Lyon's Creek Hundred circa 1756-1757 (exact dates not given). {Ref: HCC:120}

NORRIS, GEORGE (Maryland), pvt., Capt. Peregrine Brown's Company, Kent Co., on 19 Feb 1758, by which time he had enlisted, but was unable to march due to health problems. {Ref: ARMD 31:283}

NORRIS (NORRISS), JOHN (Maryland), pvt., Capt. Francis Ware's Company of MD Troops, Charles Co., circa 9 Oct 1757 to 30 Dec 1758. {Ref: MHS MS.375.1; CSOS:89} Payment to him was recorded in Col. Dagworthy's account book on 26 Feb 1763. {Ref: MHS MS.375}

NORRIS, JOSEPH (Maryland), pvt., Capt. Joseph Chapline's Company Muster Roll No. 4, Frederick Co., circa 1757-1758, exact dates not given (served 7 days); bill of credit issued or paid in his behalf to Joseph Chaplin for £0.7.0 on 5 Mar 1767. {Ref: MSA S960 or S752, p. 194; CSOS:105}

NORRIS, NATHANIEL (Maryland), b. 16 Dec 1741, St. John's P. E. Parish, Baltimore Co., second son of Thomas Norris and Avarilla Scott who m. 10 Oct 1738 and removed to Frederick Co. circa 1746; Nathaniel d. intestate in 1813. {Ref: MGSB 38:1, pp. 45-49} Cpl., Capt. Thomas Norris' Company, Frederick Co., circa 1757-1758, exact dates not given (served 30 days); bill of credit issued or paid in his behalf to William Norris on 20 May 1767 for £2. {Ref: MSA S960 or S752, pp. 176-177; CSOS:107}

NORRIS, THOMAS (Maryland), captain, Frederick Co., circa 1757-1758, exact dates not given; bill of credit issued or paid in his behalf to William Norris his exec. on 20 May 1767 for £5. {Ref: MSA S960 or S752, pp. 176-177; CSOS:107} *Identification problem:* There were two men with this name who could have served in the war: (1) Thomas Norris m. Avarilla Scott on 10 Oct 1738 in St. John's P. E. Parish, Baltimore Co., removed to Frederick Co. (now Carroll Co.) circa 1746, had children William (1739-1767), Nathaniel (1741-1813), Mary (b. 1743), and John (1746-1811), served as a county justice, 1758-1763, and d. intestate in 1763. {Ref: MGSB 38:1, pp. 45-49}; and, (2) Thomas Norris m. Sarah (N), had children Joseph and Aberilla, and d. testate by 24 Sep 1774. {Ref: WMG 4:3, pp. 119-120}

NORRIS, WILLIAM (Maryland), b. 24 Dec 1739, St. John's P. E. Parish, Baltimore Co., eldest son of Thomas Norris and Avarilla Scott (who m. 10 Oct 1738 and removed to Frederick Co. circa 1746); d. intestate in 1767. {Ref: MGSB 38:1, pp. 45-49} Pvt., Capt. Joseph Chapline's Company Muster Roll No. 1, Frederick Co., circa 1757-1758, exact dates not given (served 55 days); bill of credit issued or paid in his behalf to Joseph Chaplin for £2.15.0 on 5 Mar 1767.

{Ref: MSA S960 or S752, p. 191; CSOS:102} Pvt., Capt. Joseph Chapline's Company Muster Roll No. 4, Frederick Co., circa 1757-1758, exact dates not given (served 7 days); bill of credit issued or paid in his behalf to Joseph Chaplin for £0.7.0 on 5 Mar 1767. {Ref: MSA S960 or S752, p. 194; CSOS:105} See "Thomas Norris," q.v.

NORTH, ELLIN, see "John Moale," q.v.

NORTH, RICHARD (Delaware), m. Rachel (N), had children Thomas, John, Daniel, Ann, Mary, and Rachel, and d. testate by 16 Mar 1781. {Ref: CDSS:158} Pvt., Kent Co. Militia, Capt. John Caton's Company, 25 Apr 1757 (date of muster roll). {Ref: ARDE I:14}

NORTON, EDWARD (Delaware), pvt., Capt. Henry Vanbibber's Company of the Lower Counties on Delaware Troops at New Castle, enlisted on 21 May 1759. {Ref: ARDE I:26; ARPA (2nd Series) 2:594}

NORWOOD, ANN, see "John Connoway," q.v.

NORWOOD, RICHARD (Maryland), pvt., Capt. Elias Delashmutt's Company Muster Roll, Frederick Co., 13 Aug 1757, exact dates not given (served 52 days); also served another 30 days, exact dates not given; bill of credit issued or paid in his behalf to Elias Delashmut, Jr. on 16 Mar 1767 for £4.2.0. {Ref: MSA S960 or S752, p. 163; CSOS:94, 98}

NOWELL, JAMES (Maryland), cpl., Capt. John Dagworthy's Company of MD Troops, Frederick Co., from 9 Oct 1757 to 16 Apr 1759 when he reportedly deserted; however, payment to him was recorded in Col. Dagworthy's account book on 17 Jul 1762. {Ref: MHS MS.375; CSOS:77; MHS MS.375.1}

NOXON, BENJAMIN (Delaware), captain of a militia co. by 15 Apr 1758; resigned 13 Jun 1758. {Ref: ARDE I:16, 18; ARPA (2nd Series) 2:579}

NOYER, THOMAS (Maryland), pvt., Capt. Richard Pearis' Company of MD Troops, Frederick Co., circa 9 Oct 1757 to 31 May 1758; pvt., Capt. Joshua Beall's Company of MD Troops, Prince George's Co., from 1 Jun 1758 to 30 Dec 1758. {Ref: MHS MS.375.1; CSOS:85, 91} Payment to him was recorded in Col. Dagworthy's account book on 15 Jul 1762. {Ref: MHS MS.375}

NULL, MICHAEL (Maryland), pvt., Capt. Thomas Norris' Company, Frederick Co., circa 1757-1758, exact dates not given (served 30 days); bill of credit issued or paid in his behalf to Thomas McClune on 27 May 1767 for £1.10.0; name mistakenly listed once as "Michael Nutt." {Ref: MSA S960 or S752, p. 177; CSOS:108}

NUSSER, JACOB (Maryland), indentured servant and soldier who served in the French and Indian War some time between 1756 and 1763 (exact dates not known); his master Alexander Lawson, iron manufacturer, requested compensation from the Baltimore County Court due to the loss of use of Nusser while in the service. {Ref: MHM 94:4, p. 426, citing Baltimore Co. Court Minutes}

NUTTER, ANN, see "John Handy," q.v.

OATE, MATTHIAS (Maryland), pvt., Capt. Tobias Stansbury's Company Muster Roll, Baltimore Co., circa 1757-1758, exact dates not given; bill of credit issued or paid to him for £0.12.0 in 1767, exact date not given. {Ref: MSA S960 or S752, p. 187}

OFT (OTT), MATTHIAS (Maryland), pvt., Capt. Jonathan Hagar's Company Muster Roll, Frederick Co., circa 1757-1758, exact dates not given (served 6 days); bill of credit issued or paid to him for £0.6.0 in 1767, exact date not given. {Ref: MSA S960 or S752, p. 174; CSOS:106}

OGILVIE, JOHN (Maryland), patriot, Frederick Co., was paid £5.5.0 on 29 Jul 1758 "for his waggon attending Capt. Beall's Detachment" for the Western Expedition against Fort Duquesne. {Ref: ARMD 55:774}

OGLE, THOMAS JR. (Delaware), prob. son of Thomas Ogle (1705-1771) of Ogletown and his 1st wife Mary Livingston. {Ref: CDSS:159} Captain, Christiana Hundred, Upper Regt. of Militia, North Division, New Castle Co., 1756. {Ref: ARDE I:11; ARPA (2nd Series) 2:526; HDE I:141}

OGLEBY (OGELBY), JOHN (Maryland), pvt., Capt. Alexander Beall's Company of MD Troops, Frederick Co., from 9 Oct 1757 to 28 Jan 1758 when he reportedly died; however, payment to him was recorded in Col. Dagworthy's account book on 28 Feb 1763. {Ref: MHS MS.375; CSOS:81; MHS MS.375.1}

OGLEBY, JOHN (Maryland), pvt., Capt. Joshua Beall's Company Muster Roll, Prince George's Co., circa 1757-1758, exact dates not given; bill of credit issued or paid to him for £1.5.0 in 1767, exact date not given; one undted account indicated "Calvert County." {Ref: MSA S960 or S752, p. 185; CSOS:116}

O'GULLEN, PATRICK (Maryland), pvt., Capt. William McClellan's Company of MD Volunteers, Frederick Co., circa 1763-1764; on muster roll dated 15 Nov 1764 at Camp at the Forks of Muskingham. {Ref: ARMD 32:99}

OLIVER, DANIEL (Delaware), b. c1729, New England (age 30 in 1759); cpl., enlisted in Capt. John Wright's Company and mustered on 11 May 1759. {Ref: ARDE I:25; ARPA (2nd Series) 2:592}

ONSLOW, RICHARD, see "Richard Anslow," q.v.

ORAM, JOHN (Maryland), b. 27 Oct 1736, Baltimore Co., son of Cooper and Hannah Oram, St. Paul's P. E. Parish. {Ref: BCF:461} Pvt., Capt. Tobias Stansbury's Company Muster Roll, Baltimore Co., circa 1757-1758, exact dates not given; bill of credit or order issued and assigned to John Connoway for £3.10.0 on 6 Mar 1767. {Ref: MSA S960 or S752, p. 186}

ORCHARD, BOSTAIN (Maryland), pvt., Capt. Peter Butler's Company Muster Roll, Frederick Co., circa 1757-1758, exact dates not given (served 34 days); bill of credit or order issued to him for £1.14.0 in March 1767. {Ref: MSA S960 or S752, p. 167; CSOS:97}

ORENDUFF, CHRISTIAN (Maryland), pvt., Capt. Joseph Chapline's Company Muster Roll No. 5, Frederick Co., circa 1757-1758, exact dates not given; bill of credit or order issued in his behalf to Joseph Chaplin for £0.8.0 on 5 Mar 1767. {Ref: MSA S960 or S752, p. 195}

ORME, JAMES (Maryland), pvt., Capt. Joshua Beall's Company Muster Roll, Prince George's Co., circa 1757-1758, exact dates not given; bill of credi or order issued in his behalf to William Reynolds for £2.3.0 on 9 Mar 1767. {Ref: MSA S960 or S752, p. 184}

ORME, NATHAN (Maryland), pvt., Capt. Joshua Beall's Company Muster Roll, Prince George's Co., circa 1757-1758, exact dates not given; bill of credit issued or paid to him for £2.1.0 in 1767, exact date not given. {Ref: MSA S960 or S752, p. 185}

ORRICK, NICHOLAS (Maryland), b. 1 May 1725, Baltimore Co., son of John Orrick and Susanna Hammond, m. 1st to Hannah Cromwell and had children Ann (b. 16 Dec 1750), John (1752-1753), John (1753-1810), Margaret, Susan, Nicholas (b. 1759), Sarah, and Charles; m. 2nd to Mary Bell on 16 Mar 1769 and had children William (1779-1804) and Sydney (1771-1825). {Ref: BCF:483} On 20 Aug 1756 Capt. Samuel Gardner reported to the Governor of MD that he was "credibly informed of some of the better sort at the Church in the Forest last Sunday there was an agreement made to raise a body of about 200 men and take all my recruits from me, this town to be their rendezvous on Monday; Capt. Orrick who commands a Company of Militia in the county came on Sunday evening with about twenty horse, the men armed with clubs, and gave me to understand that they expected the whole body the next day. The captain was deputed by the rest to be their spokesman who told me they were come in a peaceable manner to demand their servants and that if they could not have them by fair means they would have them by foul. It seems some of their convict servants were run away, notwithstanding my posting up Advertisements that I would not take any convicts, they would not believe me. I gave them liberty to examine my recruits, they found none of their servants, and for the present the storm is blown over." {Ref: ARMD 6:462} In 1759 Nicholas Orrick, living near Baltimore Town, was accused of persuading James Harrod, a former servant, to desert from the military. {Ref: *MD Gazette*, 15 Mar 1759; SCWM III:151, 261}

OSBORN, ANN, see "Balsher Michael," q.v.

OSBOURN (OSBURN), THOMAS (Maryland), pvt., Capt. William Luckett's Company Muster Roll, Frederick Co., circa 1757-1758, exact dates not given (served 30 days); bill of credit issued or paid in his behalf to William Luckett, Jr. for £1.10.0 on 6 Apr 1767. {Ref: MSA S960 or S752, p. 170; CSOS:100}

OSBOURN (OSBURN), WILLIAM (Maryland), pvt., Capt. William Luckett's Company Muster Roll, Frederick Co., circa 1757-1758, exact dates not given (served 30 days); bill of credit issued or paid in his behalf to William Luckett, Jr. for £1.4.0 on 6 Apr 1767. {Ref: MSA S960 or S752, p. 169; CSOS:100}

OTT, MATTHIAS, see "Matthias Oft," q.v.

OURSLER, MARY, see "Joseph Miller," q.v.

OWEN, ISAAC (Maryland), indentured servant and soldier who served in the French and Indian War some time between 1756 and 1763 (exact dates not known); his master Brian Philpot, merchant, requested compensation from the Baltimore County Court due to the loss of use of Owen while in the service. {Ref: MHM 94:4, p. 426, citing Baltimore Co. Court Minutes}

OWEN, LAWRENCE (Maryland), patriot, Frederick Co., who was appointed one of the pressmasters of Frederick County for the ensuing year in November Court 1755. {Ref: TWL:176, citing Frederick Co. Judgment Records}

OWEN, WILLIAM (Maryland), b. c1738, MD (age about 19 in 1757); pvt., Capt. Richard Pearis' Company, Frederick Co., reported as deserted from the MD Forces in July 1757. {Ref: *MD Gazette*, 21 Jul 1757}

OWENS (OWINGS), JOHN (Maryland), pvt., Capt. Joshua Beall's Company of MD Troops, Prince George's Co., circa 9 Oct 1757 to 30 Dec 1758. {Ref: MHS MS.375.1; CSOS:85} Payment to him was recorded in Col. Dagworthy's account book on 8 Mar 1763 for work on Fort Cumberland. {Ref: MHS MS.375}

OWENS, ROBERT (Maryland), pvt., Capt. Joseph Chapline's Company Muster Roll No. 5, Frederick Co., circa 1757-1758, exact dates not given; bill of credit issued or paid in his behalf to Joseph Chaplin for £0.8.0 on 5 Mar 1767. {Ref: MSA S960 or S752, p. 195}

OWINGS, ELEANOR, see "John Long," q.v.

OWINGS (OWENS), NATHANIEL (Maryland), b. c1731, Baltimore Co., son of Henry Owings and Helen Stinchcomb, St. Thomas' P. E. Parish, and m. Urath Kelly (dau. of William Kelly) in 1763. {Ref: BCF:486} Pvt., Capt. Tobias Stansbury's Company Muster Roll, Baltimore Co., circa 1757-1758, exact dates not given; bill of credit issued or paid in his behalf to William Goodwin for £1.18.0 on 15 Apr 1767. {Ref: MSA S960 or S752, pp. 186-187}

OWINGS, THOMAS, see "Jacob Harlin," q.v.

PACA, JOHN (Maryland), b. c1712, Baltimore Co., son of Aquila Paca and Martha Phillips, m. Elizabeth Smith on 2 Nov 1732 and had children Mary (b. 3 Aug 1733), Aquila (1738-1788), William (b. 31 Oct 1740 on Bush River, Baltimore Co., became Governor of MD and a Signer of the Declaration of Independence, d. 13 Oct 1799, Queen Anne's Co.), Elizabeth (b. 8 Sep 1742), Martha (b. 3 Feb 1744/5), Susanna, and Frances. John was a patriot, planter, gentleman, captain of a horse company in 1735, commissioned Ranger of Baltimore Co. on 2 Jun 1743, member of the Lower House of the MD Assembly (1744-1774, served on the Arms and Ammunition Committee, 1762-1763), court justice (Baltimore Co., 1744-1753; Harford Co., 1774-1774), member of the Committee of Correspondence in 1774, and Judge of the Court of Appeals for Taxation in 1779; d. 2 Jan 1785, Harford Co. {Ref: BDML II:631-633; BCF:489; SCWM III:81, 222, 261} See "John Caseldine" and "Aquila Birchfield" and "Edward Hanson" and "William Mahone" and "Stephen Kimble" and "John Rice" and "Mordecai Durham" and "Benjamin Shaw," q.v.

PACK, BARTHOLOMEW (Maryland), pvt., Capt. William McClellan's Company of MD Volunteers, Frederick Co., circa 1763-1764; reported as deserted on muster roll dated 15 Nov 1764 at Camp at the Forks of Muskingham. {Ref: ARMD 32:99}

PACK, EDWARD (Maryland), pvt., Capt. Tobias Stansbury's Company Muster Roll, Baltimore Co., circa 1757-1758, exact dates not given; bill of credit issued or paid in his behalf to Robert Adair for £1.19.0 on 22 May 1767. {Ref: MSA S960 or S752, p. 187}

PACK, JACOB (Maryland), pvt., Capt. Joseph Chapline's Company Muster Roll No. 1, Frederick Co., circa 1757-1758, exact dates not given (served 17 days); bill of credit issued or paid in his behalf to Joseph Chaplin for £1.1.0 on 9 Jun 1767. {Ref: MSA S960 or S752, p. 192; CSOS:102} Pvt., Capt. Joseph Chapline's Company Muster Rolls No. 2 and 3, Frederick Co., circa 1757-1758, exact dates not given (served 5 days); bill of credit issued or paid in his behalf to Joseph

Chapline for £0.5.0 on 9 Jun 1767. {Ref: MSA S960 or S752, p. 193; CSOS:105} Pvt., Capt. Moses Chapline's Company Muster Roll No. 3, Frederick Co., circa 1757-1758, exact dates not given (served 6 days); bill of credit issued or paid in his behalf to Joseph Chaplin for £0.6.0 on 5 Mar 1767; name listed once as "Jacob Peck." {Ref: MSA S960 or S752, p. 198; CSOS:115}

PACK, JOSEPH (Maryland), pvt., Capt. Joseph Chapline's Company Muster Rolls No. 2 and 3, Frederick Co., circa 1757-1758, exact dates not given (served 5 days); bill of credit issued or paid in his behalf to Joseph Chapline for £0.5.0 on 8 Jun 1767; name listed once as "Job or Joseph Pack." {Ref: MSA S960 or S752, p. 193; CSOS:1`04}

PACK, SIMON (Maryland), pvt., Capt. Alexander Beall's Company of MD Troops, Frederick Co., from 9 Oct 1757 to 14 Sep 1758 when he was reported as killed; however, payment to him was recorded in Col. Dagworthy's account book on 7 Mar 1763. {Ref: MHS MS.375; CSOS:82; MHS MS.375.1}

PACK, THOMAS (Maryland), pvt., Capt. Elias Delashmutt's Company Muster Roll, Frederick Co., 13 Aug 1757, exact dates not given (served 52 days); bill of credit issued or paid in his behalf to Casper Shaff on 2 Mar 1767 for £2.12.0. {Ref: MSA S960 or S752, p. 162; CSOS:98}

PADGETT, JOHN (Maryland), pvt., Capt. Elias Delashmutt's Company Muster Roll, Frederick Co., circa 1757-1758, exact dates not given (served 30 days); bill of credit issued or paid in his behalf to Peter Grosh on 4 Mar 1767 for £1.10.0. {Ref: MSA S960 or S752, p. 162; CSOS:94}

PADGETT, JOSIAH (Maryland), pvt., Capt. Elias Delashmutt's Company Muster Roll, Frederick Co., circa 1757-1758, exact dates not given (served 30 days); bill of credit issued or paid in his behalf to Elias Delashmut, Jr. on 16 Mar 1767 for £1.10.0. {Ref: MSA S960 or S752, p. 162; CSOS:94}

PAGE, DANIEL (Maryland), pvt., Capt. Joshua Beall's Company Muster Roll, Prince George's Co., circa 1757-1758, exact dates not given; bill of credit issued or paid in his behalf to Thomas Contee for £2.1.0 on 22 Apr 1772. {Ref: MSA S960 or S752, p. 185}

PAGE, THOMAS (Maryland), pvt., Capt. Joshua Beall's Company of MD Troops, Prince George's Co., from 9 Oct 1757 to 17 Jan 1758 when he reportedly died; however, payment to him was recorded in Col. Dagworthy's account book on 26 Feb 1763. {Ref: MHS MS.375; CSOS:85; MHS MS.375.1}

PAIN (PAYN), THOMAS (Maryland), pvt., Capt. Moses Chapline's Company Muster Roll No. 3, Frederick Co., circa 1757-1758, exact dates not given (served 6 days); bill of credit issued or paid to him for £0.6.0 in 1767, exact date not given. {Ref: MSA S960 or S752, p. 199; CSOS:115} *Identification problem:* There were two men with this name who could have served in the war: (1) Thomas Payn m. (N), had several children (but only sons John and Flayll were mentioned in his will which he wrote on 8 Jul 1765), and d. by 16 Oct 1765; and (2), Thomas Payn, son of Flayll Payn (who d. testate by 1 Oct 1765). {Ref: WMG 2:4, pp. 163-164}

PAIRPOINT (PAIRPINT), JOHN (Maryland), pvt., Capt. Moses Chapline's Company Muster Roll No. 1, Frederick Co., circa 1757-1758, exact dates not given (served 55 days); bill of credit issued or paid in his behalf to Joseph Chaplin for £2.15.0 on 5 Mar 1767. {Ref: MSA S960 or S752, p. 196; CSOS:113} Pvt., Capt. Moses Chapline's Company Muster Roll No. 3, Frederick Co., circa 1757-1758, exact dates not given (served 6 days); bill of credit issued or paid in his behalf to Joseph Chaplin for £0.6.0 on 5 Mar 1767. {Ref: MSA S960 or S752, p. 198; CSOS:114}

PALMER, DEBORAH, see "William Wilkins," q.v.

PALSEN, PETER, see "Peter Powel," q.v.

PARDOE, JOHN (Maryland), b. c1734, MD (age 22 in 1756); pvt., Capt. Christopher Gist's Company of VA Militia, 13 Jul 1756, enlisted at Baltimore. {Ref: MSR I:37}

PARHAM, GEORGE (Delaware), b. c1741, Wales (laborer, age 18 in 1759); pvt., enlisted by Capt. James Armstrong for the PA Regt. on 6 May 1759. {Ref: ARDE I:26; ARPA (2nd Series) 2:585}

PARKER, GEORGE (Maryland), pvt., Capt. Jonathan Hagar's Company Muster Roll, Frederick Co., circa 1757-1758, exact dates not given (served 6 days); bill of credit issued or paid to him for £0.6.0 in 1767, exact date not given. {Ref: MSA S960 or S752, p. 174; CSOS:107}

PARKER, GEORGE (Maryland or Pennsylvania), Englishman (age not given); pvt. in 1757 who was hanged at Carlisle for desertion. {Ref: *MD Gazette*, 10 Nov 1757}

PARKER, THOMAS, see "Thomas Barker," q.v.

PARKS, WILL (Maryland), b. c1738, MD (age 18 in 1756); pvt., Capt. Henry Harrison's Company of VA Militia, 13 Jul 1756, enlisted in Baltimore. {Ref: MSR I:37}

PARLOT, WILLIAM, see "Johannes Brunner," q.v.

PARR, JAMES (Delaware), b. c1743, Chester, PA (laborer, age 16 in 1759); pvt., enlisted by Capt. James Armstrong for the PA Regt. on 9 May 1759. {Ref: ARDE I:26; ARPA (2nd Series) 2:585}

PARR, ZEPHANIAH (Delaware), pvt., Capt. Henry Vanbibber's Company of the Lower Counties on Delaware Troops at New Castle, enlisted on 19 May 1759. {Ref: ARDE I:26; ARPA (2nd Series) 2:594}

PARSONS (PARSON), NICHOLAS (Maryland), b. c1714, m. Sarah (N) circa 1735 in Kent Co., had children Hannah, Joseph, and John (all born in Shrewsbury Parish), and d. before 1767. {Ref: ESVR} Pvt., Capt. Peregrine Brown's Company Muster Roll, Kent Co., circa 1757-1758, exact dates not given (served 15 days); bill of credit issued in his behalf to Robert Buchanan and paid to Parsons' exec. (unnamed) on 20 May 1767 for £0.15.0. {Ref: MSA S960 or S752, p. 179; CSOS:110}

PATTERSON, ---- (Maryland), b. c1732, MD (age 24 in 1756); pvt., Capt. Christopher Gist's Company of VA Militia, 13 Jul 1756, enlisted at Baltimore. {Ref: MSR I:37}

PATTERSON, JACOB (Maryland), captain, Dorchester Co., by 1760. {Ref: ARMD 56:288}

PATTERSON, SAMUEL (Delaware), Esq., of White Clay Hundred, son of William Patterson, d. testate and unmarried by 12 May 1785. {Ref: CDSS:164}

Captain, White Clay Hundred, Upper Regt. of Militia, East Division, New Castle Co., 1756. {Ref: ARDE I:11; ARPA (2nd Series) 2:526; HDE I:141}

PATTERSON, SAMUEL (Maryland), pvt., Capt. Henry Sneavely's Company Muster Roll, Frederick Co., circa 1757-1758, exact dates not given; bill of credit issued or paid to him for £0.8.0 in 1767, exact date not given. {Ref: MSA S960 or S752, p. 190}

PATTERSON, SAMUEL (Maryland), pvt., Capt. John White's Company Muster Roll, Frederick Co., circa 1757-1758, exact dates not given (served 6 days); bill of credit issued or paid to him for £0.6.0 in 1767, exact date not given. {Ref: MSA S960 or S752, p. 165; CSOS:96}

PATTERSON, WILLIAM (Delaware), New Castle Co., patriot who served as a Justice of the Peace, Justice of the Court of Oyer and Terminer, and Justice of the Court of Common Pleas, 1756-1761. {Ref: GRSD 1:13-15} See "Samuel Patterson," q.v.

PATTON, ROBERT (Delaware), yeoman, m. Mary (N), had children William, Andrew, John, Margaret, and Mary, and d. testate by 17 May 1783. {Ref: CDSS:164} Pvt., Kent Co. Militia, Capt. John Caton's Company, 25 Apr 1757 (date of muster roll). {Ref: ARDE I:13}

PAUGH, BALSER (Maryland), pvt., Capt. Peter Butler's Company Muster Roll, Frederick Co., circa 1757-1758, exact dates not given (served 34 days); bill of credit or order issued in his behalf for £1.14.0 and paid to Casper Shaff on 2 Mar 1767. {Ref: MSA S960 or S752, p. 167; CSOS:97 listed his name twice}

PAULEN (PAULIN), ROBERT (Maryland), pvt., Capt. Richard Pearis' Company of MD Troops, Frederick Co., circa 9 Oct 1757 to 31 May 1758; pvt., Capt. John Dagworthy's Company of MD Troops, Frederick Co., from 1 Jun 1758 to 22 Jan 1759 when he reportedly deserted; however, payment to him was recorded in Col. Dagworthy's account book on 11 Jul 1762. {Ref: MHS MS.375; CSOS:77, 91; MHS MS.375.1}

PAULSON, BENJAMIN (Delaware), b. c1721, Ulster, Ireland (laborer, age 38 in 1759); pvt., enlisted by Capt. James Armstrong for the PA Regt. on 25 Apr 1759. {Ref: ARDE I:26; ARPA (2nd Series) 2:585}

PAULSON, BENJAMIN (Delaware), b. c1729, New Castle, DE (farmer, age 30 in 1759); sgt., enlisted by Capt. James Armstrong for the PA Regt. on 25 Apr 1759. {Ref: ARDE I:25; ARPA (2nd Series) 2:585}

PAYNTER, JACOB (Maryland or Pennsylvania), pvt., Capt. Culbertson's Company, was killed in "a recent battle with the Indians" in 1756 (exact date not given) in Cumberland Co., PA, after the burning of McCord's Fort. {Ref: *MD Gazette*, 29 Apr 1756}

PEACOCK, ANNE, see "William Smith," q.v.

PEACOCK, JOHN (Maryland), b. 14 Dec 1734, Baltimore Co., son of John and Frances Peacock; unmarried in 1763 (taxable bachelor in St. George's P. E. Parish). {Ref: BCF:496; Vestry Minutes} Pvt., Capt. Tobias Stansbury's Company Muster Roll, Baltimore Co., circa 1757-1758, exact dates not given; militia pay account submitted in 1758, exact date not given. {Ref: MHM 9:4, p. 366} Bill of credit issued or paid in his behalf to John Henry for £3.18.0 on 18 Mar 1767. {Ref: MSA S960 or S752, pp. 186-187}

PEARCE, ANN (Maryland), patriot, Kent Co., pay account submitted for quartering soldiers in 1757 or 1758, exact dates not given. {Ref: MHM 9:3, p. 261}

PEARCE, CHARLES (Maryland), indentured servant and soldier who served in the French and Indian War some time between 1756 and 1763 (exact dates not known); his master Robert Bryarly, planter, requested compensation from the Baltimore County Court due to the loss of use of Pearce while in the service. {Ref: MHM 94:4, p. 426, citing Baltimore Co. Court Minutes}

PEARCE, NICHOLAS (Maryland), b. 11 Apr 1735, Anne Arundel Co., son of Daniel and Elizabeth Pearce, of All Hallow's Parish. {Ref: AACR:49} Pvt., Capt. Samuel Chapman's Company Muster Roll, Anne Arundel Co., circa 1757-1758, exact dates not given; bill of credit or order issued his assignment to James Dick paid to Thomas Richardson for £1.18.0 on 21 Feb 1767. {Ref: MSA S960 or S752, p. 188}

PEARCE, NICHOLAS (Maryland), alias Nicholas Peace *[sic]*, pvt., Capt. Joseph Chapline's Company Muster Roll No. 1, Frederick Co., circa 1757-1758, exact dates not given (served 49 days); bill of credit issued or paid in his behalf to Jonathan Hagar for £2.9.0 on 10 Oct 1771. {Ref: MSA S960 or S752, p. 192; CSOS:103} Pvt., Capt. Joseph Chapline's Company Muster Rolls No. 2 and 3, Frederick Co., circa 1757-1758, exact dates not given (served 3 days); bill of credit issued or paid in his behalf to Jonathan Hagar for £0.8.0 on 10 Oct 1771. {Ref: MSA S960 or S752, p. 193; CSOS:104}

PEARIS, RICHARD (Maryland), captain, MD Troops, Frederick Co., from 9 Oct 1757 to 31 May 1758 (company roll). {Ref: MHS MS.375.1} At the end of January 1758 his company left Fort Cumberland to go to Fort Duquesne. {Ref: *MD Gazette*, 16 Feb 1758} In 1759 he was mentioned in the newspaper as "Capt. Richard Pearis, of the Pennsylvania Provincials, now recruiting in Annapolis." {Ref: *MD Gazette*, 14 Jun 1759} Payment to him was recorded in Col. Dagworthy's account book on 19 Jul 1762 and 8 Mar 1763. {Ref: MHS MS.375} He performed "sundry services at the fort" in 1763 and payment in the amount of £0.17.6 was still owed to him on 25 Nov 1763 (when reported by the Accounts Committee to the MD Assembly). {Ref: ARMD 58:400}

PEASE (PEACE), JAMES (Delaware), b. c1726, London, England (merchant, age 32 in 1758); pvt., enlisted 25 Apr 1758 "for the campaign in the lower counties" by Capt. John McClughan. {Ref: ARDE I:18; ARPA (2nd Series) 2:570}

PEASE, JAMES (Maryland or Pennsylvania), pvt., Capt. Hamilton's Company, was killed in "a recent battle with the Indians" in 1756 (exact date not given) in Cumberland Co., PA, after the burning of McCord's Fort. {Ref: *MD Gazette*, 29 Apr 1756}

PEASLEY, INGRAM, see "Thomas Franklin," q.v.

PEASLEY, RUTH, see "Thomas Franklin," q.v.

PEATON, EDWARD (Maryland), patriot, Annapolis, Anne Arundel Co., pay account submitted for quartering soldiers in 1757 or 1758, exact dates not given. {Ref: MHM 9:3, p. 261}

PECK, JACOB, see "Jacob Pack," q.v.

PECKABOUGH (PECABOUGH), LEONARD (Maryland), pvt., Capt. Peter Bainbridge's Company Muster Roll, Frederick Co., circa 1757-1758, exact dates not given (served 28 days); bill of credit issued or paid in his behalf to Jacob Young on 4 Mar 1767 for £1.8.0. {Ref: MSA S960 or S752, p. 181; CSOS:111}

PECKER, THOMAS (Maryland), patriot, Annapolis, Anne Arundel Co., pay account submitted for quartering soldiers in 1757 or 1758, exact dates not given. {Ref: MHM 9:3, p. 262}

PECKEREL (PICKEREL, PICKERILL), SAMUEL (Maryland), pvt., Capt. Richard Pearis' Company of MD Troops, Frederick Co., circa 9 Oct 1757 and 31 May 1758; pvt., Capt. Alexander Beall's Company of MD Troops, Frederick Co., from 1 Jun 1757 to 8 Nov 1758. {Ref: MHS MS.375.1; CSOS:82, 91} Payment to him was recorded in Col. Dagworthy's account book on 12 Jul 1762. {Ref: MHS MS.375}

PEDDECOAT (PEDDICORT), WILLIAM (Maryland), pvt., Capt. Alexander Beall's Company of MD Troops, Frederick Co., from 9 Oct 1757 to 30 Dec 1758; promoted to cpl. on 9 Feb 1758. {Ref: MHS MS.375.1} Payment to him was recorded in Col. Dagworthy's account book on 11 Jul 1762. {Ref: MHS MS.375}

PEDMORE, JOSEPH (Maryland), pvt., Capt. John White's Company Muster Roll, Frederick Co., circa 1757-1758, exact dates not given (served 6 days); bill of credit issued or paid in his behalf to Joseph Chaplin on 5 Mar 1767 for £0.6.0. {Ref: MSA S960 or S752, p. 164; CSOS:95}

PEDWORTH (PUDWORTH), THOMAS (Maryland), pvt. (county not stated), received £5 bounty money on 4 Aug 1757 for enlisting in the militia. {Ref: ARMD 55:265, 619}

PELLET, LEWIS, see "Lewis Pettit," q.v.

PELSER, CHRISTIAN (Maryland), pvt., Capt. John Middaugh's Company Muster Roll, Frederick Co., circa 1757-1758, exact dates not given (served 30 days); bill of credit issued or paid in his behalf to James Smith for £1.10.0 on 18 May 1767. {Ref: MSA S960 or S752, p. 172; CSOS:101}

PEMBERTON, RICHARD (Maryland), pvt., Capt. John Dagworthy's Company of MD Troops, Frederick Co., from 9 Oct 1757 to 8 Dec 1758 when he reportedly deserted; however, payment to him was recorded in Col. Dagworthy's account book on 8 Mar 1763. {Ref: MHS MS.375; CSOS:77; MHS MS.375.1}

PENDELL (PINDLE), PHILIP (Maryland), pvt., Capt. Alexander Beall's Company of MD Troops, Frederick Co., circa 9 Oct 1757 to 30 Dec 1758. {Ref: MHS MS.375.1; CSOS:82} Payment to him was recorded in Col. Dagworthy's account book on 12 Jul 1762. {Ref: MHS MS.375}

PENGROVE (PINGRAVE), FRANCIS (Maryland), pvt., Capt. John Dagworthy's Company of MD Troops, Frederick Co., from 9 Oct 1757 to 25 Jan 1759 when he reportedly died; however, payment to him was recorded in Col. Dagworthy's account book on 9 Mar 1763 for work on Fort Cumberland. {Ref: MHS MS.375; CSOS:77; MHS MS.375.1}

PENKETH, ANN, see "Samuel Chamberlaine," q.v.

PENN, ELIZABETH, see "Richard Harrison," q.v.

PENN, JOHN (Delaware), New Castle Co., lieut. governor in 1763. {Ref: GRSD 1:13}

PENN, WILLIAM, see "Richard Harrison," q.v.

PENNINGTON, WIGHLAND (Delaware), pvt., Capt. Henry Vanbibber's Company of the Lower Counties on Delaware Troops at New Castle, enlisted on 1 May 1759. {Ref: ARDE I:26; ARPA (2nd Series) 2:594}

PEPERDINE (PEPPERDINE), JAMES (Maryland), pvt., Capt. Henry Casson's Company Muster Roll, Queen Anne's Co., circa 1757-1758, exact dates not given (served 27 days); bill of credit issued or paid in his behalf to Capt. Casson on 27 Feb 1767 for £1.7.0. {Ref: MSA S960 or S752, p. 177; CSOS:109}

PEPPERAL, WILLIAM, see "Francis Graham," q.v.

PERISFIELD (PARISFIELD), RICHARD (Maryland), pvt., Capt. Joseph Chapline's Company Muster Roll No. 1, Frederick Co., circa 1757-1758, exact dates not given (served 37 days); bill of credit issued or paid in his behalf to Joseph Chaplin for £1.17.0 on 5 Mar 1767. {Ref: MSA S960 or S752, p. 190; CSOS:102}

PERKINS, BENJAMIN (Delaware), b. c1739, Cedar Creek, DE (farmer, age 19 in 1758); pvt., enlisted 4 May 1758 "for the campaign in the lower counties" by Capt. John McClughan. {Ref: ARDE I:18; ARPA (2nd Series) 2:570}

PERKINS, ELISHA (Maryland), patriot, Frederick Co., by 1758, for whom cash in the amount of £6.15.0 was retained at Fort Frederick for his heirs (unnamed) on 7 Nov 1758 "for his waggon having attended 9 days [to] the Detachment that worked on the new road to Fort Cumberland" for the Western Expedition against Fort Duquesne. {Ref: ARMD 55:776}

PERKINS, JOHN (Maryland), pvt., Capt. Richard Pearis' Company of MD Troops, Frederick Co., circa 9 Oct 1757 to 31 May 1758; pvt., Capt. Joshua Beall's Company of MD Troops, Prince George's Co., from 1 Jun 1758 to 8 Nov 1758. {Ref: MHS MS.375.1; CSOS:85, 91} Payment to him was recorded in Col. Dagworthy's account book on 14 Jul 1762. {Ref: MHS MS.375}

PERKINS, THOMAS (Maryland), pvt., Capt. Joshua Beall's Company of MD Troops, Prince George's Co., from 9 Oct 1757 to 31 May 1758 when he was discharged. {Ref: MHS MS.375.1; CSOS:85} Susannah Apple petitioned the court in November 1758, stating that she "was employed by Dr. James Brand for attending and keeping a soldier named Thomas Perkins in his sickness and had a great deal of trouble with him for the space of two weeks and then he died." She requested an allowance for her trouble. The court granted her 320 lbs. of tobacco and it was recorded in the judgment records. {Ref: TWL:188, citing Frederick Co. Judgment Records} Payment was also recorded in Col. Dagworthy's account book on 23 Jul 1762. {Ref: MHS MS.375}

PERKINS, THOMAS (Maryland), patriot and poss. soldier (rank not specified), Kent Co., militia pay account submitted in 1758, exact date not given. {Ref: MHM 9:4, p. 368}

PERKINS, WILLIAM (Maryland), pvt., Capt. Joshua Beall's Company of MD Troops, Prince George's Co., circa 9 Oct 1757 to 30 Dec 1758. {Ref: MHS MS.375.1; CSOS:85} Payment to him was recorded in Col. Dagworthy's account book on 15 Jul 1762. {Ref: MHS MS.375}

PERKINS, WILLIAM (Delaware), pvt., Capt. Henry Vanbibber's Company of the Lower Counties on Delaware Troops at New Castle, enlisted on 17 May 1759. {Ref: ARDE I:26; ARPA (2nd Series) 2:594}

PERRIE, JAMES (Maryland), patriot and poss. soldier (rank not specified), Frederick Co., militia pay account submitted in 1758, exact date not given. {Ref: MHM 9:4, p. 366}

PERRIN (PERREN), EDWARD (Maryland), ensign in Capt. Joseph Chapline's Company Muster Rolls No. 2 and 3, Frederick Co., circa 1757-1758, exact dates not given (served 8 days); bill of credit issued or paid in his behalf to Joseph Chaplin for £0.8.0 on 5 Mar 1767. {Ref: MSA S960 or S752, p. 193; CSOS:104}

PERRIN (PERREN, PERRINS), JOHN (Maryland), tanner, m. (N), had children John, Edward, Joseph, Susannah, and Mary, and d. testate by 17 Jan 1770. {Ref: WMG 3:2, p. 75} Ensign in Capt. Joseph Chapline's Company Muster Roll No. 1, Frederick Co., circa 1757-1758, exact dates not given (served 60 days); bill of credit issued or paid in his behalf to Joseph Chaplin for £6 on 5 Mar 1767. {Ref: MSA S960 or S752, p. 190; CSOS:102}

PERRIN (PERREN), JOHN JR. (Maryland), pvt., Capt. Joseph Chapline's Company Muster Roll No. 1, Frederick Co., circa 1757-1758, exact dates not given (served 39 days); bill of credit issued or paid in his behalf to Joseph Chaplin for £1.19.0 on 5 Mar 1767. {Ref: MSA S960 or S752, p. 190; CSOS:102} Pvt., Capt. Joseph Chapline's Company Muster Rolls No. 2 and 3, Frederick Co., circa 1757-1758, exact dates not given (served 8 days); bill of credit issued or paid in his behalf to Joseph Chaplin for £0.17.0 on 5 Mar 1767. {Ref: MSA S960 or S752, p. 193; CSOS:104} Pvt., Capt. Joseph Chapline's Company Muster Roll No. 5, Frederick Co., circa 1757-1758, exact dates not given; bill of credit issued or paid in his behalf to Joseph Chaplin for £1.3.0 on 5 Mar 1767. {Ref: MSA S960 or S752, p. 195}

PERRY, ELIZABETH, see "James Price," q.v.

PERRY, JAMES (Maryland), patriot and poss. soldier (rank not specified), Frederick Co., militia pay account submitted in 1758, exact date not given. {Ref: MHM 9:4, p. 366} He was paid £3 at Fort Frederick on 11 Aug 1758 "for carrying a load of corn to Fort Frederick" and was paid £11.10.0 on 18 Aug 1758 "for carrying artillery stores to Fort Cumberland" for the Western Expedition against Fort Duquesne. {Ref: ARMD 55:774-775}

PERRY, JOHN (Delaware), b. c1733, MD (laborer, age 25 in 1758); pvt., recruited by Capt. Benjamin Noxon and enlisted on 3 May 1758. {Ref: ARDE I:19; ARPA (2nd Series) 2:485, 566}

PERRY, JOHN (Maryland), pvt., Capt. Joshua Beall's Company Muster Roll, Prince George's Co., circa 1757-1758, exact dates not given; bill of credit issued or paid to him for £2.1.0 on 30 May 1767. {Ref: MSA S960 or S752, p. 184}

PERSHING, FREDERICK (Maryland), pvt., Capt. John White's Company Muster Roll, Frederick Co., circa 1757-1758, exact dates not given (served 6 days); bill of credit issued or paid to him for £0.6.0 in 1767, exact date not given. {Ref: MSA S960 or S752, p. 165; CSOS:96}

PERSON (PEARSON), THOMAS (Maryland), pvt., Capt. Joshua Beall's Company of MD Troops, Prince George's Co., circa 9 Oct 1757 to 30 Dec 1758. {Ref: MHS MS.375.1; CSOS:85} Payment to him was recorded in Col. Dagworthy's account book on 13 Jul 1762. {Ref: MHS MS.375}

PETER, CAJA (Delaware), b. c1736, Pocomock, MD (fiddlemaker, age 22 in 1758); pvt., enlisted 8 May 1758 "for the campaign in the lower counties" by Capt. John McClughan (muster roll dated 17 May 1758; name and occupation listed once as "Peter Caja, fiddle-master"). {Ref: ARDE I:18; ARPA (2nd Series) 2:489, 570}

PETER, ROBERT, see "Uzza Posey," q.v.

PETERS, RICHARD (Delaware), New Castle Co., patriot who served as a Justice of the Peace and a Justice of the Court of Oyer and Terminer, 1756-1761. {Ref: GRSD 1:13, 15} See "John McClughan," q.v.

PETERSON, ADAM (Delaware), captain, St. George's Hundred, Lower Regt. of Militia, New Castle Co., 1756. {Ref: ARDE I:11; ARPA (2nd Series) 2:525; HDE I:141} Patriot who served as a Justice of the Peace, Justice of the Court of Oyer and Terminer, and Justice of the Court of Common Pleas, 1756. {Ref: GRSD 1:13} *Identification problem:* There were two men with this name in St. George's Hundred who could have served in the war: (1) Adam Peterson m. Veronica (N) and d. testate by 23 Jan 1763; and, (2) Adam Peterson m. Rachel (N) and d. testate by 26 Nov 1773. {Ref: CDSS:167}

PETERSON, GEORGE JR. (Delaware), pvt., Capt. Richard McWilliams' Company of Foot, New Castle Co., enlisted 28 Dec 1757. {Ref: ARDE I:14}

PETERSON, JACOB (Delaware), New Castle Co., patriot and court justice in 1761. {Ref: GRSD 1:15}

PETERSON, JOHN (Delaware), pvt., Capt. Richard McWilliams' Company of Foot, New Castle Co., enlisted 28 Dec 1757. {Ref: ARDE I:14}

PETERSON, WILLIAM (Delaware), pvt., Capt. Richard McWilliams' Company of Foot, New Castle Co., enlisted 28 Dec 1757. {Ref: ARDE I:15}

PETTICOAT, NATHAN (Maryland), pvt., Capt. Elias Delashmutt's Company Muster Roll, Frederick Co., circa 1757-1758, exact dates not given (served 30 days); bill of credit issued or paid in his behalf to Casper Shaff for Petticoat's admin. (unnamed) on 2 Mar 1767 for £2. {Ref: MSA S960 or S752, p. 162; CSOS:94}

PETTIT (PELLET?), LEWIS (Maryland), pvt., Capt. Richard Pearis' Company of MD Troops, Frederick Co., circa 9 Oct 1757 and 31 May 1758; pvt., Capt. Joshua Beall's Company of MD Troops, Prince George's Co., from 1 Jun 1758 to 8 Nov 1758. {Ref: MHS MS.375.1; CSOS:85, 91} Payment to him was recorded in Col. Dagworthy's account book on 22 Jul 1762 for work on Fort Cumberland. {Ref: MHS MS.375}

PHILIPPY, FRANCIS (Maryland), pvt., Capt. Jonathan Hagar's Company Muster Roll, Frederick Co., circa 1757-1758, exact dates not given (served 6 days); bill of credit issued or paid to him for £0.6.0 in 1767, exact date not given. {Ref: MSA S960 or S752, p. 174; CSOS:106}

PHILLIPS, JACOB (Delaware), m. Hester (N), had no children, and d. testate by 19 Apr 1762. {Ref: CDSS:168} Major, Militia Regt. of Sussex Co., 1756-1758. {Ref: ARDE I:13, 15; ARPA (2nd Series) 2:529, 579; HDE I:141}

PHILLIPS, JAMES, see "Aquila Hall," q.v.

PHILLIPS, JOHANNA, see "Aquila Hall," q.v.

PHILLIPS, MARTHA, see "John Paca," q.v.

PHILLIPS, NICHOLAS (Maryland), pvt., Capt. Moses Chapline's Company Muster Roll, Frederick Co., circa 1757-1758, exact dates not given (served 6 days). {Ref: CSOS:115}

PHILLIPS (PHILIP), RUBEN or REUBIN (Maryland), pvt., Capt. John Middaugh's Company Muster Roll, Frederick Co., circa 1757-1758, exact dates not given (served 30 days); bill of credit issued or paid in his behalf to Thomas Beatty, Jr. for £1.10.0 on 3 Apr 1767. {Ref: MSA S960 or S752, p. 172; CSOS:101}

PHILLIPS (PHILIPS), SAMUEL (Maryland), b. c1715, m. Solvolitle Boswell on 28 Sep 1749, Baltimore Co., St. John's P. E. Parish. {Ref: BCF:504} Pvt., Capt. Tobias Stansbury's Company Muster Roll, Baltimore Co., circa 1757-1758, exact dates not given; bill of credit issued or paid to him for £1.18.0 in 1767, exact date not given. {Ref: MSA S960 or S752, p. 187} In 1759 John Willmott, living in Baltimore Co., reported in the Annapolis newspaper that a servant man named Samuel Philips, about age 45, who was in the Army in the last campaign, had run away. {Ref: *MD Gazette*, 28 Jun 1759}

PHILLIPS, SOLOMON (Maryland or Virginia), b. c1739 (age about 22 in 1761); pvt. in a VA Regt. who was reported by Capt. John McNeill as having deserted and indicating he formerly lived with Henry Gassaway in Annapolis. {Ref: *MD Gazette*, 18 Jun 1761}

PHILPOT (PHILPOTT), BRYAN (Maryland), patriot and poss. soldier (rank not specified), Baltimore Co., militia pay account submitted in 1758, exact date not given. {Ref: MHM 9:4, p. 366} See "Nicholas Damilery" and "John Harrison" and "Isaac Owen," q.v.

PHIPS (PHIPPS), JOHN (Maryland), pvt., Capt. Alexander Beall's Company of MD Troops, Frederick Co., from 9 Oct 1757 to 31 May 1758 when he was discharged. {Ref: MHS MS.375.1; CSOS:82} Payment to him was recorded in Col. Dagworthy's account book on 12 Jul 1762. {Ref: MHS MS.375}

PICKAPAUGH (PICKAPAH), PETER (Maryland), pvt., Capt. Elias Delashmutt's Company Muster Roll, Frederick Co., 13 Aug 1757, exact dates not given (served 52 days); bill of credit issued or paid in his behalf to Jacob Young on 4 Mar 1767 for £2.12.0. {Ref: MSA S960 or S752, p. 162; CSOS:98}

PICKETT, ELIZABETH, see "John Jones," q.v.

PIERCE, PETER (Maryland), sgt., Capt. Francis Ware's Company of MD Troops, Charles Co., circa 9 Oct 1757 to 30 Dec 1758. {Ref: MHS MS.375.1; CSOS:89} Payment to him was recorded in Col. Dagworthy's account book on 11 Jul 1762. {Ref: MHS MS.375}

PILE, ELIZABETH, see "Edward Sprigg," q.v.

PILES, FRANCIS (Maryland), son of Leonard Piles; pvt., Capt. Joshua Beall's Company Muster Roll, Prince George's Co., circa 1757-1758, exact dates not given; bill of credit issued or paid in his behalf to John Hepburn, Jr. for £2.3.0 on 13 Apr 1767. {Ref: MSA S960 or S752, pp. 184-185}

PILES, FRANCIS (Maryland), son of Francis Piles; pvt., Capt. Joshua Beall's Company Muster Roll, Prince George's Co., circa 1757-1758, exact dates not given; bill of credit issued or paid to him for £1.8.0 in 1767, exact date not given. {Ref: MSA S960 or S752, p. 185}

PINDERGRASS, ANTHONY (Delaware), pvt., Kent Co. Militia, Capt. John Caton's Company, 25 Apr 1757 (date of muster roll). {Ref: ARDE I:13}

PINDLE, PHILIP, see "Philip Pendell," q.v.

PINKSTONE, PETER (Maryland), pvt., Capt. John Dagworthy's Company, Frederick Co., 1756-1757 (exactd dates not given), recorded his discharge in Frederick Co. Court on 22 Nov 1758. Capt. Dagworthy certified that "Peter Pinkstone, being a draft from Frederick County, served in my company to date hereof and is discharged, having first received a full and true account of all his pay, clothing and other demands. Signed at Fort Frederick, 10 Feb 1757." Peter Pinkstone signed his receipt for pay which was witnessed by Sgt. John Whitman and Sgt. Thomas Teaman. {Ref: FCLR:60}

PIPER, SAMUEL (Delaware), b. c1724, Derry, Ireland (tailor, age 35 in 1759); pvt., enlisted by Capt. James Armstrong for the PA Regt. on 4 May 1759. {Ref: ARDE I:26; ARPA (2nd Series) 2:585}

PIPER, SARAH, see "John Adams," q.v.

PITNAR (PITNER, PETNER), HENRY (Maryland), pvt., Capt. Alexander Beall's Company, 1757, recorded his discharge in Frederick Co. Court on 31 Jan 1758. "Capt. Alexander Beall, commander of one of the MD Company's of Foot, certifies that the bearer hereof, Henry Pitner, served upwards of 8 months." Signed by Alexander Beall on 10 Feb 1757 and witnessed by Sgt. Robert Leonard and Sgt. George Barrance. Henry Pitner made his "HB" mark. His discharge was recorded again on 22 Mar 1759, adding "Henry Petner served 8 months, until the time of his enlistment being expired." {Ref: FCLR:38, 70}

PITTENGER, HENRY (Maryland), pvt., Capt. Henry Sneavely's Company Muster Roll, Frederick Co., circa 1757-1758, exact dates not given; bill of credit issued or paid to him for £0.8.0 in 1767, exact date not given. {Ref: MSA S960 or S752, p. 190}

PLATER, GEORGE (Maryland), b. 8 Nov 1735, St. Mary's Company, son of George Plater and Rebecca Addison (widow of James Bowles and dau. of Thomas Addison), m. 1st to Hannah Lee on 5 Dec 1762 in Charles Co., m. 2nd to Elizabeth Rousby on 19 Jul 1764, had children Rebecca (b. 18 Sep 1765), George (b. 21 Sep 1766), John Rousby (b. 15 Oct 1767), Thomas (b. 9 May 1769), Ann or Anne (b. 23 Sep 1772), and William (birth date not given), and d. 10 Feb 1792, Annapolis (interred at "Sotterly" in St. Mary's Company); patriot, mason, gentleman, prob. a lawyer, member of the MD Assembly (1757-1766, 1771-1776), colonel by 1764, naval officer at Patuxent (1767-1777), member of the MD Council (1771-1774), member of the Council of Safety (1776-1777), delegate to the Continental Congress (1777-1780), senator (1776-

1781, President of the Senate, c1782-1790), and Governor of MD (1791-1792). {Ref: BDML II:650-652; *MD Gazette*, 16 Dec 1762, 29 Sep 1763, 16 Feb 1792; MDG II:286-287}

PLATT, SAMUEL (Delaware), lieut., White Clay Hundred, Upper Regt. of Militia, West Division, New Castle Co., 1756. {Ref: ARDE I:11; ARPA (2nd Series) 2:526; HDE I:141} *Identification problem:* This will require additional research before drawing any conclusions: (1) "Samuel Platt" served on the Boston Relief Committee in 1774 and subscribed to the Oath of Fidelity and Allegiance in 1778; (2) "Lt. Samuel Platt (1723-1798)" is buried in the White Clay Creek Cem. at Newark; and, (3) "Samuel Platt, M.D." m. Margery (N), had children Samuel, Jr. (d. 1795), George, Dinah, Margaret, Elizabeth, Ann, Martha, Jane, and Mary, and d. testate by 4 Jan 1799. {Ref: CDSS:169; RPDE:215}

PLOWMAN, JONATHAN, see "Samuel Young," q.v.

PLUMBS, SAMUEL (Maryland), pvt., Capt. Jonathan Hagar's Company Muster Roll, Frederick Co., circa 1757-1758, exact dates not given (served 6 days); bill of credit issued or paid to him for £0.6.0 in 1767, exact date not given. {Ref: MSA S960 or S752, p. 174; CSOS:107}

PLUMMER, GEORGE (Maryland), pvt., Capt. Alexander Beall's Company of MD Troops, Frederick Co., from 9 Oct 1757 to 8 Nov 1758. {Ref: MHS MS.375.1; CSOS:82} Payment to him was recorded in Col. Dagworthy's account book on 11 Jul 1762 for work on Fort Cumberland. {Ref: MHS MS.375}

PLUNKET, ROBERT (Maryland), pvt., Capt. Alexander Beall's Company of MD Troops, Frederick Co., circa 9 Oct 1757 to 30 Dec 1758. {Ref: MHS MS.375.1; CSOS:82} Payment to him was recorded in Col. Dagworthy's account book on 7 Mar 1763 for work on Fort Cumberland. {Ref: MHS MS.375}

POALING, MARY ANN, see "William Johnson," q.v.

POCOCK, ABLE or ABEL (Maryland), b. c1733, Baltimore Co., son of Daniel Pocock, Sr. (who stated in a lease in 1743 that Able was age 10). {Ref: BCF:511} Pvt., Capt. Tobias Stansbury's Company Muster Roll, Baltimore Co., circa 1757-1758, exact dates not given; bill of credit issued or paid to him for £1.18.0 in 1767, exact date not given; bill of credit issued or paid in his behalf to Robert Adair for £1.18.0 on 22 May 1767; name listed once as "Abel Peacock." {Ref: MSA S960 or S752, p. 187; CSOS:118}

POE (POO), GEORGE (Maryland), b. 1742, m. (N), had a son Jacob (1775-1860), and d. 1823; pvt., Capt. John White's Company Muster Roll, Frederick Co., circa 1757-1758, exact dates not given (served 6 days); bill of credit issued or paid to him for £0.6.0 in 1767, exact date not given. {Ref: MSA S960 or S752, p. 165; SCWM III:164, 262; CSOS:96}

POLK, WILLIAM (Maryland), pvt., Capt. William McClellan's Company of MD Volunteers, Frederick Co., circa 1763-1764; reported as deserted on muster roll dated 15 Nov 1764 at Camp at the Forks of Muskingham. {Ref: ARMD 32:99}

POLLARD, MARGARET, see "Pollard Edmondson," q.v.

POLTER (POULTER), HUGH (Maryland), pvt., Capt. Richard Pearis' Company of MD Troops, Frederick Co., circa 9 Oct 1757 to 31 May 1758; pvt., Capt. Joshua Beall's Company of MD Troops, Prince George's Co., from 1 Jun 1758 to 30 Dec 1758; pvt., Capt. John Dagworthy's Company of MD Troops,

Frederick Co., from 31 Dec 1758 to 22 Jan 1759 when he reportedly deserted; however, payment to him was recorded in Col. Dagworthy's account book on 12 Jul 1762. {Ref: MHS MS.375; CSOS:77, 85, 91; MHS MS.375.1}

PONTY, JOHN (Maryland), b. c1736, MD (age 20 in 1756); pvt., Maj. Andrew Lewis' Company of VA Militia, enlisted in 1756 in Augusta, VA. {Ref: MSR I:38}

POOLE, JAMES (Maryland), farmer; pvt., Capt. Peregrine Brown's 7th Co. of Foot Militia, Kent Co., on 19 Feb 1758, by which time he had enlisted, but reportedly refused to appear and serve in arms against the enemy; he later stated that he "has been in a very ill state of health for this eighteen months past, and constantly subject to the flux and fretting of the bowels on every slight cold he catches, and quite unfit for such a service, and tho' he was conscious how unable he was to undergo such a service and that he expected he must lose his life by the attempt, yet being terrified with the punishment he apprehended he should be made to suffer for his refusal, resolved to go with the rest and accordingly packed up his baggage, and it was proved went with Thomas Honour on board Edward Drugan's vessel in order to go." {Ref: ARMD 31:283, 287-288}

POORE, ABRAHAM (Maryland), pvt., Capt. Peter Butler's Company Muster Roll, Frederick Co., circa 1757-1758, exact dates not given (served 34 days); bill of credit or order issued in his behalf for £1.14.0 and paid to Peter Grosh on 4 Mar 1767. {Ref: MSA S960 or S752, p. 168; CSOS:97}

PORTER, ABRAHAM (Maryland), b. 20 Jun 1727, Kent Co., son of John and Catheran Porter, of Shrewsbury Parish. {Ref: ESVR} Pvt., Capt. Peregrine Brown's Company, Kent Co., on 19 Feb 1758, by which time he had enlisted, but was unable to march due to health problems. {Ref: ARMD 31:283}

PORTER, ALEXANDER (Delaware), lieut., Pencader Hundred, Lower Regt. of Militia, New Castle Co., 1756. {Ref: ARDE I:12; ARPA (2nd Series) 2:525; HDE I:141}

PORTER, ALEXANDER (Delaware), captain, New Castle Hundred, Upper Regt. of Militia, South Division New Castle Co., 1756. {Ref: ARDE I:11; ARPA (2nd Series) 2:526; HDE I:141} Served as a member of the Delaware Convention in 1776; captain by June 1777; subscribed to the Oath of Fidelity and Allegiance in 1778. Alexander Porter, Esq., m. (N), had children Alexander, Jonas, and Mary, and d. testate in 1784. {Ref: RPDE:217}

PORTER, HUGH, see "Hugh Polter," q.v.

PORTER, JAMES (Maryland), patriot and poss. soldier (rank not specified), Kent Co., militia pay account submitted in 1758, exact date not given. {Ref: MHM 9:4, p. 368}

PORTER, JOHN (Maryland), pvt., Capt. Francis Ware's Company of MD Troops, Charles Co., from 9 Oct 1757 to 2 Jul 1758 (served 266 days) when he reportedly deserted; however, payment to him was recorded in Col. Dagworthy's account book on 7 Mar 1763. {Ref: MHS MS.375; CSOS:89; MHS MS.375.1}

PORTER, JOHN, see "Abraham Porter," q.v.

POSEY, RICHARD (Maryland), b. c1734, MD (age 22 in 1756); pvt., Capt. Christopher Gist's Company of VA Militia, 13 Jul 1756, enlisted at Fredericksburg, VA. {Ref: MSR I:37}

POSEY, UZZA (Maryland), pvt., Capt. Elias Delashmutt's Company Muster Roll, Frederick Co., 13 Aug 1757, exact dates not given (served 52 days); his payment of £2.12.0 was assigned to Robert Peter in March 1767 and an allowance of £2.12.0 was paid in his behalf to William Smallwood on 9 Nov 1771. {Ref: MSA S960 or S752, p. 163; CSOS:98}

POTTER, JAMES (Maryland or Pennsylvania), ensign in Capt. Potter's Company, killed during Col. Armstrong's attack on Kittanning in 1756. {Ref: *MD Gazette*, 30 Sep 1756}

POUME, JACOB (Maryland), pvt., Capt. Thomas Norris' Company, Frederick Co., circa 1757-1758, exact dates not given (served 30 days); bill of credit issued or paid in his behalf to Charles Englas on 28 Mar 1767 for £1.10.0. {Ref: MSA S960 or S752, p. 176; CSOS:108}

POWELL (POWEL), JOHN (Maryland), pvt., Capt. Joshua Beall's Company Muster Roll, Prince George's Co., circa 9 Oct 1757 to 30 Dec 1758; pvt., Capt. Joshua Beall's Company of MD Troops, Prince George's Co., from 9 Oct 1757 to 30 Dec 1758. {Ref: MHS MS.375.1; CSOS:85} Payment to him was recorded in Col. Dagworthy's account book on 21 Jul 1762. {Ref: MHS MS.375} Bill of credit issued or paid in his behalf to David Ross for £1.19.0 on 16 Mar 1767. {Ref: MSA S960 or S752, p. 184}

POWELL (POWEL), JOHN (Maryland), pvt., Capt. Moses Chapline's Company Muster Roll No. 1, Frederick Co., circa 1757-1758, exact dates not given (served 55 days); bill of credit issued or paid in his behalf to Joseph Chaplin for £2.15.0 on 5 Mar 1767. {Ref: MSA S960 or S752, p. 196; CSOS:113} Cpl., Capt. Moses Chapline's Company Muster Roll No. 3, Frederick Co., circa 1757-1758, exact dates not given (served 6 days); bill of credit issued or paid in his behalf to Joseph Chaplin for £0.8.0 on 5 Mar 1767. {Ref: MSA S960 or S752, p. 198; CSOS:115}

POWELL (POWEL), JOHN JR. (Maryland), pvt., Capt. Joseph Chapline's Company Muster Roll No. 1, Frederick Co., circa 1757-1758, exact dates not given (served 25 days); bill of credit issued or paid in his behalf to Joseph Chaplin for £1.5.0 on 5 Mar 1767; name listed without the "Jr.". {Ref: MSA S960 or S752, p. 191; CSOS:103} Pvt., Capt. Joseph Chapline's Company Muster Roll No. 4, Frederick Co., circa 1757-1758, exact dates not given (served 6 days); bill of credit issued or paid in his behalf to Joseph Chaplin for £0.6.0 on 5 Mar 1767. {Ref: MSA S960 or S752, p. 194; CSOS:105}

POWELL (POWEL), PETER (Maryland), alias Peter Palsen *[sic]*, pvt., Capt. Stephen Rensburg's or Rensburger's Company Muster Roll, Frederick Co., circa 1757-1758, exact dates not given (served 34 days); bill of credit issued or paid in his behalf to Stephen Rensburger for £1.14.0 on 27 Mar 1767. {Ref: MSA S960 or S752, p. 183; CSOS:112}

POWELL, SAMUEL (Maryland), pvt., Charles Co., received £5 bounty money on 16 Aug 1757 for enlisting in the militia. {Ref: ARMD 55:265, 619} Pvt., Capt. Francis Ware's Company of MD Troops, Charles Co., from 9 Oct 1757 to 31 May 1758 (served 235 days) when he was discharged. {Ref: MHS MS.375.1; CSOS:89} Payment to him was recorded in Col. Dagworthy's account book on 7 Mar 1763. {Ref: MHS MS.375}

POWELL, STEPHEN (Maryland), b. c1739, Shropshire, England (flax dresser, age 21 in 1760); pvt., lately in Baltimore Co., was reported as deserted from the 1st Bttn. of the Royal American Regt. in June 1760. {Ref: *MD Gazette*, 19 Jun 1760}

POWELL (POWEL), THOMAS (Maryland), m. 1st to (N) and 2nd to Sarah (N), had children George, John [#1], Elizabeth, Mary, Ann, Thomas, Joseph, Sarah, and Rachel by his 1st wife, and John [#2] and unborn child (N) in 1776 by his 2nd wife, and d. testate by 15 Feb 1776. {Ref: WMG 4:4, p. 184} Pvt., Capt. Joshua Beall's Company of MD Troops, Prince George's Co., from 9 Oct 1757 to 29 Jan 1758 when he was discharged. {Ref: MHS MS.375.1; CSOS:85} Militia pay account submitted in 1758, exact date not given; payment to him was also recorded in Col. Dagworthy's account book on 8 Mar 1763 for work on Fort Cumberland. {Ref: MHS MS.375; MHM 9:4, p. 368}

POWELL, WILLIAM (Delaware), pvt., Kent Co. Militia, Capt. John Caton's Company, 25 Apr 1757 (date of muster roll). {Ref: ARDE I:13}

POWER, ROBERT (Maryland), b. c1736, Charles Co. (planter, age 21 in 1757); pvt., enlisted in Royal American Regt. by Mr. Decheizer (date not given) and was reported as deserted by Lieut. McBean at Annapolis. Power had a ten day furlough to go to Piscataway, but did not return. It was noted that when found he should be delivered to Daniel Wolstenholme or Sgt. Henry Seale. {Ref: *MD Gazette*, 31 Mar 1757}

PRAIG (PRAIGG), PETER (Maryland), alias Peter Brake *[sic]*, pvt., Capt. Peter Butler's Company Muster Roll, Frederick Co., circa 1757-1758, exact dates not given (served 34 days); militia pay account submitted in 1758, exact date not given. {Ref: MHM 9:4, p. 367; CSOS:97} Bill of credit or order issued to Casper Shaff in his behalf for £1.14.0 and paid to David Cumming on 18 Apr 1767. {Ref: MSA S960 or S752, p. 168}

PRAPPS, JACOB (Maryland), pvt., Capt. John Middaugh's Company Muster Roll, Frederick Co., circa 1757-1758, exact dates not given (served 30 days); bill of credit issued or paid in his behalf to Charles Beatty for £1.10.0 on 1 Jul 1773. {Ref: MSA S960 or S752, p. 172; CSOS:101}

PRATHER, HENRY (Maryland), b. -- Sep 1732, Prince George's Co., son of Thomas and Elizabeth Prather, of Queen Anne's P. E. Parish. {Ref: PGCR 1:189} 2nd lieut., Capt. Joshua Beall's Company of MD Troops, Prince George's Co., from 9 Oct 1757 to 8 Nov 1758; 1st lieut., Capt. Francis Ware's Company of MD Troops, Charles Co., from 9 Nov 1758 to 30 Dec 1758. {Ref: MHS MS.375.1; CSOS:83, 87} Payment to him was recorded in Col. Dagworthy's account book on 14 Jul 1762. {Ref: MHS MS.375}

PRATHER, JAMES (Maryland), b. 27 Jan 1735/6, Prince George's Co., son of Thomas and Elizabeth Prather, of Queen Anne's P. E. Parish. {Ref: PGCR 1:189} Pvt., Capt. Joseph Chapline's Company Muster Roll No. 4, Frederick Co., circa 1757-1758, exact dates not given (served 5 days); bill of credit issued or paid in his behalf to Joseph Chaplin for £0.5.0 on 13 Jun 1768. {Ref: MSA S960 or S752, p. 195; CSOS:105}

PRATHER, LIEUT. (Maryland), first name not given (and there were three Prathers who were lieutenants), commanded the detachment of MD troops in

August 1756 who pursued the French and Indians who had attacked Fort Granville. {Ref: *MD Gazette*, 26 Aug 1756}

PRATHER, RICHARD (Maryland), b. 1 Aug 1727, Prince George's Co., son of Thomas and Elizabeth Prather, of Queen Anne's P. E. Parish. {Ref: PGCR 1:189} Lieut. in Capt. Joseph Chapline's Company (Muster Roll No. 4), Frederick Co., circa 1757-1758, exact dates not given (served 13 days); bill of credit issued or paid in his behalf to Joseph Chaplin for £1.10.3 on 13 Jun 1768. {Ref: MSA S960 or S752, p. 195; CSOS:105}

PRATHER, THOMAS (Maryland), major, Frederick Co., paid £248.19.6 by the MD Assembly in 1756 "for the support of the ranging parties on the Western Frontier" from 13 Mar to 21 May 1756. {Ref: ARMD 52:674} Colonel and commander-in-chief of the militia in Frederick Co. by 1763. {Ref: ARMD 32:60-61, 58:342} See "Basil Croser" and "Alexander Beall" and "Henry Prather," q.v.

PRATHER, THOMAS CLAGETT (Maryland), b. 9 May 1726, Prince George's Co., son of Thomas and Elizabeth Prather, of Queen Anne's P. E. Parish. {Ref: PGCR 1:189} 1st lieut., Capt. Alexander Beall's Company of MD Troops, Frederick Co., from 9 Oct 1757 to 31 May 1758; militia pay account submitted in 1758, exact date not given. {Ref: MHM 9:4, p. 366} Transferred to Capt. Francis Ware's Company on 1 Jun 1758 and was reported as killed on 12 Oct 1758; name listed once as "Thomas Prather" (no middle name given). {Ref: MHS MS.375.1; CSOS:87} A newspaper indicated "Lieut. Prather was killed in the late battle" (exact date not given). {Ref: *MD Gazette*, 2 Nov 1758} Payment due him was recorded in Col. Dagworthy's account book on 14 Jul 1762. {Ref: MHS MS.375}

PRATT, ABRAHAM (Delaware), pvt., Capt. Richard McWilliams' Company of Foot, New Castle Co., enlisted 28 Dec 1757. {Ref: ARDE I:15}

PRATT, JEREMIAH (Delaware), pvt., Capt. Richard McWilliams' Company of Foot, New Castle Co., enlisted 28 Dec 1757. {Ref: ARDE I:15}

PREALL (PEALL), FREDERICK (Maryland), pvt., Capt. John Middaugh's Company Muster Roll, Frederick Co., circa 1757-1758, exact dates not given (served 30 days); bill of credit issued or paid in his behalf to Charles Beatty for £1.10.0 on 23 Oct 1770. {Ref: MSA S960 or S752, p. 172; CSOS:101}

PREES (PRIESE), HENRY (Maryland), pvt., Capt. Alexander Beall's Company of MD Troops, Frederick Co., from 9 Oct 1757 to 8 Nov 1758. {Ref: MHS MS.375.1; CSOS:82} Payment to him was recorded in Col. Dagworthy's account book on 12 Jul 1762 for work on Fort Cumberland. {Ref: MHS MS.375}

PRETTYMAN, THOMAS (Delaware), ensign, Northern District of Indian River Hundred, Militia Regt. of Sussex Co., 1756; ensign, Angola District, 18 Mar 1758. {Ref: ARDE I:13, 15; ARPA (2nd Series) 2:529, 579; HDE I:141} *Identification problem:* There were two men with this name who could have served in the war: (1) Thomas Prettyman, Esq., m. Comfort (N) and prob. had daus. Sarah and Mary; and, (2) Thomas Prettyman, planter, m. Elizabeth (N), had children William, George, Burton, Robert, Thomas, Hessy, Comfort, Ann, Tabitha, Mary, Patience, Sarah, Agnes, and Isabell, and d. testate by 14 Apr 1795. {Ref: CDSS:171}

PRETTYMAN, WILLIAM (Delaware), ensign, Southern District of Indian River Hundred, Militia Regt. of Sussex Co., 1756-1758. {Ref: ARDE I:13, 15; ARPA (2nd Series) 2:529, 579; HDE I:141} *Identification problem:* There were four men with this name who could have served in the war: (1) William Prettyman, b. c1710, son of Robert Prettyman and Sarah Burton, m. Sarah Herring by 1735, had children William (d. before 1766), Sarah, Magdalene, Naomi, and Margaret, and d. testate by 13 Sep 1766; (2) William Prettyman, b. c1733, son of John Prettyman (d. 1754) and prob. Comfort Leatherbury, m. 1st to Comfort Woolf and 2nd to Comfort Kollock, and d. by 1772; (3) William Prettyman, b. c1734, son of William Prettyman and Sarah Herring, m. Sarah Burton (widow of Woolsey Burton and dau. of William Burton), and d. before 1766; and, (4) William Prettyman, yeoman, d. intestate by 17 Apr 1780 at which time letters of administration were granted to Robert Prettyman. {Ref: CFD 3:160, 168, 174; CDSS:171-172}

PRICE, ANDREW, see "James Price," q.v.

PRICE, ANN, see "James Price, Jr.," q.v.

PRICE, DANIEL (Delaware), b. c1733, Elizabethtown, NJ (weaver, age 25 in 1758); pvt., enlisted 4 May 1758 "for the campaign in the lower counties" by Capt. John McClughan. {Ref: ARDE I:18; ARPA (2nd Series) 2:570}

PRICE, EDWARD, see "James Price, Jr.," q.v.

PRICE, JAMES (Maryland), farmer; pvt., Capt. Peregrine Brown's 7th Co. of Foot Militia, Kent Co., on 19 Feb 1758, by which time he had enlisted, but reportedly refused to appear and serve in arms against the enemy. {Ref: ARMD 31:283, 288} *Identification problem:* There were two men with this name who could have served in the war: (1) James Price, b. 31 Mar 1727, son of Andrew Price and Elizabeth Perry; and, (2) James Price, b. c1715, m. Sarah Reading on 11 Aug 1736 in Shrewsbury Parish. {Ref: ESVR; MDG II:493}

PRICE, JAMES JR. (Maryland), b. 30 Apr 1738, Kent Co., son of James Price and Sarah Reading, of Shrewsbury Parish. {Ref: ESVR} Farmer who enlisted as a pvt. in Capt. Peregrine Brown's 7th Co. of Foot Militia, Kent Co., by 19 Feb 1758, but reportedly refused to appear at that time and serve in arms against the enemy. {Ref: ARMD 31:283, 288} He was prob. the James Price who m. Ann (N) and d. testate by 13 Nov 1777, indicating in his will "if my wife is with child my brother Edward is to be guardian for that child until of age." {Ref: Kent Co. Wills 6:30}

PRICE, JOHN (Maryland or Pennsylvania), pvt. by 1757, was arrested in Annapolis for desertion at Carlisle and sentenced to be hanged. {Ref: *MD Gazette*, 10 Nov 1757}

PRICE, JOHN (Maryland), indentured servant and soldier who served in the French and Indian War some time between 1756 and 1763 (exact dates not known); his master Daniel Stansbury, Jr., planter, requested compensation from the Baltimore County Court due to the loss of use of Price while in the service. {Ref: MHM 94:4, p. 426, citing Baltimore Co. Court Minutes}

PRICE, JOSEPH (Maryland), cpl., Capt. Peter Butler's Company Muster Roll, Frederick Co., circa 1757-1758, exact dates not given (served 34 days); bill of credit or order issued in his behalf for £2.5.3 and paid to Casper Shaff on 2 Mar 1767. {Ref: MSA S960 or S752, p. 167; CSOS:96}

PRICE, MARY, see "Simon Wilmer" and "John Hall" and "John Clark," q.v.

PRICE, NICHOLAS (Maryland), ensign in Capt. Henry Casson's Company Muster Roll, Queen Anne's Co., circa 1757-1758, exact dates not given (served 27 days); bill of credit issued or paid in his behalf to Capt. Casson on 27 Feb 1767 for £2.14.0. {Ref: MSA S960 or S752, p. 177; CSOS:108}

PRICE, REES (Maryland), pvt., Capt. Joseph Chapline's Company Muster Roll No. 1, Frederick Co., circa 1757-1758, exact dates not given (served 20 days); bill of credit issued or paid in his behalf to Joseph Chaplin for £1 on 5 Mar 1767. {Ref: MSA S960 or S752, p. 190; CSOS:102}

PRICE, THOMAS (Maryland), b. 3 Sep 1732, son of John Price (of Philadelphia, PA) and Rebecca King, m. Mary (N), had children Benjamin, Samuel, George, William, Elizabeth, Rebecca, Mary, Susannah, Matilda, and prob. Thomas, and d. testate by 20 May 1795, Frederick Co., MD; captain in PA in 1759, county justice (Frederick Co., 1763, 1768-1775), planter, hatter, gentleman, served on Committees of Correspondence and Observation (1774-1776), captain of MD Rifle Co. in 1775, major in Smallwood's Regt. in 1776, and colonel until 1780 (resigned). {Ref: BDML II:661}

PRICE, THOMAS (Maryland), sgt., Capt. Peter Butler's Company Muster Roll, Frederick Co., circa 1757-1758, exact dates not given (served 34 days); bill of credit or order issued in his behalf for £2.5.3 and paid to Casper Shaff on 2 Mar 1767. {Ref: MSA S960 or S752, p. 167; CSOS:96}

PRICE, VINCENT (Maryland), lieut., Capt. Henry Casson's Company Muster Roll, Queen Anne's Co., circa 1757-1758, exact dates not given (served 27 days); bill of credit issued or paid in his behalf to Capt. Casson on 27 Mar 1767 for £3.3.0. {Ref: MSA S960 or S752, p. 178: CSOS:108}

PRICHARD, HENRY (Delaware), pvt., Kent Co. Militia, Capt. John Caton's Company, 25 Apr 1757 (date of muster roll). {Ref: ARDE I:13}

PRIDE, SOUTHY or SUTHY (Delaware), b. c1737, Sussex, DE (planter, age 21 in 1758); pvt., enlisted 19 Apr 1758 "for the campaign in the lower counties" by Capt. John McClughan; pvt. listed again in 1759 as age 21, b. Sussex, DE, enlisted in Capt. John Wright's Company and mustered on 11 May 1759. {Ref: ARDE I:18, 25; ARPA (2nd Series) 2:570, 592}

PRIESE, HENRY, see "Henry Prees (Priese)," q.v.

PRINCESS DOWAGER, see "Colonel Haldimand," q.v.

PRINGLE, JACOB (Maryland), pvt., Capt. John Middaugh's Company Muster Roll, Frederick Co., circa 1757-1758, exact dates not given (served 30 days); bill of credit issued or paid in his behalf to Casper Shaff for £1.10.0 on 2 Mar 1767. {Ref: MSA S960 or S752, p. 171; CSOS:101}

PROCTOR, RICHARD (Delaware), b. c1733, Lancaster, England (weaver, age 26 in 1759); pvt., enlisted by Capt. James Armstrong for the PA Regt. on 29 Apr 1759. {Ref: ARDE I:26; ARPA (2nd Series) 2:585}

PUDDIVER (PUDIVER), THOMAS (Maryland), pvt., Capt. Joshua Beall's Company of MD Troops, Prince George's Co., from 9 Oct 1757 to 8 Jun 1758 (served 243 days); name was mistakenly listed once as "Thomas Puddesen." {Ref: MHS MS.375.1; CSOS:85} Payment to him was recorded in Col. Dagworthy's account book on 23 Jul 1762. {Ref: MHS MS.375}

PULLET, RICHARD (Delaware), b. c1730, MD (age 29 in 1759); pvt., enlisted in Capt. John Wright's Company and mustered on 11 May 1759. {Ref: ARDE I:25; ARPA (2nd Series) 2:508, 592}

PURGATE, CHRISTOPHER (Maryland), pvt., Capt. John White's Company Muster Roll, Frederick Co., circa 1757-1758, exact dates not given (served 6 days); bill of credit issued or paid in his behalf to Joseph Chaplin on 5 Mar 1767 for £0.6.0. {Ref: MSA S960 or S752, p. 164; CSOS:96}

PURNELL, JOHN (Maryland), d. c1761, captain and brother of "Zadock Purnell," q.v.

PURNELL, MARY, see "John Dennis, Jr.," q.v.

PURNELL, ZADOCK (Maryland), b. c1720, Somerset Co., son of John Purnell and Elizabeth Rackcliffe, and d. testate in 1805, Worcester Co.; prob. never married; company clerk in the militia in 1748, captain by 1767, member of MD Assembly (1758-1761, 1768-1770, served on Arms and Ammunition Committee), and colonel (1777-1778). {Ref: BDML II:667}

PURNOLL (PURNALL), JOHN (Maryland), pvt., Capt. Henry Casson's Company Muster Roll, Queen Anne's Co., circa 1757-1758, exact dates not given (served 27 days); bill of credit issued or paid in his behalf to Capt. Casson on 27 Mar 1767 for £1.7.0. {Ref: MSA S960 or S752, p. 178; CSOS:109}

PURSE, ALEXANDER (Delaware), pvt., Capt. Henry Vanbibber's Company of the Lower Counties on Delaware Troops at New Castle, enlisted on 19 May 1759. {Ref: ARDE I:26; ARPA (2nd Series) 2:594}

PURSLEY, DANIEL (Maryland), patriot, Frederick Co., was paid £46.12.8 at Fort Frederick on 8 Jul 1758 "for him and other battoemen for carrying artillery stores to Fort Cumberland" for the Western Expedition against Fort Duquesne. {Ref: ARMD 55:773}

PYNER, ANN, see "Simon Wilmer," q.v.

QUEEN (QUEER), HENRY (Maryland), pvt., Capt. Peter Butler's Company Muster Roll, Frederick Co., circa 1757-1758, exact dates not given (served 34 days); bill of credit or order issued in his behalf for £1.14.0 and paid to Peter Grosh on 4 Mar 1767. {Ref: MSA S960 or S752, p. 168; CSOS:97}

QUEEN (QUIN, QUIEN), JOHN (Maryland), pvt., Capt. Elias Delashmutt's Company Muster Roll, Frederick Co., 13 Aug 1757, exact dates not given (served 52 days); also served another 30 days, exact dates not given; bill of credit issued or paid in his behalf to Elias Delashmut, Jr. on 16 Mar 1767 for £4.2.0. {Ref: MSA S960 or S752, p. 163; CSOS:94, 98}

QUEEN, RICHARD (Maryland), pvt., Capt. Richard Pearis' Company of MD Troops, Frederick Co., from 9 Oct 1757 to 4 Apr 1758 when he reportedly deserted; however, payment to him was recorded in Col. Dagworthy's account book on 8 Mar 1763. {Ref: MHS MS.375; MHS MS.375.1}

QUYNN, ALLEN (Maryland), b. c1726, Annapolis, m. Elizabeth (N) by 1765, had children William, Allen, John, Catherine, Mary, Sophia, and Elizabeth, and d.

8 Nov 1803, Anne Arundel Co.; patriot, cordwainer, land developer, gentleman, entrepreneur, constable in 1767, member of the Committee of Observation in 1775, member of the MD Assembly (1777-1802), county justice (1777-1803), Orphans Court justice (1777-1794), and mayor of Annapolis (1778-1779, 1786-1787, 1792-1793, 1795, 1799, 1801-1803). {Ref: BDML II:670-671; *MD Gazette*, 10 Nov 1803} Pay account submitted for quartering soldiers in 1757 or 1758, exact dates not given. {Ref: MHM 9:3, p. 261}

RACKCLIFFE, ELIZABETH, see "Zadock Purnell," q.v.

RACKETT (RECKETT), EDWARD (Maryland), pvt., Capt. Joseph Chapline's Company Muster Rolls No. 2 and 3, Frederick Co., circa 1757-1758, exact dates not given (served 9 days); bill of credit issued or paid in his behalf to Joseph Chaplin for £0.9.0 on 5 Mar 1767. {Ref: MSA S960 or S752, p. 193; CSOS:104} See "Edward Ricketts," q.v.

RADFORD, JOHN (Maryland), patriot and poss. soldier (rank not specified), Frederick Co., militia pay account submitted in 1758, exact date not given. {Ref: MHM 9:4, p. 367}

RADFORD, THOMAS (Maryland), alias Thomas Bradford *[sic]*, pvt., Capt. Elias Delashmutt's Company Muster Roll, Frederick Co., circa 1757-1758, exact dates not given (served 30 days); bill of credit issued or paid in his behalf to Elias Delashmut, Jr. on 16 Mar 1767 for £1.10.0. {Ref: MSA S960 or S752, p. 162; CSOS:94}

RAGAN, JOHN (Maryland), cpl., Capt. John Dagworthy's Company of MD Troops, Frederick Co., from 9 Oct 1757 to 16 Apr 1759 when he reportedly deserted; however, payment to him was recorded in Col. Dagworthy's account book on 21 Jul 1762. {Ref: MHS MS.375; CSOS:77; MHS MS.375.1}

RAIMON (RAIMAN, RAYMOND), MICHAEL (Maryland), b. c1722, m. Sarah Ackland on 24 Nov c1744, Shrewsbury Parish; children unknown; pvt., Capt. Peregrine Brown's Company Muster Roll, Kent Co., circa 1757-1758, exact dates not given (served 15 days); bill of credit issued or paid in his behalf to Robert Buchanan on 20 Feb 1767 for £0.15.0. {Ref: ESVR; MSA S960 or S752, p. 180; CSOS:110}

RAITT (RAIT), ANN (Maryland), patriot, Annapolis, Anne Arundel Co., pay account submitted for quartering soldiers in 1757 or 1758, exact dates not given. {Ref: MHM 9:3, p. 260} John Raitt, merchant and late sheriff of Anne Arundel Co., d. 30 Jun 1758; Anne Raitt, widow, was his administratrix in 1758 and Nathan Hammond, Jr. was his administrator in 1760. {Ref: *MD Gazette*, 6 Jul 1758, 27 Jul 1758 and 10 Jan 1760}

RALLY (RALLEY), ISAAC (Maryland), pvt., Capt. Richard Pearis' Company of MD Troops, Frederick Co., circa 9 Oct 1757 to 31 May 1758; pvt., Capt. Alexander Beall's Company of MD Troops, Frederick Co., from 1 Jun 1758 to 12 Oct 1758; name listed once as "Israel or Isaac Rally." {Ref: MHS MS.375.1; CSOS:82, 91} Payment to him was recorded in Col. Dagworthy's account book on 15 Jul 1762. {Ref: MHS MS.375} Another account submitted to the MD Assembly on 25 Nov 1763 indicated he was due £4.12.3 as "granted by the Act for Granting a Sum of Money as a Present to the Forces, late in the Pay and Service of this Province, and taken into his Majesty's Service by Brigadier General Forbes." {Ref: ARMD 58:401}

RAMSBURG, STEPHEN, see "Stephen Rensburg," q.v.

RAMSEY, JAMES (Delaware), b. c1738, Donegal, Ireland (laborer, age 20 in 1758); pvt., enlisted 20 Apr 1758 "for the campaign in the lower counties" by Capt. John McClughan. {Ref: ARDE I:18; ARPA (2nd Series) 2:570}

RAMSEY, JOHN (Maryland), pvt., Capt. Francis Ware's Company of MD Troops, Charles Co., from 9 Oct 1757 to 8 Jun 1758 (served 243 days). {Ref: MHS MS.375.1; CSOS:89} Payment to him was recorded in Col. Dagworthy's account book on 22 Jul 1762. {Ref: MHS MS.375}

RAMSEY, RAYNOLDS (Delaware), pvt., Capt. Richard McWilliams' Company of Foot, New Castle Co., enlisted 28 Dec 1757. {Ref: ARDE I:14}

RANDLE, PETER (Delaware), b. c1720, Inniskillen, Ireland (laborer, age 39 in 1759); pvt., enlisted by Capt. James Armstrong for the PA Regt. on 4 May 1759. {Ref: ARDE I:26; ARPA (2nd Series) 2:585}

RANKIN, GEORGE, see "Charles Wallace," q.v.

RANKIN, MARY, see "Charles Wallace," q.v.

RAPE, MICHAEL (Maryland), pvt., Capt. John White's Company Muster Roll, Frederick Co., circa 1757-1758, exact dates not given (served 6 days); bill of credit issued or paid to him for £0.6.0 in 1767, exact date not given. {Ref: MSA S960 or S752, p. 165; CSOS:96}

RASH, HANNAH, see "Renn Forkcum," q.v.

RASH, JOHN, see "Renn Forkcum," q.v.

RASH, JOHN JR. (Delaware), pvt., Kent Co. Militia, Capt. John Caton's Company, 25 Apr 1757 (date of muster roll). {Ref: ARDE I:14} *Identification problem:* There were two men with this name who could have served in the war: (1) John Rash m. (N), had children Joseph, James, William, Elizabeth, Mary, Sarah, and Hannah, and d. testate by 3 Jan 1761; and, (2) John Rash, Sr., farmer, m. (N), had children Daniel, Andrew, Martin, Joseph, Sarah, Mary, Easter, Ann, Letitia, Ansley, and Patience, and d. testate by 30 Nov 1790. {Ref: CDSS:175}

RASH, JOSEPH (Delaware), pvt., Kent Co. Militia, Capt. John Caton's Company, 25 Apr 1757 (date of muster roll). {Ref: ARDE I:14}

RASIN, JOSEPH (Maryland), ensign in Capt. Peregrine Brown's Company Muster Roll, Kent Co., circa 1757-1758, exact dates not given (served 15 days); bill of credit issued or paid in his behalf to Robert Buchanan on 20 May 1767 for £1.10.0. {Ref: MSA S960 or S752, p. 179; CSOS:109}

RASIN, WILLIAM (Maryland), b. 12 Jul 1723, prob. Kent Co., son of Thomas Rasin and Mary Warner (who were Quakers, but William was a Protestant), m. Sarah (N), had children Thomas, William, Joseph, Sarah, Susannah, and Rebecca, and d. 13 Feb 1762 in George Town, Kent Co., MD; patriot, planter, merchant, miller, gentleman, member of the MD Assembly (1751-1753, 1757-1758, served on the Arms and Ammunition Committee), and sheriff (1753-1756). {Ref: BDML II:673; *MD Gazette*, 25 Feb 1762} Pay account submitted for quartering soldiers in 1757 or 1758, exact dates not given. {Ref: MHM 9:3, p. 261}

RATHELL, AARON (Maryland), pvt., Capt. John Dagworthy's Company of MD Troops, Frederick Co., from 9 Oct 1757 to 16 Feb 1758 when he was discharged. {Ref: MHS MS.375.1; CSOS:77} Payment to him was recorded in Col. Dagworthy's account book on 8 Mar 1763. {Ref: MHS MS.375}

RATTENBURY, ANN, see "John Jones," q.v.

RATTLEDGE, JAMES (Delaware), farmer, m. Mary (N), had children John, Thomas, James, Moses, William, Elizabeth, Ruth, and Jemimah, and d. testate by 26 Jul 1773. {Ref: CDSS:175} Pvt., Kent Co. Militia, Capt. John Caton's Company, 25 Apr 1757 (date of muster roll). {Ref: ARDE I:14}

RATTLEDGE, MOSES (Delaware), pvt., Kent Co. Militia, Capt. John Caton's Company, 25 Apr 1757 (date of muster roll). {Ref: ARDE I:14}

RATTLEDGE, THOMAS (Delaware), pvt., Kent Co. Militia, Capt. John Caton's Company, 25 Apr 1757 (date of muster roll). {Ref: ARDE I:14}

RAWLINGS, ---- (Maryland), sea captain by 1757, was in command of a ship (not named) when captured by the French. {Ref: *MD Gazette*, 26 May 1757}

RAWLSTON (RALSTON), HUGH (Delaware), b. c1732, Argyle, Scotland (laborer, age 27 in 1759); pvt., enlisted 26 Apr 1758 "for the campaign in the lower counties" by Capt. John McClughan. {Ref: ARDE I:18; ARPA (2nd Series) 2:570}

RAY, JOHN (Maryland), cpl., Capt. Joshua Beall's Company Muster Roll, Prince George's Co., circa 1757-1758, exact dates not given; bill of credit issued or paid in his behalf to Joshua Beall for £2.17.4½ on 23 Feb 1767. {Ref: MSA S960 or S752, p. 184; CSOS:116} *Identification problem:* There were two men with this name who could have served in the war: (1) John Ray, b. 6 Aug c1735, Prince George's Co., son of William and Ann Ray, of Queen Anne's P. E. Parish; and, (2) John Ray, b. 24 Jun 1732, Prince George's Co., son of John and Sarah Ray, of Prince George's P. E. Parish. {Ref: PGCR 1:190, 2:120}

RAY, JOSEPH (Maryland), sgt., Capt. Elias Delashmutt's Company Muster Roll, Frederick Co., circa 1757-1758, exact dates not given (served 30 days); bill of credit issued or paid in his behalf to Elias Delashmut, Jr. on 16 Mar 1767 for £5.9.3. {Ref: MSA S960 or S752, p. 162; CSOS:94}

RAY, THOMAS (Maryland), b. 27 Dec 1722 (1723?), Prince George's Co., son of William Jr. and Elizabeth Ray, of Queen Anne's P. E. Parish. {Ref: PGCR 1:190} Pvt., Capt. Elias Delashmutt's Company Muster Roll, Frederick Co., circa 1757-1758, exact dates not given (served 30 days); bill of credit issued or paid in his behalf to Elias Delashmut, Jr. on 16 Mar 1767 for £1.10.0. {Ref: MSA S960 or S752, p. 162; CSOS:94}

RAYE, CHRISTOPHER (Delaware), pvt., Capt. Henry Vanbibber's Company of the Lower Counties on Delaware Troops at New Castle, enlisted on 23 May 1759. {Ref: ARDE I:26; ARPA (2nd Series) 2:594}

READ, GEORGE (Delaware), attorney; pvt., Capt. Richard McWilliams' Company of Foot, New Castle Co., enlisted 28 Dec 1757. {Ref: ARDE I:15}

READ, JOHN (Maryland), pvt., Capt. Samuel Chapman's Company Muster Roll, Anne Arundel Co., circa 1757-1758, exact dates not given; bill of credit issued or paid to him for £1.18.0 on 25 Feb 1767. {Ref: MSA S960 or S752, p. 188}

READ, MARY, see "Gunning Bedford," q.v.

READ (REID), WILLIAM (Delaware), ensign, White Clay Hundred, Upper Regt. of Militia, East Division, New Castle Co., 1756. {Ref: ARDE I:11; ARPA (2nd Series) 2:526; HDE I:141}

READING (REDDING, READIN), JOHN (Maryland), farmer; b. 29 Feb 1731/2, Kent Co., son of John and Sarah Readin, of Shrewsbury Parish; pvt., Capt. Peregrine Brown's 7th Co. of Foot Militia, Kent Co., on 19 Feb 1758, by which time he had enlisted, but reportedly refused to appear and serve in arms against the enemy; he later stated that at the time "he had hurt his leg much and a fever had fell into it, and it was inflamed to that degree, that he could scarce stand upon it, and was entirely unable to do duty." {Ref: ESVR; ARMD 31:283, 286, 288}

READING (READIN), SARAH, see "James Price" and "John Reading," q.v.

READING (REDDING, READIN), WILLIAM (Maryland), b. 23 Dec 1735, Kent Co., son of John and Sarah Readin, of Shrewsbury Parish; pvt., Capt. Peregrine Brown's Company Muster Roll, Kent Co., circa 1757-1758, exact dates not given (served 15 days); bill of credit issued or paid in his behalf to Robert Buchanan on 21 Mar 1767 for £0.15.0. {Ref: ESVR; MSA S960 or S752, p. 179; CSOS:110}

REDBURN, SAMUEL (Maryland), pvt., Capt. Alexander Beall's Company of MD Troops, Frederick Co., from 9 Oct 1757 to 23 Oct 1758 when he reportedly deserted; however, payment to him was recorded in Col. Dagworthy's account book on 7 Mar 1763. {Ref: MHS MS.375; CSOS:82; MHS MS.375.1}

REED (READ), GEORGE (Maryland), pvt., Capt. Joseph Chapline's Company Muster Roll No. 1, Frederick Co., circa 1757-1758, exact dates not given (served 49 days); bill of credit issued or paid in his behalf to Joseph Chaplin for £1.1.0 on 23 May 1767. {Ref: MSA S960 or S752, p. 192; CSOS:103} Pvt., Capt. Joseph Chapline's Company Muster Rolls No. 2 and 3, Frederick Co., circa 1757-1758, exact dates not given (served 3 days); bill of credit issued or paid in his behalf to Thomas Bowles for £0.3.0 on 23 May 1767. {Ref: MSA S960 or S752, p. 193; CSOS:104}

REED, JAMES (Maryland), pvt., Capt. John Middaugh's Company Muster Roll, Frederick Co., circa 1757-1758, exact dates not given (served 30 days); bill of credit issued or paid in his behalf to Thomas Beatty, Jr. for £1.10.0 on 23 Feb 1767. {Ref: MSA S960 or S752, p. 171; CSOS:101}

REED, JAMES (Maryland), patriot and poss. soldier (rank not specified), Kent Co., militia pay account submitted in 1758, exact date not given. {Ref: MHM 9:4, p. 369}

REED, TILTON (Maryland), pvt., Capt. Peregrine Brown's Company Muster Roll, Kent Co., circa 1757-1758, exact dates not given (served 15 days); bill of credit issued or paid in his behalf to Robert Buchanan on 20 Feb 1767 for £0.15.0. {Ref: MSA S960 or S752, p. 179; CSOS:110}

REED, WALTER (Delaware), pvt., Capt. French Battell's Company of Lower County Provincials, enlisted 19 May 1758. {Ref: ARDE I:16; ARPA (2nd Series) 2:555}

REES (REECE), EVAN (Delaware), prob. son of Evan Reece who m. Katrina (N) and d. testate in Mill Creek Hundred by 21 Dec 1742. {Ref: CDSS:177} Captain, Mill Creek Hundred, Upper Regt. of Militia, North Division, New Castle Co., 1756. {Ref: ARDE I:11; ARPA (2nd Series) 2:526; HDE I:141} See "Evan Rice," q.v.

REES (REESE), JOHN (Delaware), m. Esther (N), had children John, Jeremiah, Thomas, David, Mary, Lydia, and Sarah, and d. testate in Little Creek Hundred by 4 Jun 1769. {Ref: CDSS:177} Lieut. in Capt. Robert Blackshire's Company, 1747-1748, during King George's War against Canada; lieut., Upper Part of Duck Creek Hundred, Militia of Kent Co. on Delaware, 1756. {Ref: ARDE I:12; ARPA (2nd Series) 2:527-529; HDE I:141}

REETER (RETER), CONROD (Maryland), pvt., Capt. Jonathan Hagar's Company Muster Roll, Frederick Co., circa 1757-1758, exact dates not given (served 6 days); bill of credit issued or paid in his behalf to Joseph Chaplin for £0.6.0 on 24 Apr 1767. {Ref: MSA S960 or S752, pp. 173-174; CSOS:106}

REETER (RETER), JACOB (Maryland), pvt., Capt. John White's Company Muster Roll, Frederick Co., circa 1757-1758, exact dates not given (served 6 days); bill of credit issued or paid to him for £0.6.0 in 1767, exact date not given. {Ref: MSA S960 or S752, p. 165; CSOS:95}

REETER (REATER, RETER), JOHN (Maryland), pvt., Capt. Joseph Chapline's Company Muster Roll No. 1, Frederick Co., circa 1757-1758, exact dates not given (served 41 days); bill of credit issued or paid in his behalf to Joseph Chaplin for £2.1.0 on 5 Mar 1767. {Ref: MSA S960 or S752, pp. 191-192; CSOS:103} Pvt., Capt. Jonathan Hagar's Company Muster Roll, Frederick Co., circa 1757-1758, exact dates not given (served 6 days); bill of credit issued or paid in his behalf to Joseph Chaplin for £0.6.0 on 24 Apr 1767. {Ref: MSA S960 or S752, pp. 173-174; CSOS:106}

REETER (REATER), JOHN JR. (Maryland), pvt., Capt. Henry Sneavely's Company Muster Roll, Frederick Co., circa 1757-1758, exact dates not given; bill of credit issued or paid in his behalf to Joseph Chaplin for £0.8.0 on 24 Apr 1767. {Ref: MSA S960 or S752, p. 190}

REEVES, ELIZABETH, see "William Thomas," q.v.

REGESTER, JOHN (Delaware), pvt., Kent Co. Militia, Capt. John Caton's Company, 25 Apr 1757 (date of muster roll). {Ref: ARDE I:14}

REID, WILLIAM, see "William Reed," q.v.

RENCH (RENTCH), ANDREW (Maryland), pvt., Capt. Jonathan Hagar's Company Muster Roll, Frederick Co., circa 1757-1758, exact dates not given (served 6 days); bill of credit issued or paid to him for £0.6.0 on 21 Feb 1767. {Ref: MSA S960 or S752, pp. 173-174; CSOS:107}

RENCH (RENTCH), JOHN (Maryland), pvt., Capt. John White's Company Muster Roll, Frederick Co., circa 1757-1758, exact dates not given (served 6 days); militia pay account submitted in 1758, exact date not given. {Ref: MHM 9:4, p. 368} Bill of credit issued or paid in his behalf to Joseph Chaplin on 24 Apr 1767 for £0.6.0. {Ref: MSA S960 or S752, p. 164; CSOS:95}

RENCH (RENTCH), PETER (Maryland), m. Margaret (N), had children Joseph, John, Andrew, and two daus. (N), and d. testate by 16 Mar 1772. {Ref: WMG 3:4, p. 149} Patriot and poss. soldier (rank not specified), Frederick Co., militia pay account submitted in 1758, exact date not given. {Ref: MHM 9:4, p. 368}

RENSBURG (RENSBURGER, RANSBERGAR), ADAM (Maryland), pvt., Capt. Stephen Rensburg's or Rensburger's Company Muster Roll, Frederick Co., circa

1757-1758, exact dates not given (served 34 days); bill of credit issued or paid in his behalf to Stephen Rensburger for £1.14.0 on 27 Mar 1767. {Ref: MSA S960 or S752, p. 183; CSOS:112}

RENSBURG (RENSBURGER, RANSBERGAR), GEORGE (Maryland), pvt., Capt. Stephen Rensburg's or Rensburger's Company Muster Roll, Frederick Co., circa 1757-1758, exact dates not given (served 34 days); bill of credit issued or paid in his behalf to Stephen Rensburger for £1.14.0 on 27 Mar 1767. {Ref: MSA S960 or S752, p. 183; CSOS:113}

RENSBURG (RENSBURGER, RANSBERGAR), STEPHEN (Maryland), captain, Frederick Co., circa 1757-1758, e xact dates not given; militia pay account submitted in 1758, exact date not given. {Ref: MHM 9:4, pp. 366-367} Bill of credit issued or paid to him for £7 on 27 Mar 1767; name also listed as "Stephen Ransburgh" and "Stephen Ransberger." {Ref: MSA S960 or S752, pp. 182-183; CSOS:111-112}

REYMOUR, JOSEPH (Maryland), pvt., Capt. Richard Pearis' Company of MD Troops, Frederick Co., circa 9 Oct 1757 to 31 May 1758; pvt., Capt. Alexander Beall's Company of MD Troops, Frederick Co., from 1 Jun 1758 to 30 Dec 1758 (served 213 days). {Ref: MHS MS.375.1; CSOS:82, 91} Payment to him was recorded in Col. Dagworthy's account book on 15 Jul 1763. {Ref: MHS MS.375}

REYMOUR (RAYMER), MICHAEL (Maryland), lieut., Capt. Stephen Rensburg's or Rensburger's Company Muster Roll, Frederick Co., circa 1757-1758, exact dates not given (served 42 days); bill of credit issued or paid in his behalf to Peter Grosh for £4.18.0 on 4 Mar 1767. {Ref: MSA S960 or S752, p. 182; CSOS:111}

REYMOUR (RAYMER), WILLIAM (Maryland), pvt., Capt. Richard Pearis' Company of MD Troops, Frederick Co., circa 9 Oct 1757 to 31 May 1758); pvt., Capt. John Dagworthy's Company of MD Troops, Frederick Co., from 1 Jun 1758 to 16 Apr 1759 when he reportedly deserted; however, payment to him was recorded in Col. Dagworthy's account book on 13 Jul 1762; name listed once as "William Raymen." {Ref: MHS MS.375; CSOS:78, 91; MHS MS.375.1}

REYNOLDS, FRANCIS (Maryland), pvt., Capt. Joseph Chapline's Company Muster Roll No. 1, Frederick Co., circa 1757-1758, exact dates not given (served 59 days); bill of credit issued or paid in his behalf to Joseph Chaplin for £2.19.1½ on 24 Apr 1767. {Ref: MSA S960 or S752, p. 192; CSOS:102} Pvt., Capt. Joseph Chapline's Company Muster Roll No. 4, Frederick Co., circa 1757-1758, exact dates not given (served 7 days); bill of credit issued or paid in his behalf to Joseph Chaplin for £0.7.0 on 24 Apr 1767; name listed once as "Francis Raynolds." {Ref: MSA S960 or S752, pp. 192, 195; CSOS:105}

REYNOLDS, GEORGE (Maryland), pvt., Capt. John Dagworthy's Company of MD Troops, Frederick Co., from 9 Oct 1757 to 26 Dec 1758 when he reportedly deserted; however, payment to him was recorded in Col. Dagworthy's account book on 11 Jul 1762 for work on Fort Cumberland. {Ref: MHS MS.375; CSOS:78; MHS MS.375.1}

REYNOLDS, JAMES (Maryland), pvt., Capt. John Middaugh's Company Muster Roll, Frederick Co., circa 1757-1758, exact dates not given (served 30 days);

bill of credit issued or paid in his behalf to Thomas Beatty, Jr. for £1.10.0 on 23 Feb 1767. {Ref: MSA S960 or S752, p. 171; CSOS:101}

REYNOLDS, JAMES (Maryland), sgt., Capt. Joshua Beall's Company of MD Troops, Prince George's Co., from 9 Oct 1757 (reduced to pvt. on 14 Aug 1758) to 30 Dec 1758; pvt., Capt. John Dagworthy's Company of MD Troops, Frederick Co., from 31 Dec 1758 to 28 Feb 1759 when he reportedly deserted; however, payment to him was recorded in Col. Dagworthy's account book on 21 Jul 1762. {Ref: MHS MS.375; CSOS:78, 85; MHS MS.375.1}

REYNOLDS, JANE, see "John Inch," q.v.

REYNOLDS (RANNOLDS), JOHN (Maryland), pvt., Capt. Joseph Chapline's Company Muster Roll No. 5, Frederick Co., circa 1757-1758, exact dates not given; bill of credit issued or paid in his behalf to Joseph Chaplin for £0.8.0 on 5 Mar 1767. {Ref: MSA S960 or S752, p. 195}

REYNOLDS, JOHN (Delaware), prob. son of Daniel Reynolds (Reynals) and Grace Lowber, m. Elizabeth (N), had no children, and d. testate by 2 Oct 1773. {Ref: CDSS:178} Pvt., Kent Co. Militia, Capt. John Caton's Company, 25 Apr 1757 (date of muster roll). {Ref: ARDE I:13}

REYNOLDS, JOHN (Maryland or Pennsylvania), ensign in Capt. Chambers' Company, killed in "a recent battle with the Indians" in 1756 (exact date not given) in Cumberland Co., PA, after the burning of McCord's Fort. {Ref: *MD Gazette*, 29 Apr 1756}

REYNOLDS, MARGARET, see "William Reynolds," q.v.

REYNOLDS, MICHAEL (Delaware), prob. son of Daniel Reynolds (Reynals) and Grace Lowber, m. Miriam Blackshare and had children Robert, Michael, Thomas, Daniel, John, George, and Letitia. {Ref: CDSS:178} Pvt., Kent Co. Militia, Capt. John Caton's Company, 25 Apr 1757 (date of muster roll). {Ref: ARDE I:13}

REYNOLDS, THOMAS JR. (Maryland), pvt., Capt. John Middaugh's Company Muster Roll, Frederick Co., circa 1757-1758, exact dates not given (served 30 days); bill of credit issued or paid in his behalf to Thomas Beatty, Jr. for £1.10.0 on 3 Apr 1767 {Ref: MSA S960 or S752, p. 172; CSOS:101}

REYNOLDS, WILLIAM (Maryland), b. c1710, m. 1st to Deborah Syng (widow) in 1739 and had children John, Thomas, Robert, Joseph, and William; m. 2nd to Mary Howell circa 1757 and had a dau. Margaret who m. Capt. Alexander Truman in 1781; and, d. testate in 1777; hatter, merchant, innkeeper, member of the South River Club, owner of Reynolds Tavern in Annapolis, and a Revolutionary War patriot. {Ref: Henry C. Peden, Jr.'s *Revolutionary Patriots of Anne Arundel County, 1775-1783*, p. 164} William Reynolds was also a patriot in the French and Indian War; pay account submitted for quartering soldiers in 1757 or 1758 (exact dates not given). {Ref: MHM 9:3, p. 260} See "James Orme," q.v.

REYNOLDS, WILLIAM (Maryland or Pennsylvania), pvt., Capt. Culbertson's Company, was wounded in "a recent battle with the Indians" in 1756 (exact date not given) in Cumberland Co., PA, after the burning of McCord's Fort. {Ref: *MD Gazette*, 29 Apr 1756}

RHEA, MATTHEW (Delaware), lieut., Appoquinimink Hundred, Lower Regt. of Militia, New Castle Co., 1756. {Ref: ARDE I:12; ARPA (2nd Series) 2:525; HDE I:141}

RHOADES (ROAD), ADAM (Maryland), pvt., Capt. John Middaugh's Company Muster Roll, Frederick Co., circa 1757-1758, exact dates not given (served 30 days); bill of credit issued or paid to him for £1.10.0 in 1767, exact date not given. {Ref: MSA S960 or S752, p. 172; CSOS:101}

RHOADES (RHOAD), CALEB or CUTLIP (Maryland), pvt., Capt. Jonathan Hagar's Company Muster Roll, Frederick Co., circa 1757-1758, exact dates not given (served 6 days); militia pay account submitted in 1758, exact date not given; name listed once as "Cutlip Rode." {Ref: MHM 9:4, p. 367; CSOS:106} Bill of credit issued or paid in his behalf to Joseph Chaplin for £0.6.0 on 24 Apr 1767. {Ref: MSA S960 or S752, pp. 173-174}

RHOADES (ROAD), GEORGE (Maryland), pvt., Capt. Stephen Rensburg's or Rensburger's Company Muster Roll, Frederick Co., circa 1757-1758, exact dates not given (served 42 days); bill of credit or order issued to Casper Shaff and paid to David Cumming for £2.2.0 on 18 Apr 1767. {Ref: MSA S960 or S752, p. 183; CSOS:112}

RHOADES (ROADES), JOHN, see "Peter Marsh," q.v.

RHOADES (ROADS), NICHOLAS (Maryland), patriot and poss. soldier (rank not specified), Frederick Co., militia pay account submitted in 1758, exact date not given. {Ref: MHM 9:4, p. 365}

RHOADES (RHODES), WILLIAM (Delaware), Esq., m. Mary (N), had sons John and James and a dau. (N) who m. a Gerrard, and d. testate by 9 Jan 1777. {Ref: CDSS:178} Captain, Lower Part of Murderkill Hundred, Militia of Kent Co. on Delaware, 1756; elected sheriff in 1760; styled "colonel" by 1776. {Ref: ARDE I:12; ARPA (2nd Series) 2:527-529; HDE I:141, 143}

RHOAR, RUDOLPH (Maryland), pvt., Capt. Peter Butler's Company Muster Roll, Frederick Co., circa 1757-1758, exact dates not given (served 34 days); bill of credit or order issued in his behalf for £1.14.0 and paid to Peter Grosh on 4 Mar 1767. {Ref: MSA S960 or S752, p. 168; CSOS:97}

RHOARER, CHRISTIAN (Maryland), pvt., Capt. Jonathan Hagar's Company Muster Roll, Frederick Co., circa 1757-1758, exact dates not given (served 6 days); bill of credit or order issued to him for £0.6.0 in 1767, exact date not given. {Ref: MSA S960 or S752, p. 175; CSOS:107}

RHODES, EZEKIEL (Maryland), pvt., Capt. Joseph Chapline's Company Muster Roll No. 4, Frederick Co., circa 1757-1758, exact dates not given (served 7 days); bill of credit issued or paid in his behalf to Joseph Chaplin for £0.7.0 on 24 Apr 1767. {Ref: MSA S960 or S752, p. 195; CSOS:105}

RHODES, FRANCES, see "Aquila Nelson," q.v.

RHODES, THOMAS (Maryland), pvt., Capt. Richard Pearis' Company of MD Troops, Frederick Co., circa 9 Oct 1757 to 31 May 1758; pvt., Capt. Alexander Beall's Company of MD Troops, Frederick Co., from 1 Jun 1758 to 8 Nov 1758. {Ref: MHS MS.375.1; CSOS:82, 91} Payment to him was recorded in Col. Dagworthy's account book on 15 Jul 1762. {Ref: MHS MS.375}

RHOE, WILLIAM (Maryland), pvt., Capt. Tobias Stansbury's Company Muster Roll, Baltimore Co., circa 1757-1758, exact dates not given; bill of credit issued or paid in his behalf to Abraham Jarrett for £1.18.0 on 23 Apr 1770. {Ref: MSA S960 or S752, p. 187} He was prob. the William Roe (Rowe), Jr. who was b. 5 Sep 1736, son of William Roe (Rowe) and Mary Jones, Baltimore Co. {Ref: BCF:555, 557}

RICE, EVAN (Delaware), b. 1737, son of Thomas Rice and Elizabeth Ball, New Castle Co., m. Elizabeth Graham, had children Thomas, Evan, William, Washington, Solomon, and John, and d. testate by 29 Nov 1783. {Ref: CDSS:178-179} Patriot who served as a Justice of the Peace, Justice of the Court of Oyer and Terminer, and Justice of the Court of Common Pleas, 1756-1763; also Justice of the Peace, 1777-1778, and one of the petitioners in 1781 who requested that the General Assembly "adjust the militia laws in order to oblige the inhabitants to provide suitable arms, attend muster, and turn out to defend their country." {Ref: GRSD 1:13, 15; RPDE:227} See "Evan Rees," q.v.

RICE, JOHN (Maryland), b. 22 Apr 1736, Baltimore Co., son of William Rice and Elizabeth Buttram, St. George's P. E. Parish. {Ref: BCF:538} Pvt., Capt. Tobias Stansbury's Company Muster Roll, Baltimore Co., circa 1757-1758, exact dates not given; bill of credit issued or paid in his behalf to John Paca for £1.18.0 on 1 Oct 1771. {Ref: MSA S960 or S752, p. 187}

RICE, JOHN DAVID (Delaware), b. c1729, America (carpenter, age 29 in 1758); pvt., recruited by Capt. Benjamin Noxon and enlisted on 20 May 1758. {Ref: ARDE I:19; ARPA (2nd Series) 2:566}

RICE, THOMAS (Delaware), b. c1737, Ware, VA (laborer, age 21 in 1758); pvt., enlisted 12 May 1758 "for the campaign in the lower counties" by Capt. John McClughan. {Ref: ARDE I:18; ARPA (2nd Series) 2:570}

RICE, WILLIAM, see "John Rice," q.v.

RICHARDS, DANIEL (Maryland), pvt., Capt. John Middaugh's Company Muster Roll, Frederick Co., circa 1757-1758, exact dates not given (served 30 days); bill of credit issued or paid in his behalf to Thomas Beatty, Jr. for £1.10.0 on 23 Feb 1767. {Ref: MSA S960 or S752, pp. 171-172; CSOS:100}

RICHARDS, JAMES, see "John Smith," q.v.

RICHARDS, JOSEPH (Maryland), pvt., Capt. John Middaugh's Company Muster Roll, Frederick Co., circa 1757-1758, exact dates not given (served 30 days); bill of credit issued or paid in his behalf to Thomas Beatty, Jr. for £1.10.0 on 23 Feb 1767. {Ref: MSA S960 or S752, pp. 171-172; CSOS:100}

RICHARDS, ROBERT (Maryland), pvt., Capt. Joshua Beall's Company Muster Roll, Prince George's Co., circa 1757-1758, exact dates not given; bill of credit issued or paid in his behalf to Dr. Richard Brookes for £1.10.6 on 27 Feb 1767; another entry stated it was assigned to Francis Waring. {Ref: MSA S960 or S752, pp. 184-185}

RICHARDS, STEPHEN (Maryland), pvt., Capt. John Middaugh's Company Muster Roll, Frederick Co., circa 1757-1758, exact dates not given (served 30 days); bill of credit issued or paid in his behalf to Thomas Beatty, Jr. for £1.10.0 on 23 Feb 1767. {Ref: MSA S960 or S752, pp. 171-172; CSOS:100}

RICHARDSON, CYNTHIA, see "Samuel Bond," q.v.

RICHARDSON, DANIEL (Maryland), b. c1734, Scotland (tailor, age about 24 in 1758); pvt. who was reported as having deserted from the Regt. of Light Infantry and when found he should be delivered to the sheriff of Prince George's Co. {Ref: *MD Gazette*, 20 Apr 1758}

RICHARDSON, JOSEPH (Maryland), sea captain by 1757 who was in command of the ship *Lux* when captured by the French. {Ref: *MD Gazette*, 3 Mar 1757}

RICHARDSON, RICHARD (Maryland), patriot and poss. soldier (rank not specified), Frederick Co., militia pay account submitted in 1758, exact date not given. {Ref: MHM 9:4, p. 367}

RICHARDSON, STEWART, see "Arthur Charlton," q.v.

RICHARDSON, SUSANNA, see "Peter Bayard," q.v.

RICHARDSON, THOMAS (Maryland), patriot and merchant, Anne Arundel or Frederick Co.; Thomas Richardson & Company received two barrels of gunpowder from the magazine and stores of the City of Annapolis on 22 Oct 1762 (as reported by the Arms and Ammunition Committee to the MD Assembly). {Ref: ARMD 58:342} See "Nicholas Pearce" and "Thomas Allen" and "James Dick," q.v.

RICHARDSON, THOMAS (Delaware), b. c1734, PA (laborer, age 24 in 1758); pvt., recruited by Capt. Benjamin Noxon and enlisted on 3 May 1758. {Ref: ARDE I:19; ARPA (2nd Series) 2:566}

RICKETTS, CHANEY (Maryland), pvt., Capt. Moses Chapline's Company Muster Roll No. 2, Frederick Co., circa 1757-1758, exact dates not given (served 13 days); bill of credit issued or paid in his behalf to Joseph Chaplin for £0.13.0 on 5 Mar 1767. {Ref: MSA S960 or S752, p. 197; CSOS:114} Pvt., Capt. Joseph Chapline's Company Muster Roll No. 4, Frederick Co., circa 1757-1758, exact dates not given (served 5 days); bill of credit issued or paid in his behalf to Joseph Chaplin for £0.5.0 on 5 Mar 1767. {Ref: MSA S960 or S752, p. 194; CSOS:105}

RICKETTS, EDWARD (Maryland), pvt., Capt. Joseph Chapline's Company Muster Roll No. 1, Frederick Co., circa 1757-1758, exact dates not given (served 55 days); bill of credit issued or paid in his behalf to Joseph Chaplin for £2.15.0 on 5 Mar 1767. {Ref: MSA S960 or S752, p. 191; CSOS:102} Pvt., Capt. Moses Chapline's Company Muster Roll No. 1, Frederick Co., circa 1757-1758, exact dates not given (served 55 days); bill of credit issued or paid in his behalf to Joseph Chaplin for £2.15.0 on 5 Mar 1767. {Ref: MSA S960 or S752, p. 196; CSOS:113} Pvt., Capt. Moses Chapline's Company Muster Roll No. 2, Frederick Co., circa 1757-1758, exact dates not given (served 55 days); bill of credit issued or paid in his behalf to Joseph Chaplin for £0.14.0 on 5 Mar 1767. {Ref: MSA S960 or S752, p. 197; CSOS:113} Pvt., Capt. Moses Chapline's Company Muster Roll No. 3, Frederick Co., circa 1757-1758, exact dates not given (served 6 days); bill of credit issued or paid in his behalf to Joseph Chaplin for £0.6.0 on 5 Mar 1767. {Ref: MSA S960 or S752, p. 198; CSOS:114} Pvt., Capt. Joseph Chapline's Company Muster Roll No. 5, Frederick Co., circa 1757-1758, exact dates not given; bill of credit issued or paid in his behalf to Joseph Chaplin for £0.6.0 on 5 Mar 1767. {Ref: MSA S960 or S752, p. 195} See "Edward Rackett," q.v.

RICKETTS, ELIZABETH, see "Rezin Ricketts," q.v.

RICKETTS, HANNAH, see "Henry Ward," q.v.

RICKETTS, JANE, see "Philip Ricketts," q.v.

RICKETTS, JOHN (Maryland), pvt., Capt. Peregrine Brown's Company Muster Roll, Kent Co., circa 1757-1758, exact dates not given (served 15 days); bill of credit issued or paid in his behalf to Robert Buchanan on 21 Mar 1767 for £0.15.0. {Ref: MSA S960 or S752, p. 179; CSOS:110}

RICKETTS, PHILIP (Maryland), b. 8 Aug 1733, Kent Co., son of Philip and Jane Ricketts, of Shrewsbury Parish. {Ref: ESVR} Pvt. in Capt. Peregrine Brown's Company, Kent Co., on 19 Feb 1758, by which time he had enlisted, but was unable to march due to health problems. {Ref: ARMD 31:283}

RICKETTS, REZIN or REASON (Maryland), b. 1 Apr 1733, Anne Arundel Co., son of John and Elizabeth Ricketts (bapt. 28 Apr 1734, All Hallow's Parish). {Ref: AACR:48} Pvt., Capt. Richard Pearis' Company, by 1757 (age about 22), reported as deserted from the MD Forces in July 1757. {Ref: *MD Gazette*, 21 Jul 1757}

RICKETTS, SINAI, see "Jesse Hollingsworth," q.v

RICKETTS, ZACHARIAH (Maryland), pvt., Capt. Joseph Chapline's Company Muster Roll No. 5, Frederick Co., circa 1757-1758, exact dates not given; bill of credit issued or paid to him for £0.6.0 in 1767, exact date not given. {Ref: MSA S960 or S752, p. 195}

RIDENOR, MATTHIAS (Maryland), pvt., Capt. Jonathan Hagar's Company Muster Roll, Frederick Co., circa 1757-1758, exact dates not given (served 6 days); bill of credit issued or paid to him for £0.6.0 in 1767, exact date not given. {Ref: MSA S960 or S752, p. 174; CSOS:106}

RIDENOR, NICHOLAS (Maryland), pvt., Capt. Jonathan Hagar's Company Muster Roll, Frederick Co., circa 1757-1758, exact dates not given (served 6 days); bill of credit issued or paid to him for £0.6.0 in 1767, exact date not given. {Ref: MSA S960 or S752, p. 174; CSOS:107}

RIDENOR, PETER (Maryland), pvt., Capt. Jonathan Hagar's Company Muster Roll, Frederick Co., circa 1757-1758, exact dates not given (served 6 days); bill of credit issued or paid to him for £0.6.0 in 1767, exact date not given. {Ref: MSA S960 or S752, p. 174; CSOS:106}

RIDER, DOROTHY, see "John Henry," q.v.

RIDER, JOHN (Maryland), pvt., Capt. Peter Bainbridge's Company Muster Roll, Frederick Co., circa 1757-1758, exact dates not given (served 28 days); bill of credit issued or paid to him for £1.8.0 in 1767, exact date not given. {Ref: MSA S960 or S752, p. 181; CSOS:111}

RIDGE, BENJAMIN (Maryland), pvt., Capt. John Middaugh's Company Muster Roll, Frederick Co., circa 1757-1758, exact dates not given (served 30 days); bill of credit issued or paid in his behalf to Robert Wood for £1.10.0 on 4 Mar 1767. {Ref: MSA S960 or S752, p. 172; CSOS:101}

RIDGELY, ANNE, see "Brice T. B. Worthington," q.v.

RIDGELY, CHARLES (Maryland), b. c1700, Prince George's Co., son of Charles Ridgley and Deborah Dorsey, m. 1st to Rachel Howard (d. 1750) by 1724, m.

2nd to Lydia Stringer (widow of Dr. Samuel Stringer and dau. of Richard Warfield) after 1750, had children John, Charles, William, Pleasance, Achsah, and Rachel, and d. by 8 Jun 1772, Baltimore Co.; planter, merchant, ironmaster, county justice (1743-1753), major by 1754, member of the MD Assembly (1751-1754), and colonel by 1763. {Ref: BDML II:681-683}

RIDGELY, CHARLES (Maryland), b. 17 Sep 1733, Baltimore Co., son of Charles Ridgely and Rachel Howard, m. Rebecca Dorsey circa 1760, and d. 28 Jun 1790, no surviving children; mariner by 1756, taken prisoner by the French in April 1757; captain of the snow *Baltimore Town* by July 1757; master of the ship *Charming Nancy* by 1759; patriot, member of the MD Assembly (1773-1789), ironmaster and co-founder of the Nottingham Ironworks in 1761 (with his father Charles and brother John) and produced cannon, balls, shot, kettles and pig iron for the MD troops during the Revolutionary War. {Ref: BDML II:683-684} See "Jethro Lynch (Linch)" and "Samuel Gardner," q.v.

RIDGELY, ELIZABETH, see "Brice T. B. Worthington," q.v.

RIDGELY, JOHN (Maryland), poss. b. 14 Jun 1723, Baltimore Co., son of Charles Ridgely and Rachel Howard, m. Mary Dorsey by 1746, had children Charles, William, John, Edward, Deborah, Rachel, Eleanor, Achsah, and eldest son (N) d. in infancy, and d. by 1 May 1771; patriot, merchant, ironmaster, gentleman, county justice (1750-1754), and Baltimore Town commissioner in 1768. {Ref: BDML II:688-689} Patriot and poss. soldier (rank not specified), militia pay account submitted in 1758, exact date not given. {Ref: MHM 9:4, p. 369} See "John Jones," q.v.

RIDGLEY, WILLIAM (Maryland), pvt., Capt. Peter Bainbridge's Company Muster Roll, Frederick Co., circa 1757-1758, exact dates not given (served 41 days); bill of credit issued or paid in his behalf to Casper Shaff on 16 Mar 1767 for £2.1.0. {Ref: MSA S960 or S752, p. 181; CSOS:111}

RIDOUT, JOHN, see "Daniel Wolstenholme," q.v.

RIGBIE, JOHANNA, see "George Grove," q.v.

RIGGS, EDMUND (Maryland), pvt., Capt. William Luckett's Company Muster Roll, Frederick Co., circa 1757-1758, exact dates not given (served 30 days); bill of credit issued or paid in his behalf to William Luckett, Jr. for £1.4.0 on 6 Apr 1767. {Ref: MSA S960 or S752, p. 169; CSOS:100}

RIGGS, JAMES JR. (Maryland), m. Mary (N), had 8 children (only mentioned son John in his will), and d. testate by 12 Jan 1770. {Ref: WMG 3:2, p. 75} Pvt., Capt. William Luckett's Company Muster Roll, Frederick Co., circa 1757-1758, exact dates not given (served 30 days); bill of credit issued or paid in his behalf to William Luckett, Jr. for £1.4.0 on 6 Apr 1767. {Ref: MSA S960 or S752, p. 170; CSOS:100}

RIGGS, JOHN (Maryland), pvt., Capt. William Luckett's Company Muster Roll, Frederick Co., circa 1757-1758, exact dates not given (served 30 days); bill of credit issued or paid in his behalf to William Luckett, Jr. for £1.10.0 on 6 Apr 1767. {Ref: MSA S960 or S752, p. 170; CSOS:99}

RILEY, JAMES (Maryland), ensign in Capt. Joshua Beall's Company Muster Roll, Prince George's Co., circa 1757-1758, exact dates not given; bill of credit issued or paid in his behalf to John Riley for £3.14.0 on 1 Apr 1767. {Ref: MSA S960 or S752, p. 184}

RILEY, JAMES (Maryland), ensign by 1757 and lieut., Capt. Joshua Beall's Company of MD Troops, Prince George's Co., from 9 Oct 1757 to 30 Dec 1758. {Ref: MHS MS.375.1; CSOS:116} "Lieut. Riley, of Capt. Joshua Beall's Company, brought a French deserter to Annapolis last Tuesday." {Ref: *MD Gazette*, 22 Dec 1757} On 22 Dec 1758 it was certified to the MD Assembly that Lieut. James Riley had produced the scalp of an Indian enemy to a provincial magistrate on 11 Dec 1757, "said Indian enemy having been killed by a Cherokee Indian, in the English interest, on St. George's Creek." {Ref: ARMD 56:134} "Lieut. James Riley, of the MD Forces, who often distinguished himself by his bravery, lately died at Fort Frederick of smallpox." {Ref: *MD Gazette*, 8 Feb 1759} Payment due him was recorded in Col. Dagworthy's account book on 21 Jul 1762. {Ref: MHS MS.375}

RILEY, JOHN, see "James Riley," q.v.

RILEY, PETER (Delaware), pvt., Capt. French Battell's Company of Lower County Provincials, enlisted 19 May 1758. {Ref: ARDE I:16; ARPA (2nd Series) 2:555}

RINEHART, GEORGE (Maryland), pvt., Capt. Henry Sneavely's Company Muster Roll, Frederick Co., circa 1757-1758, exact dates not given; bill of credit issued or paid to him for £0.8.0 in 1767, exact date not given. {Ref: MSA S960 or S752, p. 190}

RINEHART, JOHN (Maryland), pvt., Capt. John White's Company Muster Roll, Frederick Co., circa 1757-1758, exact dates not given (served 6 day); bill of credit issued or paid to him for £0.6.0 in 1767, exact date not given. {Ref: MSA S960 or S752, p. 165; CSOS:95}

RINEHART, THOMAS (Maryland), pvt., Capt. Henry Sneavely's Company Muster Roll, Frederick Co., circa 1757-1758, exact dates not given; bill of credit issued or paid to him for £0.8.0 in 1767, exact date not given. {Ref: MSA S960 or S752, p. 190}

RINEHART, VALENTINE, see "Philip Beard" and "George Burns" and "John Lewis," q.v.

RINGGOLD, THOMAS (Maryland), b. 5 Dec 1715, Kent Co., son of Thomas Ringgold and Rebecca Wilmer, m. Anna Maria Earle on 24 Oct 1743, had a son Thomas, and d. 1 Apr 1772 in Chester Town, Kent Co.; lawyer, merchant, slave trader, factor, member of the MD Assembly (1761-1771) and member of the Stamp Act Congress in 1765. {Ref: BDML II:694-695; *MD Gazette*, 9 Apr 1772} Pay account submitted for quartering soldiers in 1757 or 1758, exact dates not given. {Ref: MHM 9:3, p. 261} Militia pay account submitted in 1758, exact date not given. {Ref: MHM 9:4, p. 366, 369}

RINGGOLD, WILLIAM (Maryland), patriot, Kent Co., pay account submitted for quartering soldiers in 1757 or 1758, exact dates not given. {Ref: MHM 9:3, p. 261} *Identification problem:* There were two men with this name who could have performed the aforementioned service: (1) William Ringgold, b. 23 Feb c1723, son of Thomas Ringgold and Rebecca Wilmer, of St. Paul's Parish, m. 1st to cousin Mary Wilmer by 1761, m. 2nd to (N) prob. Jackson, and had sons James,

John, and William Tilghman; merchant, county justice by 1754, gentleman by 1755, esquire by 1766 and, member of the MD Assembly (1771-1775); and, (2) William Ringgold, of Eastern Neck, b. 19 Jul 1729, son of James Ringgold and Mary Tovey, of St. Paul's Parish; served as county justice (1762, 1763, 1768, 1774, 1777), member of the MD Assembly (1771-1776), and lieut. colonel of militia (commissioned 1777); m. 1st to Sarah Jones on 9 Jan 1750 (name listed as William Ringgold, Jr.) and m. 2nd to Sarah Johnson (widow) by 1759; had children Jacob, William Jr., Peregrine, Mary, Sarah, Rebecca, Elizabeth, Frances, Hester, Ann, Araminta, and Henrietta; d. testate by 1 Nov 1808. {Ref: ESVR; BDML II:696-697} See "James Jackson," q.v.

RIORDAN, ---- (Maryland), indentured servant and soldier who served in the French and Indian War some time between 1756 and 1763 (exact dates not known); his master William Govane, merchant, requested compensation from the Baltimore County Court due to the loss of use of Riordan while in the service. {Ref: MHM 94:4, p. 426, citing Baltimore Co. Court Minutes}

RIPELIGH, JOHN (Maryland), pvt., Capt. Peter Butler's Company Muster Roll, Frederick Co., circa 1757-1758, exact dates not given (served 34 days); bill of credit or order issued to him for £1.14.0 in March 1767. {Ref: MSA S960 or S752, p. 168; CSOS:97}

RISE, JACOB (Maryland), pvt., Capt. John White's Company Muster Roll, Frederick Co., circa 1757-1758, exact dates not given (served 6 day); bill of credit issued or paid in his behalf to William Good on 5 Jun 1767 for £0.6.0. {Ref: MSA S960 or S752, p. 164; CSOS:95}

RISSARD (REICHARD), BARBARA, see "Balsher Michael," q.v.

RITNOR (RITTNOR), GEORGE (Maryland), pvt., Capt. Joseph Chapline's Company Muster Roll No. 1, Frederick Co., circa 1757-1758, exact dates not given (served 40 days); bill of credit issued or paid in his behalf to Joseph Chaplin for £2.9.0 on 24 Apr 1767. {Ref: MSA S960 or S752, p. 192; CSOS:103}

ROAT, PAUL (Maryland), pvt., Capt. John White's Company Muster Roll, Frederick Co., circa 1757-1758, exact dates not given (served 6 day); bill of credit issued or paid to him for £0.6.0 in 1767, exact date not given. {Ref: MSA S960 or S752, p. 165; CSOS:95}

ROBERTS, BENJAMIN (Maryland), patriot and poss. soldier (rank not specified), Baltimore or Frederick Co., militia pay account submitted in 1758, exact date not given. {Ref: MHM 9:4, p. 369}

ROBERTS (ROBERT), ISAAC (Maryland), pvt., Capt. Richard Pearis' Company of MD Troops, Frederick Co., 1757 (exact dates not given); transferred to Capt. Francis Ware's Company of MD Troops, Charles Co., from 9 Oct 1757 to 30 Dec 1758 (served 213 days). {Ref: MHS MS.375.1; CSOS:89} Payment to him was recorded in Col. Dagworthy's account book on 15 Jul 1763. {Ref: MHS MS.375}

ROBERTS, JEREMIAH (Delaware), b. c1736, DE (laborer, age 22 in 1758); pvt., recruited by Capt. Benjamin Noxon and enlisted on 29 Apr 1758. {Ref: ARDE I:19; ARPA (2nd Series) 2:566}

ROBERTS, JOHN (Delaware), b. c1731, England (laborer, age 27 in 1758); pvt., enlisted 9 May 1758 "for the campaign in the lower counties" by Capt. John McClughan. {Ref: ARDE I:18; ARPA (2nd Series) 2:570}

ROBERTS, JOHN (Maryland), pvt., Capt. Peter Bainbridge's Company Muster Roll, Frederick Co., circa 1757-1758, exact dates not given (served 36 days); bill of credit issued or paid to him for £1.16.0 in 1767, exact date not given. {Ref: MSA S960 or S752, p. 181; CSOS:111}

ROBERTS (ROBARTS), JOHN (Maryland), pvt., Capt. Moses Chapline's Company Muster Roll No. 3, Frederick Co., circa 1757-1758, exact dates not given (served 6 days); bill of credit issued or paid in his behalf to Jonathan Hagar for £0.6.0 on 10 Oct 1771. {Ref: MSA S960 or S752, p. 198; CSOS:115}

ROBERTS (ROBERT), JOHN (Maryland), pvt., Capt. Richard Pearis' Company of MD Troops, Frederick Co., circa 9 Oct 1757 to 31 May 1758; pvt., Capt. Alexander Beall's Company of MD Troops, Frederick Co., from 1 Jun 1758 to 30 Dec 1758. {Ref: MHS MS.375.1; CSOS:82, 91} Payment to him was recorded in Col. Dagworthy's account book on 15 Jul 1762. {Ref: MHS MS.375}

ROBERTS, MARY, see "William Talbot," q.v.

ROBERTS, RIGNAL (Delaware), pvt., Capt. French Battell's Company of Lower County Provincials, enlisted 17 May 1758. {Ref: ARDE I:16; ARPA (2nd Series) 2:555}

ROBERTS, WILLIAM (Maryland), patriot and poss. soldier (rank not specified), Frederick Co., militia pay account submitted in 1758, exact date not given. {Ref: MHM 9:4, p. 366}

ROBERTS, WILLIAM (Maryland), patriot, Annapolis, Anne Arundel Co., pay account submitted for quartering soldiers in 1757 or 1758, exact dates not given. {Ref: MHM 9:3, p. 260}

ROBINETT, ENOCH (Maryland), pvt., Capt. Moses Chapline's Company Muster Roll No. 3, Frederick Co., circa 1757-1758, exact dates not given (served 6 days); bill of credit issued or paid to him for £0.6.0 in 1767, exact date not given; name listed once as "Enoc Robinnett". {Ref: MSA S960 or S752, p. 199; CSOS:115}

ROBINETT (ROBINATT), GEORGE (Maryland), pvt., Capt. Joseph Chapline's Company Muster Roll No. 3, Frederick Co., circa 1757-1758, exact dates not given (served 7 days); bill of credit issued or paid to him for £0.7.0 in 1767, exact date not given. {Ref: MSA S960 or S752, p. 193; CSOS:104} Pvt., Capt. Moses Chapline's Company Muster Roll No. 3, Frederick Co., circa 1757-1758, exact dates not given (served 6 days); bill of credit issued or paid in his behalf to Joseph Chapline for £0.6.0 on 13 Jun 1768. {Ref: MSA S960 or S752, pp. 198-199; CSOS:115}

ROBINETT, NATHAN (Maryland), pvt., Capt. Moses Chapline's Company Muster Roll No. 3, Frederick Co., circa 1757-1758, exact dates not given (served 6 days); bill of credit issued or paid in his behalf to Joseph Chaplin for £0.6.0 on 24 Apr 1767. {Ref: MSA S960 or S752, p. 198; CSOS:115}

ROBINS, ELIZABETH, see "William Goldsborough," q.v.

ROBINS, GEORGE, see "William Goldsborough," q.v.

ROBINS, SUSANNA, see "Thomas Chamberlaine," q.v.

ROBINSON, ANN, see "Robert Robinson," q.v.

ROBINSON, CHARLES (Maryland), pvt., Capt. Richard Pearis' Company of MD Troops, Frederick Co., from 9 Oct 1757 to 4 Apr 1758 when he reportedly deserted; however, he was a pvt. in Capt. John Dagworthy's Company of MD Troops, Frederick Co., from 1 Jun 1758 to 8 Aug 1758; payment to him was recorded in Col. Dagworthy's account book on 8 Mar 1763. {Ref: MHS MS.375; CSOS:78; MHS MS.375.1}

ROBINSON, DANIEL (Delaware), captain, militia, Murderkill Hundred, Kent Co. on Delaware, 1756; resigned 29 Mar 1758. {Ref: ARDE I:12, 15; ARPA (2nd Series) 2:527, 577; HDE I:141; CDSS:181}

ROBINSON, ELIZABETH, see "Joseph Robinson," q.v.

ROBINSON, HANNAH, see "Matthew Lowber," q.v.

ROBINSON, JAMES (Maryland or Pennsylvania), ensign in Capt. Hamilton's Company, was wounded in "a recent battle with the Indians" in 1756 (exact date not given) in Cumberland Co., PA, after the burning of McCord's Fort. {Ref: *MD Gazette*, 29 Apr 1756}

ROBINSON, JAMES (Maryland or Pennsylvania), pvt., Capt. Hamilton's Company, was killed in "a recent battle with the Indians" in 1756 (exact date not given) in Cumberland Co., PA, after the burning of McCord's Fort. {Ref: *MD Gazette*, 29 Apr 1756}

ROBINSON, JOSEPH (Delaware), pvt., Kent Co. Militia, Capt. John Caton's Company, 25 Apr 1757 (date of muster roll). {Ref: ARDE I:14} *Identification problem:* There were two men with this name who could have served in the war: (1) Joseph Robinson m. Sarah (N) and d. intestate by 13 May 1767; and, (2) Joseph Robinson m. Elizabeth (N), had children George, John, William, Deborah, Rebecca, and Martha, and d. testate by 9 Oct 1798. {Ref: CDSS:181-182}

ROBINSON, PETER (Delaware), b. 27 Aug 1734, Sussex Co., son of Peter and Catherine Robinson (of St. George's Episcopal Church, Indian River). {Ref: CFD 2:152} Lieut., Northern District of Indian River Hundred, Militia Regt. of Sussex Co., 1756; lieut., Angola District, 1758. {Ref: ARDE I:13, 15; ARPA (2nd Series) 2:529, 579; HDE I:141}

ROBINSON, ROBERT (Delaware), b. 1734, m. Ann (N), had children Aquila, William, John, Thomas, Ebenezer, Betty, Rebecca, and Sarah, and d. testate by 10 Mar 1787; buried in Old Swedes Cem. at Wilmington. {Ref: CDSS:182; RPDE:231} Ensign, Christiana Hundred, Upper Regt. of Militia, Southeast Division, New Castle Co., 1756; subscribed to the Oath of Fidelity and Allegiance in 1778. {Ref: ARDE I:11; ARPA (2nd Series) 2:526; HDE I:141; RPDE:231}

ROBINSON, SAMUEL (Delaware), son of Samuel Robinson (d. 1747) and Hannah Bowman. {Ref: CFD 2:144} Pvt., Kent Co. Militia, Capt. John Caton's Company, 25 Apr 1757 (date of muster roll). {Ref: ARDE I:13}

ROBINSON, SAMUEL, see "Matthew Lowber," q.v.

ROBINSON, SARAH, see "Joseph Robinson," q.v.

ROBINSON, THOMAS (Delaware), New Castle Co., patriot who served as a Justice of the Peace, Justice of the Court of Oyer and Terminer, and Justice of the Court of Common Pleas, 1756. {Ref: GRSD 1:13-14}

ROBINSON, WILLIAM (Delaware), b. c1740, NY (carpenter, age 18 in 1758); pvt., recruited by Capt. Benjamin Noxon and enlisted on 8 May 1758. {Ref: ARDE I:19; ARPA (2nd Series) 2:566}

ROBY, HINES (Maryland), pvt., Capt. Joseph Hanson Harrison's Company Muster Roll, Charles Co., circa 1757-1758, exact dates not given; bill of credit issued or paid in his behalf to John McPherson for £2.9.0 on 25 Mar 1767. {Ref: MSA S960 or S752, p. 189}

ROCHNOR, HANSE JORG (Maryland), indentured servant and soldier who served in the French and Indian War some time between 1756 and 1763 (exact dates not known); his master, Elinor Duhasan, requested compensation from the Baltimore County Court due to the loss of use of Rochnor while in the service. {Ref: MHM 94:4, p. 426, citing Baltimore Co. Court Minutes}

RODDEY, MICHAEL (Maryland), pvt., Capt. Jonathan Hagar's Company Muster Roll, Frederick Co., circa 1757-1758, exact dates not given (served 6 days); bill of credit issued or paid to him for £0.6.0 in 1767, exact date not given. {Ref: MSA S960 or S752, p. 175; CSOS:107}

RODNEY (RODENEY), CAESAR (Delaware), b. 7 Oct 1728, son of Caesar Rodney and Elizabeth Crawford; a commissioner for Kent County in 1759, he became very involved in governmental affairs and was one of the Signers of the Declaration of Independence in 1776; d. testate and unmarried on 20 Jun 1784. {Ref: CFD 1:224; CDSS:183; HDE I:203} Captain, Dover Hundred, Militia of Kent Co. on Delaware, by 1756. {Ref: ARDE I:12; ARPA (2nd Series) 2:527-529; HDE I:141}

ROE, ANTHONY (Maryland), pvt., Capt. Henry Casson's Company Muster Roll, Queen Anne's Co., circa 1757-1758, exact dates not given (served 27 days); bill of credit issued or paid in his behalf to Capt. Casson on 27 Mar 1767 for £1.7.0. {Ref: MSA S960 or S752, p. 178; CSOS:109}

ROE, ELIZABETH, see "Thomas Hill," q.v.

ROE, JAMES (Maryland), patriot and poss. soldier (rank not specified), Frederick Co., militia pay account submitted in 1758, exact date not given. {Ref: MHM 9:4, p. 368}

ROE, STEPHEN (Maryland), farmer; pvt., Capt. Peregrine Brown's 7th Co. of Foot Militia, Kent Co., on 19 Feb 1758, by which time he had enlisted, but reportedly refused to appear and serve in arms against the enemy. {Ref: ARMD 31:283, 288}

ROE, THOMAS (Maryland), pvt., Capt. Henry Casson's Company Muster Roll, Queen Anne's Co., circa 1757-1758, exact dates not given (served 27 days); bill of credit issued or paid in his behalf to Capt. Casson on 27 Mar 1767 for £1.7.0. {Ref: MSA S960 or S752, p. 178; CSOS:109}

ROE (ROWE), THOMAS RICHARDSON (Maryland and Delaware), b. c1732, MD (laborer, age 26 in 1758), m. Margaret Holton on 10 Apr 1748 in Queen Anne's Co., MD, and had children Rachel (b. 10 Jan 1749) and James (b. 18 Jan 1750), St. Luke's Parish; pvt., recruited by Capt. Benjamin Noxon and enlisted on 24 Apr 1758 in Delaware. {Ref: ESVR; ARDE I:19; ARPA (2nd Series) 2:485, 566} Pvt., Capt. Henry Vanbibber's Company of the Lower Counties on Delaware Troops at New Castle, enlisted on 10 May 1759; name mistakenly transcribed once as "Thomas Richardson Roen." {Ref: ARDE I:26; ARPA (2nd Series) 2:594}

ROE, WILLIAM (Maryland), pvt., Capt. Henry Casson's Company Muster Roll, Queen Anne's Co., circa 1757-1758, exact dates not given (served 27 days); bill of credit issued or paid in his behalf to Capt. Casson on 27 Feb 1767 for £1.7.0. {Ref: MSA S960 or S752, p. 177; CSOS:109}

ROE, WILLIAM, see "William Rhoe," q.v.

ROFMAN, JOHN (Maryland), pvt., Capt. Joshua Beall's Company Muster Roll, Prince George's Co., circa 1757-1758, exact dates not given; bill of credit issued or paid in his behalf to Josias Beall, Jr. for £0.9.0 on 25 Mar 1767. {Ref: MSA S960 or S752, p. 184}

ROGERS, HUGH (Delaware), b. c1739 (laborer, age 20 in 1759); pvt., enlisted by Capt. James Armstrong for the PA Regt. on 25 Apr 1759. {Ref: ARDE I:26; ARPA (2nd Series) 2:585}

ROGERS, JAMES, see "Joseph Miller," q.v.

ROGERS, JOHN, see "Daniel of St. Thomas Jenifer," q.v.

ROGERS, WILLIAM (Delaware), b. c1723, PA (laborer, age 35 in 1758); pvt., recruited by Capt. Benjamin Noxon and enlisted on 24 Apr 1758. {Ref: ARDE I:19; ARPA (2nd Series) 2:566}

ROLAND, JOHN (Delaware), b. c1735, Silver Point, VA (farmer, age 23 in 1758); pvt., enlisted 22 Apr 1758 "for the campaign in the lower counties" by Capt. John McClughan. {Ref: ARDE I:18; ARPA (2nd Series) 2:570}

ROLTON, JOSIAH (Delaware), b. c1736, Lewistown, DE (farmer, age 22 in 1758); pvt., enlisted 4 May 1758 "for the campaign in the lower counties" by Capt. John McClughan. {Ref: ARDE I:18; ARPA (2nd Series) 2:570}

RORAR (RORRAR), FREDERICK (Maryland), pvt., Capt. John White's Company Muster Roll, Frederick Co., circa 1757-1758, exact dates not given (served 6 days); militia pay account submitted in 1758, exact date not given. {Ref: MHM 9:4, p. 366} Bill of credit issued or paid in his behalf to James Smith on 18 May 1767 for £0.6.0. {Ref: MSA S960 or S752, p. 164; CSOS:95}

RORAR (RORRAR), JOHN (Maryland), pvt., Capt. John White's Company Muster Roll, Frederick Co., circa 1757-1758, exact dates not given (served 6 days); militia pay account submitted in 1758, exact date not given. {Ref: MHM 9:4, p. 366} Bill of credit issued or paid in his behalf to James Smith on 18 May 1767 for £0.6.0. {Ref: MSA S960 or S752, p. 164; CSOS:95}

ROSS, DAVID (Maryland), doctor and patriot, Frederick Co., 1756-1758. Paid £200.19.8½ by the MD Assembly in 1756 "for victualing Major Prather's, Capt. Beall's and Capt. Dagworthy's parties" for the support of the ranging parties on the Western Frontier. Paid £376.17.6 by the MD Assembly on 26 Sep 1756 "for provisions of all sorts, to Capts. Beall and Dagworthy's Companies, from the 17th of May to the 20th of July inclusive, at 9 d. per day for each man, as by the contract will appear." Paid £5.5.6 at Fort Frederick on 30 Aug 1758 "for liquors dld. to the detachments that worked on the new road after the 11th July" and £2.14.0 "for provisions dld. to sundry waggoner at Fort Frederick" and £4.19.0 "for provisions dld. to the battoemen who carried stores to Fort Cumberland" for the Western Expedition against Fort Duquesne. {Ref: ARMD 52:609,674; 55:775} See "Jane Morgan" and "James Knopp" q.v.

ROSS, GEORGE (Maryland), patriot and poss. soldier (rank not specified), Frederick Co., was paid £6 at Fort Frederick on 28 Jun 1758 "for carrying arms" for the Western Expedition against Fort Duquesne; also paid £9.10.0 on 10 Jul 1758 at Fort Frederick "for a horse that was shot yesterday by Indians under Corporal Madden as he was going to Carlyle with a letter to Sir John St. Clair." {Ref: ARMD 55:773, 776}

ROSS, HENRY (Maryland), pvt., Capt. John Middaugh's Company Muster Roll, Frederick Co., circa 1757-1758, exact dates not given (served 30 days); bill of credit issued or paid in his behalf to Thomas Beatty, Jr. for £1.10.0 on 23 Feb 1767. {Ref: MSA S960 or S752, p. 171; CSOS:101}

ROSS, JACOB (Delaware), M.D.; pvt., Capt. Richard McWilliams' Company of Foot, New Castle Co., enlisted 28 Dec 1757. {Ref: ARDE I:15}

ROSS, JAMES (Delaware), miller; b. c1741, Brandywine Hundred, DE (age 17 in 1758); pvt., enlisted 2 May 1758 "for the campaign in the lower counties" by Capt. John McClughan. {Ref: ARDE I:18; ARPA (2nd Series) 2:570}

ROSS, JAMES (Maryland), pvt., Capt. William McClellan's Company of MD Volunteers, Frederick Co., circa 1763-1764; on muster roll dated 15 Nov 1764 at Camp at the Forks of Muskingham. {Ref: ARMD 32:99}

ROSS, JOHN (Maryland), b. c1695, d. 1766; patriot, Annapolis, Anne Arundel Co., pay account submitted for quartering soldiers in 1757 or 1758, exact dates not given. {Ref: MHM 9:3, p. 260} "John Ross, Esq., died Thurs. evening last at his house in town, one of the Alderman of this City, and Lord Baltimore's Deputy Agent, in his 71st year; he had been a widower above 20 years." {Ref: *MD Gazette*, 25 Sep 1766}

ROSS, JOSEPH (Delaware), b. c1738, Ireland (age 21 in 1759); pvt., enlisted in Capt. John Wright's Company and mustered on 11 May 1759. {Ref: ARDE I:25; ARPA (2nd Series) 2:592}

ROSSER, JOHN (Maryland), farmer; pvt., Capt. Peregrine Brown's 7th Co. of Foot Militia, Kent Co., on 19 Feb 1758, by which time he had enlisted, but reportedly refused to appear and serve in arms against the enemy. {Ref: ARMD 31:283, 288}

ROTHWELL, GARRETT (Delaware), ensign, Appoquinimink Hundred, Lower Regt. of Militia, New Castle Co., 1756. {Ref: ARDE I:11; ARPA (2nd Series) 2:525; HDE I:141}

ROUGH, JOHN (Maryland), pvt., Capt. Jonathan Hagar's Company Muster Roll, Frederick Co., circa 1757-1758, exact dates not given (served 6 days); bill of credit issued or paid to him for £0.6.0 in 1767, exact date not given. {Ref: MSA S960 or S752, p. 174; CSOS:106}

ROUGH (RUFF), MICHAEL (Maryland), pvt., Capt. Jonathan Hagar's Company Muster Roll, Frederick Co., circa 1757-1758, exact dates not given (served 6 days); pvt., Frederick Co., militia pay account submitted in 1758, exact date not given. {Ref: MHM 9:4, p. 370; CSOS:106} Bill of credit issued or paid to him for £0.6.0 in 1767, exact date not given. {Ref: MSA S960 or S752, p. 174}

ROUND O'S DAUR, Indian Chief (Maryland), Frederick Co., agreed to join with the English against the French in 1758. {Ref: ARMD 31:266}

ROUSBY, ANN, see "William Fitzhugh," q.v.

ROUSBY, ELIZABETH, see "Abraham Barnes" and "George Plater," q.v.

ROUSBY, GERTRUDE, see "Robert Jenkins Henry," q.v.

ROUT, GEORGE (Maryland), pvt., Capt. William McClellan's Company of MD Volunteers, Frederick Co., circa 1763-1764; on muster roll dated 15 Nov 1764 at Camp at the Forks of Muskingham. {Ref: ARMD 32:99}

ROWE, THOMAS (Maryland), b. c1735, MD (age 21 in 1756); pvt., Capt. Robert Stewart's Company of VA Militia, enlisted on 2 Aug 1756. {Ref: MSR I:38}

ROWE, WILLIAM, see "William Rhoe," q.v.

ROWLAND, DAVID (Delaware), ensign in Capt. Timothy Griffith's Company, 1747-1748, during King George's War against Canada; ensign, Pencader Hundred, Lower Regt. of Militia, New Castle Co., 1756. {Ref: ARDE I:7, 12; ARPA (2nd Series) 2:525; HDE I:141} David Rowland m. Jean (N) and d. testate in Pencader Hundred by 4 Aug 1767. {Ref: CDSS:185}

ROWLAND, JOHN (Delaware), b. c1735, VA (laborer; gave his age as 23 in 1758 and again in 1759; height 5 ft. 5 in.); pvt., recruited by Capt. Paul Jackson for the PA Regt. on 19 Apr 1758, enlisted in Capt. John Wright's Company and mustered on 11 May 1759. {Ref: ARDE I:25, 27; ARPA (2nd Series) 2:592}

ROWLES, FRANCIS (Maryland), pvt., Capt. Francis Ware's Company of MD Troops, Charles Co., circa 9 Oct 1757 to 30 Dec 1758. {Ref: MHS MS.375.1; CSOS:89} Payment to him was recorded in Col. Dagworthy's account book on 7 Mar 1763. {Ref: MHS MS.375}

ROWLES, JACOB, see "William Rowles," q.v.

ROWLES, JOHN (Maryland), pvt., Capt. Francis Ware's Company of MD Troops, Charles Co., from 9 Oct 1757 to 8 Nov 1758 (served 396 days). {Ref: MHS MS.375.1; CSOS:89} Payment to him was recorded in Col. Dagworthy's account book on 14 Jul 1763. {Ref: MHS MS.375}

ROWLES (ROLES), THOMAS (Maryland), pvt., Capt. Richard Pearis' Company of MD Troops, Frederick Co., circa 9 Oct 1757 to 31 May 1758; pvt., Capt. Joshua Beall's Company of MD Troops, Prince George's Co., from 1 Jun 1758 to 14 Sep 1758 when he was reported as killed. {Ref: MHS MS.375.1; CSOS:85, 91} However, such was not the case. On 30 Sep 1760 Hugh Carrigan and Thomas Roles petitioned the MD Assembly "praying some recompence for their past services as soldiers enlisted in the MD Service in 1757 who were taken prisoners by the French and sent to Mississippi and from thence to Old France." {Ref: ARMD 56:339} Payment to him was also recorded in Col. Dagworthy's account book on 21 Jul 1762 for work on Fort Cumberland. {Ref: MHS MS.375}

ROWLES, WILLIAM (Maryland), b. c1730, Baltimore Co., son of Jacob Rowles and Constance Sampson, St. Paul's P. E. Parish. {Ref: BCF:558} Pvt., Capt. Tobias Stansbury's Company Muster Roll, Baltimore Co., circa 1757-1758, exact dates not given; bill of credit or order issued and assigned to William Lux paid to Robert Adair for £1.19.0 on 1 Apr 1767. {Ref: MSA S960 or S752, pp. 186-187}

ROZEL (ROXELL), DAVID (Maryland), pvt., Capt. John Middaugh's Company Muster Roll, Frederick Co., circa 1757-1758, exact dates not given (served 30 days); bill of credit issued or paid in his behalf to Thomas Beatty, Jr. for £0.17.0 on 3 Apr 1767. {Ref: MSA S960 or S752, p. 172; CSOS:102}

RUDOLPH, TOBIAS (Maryland), patriot and poss. soldier (rank not specified), Cecil Co., militia pay account submitted in 1758, exact date not given. {Ref: MHM 9:4, p. 365}

RUFF, SABRIET (Maryland), pvt., Capt. Joshua Beall's Company of MD Troops, Prince George's Co., from 9 Oct 1757 to 30 Dec 1758; payment to him was recorded in Col. Dagworthy's account book on 13 Jul 1762. {Ref: MHS MS.375.1; CSOS:85; MHS MS.375}

RUFFNECK, WILLIAM (Maryland), pvt., Capt. Joshua Beall's Company of MD Troops, Prince George's Co., from 9 Oct 1757 to 8 May 1758 (promoted to cpl. on 9 Jan 1758). {Ref: MHS MS.375.1; CSOS:85} Payment to him was recorded in Col. Dagworthy's account book on 8 Mar 1763. {Ref: MHS MS.375}

RULE, CLEMENT (Maryland), pvt., Capt. Peter Butler's Company Muster Roll, Frederick Co., circa 1757-1758, exact dates not given (served 34 days); bill of credit or order issued to him for £1.14.0 in March 1767. {Ref: MSA S960 or S752, p. 168; CSOS:97}

RUMSEY, WILLIAM (Maryland), b. 21 Mar 1729/30, Cecil Co., son of William Rumsey and Sabina Blaidenburgh, m. Susanna (N), had children Nathan, William, John, Sabina, and Amelia, and d. testate by 12 Mar 1777; farmer, gentleman, captain by 1763, county justice (1763-1774), member of the Council of Safety in 1776, and first major (Bohemia Bttn.) in 1776; militia pay account submitted in 1758 for service rendered in French and Indian War (exact date not given). {Ref: BDML II:710; MHM 9:4, p. 369}

RUNEY, PETER (Delaware), pvt., Kent Co. Militia, Capt. John Caton's Company, 25 Apr 1757 (date of muster roll). {Ref: ARDE I:14}

RUNKEL (RUNKIL), JOSEPH (Maryland), pvt., Capt. Thomas Norris' Company, Frederick Co., circa 1757-1758, exact dates not given (served 30 days); bill of credit issued or paid in his behalf to Michael McGuire on 20 Mar 1767 for £1.10.0. {Ref: MSA S960 or S752, p. 176; CSOS:108}

RUSSELL, JOHN (Maryland), pvt., Capt. Francis Ware's Company of MD Troops, Charles Co., circa 9 Oct 1757 to 30 Dec 1758; payment to him was recorded in Col. Dagworthy's account book on 26 Feb 1762. {Ref: MHS MS.375.1; CSOS:89; MHS MS.375}

RUSSELL, THOMAS (Maryland), pvt., Capt. Francis Ware's Company of MD Troops, Charles Co., circa 9 Oct 1757 to 30 Dec 1758. {Ref: MHS MS.375.1; CSOS:89} Payment to him was recorded in Col. Dagworthy's account book on 7 Mar 1763 for work on Fort Cumberland. {Ref: MHS MS.375}

RUSSOM (RUSSON), EDWARD (Maryland), pvt., Capt. Henry Casson's Company Muster Roll, Queen Anne's Co., circa 1757-1758, exact dates not given (served 27 days); bill of credit or order issued to him for £1.7.0 in 1767, exact date not given. {Ref: MSA S960 or S752, p. 178; CSOS:109}

RUTTER, JOHN (Maryland), m. (N), had children John, William, Alexander, Edmond, Mary, and Rachel, and d. testate by 20 Sep 1769. {Ref: WMG 3:2, p. 74} Pvt., Capt. Joseph Chapline's Company Muster Roll No. 4, Frederick Co., circa 1757-1758, exact dates not given (served 7 days); pvt., Frederick Co., militia pay account submitted in 1758, exact date not given; bill of credit issued or paid in his behalf to James Smith for £0.7.0 on 18 May 1767; name listed once as "John Rutur." {Ref: MSA S960 or S752, p. 195; MHM 9:4, p. 367; CSOS:105}

RUTTER, SOLOMON (Maryland), b. 31 Aug 1730, Baltimore Co., son of Thomas and Esther Rutter. {Ref: BCF:563} Pvt., Capt. Tobias Stansbury's Company Muster Roll, Baltimore Co., circa 1757-1758, exact dates not given; bill of credit issued or paid in his behalf to Josias Bowen for £3.12.0 on 13 Mar 1767; name listed once as "Solomon Butler or Rutter." {Ref: MSA S960 or S752, p. 186; CSOS:117}

RYAN, JOHN (Delaware), b. c1742, MD (tailor, age 16 in 1758); pvt., recruited by Capt. Benjamin Noxon and enlisted on 2 May 1758. {Ref: ARDE I:19; ARPA (2nd Series) 2:485, 566}

RYNE, JOHN (Delaware), b. c1737, Ireland (laborer, age 21 in 1758); pvt., recruited by Capt. Benjamin Noxon and enlisted on 2 May 1758. {Ref: ARDE I:19; ARPA (2nd Series) 2:566}

SADDLER (SADLER), WILLIAM (Maryland), pvt., Capt. Joshua Beall's Company of MD Troops, Prince George's Co., from 9 Oct 1757 to 8 Nov 1758 (served 396 days); payment to him was recorded in Col. Dagworthy's account book on 8 Mar 1763 for work on Fort Cumberland. {Ref: MHS MS.375.1; CSOS:86; MHS MS.375}

SALISBURY, MARY, see "William Govane," q.v.

SALTWELL, JOHN (Delaware), b. c1728, England (gardener, age 30 in 1758); pvt., recruited by Capt. Benjamin Noxon and enlisted on 24 Apr 1758. {Ref: ARDE I:19; ARPA (2nd Series) 2:566}

SAMPSON, CONSTANCE, see "William Rowles," q.v.

SAMPSON, MARY, see "John Green," q.v.

SAMUEL, CONROD (Maryland), pvt., Capt. Joseph Chapline's Company Muster Roll No. 1, Frederick Co., circa 1757-1758, exact dates not given (served 21 days); bill of credit issued or paid to him for £1.1.0 in 1767, exact date not given. {Ref: MSA S960 or S752, p. 192; CSOS:103}

SAMUEL, CONROD JR. (Maryland), pvt., Capt. Joseph Chapline's Company Muster Roll No. 2, Frederick Co., circa 1757-1758, exact dates not given (served 5 days); bill of credit issued or paid to him for £0.5.0 in 1767, exact date not given. {Ref: MSA S960 or S752, p. 193; CSOS:104}

SANDERS, ANN, see "William Lux," q.v.

SANDERS, EDWARD, see "Samuel Saunders," q.v.

SANDERSON, JAMES (Delaware), b. c1731, Ireland (laborer, age 27 in 1758); pvt., recruited by Capt. Benjamin Noxon and enlisted on 2 May 1758. {Ref: ARDE I:19; ARPA (2nd Series) 2:566}

SANKEY, THOMAS (Delaware), pvt., Capt. Richard McWilliams' Company of Foot, New Castle Co., enlisted 28 Dec 1757. {Ref: ARDE I:14}

SAP (SAPP), BENJAMIN (Delaware), son of Henry Sapp (d. 1743) and wife Anne (N). {Ref: CFD 2:159} Pvt., Capt. French Battell's Company of Lower County Provincials, enlisted 20 May 1758. {Ref: ARDE I:16; ARPA (2nd Series) 2:555}

SAPP, ROBERT (Maryland), pvt., Capt. Alexander Beall's Company of MD Troops, Frederick Co., 1758; transferred from Capt. Richard Pearis' Company where he had been promoted to cpl. on 19 Nov 1757 (date mistakenly listed once as 19 Nov 1758) and served from 1 Jun 1758 to 12 Oct 1758 when he was reported as killed; however, payment to him was recorded in Col. Dagworthy's account book on 12 Jul 1762. {Ref: MHS MS.375; CSOS:82; MHS MS.375.1}

SASSER, BENJAMIN (Maryland), pvt., Capt. Richard Pearis' Company of MD Troops, Frederick Co., from 9 Oct 1757 to 23 Nov 1757 when he reportedly deserted (served 45 days); however, payment to him was recorded in Col. Dagworthy's account book on 8 Mar 1763. {Ref: MHS MS.375; CSOS:91; MHS MS.375.1}

SAUNDERS, GEORGE (Maryland), pvt., Capt. Alexander Beall's Company of MD Troops, Frederick Co., from 9 Oct 1757 to 8 Nov 1758 (served 396 days); payment to him was recorded in Col. Dagworthy's account book on 14 Jul 1762. {Ref: MHS MS.375; CSOS:82; MHS MS.375}

SAUNDERS, JOHN (Maryland), pvt., Capt. Joshua Beall's Company of MD Troops, Prince George's Co., from 9 Oct 1757 to 7 Dec 1757 (date mistakenly listed once as 7 Dec 1758) and was discharged (served 60 days); payment to him was recorded in Col. Dagworthy's account book on 24 Jul 1762. {Ref: MHS MS.375.1; CSOS:86; MHS MS.375}

SAUNDERS, ROBERT (Maryland), captain by 1757 (county not stated) and appointed sergeant-at-arms for the Lower House of the MD Assembly on 28 Sep 1757. {Ref: ARMD 55:201}

SAUNDERS, SAMUEL (Maryland), b. c1734, Baltimore Co., prob. son of Edward Sanders and Christian Beardy, of St. George's P. E. Parish. {Ref: BCF:565} Pvt., Capt. Christopher Gist's Company of VA Militia, 13 Jul 1756, enlisted at Baltimore (b. MD, age 22). {Ref: MSR I:37}

SAUNDERS, WILLIAM (Maryland), pvt., Capt. Tobias Stansbury's Company Muster Roll, Baltimore Co., circa 1757-1758, exact dates not given; bill of credit issued or paid to him for £2.12.0 in 1767, exact date not given. {Ref: MSA S960 or S752, p. 187; CSOS:117}

SAUNDERS, WILLIAM (Delaware), pvt., Capt. Henry Vanbibber's Company of the Lower Counties on Delaware Troops at New Castle, enlisted on 19 May 1759. {Ref: ARDE I:26; ARPA (2nd Series) 2:594}

SCAGGS, ISAAC (Maryland), pvt., Capt. John Dagworthy's Company of MD Troops, Frederick Co., from 9 Oct 1757 to 26 Dec 1758 when he reportedly deserted; however, payment to him was recorded in Col. Dagworthy's account book on 28 Feb 1762 and also in July 1762 for work on Fort Cumberland. {Ref: MHS MS.375; CSOS:78; MHS MS.375.1}

SCAGGS, JAMES (Maryland), pvt., Capt. John Dagworthy's Company of MD Troops, Frederick Co., from 9 Oct 1757 to 22 Jan 1759 when he reportedly deserted; however, payment to him was recorded in Col. Dagworthy's account book on 8 Mar 1763 for work on Fort Cumberland. {Ref: MHS MS.375; CSOS:78; MHS MS.375.1}

SCAGGS, RICHARD (Maryland), pvt., Capt. John Dagworthy's Company of MD Troops, Frederick Co., from 9 Oct 1757 to 26 Dec 1758 when he reportedly deserted; however, payment to him was recorded in Col. Dagworthy's account book on 11 Jul 1762. {Ref: MHS MS.375; CSOS:78; MHS MS.375.1}

SCARBOROUGH, JOHN (Maryland), b. c1694, Somerset Co., son of Matthew Scarborough and Hannah Wise, m. his first cousin Mary Cade, had children Samuel, John, Betty, Mary, Ann, Leah, and Hannah, and d. testate by 19 Sep 1775, Worcester Co.; planter by 1719, cooper by 1723, colonel by 1745, gentleman justice (1742-1775), and member of the MD Assembly (1745-1761, served on the Arms and Ammunition Committee, 1758-1761). {Ref: BDML II:711-712; ARMD 55:44, 56:13}

SCARCE (SEARCE), PHILIP (Maryland), pvt., Capt. Joshua Beall's Company Muster Roll, Prince George's Co., circa 1757-1758, exact dates not given; bill of credit issued or paid to him for £1.3.0 in 1767, exact date not given. {Ref: MSA S960 or S752, p. 185}

SCATTERDAY, GEORGE (Maryland), pvt., Capt. Thomas Norris' Company, Frederick Co., circa 1757-1758, exact dates not given (served 30 days); bill of credit issued or paid in his behalf to Thomas Owings on 15 May 1767 for £1.10.0. {Ref: MSA S960 or S752, p. 177; CSOS:108}

SCHABYMAN, SPICER (Delaware), pvt., Kent Co. Militia, Capt. John Caton's Company, 25 Apr 1757 (date of muster roll). {Ref: ARDE I:13}

SCARF, MARGARET, see "John Smith," q.v.

SCHELMAN, JOHN (Maryland), patriot and poss. soldier (rank not specified), Frederick Co., militia pay account submitted in 1758, exact date not given. {Ref: MHM 9:4, p. 366}

SCHLEY, THOMAS (Maryland), lieut., Capt. Peter Butler's Company Muster Roll, Frederick Co., circa 1757-1758, exact dates not given; bill of credit or order issued in his behalf for £3.19.3 and paid to Peter Grosh on 4 Mar 1767. {Ref: MSA S960 or S752, p. 168; CSOS:96} He was paid £24.10.0 at Fort Frederick on 2 Jul 1758 "for carryage of 6 loads of arms from Annapolis" for the Western Expedition against Fort Duquesne. {Ref: ARMD 55:773}

SCHNEBELY (SNEAVELY, SHNEBELY)), HENRY (Maryland), b. c1728, poss. immigrated from PA to Frederick Co., MD, m. 1st to Elizabeth Shaver or Sheaffer by 1755, m. 2nd to Catherine Hausman circa 1797, had children Henry, John, Jacob, David, and Elizabeth, and d. testate on 24 Jul 1805, Washington Co.; planter, doctor, gentleman, member of the MD Assembly (1777-1779), county justice (1777-1782), Orphans Court justice (1777-1782), medical purveyor for the army in 1780, and MD Senate elector (1786-1801). {Ref: BDML II:712-713} Lieut. in Capt. John White's Company, Frederick Co., circa 1757-1758, exact dates not given; militia pay account submitted in 1758, exact date not given {Ref: CSOS:94; MHM 9:4, p. 368} Bill of credit issued or paid in his behalf to Peter Grosh for £0.14.0 on 4 Mar 1767. {Ref: MSA S960 or S752, p. 164} Lieut. in Capt. Henry Sneavely's Company, Frederick Co., circa 1757-1758, exact dates not given; bill of credit issued or paid in his behalf to Peter Grosh for £1.3.0 on 4 Mar 1767. {Ref: MSA S960 or S752, p. 190}

SCHNEBELY (SNEAVELY, SHNEBELY)), LEONARD (Maryland), m. Margaretha (N), had children Elizabetha, Leonart or Leonard (youngest son), Christiana, Susannah, Catharine, and others not named in his will, and d. by 9 Feb 1767. {Ref: WMG 2:4, pp. 167-168} Pvt., Capt. Jonathan Hagar's Company

Muster Roll, Frederick Co., circa 1757-1758, exact dates not given (served 6 days); bill of credit issued or paid in his behalf to Jonathan Hagar for £0.6.0 on 10 Oct 1767. {Ref: MSA S960 or S752, pp. 174-175; CSOS:106} Leonard was the brother of "Henry Schnebely," q.v.

SCOTT, ANN, see "Daniel Smithson," q.v.

SCOTT, AVARILLA, see "Thomas Norris," q.v.

SCOTT, BAPTIST (Maryland), pvt., Capt. Jonathan Hagar's Company Muster Roll, Frederick Co., circa 1757-1758, exact dates not given (served 6 days); bill of credit issued or paid in his behalf to Joseph Chaplin for £0.6.0 on 24 Apr 1767. {Ref: MSA S960 or S752, pp. 173, 175; CSOS:107}

SCOTT, FRANCIS (Maryland or Pennsylvania), pvt., Capt. Culbertson's Company, was killed in "a recent battle with the Indians" in 1756 (exact date not given) in Cumberland Co., PA, after the burning of McCord's Fort. {Ref: *MD Gazette*, 29 Apr 1756}

SCOTT, ROBERT (Delaware), b. c1735, Rye, Ireland (spinner, age 23 in 1758); pvt., enlisted 12 May 1758 "for the campaign in the lower counties" by Capt. John McClughan. {Ref: ARDE I:18; ARPA (2nd Series) 2:570}

SCOTT, WILLIAM (Delaware), b. c1724, Ireland (laborer, age 35 in 1759); pvt., enlisted by Capt. James Armstrong for the PA Regt. on 3 May 1759. {Ref: ARDE I:26; ARPA (2nd Series) 2:585}

SCOTT, ZACHARIAH (Maryland), pvt., Capt. Francis Ware's Company of MD Troops, Charles Co., from 9 Oct 1757 to 30 Dec 1758 (promoted to cpl. on 13 Oct 1758). {Ref: MHS MS.375.1; CSOS:89} Payment to him was recorded in Col. Dagworthy's account book on 22 Feb 1763. {Ref: MHS MS.375} Zachariah Scott, of Prince George's Co., m. (N), had children William, James, Charles, Amy, and Jemima, and d. testate by 8 May 1775. {Ref: MCW 16:71-72}

SCRIVENER, JOSEPH (Maryland), patriot and poss. soldier (rank not specified), Frederick Co., militia pay account submitted in 1758, exact date not given. {Ref: MHM 9:4, p. 368}

SEAL, THOMAS (Maryland), b. c1724, MD (age 32 in 1756); pvt., Capt. Henry Harrison's Company of VA Militia, 13 Jul 1756, enlisted in Suffolk, VA. {Ref: MSR I:37}

SEALE, HENRY (Maryland), sgt., Royal American Regt., by 1757; served with Lieut. Alexander McBean at Annapolis. {Ref: *MD Gazette*, 31 Mar 1757}

SEALON, JOHN (Maryland), pvt., Capt. William McClellan's Company of MD Volunteers, Frederick Co., circa 1763-1764; on muster roll dated 15 Nov 1764 at Camp at the Forks of Muskingham. {Ref: ARMD 32:99}

SEAMAR, GEORGE (Maryland), pvt., Capt. Peter Butler's Company Muster Roll, Frederick Co., circa 1757-1758, exact dates not given (served 34 days); bill of credit or order issued in his behalf for £1.14.0 and paid to Peter Grosh on 4 Mar 1767. {Ref: MSA S960 or S752, p. 168; CSOS:97}

SEANY, JOHN (Delaware), pvt., Kent Co. Militia, Capt. John Caton's Company, 25 Apr 1757 (date of muster roll). {Ref: ARDE I:14}

SEAR (SEER), FELIX (Maryland), pvt., Capt. William McClellan's Company of MD Volunteers, Frederick Co., circa 1763-1764; reported as deserted on muster roll dated 15 Nov 1764 at Camp at the Forks of Muskingham. {Ref: ARMD 32:99}

SEARE (SEAR, SAER), WILLIAM (Maryland), pvt., Capt. William Luckett's Company Muster Roll, Frederick Co., circa 1757-1758, exact dates not given (served 30 days); bill of credit issued or paid in his behalf to William Luckett, Jr. for £1.10.0 on 6 Apr 1767. {Ref: MSA S960 or S752, p. 169; CSOS:99}

SEARES (SEARS), EDWARD (Maryland), planter; pvt., recruited by Thomas Beall, Prince George's Co. recruiting officer (age and exact date not given); reportedly deserted in July 1757. {Ref: *MD Gazette*, 4 Aug 1757} However, Gov. Horatio Sharpe wrote to the MD Assembly on 7 Dec 1757, stating in part: "One Thomas Beall, a young fellow of Prince George's Co. (who was empowered by me to enlist men for his Majesty's Service, in consequence of several Acts of Assembly lately passed in this province) is accused of having pretended to enlist the said [Edward] Seares, [Thomas] Hill and [David] Mackelfish, of treating them afterwards as deserters, of compelling Seares to pay £10 for a discharged, which he could not give, and of endeavouring to oblige the other two to purchase their discharges likewise. Mr. Beall is not present to hear what is alleged against him, yet I don't think it would be right to condemn him unheard; he is no officer that I know of, neither is he in the least dependent on me; and if the complainants can prove that he has acted illegally, I hope they may redress themselves without applying to any branch of the Legislature; but if it should, on farther enquiry, appear that they were duly enlisted, you will not, I am persuaded, take it amiss if they are apprehended and delivered up to one of his Majesty's Officers." {Ref: ARMD 55:320}

SEELY, JOHN, see "Michael McNamara," q.v.

SEHR, DANIEL (Maryland), indentured servant and soldier who served in the French and Indian War some time between 1756 and 1763 (exact dates not known); his master George Myer, planter, requested compensation from the Baltimore County Court due to the loss of use of Sehr while in the service. {Ref: MHM 94:4, p. 426, citing Baltimore Co. Court Minutes}

SELBY, JOHN (Maryland), b. c1725, Worcester Co., son of Parker Selby and Mary Watts, m. Anne Drummond, had children James, Daniel, William, John, Anne (Nancy), Polly, and Betty (Betsy), and d. testate by 10 Dec 1790, Worcester Co.; planter, gentleman, lieutenant in militia in 1748, captain by 1757, county justice (1756-1789), member of the MD Assembly in 1777, Orphans Court justice (1777-1789), member of the Committee of Observation in 1776, tax commissioner (1779-1790), and Continental Loan Officer in 1779. {Ref: BDML II:719-720; ARMD 56:288}

SELBY, PARKER (Maryland), b. c1730, Worcester Co., son of Parker Selby and Mary Watts, m. Mary (N), had children Parker, Samuel, David, John, Sarah, Mary, Leah, and Ann, and d. testate by 4 Mar 1773, Worcester Co.; planter, gentleman, captain by 1762, member of the MD Assembly (1759-1770, served on the Arms and Ammunition Committee, 1762-1763), and High Sheriff of Worcester Co. (1770-1773). {Ref: BDML II:721; *MD Gazette*, 4 Mar 1772}

SELLER, JACOB (Maryland), son of Conrad Seller; pvt., Capt. Jonathan Hagar's Company Muster Roll, Frederick Co., circa 1757-1758, exact dates not given (served 6 days); bill of credit issued or paid to him for £0.6.0 in 1767, exact date not given. {Ref: MSA S960 or S752, p. 175; CSOS:107}

SELLER, JOHN JR. (Maryland), pvt., Capt. Jonathan Hagar's Company Muster Roll, Frederick Co., circa 1757-1758, exact dates not given (served 6 days); bill of credit issued or paid in his behalf to Jonathan Hagar for £0.6.0 on 10 Oct 1767. {Ref: MSA S960 or S752, pp. 174-175; CSOS:107}

SELLER, JOHN SR. (Maryland), pvt., Capt. Jonathan Hagar's Company Muster Roll, Frederick Co., circa 1757-1758, exact dates not given (served 6 days); bill of credit issued or paid in his behalf to Jonathan Hagar for £0.6.0 on 10 Oct 1767. {Ref: MSA S960 or S752, pp. 174-175; CSOS:107}

SELLERS, SABRIT, see "Sabrit Sollers, Jr.," q.v.

SENNETT, JACOB (Maryland), sgt., Capt. Henry Casson's Company Muster Roll, Queen Anne's Co., circa 1757-1758, exact dates not given; bill of credit issued or paid in his behalf to Joseph Chaplin on 27 Mar 1767 for £1.17.3. {Ref: MSA S960 or S752, p. 178}

SERGEANT (SARGEANT), SAMUEL (Maryland), b. c1733, Baltimore Co., son of John Sargeant (d. 1750) and Elizabeth Gostwick. {Ref: BCF:566} Pvt., Capt. Tobias Stansbury's Company Muster Roll, Baltimore Co., circa 1757-1758, exact dates not given; bill of credit or order issued to his heir at law (unnamed) and paid to Robert Adair for £0.19.0 on 22 May 1767. {Ref: MSA S960 or S752, p. 187; CSOS:118}

SESSLESS, ZACHARIAH (Maryland), pvt., Capt. Joshua Beall's Company Muster Roll, Prince George's Co., circa 1757-1758, exact dates not given; bill of credit issued and ordered his assignment to Stephen West for £2.3.0 on 11 Mar 1767. {Ref: MSA S960 or S752, p. 184}

SEWELL, JOHN (Maryland), patriot, Kent Co., pay account submitted for quartering soldiers in 1757 or 1758, exact dates not given. {Ref: MHM 9:3, pp. 261-262}

SEWELL, JOHN (Maryland), patriot, Cecil Co., petitioned the MD Assembly on 14 Nov 1757 "praying an allowance may be made him for some damages done his house and fencing by the soldiers quartered in Frederick County in December last." {Ref: ARMD 55:167}

SEWELL, JOSHUA (Maryland), patriot and poss. soldier (rank not specified), Baltimore Co., militia pay account submitted in 1758, exact date not given. {Ref: MHM 9:4, p. 366}

SHAFF (SCHAFF), CASPER (Maryland), sgt., Capt. Peter Butler's Company Muster Roll, Frederick Co., circa 1757-1758, exact dates not given (served 34 days). {Ref: CSOS:96} Militia pay account submitted in 1758, exact date not given. {Ref: MHM 9:4, p. 367} Bill of credit or order issued to him for £2.5.3 on 2 Mar 1767. {Ref: MSA S960 or S752, pp. 166, 168}

SHANEFELT, WILLIAM (Maryland), pvt., Capt. John White's Company Muster Roll, Frederick Co., circa 1757-1758, exact dates not given (served 6 days); bill

of credit issued or paid to him for £0.6.0 in 1767, exact date not given. {Ref: MSA S960 or S752, p. 165; CSOS:95}

SHANEYFIELD, FREDERICK (Maryland), pvt., Capt. Jonathan Hagar's Company Muster Roll, Frederick Co., circa 1757-1758, exact dates not given (served 6 days). {Ref: CSOS:107}

SHANIFIELD, EPHRAIM (Maryland), pvt., Capt. Jonathan Hagar's Company Muster Roll, Frederick Co., circa 1757-1758, exact dates not given; bill of credit issued or paid to him for £0.6.0 in 1767, exact date not given. {Ref: MSA S960 or S752, p. 175}

SHAPHARD (SHEPEARD), JOHN (Maryland), pvt., Capt. Joseph Chapline's Company Muster Roll No. 4, Frederick Co., circa 1757-1758, exact dates not given (served 7 days); bill of credit issued or paid in his behalf to Joseph Chaplin for £0.7.0 on 5 Mar 1767. {Ref: MSA S960 or S752, p. 194; CSOS:105}

SHARP, JOSEPH (Delaware), b. c 1734, Milford, MD *[sic]* (smith, age 25 in 1759); pvt., recruited by Capt. John Martin and enlisted on 8 Jun 1759 (list of recruits dated 15 Jun 1759). {Ref: ARPA (2nd Series) 2:504}

SHARP, MARY, see "Thomas Tilton," q.v.

SHARPE, HORATIO (Maryland), b. 1718 in Hull, Yorkshire, England, son of William Sharpe and Margaret Beake, and d. 9 Nov 1790, Hampstead, England; captain of marines by 1745, lieut. colonel of foot troops, and served in the West Indies; immigrated to America on 10 Aug 1753 as Governor of MD; commander-in-chief of MD Militia, ex officio, 1753-1769; commander-in-chief of forces raised to resist the French in 1754, principally at Fort Cumberland; upon his arrival at the fort in Frederick Co. he was described as "a very good soldier, cheerful and free, of good conduct, and one who won't be trifled with;" he was supplanted by Maj. Gen. Edward Braddock who was commissioned commander-in-chief of all British forces in America in September 1754, but Sharpe continued to exercise his command until Braddock arrived in the winter of 1755; Sharpe toured defenses in western MD, VA and PA and canoed about 250 miles down the Potomac River to Alexandria; he returned to the west after Braddock's defeat to do what he could to restore order; served as Governor of MD until dismissed on 20 Jul 1768, at which time he left office upon the arrival of Gov. Robert Eden and returned to England. {Ref: BDML II:726-728} In September 1758 Gov. Sharpe marched from Fort Frederick to Fort Cumberland with over 200 volunteers from Frederick County. {Ref: *MD Gazette*, 14 Sep 1758} Refer to *Archives of Maryland*, Volumes 6, 9, 31 and 54, which contain the correspondence, letters and accounts of Gov. Sharpe from 1753 to 1765. See "Henry Casson" and "John Dagworthy" and "William Goldsborough" and "Thomas Beall" and "George Steuart," q.v.

SHARPE, JOHN (Maryland), pvt., Capt. Alexander Beall's Company of MD Troops, Frederick Co., from 9 Oct 1757 to 18 Oct 1758 when he reportedly deserted; however, payment to him was recorded in Col. Dagworthy's account book on 26 Feb 1763. {Ref: MHS MS.375; CSOS:82; MHS MS.375.1}

SHARPE (SHARP), MATTHEW (Maryland), pvt., Capt. Elias Delashmutt's Company Muster Roll, Frederick Co., 13 Aug 1757, exact dates not given (served 52 days); bill of credit issued or paid to him in March 1767 for £2.12.0. {Ref: MSA S960 or S752, p. 163; CSOS:98} On 30 Aug 1758 he was paid £3 at Fort Frederick "for carryage of a load of corn to Fort Frederick" for the Western Expedition against Fort Duquesne. {Ref: ARMD 55:775}

SHARPE (SHARP), PAUL (Maryland), pvt., Capt. Peter Butler's Company Muster Roll, Frederick Co., circa 1757-1758, exact dates not given (served 34 days); bill of credit or order issued in his behalf for £1.14.0 and paid to Casper Shaff on 2 Mar 1767. {Ref: MSA S960 or S752, p. 167; CSOS:97}

SHAVER, ELIZABETH, see "Henry Sneavely (Schnebely)," q.v.

SHAVER, HONEAL or HONERAL (Maryland), pvt., Capt. Jonathan Hagar's Company Muster Roll, Frederick Co., circa 1757-1758, exact dates not given (served 6 days); bill of credit issued or paid to him for £0.6.0 in 1767, exact date not given. {Ref: MSA S960 or S752, p. 175; CSOS:106}

SHAVER, PETER (Maryland), pvt., Capt. Stephen Rensburg's or Rensburger's Company Muster Roll, Frederick Co., circa 1757-1758, exact dates not given (served 34 days); bill of credit issued or paid in his behalf to Stephen Rensburger for Shaver's exec. (unnamed) for £1.14.0 on 27 Mar 1767. {Ref: MSA S960 or S752, p. 183; CSOS:112}

SHAVER, TEVOLT (Maryland), pvt., Capt. John White's Company Muster Roll, Frederick Co., circa 1757-1758, exact dates not given (served 6 days); bill of credit issued or paid to him for £0.6.0 in 1767, exact date not given. {Ref: MSA S960 or S752, p. 165; CSOS:95}

SHAW, ANGUISH (Maryland), pvt., Capt. Joshua Beall's Company Muster Roll, Prince George's Co., circa 1757-1758, exact dates not given; bill of credit issued and ordered his assignment to Stephen West for £1.10.6 on 11 Mar 1767; another entry stated £0.12.0 was assigned to Josiah Beall for a match coat; bill of credit issued and ordered his assignment to Joshua Beall for £0.12.0 on 13 May 1767. {Ref: MSA S960 or S752, pp. 184-185; CSOS:117}

SHAW, BENJAMIN (Maryland), b. 28 Jul 1731, Baltimore Co. (noted as "age 8 next 28 July" when indentured to James Billingsley in June 1739 (along with Mordecai Shaw who was "aged 5 next 5 March"), both to serve until age 21. {Ref: BCF:573; Baltimore Co. Court Proceedings HWS No. TR, p. 402} Pvt., Capt. Tobias Stansbury's Company Muster Roll, Baltimore Co., circa 1757-1758, exact dates not given; bill of credit issued or paid in his behalf to John Paca for £1.18.0 on 1 Oct 1771. {Ref: MSA S960 or S752, p. 187; CSOS:118}

SHAW, DANIEL (Maryland), pvt., Capt. Tobias Stansbury's Company Muster Roll, Baltimore Co., circa 1757-1758, exact dates not given; bill of credit issued or paid in his behalf to Thomas Cockey Deye for £1.18.0 on 13 Jun 1768. {Ref: MSA S960 or S752, p. 187; CSOS:118}

SHAW, ROBERT (Maryland), pvt., Capt. Richard Pearis' Company of MD Troops, Frederick Co., circa 9 Oct 1757 to 31 May 1758; pvt., Capt. Alexander Beall's Company of MD Troops, Frederick Co., from 1 Jun 1758 to 30 Dec 1758. {Ref: MHS MS.375.1; CSOS:82, 91} Payment to him was recorded in Col. Dagworthy's account book on 15 Jul 1762. {Ref: MHS MS.375}

SHAW, WAMOUTH (Maryland), pvt., Capt. Tobias Stansbury's Company Muster Roll, Baltimore Co., circa 1757-1758, exact dates not given; bill of credit or order issued to John Moale and paid to James Brooks for £1.19.0 on 22 May 1767. {Ref: MSA S960 or S752, p. 187; CSOS:119}

SHAWHIN, DANIEL (Maryland), alias Daniel Shawhorn *[sic]*, cpl., Capt. Stephen Rensburg's or Rensburger's Company Muster Roll, Frederick Co., circa 1757-1758, exact dates not given (served 42 days); bill of credit issued or paid in his behalf to Stephen Rensburger for £2.16.0 on 27 Mar 1767; name mistakenly transcribed once as "Daniel Shawkin." {Ref: MSA S960 or S752, p. 183; CSOS:112}

SHEAHORN, DAVID (Delaware), pvt., Kent Co. Militia, Capt. John Caton's Company, 25 Apr 1757 (date of muster roll). {Ref: ARDE I:14}

SHEEPHER (SHEPHERD), PETER (Maryland), pvt., Capt. Thomas Norris' Company, Frederick Co., circa 1757-1758, exact dates not given (served 30 days); bill of credit issued or paid in his behalf to Michael McGuire on 27 Mar 1767 for £1.10.0. {Ref: MSA S960 or S752, p. 176; CSOS:108}

SHEERMAN, JAMES (Delaware), b. c1738, Dublin, Ireland (age 20 in 1758); pvt., enlisted 20 Apr 1758 "for the campaign in the lower counties" by Capt. John McClughan. {Ref: ARDE I:18; ARPA (2nd Series) 2:570}

SHEKALL, BENJAMIN (Maryland), pvt., Capt. Joseph Hanson Harrison's Company Muster Roll, Charles Co., circa 1757-1758, exact dates not given; bill of credit issued or paid in his behalf to Capt. Joseph Hanson Harrison for £2.4.0 on 11 Jun 1768. {Ref: MSA S960 or S752, p. 189}

SHELBY, ---- (Maryland), lieut., Frederick Co., paid £215.15.7½ by the MD Assembly in 1756 "for the support of the ranging parties on the Western Frontier" from 14 Mar to 20 May 1756. {Ref: ARMD 52:674}

SHELBY, DAVID (Maryland), pvt., Capt. William McClellan's Company of MD Volunteers, Frederick Co., circa 1763-1764; on muster roll dated 15 Nov 1764 at Camp at the Forks of Muskingham. {Ref: ARMD 32:99}

SHELBY, EVAN (Maryland), sgt., Capt. Moses Chapline's Company Muster Roll No. 1, Frederick Co., circa 1757-1758, exact dates not given (served 62 days); bill of credit issued or paid in his behalf to Joseph Chaplin for £3.13.3 on 5 Mar 1767. {Ref: MSA S960 or S752, p. 196; CSOS:102} Sgt., Capt. Moses Chapline's Company Muster Roll No. 2, Frederick Co., circa 1757-1758, exact dates not given (served 14 days); 1st lieut., Capt. Alexander Beall's Company of MD Troops, Frederick Co., promoted 28 May 1758. {Ref: MHS MS.375.1; ARMD 31:280; CSOS:114} Bill of credit issued or paid in his behalf to Joseph Chaplin for £0.18.7½ on 5 Mar 1767. {Ref: MSA S960 or S752, p. 197} Capt., Fort Frederick, 1758; he was paid £82.3.10 on 28 Jul 1758 to equip his company of volunteers for the Western Expedition against Fort Duquesne; he was paid £4.10.0 "for his wagon's attendance on the New Road" on 30 Aug 1758. {Ref: ARMD 55:773} On 22 Dec 1758 it was certified to the MD Assembly that an Indian named Captain Charles (brother to Custoga, a Delaware Indian), commanding a party of warriors in a skirmish near Loyalbanning, was killed on 12 Nov 1758 by Capt. Evan Shelby who commanded a company of MD Volunteers. {Ref: ARMD 56:134}

Payment due him was recorded in Col. Dagworthy's account book on 16 Jul 1762. {Ref: MHS MS.375} See "Daniel Davis," q.v.

SHELBY, EVAN JR. (Maryland), pvt., Capt. Joseph Chapline's Company Muster Roll No. 1, Frederick Co., circa 1757-1758, exact dates not given; bill of credit issued or paid in his behalf to Joseph Chaplin for £4.2.7½ on 5 Mar 1767. {Ref: MSA S960 or S752, pp. 190, 193} Sgt., Capt. Joseph Chapline's Company Muster Rolls No. 2 and 3, Frederick Co., circa 1757-1758, exact dates not given (served 9 days); bill of credit issued or paid in his behalf to Joseph Chaplin for £0.17.0 on 5 Mar 1767; name sometimes listed without the "Jr." {Ref: MSA S960 or S752, p. 193; CSOS:104}

SHELBY, JOHN (Maryland), patriot, Frederick Co., was paid £3 at Fort Frederick on 30 Aug 1758 "for carryage of a load of corn to Fort Frederick" for the Western Expedition against Fort Duquesne. {Ref: ARMD 55:775}

SHELL, CHARLES (Maryland), pvt., Capt. Peter Butler's Company Muster Roll, Frederick Co., circa 1757-1758, exact dates not given (served 34 days); bill of credit or order issued in his behalf for £1.14.0 and paid to Casper Shaff on 2 Mar 1767. {Ref: MSA S960 or S752, p. 167; CSOS:97}

SHELMAN, JOHN (Maryland), patriot and poss. soldier (rank not specified), Frederick Co., militia pay account submitted in 1758, exact date not given. {Ref: MHM 9:4, p. 367}

SHELTON, WILLIAM (Maryland), cpl., Capt. William Luckett's Company Muster Roll, Frederick Co., circa 1757-1758, exact dates not given (served 30 days); bill of credit issued or paid in his behalf to William Luckett, Jr. for £2 on 6 Apr 1767. {Ref: MSA S960 or S752, p. 169; CSOS:99}

SHENYFELT, JOHN (Maryland), pvt., Capt. Jonathan Hagar's Company Muster Roll, Frederick Co., circa 1757-1758, exact dates not given (served 6 days); bill of credit issued or paid to him for £0.6.0 in 1767, exact date not given. {Ref: MSA S960 or S752, p. 175; CSOS:106}

SHEPHERD, PETER, see "Peter Sheepher," q.v.

SHEPHERD, SARAH, see "George Claypoole," q.v.

SHEPPARD, HENRY (Maryland or Pennsylvania), b. Chester Co., PA (age not given); pvt., 44th Regt. of Foot [Royal American Regt.] in 1758 who was reported as a deserter in January 1759. {Ref: *MD Gazette*, 12 Jan 1759}

SHESLER (SHESSLER), ADAM (Maryland), pvt., Capt. Peter Butler's Company Muster Roll, Frederick Co., circa 1757-1758, exact dates not given (served 34 days); bill of credit or order issued in his behalf for £1.14.0 and paid to Casper Shaff on 2 Mar 1767. {Ref: MSA S960 or S752, p. 167; CSOS:97}

SHILLS, EPHRAIM (Maryland), pvt., Capt. Jonathan Hagar's Company Muster Roll, Frederick Co., circa 1757-1758, exact dates not given; bill of credit issued or paid in his behalf to Joseph Chaplin for £0.6.0 on 24 Apr 1767. {Ref: MSA S960 or S752, pp. 173, 175}

SHILWELL (SHELWELL), JOHN (Maryland), pvt., Capt. Joseph Chapline's Company Muster Roll No. 1, Frederick Co., circa 1757-1758, exact dates not given; bill of credit issued or paid in his behalf to Joseph Chaplin for £2.17.0 on 5 Mar 1767. {Ref: MSA S960 or S752, pp. 191-192}

SHINGLES, LAWRENCE (Maryland), pvt., Capt. Thomas Norris' Company, Frederick Co., circa 1757-1758, exact dates not given (served 30 days); bill of credit issued or paid in his behalf to Stephen Rensburg or Rensburger on 27 Mar 1767 for £1.10.0; name listed once as "Lawe. Shingle." {Ref: MSA S960 or S752, p. 176; CSOS:108}

SHIPMAN, JAMES, see "James Chipman," q.v.

SHIPTON, KEZIAH, see "Michael Moore," q.v.

SHIRLEY (SHURLEY), JOHN (Maryland), pvt., Capt. Moses Chapline's Company Muster Roll No. 2, Frederick Co., circa 1757-1758, exact dates not given (served 14 days); bill of credit issued or paid in his behalf to Joseph Chaplin for £0.13.0 on 5 Mar 1767. {Ref: MSA S960 or S752, p. 197; CSOS:114} Pvt., Capt. Moses Chapline's Company Muster Roll No. 3, Frederick Co., circa 1757-1758, exact dates not given (served 6 days); bill of credit issued or paid in his behalf to Joseph Chaplin for £0.6.0 on 5 Mar 1767. {Ref: MSA S960 or S752, p. 198; CSOS:114}

SHIRLEY (SHURLEY), WILLIAM (Maryland), pvt., Capt. Moses Chapline's Company Muster Roll No. 3, Frederick Co., circa 1757-1758, exact dates not given (served 6 days); bill of credit issued or paid in his behalf to Joseph Chaplin for £0.6.0 on 5 Mar 1767. {Ref: MSA S960 or S752, p. 198; CSOS:114} Pvt., Capt. Peter Bainbridge's Company Muster Roll, Frederick Co., circa 1757-1758, exact dates not given (served 36 days); bill of credit issued or paid in his behalf to Joseph Chaplin on 24 Apr 1767 for £1.16.0. {Ref: MSA S960 or S752, p. 181; CSOS:111}

SHLAY, THOMAS (Maryland), patriot, Frederick Co., who performed "sundry services at the fort" in 1763 and payment in the amount of £2.0.4 was still owed to him on 25 Nov 1763 (when reported by the Accounts Committee to the MD Assembly). {Ref: ARMD 58:400}

SHOAB, GEORGE (Maryland), pvt., Capt. Stephen Rensburg's or Rensburger's Company Muster Roll, Frederick Co., circa 1757-1758, exact dates not given (served 34 days); bill of credit issued or paid in his behalf to Casper Shaff for £1.14.0 on 2 Mar 1767; another bill of credit was issued or paid in his behalf to Stephen Rensburger for £1.14.0 on 27 Mar 1767; name mistakenly listed as "George Shoaf" and "George Shoal." {Ref: MSA S960 or S752, pp. 182-183; CSOS:112}

SHOAB, MARTIN (Maryland), pvt., Capt. Stephen Rensburg's or Rensburger's Company Muster Roll, Frederick Co., circa 1757-1758, exact dates not given (served 34 days); bill of credit issued or paid in his behalf to Casper Shaff for £1.14.0 on 2 Mar 1767. {Ref: MSA S960 or S752, p. 182; CSOS:112} This may be the Martin Shoup who m. Sofia (N), had children George, Cathrine, Sofia, Christian, Peter, Mary, and Samuel, and d. testate by 9 Dec 1783. {Ref: WMG 6:2, pp. 84-85}

SHOAP, BASTIAN or BOSTIAN (Maryland), pvt., Capt. Jonathan Hagar's Company Muster Roll, Frederick Co., circa 1757-1758, exact dates not given (served 6 days); bill of credit issued or paid to him for £0.6.0 in 1767, exact date not given. {Ref: MSA S960 or S752, p. 175; CSOS:106}

SHOAP, BASTIAN or BOSTIAN JR. (Maryland), pvt., Capt. Jonathan Hagar's Company Muster Roll, Frederick Co., circa 1757-1758, exact dates not given (served 6 days); bill of credit issued or paid to him for £0.6.0 in 1767, exact date not given. {Ref: MSA S960 or S752, p. 175; CSOS:107}

SHOEMAKER, BENJAMIN (Delaware), New Castle Co., patriot who served as a Justice of the Peace and a Justice of the Court of Oyer and Terminer, 1756-1761. {Ref: GRSD 1:13, 15}

SHOEMAKER (SHEWMAKER), SIMON (Maryland), pvt., Capt. John Middaugh's Company Muster Roll, Frederick Co., circa 1757-1758, exact dates not given (served 30 days); bill of credit or order issued to Casper Shaff and paid to David Cumming for £1.6.0 on 18 Apr 1767. {Ref: MSA S960 or S752, p. 172; CSOS:102}

SHORT, DAVID (Maryland), pvt., Capt. John Middaugh's Company Muster Roll, Frederick Co., circa 1757-1758, exact dates not given (served 30 days); bill of credit issued or paid to him for £1.10.0 in 1767, exact date not given. {Ref: MSA S960 or S752, p. 172; CSOS:101}

SHORT, HUGH (Maryland), cpl., Capt. Joshua Beall's Company of MD Troops, Prince George's Co., from 9 Oct 1757 to 12 Oct 1758 when he was reported as killed; however, payment to him was recorded in Col. Dagworthy's account book on 26 Apr 1763. {Ref: MHS MS.375; CSOS:86; MHS MS.375.1}

SHOUP, MARTIN, see "Martin Shoab," q.v.

SHOVER, HENRY (Maryland), pvt., Capt. Peter Butler's Company Muster Roll, Frederick Co., circa 1757-1758, exact dates not given (served 34 days); bill of credit or order issued in his behalf for £1.14.0 and paid to Casper Shaff on 2 Mar 1767. {Ref: MSA S960 or S752, p. 167; CSOS:97}

SHOVER, SIMON (Maryland), m. Barbara (N), had children (mentioned, but not named in his will), and d. testate by 2 May 1774 {Ref: WMG 4:2, p. 63} Pvt., Capt. John Middaugh's Company Muster Roll, Frederick Co., circa 1757-1758, exact dates not given (served 30 days); bill of credit or order issued in his behalf to Thomas Beatty, Jr. for £1.10.0 on 3 Apr 1767. {Ref: MSA S960 or S752, p. 172; CSOS:101}

SHREINER (SHRIONER), MATHIAS (Maryland), pvt., Capt. Peter Butler's Company Muster Roll, Frederick Co., circa 1757-1758, exact dates not given (served 34 days). {Ref: CSOS:98}

SHREINER (SHRIONER), VALENTINE (Maryland), pvt., Capt. Peter Butler's Company Muster Roll, Frederick Co., circa 1757-1758, exact dates not given (served 34 days); militia pay account submitted in 1758, exact date not given. {Ref: MHM 9:4, p. 367; CSOS:97} Bill of credit or order issued in his behalf for £1.14.0 and paid to Casper Shaff on 2 Mar 1767. {Ref: MSA S960 or S752, p. 167}

SHUCK (SHUCH), LAWRENCE (Maryland), pvt., Capt. Jonathan Hagar's Company Muster Roll, Frederick Co., circa 1757-1758, exact dates not given (served 6 days); bill of credit issued or paid to him for £0.6.0 in 1767, exact date not given. {Ref: MSA S960 or S752, p. 175; CSOS:107}

SHULER, MATTHIAS (Maryland), pvt., Capt. John White's Company Muster Roll, Frederick Co., circa 1757-1758, exact dates not given (served 6 days); bill of credit issued or paid to him for £0.6.0 in 1767, exact date not given. {Ref: MSA S960 or S752, p. 165; CSOS:96}

SICKLER, HENRY (Maryland), pvt., Capt. John Middaugh's Company Muster Roll, Frederick Co., circa 1757-1758, exact dates not given (served 30 days); bill of credit issued or paid in his behalf to Thomas Beatty, Jr. for £1.10.0 on 23 Feb 1767. {Ref: MSA S960 or S752, p. 171; CSOS:101}

SIDHAM, JONAS (Delaware), pvt., Capt. Richard McWilliams' Company of Foot, New Castle Co., enlisted 28 Dec 1757. {Ref: ARDE I:14}

SILER (SILOR), JACOB (Maryland), pvt., Capt. Elias Delashmutt's Company Muster Roll, Frederick Co., circa 1757-1758, exact dates not given (served 30 days); bill of credit issued or paid in his behalf to Elias Delashmut, Jr. on 16 Mar 1767 for £1.10.0. {Ref: MSA S960 or S752, p. 162; CSOS:94}

SILSBEE, JOHN (Delaware), pvt., Capt. Richard McWilliams' Company of Foot, New Castle Co., enlisted 28 Dec 1757. {Ref: ARDE I:14}

SILSBEE (SILSBY), NATHANIEL (Delaware), bricklayer, m. (N), had children Nathaniel, Ann, and Mary, and d. testate by 29 Apr 1772. {Ref: CDSS:191; RPDE:244} Lieut., New Castle Hundred, Upper Regt. of Militia, North Division, New Castle Co., 1756. {Ref: ARDE I:11; ARPA (2nd Series) 2:526; HDE I:141}

SIM (SIMM), HENRY (Maryland), pvt., Capt. Stephen Rensburg's or Rensburger's Company Muster Roll, Frederick Co., circa 1757-1758, exact dates not given (served 34 days); bill of credit issued or paid in his behalf to Casper Shaff for £1.14.0 on 2 Mar 1767. {Ref: MSA S960 or S752, p. 182; CSOS:112}

SIM (SIMM), JACOB (Maryland), patriot and poss. soldier (rank not specified), Frederick Co., militia pay account submitted in 1758, exact date not given. {Ref: MHM 9:4, p. 366}

SIM (SIMM), JOSEPH (Maryland), b. c1725, Prince George's Co., son of Dr. Patrick Sim and Mary Brooke, m. 1st to Catherine Murdock by 1754, m. 2nd to Lettice Wardrop (widow of James Wardrop and Dr. Adam Thomson, and dau. of Philip Lee) circa 1775, had children Patrick, William, Joseph, Anthony, Thomas, Ann Addison, and Mary Brooke, and d. 27 Nov 1793, Frederick Co.; patriot, merchant, businessman, major by 1751, member of the MD Assembly (1771, 1773-1781), justice of the Provincial Court in 1773, member of the Executive Council in 1777, served on the Committee of Observation in 1775, and colonel (11th Bttn.) in 1776-1777. {Ref: BDML II:736-738}

SIM (SIMM), PATRICK, see "Joseph Sim (Simm)," q.v.

SIMMONS, HENRY (Maryland), patriot, Kent Co., pay account submitted for quartering soldiers in 1757 or 1758, exact dates not given. {Ref: MHM 9:3, p. 261}

SIMMONS, JOHN (Delaware), b. c1737, MD (laborer, age 21 in 1758); pvt., recruited by Capt. Benjamin Noxon and enlisted on 23 May 1758. {Ref: ARDE I:19; ARPA (2nd Series) 2:485, 566}

SIMMONS (SIMMONDS), JONATHAN JR. (Maryland), b. 9 Aug 1735, Prince George's Co., son of Jonathan Simmons and Elizabeth Swearingen, of Queen Anne's P. E. Parish. {Ref: PGCR 1:192} Pvt., Capt. Joshua Beall's Company Muster Roll, Prince George's Co., circa 1757-1758, exact dates not given; bill of credit issued or paid to him for £2 on 23 Feb 1767. {Ref: MSA S960 or S752, p. 184}

SIMMS, JOSEPH MILBURN (Maryland), patriot and poss. soldier (rank not specified), Charles Co., militia pay account submitted in 1758, exact date not given. {Ref: MHM 9:4, p. 366}

SIMMS, MARY (Maryland), patriot, Frederick Co., pay account submitted in 1758 for quartering 23 soldiers for 572 days, exact dates not given. {Ref: MHM 9:4, p. 370}

SIMPKINS, AVARILLA, see "Thomas Hammond," q.v.

SIMPSON, ANTHONY (Maryland), pvt., Capt. Richard Pearis' Company of MD Troops, Frederick Co., circa 9 Oct 1757 to 31 May 1758; pvt., Capt. Alexander Beall's Company of MD Troops, Frederick Co., from 1 Jun 1758 to 8 Nov 1758. {Ref: MHS MS.375.1; CSOS:82, 90} Payment to him was recorded in Col. Dagworthy's account book on 12 Jul 1762. {Ref: MHS MS.375}

SIMPSON, ARTHUR (Delaware), b. c1716, Tyrone, Ireland (schoolmaster, age 43 in 1759); pvt., enlisted by Capt. James Armstrong for the PA Regt. on 1 May 1759. {Ref: ARDE I:26; ARPA (2nd Series) 2:585}

SIMPSON, JAMES (Maryland), pvt., Capt. Francis Ware's Company of MD Troops, Charles Co., from 9 Oct 1757 to 8 Feb 1758 (served 122 days) when he reportedly died. {Ref: MHS MS.375.1; CSOS:89}

SIMPSON, JOHN (Maryland), pvt., Capt. Francis Ware's Company of MD Troops, Charles Co., from 9 Oct 1757 to 16 Feb 1758 when he was discharged; payment to him was recorded in Col. Dagworthy's account book on 7 Mar 1763. {Ref: MHS MS.375; CSOS:89; MHS MS.375.1}

SIMPSON (SIMSON), JOHN (Maryland), pvt., Capt. Peter Bainbridge's Company Muster Roll, Frederick Co., circa 1757-1758, exact dates not given (served 28 days); bill of credit or order issued to Casper Shaff and paid to David Cumming on 18 Apr 1767 for £1.8.0. {Ref: MSA S960 or S752, p. 181; CSOS:111}

SIMPSON, SAMUEL (Maryland), pvt., Capt. Joseph Chapline's Company Muster Roll No. 1, Frederick Co., circa 1757-1758, exact dates not given (served 19 days); bill of credit issued or paid in his behalf to Joseph Chaplin for £0.19.0 on 5 Mar 1767. {Ref: MSA S960 or S752, p. 191; CSOS:103}

SIMPSON, THOMAS (Maryland), b. c1722, son of Thomas Simpson (aged about 56 in 1778 deposition). {Ref: MGSB 34:2, p. 178} Pvt., Capt. Francis Ware's Company of MD Troops, Charles Co., from 23 Oct 1757 to 30 Dec 1758 (promoted to cpl. on 19 Feb 1758 and promoted to sgt. on 13 Oct 1758). {Ref: MHS MS.375.1; CSOS:89} Payment to him was recorded in Col. Dagworthy's account book on 22 Feb 1763. {Ref: MHS MS.375}

SIMPSON, THOMAS (Maryland), b. c1740, son of the Widow Simpson who lived near Piscataway in Prince George's Co.; pvt., enlisted in 1st Bttn. of the Royal American Regt. on 10 Jan 1760 (age about 20); a notice placed in the Annapolis newspaper by Ensign James Gorrell indicated Simpson left Fort Frederick on Gorrell's horse and said he was going to look for the deserter Peter Dent, but he may have deserted himself; if the horse is found, deliver it to Thomas Chittam in Bladensburg. {Ref: *MD Gazette*, 5 Jun 1760}

SIMPSON, WILLIAM (Maryland), patriot, Annapolis, Anne Arundel Co., pay account submitted for quartering soldiers in 1757 or 1758, exact dates not given. {Ref: MHM 9:3, p. 261}

SIMS, JAMES (Maryland), pvt., Capt. Francis Ware's Company of MD Troops, Charles Co., from 9 Oct 1757 to 23 Oct 1757 (served 14 days) when he reportedly died; however, payment to him was recorded in Col. Dagworthy's account book on 8 Mar 1763. {Ref: MHS MS.375; CSOS:89; MHS MS.375.1}

SIMS, SARAH WOODROP, see "Benjamin Wynkoop," q.v.

SINGLETON, JOHN (Delaware or Pennsylvania), captain and recruiting officer for PA Troops in the "Three Lower Counties on Delaware" in 1758; subscribed to the Oath of Fidelity and Allegiance in 1778. {Ref: ARDE I:27; RPDE:245}

SIPPLE, CALEB (Delaware), yeoman, son of Waitman Sipple, Jr. and Mary Hunn, m. Sarah (N), had children Nancy, John, Caleb, Mary, Thomas, Elizabeth, and Garret, and d. intestate by 10 Feb 1762. {Ref: CFD 1:234; CDSS:193} Lieut., Murderkill Hundred, Kent Co. on Delaware, 29 Mar 1758. {Ref: ARDE I:15; ARPA (2nd Series) 2:577}

SKIDMORE, EDWARD (Delaware), b. c1737, DE (laborer, age 21 in 1758); pvt., recruited by Capt. Benjamin Noxon and enlisted on 29 Apr 1758. {Ref: ARDE I:19; ARPA (2nd Series) 2:566} Pvt., Capt. Henry Vanbibber's Company of the Lower Counties on Delaware Troops at New Castle, enlisted on 21 May 1759. {Ref: ARDE I:26; ARPA (2nd Series) 2:594}

SKILES (SKILLS), WILLIAM (Maryland), pvt., Capt. Joseph Chapline's Company Muster Roll No. 1, Frederick Co., circa 1757-1758, exact dates not given (served 48 days); bill of credit issued or paid in his behalf to Joseph Chaplin for £1.1.0 on 8 Jun 1767. {Ref: MSA S960 or S752, p. 192; CSOS:103} Pvt., Capt. Joseph Chapline's Company Muster Rolls No. 2 and 3, Frederick Co., circa 1757-1758, exact dates not given (served 8 days); bill of credit issued or paid in his behalf to Joseph Chapline for £0.8.0 on 8 Jun 1767; name mistakenly transcribed once as "William Still." {Ref: MSA S960 or S752, p. 193; CSOS:104}

SKIN (SKINN), GEORGE (Maryland), pvt., Capt. Peter Butler's Company Muster Roll, Frederick Co., circa 1757-1758, exact dates not given (served 34 days); bill of credit or order issued in his behalf for £1.14.0 and paid to Thomas Bowles on 23 May 1767. {Ref: MSA S960 or S752, p. 168; CSOS:98}

SKIN (SKINN), PETER (Maryland), pvt., Capt. John White's Company Muster Roll, Frederick Co., circa 1757-1758, exact dates not given (served days); bill of credit issued or paid to him for £0.6.0 in 1767, exact date not given. {Ref: MSA S960 or S752, p. 165; CSOS:96}

SKINNER, HENRY (Maryland), pvt., Capt. Joshua Beall's Company Muster Roll, Prince George's Co., circa 1757-1758, exact dates not given; bill of credit issued or paid in his behalf to his exec. Truman Skinner for £1.3.0 on 28 Feb 1767; one undated account indicated "Calvert County." {Ref: MSA S960 or S752, p. 184; CSOS:116} Pvt., Capt. Joshua Beall's Company of MD Troops, Prince George's Co., from 31 May 1758 (promoted to cadet on 1 Jun 1758) to 30 Dec 1758 (transferred from Capt. Richard Pearis' Company where he had been an ensign).

{Ref: MHS MS.375.1; CSOS:83, 90} Payment to him was recorded in Col. Dagworthy's account book on 14 Jul 1762. {Ref: MHS MS.375}

SKINNER, MARY, see "John Goldsborough," q.v.

SKINNER, REBECCA, see "William Skinner," q.v.

SKINNER, RICHARD, see "John Goldsborough," q.v.

SKINNER, TRUMAN, see "Henry Skinner," q.v.

SKINNER, WILLIAM (Delaware), m. Rebecca (N), had children John, Thomas, Daniel, Stephen, Nelly, and Betsey, and d. testate in 1792. {Ref: CDSS:194} Pvt., Kent Co. Militia, Capt. John Caton's Company, 25 Apr 1757 (date of muster roll). {Ref: ARDE I:14}

SKYOUKER, Indian Chief (Maryland), Frederick Co., agreed to join with the English against the French in 1758. {Ref: ARMD 31:266}

SLATER, ISAAC (Maryland), pvt., Capt. Joshua Beall's Company of MD Troops, Prince George's Co., from 9 Oct 1757 to 25 Oct 1757 when he was discharged. {Ref: MHS MS.375.1; CSOS:86} Payment to him was recorded in Col. Dagworthy's account book on 8 Mar 1763. {Ref: MHS MS.375}

SLATER, JOHN (Maryland), pvt., Capt. John Dagworthy's Company of MD Troops, Frederick Co., from 9 Oct 1757 to 8 Aug 1758. {Ref: MHS MS.375.1; CSOS:78} Payment to him was recorded in Col. Dagworthy's account book on 8 Mar 1763. {Ref: MHS MS.375}

SLIGH, THOMAS (Maryland), patriot and poss. soldier (rank not specified), Frederick or Baltimore Co., militia pay account submitted in 1758, exact date not given. {Ref: MHM 9:4, p. 369}

SLIM, SIMON (Maryland), pvt., Capt. Peter Butler's Company Muster Roll, Frederick Co., circa 1757-1758, exact dates not given (served 34 days); bill of credit or order issued to him for £1.14.0 in March 1767. {Ref: MSA S960 or S752, p. 168; CSOS:97}

SLOAN, JOHN (Delaware), b. c1733, Tyrone, Ireland (weaver, age 25 in 1758); pvt., enlisted 4 May 1758 "for the campaign in the lower counties" by Capt. John McClughan. {Ref: ARDE I:18; ARPA (2nd Series) 2:570}

SLORP, PETER (Maryland), pvt., Capt. Thomas Norris' Company, Frederick Co., circa 1757-1758, exact dates not given (served 30 days); bill of credit issued or paid in his behalf to Michael McGuire on 20 Mar 1767 for £1.10.0; name listed once as "Peter Slores." {Ref: MSA S960 or S752, p. 176; CSOS:108}

SLUBEY, WILLIAM (Delaware), pvt., Capt. Richard McWilliams' Company of Foot, New Castle Co., enlisted 28 Dec 1757. {Ref: ARDE I:15}

SMALL, ADAM (Maryland), pvt., Capt. Thomas Norris' Company, Frederick Co., circa 1757-1758, exact dates not given (served 30 days); bill of credit issued or paid in his behalf to Charles Englas on 28 Mar 1767 for £1.10.0. {Ref: MSA S960 or S752, p. 176; CSOS:108}

SMALL, JAMES (Maryland), pvt., Capt. William McClellan's Company of MD Volunteers, Frederick Co., circa 1763-1764; on muster roll dated 15 Nov 1764 at Camp at the Forks of Muskingham. {Ref: ARMD 32:99}

SMALLWOOD, WILLIAM (Maryland), b. 1732, Charles Co., son of Bayne Smallwood and Priscilla Heabard, never married, and d. 14 Feb 1792 on his plantation at Mattawoman Creek; planter, gentleman, esquire, and prob. Freemason; career military officer who served in the French and Indian War (1756-1763) and commissioned colonel in 1776 and major general and commander-in-chief of MD Forces in the Revolutionary War (1776-1783); member of the MD Assembly (1761-1776, served on the Arms and Ammunition Committee, 1762-1770); served on the Committee of Observation for Charles Co. in 1774; elected delegate to the Continental Congress in 1784, but declined, choosing instead to succeed William Paca as Governor of MD (1785-1788); served as President of the MD Senate, 1791-1792. {Ref: BDML II:741-742; MDG II:354} See "Uzza Posey" and "Smallwood Thompson," q.v.

SMITH, ---- (Maryland), patriot and merchant, Chester Town, Kent Co., received two barrels of gunpowder from the magazine and stores of the City of Annapolis on 10 Nov 1762 (as reported by the Arms and Ammunition Committee to the MD Assembly). {Ref: ARMD 58:342}

SMITH, ADAM (Maryland), pvt., Capt. John Middaugh's Company Muster Roll, Frederick Co., circa 1757-1758, exact dates not given (served 30 days); bill of credit issued or paid in his behalf to Thomas Beatty, Jr. for £1.10.0 on 23 Feb 1767. {Ref: MSA S960 or S752, p. 171; CSOS:101}

SMITH, ANDREW (Maryland), m. Rebekah (N), had children Thomas, William, George, and David, and d. testate by 28 Oct 1770. {Ref: WMG 3:3, p. 111} Pvt., Capt. John Middaugh's Company Muster Roll, Frederick Co., circa 1757-1758, exact dates not given (served 30 days); bill of credit issued or paid to him for £1.10.0 on 3 Apr 1767. {Ref: MSA S960 or S752, p. 172: CSOS:101}

SMITH, ANN, see "Macarty Smith," q.v.

SMITH, ANTHONY (Maryland), bapt. 6 Mar 1727/8, All Hallow's Parish, son of Samuel and Elizabeth Smith. {Ref: AACR:42} Pvt., Capt. Samuel Chapman's Company Muster Roll, Anne Arundel Co., circa 1757-1758, exact dates not given; bill of credit issued or paid in his behalf to Stephen Watkins for £1.18.0 on 10 Mar 1767. {Ref: MSA S960 or S752, p. 188}

SMITH, BARBARA, see "Benjamin Mackall, Jr.," q.v.

SMITH, BARBERY, see "Christian Smith," q.v.

SMITH, CASPER, see "Christian Smith," q.v.

SMITH, CASSANDRA, see "William Smith," q.v.

SMITH, CHARLES, see "Joseph Smith," q.v.

SMITH, CHRISTIAN (Maryland), pvt., Capt. John Middaugh's Company Muster Roll, Frederick Co., circa 1757-1758, exact dates not given (served 30 days); bill of credit issued or paid in his behalf to Thomas Beatty, Jr. for £0.17.0 on 23 Feb 1767. {Ref: MSA S960 or S752, p. 171; CSOS:102} *Identification problem:* There were two men with this name who could have served in the war: (1) Christian Smith m. Barbery (N), had two children (only named son Casper in his will which he wrote on 3 Jan 1767), and d. by 6 May 1767; and, (2) Christian Smith was named as a son of Casper Smith and wife Christina when Casper wrote his will on 14 Dec 1770 and d. by 6 Jun 1780. {Ref: WMG 2:4, p. 170; WMG 5:4, p. 166}

SMITH, DANIEL (Maryland), pvt., Capt. John Dagworthy's Company of MD Troops, Frederick Co., from 9 Oct 1757 to 17 Jan 1759 when he reportedly died; however, payment to him was recorded in Col. Dagworthy's account book on 8 Mar 1763 for work on Fort Cumberland. {Ref: MHS MS.375; CSOS:78; MHS MS.375.1}

SMITH, DANIEL (Maryland), pvt., Capt. Elias Delashmutt's Company Muster Roll, Frederick Co., 13 Aug 1757, exact dates not given (served 52 days); bill of credit issued or paid in his behalf to Peter Grosh on 4 Mar 1767 for £2.12.0. {Ref: MSA S960 or S752, p. 162; CSOS:98}

SMITH, DANIEL (Maryland), indentured servant and soldier who served in the French and Indian War some time between 1756 and 1763 (exact dates not known); his master John McLaughlan, planter, requested compensation from the Baltimore County Court due to the loss of use of Smith while in the service. {Ref: MHM 94:4, p. 426, citing Baltimore Co. Court Minutes}

SMITH, DAVID, see "Bethuel Watson," q.v.

SMITH, ELINOR, see "John Addison," q.v.

SMITH, ELIZABETH, see "John Paca" and "William Smith" and "Anthony Smith" and "Joseph Smith" and "Bethuel Watson," q.v.

SMITH, HANNAH, see "Joseph Nicholson," q.v.

SMITH, HARRIET, see "William Smith," q.v.

SMITH, HENRY (Maryland), pvt., Capt. Peter Butler's Company Muster Roll, Frederick Co., circa 1757-1758, exact dates not given (served 34 days); militia pay account submitted in 1758, exact date not given. {Ref: MHM 9:4, p. 367} Bill of credit or order issued in his behalf for £1.14.0 and paid to Casper Shaff on 2 Mar 1767. {Ref: MSA S960 or S752, p. 167; CSOS:97} See "Joseph Smith," q.v.

SMITH, JACOB (Maryland), pvt., Capt. Stephen Rensburg's or Rensburger's Company Muster Roll, Frederick Co., circa 1757-1758, exact dates not given (served 34 days); bill of credit issued or paid in his behalf to Stephen Rensburger for £1.14.0 on 27 Mar 1767. {Ref: MSA S960 or S752, p. 183; CSOS:112}

SMITH, JACOB (Maryland), pvt., Capt. Peter Bainbridge's Company Muster Roll, Frederick Co., circa 1757-1758, exact dates not given (served 28 days); bill of credit issued or paid in his behalf to Casper Shaff on 4 Mar 1767 for £1.8.0. {Ref: MSA S960 or S752, p. 180; CSOS:111}

SMITH, JAMES (Maryland), pvt., Capt. Joshua Beall's Company of MD Troops, Prince George's Co., from 9 Oct 1757 to 28 Jun 1758 when he was discharged. {Ref: MHS MS.375.1; CSOS:85} Payment to him was recorded in Col. Dagworthy's account book on 23 Jul 1762; Ann Ashley was paid in his behalf in February 1763. {Ref: MHS MS.375}

SMITH, JAMES (Maryland), patriot, Annapolis, Anne Arundel Co., pay account submitted for quartering soldiers in 1757 or 1758, exact dates not given. {Ref: MHM 9:3, p. 261}

SMITH, JAMES, see "Francis Miller" and "Joseph Wilson" and "Jonathan Hagar" and "John Rorar" and "Christian Pelser" and "John Rutter" and "Joseph Smith," q.v.

SMITH, JOHANNA, see "John Smith" and "William Smith," q.v.

SMITH, JOHN (Maryland), patriot, Annapolis, Anne Arundel Co., pay account submitted in behalf of his exec. (unnamed) for his quartering soldiers in 1757 or 1758, exact dates not given. {Ref: MHM 9:3, p. 261}

SMITH, JOHN (Maryland), pvt., Capt. Tobias Stansbury's Company Muster Roll, Baltimore Co., circa 1757-1758, exact dates not given; bill of credit issued or paid in his behalf to James Richards for £1.18.0 on 13 May 1767. {Ref: MSA S960 or S752, p. 186} *Identification problem:* There were at least four men with this name who could have served in the war: (1) John Smith m. Margaret Scarf(?) on 18 Dec 1752; (2) John Smith m. Mary (N) before 20 Jun 1758 (date of birth of son John); (3) John Smith, a Scottish servant, ran away from Pleasance Goodwin, of Soldier's Delight Hundred, in 1752; and, (4) John Smith, son of William (d. 1746) and Johanna Smith. {Ref: BCF:591-593}

SMITH, JOHN (Maryland), pvt., Capt. Moses Chapline's Company Muster Roll No. 3, Frederick Co., circa 1757-1758, exact dates not given (served 6 days); bill of credit issued or paid in his behalf to Jonathan Hagar for £0.6.0 on 10 Oct 1771. {Ref: MSA S960 or S752, p. 198; CSOS:114}

SMITH, JOHN (Maryland), pvt., Capt. Moses Chapline's Company Muster Roll No. 3, Frederick Co., circa 1757-1758, exact dates not given (served 6 days); bill of credit issued or paid in his behalf to James Smith for £0.6.0 on 18 May 1767. {Ref: MSA S960 or S752, p. 198; CSOS:115}

SMITH, JOHN (Maryland), pvt., Capt. Joseph Chapline's Company Muster Roll No. 1, Frederick Co., circa 1757-1758, exact dates not given (served 14 days); bill of credit issued or paid in his behalf to Joseph Chaplin for £1.1.0 on 18 May 1767. {Ref: MSA S960 or S752, p. 192; CSOS:103}

SMITH, JOHN (Maryland), pvt., Capt. Stephen Rensburg's or Rensburger's Company Muster Roll, Frederick Co., circa 1757-1758, exact dates not given (served 42 days); bill of credit issued or paid in his behalf to Stephen Rensburger for £2.2.0 on 27 Mar 1767. {Ref: MSA S960 or S752, p. 183; CSOS:112}

SMITH, JOHN, see "William Smith," q.v.

SMITH, JOSEPH, see "John McAdow" and "William McCau," q.v.

SMITH, JOSEPH (Delaware), pvt., Kent Co. Militia, Capt. John Caton's Company, 25 Apr 1757 (date of muster roll). {Ref: ARDE I:13} *Identification problem:* There were three men with this name who could have served in the war: (1) Joseph Smith m. Mary (N), had children Henry, James, and Mary, and d. testate by 30 Sep 1767; (2) Joseph Smith, yeoman, m. Mary (N), had children Charles, Elizabeth, Sophiah, and Mary, and d. testate by 17 Jul 1775; and, (3) Joseph Smith, blacksmith, d. intestate by 14 Nov 1793 at which time letters of administration were granted to Mary Smith. {Ref: CDSS:195-196}

SMITH, JOSEPH (Maryland), pvt., Capt. Joseph Chapline's Company Muster Roll No. 1, Frederick Co., circa 1757-1758, exact dates not given (served 45 days); bill of credit issued or paid in his behalf to Joseph Chaplin for £2.5.0 on 24 Apr 1767. {Ref: MSA S960 or S752, p. 192; CSOS:103}

SMITH, JOSEPH (Maryland), patriot, Annapolis, Anne Arundel Co., pay account submitted for quartering soldiers in 1757 or 1758, exact dates not given. {Ref: MHM 9:3, p. 262}

SMITH, MARGARET, see "William Smith," q.v.

SMITH, MARTHA, see "William Smith" and "Emory Sudler," q.v.

SMITH, MARY, see "John Smith" and "William Smith" and "Joseph Smith" and "Nehemiah Davis," q.v.

SMITH, MATTHEW (Maryland), patriot and poss. soldier (rank not specified), Frederick Co., militia pay account submitted in 1758, exact date not given. {Ref: MHM 9:4, p. 366}

SMITH, MATTHIAS (Maryland), pvt., Capt. John Middaugh's Company Muster Roll, Frederick Co., circa 1757-1758, exact dates not given (served 30 days); bill of credit issued or paid in his behalf to Thomas Beatty, Jr. for £1.10.0 on 23 Feb 1767. {Ref: MSA S960 or S752, p. 171; CSOS:101}

SMITH, MACARTY or McCARTHY (Maryland), b. 11 Jun 1739, Anne Arundel Co., son of William and Ann Smith, of St. Margaret's (Westminster) Parish. {Ref: AACR:117} Pvt., Capt. Alexander Beall's Company of MD Troops, Frederick Co., from 9 Oct 1757 to 8 Nov 1758; payment recorded in Col. Dagworthy's account book on 28 Feb 1763. {Ref: MHS MS.375; CSOS:82; MHS MS.375.1} Pvt., age about 17 or 18, labourer, born on the Severn River in Anne Arundel Co., was reported by Lieut. Harrington Baudin, at Annapolis, as having deserted from Capt. John Leland's recruiting party in 1759. {Ref: *MD Gazette*, 15 Mar 1759}

SMITH, MICHAEL (Maryland), pvt., Capt. Henry Casson's Company Muster Roll, Queen Anne's Co., circa 1757-1758, exact dates not given (served 27 days); bill of credit issued or paid in his behalf to Capt. Casson on 27 Mar 1767 for £1.7.0. {Ref: MSA S960 or S752, p. 178; CSOS:109}

SMITH, MICHAEL LUKE (Maryland), pvt., Capt. Joshua Beall's Company of MD Troops, Prince George's Co., from 9 Oct 1757 to 31 May 1758 when he reportedly deserted; however, payment to him was recorded in Col. Dagworthy's account book on 8 Mar 1763 for work on Fort Cumberland. {Ref: MHS MS.375; CSOS:86; MHS MS.375.1}

SMITH, NATHAN, see "William Smith," q.v.

SMITH, PHILIP (Maryland), drummer, Capt. John Middaugh's Company Muster Roll, Frederick Co., circa 1757-1758, exact dates not given (served 30 days); bill of credit issued or paid in his behalf to Thomas Beatty, Jr. for £2 on 23 Feb 1767. {Ref: MSA S960 or S752, pp. 171-172; CSOS:100}

SMITH, RACHEL, see "Thomas Gantt," q.v.

SMITH, REBECCA, see "Daniel Dulany, Jr." and "Walter Dulany," q.v.

SMITH, RICHARD, see "Benjamin Mackall, Jr.," q.v.

SMITH, SAMUEL, see "Anthony Smith," q.v.

SMITH, SARAH, see "William Smith," q.v.

SMITH, SOPHIAH, see "Joseph Smith," q.v.

SMITH, SUSANNA, see "Nathan Magruder," q.v.

SMITH, THOMAS (Maryland), pvt., Capt. Moses Chapline's Company Muster Roll No. 3, Frederick Co., circa 1757-1758, exact dates not given (served 6 days); bill of credit issued or paid in his behalf to Joseph Chaplin for £0.6.0 on 5 Mar 1767. {Ref: MSA S960 or S752, p. 198; CSOS:114}

SMITH, THOMAS (Maryland), pvt., Capt. Joseph Chapline's Company Muster Roll No. 1, Frederick Co., circa 1757-1758, exact dates not given (served 21 days); bill of credit issued or paid in his behalf to Joseph Chaplin for £1.1.0 on 5 Mar 1767. {Ref: MSA S960 or S752, p. 191; CSOS:103}

SMITH, THOMAS (Maryland), pvt., Capt. Joshua Beall's Company of MD Troops, Prince George's Co., circa 9 Oct 1757 to 30 Dec 1758; pvt., Capt. John Dagworthy's Company of MD Troops, Frederick Co., from 31 Dec 1758 to 22 Jan 1759 when he reportedly deserted; however, payment to him was recorded in Col. Dagworthy's account book on 16 Jul 1762. {Ref: MHS MS.375; CSOS:78, 86; MHS MS.375.1}

SMITH, THOMAS (Maryland), pvt., Capt. John Dagworthy's Company of MD Troops, Frederick Co., from 9 May 1758 to 9 Nov 1758 when he was promoted to cpl. and served to 26 Apr 1759. {Ref: MHS MS.375.1; CSOS:78} Payment to him was recorded in Col. Dagworthy's account book on 13 Jul 1762. {Ref: MHS MS.375}

SMITH, THOMAS, see "William Smith," q.v.

SMITH, WILLIAM (Delaware), b. c1731, Bellyshannon, Ireland (baker, age 27 in 1758); pvt., enlisted 9 May 1758 "for the campaign in the lower counties" by Capt. John McClughan. {Ref: ARDE I:18; ARPA (2nd Series) 2:570}

SMITH, WILLIAM (Maryland), b. c1720, Baltimore Co., son of William Smith and Elizabeth Martin (widow of Richard Dallam of Baltimore Co. and dau. of William Martin of Calvert Co.), m. Elizabeth (N) on 23 Dec 1743, had children Winston, William, Nathan, Thomas, John, Elizabeth, Cassandra, Sarah, Martha, and Harriet, and d. by 28 Jun 1777, Harford Co.; planter, surveyor, mill owner, county justice (1746-1756), member of the MD Assembly (1750-1751, 1756-1757), captain by 1760, served on the Committee of Observation (1774-1775), and signer of the Bush Declaration on 22 Mar 1775. {Ref: BDML II:752-753}

SMITH, WILLIAM (Maryland), pvt., Capt. Alexander Beall's Company of Foot, Frederick Co., 1756-1757, recorded his discharge in Frederick Co. Court on 18 Jun 1757. Capt. Beall certified that he "hath served honestly and faithfully in my company upwards of 8 months and the time of his enlistment being expired is hereby discharged agreeable to Act of Assembly, having first received full and true account of all his pay, cloathing and all other demands. Given under my hand and seal at Fort Frederick, MD, 10 Feb 1757." Signed in German script, transcribed as "Jna Schmith" and witnessed by Sgt. Robert Lineard and Sgt. George Barrance. {Ref: FCLR:25-26}

SMITH, WILLIAM (Maryland), pvt., Capt. Joshua Beall's Company of MD Troops, Prince George's Co., circa 9 Oct 1757 to 30 Dec 1758. {Ref: MHS MS.375.1; CSOS:85} Payment to him was recorded in Col. Dagworthy's account book on 8 Mar 1763. {Ref: MHS MS.375}

SMITH, WILLIAM (Maryland), pvt., Capt. John Dagworthy's Company of MD Troops, Frederick Co., circa 9 Oct 1757 to 26 Apr 1759. {Ref: MHS MS.375.1; CSOS:78} Payment to him was recorded in Col. Dagworthy's account book on 16 Feb 1763. {Ref: MHS MS.375}

SMITH, WILLIAM (Maryland), pvt., Capt. John Middaugh's Company Muster Roll, Frederick Co., circa 1757-1758, exact dates not given (served 30 days); bill of credit issued or paid in his behalf to Thomas Beatty, Jr. for £1.10.0 on 23 Feb 1767. {Ref: MSA S960 or S752, p. 171; CSOS:101}

SMITH, WILLIAM (Maryland), pvt., Capt. Tobias Stansbury's Company Muster Roll, Baltimore Co., circa 1757-1758, exact dates not given; bill of credit issued or paid to him for £1.19.0 in 1767, exact date not given. {Ref: MSA S960 or S752, p. 187} *Identification problem:* There were five men with this name who could have served in the war: (1) William Smith, b. 27 Jul 1732, son of Zachariah and Margaret Smith; (2) William Smith, b. by 1731, son of William Smith (d. 30 Jan 1731/2) and Elizabeth Dallam; (3) William Smith, b. 12 Sep 1733, son of William and Mary Smith; (4) William Smith, son of William (d. 1746) and Johanna Smith; and, (5) William Smith m. Anne Peacock in December 1751. {Ref: BCF:587, 593}

SMITH, WILLIAM, see "John Smith" and "Macarty Smith," q.v.

SMITH, WINSTON, see "William Smith," q.v.

SMITH, ZACHARIAH, see "William Smith," q.v.

SMITHSON, DANIEL (Maryland), b. 2 Jan 1714/5, Baltimore Co., son of Thomas Smithson and Ann Scott. "On 17 Sep 1760 Daniel Smitson *[sic]*, son and heir of Thomas Smitson, Baltimore Co., conveyed 50 acres of 100 acres to Thomas Smitson, planter, for £35. I believe this is the Daniel Smithson above born in 1714 as his father Thomas Smithson died in 1732. My theory is that Daniel Smithson, son of Thomas Smithson and Ann Scott, was the one who probably served in the French and Indian War. I am not sure when he died or if he married and had children." {Ref: Christopher T. Smithson, 2004} Pvt., Capt. Joseph Chapline's Company Muster Roll No. 4, Frederick Co., circa 1757-1758, exact dates not given (served 2 days); bill of credit issued or paid to him for £0.2.0 in 1767, exact date not given. {Ref: MSA S960 or S752, p. 195; CSOS:105}

SMITHSON, ELEANOR, see "Mordecai Durham," q.v.

SMOOTE, JOHN (Maryland), pvt., Capt. Elias Delashmutt's Company Muster Roll, Frederick Co., 13 Aug 1757, exact dates not given (served 52 days); also served another 30 days, exact dates not given; bill of credit issued or paid in his behalf to Casper Shaff on 2 Mar 1767 for £4.2.0. {Ref: MSA S960 or S752, p. 162; CSOS:94, 98}

SNEAVELY, HENRY, see "Henry Schnebely," q.v.

SNIDER, CHRISTIAN (Maryland), pvt., Capt. Jonathan Hagar's Company Muster Roll, Frederick Co., circa 1757-1758, exact dates not given (served 6 days); bill of credit issued or paid in his behalf to Joseph Chaplin for £0.6.0 on 24 Apr 1767. {Ref: MSA S960 or S752, pp. 173, 175; CSOS:106}

SNIDER, CONROD (Maryland), pvt., Capt. Peter Butler's Company Muster Roll, Frederick Co., circa 1757-1758, exact dates not given (served 34 days); bill of credit or order issued in his behalf for £1.14.0 and paid to Casper Shaff on 2 Mar 1767. {Ref: MSA S960 or S752, p. 167; CSOS:97}

SNIDER, FREDERICK (Maryland), pvt., Capt. John White's Company Muster Roll, Frederick Co., circa 1757-1758, exact dates not given (served 6 days; bill of credit or order issued to him for £0.6.0 in 1767, exact date not given. {Ref: MSA S960 or S752, p. 165; CSOS:95}

SNIDER, GEORGE (Maryland), pvt., Capt. Peter Butler's Company Muster Roll, Frederick Co., circa 1757-1758, exact dates not given (served 34 days); bill of credit or order issued in his behalf for £1.14.0 and paid to Casper Shaff on 2 Mar 1767. {Ref: MSA S960 or S752, p. 167; CSOS:97}

SNIDER, JACOB (Maryland), pvt., Capt. John White's Company Muster Roll, Frederick Co., circa 1757-1758, exact dates not given (served 6 days); bill of credit or order issued to him for £0.6.0 in 1767, exact date not given; name mistakenly transcribed once as "Jacob Snidtor." {Ref: MSA S960 or S752, p. 165; CSOS:95}

SNIDER, MARTIN (Maryland), pvt., Capt. John White's Company Muster Roll, Frederick Co., circa 1757-1758, exact dates not given (served 6 days); bill of credit or order issued to him for £0.6.0 in 1767, exact date not given. {Ref: MSA S960 or S752, p. 165; CSOS:95}

SNIDER, MICHAEL (Maryland), pvt., Capt. Peter Butler's Company Muster Roll, Frederick Co., circa 1757-1758, exact dates not given (served 34 days); bill of credit or order issued in his behalf for £1.14.0 and paid to Casper Shaff on 2 Mar 1767. {Ref: MSA S960 or S752, p. 167; CSOS:97}

SNOKE (SNOKES), HENRY (Maryland), pvt., Capt. John Middaugh's Company Muster Roll, Frederick Co., circa 1757-1758, exact dates not given (served 30 days); bill of credit or order issued in his behalf to Casper Shaff for £1.10.0 and paid to David Cumming on 18 Apr 1767. {Ref: MSA S960 or S752, p. 172; CSOS:102}

SNOWDAGLE, JACOB (Maryland), pvt., Capt. Peter Butler's Company Muster Roll, Frederick Co., circa 1757-1758, exact dates not given (served 34 days); bill of credit or order issued in his behalf for £1.14.0 and paid to Casper Shaff on 2 Mar 1767. {Ref: MSA S960 or S752, p. 167; CSOS:97}

SNOWDEN, ANN, see "Henry Wright Crabb," q.v.

SOLDEN, JOHN (Maryland), pvt., Capt. Joseph Chapline's Company Muster Roll No. 1, Frederick Co., circa 1757-1758, exact dates not given (served 6 days); bill of credit or order issued to him for £0.6.0 in 1767, exact date not given. {Ref: MSA S960 or S752, p. 192; CSOS:103}

SOLLERS, ROBERT (Maryland), captain, St. Leonard's Town, commander of the militia in the lower part of Calvert Co. circa 1756-1758 (exact dates not given). {Ref: HCC:121}

SOLLERS (SELLERS), SABRIT JR. (Maryland), son of Sabrett Sollers, Baltimore Co.; never married; d. July 1786. {Ref: BCF:595} Pvt., Baltimore Co., age about 24 in 1756, enlisted in Maj. Gen. Lascelles' Regt. (exact date not given) and was reported by Capt. S. Gardner at Mr. Cary's Inn in Baltimore as a deserter who had prob. gone to Patapsco Neck where his mother and some relations lived. {Ref: *MD Gazette*, 12 Aug 1756}

SOLLERS (SOLLARS), THOMAS (Maryland), son of Sabrett Sollers, Baltimore Co.; m. Ariana Dorsey. {Ref: BCF:595} Ensign in Capt. Tobias Stansbury's Company Muster Roll, Baltimore Co., circa 1757-1758, exact dates not given;

bill of credit issued or paid to him for £3.18.0 on 20 Feb 1767. {Ref: MSA S960 or S752, p. 186; CSOS:117} See "Josias Bowen" and "William Johnson," q.v.

SOMERVELL (SOMERVILLE, SUMMERVILL), ALEXANDER (Maryland), b. 9 Aug 1734, Calvert Co., son of Dr. James Somervell and Sarah Howe, m. Rebecca Dawkins on 2 Dec 1759, had children Thomas, William, and Rebecca, and d. 1783; planter, merchant, ensign by 1757; received £20 from the MD Assembly in December 1765 for his services and expenses during the French and Indian War; served as county sheriff (1769-1772), county justice in 1773, member of the MD Assembly (1773-1778), tax commissioner (1779-1783), and lieut. colonel of militia (6 Jan 1776 - 19 Dec 1776). {Ref: BDML II:757-758; ARMD 59:251} 2nd lieut., Capt. Francis Ware's Company of MD Troops, Charles Co., from 9 Oct 1757 to 8 Nov 1758; transferred to Capt. Joshua Beall's Company of MD Troops, Prince George's Co., and served from 9 Nov 1758 to 30 Dec 1758. {Ref: MHS MS.375.1; CSOS:83} Payment to him was recorded in Col. Dagworthy's account book on 12 Jul 1762. {Ref: MHS MS.375} On 3 Dec 1765 he petitioned the Lower House of the MD Assembly; the Accounts Committee determined that "Alexander Somerville performed the recruiting service mentioned in this petition and was at a very considerable expence in carrying up his recruits to Fort Frederick having no more than one shilling per day allowed him for provision for said recruits, that after he had a commission as ensign he recruited upwards of 30 men more for the service with whom he was at a much greater charge than the sum allowed for their maintenance would defray, and that he was obliged to allow the sum of £7.7.11 for his proportion of the charge of soliciting for and receiving the pay due him and advanced by the Crown." {Ref: ARMD 59:197}

SONPOWER, MICHAEL (Maryland), pvt., Capt. Stephen Rensburg's or Rensburger's Company Muster Roll, Frederick Co., circa 1757-1758, exact dates not given (served 34 days); bill of credit issued or paid in his behalf to Stephen Rensburger for £1.14.0 on 27 Mar 1767. {Ref: MSA S960 or S752, p. 183; CSOS:113}

SOTHORON, HENRY GREENFIELD, see "Zachariah Bond," q.v.

SOUDER, PHILIP (Maryland), pvt., Capt. Stephen Rensburg's or Rensburger's Company Muster Roll, Frederick Co., circa 1757-1758, exact dates not given (served 42 days); bill of credit issued or paid in his behalf to Stephen Rensburger for £2.2.0 on 27 Mar 1767; name mistakenly transcribed once as "Philix Souder." {Ref: MSA S960 or S752, p. 183; CSOS:112}

SOUTH, THOMAS (Maryland), pvt., Capt. Joseph Chapline's Company Muster Roll No. 4, Frederick Co., circa 1757-1758, exact dates not given (served 6 days); bill of credit issued or paid in his behalf to Joseph Chaplin for £0.6.0 on 5 Mar 1767. {Ref: MSA S960 or S752, p. 194; CSOS:105}

SOUTHERLAND, JAMES (Maryland), pvt., Capt. Alexander Beall's Company of MD Troops, Frederick Co., from 21 Mar 1758 to 8 Nov 1758. {Ref: MHS MS.375.1; CSOS:82} Payment to him was recorded in Col. Dagworthy's account book on 7 Mar 1763. {Ref: MHS MS.375}

SOUTHERLAND, JOHN (Maryland), pvt., Capt. Alexander Beall's Company of MD Troops, Frederick Co., from 9 Oct 1757 to 12 Jun 1758 when he reportedly died. {Ref: MHS MS.375.1; CSOS:82} However, payment to him was recorded in Col. Dagworthy's account book on 7 Mar 1763. {Ref: MHS MS.375}

SOUTHERLAND, JOHN (Maryland), pvt., Capt. Joseph Hanson Harrison's Company Muster Roll, Charles Co., circa 1757-1758, exact dates not given; bill of credit issued or paid in his behalf to Capt. Joseph Hanson Harrison for £2.12.0 on 29 Nov 1771. {Ref: MSA S960 or S752, p. 189}

SOWARD, DANIEL (Delaware), pvt., Kent Co. Militia, Capt. John Caton's Company, 25 Apr 1757 (date of muster roll). {Ref: ARDE I:13}

SOWARD, ISAAC (Delaware), pvt., Kent Co. Militia, Capt. John Caton's Company, 25 Apr 1757 (date of muster roll). {Ref: ARDE I:13}

SPANGLER, MATTHIAS (Maryland), pvt., Capt. Peter Butler's Company Muster Roll, Frederick Co., circa 1757-1758, exact dates not given (served 34 days); bill of credit or order issued in his behalf for £1.14.0 and paid to Casper Shaff on 2 Mar 1767. {Ref: MSA S960 or S752, p. 167; CSOS:97}

SPARKS, JOHN (Maryland), patriot and poss. soldier (rank not specified), Queen Anne's Co., militia pay account submitted in 1758, exact date not given. {Ref: MHM 9:4, p. 367}

SPARKS, WILLIAM (Maryland), pvt., Capt. William McClellan's Company of MD Volunteers, Frederick Co., circa 1763-1764; on muster roll dated 15 Nov 1764 at Camp at the Forks of Muskingham. {Ref: ARMD 32:99}

SPEAKMAN, ----, see "David Wolstenholme." q.v.

SPEAR, CHARLES (Delaware), b. c1734, Faughboyne, Ireland (age 24 in 1758); pvt., enlisted in Apr or May (exact date not given) 1758 "for the campaign in the lower counties" by Capt. John McClughan. {Ref: ARDE I:18; ARPA (2nd Series) 2:570}

SPECK, GEORGE (Maryland), pvt., Capt. Jonathan Hagar's Company Muster Roll, Frederick Co., circa 1757-1758, exact dates not given (served 6 days); bill of credit issued or paid to him for £0.6.0 in 1767, exact date not given. {Ref: MSA S960 or S752, p. 175; CSOS:106}

SPENCE, ADAM (Maryland), captain, Worcester Co., by 1760. {Ref: ARMD 56:288}

SPENCER, ---- (Maryland), pvt., Frederick Co., by 1758; was paid £1.2.6 on 7 Nov 1758 "for going to Carlyle express with a letter to Sir John St. Clair" during the Western Expedition against Fort Duquesne. {Ref: ARMD 55:776}

SPENCER, FRANCIS (Maryland), pvt., Capt. Joshua Beall's Company of MD Troops, Prince George's Co., from 9 Oct 1757 to 29 Jan 1758 when he was discharged. {Ref: MHS MS.375.1; CSOS:85} Payment to him was recorded in Col. Dagworthy's account book on 13 Jul 1762. {Ref: MHS MS.375}

SPENCER, THOMAS (Maryland), b. 12 Jun c1731, Kent Co., son of Henry and Sarah Spencer, of Shrewsbury Parish; patriot and poss. soldier (rank not specified), Kent Co., militia pay account submitted in 1758, exact date not given. {Ref: ESVR; MHM 9:4, p. 369}

SPENCER, WILLIAM (Delaware), pvt., Capt. Richard McWilliams' Company of Foot, New Castle Co., enlisted 28 Dec 1757. {Ref: ARDE I:15}

SPENCER, WILLIAM JR. (Delaware), pvt., Capt. Richard McWilliams' Company of Foot, New Castle Co., enlisted 28 Dec 1757. {Ref: ARDE I:14}

SPICER, DINAH, see "John Hall," q.v.

SPIKERNAL (SPEKERNEL), ROBERT (Maryland), pvt., Capt. Richard Pearis' Company of MD Troops, Frederick Co., from 9 Oct 1757 to 22 Oct 1757 when he reportedly died; however, payment to him was recorded in Col. Dagworthy's account book on 8 Mar 1763. {Ref: MHS MS.375; MHS MS.375.1}

SPRIGG, ANNE, see "Joseph Belt," q.v.

SPRIGG, EDWARD (Maryland), b. 12 Jun 1723, Prince George's Co., son of Edward Sprigg and Elizabeth Pile, of Queen Anne's P. E. Parish, m. Eleanor (N) by 1746, had a son Edward (poss. others), and died some time between 20 Sep 1758 and 19 Oct 1758 in the explosion of a powder magazine at Fort Cumberland; planter, gentleman, member of the MD Assembly (1754-1757), and captain by 1758. {Ref: BDML II:761-762; *MD Gazette*, 19 Oct 1758; PGCR 1:192}

SPRIGG, ELEANOR, see "William Murdock," q.v.

SPRIGG, MARGARET, see "William Bowie," q.v.

SPRIGG, PRISCILLA, see "Henry Wright Crabb," q.v.

SPRING, DOUGLAS (Maryland), pvt., Capt. Alexander Beall's Company of MD Troops, Frederick Co., circa 9 Oct 1757 to 30 Dec 1758. {Ref: MHS MS.375.1; CSOS:82} Payment to him was recorded in Col. Dagworthy's account book on 14 Jul 1762. {Ref: MHS MS.375}

SPRINGER, CHARLES (Delaware), pvt., Capt. Richard McWilliams' Company of Foot, New Castle Co., enlisted 28 Dec 1757. {Ref: ARDE I:15}

SPRINGER, CHARLES (Maryland), pvt., Capt. John Middaugh's Company Muster Roll, Frederick Co., circa 1757-1758, exact dates not given (served 30 days); bill of credit issued or paid in his behalf to Casper Shaff for £2 on 2 Mar 1767. {Ref: MSA S960 or S752, p. 171; CSOS:100}

SPRINGER, JACOB (Maryland), pvt., Capt. Stephen Rensburg's or Rensburger's Company Muster Roll, Frederick Co., circa 1757-1758, exact dates not given (served 42 days); bill of credit issued or paid in his behalf to Stephen Rensburger for £2.2.0 on 27 Mar 1767. {Ref: MSA S960 or S752, p. 183; CSOS:112}

SPROUL, THOMAS (Delaware), pvt., Capt. Richard McWilliams' Company of Foot, New Castle Co., enlisted 28 Dec 1757. {Ref: ARDE I:14}

SPURGEN (SPURGIN, SPURGENS), JAMES (Maryland), pvt., Capt. Peter Bainbridge's Company Muster Roll, Frederick Co., circa 1757-1758, exact dates not given (served 41 days); bill of credit issued or paid in his behalf to Joseph Chaplin on 24 Apr 1767 for £2.1.0. {Ref: MSA S960 or S752, p. 181; CSOS:111} Pvt., Capt. Moses Chapline's Company Muster Roll No. 1, Frederick Co., circa 1757-1758, exact dates not given (served 55 days); bill of credit issued or paid in his behalf to Joseph Chaplin for £2.15.0 on 24 Apr 1767. {Ref: MSA S960 or S752, p. 196; CSOS:113} Pvt., Capt. Joseph Chapline's Company Muster Roll No. 1, Frederick Co., circa 1757-1758, exact dates not given (served 30 days); bill of credit issued or paid in his behalf to Joseph Chaplin for £1.10.0 on 24 Apr 1767. {Ref: MSA S960 or S752, p. 192; CSOS:102}

SPURGEN (SPURGIN), JOHN (Maryland), pvt., Capt. Joseph Chapline's Company Muster Roll No. 1, Frederick Co., circa 1757-1758, exact dates not given (served 54 days); bill of credit issued or paid in his behalf to Joseph Chaplin for £2.14.0 on 5 Mar 1767. {Ref: MSA S960 or S752, p. 190; CSOS:102} Pvt., Capt. Joseph Chapline's Company Muster Rolls No. 2 and 3, Frederick Co., circa 1757-1758, exact dates not given (served 9 days); bill of credit issued or paid in his behalf to Joseph Chaplin for £0.14.0 on 5 Mar 1767. {Ref: MSA S960 or S752, p. 193; CSOS:104} Pvt., Capt. Joseph Chapline's Company Muster Roll No. 4, Frederick Co., circa 1757-1758, exact dates not given (served 5 days); bill of credit issued or paid in his behalf to Joseph Chaplin for £0.5.0 on 5 Mar 1767. {Ref: MSA S960 or S752, p. 194; CSOS:104} Cpl., Capt. Moses Chapline's Company Muster Roll No. 1, Frederick Co., circa 1757-1758, exact dates not given (served 55 days); bill of credit issued or paid in his behalf to Joseph Chaplin for £3.13.3 on 5 Mar 1767. {Ref: MSA S960 or S752, p. 196; CSOS:113}

SPURGEN (SPURGIN, SPURGENS), SAMUEL (Maryland), pvt., Capt. Peter Bainbridge's Company Muster Roll, Frederick Co., circa 1757-1758, exact dates not given (served 41 days); bill of credit issued or paid in his behalf to Joseph Chaplin on 24 Apr 1767 for £2.1.0. {Ref: MSA S960 or S752, p. 181; CSOS:110} Pvt., Capt. Joseph Chapline's Company Muster Roll No. 1, Frederick Co., circa 1757-1758, exact dates not given (served 19 days); bill of credit issued or paid in his behalf to Joseph Chaplin for £0.19.0 on 5 Mar 1767. {Ref: MSA S960 or S752, p. 191; CSOS:103} Cpl., Capt. Moses Chapline's Company Muster Roll No. 1, Frederick Co., circa 1757-1758, exact dates not given (served 55 days); bill of credit issued or paid in his behalf to Joseph Chaplin for £2.15.0 on 24 Apr 1767. {Ref: MSA S960 or S752, p. 196; CSOS:113}

SPURGEN (SPURGIN, SPURGENS), WILLIAM (Maryland), pvt., Capt. Joseph Chapline's Company Muster Roll No. 1, Frederick Co., circa 1757-1758, exact dates not given (served 19 days); bill of credit issued or paid in his behalf to Joseph Chaplin for £0.19.0 on 24 Apr 1767. {Ref: MSA S960 or S752, p. 192; CSOS:103} Pvt., Capt. Moses Chapline's Company Muster Roll No. 1, Frederick Co., circa 1757-1758, exact dates not given (served 55 days); bill of credit issued or paid in his behalf to Joseph Chaplin for £2.15.0 on 24 Apr 1767. {Ref: MSA S960 or S752, p. 196; CSOS:113} Pvt., Capt. Peter Bainbridge's Company Muster Roll, Frederick Co., circa 1757-1758, exact dates not given (served 41 days); bill of credit issued or paid in his behalf to Joseph Chaplin on 24 Apr 1767 for £2.1.0. {Ref: MSA S960 or S752, p. 181; CSOS:110}

SQUIRES, RICHARD (Delaware), b. c1734, Bristol, PA (age 25 in 1759); drummer, enlisted in Capt. John Wright's Company and mustered on 11 May 1759; also, drummer, Capt. John Woodgate's Company, Flying Camp, stationed at Port Amboy, September 1776, during Revolutionary War. {Ref: ARDE I:25; ARPA (2nd Series) 2:592; RPDE:252}

ST. CLAIR, SIR JOHN, see "Mordecai Madding" and "George Ross" and "---- Spencer," q.v.

ST. CLEAR, ROBERT (Maryland), pvt., Capt. Joshua Beall's Company Muster Roll, Prince George's Co., circa 1757-1758, exact dates not given; bill of credit issued or paid to him for £1.10.6 on 22 Oct 1771. {Ref: MSA S960 or S752, p. 185}

STAB, MARY PHILIPPINA, see "Balsher Michael," q.v.

STALCUP, ISRAEL (Delaware), pvt., Capt. Richard McWilliams' Company of Foot, New Castle Co., enlisted 28 Dec 1757. {Ref: ARDE I:14}

STALEY, JACOB (Maryland), pvt., Capt. Peter Bainbridge's Company Muster Roll, Frederick Co., circa 1757-1758, exact dates not given (served 28 days); militia pay account submitted in 1758, exact date not given; name mistakenly transcribed once as "Jacob Haley." {Ref: MHM 9:4, p. 367; CSOS:111} Bill of credit or order issued to Casper Shaff and paid to David Cumming on 18 Apr 1767 for £1.8.0. {Ref: MSA S960 or S752, p. 181}

STALEY, JACOB (Maryland), pvt., Capt. Stephen Rensburg's or Rensburger's Company Muster Roll, Frederick Co., circa 1757-1758, exact dates not given (served 42 days); bill of credit issued or paid in his behalf to Stephen Rensburger for Staley's exec. (unnamed) for £2.2.0 on 27 Mar 1767. {Ref: MSA S960 or S752, p. 183; CSOS:112}

STALEY, MELCOR (Maryland), pvt., Capt. Stephen Rensburg's or Rensburger's Company Muster Roll, Frederick Co., circa 1757-1758, exact dates not given (served 34 days); bill of credit issued or paid in his behalf to Casper Shaff for £1.14.0 on 2 Mar 1767. {Ref: MSA S960 or S752, p. 182; CSOS:112}

STALLINGS, ABSOLOM (Maryland), sgt., Calvert Co., Capt. Edward Gantt's Militia Co., Lyon's Creek Hundred circa 1756-1757 (exact dates not given). {Ref: HCC:120}

STANDIFORD, WILLIAM (Maryland), b. 13 Feb 1736/7, Baltimore Co., son of Skelton Standiford (d. 1752) and Esther Fuller. {Ref: BCF:600} Pvt., Capt. Tobias Stansbury's Company Muster Roll, Baltimore Co., circa 1757-1758, exact dates not given; bill of credit issued or paid to him for £1.18.0 on 1 Apr 1767. {Ref: MSA S960 or S752, p. 186}

STANSBURY, DANIEL JR., see "John Price," q.v.

STANSBURY, EDMUND or EDMOND (Maryland), b. 13 Jan 1724/5, son of Thomas Stansbury and Jane Dixon, m. Keziah Gostwick (1753-1809) circa 1775, had children Jane (b. 3 Oct 1776), Mary (b. 30 Oct 1778), and Keziah (b. 22 Feb 1780), and d. intestate on 22 Apr 1780 (his widow m. Joseph Cromwell). {Ref: BCF:605; MDG II:402, 409} Pvt., Capt. Tobias Stansbury's Company Muster Roll, Baltimore Co., circa 1757-1758, exact dates not given; bill of credit or order issued in his behalf and paid to to Thomas Cockey Deye for £3.12.0 on 13 Jun 1768. {Ref: MSA S960 or S752, p. 187}

STANSBURY, TOBIAS (Maryland), b. 23 Mar 1718/9, Baltimore Co., son of Luke and Jane Stansbury, m. Mary Hammond (dau. of Thomas Hammond and Catherine Emerson) on 27 Apr 1746, had children Henrietta Maria (b. 26 Feb 1747/8), Catherine (b. 28 Mar 1749), Rebecca (b. 22 Apr 1751), Jane (b. 9 Jun 1753), Mary and Sarah (twins, b. 12 Sep 1755), and Tobias Emerson (1757-1849), and d. testate circa 15 October 1757. {Ref: BCF:605; MDG II:409; *MD Gazette*, 20 Oct 1757} Captain in the militia by 1756; bill of credit issued or paid in his behalf to his admx. Mary Stansbury for £8.9.0 on 20 Feb 1767. {Ref: MSA S960 or S752, p. 186; ARMD 55:261} See "William Holmes," q.v.

STANT, JOSEPH (Delaware), pvt., Capt. French Battell's Company of Lower County Provincials, enlisted 19 May 1758. {Ref: ARDE I:17; ARPA (2nd Series) 2:555}

STANTON, ---- (Maryland), captain, Cecil County, quartered at Charlestown in March, 1757. {Ref: ARMD 31:230}

STANWIX, BRIG. GEN., see "Capt. ---- Cochran," q.v.

STAPLER, JOHN (Delaware), New Castle Co., patriot and court justice in 1761. {Ref: GRSD 1:15}

STARNORDER, FRANCIS (Maryland), pvt., Capt. John White's Company Muster Roll, Frederick Co., circa 1757-1758, exact dates not given (served 6 days); bill of credit issued or paid to him for £0.6.0 in 1767, exact date not given. {Ref: MSA S960 or S752, p. 165; CSOS:95}

STAVELY, REBECCA, see "James Greenwood," q.v.

STEEL, ANDREW (Delaware), pvt., Capt. Henry Vanbibber's Company of the Lower Counties on Delaware Troops at New Castle, enlisted on 20 May 1759. {Ref: ARDE I:26; ARPA (2nd Series) 2:594}

STEEL, ARTHUR (Delaware), b. c1736, Kent, DE (age 23 in 1759); pvt., enlisted in Capt. John Wright's Company and mustered on 11 May 1759. {Ref: ARDE I:25; ARPA (2nd Series) 2:592}

STEEL, HUGH (Delaware), b. c1731, Ireland (laborer, age 27 in 1758); pvt., recruited by Capt. Benjamin Noxon and enlisted on 1 May 1758; subscribed to the Oath of Fidelity and Allegiance in 1778. {Ref: ARDE I:19; ARPA (2nd Series) 2:566; RPDE:254}

STEEL, JAMES (Delaware), pvt., Capt. French Battell's Company of Lower County Provincials, enlisted 24 May 1758. {Ref: ARDE I:17; ARPA (2nd Series) 2:555}

STEEL, JOHN (Maryland), pvt., Capt. Joshua Beall's Company of MD Troops, Prince George's Co., circa 9 Oct 1757 to 30 Dec 1758. {Ref: MHS MS.375.1; CSOS:86} Payment to him was recorded in Col. Dagworthy's account book on 14 Jul 1762. {Ref: MHS MS.375}

STEPHENS (STEVENS), SOLOMON (Maryland), pvt., Capt. Richard Pearis' Company of MD Troops, Frederick Co., from 9 Oct 1757 to 31 May 1758. {Ref: MHS MS.375.1} Payment to him was recorded in Col. Dagworthy's account book on 15 Jul 1762. {Ref: MHS MS.375}

STEPHENSON, JOHN (Maryland), ironmaster and patriot, Baltimore Co., who was paid £54 on 7 Aug 1758 "for two ton of bar iron" to be used at Fort Frederick for the Western Expedition against Fort Duquesne. {Ref: ARMD 55:774}

STERLING, CHRISTIAN, see "Robert Adair," q.v.

STERLING, ROBERT (Maryland), lieut., 48th Regt. of His Majesty's Foot Soldiers, and recruiting officer in Kent County in 1757. {Ref: ARMD 31:205-208}

STERN, JOHN (Maryland), cpl., Capt. Stephen Rensburg's or Rensburger's Company Muster Roll, Frederick Co., circa 1757-1758, exact dates not given (served 42 days); bill of credit issued or paid in his behalf to Thomas Schley for Stern's exec. (unnamed) £2.16.0 on 23 Mar 1767. {Ref: MSA S960 or S752, p. 182; CSOS:112}

STERRUM, ISAAC (Maryland), patriot and poss. soldier (rank not specified), Frederick Co., militia pay account submitted in 1758, exact date not given. {Ref: MHM 9:4, p. 366}

STEUART, GEORGE (Maryland), b. 1700, Perthshire, Scotland, immigrated to Maryland circa 1721 as a free adult, m. Anne Digges circa 1743, and had children George Hume, James, David, Charles, William, Susannah, Ann, and Jane; served as riding surveyor of Pocomoke (1743-1746), commissioner, Paper Currency Office (1746-1766), judge, Land Office (1747-1775), justice, Provincial Court (1749-c1766), Deputy Secretary of Maryland (1755-1756); doctor and patriot, Annapolis, Anne Arundel Co., pay account submitted for quartering soldiers in 1757 or 1758, exact dates not given; served as lieutenant colonel of the Horse Militia at the time Horatio Sharpe was governor of MD; also served in the MD Assembly (1745, 1758-1763) and MD Council (1769-1774), Mayor of Annapolis (175-1763), and Commissary, Court of Vice Admiralty (commissioned in 1773), among other offices; closely allied with proprietary interests, he left MD at the outset of the Revolutionary War in 1775 and returned to Perthshire, Scotland where he died by 2 Aug 1784. {Ref: BMDL II:773-774; SLMH II:225-227; MHM 9:3, p. 262}

STEUART, JOHN (Delaware), pvt., Capt. Richard McWilliams' Company of Foot, New Castle Co., enlisted 28 Dec 1757. {Ref: ARDE I:14}

STEVENS, JAMES (Maryland), alias James Stevenson *[sic]*, pvt., Capt. John Middaugh's Company Muster Roll, Frederick Co., circa 1757-1758, exact dates not given (served 30 days); bill of credit or order issued to Casper Shaff and paid to David Cumming for £1.10.0 on 18 Apr 1767. {Ref: MSA S960 or S752, p. 172; CSOS:101}

STEVENS, MARY, see "Thomas MacKeele," q.v.

STEVENS, SAMUEL (Maryland), patriot, Frederick Co., who performed "sundry services at the fort" in 1763 and payment in the amount of £0.16.7½ was still owed to him on 25 Nov 1763 (when reported by the Accounts Committee to the MD Assembly). {Ref: ARMD 58:400}

STEVENSON, HENRY (Maryland), pvt., Capt. Tobias Stansbury's Company Muster Roll, Baltimore Co., circa 1757-1758, exact dates not given; bill of credit issued or paid in his behalf to Josias Bowen for £3.16.0 on 13 Mar 1767. {Ref: MSA S960 or S752, p. 186} *Identification problem:* There were two men with this name who could have served in the war: (1) Henry Stevenson, b. 27 Jun 1737, son of Edward and Stevenson and Susan Tracey(?); and, (2) Henry Stevenson, b. 2 Mar 1739, son of Henry Stevenson and Jemima Merryman. {Ref: BCF:609}

STEVENSON, JAMES (Maryland), lieut., 47th Regt. of Foot, was in Annapolis in February 1759 and reported the name of a deserter in the local newspaper. {Ref: *MD Gazette*, 15 Feb 1759}

STEVENSON, JOHN (Maryland), patriot and merchant, Baltimore County, along with William Walton, merchant, New York, who contracted with the Governor of MD and the Royal Officers of the Spanish Garrison at St. Augustine to furnish the garrison with three thousand barrels of flour for the year 1757, of which Stevenson was to furnish one thousand barrels, to be delivered on the sloop *Lena* commanded by Jonathan Lawrence. {Ref: ARMD 31:192}

STEWART, ALEXANDER (Maryland), sgt., Capt. Henry Casson's Company Muster Roll, Queen Anne's Co., circa 1757-1758, exact dates not given (served 3 days); bill of credit issued to him for £0.4.0 in 1767, exact date not given. {Ref: MSA S960 or S752, p. 178; CSOS:108}

STEWART, ANTHONY, see "James Dick," q.v.

STEWART, ASAEL (Maryland), b. c 1739, MD (age 17 in 1756); pvt., Capt. Christopher Gist's Company of VA Militia, 13 Jul 1756, enlisted at Baltimore. {Ref: MSR I:37}

STEWART, EDWARD (Maryland), pvt., Capt. Samuel Chapman's Company Muster Roll, Anne Arundel Co., circa 1757-1758, exact dates not given; bill of credit issued or paid in his behalf to Henry Hall for £2.10.7½ on 12 Mar 1767. {Ref: MSA S960 or S752, p. 189}

STEWART, ROBERT, see "George Clancy" and "John Huff" and "Thomas Rowe," q.v.

STEWART, WILLIAM (Delaware), pvt., Capt. French Battell's Company of Lower County Provincials, enlisted 23 May 1758. {Ref: ARDE I:17; ARPA (2nd Series) 2:555}

STIFLER (STRIFLER), VALENTINE (Maryland), pvt., Capt. Peter Butler's Company Muster Roll, Frederick Co., circa 1757-1758, exact dates not given (served 34 days); bill of credit or order issued in his behalf for £1.14.0 and paid to Casper Shaff on 2 Mar 1767. {Ref: MSA S960 or S752, p. 167; CSOS:98}

STIGAR (STIGER), ANDREW, see "William Egle" and "Jacob Bauman," q.v.

STILL, RICHARD (Delaware), pvt., Kent Co. Militia, Capt. John Caton's Company, 25 Apr 1757 (date of muster roll). {Ref: ARDE I:13}

STILLEY, PETER (Maryland), sgt., Capt. Stephen Rensburg's or Rensburger's Company Muster Roll, Frederick Co., circa 1757-1758, exact dates not given (served 42 days); bill of credit issued or paid in his behalf to Casper Shaff for Stilley's exec. (unnamed) for £2.5.3 on 2 Mar 1767. {Ref: MSA S960 or S752, p. 182; CSOS:111}

STILLS, EPHRAIM (Maryland), pvt., Capt. Jonathan Hagar's Company Muster Roll, Frederick Co., circa 1757-1758, exact dates not given (served 6 days). {Ref: CSOS:107}

STILLWELL, NATHANIEL (Maryland), pvt., Capt. John Dagworthy's Company of MD Troops, Frederick Co., from 9 Oct 1757 to 16 Apr 1759 when he reportedly deserted; however, payment to him was recorded in Col. Dagworthy's account book on 8 Mar 1763 for work on Fort Cumberland. {Ref: MHS MS.375; CSOS:78; MHS MS.375.1}

STILLWORTH, JOHN (Maryland), pvt., Capt. Richard Pearis' Company of MD Troops, Frederick Co., from 9 Oct 1757 to 4 Apr 1758 when he reportedly deserted; however, payment to him was recorded in Col. Dagworthy's account book on 8 Mar 1763. {Ref: MHS MS.375; MHS MS.375.1}

STIMPSON, COMFORT, see "John Hammond Dorsey," q.v.

STINCHCOMB, HELEN, see "Nathaniel Owings," q.v.

STINCHCOMB, NORMAN (Maryland), b. 26 Sep 1735, Baltimore Co., son of John Stinchcomb and Catherine McLean, St. Paul's P. E. Parish. {Ref: BCF:611} Pvt., Capt. Tobias Stansbury's Company Muster Roll, Baltimore Co., circa 1757-1758, exact dates not given; bill of credit issued or paid to him for £3.10.0 on 17 Oct 1770 (name listed as "Normand Stinchicomb"). {Ref: MSA S960 or S752, p. 187}

STOAKLEY, SOLOMON (Delaware), b. c1736, Sussex, DE (age 23 in 1759); pvt., enlisted in Capt. John Wright's Company and mustered on 11 May 1759. {Ref: ARDE I:25; ARPA (2nd Series) 2:592}

STOCKETT, ELEANOR, see "Joseph Williams," q.v.

STOCKETT, LEWIS (Maryland), m. 1st to Katharine (N) circa 1756 and 2nd to Ann Ijams on 10 Jun 1763(?); had children Milcah (b. 26 May 1757), Henry (b. 30 Jan 1759), Thomas (b. 19 Jul 1761), Mary (b. 26 Mar 1763), and John (b. 17 Nov 1767), all born in All Hallow's Parish. {Ref: AACR:55-57} Pvt., Capt. Samuel Chapman's Company Muster Roll, Anne Arundel Co., circa 1757-1758, exact dates not given; bill of credit issued or paid to him for £1.18.0 on 11 Mar 1767. {Ref: MSA S960 or S752, p. 188}

STOCKETT, THOMAS JR. (Maryland), b. 14 Jul 1733, Anne Arundel Co., son of Thomas and Elizabeth Stockett (bapt. 7 Sep 1733, All Hallow's Parish). {Ref: AACR:47} Pvt., Capt. Samuel Chapman's Company Muster Roll, Anne Arundel Co., circa 1757-1758, exact dates not given; bill of credit issued or paid to him for £1.18.0 on 27 Feb 1767. {Ref: MSA S960 or S752, p. 188}

STOCKSTILL, WILLIAM (Maryland), b. c1739, MD (age 17 in 1756); pvt., Capt. Christopher Gist's Company of VA Militia, 13 Jul 1756, enlisted at Baltimore. {Ref: MSR I:37}

STODDART (STODDERT), THOMAS (Maryland), lieut., Charles Co., paid £62.0.7 by the MD Assembly in 1756 "for the support of the ranging parties on the Western Frontier" from 22 Mar to 16 May 1756. {Ref: ARMD 52:674} 1st lieut., Capt. Francis Ware's Company of MD Troops, from 9 Oct 1757 to 31 May 1758 when he resigned. {Ref: MHS MS.375.1; CSOS:87}

STOKES (STOAKES), JEREMIAH (Maryland), pvt., Capt. William Luckett's Company Muster Roll, Frederick Co., circa 1757-1758, exact dates not given (served 23 days); bill of credit issued or paid in his behalf to William Luckett, Jr. for £1.3.0 on 6 Apr 1767. {Ref: MSA S960 or S752, pp. 169-170; CSOS:100}

STOKES, PETER (Maryland), pvt., Capt. Joshua Beall's Company of MD Troops, Prince George's Co., circa 9 Oct 1757 to 30 Dec 1758; pvt., Capt. John Dagworthy's Company of MD Troops, Frederick Co., from 31 Dec 1758 to 24 Jan 1759 when he reportedly died; however, payment to him was recorded in Col. Dagworthy's account book on 26 Feb 1763. {Ref: MHS MS.375; CSOS:78, 86; MHS MS.375.1}

STOKES (STOAKES), THOMAS (Maryland), pvt., Capt. William Luckett's Company Muster Roll, Frederick Co., circa 1757-1758, exact dates not given (served 30 days); pvt., Capt. Joshua Beall's Company of MD Troops, Prince George's Co., from 9 Oct 1757 to 29 Jan 1758 (served 113 days) when he was discharged. {Ref: MHS MS.375.1; CSOS:86, 100} Payment to him was recorded in

Col. Dagworthy's account book on 23 Jul 1762. {Ref: MHS MS.375} Bill of credit issued or paid in his behalf to William Luckett, Jr. for £1.3.0 on 6 Apr 1767. {Ref: MSA S960 or S752, pp. 169-170}

STONE, JOHN (Maryland), cpl., Calvert Co., Capt. Edward Gantt's Militia Co., Lyon's Creek Hundred circa 1756-1757 (exact dates not given). {Ref: HCC:120}

STONE, VERLINDA, see "Joseph Hanson Harrison" and "Richard Harrison," q.v.

STONE, WILLIAM (Maryland), b. c1732 (aged about 42 in 1774 deposition). {Ref: MGSB 34:2, p. 181} Ensign in Capt. Joseph Hanson Harrison's Company, Charles Co., circa 1757-1758, exact dates not given; bill of credit issued or paid in his behalf to John Hanson, Jr. for £6.15.0 on 21 Feb 1767. {Ref: MSA S960 or S752, p. 189}

STONER, JACOB (Maryland), pvt., Capt. Peter Butler's Company Muster Roll, Frederick Co., circa 1757-1758, exact dates not given (served 34 days); bill of credit or order issued in his behalf for £1.14.0 and paid to Casper Shaff on 2 Mar 1767; name mistakenly transcribed once as "Jacob Stone." {Ref: MSA S960 or S752, p. 167; CSOS:97}

STONER, JOHN (Maryland), m. Anneh (N), had children John, David, Jacob, Daniel, Samuel, Cathrine, Anna, and Susannah, and d. testate by 8 Jul 1774. {Ref: WMG 4:2, p. 65} Pvt., Capt. Stephen Rensburg's or Rensburger's Company Muster Roll, Frederick Co., circa 1757-1758, exact dates not given (served 42 days); militia pay account submitted in 1758, exact date not given; bill of credit or order issued to him for £2.2.0 on 11 Mar 1767; bill of credit or order issued to him for £1.14.0 in 1767, exact date not given. {Ref: MSA S960 or S752, pp. 177, 182; MHM 9:4, p. 367; CSOS:113}

STOODAY, MARTIN (Maryland), pvt., Capt. Thomas Norris' Company, Frederick Co., circa 1757-1758, exact dates not given (served 30 days); bill of credit issued or paid in his behalf to Charles Englas on 28 Mar 1767 for £1.10.0. {Ref: MSA S960 or S752, p. 176; CSOS:108}

STOOP, CHRISTOPHER (Delaware), pvt., Capt. Richard McWilliams' Company of Foot, New Castle Co., enlisted 28 Dec 1757. {Ref: ARDE I:14}

STOOP, JOHN JR. (Delaware), pvt., Capt. Richard McWilliams' Company of Foot, New Castle Co., enlisted 28 Dec 1757. {Ref: ARDE I:14}

STOUT, JACOB (Delaware), lieut., militia, Lower Part of Duck Creek Hundred, Kent Co. on Delaware, 1756. {Ref: ARDE I:12; ARPA (2nd Series) 2:527-529; HDE I:141}

STRAGHAN, JOHN (Delaware), b. c1734, Derry, Ireland (laborer, age 24 in 1758); pvt., enlisted 18 Apr 1758 "for the campaign in the lower counties" by Capt. John McClughan. {Ref: ARDE I:18; ARPA (2nd Series) 2:570}

STREBACK, GEORGE (Maryland), patriot and poss. soldier (rank not specified), Frederick Co., militia pay account submitted in 1758, exact date not given. {Ref: MHM 9:4, p. 366}

STREEP, WILLIAM (Delaware), m. Rachel (N) and d. intestate by 9 Jan 1771. {Ref: CDSS:202} Pvt., Kent Co. Militia, Capt. John Caton's Company, 25 Apr 1757 (date of muster roll). {Ref: ARDE I:13}

STREET, ---- (Maryland or Pennsylvania), drummer, Capt. Ward's Company, was captured by the Indians at Fort Granville in 1756 (exact date not given) and escaped to Conococheague in the summer of 1757. {Ref: *MD Gazette*, 14 Jul 1757}

STREET, DAVID (Delaware), b. c1736, Sussex, DE (age 23 in 1759); pvt., enlisted in Capt. John Wright's Company and mustered on 11 May 1759. {Ref: ARDE I:25; ARPA (2nd Series) 2:592}

STREET, EZEKIEL (Delaware), b. c1736, Black Swamp, DE (planter, age 22 in 1758); pvt., enlisted 10 Apr 1758 "for the campaign in the lower counties" by Capt. John McClughan. {Ref: ARDE I:18; ARPA (2nd Series) 2:570}

STRETTELL, ROBERT (Delaware), New Castle Co., patriot who served as a Justice of the Peace and a Justice of the Court of Oyer and Terminer in 1756. {Ref: GRSD 1:13}

STRINGER, LYDIA, see "Charles Ridgely," q.v.

STRINGER, RACHEL, see "Nehemiah Davis," q.v.

STRINGER, SAMUEL, see "Charles Ridgely," q.v.

STRINGER, WILLIAM (Delaware), pvt., Capt. Henry Vanbibber's Company of the Lower Counties on Delaware Troops at New Castle, enlisted on 1 May 1759. {Ref: ARDE I:26; ARPA (2nd Series) 2:594}

STRINGER, WILLIAM (Delaware), b. c1736, England (laborer, age 22 in 1758); pvt., recruited by Capt. Benjamin Noxon and enlisted on 29 May 1758. {Ref: ARDE I:19; ARPA (2nd Series) 2:566}

STRUM, JACOB, see "Jacob Sturm," q.b.

STUART, DAVID (Delaware), b. c1738, Sussex, DE (age 21 in 1759); pvt., enlisted in Capt. John Wright's Company and mustered on 11 May 1759. {Ref: ARDE I:25; ARPA (2nd Series) 2:592}

STUCKEY (STUKEY), PETER (Maryland), pvt., Capt. Jonathan Hagar's Company Muster Roll, Frederick Co., circa 1757-1758, exact dates not given (served 6 days); bill of credit issued or paid to him for £0.6.0 in 1767, exact date not given. {Ref: MSA S960 or S752, p. 175; CSOS:107}

STULL, JOHN (Maryland), b. 1733, prob. Germany, son of John and Martha Stull, and stepson of John White (q.v.), m. 1st to Sarah (N) by 1749, m. 2nd to Mercy Williams after 1770, had children Daniel, Johannes Isaac, Otho Holland Williams, Prudence Rose, Matilda, Holland, Martha, Susannah, Letitia, and Mercy, and d. 9 Apr 1791, Elizabeth Town (now Hagerstown), Washington Co.; farmer, miller, distiller, Frederick County justice (1773-1775), member of the Frederick Co. Committees of Correspondence and Observation (1774-1775), colonel by 1776 (resigned 1779), Washington Co. justice (1777-1791), and member of the MD Assembly (1779-1789). {Ref: BDML II:792-793} Company clerk (prob. cpl.), Capt. John White's Company Muster Roll, Frederick Co., circa 1757-1758, exact dates not given (served 6 days); bill of credit issued or paid to him for £0.6.0 in 1767, exact date not given. {Ref: MSA S960 or S752, p. 165; CSOS:95}

STULL, PETER (Maryland), pvt., Capt. John Middaugh's Company Muster Roll, Frederick Co., circa 1757-1758, exact dates not given (served 30 days); bill of credit or order issued to Casper Shaff and paid to David Cumming for £1.10.0 on 18 Apr 1767. {Ref: MSA S960 or S752, p. 172; CSOS:101}

STULLWELL, JOHN (Maryland), pvt., Capt. Joseph Chapline's Company, Frederick Co., circa 1757-1758, exact dates not given (served 57 days). {Ref: CSOS:102}

STULMAN, JOHN (Maryland), pvt., Capt. Thomas Norris' Company, Frederick Co., circa 1757-1758, exact dates not given (served 30 days); bill of credit issued or paid in his behalf to Jacob Yingland on 10 Apr 1767 for £1.10.0. {Ref: MSA S960 or S752, p. 176; CSOS:108}

STUMP, ADAM (Maryland), pvt., Capt. Jonathan Hagar's Company Muster Roll, Frederick Co., circa 1757-1758, exact dates not given (served 6 days); bill of credit issued or paid to him for £0.6.0 in 1767, exact date not given. {Ref: MSA S960 or S752, p. 175; CSOS:106}

STUMP (STUMPF), MICHAEL (Maryland), pvt., Capt. Peter Butler's Company Muster Roll, Frederick Co., circa 1757-1758, exact dates not given (served 34 days); bill of credit or order issued in his behalf for £1.14.0 and paid to Casper Shaff on 2 Mar 1767. {Ref: MSA S960 or S752, p. 167; CSOS:97}

STURANE, JACOB (Maryland), pvt., Capt. Joseph Chapline's Company Muster Roll No. 5, Frederick Co., circa 1757-1758, exact dates not given; bill of credit or order issued in his behalf to Joseph Chaplin for £0.8.0 on 5 Mar 1767. {Ref: MSA S960 or S752, p. 195}

STURGIS, STOKELY (Delaware), yeoman, m. (N), had children Stokley and Sarah, and d. testate by 14 May 1787. {Ref: CDSS:203} Ensign, Lower Part of Little Creek Hundred, Militia of Kent Co. on Delaware, 1756. {Ref: ARDE I:12; ARPA (2nd Series) 2:527-529; HDE I:141}

STURM (STURN, STRUM), JACOB (Maryland), pvt., Capt. Peter Bainbridge's Company Muster Roll, Frederick Co., circa 1757-1758, exact dates not given (served 35 days); bill of credit issued or paid in his behalf to Jacob Young on 4 Mar 1767 for £1.15.0. {Ref: MSA S960 or S752, p. 181; CSOS:111}

STURRON (STURROM), JOHN (Maryland), pvt., Capt. Thomas Norris' Company, Frederick Co., circa 1757-1758, exact dates not given (served 30 days); bill of credit issued or paid in his behalf to Charles Englas on 28 Mar 1767 for £1.10.0. {Ref: MSA S960 or S752, p. 176; CSOS:108}

STYGER, ANDREW (Maryland), patriot and poss. soldier (rank not specified), Baltimore Co., militia pay account submitted in 1758, exact date not given. {Ref: MHM 9:4, p. 366}

SUDITH, JAMES (Maryland), pvt., Capt. Joseph Hanson Harrison's Company Muster Roll, Charles Co., circa 1757-1758, exact dates not given; bill of credit issued or paid to him for £2.12.0 in 1767, exact date not given. {Ref: MSA S960 or S752, p. 189}

SUDLER, EMORY (Maryland), b. 1725, prob. Queen Anne's Co., son of Joseph Sudler and Ann Emory, m. Martha Smith, had daus. Mary and Anna and prob. son Emory, and d. intestate by 24 Feb 1797, Kent Co.; planter, merchant, member of the MD Assembly (1757-1758, served on the Arms and Ammunition

Committee; 1773-1774), Committee of Correspondence in 1774, and was a commissioned officer in the militia (resigned 1776). {Ref: BDML II:793-794}

SUITOR, CHARLES, see "Charles Sutter (Sueter)," q.v.

SULLIVAN, PETER (Maryland), indentured servant and soldier who served in the French and Indian War some time between 1756 and 1763 (exact dates not known); his master, Rev. Andrew Lendrum, requested compensation from the Baltimore County Court due to the loss of use of Sullivan while in the service. {Ref: MHM 94:4, p. 426, citing Baltimore Co. Court Minutes}

SUMMERS (SUMMER), JOHN (Maryland), m. Ann (N), had children John, Jacob, and Mary, and d. testate by 29 Apr 1780. {Ref: WMG 5:4, p. 167} Pvt., Capt. Peter Butler's Company Muster Roll, Frederick Co., circa 1757-1758, exact dates not given (served 34 days); bill of credit or order issued in his behalf for £1.14.0 to Casper Shaff and paid to David Cumming on 18 Apr 1767. {Ref: MSA S960 or S752, p. 168; CSOS:98}

SUMMERSFIELD, JOHN (Maryland), pvt., Capt. John Dagworthy's Company of MD Troops, Frederick Co., from 9 Oct 1757 to 16 Apr 1759 when he reportedly deserted; however, payment to him was recorded in Col. Dagworthy's account book on 8 Mar 1763. {Ref: MHS MS.375; CSOS:78; MHS MS.375.1}

SUMNER, JOHN (Maryland), pvt., Capt. Joshua Beall's Company of MD Troops, Prince George's Co., from 9 Oct 1757 to 8 Jun 1758. {Ref: MHS MS.375.1; CSOS:86} Payment to him was recorded in Col. Dagworthy's account book on 23 Jul 1762. {Ref: MHS MS.375}

SUNFRANK, JACOB (Maryland), pvt., Capt. Peter Butler's Company Muster Roll, Frederick Co., circa 1757-1758, exact dates not given (served 34 days); bill of credit or order issued in his behalf for £1.14.0 and paid to Casper Shaff on 2 Mar 1767. {Ref: MSA S960 or S752, p. 167; CSOS:97}

SURRATT (SURATT), JOSEPH (Maryland), pvt., Capt. Richard Pearis' Company of MD Troops, Frederick Co., circa 9 Oct 1757 to 31 May 1758); pvt., Capt. Joshua Beall's Company of MD Troops, Prince George's Co., from 1 Jun 1758 to 30 Dec 1758; pvt., Capt. John Dagworthy's Company of MD Troops, Frederick Co., from 31 Dec 1758 to 28 Feb 1758 when he reportedly deserted; however, payment to him was recorded in Col. Dagworthy's account book on 12 Jul 1762. {Ref: MHS MS.375; CSOS:78, 86; MHS MS.375.1}

SUTTER (SUETER, SUITOR), CHARLES (Maryland), pvt., Capt. Richard Pearis' Company of MD Troops, Frederick Co., circa 9 Oct 1757 and to May 1758; pvt., Capt. Alexander Beall's Company of MD Troops, Frederick Co., from 1 Jun 1758 to 30 Dec 1758. {Ref: MHS MS.375.1; CSOS:82, 91} Pvt., Capt. Joshua Beall's Company Muster Roll, Prince George's Co., circa 1757-1758, exact dates not given; bill of credit issued or paid to him for £1.6.9 in 1767, exact date not given. {Ref: MSA S960 or S752, p. 185} Payment to him was also recorded in Col. Dagworthy's account book on 15 Jul 1762. {Ref: MHS MS.375; CSOS:116}

SUTTON, JOHN (Delaware), b. c1730, Wilts, England (weaver, age 28 in 1758); pvt., enlisted 30 Apr 1758 "for the campaign in the lower counties" by Capt. John McClughan. {Ref: ARDE I:18; ARPA (2nd Series) 2:570}

SWAFORD, WIDOW, see "John Hawkins," q.v.

SWAGLER, GEORGE, see "George Sweagler," q.v.

SWAILES, WILLIAM (Maryland or Pennsylvania), ensign in Capt. Hamilton's Company, wounded in "a recent battle with the Indians" in 1756 (exact date not given) in Cumberland Co., PA, after the burning of McCord's Fort. {Ref: *MD Gazette*, 29 Apr 1756}

SWAN, ROBERT (Maryland), b. c1720, d. 4 May 1764, Annapolis, Anne Arundel Co.; merchant and patriot whose pay account was submitted for quartering soldiers in 1757 or 1758 (exact dates not given). {Ref: MHM 9:3, p. 260} "Mr. Robert Swan, merchant, died here on Fri. last in his 44th year; one of the Common Council of this city." {Ref: *MD Gazette*, 10 May 1764}

SWANEY, EDWARD (Maryland), farmer; pvt., Capt. Peregrine Brown's 7th Co. of Foot Militia, Kent Co., on 19 Feb 1758, by which time he had enlisted, but reportedly refused to appear and serve in arms against the enemy. {Ref: ARMD 31:283, 288} It should be noted that an Edward Swany, farmer, m. Lydia (N), had children William, Edward, Anne, Lydia, and Margaret, and d. testate in Frederick Co. by 31 Jul 1779. {Ref: WMG 5:3, p. 136}

SWANN (SWAN), JOHN (Maryland), pvt., Capt. Joseph Chapline's Company Muster Roll No. 4, Frederick Co., circa 1757-1758, exact dates not given (served 5 days); bill of credit issued or paid in his behalf to Joseph Chaplin for £0.5.0 on 5 Mar 1767. {Ref: MSA S960 or S752, p. 194; CSOS:105}

SWEAGLER (SWAGLER), GEORGE (Maryland), m. Elizabeth (N), had sons Jacob and Joshua, and d. testate by 15 Nov 1770. {Ref: WMG 3:3, p. 111} Pvt., Capt. Jonathan Hagar's Company Muster Roll, Frederick Co., circa 1757-1758, exact dates not given (served 6 days); bill of credit issued or paid to him for £0.6.0 in 1767, exact date not given. {Ref: MSA S960 or S752, p. 175; CSOS:107}

SWEAGLER (SWAGLER), JACOB (Maryland), pvt., Capt. Jonathan Hagar's Company Muster Roll, Frederick Co., circa 1757-1758, exact dates not given (served 6 days); bill of credit issued or paid to him for £0.6.0 in 1767, exact date not given. {Ref: MSA S960 or S752, p. 175; CSOS:106}

SWEARINGEN, CHARLES (Maryland), pvt., Capt. Joseph Chapline's Company Muster Roll No. 4, Frederick Co., circa 1757-1758, exact dates not given (served 6 days); bill of credit issued or paid in his behalf to Joseph Chaplin for £0.6.0 on 5 Mar 1767. {Ref: MSA S960 or S752, p. 194; CSOS:105}

SWEARINGEN, ELIZABETH, see "Jonathan Simmons, Jr.," q.v.

SWEARINGEN, JOHN (Maryland), ensign in Capt. Moses Chapline's Company Muster Roll No. 2, Frederick Co., circa 1757-1758, exact dates not given (served 14 days); bill of credit issued or paid in his behalf to Joseph Chaplin for £1.8.0 on 5 Mar 1767. {Ref: MSA S960 or S752, p. 197; CSOS:114}

SWEARINGEN, JOHN (Maryland), pvt., Capt. Joseph Chapline's Company Muster Rolls No. 2 and 3, Frederick Co., circa 1757-1758, exact dates not given (served 7 days); bill of credit issued or paid in his behalf to Joseph Chaplin for £0.7.0 on 5 Mar 1767. {Ref: MSA S960 or S752, p. 193; CSOS:104}

SWEARINGEN, JOHN (Maryland), ensign in Capt. Moses Chapline's Company Muster Roll No. 3, Frederick Co., circa 1757-1758, exact dates not given (served 6 days); bill of credit issued or paid in his behalf to Joseph Chaplin for £0.12.0 on 5 Mar 1767. {Ref: MSA S960 or S752, p. 198; CSOS:115}

SWEARINGEN, THOMAS JR. (Maryland), pvt., Capt. Joseph Chapline's Company Muster Roll No. 4, Frederick Co., circa 1757-1758, exact dates not given (served 5 days); bill of credit issued or paid in his behalf to Joseph Chaplin for £0.5.0 on 5 Mar 1767. {Ref: MSA S960 or S752, p. 194; CSOS:105}

SWEARINGEN, VAN SR. (Maryland), patriot and poss. soldier (rank not specified), Frederick Co., militia pay account submitted in 1758, exact date not given. {Ref: MHM 9:4, p. 369} Van, Sr. was still living on 5 Mar 1784 when his son Van, Jr. wrote his will and stated "if my father Van Swearingen should be destitute of a living, he should be brought to my house and taken care of." {Ref: WMG 6:3, p. 121}

SWEARINGEN, VAN JR. (Maryland), m. Margaret (N), had children Joseph, Thomas Van, John Van, Isaac Stull, Eleanor, Margaret, Mary, Drusilla, and Elizabeth, and d. testate by 6 Apr 1784. {Ref: WMG 6:3, p. 121} Patriot and poss. soldier (rank not specified), Frederick Co., militia pay account submitted in 1758, exact date not given. {Ref: MHM 9:4, p. 369}

SWEATNAM, ESTHER, see "William Hopper," q.v.

SWEET, BENJAMIN (Maryland), patriot, Frederick Co., was paid on 10 Jul 1758 at Fort Frederick "for sawing plank to make coffins for the N Carolina and Pensa. soldiers that died at Fort Frederick." {Ref: ARMD 55:773}

SWEM (SWIM), WILLIAM (Maryland), pvt., Capt. Moses Chapline's Company Muster Roll No. 1, Frederick Co., circa 1757-1758, exact dates not given (served 55 days); bill of credit issued or paid in his behalf to Joseph Chaplin for £2.15.0 on 24 Apr 1767. {Ref: MSA S960 or S752, p. 196; CSOS:113} Pvt., Capt. Moses Chapline's Company Muster Roll No. 3, Frederick Co., circa 1757-1758, exact dates not given (served 6 days); bill of credit issued or paid in his behalf to Joseph Chaplin for £0.6.0 on 25 Apr 1767; name mistakenly transcribed once as "George Swinn." {Ref: MSA S960 or S752, pp. 198-199; CSOS:115}

SWOBE, LAWRENCE (Maryland), pvt., Capt. Jonathan Hagar's Company Muster Roll, Frederick Co., circa 1757-1758, exact dates not given (served 6 days); bill of credit issued or paid to him for £0.6.0 in 1767, exact date not given. {Ref: MSA S960 or S752, p. 175; CSOS:106}

SYKES, JAMES (Delaware), m. Agnes (N), had children James, Stephen, George, Nathaniel, Mary, Ann, Lucy Matilda, and Harriott, and d. testate by 16 Apr 1792. {Ref: CDSS:205} Lieut., Dover Hundred, Militia of Kent Co. on Delaware, 1756. {Ref: ARDE I:12; ARPA (2nd Series) 2:527-529; HDE I:141}

SYNG, DEBORAH, see "William Reynolds," q.v.

TALBOT (TALBOTT), HENRY (Maryland), pvt., Capt. Peregrine Brown's Company Muster Roll, Kent Co., circa 1757-1758, exact dates not given (served 15 days); bill of credit issued or paid in his behalf to Robert Buchanan on 20 Feb 1767 for £0.15.0. {Ref: MSA S960 or S752, p. 179; CSOS:110}

TALBOT (TALBUTT), HENRY (Maryland), pvt., Capt. William Luckett's Company Muster Roll, Frederick Co., circa 1757-1758, exact dates not given (served 30 days); bill of credit issued or paid in his behalf to William Luckett, Jr. for £1.10.0 on 6 Apr 1767. {Ref: MSA S960 or S752, pp. 169-170; CSOS:99}

TALBOT (TALBUTT), RICHARD (Maryland), pvt., Capt. William Luckett's Company Muster Roll, Frederick Co., circa 1757-1758, exact dates not given (served 30 days); bill of credit issued or paid in his behalf to William Luckett, Jr. for £1.4.0 on 6 Apr 1767. {Ref: MSA S960 or S752, pp. 169-170; CSOS:100}

TALBOT, WILLIAM (Maryland), b. 10 Feb 1734/5, Baltimore Co., son of William Talbot and Mary Roberts. {Ref: BCF:621} Pvt., Capt. Christopher Gist's Company of VA Militia, 13 Jul 1756, enlisted at Baltimore (b. MD, age 22). {Ref: MSR I:37}

TALBOTT, JOHN, see "William Allnutt," q.v.

TALBOTT, SARAH, see "William Allnutt," q.v.

TALBOURT, JOHN (Delaware), pvt., Kent Co. Militia, Capt. John Caton's Company, 25 Apr 1757 (date of muster roll). {Ref: ARDE I:14}

TALKINGTON (TALKINTON), STEPHEN (Delaware), b. c1738, PA (cooper, age 20 in 1758); pvt., recruited by Capt. Benjamin Noxon and enlisted on 29 Apr 1758. {Ref: ARDE I:19; ARPA (2nd Series) 2:566} Pvt., Capt. Henry Vanbibber's Company of the Lower Counties on Delaware Troops at New Castle, enlisted on 19 May 1759; on roll dated 4 Jun 1759. {Ref: ARDE I:26; ARPA (2nd Series) 2:594}

TAMER, ANDREW (Maryland), alias Andrew Damer *[sic]*, pvt., Capt. Thomas Norris' Company, Frederick Co., circa 1757-1758, exact dates not given (served 30 days); bill of credit issued or paid in his behalf to Michael McGuire on 11 Apr 1767 for £1.10.0; name mistakenly listed once as "Andrew Tanner." {Ref: MSA S960 or S752, p. 176; CSOS:108}

TAMERL (TAMAB?), LODOWICK (Maryland), pvt., Capt. John White's Company Muster Roll, Frederick Co., circa 1757-1758, exact dates not given (served 6 days); bill of credit issued or paid to him for £0.6.0 in 1767, exact date not given. {Ref: MSA S960 or S752, p. 165; CSOS:96}

TANDY, RICHARD (Maryland), pvt., Capt. Francis Ware's Company of MD Troops, Charles Co., circa 9 Oct 1757 to 30 Dec 1758. {Ref: MHS MS.375.1; CSOS:89} Payment to him was recorded in Col. Dagworthy's account book on 7 Mar 1763. {Ref: MHS MS.375}

TANNER, ANDREW, see "Andrew Tamer," q.v.

TANNIHIL, ANDREW (Maryland), alias Andrew Fanchil or Franchill *[sic]*, pvt., Capt. Elias Delashmutt's Company Muster Roll, Frederick Co., 13 Aug 1757, exact dates not given (served 52 days); bill of credit issued or paid in his behalf to Elias Delashmut, Jr. on 16 Mar 1767 for £2.12.0. {Ref: MSA S960 or S752, p. 163; CSOS:98}

TANNIHILL, CARLTON (Maryland), pvt., Capt. Elias Delashmutt's Company Muster Roll, Frederick Co., circa 1757-1758, exact dates not given (served 30 days); bill of credit issued or paid in his behalf to Robert Couden on 5 Jun 1767 for £1.10.0. {Ref: MSA S960 or S752, p. 163; CSOS:94}

TANNIHILL, PHILIP (Maryland), pvt., Capt. Joshua Beall's Company Muster Roll, Prince George's Co., circa 1757-1758, exact dates not given; bill of credit issued and ordered his assignment to John Tolson for £1.10.6 on 13 Apr 1767; name listed once as "Philip Tanneyhill, Jr." {Ref: MSA S960 or S752, p. 184}

TANSEY (TANSER), ABRAHAM (Maryland), alias Abraham Falsey *[sic]*, pvt., Capt. Elias Delashmutt's Company Muster Roll, Frederick Co., circa 1757-1758, exact dates not given (served 30 days); bill of credit issued or paid in his behalf to Elias Delashmut, Jr. on 16 Mar 1767 for £4.2.0. {Ref: MSA S960 or S752, pp. 162-163; CSOS:94} Pvt., Capt. Peter Bainbridge's Company Muster Roll, Frederick Co., circa 1757-1758, exact dates not given (served 30 days); bill of credit issued or paid in his behalf to Elias Delashmut, Jr. on 16 Mar 1767 for £1.10.0. {Ref: MSA S960 or S752, p. 181; CSOS:111}

TANSEY (TANSER), EDWARD (Maryland), alias Edward Falsey *[sic]*, pvt., Capt. Elias Delashmutt's Company Muster Roll, Frederick Co., circa 1757-1758, exact dates not given; bill of credit issued or paid in his behalf to Casper Shaff on 2 Mar 1767 for £2.12.0. {Ref: MSA S960 or S752, p. 162} Pvt., Capt. Peter Bainbridge's Company Muster Roll, Frederick Co., circa 1757-1758, exact dates not given (served 30 days); bill of credit issued or paid in his behalf to Casper Shaff on 2 Mar 1767 for £0.9.0. {Ref: MSA S960 or S752, p. 180; CSOS:111}

TANSEY (TONSEY), SAMUEL (Maryland), farmer; pvt., Capt. Peregrine Brown's 7th Co. of Foot Militia, Kent Co., 19 Feb 1758, by which time he had enlisted, but reportedly refused to appear and serve in arms against the enemy. {Ref: ARMD 31:283, 288}

TARMAN, ANN, see "Benjamin Nearn," q.v.

TARR, HENRY (Maryland), pvt., Capt. Tobias Stansbury's Company Muster Roll, Baltimore Co., circa 1757-1758, exact dates not given; bill of credit or order issued and assigned to William Lux paid to Robert Adair for £1.18.0 on 1 Apr 1767. {Ref: MSA S960 or S752, pp. 186, 188}

TARVEN (TARVIN), RICHARD (Maryland), pvt., Capt. Alexander Beall's Company of MD Troops, Frederick Co., from 9 Oct 1757 to 18 Oct 1758 when he reportedly deserted; however, payment to him was recorded in Col. Dagworthy's account book on 16 Jul 1762. {Ref: MHS MS.375; CSOS:82; MHS MS.375.1}

TASKER, BENJAMIN (Maryland), b. c1690, prob. Calvert Co., son of Thomas Tasker and Rebecca Isaacs Brooke, m. Anne Bladen on 31 Jul 1711, had children William, Benjamin, Bladen (three sons by this name all died in infancy), Anne, Rebecca, Elizabeth, and Frances, and d. 19 Jun 1768, Annapolis; patriot, gentleman, ironmaster, clerk of the Prerogative Office (1714-1718), Anne Arundel Co. justice (1714-1717), county sheriff (1717-1720), surveyor and searcher (1718-1734), member of the MD Assembly (1715-1761), naval officer at Annapolis (by 1719 and 1733-1742), mayor of Annapolis (1720-1721, 1725-1726, 1747-1748, 1757-1758), rent roll keeper of the Western Shore (1733-1752), joint commissary general (1733-1734, 1754-1756), sole commissary general (1756-1758), agent and receiver general (1734, 1742-1753), justice of the Provincial Court (1726-1731), member of the MD Council (1722-1768, President 1737, 1741, 1742-1768, and Chief Executive of MD in the absence of the Governor). {Ref: BDML II:799-801; *MD Gazette*, 23 Jun 1768} Pay account submitted for quartering soldiers in 1757 or 1758, exact dates not given.

{Ref: M HM 9:3, p. 262} See "George Dale" and "Thomas Ivory" and "Francis Watkinson," q.v.

TASKER, BENJAMIN JR. (Maryland), b. 14 Feb 1720/1, Annapolis, son of Benjamin Tasker and Anne Bladen, of St. Anne's Parish, and d. 17 Oct 1760 "of a slow fever;" gentleman, planter, ironmaster, merchant, slave trader, member of the MD Assembly and MD Council (1742-1760), naval officer at Annapolis (1742-1755), riding surveyor (1743-1760), surveyor general of the Eastern Shore (1747-1755), deputy secretary of MD (1755-1760), mayor of Annapolis (1754-1755), colonel in the militia by 1744 and one of the two principal field officers of Anne Arundel County in 1756; never married. {Ref: BDML II:801-802; ARMD 56:xxxvii; *MD Gazette*, 23 Oct 1760; AACR:87}

TASKER, REBECCA, see "Daniel Dulany," q.v.

TATE, JAMES (Maryland), pvt., Capt. Joshua Beall's Company of MD Troops, Prince George's Co., circa 9 Oct 1757 to 30 Dec 1758. {Ref: MHS MS.375.1; CSOS:86} Payment to him was recorded in Col. Dagworthy's account book on 7 Mar 1763 for work on Fort Cumberland. {Ref: MHS MS.375}

TATLOW, JOSEPH (Delaware), pvt., Capt. Richard McWilliams' Company of Foot, New Castle Co., enlisted 28 Dec 1757. {Ref: ARDE I:14}

TAXER, MATTHIAS (Maryland), pvt., Capt. John Middaugh's Company Muster Roll, Frederick Co., circa 1757-1758, exact dates not given (served 30 days); bill of credit issued or paid in his behalf to Thomas Beatty, Jr. for £1.10.0 on 23 Feb 1767. {Ref: MSA S960 or S752, p. 171; CSOS:101}

TAYLOR, CHRISTIAN (Maryland), pvt., Capt. Joseph Chapline's Company Muster Roll No. 1, Frederick Co., circa 1757-1758, exact dates not given (served 50 days); bill of credit issued or paid in his behalf to Joseph Chaplin for £2.10.0 on 5 Mar 1767. {Ref: MSA S960 or S752, p. 191; CSOS:102}

TAYLOR, EDWARD (Maryland), pvt., Capt. Joshua Beall's Company Muster Roll, Prince George's Co., circa 1757-1758, exact dates not given; bill of credit issued or paid to him for £2.1.0 in 1767, exact date not given. {Ref: MSA S960 or S752, p. 185}

TAYLOR, ELIZABETH, see "Bartholomew Ennalls," q.v.

TAYLOR, GARRETT (Maryland), pvt., Capt. John Middaugh's Company Muster Roll, Frederick Co., circa 1757-1758, exact dates not given (served 30 days); bill of credit issued or paid in his behalf to William Beatty for £1.10.0 on 14 Sep 1770. {Ref: MSA S960 or S752, p. 172; CSOS:101} See "William Taylor," q.v.

TAYLOR (TAYLER), JAMES (Maryland), pvt., Capt. John Dagworthy's Company of MD Troops, Frederick Co., from 9 Oct 1757 to 22 Feb 1759 when he reportedly deserted; however, payment to him was recorded in Col. Dagworthy's account book on 8 Mar 1763 for work on Fort Cumberland. {Ref: MHS MS.375; CSOS:78; MHS MS.375.1}

TAYLOR, JOHN (Delaware), pvt., Capt. French Battell's Company of Lower County Provincials, enlisted 10 May 1758. {Ref: ARDE I:17; ARPA (2nd Series) 2:555}

TAYLOR, JOHN (Maryland), pvt., Capt. Elias Delashmutt's Company Muster Roll, Frederick Co., circa 1757-1758, exact dates not given (serve 30 days); bill of credit issued or paid in his behalf to Casper Shaff on 2 Mar 1767 for £1.10.0. {Ref: MSA S960 or S752, p. 162; CSOS:94}

TAYLOR, WILLIAM, see "Bartholomew Ennalls," q.v.

TAYLOR, WILLIAM (Maryland), son of Garrett Taylor; pvt., Capt. John Middaugh's Company Muster Roll, Frederick Co., circa 1757-1758, exact dates not given (served 30 days); bill of credit issued or paid in his behalf to William Beatty for £1.10.0 on 14 Sep 1770. {Ref: MSA S960 or S752, p. 172; CSOS:101}

TAYLOR, WILLIAM (Maryland), pvt., Capt. John Middaugh's Company Muster Roll, Frederick Co., circa 1757-1758, exact dates not given (served 30 days); bill of credit issued or paid in his behalf to Thomas Beatty, Jr. for £1.10.0 on 3 Apr 1767. {Ref: MSA S960 or S752, p. 172: CSOS:101}

TEAGARDEN, WILLIAM (Maryland), pvt., Capt. Jonathan Hagar's Company Muster Roll, Frederick Co., circa 1757-1758, exact dates not given (served 6 days). {Ref: CSOS:107} Militia pay account submitted in 1758, exact date not given. {Ref: MHM 9:4, p. 370} Bill of credit issued or paid in his behalf to Joseph Chaplin for £0.6.0 on 5 Mar 1767; name misspelled once as "Willm. Teegarder" and once as "William Tegarden." {Ref: MSA S960 or S752, pp. 173, 175} Paid £3 at Fort Frederick on 26 Jun 1758 for carrying arms for the Western Expedition against Fort Duquesne. {Ref: ARMD 55:773}

TEAL, EDWARD (Maryland), pvt., Capt. Tobias Stansbury's Company Muster Roll, Baltimore Co., circa 1757-1758, exact dates not given; bill of credit issued or paid to him for £0.5.0 in 1767, exact date not given. {Ref: MSA S960 or S752, p. 188} *Identification problem:* There were two men with this name who could have served in the war: (1) Edward Teal, b. before 1722, son of John and Jane Teal; and, (2) Edward Teal, b. 17 Apr 1726, son of William and Christian Teal. {Ref: BCF:630-631}

TEAL, PHILIP (Maryland), pvt., Capt. John Middaugh's Company Muster Roll, Frederick Co., circa 1757-1758, exact dates not given (served 30 days); bill of credit issued or paid to him for £1.10.0 in 1767, exact date not given. {Ref: MSA S960 or S752, p. 172: CSOS:101}

TEAL, SAMUEL (Maryland), pvt., Capt. John Middaugh's Company Muster Roll, Frederick Co., circa 1757-1758, exact dates not given (erved 30 days); bill of credit issued or paid to him for £0.17.0 in 1767, exact date not given. {Ref: MSA S960 or S752, p. 173; CSOS:102}

TEAL, WILLIAM, see "Edward Teal," q.v.

TEAMAN, THOMAS (Maryland), sgt., Capt. John Dagworthy's Company, Frederick Co., by 10 Feb 1757 at which time he was stationed at Fort Frederick. {Ref: FCLR:60}

TEATER, GEORGE (Maryland), pvt., Capt. Alexander Beall's Company of MD Troops, Frederick Co., circa 9 Oct 1757 to 30 Dec 1758; pvt., Capt. John Dagworthy's Company of MD Troops, Frederick Co., from 31 Dec 1758 to 26 Apr 1759; name mistakenly transcribed once as "Geo: Tealer." {Ref: MHS MS.375.1; CSOS:78, 82} Payment to him was recorded in Col. Dagworthy's account book on 11 Jul 1762. {Ref: MHS MS.375}

TEATER, SAMUEL (Maryland), pvt., Capt. Joshua Beall's Company of MD Troops, Prince George's Co., circa 9 Oct 1757 to 30 Dec 1758; pvt., Capt. John Dagworthy's Company of MD Troops, Frederick Co., from 31 Dec 1758 to 26 Apr 1759. {Ref: MHS MS.375.1; CSOS:78, 86} Payment to him was recorded in Col. Dagworthy's account book on 8 Mar 1763 for work on Fort Cumberland. {Ref: MHS MS.375}

TEGAN, PETER (Maryland), pvt., Capt. Peter Butler's Company Muster Roll, Frederick Co., circa 1757-1758, exact dates not given (served 34 days); bill of credit or order issued in his behalf for £1.14.0 to Casper Shaff and paid to David Cumming on 18 Apr 1767. {Ref: MSA S960 or S752, p. 168; CSOS:98}

TEMPLE, SUSANNA, see "James Munday," q.v.

TENALLY (TENNELLY), THOMAS (Maryland), pvt., Capt. Elias Delashmutt's Company Muster Roll, Frederick Co., 1757, exact dates not given (served 30 days); cpl. by 13 Aug 1757 (served 52 days); bill of credit issued or paid in his behalf to Casper Shaff for Tenally's admin. (unnamed) on 18 Apr 1767 for £4.19.3. {Ref: MSA S960 or S752, p. 163; CSOS:94, 98}

TERRELL, JOHN (Maryland), pvt., Capt. Alexander Beall's Company of MD Troops, Frederick Co., from 9 Oct 1757 to 14 Sep 1758 when he was reported as killed; however, payment to him was recorded in Col. Dagworthy's account book on 11 Jul 1763. {Ref: MHS MS.375; CSOS:82; MHS MS.375.1} An account submitted to the MD Assembly on 25 Nov 1763 indicated he was due £4.12.3 as "granted by the Act for Granting a Sum of Money as a Present to the Forces, late in the Pay and Service of this Province, and taken into his Majesty's Service by Brigadier General Forbes." {Ref: ARMD 58:401}

TERRITEHE, Indian Chief (Maryland), Frederick Co., agreed to join with the English against the French in 1758. {Ref: ARMD 31:266}

TEST, JOSEPH (Delaware), pvt., Capt. French Battell's Company of Lower County Provincials, enlisted 10 May 1758. {Ref: ARDE I:17; ARPA (2nd Series) 2:555}

TETER, ABRAHAM (Maryland), pvt., Capt. Jonathan Hagar's Company Muster Roll, Frederick Co., circa 1757-1758, exact dates not given (served 6 days); bill of credit issued or paid to him for £0.6.0 in 1767, exact date not given. {Ref: MSA S960 or S752, p. 175; CSOS:106}

TETER, JOHN (Maryland), pvt., Capt. Jonathan Hagar's Company Muster Roll, Frederick Co., circa 1757-1758, exact dates not given (served 6 days); bill of credit issued or paid to him for £0.6.0 in 1767, exact date not given. {Ref: MSA S960 or S752, p. 175; CSOS:106}

TETERICK, HENRY (Maryland), pvt., Capt. Thomas Norris' Company, Frederick Co., circa 1757-1758, exact dates not given (served 30 days); bill of credit issued or paid to him for £1.10.0 in 1767, exact date not given. {Ref: MSA S960 or S752, p. 177; CSOS:108}

THARP, HENRY (Delaware), b. Kent Co., DE, laborer, age not given (height 5 ft. 6 in.); pvt., enlisted by Capt. John Blackwood in Philadelphia on 15 May 1758. {Ref: ARDE I:27}

THERNBURGH, THOMAS (Maryland), patriot, Frederick Co., who performed "sundry services at the fort" in 1763 and payment in the amount of £4.10.0 was still owed to him on 25 Nov 1763 (when reported by the Accounts Committee to the MD Assembly). {Ref: ARMD 58:400}

THOMAS, BENJAMIN (Delaware), pvt., Kent Co. Militia, Capt. John Caton's Company, 25 Apr 1757 (date of muster roll). {Ref: ARDE I:14}

THOMAS, CHRISTIAN (Maryland), m. (N), had children Henry, Barbara, Mary, and Christian, and d. testate by 24 Dec 1777, Frederick Co. {Ref: WMG 5:2, p. 82} Patriot who was paid £3 at Fort Frederick on 30 Aug 1758 "for carryage of a load of corn to Fort Frederick" for the Western Expedition against Fort Duquesne; pay account submitted in 1758, exact date not given. {Ref: ARMD 55:775; MHM 9:4, p. 368}

THOMAS, CHRISTOPHER (Maryland), pvt., Capt. Elias Delashmutt's Company Muster Roll, Frederick Co., 13 Aug 1757, exact dates not given (served 52 days); also served another 30 days, exact dates not given; bill of credit issued or paid in his behalf to Elias Delashmut, Jr. on 16 Mar 1767 for £4.2.0. {Ref: MSA S960 or S752, p. 163; CSOS:94, 98}

THOMAS, EDWARD (Maryland), pvt., Capt. Elias Delashmutt's Company Muster Roll, Frederick Co., circa 1757-1758, exact dates not given (served 30 days); bill of credit issued or paid in his behalf to Casper Shaff on 2 Mar 1767 for £1.10.0. {Ref: MSA S960 or S752, p. 162; CSOS:94}

THOMAS, FELTY (Maryland), pvt., Capt. Elias Delashmutt's Company Muster Roll, Frederick Co., circa 1757-1758, exact dates not given (served 30 days); bill of credit issued or paid in his behalf to Elias Delashmut, Jr. on 16 Mar 1767 for £1.10.0. {Ref: MSA S960 or S752; CSOS:94}

THOMAS, JAMES (Delaware), pvt., Kent Co. Militia, Capt. John Caton's Company, 25 Apr 1757 (date of muster roll). {Ref: ARDE I:13}

THOMAS, JOHN (Maryland), pvt., Capt. Elias Delashmutt's Company Muster Roll, Frederick Co., circa 1757-1758, exact dates not given (served 30 days); bill of credit issued or paid in his behalf to Elias Delashmut, Jr. on 16 Mar 1767 for £1.10.0. {Ref: MSA S960 or S752, p. 162; CSOS:94}

THOMAS, LEWIS (Delaware), captain, Pencader Hundred, Lower Regt. of Militia, New Castle Co., 1756. {Ref: ARDE I:12; ARPA (2nd Series) 2:525; HDE I:141}

THOMAS, MICHA (Delaware), b. c1727, PA (carpenter, age 31 in 1758); pvt., recruited by Capt. Benjamin Noxon and enlisted on 13 May 1758. {Ref: ARDE I:19; ARPA (2nd Series) 2:566}

THOMAS, NOTLEY (Maryland), pvt., Capt. Elias Delashmutt's Company Muster Roll, Frederick Co., circa 1757-1758, exact dates not given (served 30 days); bill of credit issued or paid in his behalf to Casper Shaff on 2 Mar 1767 for £1.10.0. {Ref: MSA S960 or S752, p. 162; CSOS:94}

THOMAS, PHILOMAN (Maryland), patriot and poss. soldier (rank not specified), Frederick Co., militia pay account submitted in 1758, exact date not given. {Ref: MHM 9:4, p. 368}

THOMAS, RICHARD (Maryland), pvt., Capt. Francis Ware's Company of MD Troops, Charles Co., circa 9 Oct 1757 to 30 Dec 1758. {Ref: MHS MS.375.1; CSOS:89} Payment to him was recorded in Col. Dagworthy's account book on 11 Jul 1762 for work on Fort Cumberland. {Ref: MHS MS.375}

THOMAS, WILLIAM (Maryland), b. 1714, Charles Co., son of John Thomas and prob. Anne Atkinson (widow of William Atkinson), m. Elizabeth Reeves by 1751, had children William, John, George, James, and Elizabeth, and d. 25 Mar 1795, St. Mary's Company; planter, gentleman, major by 1754, and member of the MD Assembly (1760-1761, 1768-1771, 1777). {Ref: BDML II:814}

THOMAS, WILLIAM JR. (Maryland), pvt., Capt. Elias Delashmutt's Company Muster Roll, Frederick Co., circa 1757-1758, exact dates not given (served 30 days); bill of credit issued or paid in his behalf to Elias Delashmut, Jr. on 16 Mar 1767 for £1.10.0. {Ref: MSA S960 or S752, pp. 162-163; CSOS:94}

THOMPKINS (TOMKINS), THOMAS (Maryland), cpl., Capt. Moses Chapline's Company Muster Roll No. 2, Frederick Co., circa 1757-1758, exact dates not given (served 14 days); bill of credit issued or paid in his behalf to Joseph Chaplin for £0.13.0 on 5 Mar 1767. {Ref: MSA S960 or S752, p. 197; CSOS:114} Cpl., Capt. Moses Chapline's Company Muster Roll No. 3, Frederick Co., circa 1757-1758, exact dates not given (served 6 days); bill of credit issued or paid in his behalf to Joseph Chaplin for £0.8.0 on 5 Mar 1767. {Ref: MSA S960 or S752, pp. 198-199; CSOS:115}

THOMPSON, CAPTAIN, see "David Wolstenholme," q.v.

THOMPSON (THOMSON), ADAM, see "Joseph Sim (Simm)," q.v.

THOMPSON, ANDREW (Maryland), patriot, Annapolis, Anne Arundel Co., pay account submitted for quartering soldiers in 1757 or 1758, exact dates not given. {Ref: MHM 9:3, p. 261}

THOMPSON, COLLIN (Maryland), pvt., Capt. Francis Ware's Company of MD Troops, Charles Co., from 9 Oct 1757 to 4 Jun 1758 when he was "transferred to Virginians as a deserter" (served 239 days). {Ref: MHS MS.375.1; CSOS:89} However, payment to him was recorded in Col. Dagworthy's account book on 7 Mar 1763. {Ref: MHS MS.375}

THOMPSON, COTTON (Maryland), pvt., Capt. Joseph Hanson Harrison's Company Muster Roll, Charles Co., circa 1757-1758, exact dates not given; bill of credit issued or paid in his behalf to Capt. Joseph Hanson Harrison for £2.9.0 on 29 Nov 1771. {Ref: MSA S960 or S752, p. 189}

THOMPSON (THOMSON), FRANCIS (Maryland), patriot, Frederick Co., 1758; he and several others were called "battomen" when paid on 6 Oct 1758 "for carrying up baggage belonging to the militia that garrisoned Fort Cumberland." {Ref: ARMD 55:775} He performed "sundry services at the fort" in 1763 and payment in the amount of £0.4.6 was still owed to him on 25 Nov 1763 (when reported by the Accounts Committee to the MD Assembly). {Ref: ARMD 58:400}

THOMPSON, JAMES (Delaware), b. c1740, Ireland (linen printer, age 18 in 1758); pvt., recruited by Capt. Benjamin Noxon and enlisted on 28 Apr 1758. {Ref: ARDE I:19; ARPA (2nd Series) 2:566}

THOMPSON, JAMES (Maryland), pvt., Capt. John Dagworthy's Company of MD Troops, Frederick Co., from 9 Oct 1757 to 11 Oct 1758 when he was reported as killed; however, payment to him was recorded in Col. Dagworthy's account book on 8 Mar 1763 for work on Fort Cumberland. {Ref: MHS MS.375; CSOS:78; MHS MS.375.1} An account submitted to the MD Assembly on 25 Nov 1763 indicated he was due £4.12.3 as "granted by the Act for Granting a Sum of Money as a Present to the Forces, late in the Pay and Service of this Province, and taken into his Majesty's Service by Brigadier General Forbes." {Ref: ARMD 58:401}

THOMPSON, JAMES (Maryland), patriot, Frederick Co., who performed "sundry services at the fort" in 1763 and payment in the amount of £0.17.6 was still owed to him on 25 Nov 1763 (when reported by the Accounts Committee to the MD Assembly). {Ref: ARMD 58:400}

THOMPSON, JOHN (Delaware), pvt., Capt. Richard McWilliams' Company of Foot, New Castle Co., enlisted 28 Dec 1757. {Ref: ARDE I:14}

THOMPSON, JOHN (Maryland), pvt., Capt. John Dagworthy's Company of MD Troops, Frederick Co., from 9 Oct 1757 to 16 Apr 1759 when he reportedly deserted; however, payment to him was recorded in Col. Dagworthy's account book on 26 Feb 1763. {Ref: MHS MS.375; CSOS:78; MHS MS.375.1}

THOMPSON, JOHN (Maryland), m. Elizabeth Ward on 27 Dec 1726, St. Anne's Parish. {Ref: AACR:93} Patriot, Annapolis, Anne Arundel Co., pay account submitted for quartering soldiers in 1757 or 1758, exact dates not given. {Ref: MHM 9:3, p. 260}

THOMPSON, JOHN JR. (Maryland), b. 8 Jul 1733, Annapolis, son of John Thompson and Elizabeth Ward, St. Anne's Parish. {Ref: AACR:97} Patriot, Annapolis, Anne Arundel Co., pay account submitted for quartering soldiers in 1757 or 1758, exact dates not given. {Ref: MHM 9:3, p. 260}

THOMPSON, LUKE (Maryland), patriot, Frederick Co., who performed "sundry services at the fort" in 1763 and payment in the amount of £0.4.6 was still owed to him on 25 Nov 1763 (when reported by the Accounts Committee to the MD Assembly). {Ref: ARMD 58:400}

THOMPSON, RICHARD (Delaware), pvt., Capt. French Battell's Company of Lower County Provincials, enlisted 12 May 1758. {Ref: ARDE I:17; ARPA (2nd Series) 2:555}

THOMPSON, ROBERT (Delaware), pvt., Capt. French Battell's Company of Lower County Provincials, enlisted 15 May 1758. {Ref: ARDE I:17; ARPA (2nd Series) 2:555}

THOMPSON, SMALLWOOD (Maryland), pvt., Capt. Joseph Hanson Harrison's Company Muster Roll, Charles Co., circa 1757-1758, exact dates not given; bill of credit issued or paid in his behalf to William Smallwood for £2.9.0 on 20 Feb 1767. {Ref: MSA S960 or S752, p. 189}

THOMPSON, WILLIAM (Delaware), pvt., Capt. Henry Vanbibber's Company of the Lower Counties on Delaware Troops at New Castle, enlisted on 1 May 1759. {Ref: ARDE I:26; ARPA (2nd Series) 2:594}

THOMPSON, WILLIAM (Maryland), pvt., Capt. Alexander Beall's Company of MD Troops, Frederick Co., circa 9 Oct 1757 to 30 Dec 1758. {Ref: MHS MS.375.1; CSOS:82} Payment to him was recorded in Col. Dagworthy's account book on 11 Jul 1762 for work on Fort Cumberland. {Ref: MHS MS.375} Also performed "sundry services at the fort" in 1763 and payment in the amount of £1.1.0 was still owed to him on 25 Nov 1763 (when reported by the Accounts Committee to the MD Assembly). {Ref: ARMD 58:400}

THOMPSON, WILLIAM (Maryland), pvt., Capt. William Luckett's Company Muster Roll, Frederick Co., circa 1757-1758, exact dates not given (served 30 days); bill of credit or order issued in his behalf to William Luckett, Jr. for £1.10.0 on 6 Apr 1767. {Ref: MSA S960 or S752, p. 169; CSOS:99}

THORNTON, WILLIAM (Maryland), d. 3 Feb 1769, Annapolis, Anne Arundel Co. patriot; pay account submitted for quartering soldiers in 1757 or 1758, exact dates not given. {Ref: MHM 9:3, p. 260} "William Thornton died Fri. last at Baltimore Town, formerly sheriff of Anne Arundel Co." {Ref: *MD Gazette*, 9 Feb 1769}

THRAMPTON (TRAMPTON), WILLIAM (Maryland), pvt., Capt. Henry Casson's Company Muster Roll, Queen Anne's Co., circa 1757-1758, exact dates not given (served 27 days); bill of credit or order issued to him for £1.7.0 in 1767, exact date not given. {Ref: MSA S960 or S752, p. 178; CSOS:109}

THREASHER, JOHN (Maryland), pvt., Capt. Alexander Beall's Company of MD Troops, Frederick Co., from 9 Oct 1757 to 23 Oct 1758 when he reportedly deserted; however, payment to him was recorded in Col. Dagworthy's account book on 26 Feb 1763. {Ref: MHS MS.375; CSOS:82; MHS MS.375.1}

THROP, SAMUEL (Delaware), pvt., Capt. French Battell's Company of Lower County Provincials, enlisted 16 May 1758. {Ref: ARDE I:17; ARPA (2nd Series) 2:555}

THURSEL, GOODHERT (Maryland), pvt., Capt. John White's Company Muster Roll, Frederick Co., circa 1757-1758, exact dates not given (served 6 days); bill of credit issued or paid to him for £0.6.0 in 1767, exact date not given. {Ref: MSA S960 or S752, p. 165; CSOS:95}

TILDEN, JOHN (Maryland), b. 1 Jul 1725, Kent Co., son of John Tilden and Catherine Blay, of Shrewsbury Parish, m. Elizabeth (N), had a son John, and d. by 23 Feb 1764; planter, gentleman, county justice (1756-1760), member of the MD Assembly (1757-1761), and captain by 1758. {Ref: BDML II:818; *MD Gazette*, 28 Sep 1758}

TILDEN, MARTHA, see "John Hyland," q.v.

TILGHMAN, ANNA MARIA, see "William Hemsley," q.v.

TILGHMAN, EDWARD (Maryland), b. 3 Jul 1713, Queen Anne's Co., son of Richard Tilghman and Anna Maria Lloyd; m. 1st to Anna Maria Turbutt circa 1738, had dau. Anna Maria; m. 2nd to Elizabeth Chew in 1749, had children Richard, Edward (1750/1-1815), Benjamin, Elizabeth, and Anna Maria [one source indicated Edward had a son Paul (b. 1750), but two other sources did not mention him]; m. 3rd to Juliana Carroll in 1759, had children Matthew, Benjamin (b. 1764), Mary, and Susanna; and, d. 9 Oct 1785; patriot, planter, gentleman by 1737, esquire by 1740, sheriff (1739-1742), county justice (1743-1749), member of the MD Assembly (1745-1749, 1754-1771, Speaker of the House), Rent Roll Keeper of the Eastern Shore (1750-1756), captain by 1746, and colonel by 1755. {Ref: BDML II:820-822; ARMD 55:44; *MD Gazette*, 28 Sep 1758; SCWM III:49, 268; MDG II:450-451} Militia pay account submitted in 1758, exact date not given. {Ref: MHM 9:4, p. 368}

TILGHMAN, MARGARET, see "Charles Carroll, Esq.," q.v.

TILGHMAN, MATTHEW (Maryland), b. 17 Feb 1717/8, Queen Anne's Co., son of Richard Tilghman and Anna Maria Lloyd; adopted at age 15 by his childless cousin Maj. Gen. Matthew Tilghman Ward; m. his cousin Anne or Anna Lloyd (1723-1794) on 6 Apr 1741, had children Margaret (1742-1817), Matthew Ward (1743-1753), Richard (1746-1805), Lloyd (1748-1811), and Anna Maria (1755-1843), and d. 4 May 1790, Talbot Co., of a paralytic stroke; planter, merchant, gentleman, captain of a troop of horse by 1741, county justice (1741-1775), member of the MD Assembly (represented Talbot County 1751-1758, Queen Anne's County 1760-1761, and Talbot County 1768-1774, including Speaker of the House 1773-1774), President of the MD Senate (1773-1774), member of the Committee of Correspondence in 1774 and Council of Safety in 1775, member of Congress (1774-1777), and Chairman of the Provincial Conventions (1774-1776). {Ref: BDML II:825-827; MDG II:453-454}

TILGHMAN, RICHARD, see "William Goldsborough," q.v.

TILGHMAN, WILLIAM (Maryland), b. 22 Sep 1711, Queen Anne's Co., son of Richard Tilghman and Anna Maria Lloyd, m. his cousin Margaret Lloyd on 2 Aug 1736, had children Anna Maria (1737-1768), Richard Jr. (1740-1809), James (b. 1742), Margaret (b, 1744), Henrietta Maria (b. 1749), and Mary (b. 1753), and d. testate by 31 Oct 1782, Talbot Co.; patriot, planter, gentleman, deputy commissary (1738-1758), major by 1744, member of the MD Assembly (1734-1737), county justice (1734-1760), and deputy commissary (1738-1758). {Ref: BDML II:832-833; MDG II:449-450}

TILL, THOMAS (Delaware), captain, Southern District of Cedar Creek Hundred, Militia Regt. of Sussex Co., 1756; capt., Slaughter Neck District, 1758 (name mistakenly listed once as "Thomas Hill"). {Ref: ARDE I:13, 15; ARPA (2nd Series) 2:529, 579; HDE I:141}

TILL, WILLIAM (Delaware), New Castle Co., patriot who served as a Justice of the peace, Justice of the Court of Oyer and Terminer, and Justice of the Supreme Court, 1756-1761. {Ref: GRSD 1:13-14}

TILLINGER, GEORGE (Delaware), b. c1740, Germany (saddler, age 19 in 1759); pvt., enlisted by Capt. James Armstrong for the PA Regt. on 5 May 1759. {Ref: ARDE I:26; ARPA (2nd Series) 2:585}

TILTON, THOMAS (Delaware), son of John Tilton (d. 1746) and Mary Sharp, of Duck Creek Hundred, m. Sabrah Allee (d. 1797), had children James, Abraham, Thomas, Rachel, and Nancy, and d. testate by 9 Nov 1789. {Ref: CFD 2:174-176; CDSS:209} Ensign, Lower Part of Duck Creek Hundred, Militia of Kent Co. on Delaware, 1756; captain and member of the Council of Safety in Kent Co. on 8 Jan 1776. {Ref: ARDE I:12; ARPA (2nd Series) 2:527-529; HDE I:141; RPDE:265}

TIPPEN, ISAAC (Maryland), patriot and poss. soldier (rank not specified), Frederick Co., militia pay account submitted in 1758, exact date not given. {Ref: MHM 9:4, p. 368}

TIPTON (TIPTEN), SILVESTER (Maryland), cpl., Capt. Joseph Chapline's Company Muster Roll No. 1, Frederick Co., circa 1757-1758, exact dates not given (served 20 days); bill of credit issued or paid in his behalf to Joseph Chaplin for £1.6.7½ on 5 Mar 1767. {Ref: MSA S960 or S752, pp. 190, 192; CSOS:102}

TOBIN, THOMAS (Delaware), lieut., Red Lion Hundred, Lower Regt. of Militia, New Castle Co., 1756 (name misspelled once as "Thomas Tabin"). {Ref: ARDE I:12; ARPA (2nd Series) 2:525; HDE I:141} Court Justice, 1761. {Ref: GRSD 1:15}

TODD, CATHERINE, see "John Green," q.v.

TODD, SARAH, see "Charles Dorsey," q.v.

TOIL, ADAM (Maryland), pvt., Capt. John White's Company Muster Roll, Frederick Co., circa 1757-1758, exact dates not given (served 6 days); bill of credit issued or paid to him for £0.6.0 in 1767, exact date not given. {Ref: MSA S960 or S752, p. 165; CSOS:95}

TOLE, TIMOTHY (Maryland), b. c1733, MD (age 23 in 1756); pvt., Capt. Christopher Gist's Company of VA Militia, 13 Jul 1756, enlisted at Fredericksburg, VA. {Ref: MSR I:37}

TOLLEY, WALTER (Maryland), b. c1710, Baltimore Co., son of Thomas Tolley and Mary Freeborn, m. 1st to Mary Garrettson in 1735, m. 2nd to Martha Hall in 1751, had children Thomas (d. young), Walter, James, Thomas Garrettson, Edward Carvil, Elizabeth, Mary, Sophia, Martha, and Ann, and d. 29 Mar 1783; planter, gentleman by 1752, court justice (1754-1773), captain by 1756, member of the MD Assembly (1751, 1754-1757), and member of the Committee of Observation in 1774 {Ref: BDML II:837; ARMD 55:44; Baltimore Co. Court Minutes, August 1759}

TOLSON (TOALSON, TOLESON), ANDREW (Maryland), b. c1725, m. Hannah (N) by 1748 and had a son Nathaniel (b. 6 Jan 1748/9), Shrewsbury Parish. {Ref: ESVR} Pvt., Capt. Peregrine Brown's Company Muster Roll, Kent Co., circa 1757-1758, exact dates not given (served 15 days); bill of credit issued or paid in his behalf to Robert Buchanan on 20 May 1767 for £0.15.0. {Ref: MSA S960 or S752, p. 179; CSOS:110}

TOLSON, JOHN, see "John Lowebean" and "Philip Tannihill," q.v.

TOMAS, THOMAS (Delaware), pvt., Kent Co. Militia, Capt. John Caton's Company, 25 Apr 1757 (date of muster roll). {Ref: ARDE I:13}

TOMBS, CHARLES (Maryland), pvt., Capt. Peregrine Brown's Company Muster Roll, Kent Co., circa 1757-1758, exact dates not given (served 15 days); bill of credit issued or paid in his behalf to Robert Buchanan on 20 Feb 1767 for £0.15.0. {Ref: MSA S960 or S752, p. 179; CSOS:110}

TOMLINSON, JOSEPH (Maryland), pvt., Capt. Joseph Chapline's Company Muster Roll No. 1, Frederick Co., circa 1757-1758, exact dates not given (served 31 days); bill of credit issued or paid in his behalf to Joseph Chaplin for £1.1.0 on 8 May 1767. {Ref: MSA S960 or S752, p. 192; CSOS:102} He was paid £9.15.0 on 17 Jul 1758 at Fort Frederick "for his waggon's attending the Pensilvania Detachments under the command of Major Wells on the New Road" for the Western Expedition against Fort Duquesne. {Ref: ARMD 55:774}

TOMLINSON (TOMBLINSON), NATHANIEL (Maryland), patriot and poss. soldier (rank not specified), Frederick Co., militia pay account submitted in 1758, exact date not given. {Ref: MHM 9:4, p. 366} "Nathaniel Tomlinson was killed lately by Indians in the back country" (exact date not given). {Ref: *MD Gazette*, 29 Apr 1762}

TOMLINSON, RICHARD (Maryland), pvt., Capt. Francis Ware's Company of MD Troops, Charles Co., from 9 Oct 1757 to 8 Nov 1758 (served 395 days) when he reportedly deserted; however, payment to him was recorded in Col. Dagworthy's account book on 7 Mar 1763 for work on Fort Cumberland. {Ref: MHS MS.375; CSOS:89; MHS MS.375.1}

TONIER (TONSER), CHRISTOPHER (Maryland), pvt., Capt. Thomas Norris' Company, Frederick Co., circa 1757-1758, exact dates not given (served 30 days); bill of credit issued or paid in his behalf to Michael McGuire on 20 Mar 1767 for £1.10.0. {Ref: MSA S960 or S752, p. 176; CSOS:108}

TOOLE, ARTHUR (Maryland), patriot, Frederick Co., was paid £6.10.0 on 16 Jul 1758 at Fort Frederick "for carrying swords, holstors, etc. to Winchester" for the Western Expedition against Fort Duquesne. {Ref: ARMD 55:773}

TOONE, ROBERT (Maryland), pvt., Capt. Elias Delashmutt's Company Muster Roll, Frederick Co., circa 1757-1758, exact dates not given (served 30 days); bill of credit issued or paid in his behalf to Elias Delashmut, Jr. on 16 Mar 1767 for £1.10.0. {Ref: MSA S960 or S752, p. 162; CSOS:94}

TOOTELL (TOOTLE), ABNER (Maryland), pvt., Capt. Henry Casson's Company Muster Roll, Queen Anne's Co., circa 1757-1758, exact dates not given (served 27 days); bill of credit issued or paid in his behalf to Capt. Casson on 27 Mar 1767 for £1.7.0. {Ref: MSA S960 or S752, p. 178; CSOS:109}

TOOTELL, HELLEN or HELEN (Maryland), patriot, Annapolis, Anne Arundel Co., pay account submitted for quartering soldiers in 1757 or 1758, exact dates not given. {Ref: MHM 9:3, p. 261} Hellen Tootell was the 2nd wife of Richard Tootell (c1690-1745); had children Eliner, Marshall [#1], Richard, Marshall [#2], Nicholas, and James, all born in St. Anne's Parish. Helen Tootell, widow, aged 73, one of the oldest inhabitants of Annapolis, d. 22 Sep 1763. {Ref: AACR:85-95; *MD Gazette*, 29 Sep 1763}

TOOTELL, RICHARD (Maryland), b. 16 Dec 1721, Annapolis, son of Richard and Hellen Tootell, St Anne's Parish, m. Elizabeth Frazier and had children Hellen, Richard, Elizabeth, and Priscilla; physician who served as a surgeon in the Revolutionary War; d. testate by 4 Jan 1782. {Ref: AA Co. Wills TG 1:34, pp. 40-41} Dr. Tootell was also a patriot in the French and Indian War; pay account submitted for quartering soldiers in 1757 or 1758, exact dates not given. {Ref: MHM 9:3, p. 260}

TOVEY, MARY, see "William Ringgold," q.v.

TOWLAND, WILLIAM (Delaware), b. c1736, DE (laborer, age 22 in 1758); pvt., recruited by Capt. Benjamin Noxon and enlisted on 25 Apr 1758. {Ref: ARDE I:19; ARPA (2nd Series) 2:566}

TOWLAND, WILLIAM (Delaware), b. c1736, New Castle Co., DE (laborer, age 22 in 1758); pvt., prob. in Capt. John McClughan's Company, 15 Apr 1758. {Ref: ARDE I:18; ARPA (2nd Series) 2:570}

TOWNEY, ARCHIBALD (Delaware), lieut., Kent Co., commissioned 23 May 1759. {Ref: ARDE I:20; ARPA (2nd Series) 2:582}

TOWNSHEND (TOWNSEND), SOLOMON (Maryland), pvt., Capt. Henry Casson's Company Muster Roll, Queen Anne's Co., circa 1757-1758, exact dates not given (served 27 days); bill of credit issued or paid in his behalf to Capt. Casson for Townshend's mother (unnamed) on 27 Mar 1767 for £1.7.0. {Ref: MSA S960 or S752, p. 178; CSOS:109}

TOWNSHEND (TOWNSEND), THOMAS (Maryland), pvt., Capt. Henry Casson's Company Muster Roll, Queen Anne's Co., circa 1757-1758, exact dates not given (served 27 days); bill of credit issued or paid in his behalf to Capt. Casson on 27 Feb 1767 for £1.7.0. {Ref: MSA S960 or S752, p. 177; CSOS:109}

TOWNSON, JOHN (Delaware), pvt., Kent Co. Militia, Capt. John Caton's Company, 25 Apr 1757 (date of muster roll). {Ref: ARDE I:13}

TRACEY, SUSAN, see "Henry Stevenson," q.v.

TRACY (TRACEY), PIERCE (Maryland), pvt., Capt. John Dagworthy's Company of MD Troops, Frederick Co., from 9 Oct 1757 to 16 Apr 1759 when he reportedly deserted; however, payment to him was recorded in Col. Dagworthy's account book on 8 Mar 1763 for work on Fort Cumberland. {Ref: MHS MS.375; CSOS:78; MHS MS.375.1}

TRAHAN, NEHEMIAH (Maryland), pvt., Capt. Joshua Beall's Company Muster Roll, Prince George's Co., circa 1757-1758, exact dates not given; bill of credit issued or paid in his behalf to Joshua Beall for £2.3.0 on 12 Dec 1769. {Ref: MSA S960 or S752, p. 185}

TRAIN, HAMILTON (Delaware), son of Roger Train (d. 1737) and his wife Mary (d. 1755), poss. m. Alice (N), had an only child John, and d. by 19 May 1768. {Ref: CFD 2:184} Pvt., Kent Co. Militia, Capt. John Caton's Company, 25 Apr 1757 (date of muster roll). {Ref: ARDE I:13}

TRAIT, GEORGE ADAM (Maryland), pvy., Capt. Jonathan Hager's Company, circa 1757-1758, exact dates not given (served 6 days). {Ref: CSOS:107}

TRAUBERG, ANDREW (Delaware), captain, Christiana Hundred, Upper Regt. of Militia, Southeast Division, New Castle Co., 1756. {Ref: HDE I:141}

TRAVERS (TRAVERSE), HENRY (Maryland), b. c1705, Dorchester Co., son of Matthew Travers and Elizabeth (N), m. his half first cousin Ann Hicks by 1729 (Ann's mother and Henry's mother were half sisters), had children Levin, Henry Jr., John Hicks, William Hicks, Mary, Nancey, Emelia, Priscilla, and Rebecca, and d. by 18 Dec 1765, Annapolis, of smallpox; merchant, land commissioner in 1728, gentleman by 1738, county justice (1734-1765), captain by 1750, esquire by 1751, member of MD Assembly (1749-1761, 1765), major by 1756 and colonel by 1765. {Ref: BDML II:839-840}

TRAVERS, ELIZABETH, see "Joseph Chapline," q.v.

TREADWAY, THOMAS, see "Thomas Brown," q.v.

TREBECK, GEORGE (Maryland), patriot, Baltimore Co., was paid £10.10.0 on 7 Aug 1758 "for carryage of two ton of bar iron" from Baltimore to Fort Frederick for the Western Expedition against Fort Duquesne. {Ref: ARMD 55:774}

TREMBLE, MOSES (Maryland), pvt., Capt. John Dagworthy's Company of MD Troops, Frederick Co., from 9 Oct 1757 to 16 Apr 1759 when he reportedly deserted; however, payment to him was recorded in Col. Dagworthy's account book on 26 Feb 1763. {Ref: MHS MS.375; CSOS:78; MHS MS.375.1}

TRENNELL, JOHN (Maryland), pvt. (age about 19 in 1757) in Capt. Francis Ware's Company of MD Troops, Charles Co., reported as deserted in August 1757. {Ref: *MD Gazette*, 1 Sep 1757}

TRIGGS, BENJAMIN (Maryland), pvt., Capt. Joshua Beall's Company Muster Roll, Prince George's Co., circa 1757-1758, exact dates not given; bill of credit issued or paid to him for £1.10.6 in 1767, exact date not given. {Ref: MSA S960 or S752, p. 185}

TRIPPE, HENRY, see "Bartholomew Ennalls," q.v.

TRIPPE, MARY, see "Jacob Hindman," q.v.

TRIPPIT, DANIEL (Delaware), pvt., Kent Co. Militia, Capt. John Caton's Company, 25 Apr 1757 (date of muster roll). {Ref: ARDE I:14}

TROOSBURGH, NICHOLAS (Maryland), patriot and poss. soldier (rank not specified), Frederick Co., militia pay account submitted in 1758, exact date not given. {Ref: MHM 9:4, p. 366}

TROUTWINE, GEORGE JACOB (Maryland), patriot and poss. soldier (rank not specified), Frederick Co., militia pay account submitted in 1758, exact date not given. {Ref: MHM 9:4, p. 366}

TRUET, LODWICK (Delaware), pvt., Kent Co. Militia, Capt. John Caton's Company, 25 Apr 1757 (date of muster roll). {Ref: ARDE I:14}

TRUET, ROUNS (Delaware), pvt., Kent Co. Militia, Capt. John Caton's Company, 25 Apr 1757 (date of muster roll). {Ref: ARDE I:14}

TRUGATE (FRUGATE?), PETER (Maryland), pvt., Capt. John White's Company Muster Roll, Frederick Co., circa 1757-1758, exact dates not given (served 6 days). {Ref: CSOS:96}

TRULOCK, HENRY (Maryland), sgt., Capt. Peregrine Brown's Company Muster Roll, Kent Co., circa 1757-1758, exact dates not given (served 15 days); bill of credit issued or paid to him on 20 Feb 1767 for £1. {Ref: MSA S960 or S752, p. 179; CSOS:110} Henry Trulock, of Kent Co., m. (N), had sons Henry Jr., Philip, and Samuel (and poss. other children not named in his will), and d. testate by 31 May 1785. {Ref: Kent Co. Wills 7:104}

TRULOCK, JACOB (Maryland), pvt., Capt. Peregrine Brown's Company Muster Roll, Kent Co., circa 1757-1758, exact dates not given (served 15 days); bill of credit issued or paid in his behalf to Robert Buchanan on 21 Mar 1767 for £0.15.0. {Ref: MSA S960 or S752, p. 179; CSOS:110}

TRULOCK, JAMES (Maryland), pvt., Capt. Peregrine Brown's Company, Kent Co., on 19 Feb 1758, by which time he had enlisted, but was unable to march due to health problems. {Ref: ARMD 31:283}

TRULOCK, JOSEPH (Maryland), sgt., Capt. Peregrine Brown's Company Muster Roll, Kent Co., circa 1757-1758, exact dates not given (served 15 days); bill of credit issued or paid to him for £1 in 1767, exact date not given. {Ref: MSA S960 or S752, p. 180; CSOS:110}

TRUMAN, ALEXANDER, see "William Reynolds," q.v.

TRUMAN, FURGUSON (Maryland), pvt., Capt. Joshua Beall's Company Muster Roll, Prince George's Co., circa 1757-1758, exact dates not given; bill of credit issued or paid to him for £1.3.0 in 1767 (exact date not given); one source indicated "Calvert County" after his name, which was mistakenly transcribed as "Ferguson Freeman." {Ref: MSA S960 or S752, p. 185; CSOS:116}

TRUMAN, RICHARD (Maryland), pvt., Capt. Francis Ware's Company of MD Troops, Charles Co., circa 9 Oct 1757 to 30 Dec 1758. {Ref: MHS MS.375.1; CSOS:89} Payment to him was recorded in Col. Dagworthy's account book on 7 Mar 1763. {Ref: MHS MS.375}

TRUNER, JACOB, see "Jacob Turner," q.v.

TRYER, FREDERICK (Maryland), ensign in Capt. Thomas Norris' Company, Frederick Co., circa 1757-1758, exact dates not given (served 30 days); bill of credit issued or paid to him on 27 Mar 1767 for £3. {Ref: MSA S960 or S752, p. 176; CSOS:107}

TRYSE, JAMES (Maryland), alias James Fyse *[sic]*, pvt., Capt. William Luckett's Company Muster Roll, Frederick Co., circa 1757-1758, exact dates not given; bill of credit issued or paid in his behalf to William Luckett, Jr. for £1.10.0 on 6 Apr 1767. {Ref: MSA S960 or S752, pp. 169-170}

TUCKER, GEORGE (Maryland), sgt., Capt. Peter Bainbridge's Company Muster Roll, Frederick Co., circa 1757-1758, exact dates not given (served 41 days); bill of credit issued or paid in his behalf to Joseph Chaplin on 13 Jun 1768 for £2.14.7½. {Ref: MSA S960 or S752, p. 181; CSOS:110}

TUCKER, JAMES (Maryland), cpl., Capt. Joshua Beall's Company of MD Troops, Prince George's Co., from 9 Oct 1757 to 30 Dec 1758 (promoted to sgt. on 15 Aug 1758). {Ref: MHS MS.375.1} Payment to him was recorded in Col. Dagworthy's account book on 7 Mar 1763. {Ref: MHS MS.375}

TUCKER, JOHN (Maryland), pvt., Capt. John Dagworthy's Company of MD Troops, Frederick Co., from 9 Oct 1757 to 8 Apr 1758 when he was discharged. {Ref: MHS MS.375.1; CSOS:78} Payment to him was recorded in Col. Dagworthy's account book on 8 Mar 1763. {Ref: MHS MS.375}

TUCKER, JOHN (Maryland), pvt., Capt. Joshua Beall's Company of MD Troops, Prince George's Co., from 9 Oct 1757 to 16 Oct 1758 when he was discharged; one undated account indicated "Calvert County." {Ref: MHS MS.375.1; CSOS:86, 116} Payment to him was recorded in Col. Dagworthy's account book on 12 Jul 1762. {Ref: MHS MS.375} Bill of credit issued or paid in his behalf to Joseph Chaplin for £1.3.0 on 13 Jun 1767 or 1768. {Ref: MSA S960 or S752, p. 185}

TUCKER, LITTLETON (Maryland), pvt., Capt. Joshua Beall's Company of MD Troops, Prince George's Co., from 9 Oct 1757 to 14 Sep 1758 when he was reported as killed; however, payment to him was recorded in Col. Dagworthy's account book on 26 Feb 1762. {Ref: MHS MS.375; CSOS:86; MHS MS.375.1}

TUCKER, STEPHEN (Maryland), pvt., Capt. Francis Ware's Company of MD Troops, Charles Co., circa 9 Oct 1757 to 30 Dec 1758. {Ref: MHS MS.375.1; CSOS:89} Payment to him was recorded in Col. Dagworthy's account book on 12 Jul 1762 for work on Fort Cumberland. {Ref: MHS MS.375}

TUCKWELL, JOHN (Maryland), pvt., Capt. Peregrine Brown's Company Muster Roll, Kent Co., circa 1757-1758, exact dates not given (served 15 days); bill of credit issued or paid in his behalf to Robert Buchanan on 20 Feb 1767 for £0.15.0. {Ref: MSA S960 or S752, p. 180; CSOS:110}

TUDAR (FUDAR?), JOHN (Maryland), pvt., Capt. Elias Delashmutt's Company Muster Roll, Frederick Co., 13 Aug 1757, exact dates not given (served 52 days); bill of credit issued or paid in his behalf to Elias Delashmut, Jr. on 16 Mar 1767 for £2.12.0. {Ref: MSA S960 or S752, p. 163; CSOS:98}

TUFFREY, SIMON (Delaware), pvt., Capt. Henry Vanbibber's Company of the Lower Counties on Delaware Troops at New Castle, enlisted on 21 May 1759. {Ref: ARDE I:26; ARPA (2nd Series) 2:594}

TURBERVILLE, GEORGE, see "William Fitzhugh," q.v.

TURBUTT, ANNA MARIA, see "Edward Tilghman," q.v.

TURBUTT, ANNE, see "John Goldsborough," q.v.

TURNER, EDWARD (Delaware), pvt., Capt. French Battell's Company of Lower County Provincials, enlisted 15 May 1758. {Ref: ARDE I:17; ARPA (2nd Series) 2:555}

TURNER, EPHRAIM (Delaware), b. c1741, Sussex, DE (age 18 in 1759); pvt., enlisted in Capt. John Wright's Company and mustered on 11 May 1759. {Ref: ARDE I:25; ARPA (2nd Series) 2:592}

TURNER, GIDEON (Maryland), lieut., Capt. Robert Sollers' Militia Co. in the lower part of Calvert Co. circa 1756-1757 (exact dates not given). {Ref: HCC:121}

TURNER, JONATHAN (Maryland), b. c1720, m. 1st to Sarah Greenwood on 29 Dec 1743 in Shrewsbury Parish, Kent Co., m. 2nd to Martha (N), had children Daniel, William, John, Martha, Elizabeth, Sarah, Araminta, Joseph, Ebenezer, Susannah, and Mary, and d. testate by 24 Jul 1784. {Ref: ESVR; Kent Co. Wills 7:61} Pvt., Capt. Peregrine Brown's Company, Kent Co., on 19 Feb 1758, by which time he had enlisted, but was unable to march due to health problems. {Ref: ARMD 31:283}

TURNER (TRUNER), JACOB, (Maryland), pvt., Capt. Peter Bainbridge's Company Muster Roll, Frederick Co., circa 1757-1758, exact dates not given; bill of credit issued or paid in his behalf to Jacob Young on 4 Mar 1767 for £1.8.0. {Ref: MSA S960 or S752, p. 181}

TURNER, JOSEPH (Delaware), New Castle Co., patriot who served as a Justice of the Peace and a Justice of the Court of Oyer and Terminer, 1756-1761. {Ref: GRSD 1:13, 15}

TURNER, SAMUEL BEVENS or BEVANS (Delaware), m. Jean Huet, had children Benjamin, Samuel, George, Jesse, Elias, Polly, Levicy, Nicy, and Sally, and d. testate by 31 Aug 1793. {Ref: CDSS:213} Ensign, Middle Part of Mispillion Hundred, Militia of Kent Co. on Delaware, 1756. {Ref: ARDE I:12; ARPA (2nd Series) 2:527-529; HDE I:141}

TURNEY, CHARLES (Maryland), pvt., Capt. Richard Pearis' Company of MD Troops, Frederick Co., circa 9 Oct 1757 to 31 May 1758; pvt., Capt. Alexander Beall's Company of MD Troops, Frederick Co., from 1 Jun 1758 to 30 Dec 1758; pvt., Capt. John Dagworthy's Company of MD Troops, Frederick Co., from 31 Dec 1758 to 16 Apr 1759 when he reportedly deserted; however, payment to him was recorded in Col. Dagworthy's account book on 13 Jul 1762. {Ref: MHS MS.375; CSOS:78, 82, 91; MHS MS.375.1}

TURNWOOLF, FREDERICK (Maryland), pvt., Capt. Peter Butler's Company Muster Roll, Frederick Co., circa 1757-1758, exact dates not given (served 34 days); bill of credit or order issued in his behalf for £1.14.0 and paid to Casper Shaff on 2 Mar 1767. {Ref: MSA S960 or S752, p. 167; CSOS:98}

TUSEY (TUSSEY), STEPHEN (Delaware), b. c1732, Brandywine Hundred, DE (laborer, age 26 in 1758); pvt., enlisted 24 Apr 1758 "for the campaign in the lower counties" by Capt. John McClughan. {Ref: ARDE I:18; ARPA (2nd Series) 2:570}

TWIGG, ROBERT (Maryland), pvt., Capt. Moses Chapline's Company Muster Roll No. 3, Frederick Co., circa 1757-1758, exact dates not given (served 6 days); bill of credit issued or paid in his behalf to Joseph Chaplin for £0.6.0 on 5 Mar 1767. {Ref: MSA S960 or S752, p. 198; CSOS:115}

TYBOUT, JAMES (Delaware), son of James Tybout (d. 1743) and Rachel Martin (widow of George Martin; Rachel Martin Tybout d. 1746), m. Comfort (N). {Ref: CFD 2:185-186} Lieut., Upper Part of Little Creek Hundred, Militia of Kent Co. on Delaware, 1756. {Ref: ARDE I:12; ARPA (2nd Series) 2:527-529; HDE I:141}

TYE, GEORGE (Maryland), pvt., Capt. Thomas Norris' Company, Frederick Co., circa 1757-1758, exact dates not given (served 30 days); bill of credit issued or paid in his behalf to Thomas Owings on 15 May 1767 for £1.10.0. {Ref: MSA S960 or S752, p. 177; CSOS:107}

TYRES (TYCER?), JOHN (Maryland), pvt., Capt. Richard Pearis' Company of MD Troops, Frederick Co., circa 9 Oct 1757 to 31 May 1758; pvt., Capt. Joshua Beall's Company of MD Troops, Prince George's Co., from 1 Jun 1758 to 14 Sep 1758 when he was reported as killed; however, payment to him was recorded in Col. Dagworthy's account book on 14 Jul 1762. {Ref: MHS MS.375; CSOS:86, 91; MHS MS.375.1}

UNDERHILL, JAMES (Maryland), farmer; pvt., Capt. Peregrine Brown's 7th Co. of Foot Militia, Kent Co., on 19 Feb 1758, by which time he had enlisted, but reportedly refused to appear and serve in arms against the enemy. {Ref: ARMD 31:283, 288}

UNDERICH (UNDERICK), MELCHOR (Maryland), pvt., Capt. Jonathan Hagar's Company Muster Roll, Frederick Co., circa 1757-1758, exact dates not given (served 6 days); bill of credit issued or paid to him for £0.6.0 in 1767, exact date not given. {Ref: MSA S960 or S752, p. 175; CSOS:106}

UNGRIE, ANDREW (Maryland), indentured servant and soldier who served in the French and Indian War some time between 1756 and 1763 (exact dates not known); his masters, Daniel Charmier and John Carnan, merchants, requested compensation from the Baltimore County Court due to the loss of use of Ungrie while in the service. {Ref: MHM 94:4, p. 426, citing Baltimore Co. Court Minutes}

UNNECUNOWE, Indian Chief (Maryland), Frederick Co., agreed to join with the English against the French in 1758. {Ref: ARMD 31:266}

UNSELF, FREDERICK (Maryland), pvt., Capt. Jonathan Hagar's Company Muster Roll, Frederick Co., circa 1757-1758, exact dates not given (served 6 days); bill of credit issued or paid to him for £0.6.0 in 1767, exact date not given; name misspelled once as "Frederick Unselt." {Ref: MSA S960 or S752, p. 175; CSOS:106}

USULMAN, VAL. (Maryland), patriot, Frederick Co., who performed "sundry services at the fort" in 1763 and payment in the amount of £1.10.0 was still owed to him on 25 Nov 1763 (when reported by the Accounts Committee to the MD Assembly). {Ref: ARMD 58:400}

UPHAM, ABRAM (Maryland), indentured servant and soldier who served in the French and Indian War some time between 1756 and 1763 (exact dates not known); his master William Lux, merchant, requested compensation from the Baltimore County Court due to the loss of use of Upham while in the service. {Ref: MHM 94:4, p. 426, citing Baltimore Co. Court Minutes}

UTOSSITE, ROUND O, Indian Chief (Maryland), Frederick Co., agreed to join with the English against the French in 1758. {Ref: ARMD 31:266-271}

VANBIBBER (VAN BEBBER), HENRY (Delaware), 2nd lieut., New Castle Co., 21 Apr 1758; promoted to adjutant 4 Jun 1758 and to 1st lieut. 13 Jun 1758; captain, 3rd Bttn. of PA Regt., commissioned 23 May 1759; subscribed to the Oath of Fidelity and Allegiance in 1778. {Ref: ARDE I:16, 20, 26; ARPA (2nd Series) 2:579, 582, 594; CDSS:214; RPDE:272}

VANBIBBER (VAN BEBBER), JACOB (Delaware), m. Mary (N), had children William and Sarah, and d. testate in Red Lion Hundred by 28 Apr 1768. {Ref: CDSS:214} Lieut. in Capt. John Gooding's Company, 1747; promoted to major during King George's War against Canada, 1747-1748; colonel, Lower Regt. of Militia, New Castle Co., 1756. {Ref: ARDE I:11; ARPA (2nd Series) 2:525; HDE I:141; CDSS:214} Patriot who served as a Justice of the Peace, Justice of the Court of Oyer and Terminer, and Justice of the Court of Common Pleas, 1756-1761. {Ref: GRSD 1:13}

VANBUSKART, MICHAEL (Maryland), lieut., Capt. Beall's Company, Frederick Co., was paid £43.2.6 by the MD Assembly on 23 Sep 1756 "for his charge of enlisting men." {Ref: ARMD 52:608}

VANCE, JOHN (Delaware), captain, St. George's Hundred, Lower Regt. of Militia, New Castle Co., 1756. {Ref: ARDE I:11; ARPA (2nd Series) 2:525; HDE I:141}

VANDERFORD, CHARLES (Delaware), pvt., Kent Co. Militia, Capt. John Caton's Company, 25 Apr 1757 (date of muster roll). {Ref: ARDE I:13}

VANDIKE, ANDREW (Delaware), b. c1738, DE (laborer, age 20 in 1758); pvt., recruited by Capt. Benjamin Noxon and enlisted on 2 May 1758. {Ref: ARDE I:19; ARPA (2nd Series) 2:566}

VANDIVER, JACOB (Delaware), b. c1741, Wilmington, DE (laborer, age 18 in 1759); pvt., enlisted by Capt. James Armstrong for the PA Regt. on 2 May 1759. {Ref: ARDE I:26; ARPA (2nd Series) 2:585}

VANDIVER (VANDEAVER, VANDEVEER), JOHN (Maryland), pvt., Capt. Peter Bainbridge's Company Muster Roll, Frederick Co., circa 1757-1758, exact dates not given (served 33 days); bill of credit issued or paid in his behalf to Joseph Chaplin on 9 Jun 1767 for £1.13.0. {Ref: MSA S960 or S752, p. 181; CSOS:111} Pvt., Capt. Joseph Chapline's Company Muster Roll No. 1, Frederick Co., circa 1757-1758, exact dates not given (served 39 days); bill of credit issued or paid in his behalf to Joseph Chaplin for £1.19.0 on 5 Mar 1767. {Ref: MSA S960 or S752, p. 190; CSOS:102} Pvt., Capt. Moses Chapline's Company Muster Roll No. 2, Frederick Co., circa 1757-1758, exact dates not given (served 13 days); bill of credit issued or paid in his behalf to Joseph Chaplin for £0.13.0 on 5 Mar 1767. {Ref: MSA S960 or S752, p. 197; CSOS:107} Pvt., Capt. Moses Chapline's Company Muster Roll No. 3, Frederick Co., circa 1757-1758, exact dates not given (served 6 days); bill of credit issued or paid in his behalf to Joseph Chaplin for £0.6.0 on 5 Mar 1767. {Ref: MSA S960 or S752, p. 198; CSOS:114}

VANDYKE (VAN DIKE), JOHN (Delaware), m. Margaret (N), had children Isaac and Ann, and d. testate in St. George's Hundred by 26 Dec 1759. {Ref: CDSS:214} Lieut. in Capt. John Vance's Company, 1747-1748, during King George's War against Canada; lieut., St. George's Hundred, Lower Regt. of Militia, New Castle Co., 1756. {Ref: ARDE I:7, 11; ARPA (2nd Series) 2:525; HDE I:141}

VANLEUVENIGH, PHILIP (Delaware), son of Philip (d. 1745) and Eleanor Vanleuvenigh. {Ref: CDSS:216} Pvt., Capt. Richard McWilliams' Company of Foot, New Castle Co., enlisted 28 Dec 1757. {Ref: ARDE I:14}

VANLEUVENIGH, SAMUEL (Delaware), shopkeeper, prob. son of Samuel (d. 1754), never married and d. testate by 27 Dec 1759. {Ref: CDSS:216} Pvt., Capt. Richard McWilliams' Company of Foot, New Castle Co., enlisted 28 Dec 1757. {Ref: ARDE I:14}

VANLEUVENIGH, ZACHARIAH (Delaware), tanner, prob. son of Samuel (d. 1754), m. Ann (N), had children George, John, William, Elizabeth, Rebecca, and Mary, and d. testate by 13 Mar 1789. {Ref: CDSS:216} Ensign, New Castle Hundred, Upper Regt. of Militia, North Division, New Castle Co., 1756 (name mistakenly transcribed once as "Zachariah Vanlunanigh" and once as "Zachariah Luwanigh"). {Ref: ARDE I:11; ARPA (2nd Series) 2:526; HDE I:141}

VASHAN, MICHAEL (Delaware), b. c1729, Armagh, Ireland (laborer, age 30 in 1759); pvt., enlisted by Capt. James Armstrong for the PA Regt. on 7 May 1759. {Ref: ARDE I:26; ARPA (2nd Series) 2:585}

VAUGHAN, ABRAHAM (Maryland), b. c1732, son of Abraham and Caty or Laty Vaughan, of Patapsco Hundred. {Ref: BCF:657} Pvt., Capt. Tobias Stansbury's Company Muster Roll, Baltimore Co., circa 1757-1758, exact dates not given; bill of credit issued or paid to him for £3.16.0 on 25 Mar 1767. {Ref: MSA S960 or S752, p. 186}

VAUGHAN, GIST (Maryland), b. c1735, MD, son of Abraham and Caty or Laty Vaughan, of Patapsco Hundred. {Ref: BCF:657} Pvt., Capt. Christopher Gist's Company of VA Militia, 13 Jul 1756, enlisted at Baltimore (b. MD, age 21). {Ref: MSR I:37}

VAUGHAN, THOMAS (Maryland), pvt., Capt. William McClellan's Company of MD Volunteers, Frederick Co., circa 1763-1764; on muster roll dated 15 Nov 1764 at Camp at the Forks of Muskingham. {Ref: ARMD 32:99}

VAUGHAN, WILLIAM (Maryland), pvt., Capt. Alexander Beall's Company of MD Troops, Frederick Co., from 1 Jun 1758 (transferred from Capt. Richard Pearis' Company where he had been a sgt.) and served to 8 Nov 1758 when he was reported as discharged; sgt., Capt. John Dagworthy's Company of MD

Troops, Frederick Co., from 31 Dec 1758 to 28 Feb 1759, having transferred from Capt. Alexander Beall's Company, and reportedly deserted; however, payment to him was recorded in Col. Dagworthy's account book on 15 Jul 1762. {Ref: MHS MS.375; CSOS:78, 82; MHS MS.375.1}

VEARS, WILLIAM (Maryland), pvt., Capt. William Luckett's Company Muster Roll, Frederick Co., circa 1757-1758, exact dates not given (served 30 days); bill of credit issued or paid in his behalf to William Luckett, Jr. for £1.10.0 on 6 Apr 1767. {Ref: MSA S960 or S752, p. 170; CSOS:99}

VEAST, JACOB (Maryland), pvt., Capt. John Middaugh's Company Muster Roll, Frederick Co., circa 1757-1758, exact dates not given (served 30 days); bill of credit issued or paid to him for £1.10.0 in 1767, exact date not given. {Ref: MSA S960 or S752, p. 173; CSOS:101}

VEATCH, JAMES (Maryland), pvt., Capt. William Luckett's Company Muster Roll, Frederick Co., circa 1757-1758, exact dates not given (served 30 days); bill of credit issued or paid in his behalf to William Luckett, Jr. for £1.10.0 on 6 Apr 1767; name mistakenly transcribed once as "James Neatch." {Ref: MSA S960 or S752, p. 169; CSOS:99}

VEAZEY, JOHN (Maryland), b. 12 Feb 1701/2, Cecil Co., son of Edward Veazey and Susanna (N), m. Rebecca Ward, had children Edward, John Ward, William, Thomas Brockus, and Rebecca, and d. 4 May 1777, Cecil Co., of smallpox; planter, gentleman by 1724, deputy surveyor in 1734, county justice (1734-1754), captain by 1736, naval officer of Cecil County District (1743-1754), major in the militia by 1748, esquire by 1752, colonel by 1756, county commander in 1758, and member of MD Assembly (1761, 1768-1774, served on the Arms and Ammunition Committee). {Ref: BDML II:850; ARMD 31:244} Militia pay account submitted in 1758, exact date not given. {Ref: MHM 9:4, p. 370} See "Henry Ward," q.v.

VENABLES, LAWRENCE (Maryland), pvt., Capt. Joshua Beall's Company Muster Roll, Prince George's Co., circa 1757-1758, exact dates not given; bill of credit issued or paid to him for £1.6.0 in 1767, exact date not given. {Ref: MSA S960 or S752, p. 185}

VERNOR (VENOR), GEORGE (Maryland), pvt., Capt. Thomas Norris' Company, Frederick Co., circa 1757-1758, exact dates not given (served 30 days); bill of credit issued or paid in his behalf to Jacob Yingland on 10 Apr 1767 for £1.10.0. {Ref: MSA S960 or S752, p. 176; CSOS:108}

VICKERS (VICARS), JOSEPH (Maryland), pvt., Capt. Henry Casson's Company Muster Roll, Queen Anne's Co., circa 1757-1758, exact dates not given (served 27 days); bill of credit issued to him for £1.7.0 in 1767, exact date not given. {Ref: MSA S960 or S752, p. 178; CSOS:109}

VINE, GODFREY (Maryland), b. 5 Jul 1733, Baltimore Co., son of Godfrey Vine and Sarah Beddoes (who m. 17 Feb 1732/3 in Queen Anne's Co., St. Paul's P. E. Parish, and subsequently removed to Baltimore Co., St. George's P. E. Parish). {Ref: BCF:658} Pvt., Capt. Tobias Stansbury's Company, Baltimore Co., circa 1757-1758, exact dates not given; bill of credit issued or paid to him for £1.18.0 in 1767, exact date not given. {Ref: MSA S960 or S752, p. 188}

VINING, JOHN (Delaware), colonel, Regt. of Militia for Kent Co. on Delaware, 1756. {Ref: ARDE I:12; ARPA (2nd Series) 2:527-529; HDE I:141} Patriot who served as a Justice of the Peace and a Justice of the Supreme Court, 1756-1761; d. 1793, buried in the Episcopal Cem. at New Castle. {Ref: GRSD 1:14; RPDE:276}

VINNEY, PETER (Delaware), b. c1734, Newport, DE (shoemaker, age 24 in 1758); pvt., enlisted 24 Apr 1758 "for the campaign in the lower counties" by Capt. John McClughan. {Ref: ARDE I:18; ARPA (2nd Series) 2:570}

VOLGAMOT, JOSEPH, see "Joseph Wolgamot," q.v.

WAGGAMAN, HENRY (Maryland), b. c1715, prob. Accomack Co., VA, son of Jonathan Waggaman and Margaret Eliot, m. Mary Woolford circa 1740, had children John Elliott, William Elliott, George, Henry, Sarah, Elizabeth, and Mary, and d. by 15 Apr 1761, Somerset Co., MD; mariner, merchant, captain by 1745, county justice (1746-1760), member of the MD Assembly (1749-1760), and major by 1759. {Ref: BDML II:851-852; ARMD 55:64; *MD Gazette*, 11 Dec 1760}

WAHACKEY, Indian Chief, see "Daniel Wolstenholme," q.v.

WALDRAVEN, TOBIAS (Delaware), b. c1739, New Castle, DE (tanner, age 20 in 1759); pvt., enlisted by Capt. James Armstrong for the PA Regt. on 26 Apr 1759. {Ref: ARDE I:26; ARPA (2nd Series) 2:585}

WALHATTER (WALHATTERS), GEORGE (Maryland), pvt., Capt. John White's Company Muster Roll, Frederick Co., circa 1757-1758, exact dates not given (served 6 days); bill of credit issued or paid to him for £0.6.0 in 1767, exact date not given. {Ref: MSA S960 or S752, p. 166; CSOS:96}

WALKER, AGNES, see "William Lux," q.v.

WALKER, CHARLES (Maryland), pvt., Capt. Moses Chapline's Company Muster Roll No. 3, Frederick Co., circa 1757-1758, exact dates not given (served 6 days); bill of credit issued or paid in his behalf to Joseph Chaplin for £0.6.0 on 24 Apr 1767. {Ref: MSA S960 or S752, p. 198; CSOS:115}

WALKER, JAMES (Delaware), lieut., Mill Creek Hundred, Upper Regt. of Militia, North Division, New Castle Co., 1756. {Ref: ARDE I:11; ARPA (2nd Series) 2:526; HDE I:141}

WALKER, JOHN (Maryland), pvt., Capt. Moses Chapline's Company Muster Roll, Frederick Co., circa 1757-1758, exact dates not given (served 6 days). {Ref: CSOS:115}

WALKER, NATHAN (Maryland), pvt., Capt. John Dagworthy's Company of MD Troops, Frederick Co., circa 9 Oct 1757 to 26 Apr 1759. {Ref: MHS MS.375.1; CSOS:79} payment recorded in Col. Dagworthy's account book on 11 Jul 1762 for work on Fort Cumberland. {Ref: MHS MS.375}

WALKER, RICHARD (Maryland), pvt., Capt. Joshua Beall's Company Muster Roll, Prince George's Co., circa 1757-1758, exact dates not given; bill of credit issued or paid to him for £2.3.0 on 15 Apr 1767; name listed once as "Richard Walker, Jr." {Ref: MSA S960 or S752, pp. 184-185; CSOS:117}

WALKER, WILLIAM (Delaware), pvt., Capt. Richard McWilliams' Company of Foot, New Castle Co., enlisted 28 Dec 1757. {Ref: ARDE I:14}

WALKER, ZACHARIAH (Maryland), pvt., Capt. Peter Bainbridge's Company Muster Roll, Frederick Co., circa 1757-1758, exact dates not given (served 28 days); bill of credit issued or paid in his behalf to Joseph Chaplin on 5 Mar 1767 for £1.8.0. {Ref: MSA S960 or S752, p. 181; CSOS:111} Pvt., Capt. Joseph Chapline's Company Muster Roll No. 1, Frederick Co., circa 1757-1758, exact dates not given (served 32 days); bill of credit issued or paid in his behalf to Joseph Chaplin for £1.12.0 on 5 Mar 1767. {Ref: MSA S960 or S752, p. 191; CSOS:103} Pvt., Capt. Moses Chapline's Company Muster Roll No. 1, Frederick Co., circa 1757-1758, exact dates not given (served 55 days); bill of credit issued or paid in his behalf to Joseph Chaplin for £2.15.0 on 5 Mar 1767. {Ref: MSA S960 or S752, p. 196; CSOS:113}

WALL, HENRY (Maryland), pvt., Capt. John White's Company Muster Roll, Frederick Co., circa 1757-1758, exact dates not given (served 6 days); bill of credit issued or paid to him for £0.6.0 in 1767, exact date not given. {Ref: MSA S960 or S752, p. 166; CSOS:96}

WALLACE, CHARLES (Maryland), b. 27 Apr 1727, Anne Arundel Co., son of John Wallace and Anne (N), St. Anne's Parish, m. 1st to Catherine (N) circa 1749, m. 2nd to Mary Rankin (widow of George Rankin and dau. of Constantine Bull) on 26 Apr 1798, poss. had children Charles, Catherine, and others who did not survive him, and d. 13 Feb 1812 at his home near South River; patriot, staymaker, tavern keeper, land developer, merchant, gentleman, Annapolis councilman (1757-1765), chairman of the Committee of Observation in 1775, tax commissioner (1778-1783), Judge of the Court of Appeals in 1786, paymaster for the MD troops (1776-1780), and member of the Executive Council (1783-1785). {Ref: BDML II:854-856; AACR:94} Pay account submitted for quartering soldiers in 1757 or 1758, exact dates not given. {Ref: MHM 9:3, p. 261}

WALLACE, ELIZABETH AND HANNA, see "William Wallace," q.v.

WALLACE, RICHARD JR. (Delaware), pvt., Kent Co. Militia, Capt. John Caton's Company, 25 Apr 1757 (date of muster roll). {Ref: ARDE I:13}

WALLACE, SAMUEL (Maryland), pvt., Capt. William Luckett's Company Muster Roll, Frederick Co., circa 1757-1758, exact dates not given (served 30 days); bill of credit issued or paid in his behalf to William Luckett, Jr. for £1.4.0 on 6 Apr 1767. {Ref: MSA S960 or S752, p. 169; CSOS:100}

WALLACE, WILLIAM (Delaware), pvt., Kent Co. Militia, Capt. John Caton's Company, 25 Apr 1757 (date of muster roll). {Ref: ARDE I:14} *Identification problem:* There were three men with this name who could have served in the war: (1) William Wallace d. intestate by 27 Aug 1779 at which time letters of administration were granted to Hannah Wallace and Layton Jones; (3) William Wallace d. intestate by 2 Oct 1783 at which time letters of admin. were granted to Jonathan Clampit; and, (3) William Wallace d. intestate by 8 Oct 1789 at which time letters of administration were granted to Elizabeth Wallace. {Ref: CDSS:220}

WALLER, JOHN (Maryland), pvt., Capt. Joseph Chapline's Company Muster Roll No. 4, Frederick Co., circa 1757-1758, exact dates not given (served 7 days); bill of credit issued or paid in his behalf to Joseph Chaplin for £0.7.0 on 5 Mar

1767; name transcribed once as "John Walter." {Ref: MSA S960 or S752, p. 194; CSOS:105} Pvt., Capt. Joseph Chapline's Company Muster Roll No. 5, Frederick Co., circa 1757-1758, exact dates not given; bill of credit issued or paid in his behalf to Joseph Chaplin for £0.8.0 on 5 Mar 1767. {Ref: MSA S960 or S752, p. 195}

WALLING, DELASHMUT (Maryland), pvt., Capt. Elias Delashmutt's Company Muster Roll, Frederick Co., 13 Aug 1757, exact dates not given (served 52 days); bill of credit issued or paid in his behalf to Joseph Chapline on 8 Jun 1767 for £2.12.0. {Ref: MSA S960 or S752, p. 163; CSOS:98} Pvt., Capt. John White's Company Muster Roll, Frederick Co., circa 1757-1758, exact dates not given (served 6 days); bill of credit issued or paid in his behalf to Joseph Chaplin on 9 Jun 1767 for £0.6.0; name mistakenly listed once as "Elashmut Walling." {Ref: MSA S960 or S752, p. 164; CSOS:95}

WALLING, JAMES SR. (Maryland), patriot and poss. soldier (rank not specified), Frederick Co., militia pay account submitted in 1758, exact date not given. {Ref: MHM 9:4, p. 370}

WALSH, EDWARD (Maryland), indentured servant and soldier who served in the French and Indian War some time between 1756 and 1763 (exact dates not known); his master Gilbert Crocket, planter, requested compensation from the Baltimore County Court due to the loss of use of Walsh while in the service. {Ref: MHM 94:4, p. 426, citing Baltimore Co. Court Minutes}

WALTER, DANIEL (Maryland), m. Sarah (N), had children Sarah, Levi, John, David, Clement, Samuel, Ann, Walter, and William, and d. testate by 12 Apr 1768. {Ref: WMG 3:1, p. 40} Pvt., Capt. William Luckett's Company Muster Roll, Frederick Co., circa 1757-1758, exact dates not given (served 30 days); bill of credit issued or paid in his behalf to William Luckett, Jr. for £1.10.0 on 6 Apr 1767. {Ref: MSA S960 or S752, p. 170; CSOS:100}

WALTER, DAVID (Maryland), pvt., Capt. William Luckett's Company Muster Roll, Frederick Co., circa 1757-1758, exact dates not given (served 30 days); bill of credit issued or paid in his behalf to William Luckett for £1.4.0 on 18 Jun 1768; name mistakenly transcribed once as "David Walton." {Ref: MSA S960 or S752, p. 170; CSOS:100}

WALTER, JACOB (Maryland), pvt., Capt. Thomas Norris' Company, Frederick Co., circa 1757-1758, exact dates not given (served 30 days); bill of credit issued or paid in his behalf to Valentine Rinehart on 6 May 1767 for £1.10.0. {Ref: MSA S960 or S752, p. 176; CSOS:108}

WALTER, JACOB (Maryland), pvt., Capt. John Middaugh's Company Muster Roll, Frederick Co., circa 1757-1758, exact dates not given (served 30 days); bill of credit issued or paid in his behalf to Casper Shaff for £1.10.0 on 2 Mar 1767. {Ref: MSA S960 or S752, p. 171; CSOS:101}

WALTER, JOHN (Maryland), pvt., Capt. William Luckett's Company Muster Roll, Frederick Co., circa 1757-1758, exact dates not given (served 30 days); bill of credit issued or paid in his behalf to William Luckett, Jr. for £1.10.0 on 6 Apr 1767. {Ref: MSA S960 or S752, p. 169; CSOS:99}

WALTER, SAMUEL (Maryland), pvt., Capt. William Luckett's Company Muster Roll, Frederick Co., circa 1757-1758, exact dates not given (served 30 days);

bill of credit issued or paid in his behalf to William Luckett, Jr. for £1.10.0 on 6 Apr 1767. {Ref: MSA S960 or S752, p. 170; CSOS:99}

WALTERS, JACOB (Maryland), captain, Baltimore Co., by 1762; wife Sarah Walters d. 29 Sep 1762 at Patapsco in her 38th year. {Ref: *MD Gazette*, 7 Oct 1762}

WALTON (WALLEN?), JOHN (Maryland), pvt., Capt. John White's Company Muster Roll, Frederick Co., circa 1757-1758, exact dates not given (served 6 days); bill of credit issued or paid to him for £0.6.0 in 1767, exact date not given; name transcribed once as "John Wallen." {Ref: MSA S960 or S752, p. 165; CSOS:95}

WALTON, WILLIAM, see "John Stevenson," q.v.

WAPLES, BURTON (Delaware), b. 10 Feb 1719/20, son of William and Mary Waples, of St. George's Episcopal Church, m. Comfort Burton circa 1743 and had children Woolsey (b. 11 May 1744), Burton (b. 18 Jan 1745/6), Agness (b. 6 May 1747), William (1749-1752), Cornelius (b. 29 Dec 1750), Anne (1753-1758?), William (b. 3 Jul 1755), Comfort (b. 8 May 1757), and Patience (b. 6 Aug 1759); prob. died in 1796; captain who was paid in 1776 "for answering an alarm" and served as a Justice of the Peace in 1778. {Ref: CFD 2:201; RPDE:279} Captain, Southern District of Indian River Hundred, Militia Regt. of Sussex Co., 1756-1758. {Ref: ARDE I:13, 15; ARPA (2nd Series) 2:529, 579; HDE I:141; CDSS:220}

WARD, ELIZABETH, see "John Thompson," q.v.

WARD, HENRY (Maryland), b. c1710, Cecil Co., son of John Ward and Mary (N), m. Hannah Ricketts on 9 May 1739, had sons Henry and John, and d. by 17 Jul 1760 of smallpox; planter, county coroner in 1746, captain by 1758 (dates of service not indicated), and member of the MD Assembly (1754-1760, served on the Arms and Ammunition Committee). {Ref: BDML II:859; ARMD 56:xxxvii; *MD Gazette*, 28 Sep 1758 and 17 Jul 1760}

WARD, JOHN (Delaware), b. c1739, Donegal, Ireland (miller, age 20 in 1759); pvt., enlisted by Capt. James Armstrong for the PA Regt. on 6 May 1759. {Ref: ARDE I:26; ARPA (2nd Series) 2:585}

WARD, JOHN (Delaware), b. c1719, Jersey (age 40 in 1759); pvt., enlisted in Capt. John Wright's Company and mustered on 11 May 1759. {Ref: ARDE I:25; ARPA (2nd Series) 2:592}

WARD, MATTHEW TILGHMAN, see "Matthew Tilghman," q.v.

WARD, NICHOLAS (Maryland), recruiting officer for the regt. of Light Infantry in 1758, reported that Daniel Richardson had deserted and when found he should be delivered to the sheriff of Prince George's Co. {Ref: *MD Gazette*, 20 Apr 1758}

WARD, REBECCA, see "John Veazey," q.v.

WARD, SAMUEL (Maryland), pvt., Capt. Joshua Beall's Company of MD Troops, Prince George's Co., from 9 Oct 1757 to 7 Dec 1757 when he was discharged. {Ref: MHS MS.375.1; CSOS:86} Payment to him was recorded in Col. Dagworthy's account book on 24 Jul 1762. {Ref: MHS MS.375}

WARDROP, JAMES, see "Joseph Sim," q.v.

WARDROP, LETTICE, see "Joseph Sim," q.v.

WARE, FRANCIS (Maryland), b. c1732, prob. Charles Co. (aged about 42 in 1774 deposition and aged about 47 in 1779 deposition), son of Francis Ware, m. Ann (N) by 1764 (no known children), and d. after 1798, Charles Co.; planter, captain by 1756, gentleman by 1764, esquire by 1776, member of the MD Assembly (1765-1776, 1783-1784), served in the Revolutionary War (captain, 1775; lieut. colonel, 1776; county lieutenant, 1777-1782, and colonel by 1780), and sheriff (1785-1788). {Ref: BDML II:861; MGSB 34:3, p. 273} Capt., MD Troops, Charles Co., from 9 Oct 1757 to 30 Dec 1758 (muster roll); payment to him was recorded in Col. Dagworthy's account book on 13 Jul 1762 and 26 Feb 1763. {Ref: MHS MS.375; CSOS:87; MHS MS.375.1} He also received £250 from the MD Assembly in December 1765 for his services and expenses during the French and Indian War. {Ref: ARMD 59:196, 251} See "Bennett Jackson" and "Edward Hubbart," q.v.

WARE, JAMES (Maryland), pvt., Capt. William McClellan's Company of MD Volunteers, Frederick Co., circa 1763-1764; on muster roll dated 15 Nov 1764 at Camp at the Forks of Muskingham. {Ref: ARMD 32:99}

WARFIELD, ELINOR, see "Edward Dorsey," q.v.

WARFIELD, RICHARD, see "Charles Ridgely," q.v.

WARING, BASIL, see "Joshua Beall," q.v.

WARING, ELIZABETH, see "Joshua Beall," q.v.

WARING, FRANCIS (Maryland), major, Prince George's Co., by 1760, chief justice and one of the representatives of his county, d. 1769 at his home. {Ref: ARMD 56:288; *MD Gazette*, 23 Feb 1769} See "Robert Richards," q.v.

WARNER, MARY, see "William Rasin," q.v.

WARNER, SAMUEL (Maryland), pvt., Capt. Peregrine Brown's Company Muster Roll, Kent Co., circa 1757-1758, exact dates not given (served 15 days); bill of credit issued or paid in his behalf to Robert Buchanan on 21 Mar 1767 for £0.15.0; name listed once as "Samuel Warner or Warren." {Ref: MSA S960 or S752, pp. 179-180; CSOS:110}

WARREN, BASIL (Maryland), pvt., Capt. Henry Casson's Company Muster Roll, Queen Anne's Co., circa 1757-1758, exact dates not given (served 27 days); bill of credit issued and ordered "his assignment to J. Lockerman paid his adm." (unnamed) on 2 Nov 1773 for £1.7.0. {Ref: MSA S960 or S752, p. 178; CSOS:109}

WARREN, BENJAMIN JR. (Delaware), ensign, Murderkill Hundred, Militia of Kent Co. on Delaware, 1756; resigned in March 1758; pvt. in Capt. Thomas Rodney's Dover Light Infantry Co. in 1776, commissioned lieut. in the 2nd Regt., Kent Co. Militia, on 7 Aug 1780, and served in the Continental Army until 1 Nov 1780. {Ref: ARDE I:12, 15; ARPA (2nd Series) 2:527, 577; HDE I:141; RPDE:280-281}

WARRINGTON, ZACHARIAH (Delaware), b. c1740, Angola Hundred, DE (planter, age 18 in 1758); pvt., enlisted 20 Apr 1758 "for the campaign in the lower counties" by Capt. John McClughan. {Ref: ARDE I:18; ARPA (2nd Series) 2:570}

WASHINGTON, GEORGE, see "Christopher Gist" and "William Fitzhugh," q.v.

WATERS, ESTHER, see "Henry Lowes," q.v.

WATERS, JAMES (Maryland), pvt., Capt. Richard Pearis' Company of MD Troops, Frederick Co., circa 9 Oct 1757 to 31 May 1758; pvt., Capt. Joshua Beall's Company of MD Troops, Prince George's Co., from 1 Jun 1758 to 10 Oct 1758, having transferred from Capt. Richard Pearis' Company (name listed as "James Waters, Jr."). {Ref: MHS MS.375.1; CSOS:86, 91} Payment to him was recorded in Col. Dagworthy's account book on 15 Jul 1762. {Ref: MHS MS.375}

WATERS, NATHAN (Maryland), patriot, Annapolis, Anne Arundel Co., pay account submitted for quartering soldiers in 1757 or 1758, exact dates not given. {Ref: MHM 9:3, p. 260}

WATKINS, ELIZABETH, see "Henry Hall," q.v.

WATKINS, FRANCES, see "John Hammond Dorsey," q.v.

WATKINS, GASSAWAY (Maryland), b. 25 Apr 1733, Anne Arundel Co., son of Nicholas and Margaret Watkins, St. Anne's Parish. {Ref: AACR:49} Pvt., Capt. Samuel Chapman's Company Muster Roll, Anne Arundel Co., circa 1757-1758, exact dates not given; bill of credit issued or paid to him for £1.18.0 on 11 Mar 1767. {Ref: MSA S960 or S752, p. 188}

WATKINS, JAMES (Delaware), b. c1732, England (laborer, age 26 in 1758); pvt., recruited by Capt. Benjamin Noxon and enlisted on 3 May 1758. {Ref: ARDE I:19; ARPA (2nd Series) 2:566}

WATKINS, JOHN, see "Henry Hall," q.v.

WATKINS, JOSEPH (Maryland), b. 23 Feb 1734/5, Anne Arundel Co., son of Nicholas and Margaret Watkins, St. Anne's Parish. {Ref: AACR:49} Pvt., Capt. Samuel Chapman's Company Muster Roll, Anne Arundel Co., circa 1757-1758, exact dates not given; bill of credit issued or paid to him for £1.18.0 on 11 Mar 1767. {Ref: MSA S960 or S752, p. 188} See "Samuel Gardner," q.v.

WATKINS, NICHOLAS, see "Gassaway Watkins," q.v.

WATKINS, ROBERT (Maryland), pvt., Capt. Elias Delashmutt's Company Muster Roll, Frederick Co., circa 1757-1758, exact dates not given (served 30 days); bill of credit issued or paid in his behalf to Elias Delashmut, Jr. on 16 Mar 1767 for £1.10.0. {Ref: MSA S960 or S752, p. 162; CSOS:94}

WATKINS, SAMUEL (Maryland), pvt., Capt. Samuel Chapman's Company Muster Roll, Anne Arundel Co., circa 1757-1758, exact dates not given; bill of credit issued or paid to him for £1.18.0 on 11 Mar 1767. {Ref: MSA S960 or S752, p. 188}

WATKINS, STEPHEN (Maryland), pvt., Capt. Samuel Chapman's Company Muster Roll, Anne Arundel Co., circa 1757-1758, exact dates not given; bill of credit issued or paid to him for £1.18.0 on 10 Mar 1767. {Ref: MSA S960 or S752, p. 188} See "Anthony Smith," q.v.

WATKINS, THOMAS (Maryland), b. 14 Feb 1736/7, Anne Arundel Co., son of Nicholas and Margaret Watkins, St. Anne's Parish. {Ref: AACR:49} Pvt., Capt. Samuel Chapman's Company Muster Roll, Anne Arundel Co., circa 1757-1758, exact dates not given; bill of credit issued or paid to him for £1.18.0 on 11 Mar 1767. {Ref: MSA S960 or S752, p. 188}

WATKINSON, FRANCIS (Maryland), indentured servant and soldier who served in the French and Indian War some time between 1756 and 1763 (exact dates not known); his master Benjamin Tasker, iron manufacturer, requested compensation from the Baltimore County Court due to the loss of use of Watkinson while in the service. {Ref: MHM 94:4, p. 426, citing Baltimore Co. Court Minutes}

WATSON, BETHUEL (Delaware), son of Bethuel Watson (of Isaac) and Elizabeth Smith (dau. of David Smith), was still living in 1794 at which time his father wrote his will and named him the executor (probated 12 Sep 1797). {Ref: CFD 1:252} Lieut., Northern District of Cedar Creek Hundred, Militia Regt. of Sussex Co., 1756-1758. {Ref: ARDE I:13, 15; ARPA (2nd Series) 2:529, 579; HDE I:141}

WATSON, GEORGE (Maryland), pvt., Capt. John White's Company Muster Roll, Frederick Co., circa 1757-1758, exact dates not given (served 6 days); bill of credit issued or paid to him for £0.6.0 in 1767, exact date not given. {Ref: MSA S960 or S752, p. 166; CSOS:96} Pvt., Capt. Joseph Chapline's Company Muster Rolls No. 2 and 3, Frederick Co., circa 1757-1758, exact dates not given (served 4 days); bill of credit issued or paid in his behalf to Joseph Chaplin for £0.4.0 on 5 Mar 1767. {Ref: MSA S960 or S752, p. 193; CSOS:104}

WATSON, ISAAC (Delaware), prob. son of Isaac Watson (d. 1773) and Mary (N). {Ref: CFD 1:254} Lieut., Southern District of Cedar Creek Hundred, Militia Regt. of Sussex Co., 1756; lieut., Slaughter Neck District, 1758. {Ref: ARDE I:13, 15; ARPA (2nd Series) 2:529, 579; HDE I:141}

WATSON (WATTSON), JOHN (Maryland), pvt., Capt. Moses Chapline's Company Muster Roll No. 2, Frederick Co., circa 1757-1758, exact dates not given (served 13 days); bill of credit issued or paid in his behalf to Joseph Chaplin for £0.13.0 on 5 Mar 1767. {Ref: MSA S960 or S752, p. 197; CSOS:114} Pvt., Capt. Joseph Chapline's Company Muster Roll No. 4, Frederick Co., circa 1757-1758, exact dates not given (served 6 days); bill of credit issued or paid in his behalf to Joseph Chaplin for £0.6.0 on 5 Mar 1767. {Ref: MSA S960 or S752, p. 195; CSOS:105}

WATSON, WALTER (Maryland), pvt., Capt. Joshua Beall's Company Muster Roll, Prince George's Co., circa 1757-1758, exact dates not given; bill of credit issued or paid to him for £1.6.0 in 1767, exact date not given. {Ref: MSA S960 or S752, p. 185}

WATSON, WILLIAM (Maryland), pvt., Capt. Tobias Stansbury's Company Muster Roll, Baltimore Co., circa 1757-1758, exact dates not given; bill of credit issued or paid to him for £1.10.0 in 1767, exact date not given. {Ref: MSA S960 or S752, p. 188}

WATTS, HENRY (Maryland), pvt., Capt. John Dagworthy's Company of MD Troops, Frederick Co., from 9 Oct 1757 to 9 Nov 1758. {Ref: MHS MS.375.1; CSOS:79} He was paid £1 at Fort Frederick on 7 Nov 1758 "for coming express with a letter from the General at Rays Town" for the Western Expedition against Fort Duquesne. {Ref: ARMD 55:776} On 16 Apr 1761 he petitioned the MD Assembly for relief as a maimed soldier of the MD Service. {Ref: ARMD 56:408, 451} Payment to him was recorded in Col. Dagworthy's account book on 13 Jul 1762. {Ref: MHS MS.375}

WATTS, MARY, see "John Selby" and "Parker Selby," q.v.

WATTS, SAMUEL (Maryland), pvt., Capt. Richard Pearis' Company of MD Troops, Frederick Co., circa 9 Oct 1757 to 31 May 1758; pvt., Capt. Joshua Beall's Company of MD Troops, Prince George's Co., from 1 Jun 1758 to 30 Dec 1758 when he was discharged. {Ref: MHS MS.375.1; CSOS:86, 91} Payment to him was recorded in Col. Dagworthy's account book on 14 Jul 1762. {Ref: MHS MS.375}

WATTSON, HENRY (Maryland), pvt., Capt. John Dagworthy's Company of MD Troops, Frederick Co., circa 9 Oct 1757 to 26 Apr 1759. {Ref: MHS MS.375.1; CSOS:79} Payment to him was recorded in Col. Dagworthy's account book on 21 Jul 1762. {Ref: MHS MS.375}

WATTSON, MARY, see "Nehemiah Davis," q.v.

WATTSON, THOMAS, see "Nehemiah Davis," q.v.

WATTSON, WALTER (Maryland), pvt., Capt. Richard Pearis' Company of MD Troops, Frederick Co., circa 9 Oct 1757 to 31 May 1758; pvt., Capt. Joshua Beall's Company of MD Troops, Prince George's Co., from 1 Jun 1758 to 14 Sep 1758 when he was reported as killed; however, payment to him was recorded in Col. Dagworthy's account book on 15 Jul 1762. {Ref: MHS MS.375; CSOS:86, 91; MHS MS.375.1}

WATTWOOD, GEORGE (Delaware), b. Ireland (age not given); pvt. in 1756, who was reported by Lieut. Brehm at Frederick Town in Frederick Co., MD, as being a deserter from His Majesty's Royal American Regiment, and noting he had lived some time in and about New Castle, DE. {Ref: *MD Gazette*, 26 Aug 1756}

WAUGH, CATHERINE, see "Elias Delashmut, Jr.," q.v.

WAUGH, WILLIAM (Maryland), pvt., Capt. Peter Butler's Company Muster Roll, Frederick Co., circa 1757-1758, exact dates not given (served 34 days); bill of credit or order issued in his behalf for £1.14.0 and paid to Casper Shaff on 2 Mar 1767. {Ref: MSA S960 or S752, p. 167; CSOS:98}

WAUGHOP, ANN, see "Robert Chesley," q.v.

WAY, JOHN (Maryland), pvt. (age 25 in 1757) in Capt. Francis Ware's Company of MD Troops, Charles Co., reported as deserted in August 1757. {Ref: *MD Gazette*, 1 Sep 1757}

WEANER, CHRISTOPHER (Maryland), indentured servant and soldier who served in the French and Indian War some time between 1756 and 1763 (exact dates not known); his master Alexander Lawson, iron manufacturer, requested compensation from the Baltimore County Court due to the loss of use of Weaner while in the service. {Ref: MHM 94:4, p. 426, citing Baltimore Co. Court Minutes}

WEBB, ANN, see "John Webb," q.v.

WEBB, EDGAR (Maryland), pvt., Capt. Henry Casson's Company Muster Roll, Queen Anne's Co., circa 1757-1758, exact dates not given (served 27 days); bill of credit issued or paid in his behalf to Capt. Casson on 27 Mar 1767 for £1.7.0. {Ref: MSA S960 or S752, pp. 178-179; CSOS:109}

WEBB, JAMES (Maryland), pvt., Capt. Alexander Beall's Company of MD Troops, Frederick Co., circa 9 Oct 1757 to 30 Dec 1758. {Ref: MHS MS.375.1; CSOS:82} Payment to him was recorded in Col. Dagworthy's account book on 26 Feb 1763. {Ref: MHS MS.375}

WEBB, JOHN (Maryland), pvt., Capt. John White's Company Muster Roll, Frederick Co., circa 1757-1758, exact dates not given (served 6 days); bill of credit issued or paid to him for £0.6.0 in 1767, exact date not given. {Ref: MSA S960 or S752, p. 166; CSOS:95}

WEBB, JOHN (Delaware), m. Ann (N), had children Caleb, Daniel, Elizabeth, and Sarah, and d. testate by 1 Dec 1760. {Ref: CDSS:223} Pvt., Kent Co. Militia, Capt. John Caton's Company, 25 Apr 1757 (date of muster roll). {Ref: ARDE I:14}

WEBB, MARGARET (Maryland), patriot or poss. widow of soldier (unnamed), Frederick Co., pay account submitted in 1758, exact date not given. {Ref: MHM 9:4, pp. 366, 368}

WEBB, SAMUEL, see "Michael McDaniel," q.v.

WEBB, THOMAS (Maryland), b. 18 Sep 1736, Prince George's Co., son of Thomas Webb and Elizabeth Child, of Queen Anne's P. E. Parish. {Ref: PGCR 1:196} Pvt., Capt. Joshua Beall's Company Muster Roll, Prince George's Co., circa 1757-1758, exact dates not given; bill of credit issued or paid to him for £1.10.6 on 1 Jun 1767. {Ref: MSA S960 or S752, p. 184}

WEBB, WILLIAM (Maryland), pvt., Capt. Henry Casson's Company Muster Roll, Queen Anne's Co., circa 1757-1758, exact dates not given (served 27 days); bill of credit issued or paid in his behalf to Capt. Casson on 27 Mar 1767 for £1.7.0. {Ref: MSA S960 or S752, pp. 178-179; CSOS:109}

WEBSTER, ALICEANNA, see "Samuel Bond," q.v.

WEHAUN, HENRY (Maryland), pvt., Capt. Peter Butler's Company Muster Roll, Frederick Co., circa 1757-1758, exact dates not given (served 34 days); bill of credit or order issued in his behalf for £1.14.0 and paid to Thomas Cresap on 13 Mar 1767. {Ref: MSA S960 or S752, p. 168; CSOS:98}

WELDING, CHARLES JR. (Maryland), farmer; pvt., Capt. Peregrine Brown's 7th Co. of Foot Militia, Kent Co., on 19 Feb 1758, by which time he had enlisted, but reportedly refused to appear and serve in arms against the enemy. {Ref: ARMD 31:283, 288}

WELDON, DANIEL (Delaware), ensign, Appoquinimink Hundred, Lower Regt. of Militia, New Castle Co., 1756. {Ref: ARDE I:11; ARPA (2nd Series) 2:525; HDE I:141}

WELFLEY (WELSLEY?), CHARLES (Maryland), pvt., Capt. Stephen Rensburg's or Rensburger's Company Muster Roll, Frederick Co., circa 1757-1758, exact dates not given (served 34 days); bill of credit issued or paid in his behalf to Stephen Rensburger for £1.14.0 on 27 Mar 1767. {Ref: MSA S960 or S752, p. 183; CSOS:112}

WELLS, ALEXANDER, see "Charles Gosnell" and "William Igoe" and "William Bailey," q.v.

WELLS, ANN, see "George Wells" and "James Wells," q.v.

WELLS, BENJAMIN (Maryland), pvt., Capt. Joseph Chapline's Company Muster Roll No. 4, Frederick Co., circa 1757-1758, exact dates not given (served 6 days); bill of credit issued or paid in his behalf to Joseph Chaplin for £0.6.0 on 5 Mar 1767. {Ref: MSA S960 or S752, p. 195; CSOS:105}

WELLS, GEORGE (Maryland), patriot and poss. soldier (rank not specified), Frederick Co., militia pay account submitted in 1758, exact date not given. {Ref: MHM 9:4, p. 368}

WELLS, GEORGE (Delaware), prob. son of Thomas and Ann Wells, m. Hannah Cummins by 1757. {Ref: CFD 2:210-211} Pvt., New Castle Co. Militia, by 1758; promoted to ensign on 16 Jun 1758. {Ref: ARDE I:16; ARPA (2nd Series) 2:579}

WELLS, JAMES (Delaware), prob. son of Thomas and Ann Wells, m. Rebecca (N) by 1748 and had a son Thomas. {Ref: CFD 2:209-210} Ensign, Town of Dover, Militia of Kent Co. on Delaware, 1756. {Ref: ARDE I:12; ARPA (2nd Series) 2:527-529; HDE I:141}

WELLS, JAMES (Maryland), pvt., Capt. Thomas Norris' Company, Frederick Co., circa 1757-1758, exact dates not given (served 30 days); bill of credit issued or paid in his behalf to Michael McGuire on 27 Mar 1767 for £1.10.0. {Ref: MSA S960 or S752, p. 176; CSOS:108}

WELLS, JEREMIAH (Maryland), pvt., Capt. Joseph Chapline's Company Muster Roll No. 1, Frederick Co., circa 1757-1758, exact dates not given (served 7 days); bill of credit issued or paid in his behalf to Joseph Chaplin for £0.7.0 on 5 Mar 1767. {Ref: MSA S960 or S752, p. 191; CSOS:103} Pvt., Capt. Joseph Chapline's Company Muster Roll No. 4, Frederick Co., circa 1757-1758, exact dates not given (served 5 days); bill of credit issued or paid in his behalf to Joseph Chaplin for £0.5.0 on 5 Mar 1767; name transcribed once as "Jerome Wells." {Ref: MSA S960 or S752, p. 194; CSOS:105}

WELLS, MAJOR, see "Thomas Mains," q.v.

WELLS (WILLS), NATHANIEL (Maryland), pvt., Capt. Elias Delashmutt's Company Muster Roll, Frederick Co., circa 1757-1758, exact dates not given (served 30 days); bill of credit issued or paid in his behalf to Elias Delashmut, Jr. on 16 Mar 1767 for £1.10.0. {Ref: MSA S960 or S752, pp. 162-163; CSOS:94}

WELLS, RICHARD (Maryland), lieut., Capt. Thomas Norris' Company, Frederick Co., circa 1757-1758, exact dates not given (served 30 days); bill of credit issued or paid in his behalf to Thomas Owings on 15 May 1767 for £3.10.0. {Ref: MSA S960 or S752, pp. 176-177; CSOS:107}

WELLS, RICHARD (Delaware), Esq., m. (N), had a son Thomas (minor in 1767), and d. testate by 20 May 1767. {Ref: CDSS:224} Ensign in Capt. John Vining's Company, 1747-1748, during King George's War against Canada; captain, Kent Co., 17 Apr 1758; promoted to major "of the lower government on Delaware" in June 1758. {Ref: ARDE I:8, 16; ARPA (2nd Series) 2:579-580}

WELLS, THOMAS, see "George Wells" and "James Wells," q.v.

WELLS, WILLIAM (Maryland), pvt., Capt. Jonathan Hagar's Company Muster Roll, Frederick Co., circa 1757-1758, exact dates not given (served 6 days); bill of credit issued or paid to him for £0.6.0 in 1767, exact date not given. {Ref: MSA S960 or S752, p. 175; CSOS:106}

WELSH, ROBERT (Delaware), pvt., Capt. French Battell's Company of Lower County Provincials, enlisted 12 May 1758. {Ref: ARDE I:17; ARPA (2nd Series) 2:555}

WERTINBURGER (WITENBARKER), BARNET (Maryland), pvt., Capt. Peter Bainbridge's Company Muster Roll, Frederick Co., circa 1757-1758, exact dates not given (served 28 days); bill of credit issued or paid in his behalf to Casper Shaff on 4 Mar 1767 for £1.8.0. {Ref: MSA S960 or S752, pp. 180-181; CSOS:111}

WEST, STEPHEN, see "William Brown," q.v.

WEST, WILLIAM (Maryland), pvt., Capt. Alexander Beall's Company of MD Troops, Frederick Co., from 9 Oct 1757 to 23 Oct 1758 when he reportedly deserted; however, payment to him was recorded in Col. Dagworthy's account book on 13 Jul 1762. {Ref: MHS MS.375; CSOS:82; MHS MS.375.1}

WESTCOTT, THOMAS (Delaware), b. c1735, Indian River, MD (farmer, age 23 in 1758); pvt., enlisted 4 May 1758 "for the campaign in the lower counties" by Capt. John McClughan (muster roll dated 17 May 1758). {Ref: ARDE I:18; ARPA (2nd Series) 2:489, 570}

WESTFIELD, WILLIAM (Maryland), pvt., Capt. Tobias Stansbury's Company Muster Roll, Baltimore Co., circa 1757-1758, exact dates not given; bill of credit issued or paid in his behalf to Edmund Talbut for £1.19.0 on 20 Feb 1767. {Ref: MSA S960 or S752, p. 186}

WHEATLEY, NATHAN (Maryland), pvt., Capt. Henry Casson's Company Muster Roll, Queen Anne's Co., circa 1757-1758, exact dates not given (served 27 days); bill of credit issued or paid in his behalf to Capt. Casson on 27 Mar 1767 for £1.7.0. {Ref: MSA S960 or S752, p. 178; CSOS:109}

WHEELER, ALICE, see "William Wheeler," q.v.

WHEELER, ANNE, see "Owen Wheeler," q.v.

WHEELER, CHARLES (Maryland), cpl., Capt. John Dagworthy's Company of MD Troops, Frederick Co., from 9 Oct 1757 to 28 Jan 1759 when he reportedly deserted; however, payment to him was recorded in Col. Dagworthy's account book on 28 Feb 1763. {Ref: MHS MS.375; CSOS:78; MHS MS.375.1}

WHEELER, DINAH, see "John Cross," q.v.

WHEELER, ELIZABETH, see "Edward Gantt" and "William Wheeler," q.v.

WHEELER (WHELOR), OWEN (Delaware), m. Anne (N) and d. intestate by 11 May 1774. {Ref: CDSS:225} Pvt., Kent Co. Militia, Capt. John Caton's Company, 25 Apr 1757 (date of muster roll). {Ref: ARDE I:13}

WHEELER (WHELOR), WILLIAM (Delaware), pvt., Kent Co. Militia, Capt. John Caton's Company, 25 Apr 1757 (date of muster roll). {Ref: ARDE I:14} *Identification problem:* There were two men with this name who could have served in the war: (1) William Wheeler, shoemaker, m. Elizabeth (N), had sons William, Joseph, and Jesse, and d. testate by 9 Nov 1774; and, (2) William Wheeler m. Alice (N), had daus. Sarah and Mary, and d. intestate by 28 Aug 1782. {Ref: CDSS:225}

WHELLAN, LUKE (Delaware), b. c1723, Waterford, Ireland (miller, age 35 in 1758); pvt., enlisted 22 Apr 1758 "for the campaign in the lower counties" by Capt. John McClughan. {Ref: ARDE I:18; ARPA (2nd Series) 2:570}

WHETHERFORD (WHITHERFORD), THOMAS (Maryland), pvt., Capt. John Dagworthy's Company of MD Troops, Frederick Co., from 9 Oct 1757 to 26 Apr 1759. {Ref: MHS MS.375.1; CSOS:79} Payment to him was recorded in Col. Dagworthy's account book on 11 Jul 1762. {Ref: MHS MS.375}

WHETSTONE, CONROD (Maryland), pvt., Capt. John Middaugh's Company Muster Roll, Frederick Co., circa 1757-1758, exact dates not given (served 30 days); bill of credit issued or paid in his behalf to George Devilbiss for £1.10.0 on 22 May 1767. {Ref: MSA S960 or S752, p. 172; CSOS:101}

WHETSTONE, PETER (Maryland), pvt., Capt. Joseph Chapline's Company Muster Roll No. 1, Frederick Co., circa 1757-1758, exact dates not given (served 49 days); bill of credit issued or paid in his behalf to Joseph Chaplin for £2.9.0 on 13 Jun 1768. {Ref: MSA S960 or S752, p. 192; CSOS:103}

WHITAKER (WHITTAKER), ABRAHAM (Maryland), b. 1 Aug 1737, Baltimore Co., son of Charles and Mary Whitaker. {Ref: BCF:684} Pvt., Capt. Christopher Gist's Company of VA Militia, 13 Jul 1756, enlisted at Baltimore (age 19). {Ref: MSR I:37}

WHITAKER, BLANCH, see "John Long," q.v.

WHITAKER (WHITACRE, WHITEACRE), ISAAC (Maryland), b. 5 May 1735, Baltimore Co., son of Charles and Mary Whitaker, m. Sarah (N), and d. circa 1765. {Ref: BCF:684-685} Pvt., Capt. Christopher Gist's Company of VA Militia, 13 Jul 1756, enlisted at Baltimore, age 21. {Ref: MSR I:37} Pvt., Capt. Tobias Stansbury's Company Muster Roll, Baltimore Co., circa 1757-1758, exact dates not given; bill of credit or order issued to his admin. (unnamed) and paid to Abraham Jarrett for £1.18.0 on 11 Sep 1771. {Ref: MSA S960 or S752, pp. 187-188; CSOS:118}

WHITAKER, SARAH, see "Isaac Whitaker," q.v.

WHITAKER (WHITTACRE), WILLIAM (Maryland), pvt., Capt. Joshua Beall's Company Muster Roll, Prince George's Co., circa 1757-1758, exact dates not given; bill of credit issued or paid in his behalf to Robert Whitaker his exec. for £2.1.0 on 1 Apr 1767. {Ref: MSA S960 or S752, pp. 184-185; CSOS:116}

WHITAKER, ROBERT, see "William Whitaker" and "William White," q.v.

WHITE, BENJAMIN, see "William White," q.v.

WHITE, EDWARD (Maryland), pvt., Capt. Francis Ware's Company of MD Troops, Charles Co., from 9 Oct 1757 to 8 Jun 1758 (served 243 days). {Ref: MHS MS.375.1; CSOS:89} Payment to him was recorded in Col. Dagworthy's account book on 7 Mar 1763 for work on Fort Cumberland. {Ref: MHS MS.375}

WHITE, ELIZABETH, see "Richard White," q.v.

WHITE, JAMES (Maryland), ensign in Capt. Jonathan Hagar's Company Muster Roll, Frederick Co., circa 1757-1758, exact dates not given (served 6 days); bill of credit issued or paid to him for £0.12.0 in 1767, exact date not given. {Ref: MSA S960 or S752, p. 173; CSOS:106}

WHITE, JAMES (Maryland), sgt., Capt. Joshua Beall's Company Muster Roll, Prince George's Co., circa 1757-1758, exact dates not given; bill of credit issued or paid in his behalf to Davis Ross for £2.8.0 on 16 Mar 1767. {Ref: MSA S960 or S752, p. 184}

WHITE, JOHN (Maryland), captain, Frederick Co., circa 1757-1758, exact dates not given; militia pay account submitted in 1758, exact date not given. {Ref: CSOS:94; MHM 9:4, p. 368; CSOS:94} Bill of credit issued in his behalf to Joseph

Chaplin for £1 and paid to White's exec. (unnamed) on 5 Mar 1767. {Ref: MSA S960 or S752, p. 164} See "John Stull," q.v.

WHITE, JOHN (Maryland), pvt., Charles Co., received £5 bounty money on 15 Aug 1757 for enlisting in the militia. {Ref: ARMD 55:265, 619} Cpl., Capt. Francis Ware's Company of MD Troops, Charles Co., from 9 Oct 1757 (promoted to cpl. on 4 Nov 1757) to 16 Feb 1758 when he was discharged. {Ref: MHS MS.375.1; CSOS:89} Payment to him was recorded in Col. Dagworthy's account book on 7 Mar 1763. {Ref: MHS MS.375}

WHITE, LEONARD (Maryland), sgt., Capt. John White's Company Muster Roll, Frederick Co., circa 1757-1758, exact dates not given (served 6 days); bill of credit issued or paid to him for £0.8.0 in 1767, exact date not given. {Ref: MSA S960 or S752, p. 165; CSOS:95} Sgt., Capt. Henry Sneavely's Company Muster Roll, Frederick Co., circa 1757-1758, exact dates not given; bill of credit issued or paid to him for £0.8.0 in 1767, exact date not given. {Ref: MSA S960 or S752, p. 190}

WHITE, LYDIA, see "Richard White," q.v.

WHITE, MARTHA AND MARY, see "Richard White, " q.v.

WHITE, PETER (Maryland), ensign in Capt. John White's Company Muster Roll, Frederick Co., circa 1757-1758, exact dates not given; bill of credit issued or paid to him for £0.6.0 in 1767, exact date not given. {Ref: CSOS:94; MSA S960 or S752, p. 164}

WHITE, RACHEL AND REBECCA, see "Richard White," q.v.

WHITE, RICHARD (Delaware), pvt., Kent Co. Militia, Capt. John Caton's Company, 25 Apr 1757 (date of muster roll). {Ref: ARDE I:14} *Identification problem:* There were two men with this name who could have served in the war: (1) Richard White, the younger, m. Rebecca (N) and d. testate by 15 Feb 1777; and, (2) Richard White m. (N), had children William, Thomas, Martha, Lydia, Sarah, Mary, Rachel, and Elizabeth, and d. testate by 20 Jan 1794. {Ref: CDSS:226}

WHITE, SARAH, see "Richard White," q.v.

WHITE, THOMAS, see "Aquila Hall" and "Richard White," q.v.

WHITE, WILLIAM (Delaware), pvt., Kent Co. Militia, Capt. John Caton's Company, 25 Apr 1757 (date of muster roll). {Ref: ARDE I:14} *Identification problem:* There were three men with this name who could have served in the war: (1) William White m. Sarah (N) and d. intestate by 1 Nov 1762; (2) William White d. intestate by 28 Feb 1778 at which time letters of administration were granted to John Darrach; and, (2) William White m. Deborah (N) and d. intestate by 16 Feb 1793. {Ref: CDSS:226}

WHITE, WILLIAM (Delaware), b. c1734, Cedar Creek, DE (farmer, age 24 in 1758); pvt., enlisted 4 May 1758 "for the campaign in the lower counties" by Capt. John McClughan. {Ref: ARDE I:18; ARPA (2nd Series) 2:570} Also see the other William White above.

WHITE, WILLIAM (Maryland), b. 29 Jul 1735, Prince George's Co., son of Benjamin White and Ann Hilliard, of Queen Anne's P. E. Parish. {Ref: PGCR 1:198} Pvt., Capt. Joshua Beall's Company Muster Roll, Prince George's Co., circa 1757-1758, exact dates not given; bill of credit issued or paid in his behalf to Robert Whitaker for £2.3.0 on 1 Apr 1767. {Ref: MSA S960 or S752, p. 184}

WHITEHEAD, JOSIAH (Delaware), pvt., Kent Co. Militia, Capt. John Caton's Company, 25 Apr 1757 (date of muster roll). {Ref: ARDE I:13}

WHITEMAN (WHITMAN), FREDERICK (Maryland), pvt., Capt. Stephen Rensburg's or Rensburger's Company Muster Roll, Frederick Co., circa 1757-1758, exact dates not given (served 42 days); bill of credit issued or paid in his behalf to Casper Shaff for £2.2.0 on 2 Mar 1767. {Ref: MSA S960 or S752, p. 182; CSOS:112}

WHITEMORE (WHITMORE), JOHN (Maryland), pvt., Capt. Peter Butler's Company Muster Roll, Frederick Co., circa 1757-1758, exact dates not given (served 34 days); bill of credit or order issued in his behalf for £1.14.0 and paid to Casper Shaff on 2 Mar 1767. {Ref: MSA S960 or S752, p. 167; CSOS:98}

WHITFALL, HENRY or MARTIN (Maryland), pvt., Capt. Peter Butler's Company Muster Roll, Frederick Co., circa 1757-1758, exact dates not given; bill of credit or order issued to him for £1.14.0 on 20 Mar 1767 (one entry listed him as "Martin Whitfall" and another as "Henry or Martin Whitfall"). {Ref: MSA S960 or S752, p. 168}

WHITFORD, JOHN (Delaware), pvt., Capt. French Battell's Company of Lower County Provincials, enlisted 13 May 1758. {Ref: ARDE I:17; ARPA (2nd Series) 2:555}

WHITMAN, JOHN (Maryland), pvt., Capt. John Dagworthy's Company of MD Troops, Frederick Co., from 9 Oct 1757 to 8 Apr 1758, deserted on 3 Dec 1757, retaken on 9 Dec 1757 and discharged (exact date not given). {Ref: MHS MS.375.1; CSOS:79} Payment to him was recorded in Col. Dagworthy's account book on 8 Mar 1763. {Ref: MHS MS.375}

WHITMAN, JOHN (Maryland), sgt., Capt. John Dagworthy's Company, Frederick Co., by 10 Feb 1757 at which time he was stationed at Fort Frederick. {Ref: FCLR:60}

WHITNAL (WHITMALL), ROBERT (Maryland), clerk, Capt. John Middaugh's Company Muster Roll, Frederick Co., circa 1757-1758, exact dates not given (served 30 days); bill of credit issued or paid in his behalf to Thomas Beatty, Jr. for £1.10.0 on 3 Apr 1767. {Ref: MSA S960 or S752, pp. 172-173; CSOS:100}

WHITTEL (WHITTLE), WILLIAM (Delaware), lieut., St. George's Hundred, Lower Regt. of Militia, New Castle Co., 1756. {Ref: ARDE I:11; ARPA (2nd Series) 2:525; HDE I:141}

WHITTILO, DAVID (Delaware), pvt., Capt. Richard McWilliams' Company of Foot, New Castle Co., enlisted 28 Dec 1757. {Ref: ARDE I:15}

WHITTINGTON, BETTY, see "Benton Harris," q.v.

WHITTINGTON, WILLIAM (Maryland), pvt., Capt. Joshua Beall's Company of MD Troops, Prince George's Co., from 9 Oct 1757 to 29 Nov 1757 when he was discharged. {Ref: MHS MS.375.1; CSOS:86} Payment to him was recorded in Col. Dagworthy's account book on 24 Jul 1762. {Ref: MHS MS.375} See "Benton Harris," q.v.

WICKES, MARTHA, see "William Hynson," q.v.

WICKHAM, NATHANIEL (Maryland), m. (N), had children John, Robert, Joseph, Nathaniel, Elizabeth, and Sarah, and d. testate by 1 Dec 1778. {Ref: WMG 5:3, p. 132} Justice, colonel, and commander-in-chief of the militia in Frederick Co. by 1755. {Ref: ARMD 31:73-75}

WIDRUCK (WIDRICK), MARTIN (Maryland), pvt., Capt. Stephen Rensburg's or Rensburger's Company Muster Roll, Frederick Co., circa 1757-1758, exact dates not given (served 34 days); bill of credit issued or paid in his behalf to Stephen Rensburger for £1.14.0 on 27 Mar 1767. {Ref: MSA S960 or S752, p. 183; CSOS:112}

WIGGERS, ---- (Maryland), patriot, Frederick Co., was paid £1.6.0 on 7 Nov 1758 "for advising and assisting in laying out the new road" to Fort Frederick during the Western Expedition against Fort Duquesne. {Ref: ARMD 55:776}

WIGGINS, PHILIP (Maryland), pvt., Capt. Moses Chapline's Company Muster Roll No. 1, Frederick Co., circa 1757-1758, exact dates not given (served 55 days); bill of credit issued or paid in his behalf to Thomas Cresap for £2.15.0 on 13 Mar 1767. {Ref: MSA S960 or S752, p. 196; CSOS:113} Pvt., Capt. Moses Chapline's Company Muster Roll No. 3, Frederick Co., circa 1757-1758, exact dates not given (served 6 days); bill of credit issued or paid in his behalf to Thomas Cresap for £0.6.0 on 113 Mar 1767. {Ref: MSA S960 or S752, p. 198; CSOS:115}

WIGGINS, THOMAS (Maryland), pvt., Capt. Moses Chapline's Company Muster Roll No. 3, Frederick Co., circa 1757-1758, exact dates not given (served 6 days); bill of credit issued or paid in his behalf to Joseph Chapline for £0.6.0 on 8 Jun 1767. {Ref: MSA S960 or S752, p. 198; CSOS:115}

WIGGINS, THOMAS JR. (Maryland), pvt., Capt. Joseph Chapline's Company Muster Roll No. 1, Frederick Co., circa 1757-1758, exact dates not given (served 17 days); bill of credit issued or paid in his behalf to Michael Cresap for £0.17.0 on 20 Apr 1767. {Ref: MSA S960 or S752, p. 191; CSOS:103}

WILBURN, JOHN (Maryland), pvt., Capt. Joshua Beall's Company Muster Roll, Prince George's Co., circa 1757-1758, exact dates not given; bill of credit issued or paid to him for £1.6.0 in 1767, exact date not given. {Ref: MSA S960 or S752, p. 185}

WILBURN (WILBOURN), JOHN JR. (Maryland), pvt., Capt. Joshua Beall's Company Muster Roll, Prince George's Co., circa 1757-1758, exact dates not given; bill of credit issued or paid in his behalf to Dr. Richard Brookes for £1.10.6 on 13 Apr 1767. {Ref: MSA S960 or S752, p. 184}

WILCOCKS, ISAAC (Maryland), pvt., Capt. William McClellan's Company of MD Volunteers, Frederick Co., circa 1763-1764; on muster roll dated 15 Nov 1764 at Camp at the Forks of Muskingham. {Ref: ARMD 32:99}

WILCOXON, JOHN (Maryland), b. c1718, son of John Wilcoxon (d. by 1757), Frederick Co. (gave his age as 39 in a 1757 deposition). {Ref: FCLR:79-80} Pvt., Capt. Elias Delashmutt's Company Muster Roll, Frederick Co., circa 1757-1758, exact dates not given (served 30 days); bill of credit issued or paid in his behalf to William Luckett his admin. on 18 Jun 1768 for £1.10.0. {Ref: MSA S960 or S752, p. 163; CSOS:94}

WILES, GEORGE (Maryland), pvt., Capt. John White's Company Muster Roll, Frederick Co., circa 1757-1758, exact dates not given (served 6 days); bill of credit issued or paid to him for £0.6.0 in 1767, exact date not given. {Ref: MSA S960 or S752, p. 165; CSOS:95}

WILES, WILLIAM (Maryland), pvt., Capt. John White's Company Muster Roll, Frederick Co., circa 1757-1758, exact dates not given (served 6 days); bill of credit issued or paid to him for £0.6.0 in 1767, exact date not given. {Ref: MSA S960 or S752, p. 166; CSOS:95}

WILKINS, GABRIEL (Maryland), pvt., Capt. Joseph Chapline's Company Muster Roll No. 4, Frederick Co., circa 1757-1758, exact dates not given (served 6 days); bill of credit issued or paid in his behalf to Joseph Chaplin for Wilkins' exec. (unnamed) for £0.6.0 on 5 Mar 1767. {Ref: MSA S960 or S752, p. 195; CSOS:105}

WILKINS, THOMAS (Maryland), pvt., Capt. Moses Chapline's Company Muster Roll No. 1, Frederick Co., circa 1757-1758, exact dates not given (served 55 days); bill of credit issued or paid in his behalf to Joseph Chaplin for £2.15.0 on 5 Mar 1767. {Ref: MSA S960 or S752, p. 196; CSOS:113} Pvt., Capt. Joseph Chapline's Company Muster Roll No. 4, Frederick Co., circa 1757-1758, exact dates not given (served 7 days); bill of credit issued or paid in his behalf to Joseph Chaplin for £0.7.0 on 5 Mar 1767. {Ref: MSA S960 or S752, p. 194; CSOS:105}

WILKINS, THOMAS JR. (Maryland), pvt., Capt. Joseph Chapline's Company Muster Roll No. 1, Frederick Co., circa 1757-1758, exact dates not given (served 39 days); bill of credit issued or paid in his behalf to Joseph Chaplin for £1.19.0 on 5 Mar 1767; name listed once without the "Jr." {Ref: MSA S960 or S752, p. 191; CSOS:102}

WILKINS, WILLIAM (Maryland), m. Deborah Palmer on 19 Apr 1735 and had children Sarah (b. 22 Feb 1735/6) and William (b. 19 Jun 1737), St. Anne's Parish. {Ref: AACR:97-98} Patriot, Annapolis, Anne Arundel Co., pay account submitted for quartering soldiers in 1757 or 1758, exact dates not given. {Ref: MHM 9:3, p. 260}

WILKINSON (WILKENSON), ALEXANDER (Maryland), pvt., Capt. Francis Ware's Company of MD Troops, Charles Co., circa 9 Oct 1757 to 30 Dec 1758. {Ref: MHS MS.375.1; CSOS:89} Payment to him was recorded in Col. Dagworthy's account book on 12 Jul 1762. {Ref: MHS MS.375}

WILKINSON, JOHN (Maryland), patriot, Annapolis, Anne Arundel Co., pay account submitted for quartering soldiers in 1757 or 1758, exact dates not given. {Ref: MHM 9:3, p. 260}

WILKINSON, PHILIP (Maryland), pvt., Capt. Tobias Stansbury's Company Muster Roll, Baltimore Co., circa 1757-1758, exact dates not given; bill of credit or order issued and assigned to William Lux paid to Robert Adair for £1.19.0 on 1 Apr 1767. {Ref: MSA S960 or S752, pp. 186, 188}

WILKINSON, SUSANNAH, see "John Addison," q.v.

WILLIAMS, DERRICK (Delaware), lieut., Appoquinimink Hundred, Lower Regt. of Militia, New Castle Co., 1756; subscribed to the Oath of Fidelity and Allegiance in 1778. {Ref: ARDE I:11; ARPA (2nd Series) 2:525; RPDE:289}

WILLIAMS, DUNBAR or DUNBARR (Maryland), pvt., Capt. Joshua Beall's Company of MD Troops, Prince George's Co., from 9 Oct 1757 to 29 Nov 1757 when he was discharged. {Ref: MHS MS.375.1; CSOS:86} Payment to him was recorded in Col. Dagworthy's account book on 24 Jul 1762. {Ref: MHS MS.375}

WILLIAMS, GEORGE (Maryland), pvt., Capt. Joseph Chapline's Company Muster Roll No. 4, Frederick Co., circa 1757-1758, exact dates not given (served 6 days); bill of credit issued or paid in his behalf to Joseph Chaplin for £0.6.0 on 24 Apr 1767. {Ref: MSA S960 or S752, p. 195; CSOS:105}

WILLIAMS, JOHN (Delaware), cooper; pvt., Wilmington Township, enlisted by Capt. Samuel Grubb for the PA Regt. in 1759. {Ref: ARDE I:27}

WILLIAMS, JOHN (Delaware), b. c1739, Wales (laborer, age 20 in 1759); pvt., enlisted by Capt. James Armstrong for the PA Regt. on 5 May 1759. {Ref: ARDE I:26; ARPA (2nd Series) 2:585}

WILLIAMS, JOHN (Maryland), pvt., Capt. Richard Pearis' Company of MD Troops, Frederick Co., circa 9 Oct 1757 to 31 May 1758); pvt., Capt. Joshua Beall's Company of MD Troops, Prince George's Co., from 1 Jun 1758 to 30 Dec 1758 (reported as discharged, but actually transferred to another company); pvt., Capt. John Dagworthy's Company of MD Troops, Frederick Co., from 31 Dec 1758 to 22 Jan 1759 when he reportedly deserted; however, payment to him was recorded in Col. Dagworthy's account book on 7 Mar 1763. {Ref: MHS MS.375; CSOS:79, 91; MHS MS.375.1}

WILLIAMS, JOHN (Maryland), constable; pvt., Capt. Peregrine Brown's Company, Kent Co., on 19 Feb 1758, by which time he had enlisted, but reportedly refused to appear and serve in arms against the enemy. {Ref: ARMD 31:283}

WILLIAMS, JOHN, see "Peter Williams," q.v.

WILLIAMS, JOSEPH (Maryland), pvt., Capt. Jonathan Hagar's Company Muster Roll, Frederick Co., circa 1757-1758, exact dates not given (served 6 days); bill of credit issued or paid to him for £0.6.0 in 1767, exact date not given. {Ref: MSA S960 or S752, p. 175; CSOS:107}

WILLIAMS, JOSEPH (Maryland), pvt., Capt. Joshua Beall's Company of MD Troops, Prince George's Co., from 9 Oct 1757 to 30 Dec 1758; name listed once as "Joseph William." {Ref: MHS MS.375.1; CSOS:86} Payment to him was recorded in Col. Dagworthy's account book on 7 Mar 1763 for work on Fort Cumberland. {Ref: MHS MS.375}

WILLIAMS, JOSEPH (Maryland), b. 3 Mar 1727/8, Anne Arundel Co., son of Richard Williams and Eleanor Stockett, of All Hallow's Parish. {Ref: AACR:42} Pvt., Capt. Samuel Chapman's Company Muster Roll, Anne Arundel Co., circa 1757-1758, exact dates not given; bill of credit issued or paid in his behalf to Thomas Ijams for £1.18.0 on 12 Mar 1767. {Ref: MSA S960 or S752, p. 189}

WILLIAMS, MATTHEW (Maryland), pvt., Capt. Henry Casson's Company Muster Roll, Queen Anne's Co., circa 1757-1758, exact dates not given (served 27 days); bill of credit issued or paid in his behalf to Capt. Casson on 27 Mar 1767 for £1.7.0; name listed once as "Martin or Matthew Williams." {Ref: MSA S960 or S752, p. 178; CSOS:109}

WILLIAMS, MERCY, see "John Stull," q.v.

WILLIAMS, MORRIS (Maryland), pvt., Capt. Alexander Beall's Company, Frederick Co., by 1758. "In a suit by the Lord Proprietary against Daniel Cresap for 'buying an ammunition blanket from Morris Williams a soldier belonging to Captain Alexander Beall's Company' he was discharged upon paying the costs" in June Court 1758. {Ref: TWL:179, citing Frederick Co. Judgment Records}

WILLIAMS (WILLIAM), PETER (Maryland), b. 21 Jan 1736/7, Baltimore Co., son of John Williams and Margaret Clark, of St. George's P. E. Parish. {Ref: BCF:692} Pvt., Capt. Christopher Gist's Company of VA Militia, 13 Jul 1756, enlisted at Baltimore (b. MD, age 20). {Ref: MSR I:37}

WILLIAMS, RICHARD, see "Joseph Williams," q.v.

WILLIAMS, RUHAMAH, see "Joseph Chapline," q.v.

WILLIAMS, THOMAS (Maryland), pvt., Capt. Francis Ware's Company of MD Troops, Charles Co., circa 9 Oct 1757 and 30 Dec 1758; payment to him was recorded in Col. Dagworthy's account book on 12 Jul 1762. {Ref: MHS MS.375; CSOS:89; MHS MS.375.1}

WILLIAMS, THOMAS (Maryland), pvt., Capt. William McClellan's Company of MD Volunteers, Frederick Co., circa 1763-1764; on muster roll dated 15 Nov 1764 at Camp at the Forks of Muskingham. {Ref: ARMD 32:99}

WILLIAMS, WILLIAM (Delaware), captain, Appoquinimink Hundred, Lower Regt. of Militia, New Castle Co., 1756. {Ref: ARDE I:11; ARPA (2nd Series) 2:525; HDE I:141} Patriot who served as a Justice of the Peace, Justice of the Court of Oyer and Terminer, and Justice of the Court of Common Pleas, 1756-1761. {Ref: GRSD 1:13, 15}

WILLIAMSON, ALEXANDER (Maryland), captain by 1758, Kent Co. {Ref: *MD Gazette*, 28 Sep 1758}

WILLIAMSON, ELIZABETH, see "John Hall," q.v.

WILLIAMSON, JACOB (Delaware), pvt., Kent Co. Militia, Capt. John Caton's Company, 25 Apr 1757 (date of muster roll). {Ref: ARDE I:13}

WILLIAMSON, JOHN (Maryland), patriot, Kent Co., pay account submitted for quartering soldiers in 1757 or 1758, exact dates not given. {Ref: MHM 9:3, p. 261}

WILLIAMSON, MOSES (Maryland), pvt., Capt. Joseph Chapline's Company Muster Roll No. 4, Frederick Co., circa 1757-1758, exact dates not given (served 7 days); bill of credit issued or paid to him for £0.7.0 in 1767, exact date not given. {Ref: MSA S960 or S752, p. 195; CSOS:105}

WILLIAMSON, SARAH, see "William Hemsley," q.v.

WILLIAMSON, THOMAS (Delaware), ensign, White Clay Hundred, Upper Regt. of Militia, West Division, New Castle Co., 1756. {Ref: ARDE I:11; ARPA (2nd Series) 2:526; HDE I:141}

WILLIAMSON, THOMAS (Maryland), patriot, Annapolis, Anne Arundel Co., pay account submitted for quartering soldiers in 1757 or 1758, exact dates not given. {Ref: MHM 9:3, pp. 260-261}

WILLIARD (WILLYARD), ELIAS (Maryland), eldest son of Dawalt Williard (as named in his will written on 26 Nov 1781). {Ref: WMG 5:4, p. 170} Pvt., Capt. Peter Bainbridge's Company Muster Roll, Frederick Co., circa 1757-1758, exact dates not given; bill of credit issued or paid in his behalf to Casper Shaff on 2 Mar 1767 for £1.10.0; name listed once as "Elias Williar." {Ref: MSA S960 or S752, pp. 180-181; CSOS:111} Pvt., Capt. Moses Chapline's Company Muster Roll No. 1, Frederick Co., circa 1757-1758, exact dates not given (served 55 days); bill of credit issued or paid in his behalf to Casper Shaff for £2.15.0 on 2 Mar 1767. {Ref: MSA S960 or S752, p. 196; CSOS:113}

WILLIS, JOHN (Maryland), pvt., Capt. John Dagworthy's Company of MD Troops, Frederick Co. (transferred from Capt. Richard Pearis' Company where he had been a cpl.), from 1 Jun 1758 to 26 Dec 1758 when he reportedly deserted; however, payment to him was recorded in Col. Dagworthy's account book on 17 Jul 1762. {Ref: MHS MS.375; CSOS:79, 91; MHS MS.375.1}

WILLIS, THOMAS (Delaware), b. c1742, Sussex, DE (age 17 in 1759); pvt., enlisted in Capt. John Wright's Company and mustered on 11 May 1759. {Ref: ARDE I:25; ARPA (2nd Series) 2:592}

WILLMOTT, JOHN, see "Samuel Phillips," q.v.

WILLS, CALEB (Delaware), b. c1738, Sussex, DE (age 21 in 1759); pvt., enlisted in Capt. John Wright's Company and mustered on 11 May 1759. {Ref: ARDE I:25; ARPA (2nd Series) 2:592}

WILLS, LAWRENCE (Delaware), b. c1738, Sussex, DE (age 21 in 1759); pvt., enlisted in Capt. John Wright's Company and mustered on 11 May 1759. {Ref: ARDE I:25; ARPA (2nd Series) 2:592}

WILLSON, JOHN (Maryland), cpl., Capt. Joshua Beall's Company of MD Troops, Prince George's Co., from 9 Oct 1757 to 30 Dec 1758 (reduced to pvt. on 14 Oct 1757 and promoted to cpl. again on 14 Oct 1758). {Ref: MHS MS.375.1; CSOS:86} Payment to him was recorded in Col. Dagworthy's account book on 22 Jul 1762

WILLSON, JOHN (Delaware), m. Susannah (N), had children Nathan, Mary, Susannah, Hannah, Sarah, Ruth, Rachel, Elizabeth, Mariam, Margaret, Ann, and Lutisi, and d. testate by 30 Jul 1781. {Ref: CDSS:230} Pvt., Kent Co. Militia, Capt. John Caton's Company, 25 Apr 1757 (date of muster roll). {Ref: ARDE I:13}

WILLSON, JONATHAN (Maryland), b. c1715, Charles Co., son of John Willson and (N), m. Martha Briscoe in 1737, had a son John, and d. testate by 18 Oct 1806, Montgomery Co.; planter, gentleman, member of the MD Assembly (1749-1751), Frederick Co. justice (1763-1769), served on the Committee of Observation in 1774, tax commissioner in Montgomery Co. in 1777, and Judge of the Court of Appeals in 1778. {Ref: BDML II:893-894} Patriot and poss. soldier, Frederick Co., militia pay account submitted in 1758, exact date not given. {Ref: MHM 9:4, p. 366}

WILLSON, PETER (Maryland), pvt., Capt. John Dagworthy's Company of MD Troops, Frederick Co., from 9 Oct 1757 to 26 Dec 1758 when he reportedly deserted; however, payment to him was recorded in Col. Dagworthy's account book on 17 Jul 1762. {Ref: MHS MS.375; CSOS:79; MHS MS.375.1}

WILLSON, SUSANNAH, see "John Willson," q.v.

WILLSON, THOMAS JR. (Maryland), pvt., Capt. Richard Pearis' Company of MD Troops, Frederick Co., from 26 Oct 1757 to 31 May 1758; pvt., Capt. John

Dagworthy's Company of MD Troops, Frederick Co., from 1 Jun 1758 to 16 Apr 1759 when he reportedly deserted; however, payment to him was recorded in Col. Dagworthy's account book on 11 Jul 1762. {Ref: MHS MS.375; CSOS:79; MHS MS.375.1}

WILLSON, THOMAS SR. (Maryland), pvt., Capt. John Dagworthy's Company of MD Troops, Frederick Co., from 9 Oct 1757 to 18 Dec 1757 when he reportedly deserted; however, payment to him was recorded in Col. Dagworthy's account book on 26 Feb 1762 for work on Fort Cumberland. {Ref: MHS MS.375; CSOS:79; MHS MS.375.1}

WILLY, WAITMAN (Delaware), b. c1734, MD (age 25 in 1759); pvt., enlisted in Capt. John Wright's Company and mustered on 11 May 1759. {Ref: ARDE I:25; ARPA (2nd Series) 2:508, 592}

WILMER, EDWARD (Maryland), lieut., Capt. Jesse Hollingsworth's Company, by 1758; militia company departed Head of Elk in Cecil County and marched to Fort Frederick on 16 Aug 1758. {Ref: *MD Gazette*, 7 Sep 1758}

WILMER, MARY, see "William Ringgold," q.v.

WILMER, REBECCA, see "Thomas Ringgold" and "William Ringgold," q.v.

WILMER, SIMON (Maryland), b. 12 Apr 1713, Kent Co., son of Lambert Wilmer and Ann Pyner, m. Mary Price on 16 Sep 1735, had children Edward Price, Simon, John Lambert, James Jones, Mary, and Ann, and d. by 19 Jan 1769; planter, gentleman by 1741, sheriff (1738-1741), county justice (1744-1764), esquire by 1760, and member of the MD Assembly (1749-1751, 1762-1763). {Ref: ESVR; BDML II:896-897} Patriot and poss. soldier, militia pay account submitted in 1758, exact date not given. {Ref: MHM 9:4, p. 369}

WILSON, ADAM (Maryland), pvt., Capt. Joseph Chapline's Company Muster Roll No. 1, Frederick Co., circa 1757-1758, exact dates not given (served 21 days); bill of credit issued or paid in his behalf to Joseph Chaplin for £1.1.0 on 5 Mar 1767. {Ref: MSA S960 or S752, p. 191; CSOS:103} Pvt., Capt. Moses Chapline's Company Muster Roll No. 1, Frederick Co., circa 1757-1758, exact dates not given (served 55 days); bill of credit issued or paid in his behalf to Joseph Chaplin for £2.15.0 on 5 Mar 1767. {Ref: MSA S960 or S752, p. 196; CSOS:113} Pvt., Capt. Moses Chapline's Company Muster Roll No. 3, Frederick Co., circa 1757-1758, exact dates not given (served 6 days); bill of credit issued or paid in his behalf to Joseph Chaplin for £0.6.0 on 5 Mar 1767. {Ref: MSA S960 or S752, p. 198; CSOS:115}

WILSON, ALLAN (Delaware), pvt., Capt. Richard McWilliams' Company of Foot, New Castle Co., enlisted 28 Dec 1757. {Ref: ARDE I:14}

WILSON, AQUILLA (Maryland), b. c1735, MD; pvt., Capt. Christopher Gist's Company of VA Militia, 13 Jul 1756, enlisted at Baltimore (age 21). {Ref: MSR I:37}

WILSON, CORNELIUS (Maryland), pvt., Capt. Moses Chapline's Company Muster Roll No. 3, Frederick Co., circa 1757-1758, exact dates not given (served 6 days); bill of credit issued or paid in his behalf to Joseph Chaplin for £0.6.0 on 24 Apr 1767; name was listed once as "Cornelius Wilson or Wooleson." {Ref: MSA S960 or S752, p. 198; CSOS:115}

WILSON, GEORGE (Maryland), pvt., Capt. William Luckett's Company Muster Roll, Frederick Co., circa 1757-1758, exact dates not given (served 30 days); bill of credit issued or paid in his behalf to William Luckett, Jr. for £1.10.0 on 6 Apr 1767. {Ref: MSA S960 or S752, p. 169; CSOS:99}

WILSON, HILLARY (Maryland), sgt., Calvert Co., Capt. Sutton Isaac's Militia Co. in the Upper Hundred of the Cliffs; sent to the Western Frontier to help defend against the Indians circa 1756-1757 (exact dates not given). {Ref: HCC:121-122}

WILSON, JAMES (Maryland), pvt., Capt. Peter Bainbridge's Company Muster Roll, Frederick Co., circa 1757-1758, exact dates not given (served 36 days); bill of credit issued or paid in his behalf to Joseph Chaplin on 25 Apr 1767 for £1.16.0. {Ref: MSA S960 or S752, p. 181; CSOS:111}

WILSON, JAMES (Maryland), pvt., Capt. Moses Chapline's Company Muster Roll No. 1, Frederick Co., circa 1757-1758, exact dates not given (served 55 days); bill of credit issued or paid in his behalf to Joseph Chaplin for £2.15.0 on 5 Mar 1767. {Ref: MSA S960 or S752, p. 196; CSOS:113} Pvt., Capt. Moses Chapline's Company Muster Roll No. 2, Frederick Co., circa 1757-1758, exact dates not given (served 14 days); bill of credit issued or paid in his behalf to Joseph Chaplin for £0.14.0 on 5 Mar 1767. {Ref: MSA S960 or S752, p. 197; CSOS:114} Pvt., Capt. Moses Chapline's Company Muster Roll No. 3, Frederick Co., circa 1757-1758, exact dates not given (served 6 days); bill of credit issued or paid in his behalf to Joseph Chaplin for £0.6.0 on 5 Mar 1767. {Ref: MSA S960 or S752, p. 198; CSOS:115} Pvt., Capt. Joseph Chapline's Company Muster Roll No. 1, Frederick Co., circa 1757-1758, exact dates not given (served 3 days); bill of credit issued or paid in his behalf to Joseph Chaplin for £0.3.0 on 5 Mar 1767. {Ref: MSA S960 or S752, p. 191; CSOS:103}

WILSON, JOSEPH (Maryland), pvt., Capt. Elias Delashmutt's Company Muster Roll, Frederick Co., 13 Aug 1757, exact dates not given (served 52 days); bill of credit issued or paid in his behalf to James Smith on 18 May 1767 for £2.12.0. {Ref: MSA S960 or S752, p. 163; CSOS:98} Pvt., Capt. Moses Chapline's Company Muster Roll No. 2, Frederick Co., circa 1757-1758, exact dates not given (served 14 days); bill of credit issued or paid in his behalf to James Smith for £0.14.0 on 18 May 1767. {Ref: MSA S960 or S752, p. 197; CSOS:114}

WILSON, JOSEPH, see "Samuel Wilson," q.v.

WILSON, JOSIAH (Maryland), pvt., Capt. William Luckett's Company Muster Roll, Frederick Co., circa 1757-1758, exact dates not given (served 30 days); bill of credit issued or paid in his behalf to William Luckett, Jr. for £1.10.0 on 6 Apr 1767. {Ref: MSA S960 or S752, p. 170; CSOS:100}

WILSON, JOSIAS (Maryland), lieut., Calvert Co., Capt. Sutton Isaac's Militia Co. in the Upper Hundred of the Cliffs; sent to the Western Frontier to help defend against the Indians circa 1756-1757 (exact dates not given). {Ref: HCC:121-122}

WILSON, NATHAN (Maryland), pvt., Capt. Henry Casson's Company Muster Roll, Queen Anne's Co., circa 1757-1758, exact dates not given (served 27 days); bill of credit issued or paid in his behalf to Capt. Casson for Wilson's exec. (unnamed) on 27 Mar 1767 for £1.7.0. {Ref: MSA S960 or S752, p. 178; CSOS:109}

WILSON, SAMUEL (Delaware), b. c1743, Kennett, PA (laborer, age 15 in 1758); pvt., enlisted 12 May 1758 "for the campaign in the lower counties" by Capt. John McClughan. {Ref: ARDE I:18; ARPA (2nd Series) 2:570}

WILSON, SAMUEL (Delaware), pvt., Kent Co. Militia, Capt. John Caton's Company, 25 Apr 1757 (date of muster roll). {Ref: ARDE I:14}

WILSON, SAMUEL (Maryland), b. c1736 (aged 40 in 1776), son of Joseph Wilson and Hannah Farmer, of St. George's P. E. Parish, and d. by 7 Feb 1785. {Ref: BCF:697} Pvt., Capt. Christopher Gist's Company of VA Militia, 13 Jul 1756, enlisted at Baltimore (b. MD, age 19). {Ref: MSR I:37}

WILSON, SARAH, see "William Wilson," q.v.

WILSON, SOLOMON (Delaware), b. c1740, Chester River, MD (laborer, age 18 in 1758); pvt., enlisted 1 May 1758 "for the campaign in the lower counties" by Capt. John McClughan (muster roll dated 17 May 1758). {Ref: ARDE I:18; ARPA (2nd Series) 2:489, 570}

WILSON, WILL (Maryland), b. c1738, MD; pvt., Capt. Henry Harrison's Company of VA Militia, 13 Jul 1756, enlisted in Baltimore (age 18). {Ref: MSR I:37}

WILSON, WILLIAM (Maryland), pvt., Capt. John Middaugh's Company Muster Roll, Frederick Co., circa 1757-1758, exact dates not given (served 30 days); bill of credit issued or paid in his behalf to Thomas Beatty, Jr. for £1.10.0 on 23 Feb 1767. {Ref: MSA S960 or S752, p. 171; CSOS:100}

WILSON, WILLIAM (Maryland), pvt., Capt. William Luckett's Company Muster Roll, Frederick Co., circa 1757-1758, exact dates not given (served 30 days); bill of credit issued or paid in his behalf to William Luckett, Jr. for £1.10.0 on 6 Apr 1767. {Ref: MSA S960 or S752, p. 170; CSOS:100}

WILSON, WILLIAM (Maryland), pvt., Capt. Tobias Stansbury's Company Muster Roll, Baltimore Co., circa 1757-1758, exact dates not given; bill of credit issued or paid in his behalf to Robert Cummins for £1.18.0 on 1 Oct 1776 *[sic]*. {Ref: MSA S960 or S752, p. 187} *Identification problem:* There were four men with this name who could have served in the war: (1) William Wilson, of Pipe Creek Hundred, in 1750; (2) William Wilson, of Soldier's Delight Hundred, in 1750; (3) William Wilson, Jr., who owned land called *Rush Grove* in 1750; and, (4) William Wilson, b. 1 Jul 1738, son of William and Sarah Wilson. {Ref: BCF:698}

WILSON (WILLSON), WILLIAM (Maryland), pvt., Capt. Thomas Norris' Company, Frederick Co., circa 1757-1758, exact dates not given (served 30 days); bill of credit issued or paid in his behalf to Michael McGuire on 27 Mar 1767 for £1.10.0. {Ref: MSA S960 or S752, p. 176; CSOS:108}

WINCHESTER, WILLIAM (Maryland), b. 1710, son William Winchester II (1750-1812), and d. 1790; company clerk, Capt. Thomas Norris' Company, Frederick Co., circa 1757-1758, exact dates not given (served 30 days); bill of credit issued or paid in his behalf to Michael McGuire on 27 Mar 1767 for £1.10.0. {Ref: SCWM III:110, 271; MSA S960 or S752, pp. 176-177; CSOS:107}

WINDER (WINDERS), JAMES (Maryland), pvt., Capt. John White's Company Muster Roll, Frederick Co., circa 1757-1758, exact dates not given (served 6 days); bill of credit issued or paid to him for £0.6.0 in 1767, exact date not given. {Ref: MSA S960 or S752, p. 165; CSOS:95} Pvt., Capt. Henry Sneavely's

Company Muster Roll, Frederick Co., circa 1757-1758, exact dates not given; bill of credit issued or paid to him for £0.8.0 in 1767, exact date not given. {Ref: MSA S960 or S752, p. 190}

WINGFIELD, THOMAS (Maryland), pvt., Capt. Alexander Beall's Company of MD Troops, Frederick Co., circa 9 Oct 1757 to 30 Dec 1758; pvt., Capt. John Dagworthy's Company of MD Troops, Frederick Co., from 31 Dec 1758 to 22 Jan 1759 when he reportedly deserted; however, payment to him was recorded in Col. Dagworthy's account book on 7 Mar 1763 (name listed once as "Thomas Winfield"). {Ref: MHS MS.375; CSOS:79, 82; MHS MS.375.1}

WINROD, JACOB (Maryland), pvt., Capt. John Middaugh's Company Muster Roll, Frederick Co., circa 1757-1758, exact dates not given (served 30 days); bill of credit issued or paid in his behalf to Casper Shaff for £1.10.0 on 2 Mar 1767. {Ref: MSA S960 or S752, p. 171; CSOS:101}

WINSHART, JOHN (Maryland), patriot, Frederick Co., who performed "sundry services at the fort" in 1763 and payment in the amount of £3.19.6 was still owed to him on 25 Nov 1763 (when reported by the Accounts Committee to the MD Assembly). {Ref: ARMD 58:400}

WINTER (WINTERS), GEORGE (Maryland), pvt., Capt. John White's Company Muster Roll, Frederick Co., circa 1757-1758, exact dates not given (served 6 days); militia pay account submitted in 1758, exact date not given. {Ref: MHM 9:4, p. 366} Bill of credit issued or paid to him for £0.6.0 in 1767, exact date not given. {Ref: MSA S960 or S752, p. 166; CSOS:95}

WISE, ABRAHAM (Maryland), pvt., Capt. John Middaugh's Company Muster Roll, Frederick Co., circa 1757-1758, exact dates not given (served 30 days); bill of credit issued or paid in his behalf to Casper Shaff for £1.10.0 on 2 Mar 1767. {Ref: MSA S960 or S752, p. 171; CSOS:101}

WISE, DANIEL (Maryland), pvt., Capt. John Middaugh's Company Muster Roll, Frederick Co., circa 1757-1758, exact dates not given (served 30 days); bill of credit issued or paid in his behalf to Peter Bainbridge for £1.10.0 on 13 Apr 1767. {Ref: MSA S960 or S752, p. 172; CSOS:101}

WISE, GEORGE (Maryland), pvt., Capt. Stephen Rensburg's or Rensburger's Company Muster Roll, Frederick Co., circa 1757-1758, exact dates not given (served 42 days); bill of credit issued or paid in his behalf to Casper Shaff for £2.2.0 on 2 Mar 1767. {Ref: MSA S960 or S752, p. 182; CSOS:112}

WISE, HANNAH, see "John Scarborough," q.v.

WISE, HENRY (Maryland), pvt., Capt. Tobias Stansbury's Company Muster Roll, Baltimore Co., circa 1757-1758, exact dates not given; bill of credit issued or paid in his behalf to Thomas Cockey Deye for £1.19.0 on 13 Jun 1768. {Ref: MSA S960 or S752, p. 187}

WISE, HENRY (Maryland), pvt., Capt. Peter Butler's Company Muster Roll, Frederick Co., circa 1757-1758, exact dates not given (served 34 days); bill of credit or order issued in his behalf for £1.14.0 and paid to Casper Shaff on 2 Mar 1767. {Ref: MSA S960 or S752, p. 167; CSOS:98}

WISE, JOHN (Maryland), pvt., Capt. Stephen Rensburg's or Rensburger's Company Muster Roll, Frederick Co., circa 1757-1758, exact dates not given (served 42 days); bill of credit or order issued in his behalf to Casper Shaff for £2.2.0 and paid to David Cumming on 18 Apr 1767. {Ref: MSA S960 or S752, p. 183; CSOS:112}

WISE, PETER (Maryland), pvt., Capt. John Middaugh's Company Muster Roll, Frederick Co., circa 1757-1758, exact dates not given (served 30 days); bill of credit issued or paid in his behalf to Peter Bainbridge for £1.10.0 on 13 Apr 1767. {Ref: MSA S960 or S752, p. 172; CSOS:101}

WISE, VALENTINE (Maryland), pvt., Capt. John Middaugh's Company Muster Roll, Frederick Co., circa 1757-1758, exact dates not given (served 30 days); bill of credit issued or paid in his behalf to Casper Shaff for £1.10.0 on 2 Mar 1767. {Ref: MSA S960 or S752, p. 171; CSOS:101}

WITHERS, WILLIAM (Maryland), alias William Deloney *[sic]*, an Irishman and soldier, Frederick Co. (age about 34 in 1756), was reported by Capt. Dagworthy as being a deserter from the MD Forces at Fort Frederick in July 1756. {Ref: *MD Gazette*, 5 Aug 1756}

WITHERS, WILLIAM (Maryland), ensign in Capt. Jesse Hollingsworth's Company, by 1758; militia company departed Head of Elk in Cecil County and marched to Fort Frederick on 16 Aug 1758. {Ref: *MD Gazette*, 7 Sep 1758}

WITHERSPOON (WETHERSPOON), DAVID (Delaware), lieut. colonel, Lower Regt. of Militia, New Castle Co., 1756. {Ref: ARDE I:11; ARPA (2nd Series) 2:525; HDE I:141} Patriot who served as a Justice of the Peace, Justice of the Court of Oyer and Terminer, and Justice of the Court of Common Pleas in 1756. {Ref: GRSD 1:13}

WITHERSPOON, ROBERT (Delaware), b. c1737, Down, Ireland (weaver, age 22 in 1759); pvt., enlisted by Capt. James Armstrong for the PA Regt. on 1 May 1759. {Ref: ARDE I:26; ARPA (2nd Series) 2:585}

WOGAN, HENRY (Maryland), cpl., Capt. Joshua Beall's Company of MD Troops, Prince George's Co., from 9 Oct 1757 to 8 Nov 1758. {Ref: MHS MS.375.1; CSOS:86} Payment to him was recorded in Col. Dagworthy's account book on 12 Jul 1762 for work on Fort Cumberland. {Ref: MHS MS.375}

WOLF, REES or RICE (Delaware), lieut., Southern District of Lewes and Rehoboth Hundred, Militia Regt. of Sussex Co., 1756-1758 (name listed once as "Rees Woolf, Sr."). {Ref: ARDE I:13, 15; ARPA (2nd Series) 2:529, 579; HDE I:141} *Identification problem:* There were two men with this name who could have served in the war: (1) Rees Wolf, innholder, m. (N), had a dau. Mary, and d. testate in Lewes by 21 Apr 1773; and, (2) Reece Wolfe m. Mary (N), had children Reece, William, Daniel, Harry, George, Benjamin, David, Comfort, Sarah, and Jane, and d. testate by 10 May 1797. {Ref: CDSS:232}

WOLFE, JOHN (Maryland), indentured servant and soldier who served in the French and Indian War some time between 1756 and 1763 (exact dates not known); his master Alexander Lawson, iron manufacturer, requested compensation from the Baltimore County Court due to the loss of use of Wolfe while in the service. {Ref: MHM 94:4, p. 426, citing Baltimore Co. Court Minutes}

WOLGAMOTT (WOLGOMAT), JOHN (Maryland), m. Mary (N), had children John, Joseph, Susanna, and Mary, and d. testate by 18 Jul 1774. {Ref: WMG 4:2, p. 65} Captain, MD Volunteers, Frederick Co., circa 1763-1764; on muster roll dated 15 Nov 1764 at Camp at the Forks of Muskingham. {Ref: ARMD 32:99} See "Henry Bouquet," q.v.

WOLGAMOTT (WOLGOMAT), JOHN (Maryland), pvt., Capt. Joseph Chapline's Company Muster Roll No. 1, Frederick Co., circa 1757-1758, exact dates not given (served 18 days); bill of credit issued or paid in his behalf to Joseph Chaplin for £0.18.0 on 24 Apr 1767. {Ref: MSA S960 or S752, p. 192; CSOS:103}

WOLGAMOTT (WOLGOMOT), JOSEPH (Maryland), m. Catherine (N), had children Joseph, David, Ann, Hester, Elizabeth, and Sarah, and d. testate by 12 Jan 1775. {Ref: WMG 4:3, p. 122} Pvt., Capt. Jonathan Hagar's Company Muster Roll, Frederick Co., circa 1757-1758, exact dates not given (served 6 days); bill of credit issued or paid in his behalf to Joseph Chaplin for £0.6.0 on 24 Apr 1767; name misspelled once as "Joseph Volgamot." {Ref: MSA S960 or S752, pp. 173, 175; CSOS:106} Militia pay account submitted in 1758, exact date not given; pay account submitted "for provisions found for Capt. Joseph Chapline's Company for 244 days," exact dates not given; name listed once as "Joseph Wolgemot" and once as "Joseph Vulgamott." {Ref: MHM 9:4, pp. 367-368} He was paid £4.15.0 at Fort Frederick on 14 Jun 1758 for carrying arms for the Western Expedition against Fort Duquesne. {Ref: ARMD 55:773}

WOLSTAD, MARY, see "Joshua Beall," q.v.

WOLSTENHOLME, DANIEL (Maryland), b. c1730, prob. in England, immigrated to MD by 1750, resided in Annapolis, m. Deborah (N) after 1763 (no known children), and d. testate by 22 Oct 1795, St. Mary's Company; planter, merchant, factor, supply agent in 1756; Indian agent appointed by the governor to treat with the Cherokee Indians at Fort Frederick in 1757; Collector of North Potomac (1760-1775); and, a loyalist during the Revolutionary War who refused to sign the Association of Freemen of Maryland in 1775. {Ref: BDML II:905-906; ARMD 203-204} He was paid £41.3.7½ by the MD Assembly in 1756 "for 80 blanketts for the ranging parties" for the support of the ranging parties on the Western Frontier. {Ref: ARMD 52:674} Pay account submitted for quartering soldiers in 1757 or 1758, exact dates not given. {Ref: MHM 9:3, p. 262} On 25 May 1757 Daniel Wolstenholme and John Ridout reported to the Governor of MD that "they arrived nine miles beyond Conegocheague near Fort Frederick on the 19th, were well received by the Cherokee Indians under Chief Wahackey ... Indians agreed to fight for the English against the French and the enemy Indians." {Ref: CMSP-The Black Books:135} In September 1758 "Daniel Wolstenholme, merchant in Annapolis, reported a prisoner who escaped from Shippensburg, a slave named Jack, who left with a deserter named Speakman, from Capt. Thompson's Light Horse." {Ref: *MD Gazette*, 14 Sep 1758} See "Robert Power," q.v.

WOOD, ABRAHAM (Maryland), patriot and poss. soldier (rank not specified), Kent Co., militia pay account submitted in 1758, exact date not given. {Ref: MHM 9:4, p. 369}

WOOD, DAVID (Maryland), farmer; pvt., Capt. Peregrine Brown's 7th Co. of Foot Militia, Kent Co., on 19 Feb 1758, by which time he had enlisted, but reportedly refused to appear and serve in arms against the enemy. {Ref: ARMD 31:283, 288}

WOOD, GABRIEL (Maryland), cpl., Capt. Joshua Beall's Company of MD Troops, Prince George's Co., from 9 Oct 1757 to 31 May 1758 when he reportedly deserted; however, payment to him was recorded in Col. Dagworthy's account book on 8 Mar 1763; name listed once as "Gabriel or Sabriet Wood." {Ref: MHS MS.375; CSOS:86; MHS MS.375.1}

WOOD, JOHN (Maryland), b. 14 Feb 1736/7, son of Joshua Wood and Mary Garrett, prob. m. Sarah (N) and had children Rebecca (b. 18 Oct 1759), Mary (b. 13 Jan 1762), Susanna (b. 18 Apr 1764), Sarah (b. 3 Apr 1768), Elizabeth (b, 9 Mar 1768), Joshua (b. 16 Mar 1773), and John (b. 19 Aug 1776). {Ref: BCF:701-702} Pvt., Capt. Tobias Stansbury's Company Muster Roll, Baltimore Co., circa 1757-1758, exact dates not given; bill of credit issued or paid in his behalf to John Hall, Jr. for £3.16.0 on 30 Apr 1767. {Ref: MSA S960 or S752, p. 186; CSOS:118}

WOOD, JOHN (Maryland), patriot, Frederick Co., who performed "sundry services at the fort" in 1763 and payment in the amount of £4.18.10 was still owed to him on 25 Nov 1763 (when reported by the Accounts Committee to the MD Assembly). {Ref: ARMD 58:400}

WOOD, JOHN (Maryland), patriot, Frederick Co., to whom £3 cash was issued at Fort Frederick on 7 Nov 1758 "to buy necessaries for the 3 people who were sent down the country in the smallpox from Fort Frederick to prevent the distemper's being communicated to the soldiers" during the Western Expedition against Fort Duquesne. {Ref: ARMD 55:776}

WOOD, ROBERT (Maryland), clerk, Capt. Peter Butler's Company Muster Roll, Frederick Co., circa 1757-1758, exact dates not given (served 34 days); bill of credit or order issued to him for £1.14.0 on 4 Mar 1767. {Ref: MSA S960 or S752, p. 167; CSOS:96} See "George Beatty," q.v.

WOOD, SARAH, see "John Wood," q.v.

WOOD, WILLIAM (Maryland), pvt., Capt. John Dagworthy's Company of MD Troops, Frederick Co., from 9 Oct 1757 to 11 Jul 1758. {Ref: MHS MS.375.1; CSOS:79} Payment to him was recorded in Col. Dagworthy's account book on 8 Mar 1763 for work on Fort Cumberland. {Ref: MHS MS.375}

WOODWARD, HENRY (Maryland), b. 21 Nov 1733, Anne Arundel Co., son of Amos Woodward and Acca or Achsah Dorsey (dau. of Caleb Dorsey), m. Mary Young on 8 Jan 1755, had daus. Rebecca, Achsah, Mary, and Harriet, and d. 16 Sep 1761; patriot, planter, merchant, businessman, horse breeder, gentleman by 1756, esquire by 1759, and member of the MD Assembly (1757-1758). {Ref: BDML II:906-907; *MD Gazette*, 24 Sep 1761; AACR:94-97} Pay account submitted for quartering soldiers in 1757 or 1758, exact dates not given. {Ref: MHM 9:3, p. 260}

WOOLEN (WOOLLEN), JAMES (Maryland), pvt., Capt. John White's Company Muster Roll, Frederick Co., circa 1757-1758, exact dates not given (served 6 days); bill of credit issued or paid to him for £0.6.0 in 1767, exact date not given. {Ref: MSA S960 or S752, p. 165; CSOS:95}

WOOLEN (WOOLLEN), JAMES JR. (Maryland), sgt., Capt. John White's Company Muster Roll, Frederick Co., circa 1757-1758, exact dates not given (served 6 days); bill of credit issued or paid in his behalf to Samuel Buzzard on 9 Jun 1767 for £0.6.0. {Ref: MSA S960 or S752, pp. 164-165; CSOS:94}

WOOLESON, CORNELIUS (Maryland), pvt., Capt. Moses Chapline's Company Muster Roll No. 3, Frederick Co., circa 1757-1758, exact dates not given (served 6 days); bill of credit issued or paid in his behalf to Joseph Chaplin for £0.6.0 on 24 Apr 1767; name was listed once as "Cornelius Wilson or Wooleson." {Ref: MSA S960 or S752, p. 198; CSOS:115}

WOOLEY, HANNAH, see "John Jones," q.v.

WOOLF (WOLF), ADAM (Maryland), pvt., Capt. Elias Delashmutt's Company Muster Roll, Frederick Co., circa 1757-1758, exact dates not given (served 30 days); bill of credit issued or paid in his behalf to Elias Delashmut, Jr. on 16 Mar 1767 for £1.10.0. {Ref: MSA S960 or S752, p. 163; CSOS:94} Pvt., Capt. Jonathan Hagar's Company Muster Roll, Frederick Co., circa 1757-1758, exact dates not given (served 6 days); bill of credit issued or paid to him for £0.6.0 in 1767, exact date not given. {Ref: MSA S960 or S752, p. 175; CSOS:106}

WOOLF, COMFORT, see "William Prettyman," q.v.

WOOLF, JOHN (Maryland), cpl., Capt. Jonathan Hagar's Company Muster Roll, Frederick Co., circa 1757-1758, exact dates not given (served 6 days); bill of credit issued or paid in his behalf to his exec. (unnamed) for £0.8.0 on 24 Apr 1767. {Ref: MSA S960 or S752, pp. 173, 175; CSOS:106} Cpl., Capt. Joseph Chapline's Company Muster Roll No. 1, Frederick Co., circa 1757-1758, exact dates not given (served 25 days); bill of credit issued or paid in his behalf to Joseph Chaplin for Woolf's exec. (unnamed) for £1.5.0 on 24 Apr 1767. {Ref: MSA S960 or S752, p. 192; CSOS:103}

WOOLF, NICHOLAS (Maryland), pvt., Capt. Jonathan Hagar's Company Muster Roll, Frederick Co., circa 1757-1758, exact dates not given (served 6 days); bill of credit issued or paid in his behalf to Joseph Chaplin for £0.6.0 on 8 Jun 1767. {Ref: MSA S960 or S752, pp. 173, 175; CSOS:106} Pvt., Capt. Joseph Chapline's Company Muster Roll No. 1, Frederick Co., circa 1757-1758, exact dates not given (served 31 days); bill of credit issued or paid in his behalf to Joseph Chaplin for £1.11.0 on 5 Mar 1767. {Ref: MSA S960 or S752, p. 191; CSOS:103}

WOOLF (WOLF, WOLFE), PAUL (Maryland), pvt., Capt. John Middaugh's Company Muster Roll, Frederick Co., circa 1757-1758, exact dates not given (served 30 days); bill of credit issued or paid in his behalf to Thomas Beatty, Jr. for £1.10.0 on 3 Apr 1767. {Ref: MSA S960 or S752, p. 172; CSOS:101}

WOOLF, SIMON (Maryland), pvt., Capt. Moses Chapline's Company Muster Roll No. 3, Frederick Co., circa 1757-1758, exact dates not given (served 6 days); bill of credit issued or paid in his behalf to James Smith for £0.6.0 on 18 May 1767. {Ref: MSA S960 or S752, p. 198; CSOS:115}

WOOLFORD, JAMES, see "Joseph Cox Gray," q.v.

WOOLFORD, MARY, see "Henry Waggaman," q.v.

WOOLRIDGE (WOOLDRIDGE), ROGER (Maryland), pvt., Capt. Richard Pearis' Company of MD Troops, Frederick Co., circa 9 Oct 1757 to 31 May 1758; pvt., Capt. Joshua Beall's Company of MD Troops, Prince George's Co., from 1 Jun 1758 to 1 Nov 1758 when he reportedly deserted; However, payment to him was recorded in Col. Dagworthy's account book on 15 Jul 1762. {Ref: MHS MS.375; CSOS:86, 91; MHS MS.375.1}

WOOTTARS, JOHN (Maryland), pvt., Capt. Henry Casson's Company Muster Roll, Queen Anne's Co., circa 1757-1758, exact dates not given (served 27 days); bill of credit issued or paid in his behalf to Capt. Casson on 27 Mar 1767 for £1.7.0; name listed once as "John Woollars." {Ref: MSA S960 or S752, p. 178; CSOS:109}

WOOTTON, THOMAS (Maryland), pvt., Capt. Samuel Chapman's Company Muster Roll, Anne Arundel Co., circa 1757-1758, exact dates not given; bill of credit issued or paid to him for £1.18.0 on 11 Mar 1767. {Ref: MSA S960 or S752, p. 188}

WOOTTON, WILLIAM TURNOR, see "Samuel Chapman," q.v.

WORBLE, JOHN (Maryland), pvt., Capt. Thomas Norris' Company, Frederick Co., circa 1757-1758, exact dates not given (served 30 days). {Ref: CSOS:108}

WORLEY, MICHAEL (Maryland), pvt., Capt. Thomas Norris' Company, Frederick Co., circa 1757-1758, exact dates not given (served 30 days); bill of credit issued or paid to him for £1.10.0 in 1767, exact date not given. {Ref: MSA S960 or S752, p. 177; CSOS:108}

WORT, ---- (Maryland), Frederick Co. "The little Pedler, well known by the name of Capt. Wort, who kept a store at Fort Frederick, and three of his associates, were lately killed by the enemy near Loyalhannon." {Ref: *MD Gazette*, 24 May 1759}

WORTENBURGER (WORTENBAKER), ADAM (Maryland), pvt., Capt. Peter Butler's Company Muster Roll, Frederick Co., circa 1757-1758, exact dates not given (served 34 days); bill of credit or order issued in his behalf for £1.14.0 and paid to Casper Shaff on 2 Mar 1767. {Ref: MSA S960 or S752, p. 167; CSOS:98}

WORTHINGTON, BRICE THOMAS BEALE (Maryland), b. 2 Nov 1727, Anne Arundel Co., son of Thomas Worthington and Elizabeth Ridgely, of St. Anne's Parish, m. his first cousin Anne Ridgely, had children Henry, John, Brice Thomas Beale Jr., Elizabeth, Sarah, Henrietta, and Polly, and d. 17 Jul 1794 at his plantation near Annapolis; miller, planter, gentleman, merchant by 1752, captain by 1756, member of the MD Assembly (1756-1774, 1781-1790), member of the MD Senate (1777-1781, 1791-1794), and member of the Committee of Observation (1775-1776) and Council of Safety (1776-1777). {Ref: BDML II:912-913; SCWM III:161, 272; ARMD 52:604; AACR:94}

WRIGHT, ABRAHAM (Maryland), pvt., Capt. William Luckett's Company Muster Roll, Frederick Co., circa 1757-1758, exact dates not given (served 30 days); bill of credit issued or paid in his behalf to William Luckett, Jr. for £1.10.0 on 6 Apr 1767. {Ref: MSA S960 or S752, p. 170; CSOS:99}

WRIGHT, EDWARD, see "Nathan or Nathaniel Wright," q.v.

WRIGHT, EZEKIEL (Delaware), pvt., Capt. Henry Vanbibber's Company of the Lower Counties on Delaware Troops at New Castle, enlisted on 10 May 1759. {Ref: ARDE I:26; ARPA (2nd Series) 2:594}

WRIGHT, GEORGE (Maryland), pvt., Capt. Francis Ware's Company of MD Troops, Charles Co., from 9 Oct 1757 to 8 Nov 1758 (served 396 days). {Ref:

MHS MS.375.1; CSOS:89} Payment to him was recorded in Col. Dagworthy's account book on 22 Feb 1763. {Ref: MHS MS.375}

WRIGHT, JOHN (Delaware), b. c1736, MD (laborer, age 22 in 1758); pvt., recruited by Capt. Benjamin Noxon and enlisted on 2 May 1758. {Ref: ARDE I:19; ARPA (2nd Series) 2:485, 566}

WRIGHT, JOHN (Delaware), 1st lieut., New Castle Co., 19 Apr 1758; capt., commissioned 24 May 1759. {Ref: ARDE I:16, 20; ARPA (2nd Series) 2:580, 582}

WRIGHT, MARY ANNE, see "William Hopper," q.v.

WRIGHT, NATHAN or NATHANIEL (Maryland), patriot and poss. soldier (rank not specified), Queen Anne's Co., militia pay account submitted in 1758, exact date not given. {Ref: MHM 9:4, p. 367} *Identification problem:* There were two men with this name who could have served in the war: (1) Nathaniel Wright (d. 1770, son of Solomon Wright); and, (2) Nathaniel Wright (d. 1794, son of Edward Wright). {Ref: BDML II:919-920}

WRIGHT, SOLOMON, see "Nathan or Nathaniel Wright," q.v.

WYCHEL, ADAM (Maryland), pvt., Capt. Peter Butler's Company Muster Roll, Frederick Co., circa 1757-1758, exact dates not given (served 34 days); bill of credit or order issued to him for £1.14.0 in March 1767. {Ref: MSA S960 or S752, p. 168; CSOS:98}

WYCHEL, BASTIAN (Maryland), pvt., Capt. Peter Butler's Company Muster Roll, Frederick Co., circa 1757-1758, exact dates not given (served 34 days); bill of credit or order issued in his behalf for £1.14.0 and paid to Peter Grosh on 4 Mar 1767. {Ref: MSA S960 or S752, p. 168; CSOS:98}

WYMER, FREDERICK (Maryland), pvt., Capt. Jonathan Hagar's Company Muster Roll, Frederick Co., circa 1757-1758, exact dates not given (served 6 days); bill of credit issued or paid to him for £0.6.0 in 1767, exact date not given. {Ref: MSA S960 or S752, p. 175; CSOS:106}

WYMORD, GEORGE (Maryland), pvt., Capt. Henry Sneavely's Company Muster Roll, Frederick Co., circa 1757-1758, exact dates not given; bill of credit issued or paid to him for £0.8.0 in 1767, exact date not given. {Ref: MSA S960 or S752, p. 190}

WYNKOOP (WYNCOOP), BENJAMIN (Delaware), b. 1734, son of Benjamin Wynkoop and Esther Fisher, removed to Philadelphia (merchant), m. Sarah Woodrop Sims by 1767, and d. after 1790. {Ref: CFD 4:235} Captain, Northern District of Cedar Creek Hundred, Militia Regt. of Sussex Co., 1756-1758. {Ref: ARDE I:13, 15; ARPA (2nd Series) 2:529, 579; HDE I:141}

YARDLEY, JOYCE, see "Nathan Baker," q.v.

YATES, ROBERT, see "Arthur Lee," q.v.

YEA, HENRY (Maryland), pvt., Capt. Alexander Beall's Company, Frederick Co., 1756-1757, recorded his discharge in Frederick Co. Court on 10 Aug 1757. Capt. Beall certified his service of 8 months and his receipt for clothing and pay was signed by Sgt. Robert Lenart and Sgt. George Barrance. Henry Yea made his "X" mark. {Ref: FCLR:30}

YEAST, GEORGE (Maryland), pvt., Capt. Peter Bainbridge's Company Muster Roll, Frederick Co., circa 1757-1758, exact dates not given (served 28 days);

bill of credit issued or paid in his behalf to Jacob Young on 4 Mar 1767 for £1.8.0. {Ref: MSA S960 or S752, p. 181; CSOS:111}

YELDELL, WILLIAM (Maryland), patriot, Annapolis, Anne Arundel Co., paid £11.10.0 by the MD Assembly in 1756 "for carting ammunition and blanketts" for the support of the ranging parties on the Western Frontier. {Ref: ARMD 52:674} Pay account submitted for quartering soldiers in 1757 or 1758, exact dates not given. {Ref: MHM 9:3, p. 261} Militia pay account submitted in 1758, exact date not given. {Ref: MHM 9:4, p. 368}

YINGLING (YINGLAND), JOHN (Maryland), patriot and poss. soldier in Capt. Thomas Norris' Company, Frederick Co., circa 1757-1758 (service and exact dates not given); bills of credit were issued to Jacob Yingland on 10 Apr 1767 for £1.10.0 each for soldiers "Paul Beard" and "John Stulman" and "George Vernor," q.v. {Ref: MSA S960 or S752, p. 176}

YINGLING (YINGLAND), ABRAHAM (Maryland), pvt., Capt. Thomas Norris' Company, Frederick Co., circa 1757-1758, exact dates not given (served 30 days); bill of credit was issued to Abraham Yingland for £1.10.0 and paid to Robert Davis on 15 Mar 1767. {Ref: MSA S960 or S752, p. 176; CSOS:108}

YOAKLEY (YOARKLEY), JOHN (Maryland), pvt., Capt. Peregrine Brown's Company Muster Roll, Kent Co., circa 1757-1758, exact dates not given (served 15 days); bill of credit issued or paid in his behalf to Robert Buchanan on 20 Feb 1767 for £0.15.0. {Ref: MSA S960 or S752, p. 180; CSOS:110}

YORK (YORKE, YOURK), JEREMIAH (Maryland), pvt., Capt. Moses Chapline's Company Muster Roll No. 2, Frederick Co., circa 1757-1758, exact dates not given (served 13 days); bill of credit issued or paid in his behalf to Joseph Chaplin for £0.13.0 on 5 Mar 1767. {Ref: MSA S960 or S752, p. 197; CSOS:114} Pvt., Capt. Joseph Chapline's Company Muster Roll No. 3, Frederick Co., circa 1757-1758, exact dates not given (served 7 days); bill of credit issued or paid to him for £0.7.0 in 1767, exact date not given; name mistakenly transcribed once as "Jerome York." {Ref: MSA S960 or S752, p. 193; CSOS:104} Pvt., Capt. John White's Company Muster Roll, Frederick Co., circa 1757-1758, exact dates not given (served 6 days); bill of credit issued or paid to him for £0.6.0 in 1767, exact date not given. {Ref: MSA S960 or S752, p. 166; CSOS:95}

YORKSON, JOHN (Delaware), b. c1738, MD (carpenter, age 20 in 1758); pvt., recruited by Capt. Benjamin Noxon and enlisted on 2 May 1758. {Ref: ARDE I:19; ARPA (2nd Series) 2:485, 566}

YOST, GEORGE (Maryland), alias George Yose or Gose *[sic]*, pvt., Capt. John Middaugh's Company Muster Roll, Frederick Co., circa 1757-1758, exact dates not given (served 30 days); bill of credit issued or paid in his behalf to Casper Shaff for £1.10.0 on 2 Mar 1767. {Ref: MSA S960 or S752, p. 171; CSOS:101}

YOUCHEY (YOUTCHEY), PETER (Maryland), pvt., Capt. Stephen Rensburg's or Rensburger's Company Muster Roll, Frederick Co., circa 1757-1758, exact dates not given (served 34 days); bill of credit issued or paid in his behalf to Jacob Young for £1.14.2 on 4 Mar 1767. {Ref: MSA S960 or S752, p. 182; CSOS:112}

YOUNG, BENJAMIN (Maryland), son of Hon. Benjamin Young; m. Mary Dulany, youngest dau. of Hon. Daniel Dulany, of Annapolis, on 10 Aug 1757; colonel, Baltimore Co., by 1757. {Ref: ARMD 56:316; *MD Gazette*, 18 Aug 1757}

YOUNG, GOODMAN (Delaware), b. c1736, Ireland (weaver, age 22 in 1758); pvt., recruited by Capt. Benjamin Noxon and enlisted on 3 May 1758. {Ref: ARDE I:19; ARPA (2nd Series) 2:566}

YOUNG, ISAAC (Delaware), b. c1739, Down, Ireland (laborer, age 20 in 1759); pvt., enlisted by Capt. James Armstrong for the PA Regt. on 7 May 1759. {Ref: ARDE I:26; ARPA (2nd Series) 2:585}

YOUNG, JACOB (Maryland), ensign in Capt. Peter Bainbridge's Company Muster Roll, Frederick Co., circa 1757-1758, exact dates not given (served 28 days); bill of credit issued or paid to him on 4 Mar 1767 for £2.16.0. {Ref: MSA S960 or S752, p. 180; CSOS:110}

YOUNG, JACOB (Maryland), weaver; pvt., Capt. Peter Bainbridge's Company Muster Roll, Frederick Co., circa 1757-1758, exact dates not given (served 30 days); bill of credit issued or paid to him for £1.10.0 in 1767, exact date not given; name mistakenly transcribed once as "Jacob Young Weaver." {Ref: MSA S960 or S752, p. 181; CSOS:111}

YOUNG, JAMES (Delaware or Pennsylvania), "Commiss. of the Musters" in the 3rd Bttn. of PA Regt. under Col. Hugh Mercer on 13 Jun 1759, including the three companies "of the lower counties" on Delaware. {Ref: ARDE I:20; CDSS:234}

YOUNG, JAMES (Delaware), pvt., Capt. Henry Vanbibber's Company of the Lower Counties on Delaware Troops at New Castle, enlisted on 23 May 1759. {Ref: ARDE I:26; ARPA (2nd Series) 2:594}

YOUNG, JAMES (Delaware), b. c1738, New England (weaver, age 20 in 1758); pvt., recruited by Capt. Benjamin Noxon and enlisted on 15 May 1758. {Ref: ARDE I:19; ARPA (2nd Series) 2:566}

YOUNG, JOHN (Delaware), pvt., Capt. French Battell's Company of Lower County Provincials, enlisted 15 May 1758. {Ref: ARDE I:17; ARPA (2nd Series) 2:555}

YOUNG, JOHN (Delaware), b. c1739, Ireland (weaver, age 20 in 1759); pvt., enlisted in Capt. John Wright's Company and mustered on 11 May 1759. {Ref: ARDE I:25; ARPA (2nd Series) 2:592}

YOUNG, JOHN (Maryland), pvt., Capt. Joshua Beall's Company Muster Roll, Prince George's Co., circa 1757-1758, exact dates not given; bill of credit issued or paid to him for £2.3.0 in 1767, exact date not given. {Ref: MSA S960 or S752, p. 185} He may have been the John Young who m. Anna Maria (N), had children George, Lodwick, Eve, Margrata, Catarina, and Maria, and d. testate by 27 Mar 1776 in Frederick Co. {Ref: WMG 5:1, p. 17}

YOUNG, JOSHUA (Maryland), pvt., Capt. William McClellan's Company of MD Volunteers, Frederick Co., circa 1763-1764; on muster roll dated 15 Nov 1764 at Camp at the Forks of Muskingham. {Ref: ARMD 32:99}

YOUNG, LODWICK or LODOWICK (Maryland), son of John (d. 1776) and Anna Maria Young. {Ref: WMG 5:1, p. 17} Pvt., Capt. Peter Butler's Company Muster Roll, Frederick Co., circa 1757-1758, exact dates not given (served 34 days);

bill of credit or order issued in his behalf to Casper Shaff for £1.14.0 and paid to David Cumming on 18 Apr 1767. {Ref: MSA S960 or S752, p. 168; CSOS:98}

YOUNG, MARY, see "Henry Woodward," q.v.

YOUNG, SAMUEL (Maryland), farmer, m. Elizabeth (N), had children Martha, Mary, John, and Alexander, and d. testate by 22 Aug 1781. {Ref: WMG 5:4, pp. 168-169} Lieut. in Capt. Tobias Stansbury's Company, Baltimore Co., circa 1757-1758, exact dates not given; bill of credit issued or paid in his behalf to Jonathan Plowman for £4.10.0 on 23 Feb 1767. {Ref: MSA S960 or S752, p. 187; CSOS:117}

YOUNG, WILLIAM (Maryland), colonel, Baltimore Co., by 1757; deputy commissary by 1757; and, court justice by 1759. {Ref: ARMD 55:63; Baltimore Co. Court Minutes, August 1759}

YOUNGER, GILBERT (Maryland), pvt., Capt. Joshua Beall's Company of MD Troops, Prince George's Co., from 9 Oct 1757 to 14 Sep 1758 when he was reported as killed; however, payment to him was recorded in Col. Dagworthy's account book on 26 Jul 1763. {Ref: MHS MS.375; CSOS:86; MHS MS.375.1}

ZERICK (ZERECK), ANTHONY (Maryland), m. (N), had children Daniel, Jacob, John, Catharine, and Betsy, and d. testate by 7 Dec 1782. {Ref: WMG 6:1, p. 31} Pvt., Capt. Peter Butler's Company Muster Roll, Frederick Co., circa 1757-1758, exact dates not given (served 34 days); bill of credit or order issued in his behalf for £1.14.0 and paid to Casper Shaff on 2 Mar 1767. {Ref: MSA S960 or S752, p. 167; CSOS:98}

Heritage Books by Henry C. Peden, Jr.:

A Closer Look at St. John's Parish Registers [Baltimore County, Maryland], 1701–1801

A Collection of Maryland Church Records

A Guide to Genealogical Research in Maryland: 5th Edition, Revised and Enlarged

Abstracts of Marriages and Deaths in Harford County, Maryland, Newspapers, 1837–1871

Abstracts of the Ledgers and Accounts of the Bush Store and Rock Run Store, 1759–1771

Abstracts of the Orphans Court Proceedings of Harford County, 1778–1800

Abstracts of Wills, Harford County, Maryland, 1800–1805

Anne Arundel County, Maryland, Marriage References 1658–1800
Henry C. Peden, Jr. and Veronica Clarke Peden

Baltimore City [Maryland] Deaths and Burials, 1834–1840

Baltimore County, Maryland, Overseers of Roads, 1693–1793

Bastardy Cases in Baltimore County, Maryland, 1673–1783

Bastardy Cases in Harford County, Maryland, 1774–1844

Bible and Family Records of Harford County, Maryland, Families: Volume V

Cecil County, Maryland Marriage References, 1674–1824
Henry C. Peden, Jr. and Veronica Clarke Peden

Children of Harford County: Indentures and Guardianships, 1801–1830

Colonial Delaware Soldiers and Sailors, 1638–1776

Colonial Families of the Eastern Shore of Maryland Volumes 5, 6, 7, 8, 9, 11, 12, 13, 14, 16, and 19
Henry C. Peden, Jr. and F. Edward Wright

Colonial Families of the Eastern Shore of Maryland Volume 21 and Volume 23

Colonial Maryland Soldiers and Sailors, 1634–1734

Colonial Tavern Keepers of Maryland and Delaware, 1634–1776

Dorchester County, Maryland, Marriage References, 1669–1800
Henry C. Peden, Jr. and Veronica Clarke Peden

Dr. John Archer's First Medical Ledger, 1767–1769, Annotated Abstracts

Early Anglican Records of Cecil County

Early Harford Countians, Individuals Living in Harford County, Maryland in Its Formative Years Volume 1: A to K, Volume 2: L to Z, and Volume 3: Supplement

Family Cemeteries and Grave Sites in Harford County, Maryland

First Presbyterian Church Records, Baltimore, Maryland, 1840–1879

Frederick County, Maryland, Marriage References and Family Relationships, 1748–1800
Henry C. Peden, Jr. and Veronica Clarke Peden

Genealogical Gleanings from Harford County, Maryland, Medical Records, 1772–1852
Winner of the Norris Harris Prize from MHS for the best genealogical reference book in 2016!

Harford (Maryland) Homicides

Harford County Taxpayers in 1870, 1872 and 1883

Harford County, Maryland Death Records, 1849–1899

Harford County, Maryland Deponents, 1775–1835

Harford County, Maryland Divorces and Separations, 1823–1923

Harford County, Maryland, Death Certificates, 1898–1918: An Annotated Index

Harford County, Maryland, Divorce Cases, 1827–1912: An Annotated Index

Harford County, Maryland, Inventories, 1774–1804

Harford County, Maryland, Marriage References and Family Relationships, 1774–1824
Henry C. Peden, Jr. and Veronica Clarke Peden

Harford County, Maryland, Marriage References and Family Relationships, 1825–1850

Harford County, Maryland, Marriage References and Family Relationships, 1851–1860
Henry C. Peden, Jr. and Veronica Clarke Peden

Harford County, Maryland, Marriage References and Family Relationships, 1861–1870
Henry C. Peden, Jr. and Veronica Clarke Peden

Harford County, Maryland, Marriage References and Family Relationships, 1871–1875

Harford (Old Brick Baptist) Church, Harford County, Maryland, Records and Members (1742–1974), Tombstones, Burials (1775–2009) and Family Relationships

Heirs and Legatees of Harford County, Maryland, 1774–1802

Heirs and Legatees of Harford County, Maryland, 1802–1846

Inhabitants of Baltimore County, Maryland, 1763–1774

Inhabitants of Cecil County, Maryland 1774–1800

Inhabitants of Cecil County, Maryland, 1649–1774

Inhabitants of Harford County, Maryland, 1791–1800

Inhabitants of Kent County, Maryland, 1637–1787

Joseph A. Pennington & Co., Havre De Grace, Maryland, Funeral Home Records: Volume II, 1877–1882, 1893–1900

Kent County, Maryland Marriage References, 1642–1800
Henry C. Peden, Jr. and Veronica Clarke Peden

Marriages and Deaths from Baltimore Newspapers, 1817–1824

Maryland Bible Records, Volume 1: Baltimore and Harford Counties

Maryland Bible Records, Volume 2: Baltimore and Harford Counties

Maryland Bible Records, Volume 3: Carroll County

Maryland Bible Records, Volume 4: Eastern Shore

Maryland Bible Records, Volume 5: Harford, Baltimore and Carroll Counties

Maryland Bible Records, Volume 7: Baltimore, Harford and Frederick Counties

Maryland Deponents, 1634–1799

Maryland Deponents: Volume 3, 1634–1776

Maryland Prisoners Languishing in Goal, Volume 1: 1635–1765

Maryland Prisoners Languishing in Goal, Volume 2: 1766–1800

*Maryland Public Service Records, 1775–1783:
A Compendium of Men and Women of Maryland
Who Rendered Aid in Support of the American Cause
against Great Britain during the Revolutionary War*

Marylanders and Delawareans in the French and Indian War, 1756–1763

*Marylanders to Carolina: Migration of Marylanders to
North Carolina and South Carolina prior to 1800*

Marylanders to Kentucky, 1775–1825

Marylanders to Ohio and Indiana, Migration Prior to 1835

Marylanders to Tennessee

Methodist Records of Baltimore City, Maryland: Volume 1, 1799–1829

Methodist Records of Baltimore City, Maryland: Volume 2, 1830–1839

*Methodist Records of Baltimore City, Maryland: Volume 3, 1840–1850
(East City Station)*

More Maryland Deponents, 1716–1799

*More Marylanders to Carolina: Migration of Marylanders to
North Carolina and South Carolina prior to 1800*

More Marylanders to Kentucky, 1778–1828

More Marylanders to Ohio and Indiana: Migrations Prior to 1835

Orphans and Indentured Children of Baltimore County, Maryland, 1777–1797

Outpensioners of Harford County, Maryland, 1856–1896

Presbyterian Records of Baltimore City, Maryland, 1765–1840

Quaker Records of Baltimore and Harford Counties, Maryland, 1801–1825

Quaker Records of Northern Maryland, 1716–1800

Quaker Records of Southern Maryland, 1658–1800

Revolutionary Patriots of Anne Arundel County, Maryland, 1775–1783

Revolutionary Patriots of Baltimore Town and Baltimore County, 1775–1783

*Revolutionary Patriots of Calvert
and St. Mary's Counties, Maryland, 1775–1783*

Revolutionary Patriots of Caroline County, Maryland, 1775–1783

Revolutionary Patriots of Cecil County, Maryland, 1775–1783

Revolutionary Patriots of Charles County, Maryland, 1775–1783

Revolutionary Patriots of Delaware, 1775–1783

Revolutionary Patriots of Dorchester County, Maryland, 1775–1783

Revolutionary Patriots of Frederick County, Maryland, 1775–1783

Revolutionary Patriots of Harford County, Maryland, 1775–1783

Revolutionary Patriots of Kent and Queen Anne's Counties, 1775–1783

Revolutionary Patriots of Lancaster County, Pennsylvania, 1775–1783

Revolutionary Patriots of Maryland, 1775–1783: A Supplement

Revolutionary Patriots of Maryland, 1775–1783: Second Supplement

Revolutionary Patriots of Montgomery County, Maryland, 1776–1783

Revolutionary Patriots of Prince George's County, Maryland, 1775–1783

Revolutionary Patriots of Talbot County, Maryland, 1775–1783

Revolutionary Patriots of Washington County, Maryland, 1776–1783

Revolutionary Patriots of Worcester and Somerset Counties, Maryland, 1775–1783

St. George's (Old Spesutia) Parish, Harford County, Maryland Church and Cemetery Records, 1820–1920

St. John's and St. George's Parish Registers, 1696–1851

Survey Field Book of David and William Clark in Harford County, Maryland, 1770–1812

Talbot County, Maryland Marriage References, 1662–1800
Henry C. Peden, Jr. and Veronica Clarke Peden

The Crenshaws of Kentucky, 1800–1995

The Delaware Militia in the War of 1812

Union Chapel United Methodist Church Cemetery Tombstone Inscriptions, Wilna, Harford County, Maryland